lonely

Austria

Vienna
p60

Upper Austria
p158

Lower Austria
& Burgenland
p121

The
Salzkammergut
p207

Salzburg &
Salzburgerland
p227

Styria
p179

Tyrol & Vorarlberg
p291

Carinthia
p269

THIS EDITION WRITTEN AND RESEARCHED BY
Marc Di Duca,
Kerry Christiani, Catherine Le Nevez, Donna Wheeler

Contents

ACHENSEE, P310

MRGB/SHUTTERSTOCK ©

SCHLOSS MIRABELL, P231

ANIBAL TREJO/SHUTTERSTOCK ©

Contents

UNDERSTAND

SURVIVAL GUIDE

SPECIAL FEATURES

Welcome to Austria

No country waltzes so effortlessly between the urban and the outdoors as Austria. One day you're cresting alpine summits, the next you're swanning around imperial Vienna.

Cue High Culture

You'll still feel the immense wealth of the Habsburg culture reverberating through Austria today – be it watching Lipizzaner stallions prance at the Spanish Riding School, or crossing the Hofburg to eyeball Rubens masterpieces in the Kunsthistorisches Museum. The work of classical pop stars such as Mozart, Strauss, Mahler, Haydn and Schubert echo as loudly as ever at lavishly gilded concert halls, and music festivals like Salzburg Festival and Bregenzer Festspiele are staged against uplifting lakeside or mountain backdrops.

River Deep, Mountain High

The journey really is the destination in Austria. Perhaps yours will be a meandering one through deeply carved valleys, on railways that unzip the Alps to thread improbably along sheer mountain flanks, past glaciers and through flower-flecked meadows. Such lyrical landscapes may have you itching to leap onto a bicycle saddle or lace up hiking boots to reach those enticingly off-the-radar corners of the country. In winter, the slopes hum with skiers and boarders, while summer beckons whitewater rafters and canyoners to glacial rivers and lakes that sparkle like gemstones. *Der Berg ruft* – the mountain calls!

Baroque & Beyond

Austria might conjure visions of baroque churches, palatial Habsburg headquarters like Schloss Schönbrunn, and Gothic crowning glories like the Stephansdom. But the country is more than pomp and palaces. A fresh breath of architectural air and a feel of new-found cool is sweeping through the cities, bringing with it a happy marriage of the contemporary and historic. Some of the most eye-catching icons are actually the newbies: Vienna's MuseumsQuartier in revamped imperial stables, the colour-shifting giant Rubik's Cube of Ars Electronica in Linz and the sci-fi ready Kunsthaus Graz.

Food at the Source

Guess what? There's more to Austrian cuisine than schnitzels and dumplings. The country has come on in culinary leaps and bounds, while staying true to its ethos of careful local sourcing. Vegan, organic, foraged, Slow Food: they are more than just buzzwords. Whether you're at a farmers market, a retro-style deli, a cool new brunch spot or a Michelin-starred restaurant, the love of the land shines through time and again. Asparagus in spring, *Marille* (apricots) in summer, mushrooms, game and new wine in autumn – Austria likes its food to swing with the seasons and taste of the source.

Why I Love Austria
By Kerry Christiani, Writer

Austria looks small on the map, but most of it is vertical, so there's always another hairpin-riddled lane, off-the-radar village or knockout alpine view to discover. As a hiker, I'm never happier than when dangling off a 2000m precipice on a trail in Tyrol or Salzburgerland – watching the spring-time eruption of wildflowers, say, or the last light creep down immense peaks of limestone. *Alpenglühen*, they call it. Then there are Vienna's fabulous coffee houses and phenomenal art, the romance of the vine-laced Wachau, the crystal-clear lakes of Salzkammergut and Carinthia's medieval villages, not to mention the castles, abbeys and cakes everywhere. What's not to love?

For more about our writers, see p416.

Above: Mountain vista, Salzburg region (p250)

Austria

Salzburg
Indulge in Mozart and celestial architecture (p229)

Eisriesenwelt
Drop into this glittering ice empire (p252)

Innsbruck
Enjoy culture infused with Tyrolean nature (p293)

Krimmler Wasserfälle
Austria's spectacular 360m-high waterfall (p267)

Pinzgauer Spaziergang
Walk one of Austria's great alpine trails (p263)

Grossglockner Road
Europe's sensational alpine drive (p265)

GERMANY

SWITZERLAND

ITALY

ELEVATION

4500m
3000m
1500m
1000m
750m
500m
250m
0

Adriatic Sea

Stuttgart
Regensburg
Munich
Memmingen
Braunau am Inn
Salzburg
Bad Reichenhall
Bregenz
Dornbirn
Hohenems
Schwarzenberg
Oberstdorf
Zugspitze (2963m)
Kufstein
Wörgl
SALZBURG (SALZBURGERLAND)
Tennengebirg
Cintui
Werfen
Vaduz
Feldkirch
St Anton am Arlberg
Hall
Kitzbühel
Saalfelden
Zell am See
Zeller See
Grossglockner Rd
Alberg Pass
Stanz
Innsbruck
Schwaz
Pinzgauer Spaziergang
Bludenz
Landeck
Ötz
Mayrhofen
Edelweiss Spitze (2577m)
Grossglockner (3798m)
Bad Gastein
VORARLBERG
TYROL
Krimmler Wasserfälle
Kaiser-Franz-Josefs-Höhe (2369m)
Davos
Wildspitze (3774m)
Brenner Pass (1374m)
Hohe Tauern National Park
Reschen Pass (1508m)
Timmelsjoch Pass
Lienz
Bodensee (Lake Constance)
Bregenzerwald
Hohenems
Trento
Udine
Portogruaro

CZECH REPUBLIC

The Wachau
Hike, dine or cycle
in the valley (p124)

Vienna
Explore Vienna's
imperial palaces (p60)

Stift Melk
Austria's glorious
Benedictine abbey (p131)

Brno

Passau

Drosendorf

Znojmo

Retz

Horn

Freistadt

Krems an
der Donau

Hollabrunn

UPPER AUSTRIA

LOWER AUSTRIA

Stockerau

SLOVAKIA

Linz

Traun

The Wachau

Tulln

Ansfelden

Melk

St Pölten

Vienna

Wels

Amstetten

Perchtoldsdorf

Mödling

Schwechat

Bratislava

Steyr

Baden bei Wien

Bad Vöslau

Neusiedl
am See

Gmunden

Waidhofen an
der Ybbs

Schneeberg
(2076m)

Wiener
Neustadt

*Neusiedler
See*

Mondsee

Traunkirchen

Mariazell

Neunkirchen

Eisenstadt

Ebensee

Hoher
Nock
(1963m)

Ternitz

Sopron

St
Gilgen

Bad
Ischl

**THE
SALZKAMMERGUT**

**Nationalpark
Kalkalpen**

Semmering

Gloggnitz

Bad Aussee

Eisenerz

Mürzzuschlag

Oberpullendorf

Hallstatt

Stainach-
Irdning

Admont

Kapfenberg

Haus

Leoben

Radstadt

STYRIA

Bruck an
der Mur

Oberwart

Tamsweg

Unzmarkt-
Frauenburg

BURGENLAND

Szombathely

Rennweg

Murau

Judenburg

Köflach

Graz

Güssing

CARINTHIA

Voitsberg

Feldbach

Bad
Blumau

HUNGARY

Spittal an
der Drau

Wolfsberg

Bad
Radkersburg

Feldkirchen

St Veit an
der Glan

St Andrä

Klagenfurt

Drau

Ehrenhausen

Villach

Völkermarkt

Wörthersee

Semmeringbahn
Ride the spectacular
railway to Semmering (p147)

Hallstätter See
Dip into refreshing
Salzkammergut lakes (p211)

Admont
Fascinating exhibitions set
in historic architecture (p201)

Nova
Gorica

Ljubljana

Sava

CROATIA

Drava

Zagreb

SLOVENIA

0   100 km
0   50 miles

Austria's
Top 23

1

Grossglockner Road

1 Hairpin bends: 36. Length: 48km. Average slope gradient: 9%. Highest viewpoint: Edelweiss Spitze (2571m). Grossglockner Road (p265) is one of Europe's greatest drives and the showpiece of Hohe Tauern National Park. The scenery unfolds as you climb higher on this serpentine road. And what scenery! Snow-capped mountains, plunging waterfalls and lakes scattered like gemstones are just the build-up to Grossglockner (3798m), Austria's highest peak, and the Pasterze Glacier. Start early and allow enough time, as there's a stop-the-car-and-grab-the-camera view on every corner.

Imperial Palaces of Vienna

2 Imagine what you could do with unlimited riches and Austria's top architects at hand for 640 years and you'll have the Vienna of the Habsburgs. The monumentally graceful Hofburg (p61) whisks you back to the age of empires; marvel at the treasury's imperial crowns, the equine ballet of the Spanische Hofreitschule and the chandelier-lit apartments fit for Empress Elisabeth. The palace is rivalled in grandeur only by the 1441-room Schloss Schönbrunn (pictured; p87), a Unesco World Heritage site, and baroque Schloss Belvedere, both set in exquisite gardens.

MARIUSZ NIEDZWIEDZKI/SHUTTERSTOCK ©

MARTIN HOLLAUS/500PX ©

Skiing in the Alps

3 In a country where three-year-olds can snowplough, 70-year-olds still slalom and the tiniest speck of a village has its own lift system, skiing is more than just a sport – it's a way of life. Why? Just look around you. There's St Anton am Arlberg (p324) for off-piste and après-ski, Mayrhofen for freestyle boarding and its epic Harakiri, Kitzbühel for its perfect mix – the scope is limitless and the terrain fantastic. Cross-country or back-country, downhill or glacier, whatever your ski style, Austria has a piste with your name on it.

Cafe Culture in Vienna

4 A pianist plays and bow-tied waiters bustle to and fro with cakes and encyclopaedic coffee menus. Ahhh, this is what the Viennese mean by *Gemütlichkeit* (cosiness), you realise, as you sip your *melange* (milky coffee), rustle your newspaper and watch life go decadently by. Café Sacher (p113) for the richest of chocolate cakes, Café Jelinek for its quirky vibe, Café Leopold Hawelka for bohemian flavour – Vienna has a coffee house for every mood and occasion. Indulge, talk, read and dream; just as Trotsky and Freud, Hundertwasser and Warhol once did. Café Sperl

Festung Hohensalzburg

5 Work up a sweat on the steep walk or step into the funicular and sway up to Salzburg's glorious fortress, Festung Hohensalzburg (p229), beckoning on a forested peak above the city. As you make your way around Europe's best-preserved fortress, glide through the Golden Hall, with its celestial ceiling capturing the starlit heavens. After all this beauty, you will find yourself cast among a chilling array of medieval torture instruments in the Fortress Museum, and don't miss the 360-degree views from the tower. View over the cathedral to the fortress

FRANZ PRITZ/GETTY IMAGES ©

6

7

The Wachau

6 When Strauss composed 'The Blue Danube', he surely had the Wachau in mind. Granted Unesco World Heritage status for its harmonious natural and cultural beauty, this romantic stretch of the Danube Valley (p124) waltzes you through poetic landscapes of terraced vineyards, forested slopes and apricot orchards. Beyond the highlight attraction of Stift Melk, Dürnstein's Kuenringerburg (p128) begs exploration. This ruined hilltop castle is where the troubadour Blondel attempted to rescue Richard the Lionheart from the clutches of Duke Leopold V.

Salzburg Festival

7 No country can outshine Austria when it comes to classical music. The country was a veritable production line of great composers in the 18th and 19th centuries. And there's always a reason to celebrate that great heritage, especially at the much-lauded Salzburg Festival (p239), held late July to August, which was staged for the first time in 1920 and is today a highlight of Austria's cultural calendar. As well as concerts featuring illustrious composers such as homegrown Mozart, make sure you catch an opera and a theatre performance or two.

Hiking the Pinzgauer Spaziergang

8 You're on the Pinzgauer Spaziergang (p263), a crisp blue sky overhead, snowy peaks crowding the horizon. You're waking up to a rose-tinted sunrise in the Dolomites. Or perhaps tramping along the Zillertal Circuit, its highest peaks frosted with glaciers. You're thanking your lucky stars you packed your walking boots... Locals delight in telling you that the best – no, no, the only – way to see the Austrian Alps is on foot. And they're right. Here a peerless network of trails and alpine huts brings you that bit closer to nature.

AVAR NIKKYA/ALAMY ©

Eisriesenwelt

9 The twinkling chambers and passageways of Eisriesenwelt (p252) are like something out of Narnia under the White Witch. Sculpted drip by drip over millennia, the icy underworld of the limestone Tennengebirge range is billed as the world's largest accessible ice cave. Otherworldly sculptures, shimmering lakes and a cavernous *Eispalast* (ice palace) appear as you venture deep into the frozen heart of the mountain, carbide lamp in hand. Even in summer, temperatures down here are subzero, so wrap up warm.

MILOSLAV VANEK/PROFIMEDIA.CZ A.S./ALAMY ©

The Sound of Music

10 Salzburg is a celebrity for those who have never even set foot in the city, thanks to its star appearance in *The Sound of Music*. Should you wish, you can fine-tune your own tour of the film locations. The sculpture-dotted Mirabellgarten (pictured; p231) of 'Do-Re-Mi' fame, the Benedictine nunnery Stift Nonnberg, the 'Sixteen Going on Seventeen' pavilion in Hellbrunn Park – it's enough to make you yodel out loud. For the truth behind the celluloid legend, stay the night at the original Villa Trapp, a 19th-century mansion in the Aigen district.

Stift Melk

11 Austria's greatest works of art are those wrought for God, some say. Gazing up at the golden glory of Stift Melk (p131), Austria's must-see Benedictine abbey-fortress, you can't help but agree. The twin-spired monastery church is a baroque tour de force, swirling with prancing angels, gilt flourishes and Johann Michael Rottmayr's ceiling paintings. Such opulence continues in the library and marble hall, both embellished with illusionary *trompe l'oeil* tiers by Paul Troger. If you can, stay to see the monarch of monasteries strikingly lit at night.

CANADASTOCK/SHUTTERSTOCK ©

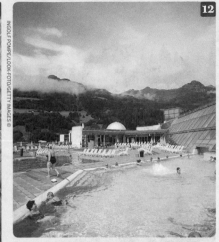

Spa Sensations

12 With its crisp mountain air and thermal springs, Austria positively radiates good health. For an otherworldly spa experience, drift off in flying-saucer-shaped pools at crystalline Aqua Dome (p318) at the foot of the Ötztaler Alps, or in the fantastical hot springs of Hundertwasser's technicolor Rogner-Bad Blumau. History bubbles to the surface in the Wienerwald's Römertherme, where Romans once took the sulphuric waters. The Victorians favoured belle-époque Bad Gastein, whose radon-laced springs reputedly cure a multitude of ills. Alpentherme (p261)

MuseumsQuartier

13 Once the imperial stables, now one of the world's biggest exhibition spaces, Vienna's 60,000-sq-metre MuseumsQuartier (p77) contains more art than some small countries. Emotive works by Klimt and Schiele hang out in the Leopold Museum, while the basalt MUMOK (pictured; p80) highlights provocative Viennese Actionists, and the Kunsthalle new media. Progressive boutiques, workshops and cafes take creativity beyond the canvas. On warm days, Viennese gather in the huge courtyard to chat, drink and watch the world go by.

WILCO SNOEIJER/SHUTTERSTOCK ©

VADIM PETRAKOV/SHUTTERSTOCK ©

LOU JONES/GETTY IMAGES ©

Krimmler Wasserfälle

14 No doubt you'll hear the thunderous roar of the 380m-high Krimmler Wasserfälle (p267), Europe's highest waterfall, before you see it. You can't help but feel insignificant when confronted with the sheer force and scale of this cataract, which thrashes immense boulders and produces the most photogenic of rainbows. As with all natural wonders, this one looks best from certain angles, namely from the Wasserfallweg (Waterfall Trail). The path zigzags up through moist, misty forest to viewpoints that afford close-ups of the three-tiered falls and a shower in its fine spray.

Outdoor Adventure in Tyrol

15 Anywhere where there's foaming water, a tall mountain or a sheer ravine, there are heart-pumping outdoor escapades in Austria. For a summertime buzz, you can't beat throwing yourself down raging rivers such as the Inn and Sanna in Tyrol, Austria's rafting (p296) mecca. Or strap into your harness and be blown away by the alpine scenery while paragliding in the Zillertal. Cyclists use the cable-car network to access the many high-altitude and downhill routes. Paragliding in Mayrhofen (p308)

Wine Tasting in Heurigen

16 If you see an evergreen branch hanging on a door on Vienna's outskirts and Burgenland, especially around the Neusiedler See where there's a growing number of young, innovative winemakers, you've probably stumbled across a *Heuriger* (p54). Pull up a chair in one of these cosy wine taverns to taste the local vintage of crisp white Grüner Veltliner and spicy Blaufränkisch wines. The experience is partly to do with the wine and partly what surrounds it – the atmosphere, the scenery, the chatty locals, the hearty food. September is the month for new wine and golden vineyard strolls.

Mozart's Salzburg

17 Mozart's spiritual home may have been Vienna, but the musical prodigy was born and bred in Salzburg's baroque Altstadt. Here you can see where the 18th-century superstar lived, loved and composed (p229). Orchestras wish the late Amadeus a happy (if rather belated) birthday at Mozartwoche in late January. Year-round there are chamber concerts of Mozart's music in the exquisite surrounds of the Marmorsaal (Marble Hall) at Schloss Mirabell. Marionettes bring his operas magically to life at the nearby Salzburger Marionettentheater (pictured).

Semmeringbahn

18 The monumental Semmeringbahn (p147), or Semmering Railway, is a panoramic journey through the Eastern Alps and a nostalgic trip back to early rail travel. Some 20,000 workers toiled to create the railway, an alpine first, in a feat of 19th-century engineering that is now a Unesco World Heritage site. Though steam has been replaced by electricity, you can still imagine the wonder of the first passengers as the train curves around 16 viaducts, burrows through 15 tunnels and glides across 100 stone bridges. The grandeur of the railway and landscapes is timeless.

17

RON7000G/SHUTTERSTOCK ©

18

TRABANTOS/SHUTTERSTOCK ©

Admont's Benedictine Abbey

19 Situated deep in the rifts of the Gesäuse mountains in Styria, Admont's Benedictine Abbey (p201) is a remarkable fusion of landscape, architecture and museum space. The Benedictine Abbey's baroque library, with its ceiling frescoes from the 18th century, should be sufficient to lure you into this remote region of gurgling streams and soaring peaks. But take the time to stroll around the abbey's museums, which bring together the region's natural history with contemporary art and works from past ages. From a glass staircase you can revel in the spectacular view to the Nationalpark Gesäuse.

Vienna's Naschmarkt

20 Austrians pride themselves on home-grown flavours, with almost every region producing mouth-watering surprises. And most of these find their way to Vienna's largest and most famous market, the Naschmarkt (p101) – fresh cheeses from the Kemptal in Lower Austria or the Bregenzerwald, or Thum ham from the Mangalitza breed. But a stroll through the market takes you not only through the culinary regions of Austria, but also into a sensory world of exotic spices. Drop into the food stalls – some as large as restaurants – where you can rest your feet and fill up on some of the capital's best food.

Innsbruck

21 Set against an impressive backdrop of the Nordkette Alps, Tyrol's capital (p293) is the kind of place where at one moment you are celebrating cultural achievement in elegant state apartments or the Gothic Hofkirche, and the next whizzing up into the Alps inside Zaha Zadid's futuristic funicular or heading out for the ski pistes. Culture is folded neatly here into the crevices of the landscape. If clinging to a fixed rope on the Innsbrucker Klettersteig while you make your way across seven peaks sounds too head-swirling, try the marginally less vertiginous Nordkette Singletrail mountain-bike track.

Lakes of the Salzkammergut

22 With its sparkling alpine lakes, the Salzkammergut (p207) is one of Austria's finest regions for washing away the dust of travel. Hallstätter See, set at the foot of the rugged Dachstein Mountains, is one spectacular place to enjoy the lakes. While Hallstatt draws the crowds, across the lake in Obertraun the lake shore retains a sleepy air. A stroll or bike ride around the warmer and gentler Wolfgangsee is within easy reach of small towns like Bad Aussee and Bad Ischl. Or unfurl the sails and let the breeze carry you along on the Mondsee. Hallstatt

Graz

23 Austria's largest city after Vienna is also one the country's most relaxed. After you have visited Schloss Eggenberg and climbed the Schlossberg for magnificent views over the red rooftops of town – perhaps sipping a long drink or two on a warm afternoon at the Aiola Upstairs – set your sights upon the south Styrian wine roads. This wine-growing region about 50km south of Graz (p181) is a treat to the tastebuds as well as to the eyes: rolling, verdant hills and picturesque vineyards unfolding to the Slovenian border. Schloss Eggenberg

Need to Know

For more information, see Survival Guide (p383).

Currency
Euro (€)

Language
German

Visas
Austria is part of the Schengen Agreement. A visa generally isn't necessary for stays of up to three months, but some nationalities need a Schengen visa.

Money
ATMs widely available. Maestro direct debit and Visa and MasterCard credit cards are accepted in most hotels and midrange restaurants. Expect to pay cash elsewhere. Travellers cheques not accepted.

Mobile Phones
Local SIM cards (about €15) are easily purchased for 'unlocked' phones.

Time
Central European Time (GMT/UTC plus one hour)

When to Go

Mild to hot summers, cold winters
Warm to hot summers, mild winters
Mild year-round
Cold climate

Vienna
GO Late Mar–Oct

Kitzbühel
GO Jun–Sep & Dec–Mar

Salzburg
GO Jul & Aug

Innsbruck
GO Jun–Sep & Dec–Mar

Graz
GO Apr–Oct

High Season
(Apr–Oct)

➡ High season peaks from July to August.

➡ In lake areas, the peak is June to September.

➡ Prices rise over Christmas and Easter.

➡ Salzburg is busiest in July and August for the Salzburg Festival.

Shoulder
(late Mar–May & late Sep–Oct)

➡ The weather's changeable, the lakes are chilly and the hiking's excellent.

➡ Sights are open and less crowded.

Low Season
(Nov–Mar)

➡ Many sights are closed at this time of year.

➡ There's a cultural focus in Vienna and the regional capitals.

➡ Ski resorts open from mid-December.

➡ High season for skiing is mid-December to March.

Useful Websites

Embassy of Austria (www.austria.org) US-based website with current affairs and information.

Lonely Planet (www.lonelyplanet.com/austria) Destination information, hotel bookings, traveller forum and more.

Österreich Werbung (www.austria.info) National tourism authority.

Tiscover (www.tiscover.com) Information and accommodation booking.

Important Numbers

To dial listings from outside Austria, dial your international access code, the country code, the city code and then the number.

Austria's country code	☑43
Emergency (police, fire, ambulance)	☑112
International access code	☑00
International operator & information	☑11 88 77 (inland, EU & neighbouring countries); ☑0900 11 88 77 (other countries)
Mountain rescue	☑140

Exchange Rates

Australia	A$1	€0.70
Canada	C$1	€0.72
Japan	¥100	€0.82
New Zealand	NZ$	€0.67
Russia	RUB1	€0.01
UK	UK£1	€1.19
USA	US$1	€0.94

For current exchange rates see www.xe.com.

Daily Costs

Budget: Less than €80

➡ Dorm beds or cheap doubles: about €25 per person

➡ Self-catering or lunch specials: €6–12

➡ Cheap museums: €4

Midrange: €80–160

➡ Hotel singles: €60–90 per person

➡ Two-course meal with glass of wine: €30

➡ High-profile museums: €12

Top end: More than €160

➡ Plush suites and doubles in major cities: from €200

➡ Pampering at spa facilities: €40–100

➡ Fine dining and wine pairing: €70

Opening Hours

Banks 8am or 9am to 3pm weekdays (to 5.30pm Thursdays).

Cafes 7am or 8am to 11pm or midnight.

Government offices 8am to 3.30pm, 4pm or 5pm Monday to Friday.

Post offices 8am to noon and 2pm to 6pm Monday to Friday.

Restaurants 11am to 2.30pm or 3pm and 6pm to 11pm or midnight.

See p389 for more details.

Arriving in Austria

Vienna International Airport The City Airport Train (CAT) runs to Wien-Mitte every 30 minutes from 5.36am to 11.06pm and takes 16 minutes. A single/return costs €11/17. Vienna Airport Lines buses run every 30 minutes 24/7; it's 20 minutes to Schwedenplatz (central Vienna). A single costs €8.

Vienna Hauptbahnhof Vienna's shiny new main train station was completed in 2015. Other services arrive in Wien-Meidling and Westbahnhof.

Graz Airport Trains leave the airport from 4.47am to 11.45pm Monday to Saturday, and from 5.10am Sunday, at least hourly. Buses 630 and 631 to the *Hauptbahnhof* run less frequently and take around 30 minutes. An hour's ticket valid for either costs €2.20.

Innsbruck Airport Bus F serves the airport. Buses depart every 15 or 20 minutes from Maria-Theresien-Strasse (€2.30, 16 minutes); taxis charge about €10 for the same trip.

Salzburg Airport Buses 2, 8 and 27 (€2, 19 minutes) depart from outside the terminal roughly every 10 to 15 minutes and make several central stops near the Altstadt; buses 2 and 27 terminate at the *Hauptbahnhof*. Services operate roughly from 5.30am to 11pm.

Getting Around

Car Small towns and even small cities often have limited or no car-hire services, so reserve ahead from major cities.

Train & Bus Austria's national railway system is integrated with the Postbus bus services. Plan your route using the ÖBB (p394) or Postbus (p397) websites.

For much more on **getting around**, see p397.

First Time Austria

For more information, see Survival Guide (p384).

Checklist

➡ Make sure your passport is valid for at least six months from your arrival date

➡ Make sure you have a visa if you need one

➡ Arrange travel insurance, and medical insurance if needed (see p388)

➡ Check credit/debit card can be used with ATMs internationally

➡ Make copies of all important documents and cards (store online or in hard copy)

➡ Turn off data roaming on mobile (cell) phone

What to Pack

➡ Hiking boots (with profile for snow), plus one pair of dress shoes

➡ Waterproof jacket (summer) or winter jacket

➡ Day pack

➡ Electrical adapter if needed

Top Tips for Your Trip

➡ Explore towns and cities at night or consider an easy night hike on a forestry track for a totally different perspective.

➡ Choose a convenient city, small town or village as a regional hub and explore on day trips – save time and lugging bags.

➡ Factor in time for lingering in coffee houses or *Beisl* (small tavern/restaurant) visits in Vienna and Salzburg, or for sitting around in a park or square to soak up the 'feel' of the place.

➡ Book train tickets in advance online to save time and look out for discounted *Sparschiene* tickets.

What to Wear

Winter can be cold and the ground icy, so several layers of warm clothing and good shoes are essential, along with gloves, scarf and a woollen cap or a hat. In summer, wear layers you can peel off and make sure you have something for occasional rain showers. Especially in larger cities, Austrians tend to dress up well in the evening or for good restaurants, but fashion jeans are fine even for upmarket clubs and restaurants if combined with a good shirt or blouse and a men's sports coat *(Sakko)* or women's summer jacket.

Sleeping

Tourist offices invariably keep lists and details of accommodation; some arrange bookings (free, or for a small fee).

➡ **Hotels** Swing from budget to five-star luxury in palatial surrounds.

➡ **B&Bs** Also called pensions and *Gasthöfe*; range from simple city digs to rustic chalets in the mountains.

➡ **Private Rooms** *Privatzimmer* usually represent great value (doubles go for as little as €50).

➡ **Farmstays** Well geared towards families. Some only operate during the summer months.

➡ **Alpine Huts** Opening with the snow from roughly late June to mid-September. Advance bookings essential.

➡ **Camping** Most resorts and cities have camp grounds, usually in pretty natural settings.

Money

ATMs are widely available. Maestro direct debit and Visa and MasterCard credit cards are accepted in most hotels and in midrange restaurants. Expect to pay cash elsewhere. Travellers cheques are not accepted.

Bargaining

Bargaining in shops is not really a part of Austrian culture. Flea markets are the exception; or when negotiating a longer than usual period of rental for, say, a kayak or a bicycle, you can ask whether there's a cheaper rate they can offer.

Tipping

➡ **Hotels** One or two euros per suitcase for porters and for valet parking in top-end hotels.

➡ **Restaurants** About 10% (unless service is abominable).

➡ **Bars** About 5% at the bar and 10% at a table.

➡ **Taxis** About 10%.

JEAN-PIERRE LESCOURRET/GETTY IMAGES ©

Relaxing in a cafe in Vienna

Etiquette

Austrians are fairly formal and use irony to alleviate social rules and constraints rather than debunk or break them overtly.

➡ **Telephone** Always give your name at the start of a telephone call, especially when making reservations. When completing the call, say *auf Wiederhören* ('goodbye'), the customary telephone form.

➡ **Greetings** Use the *Sie* (formal 'you') form unless you're youngish (in your 20s) and among peers, or your counterpart starts using *du* (informal 'you'). Acknowledge fellow hikers on trails with a *Servus*, *Grüss di* (or the informal *Grüss dich*) or *Grüss Gott* (all ways of saying 'hello!').

➡ **Eating & Drinking** Bring chocolate or flowers as a gift if invited into a home. Before starting to eat, say *Guten Appetit*. To toast say *Zum Wohl* (if drinking wine) or *Prost!* (beer), and look your counterpart in the eye – not to do so is impolite and reputedly brings seven years of bad sex.

Language

In Vienna, the regional capitals and tourist areas (such as around lakes or in resorts) you'll find that many people speak English, especially in restaurants and hotels. In much of the countryside, however, it's a slightly different picture, and you should equip yourself with a few necessary phrases.

Conductors on trains and many bus drivers know enough English to help with necessities.

If You Like...

Museums & Palaces

MuseumsQuartier Where baroque stables have morphed into Europe's finest modern museum quarter. (p77)

Vienna's Hofburg Habsburg HQ for over 600 years and now host to phenomenal museums. (p61)

Schloss Belvedere Prince Eugene's Viennese masterpiece, with sensational art collections. (p83)

Schloss Schönbrunn Vienna's premier palace and gardens where the Habsburg story is told. (p87)

Schloss Eggenberg Graz' magnificent Renaissance palace, with museums and gardens. (p185)

Festung Hohensalzburg Salzburg's mighty 900-year-old fortress, complete with torture chamber. (p229)

Salzburg's Residenzplatz Opulence coupled with European grand masters. (p230)

Hiking

Pinzgauer Spaziergang An alpine walk affording mesmerising views of the snowcapped Hohe Tauern National Park and Kitzbühel Alps.

Ranger Walks Back-to-nature guided walks in Hohe Tauern with clued-up rangers – from glacier trekking to wildlife spotting. (p256)

Zillertal Circuit A classic alpine day hike starting at a jewel-coloured reservoir and offering fantastic views of the Zillertal Alps. (p307)

Radsattel Circuit One of Vorarlberg's most spectacular hikes, through valleys and high into the realms of glaciers and 3000m mountains. (p344)

Contemporary Eating & Drinking

Café Drechsler Classic goulash in an ultra-cool coffee house with DJs. (p111)

Der Steirer Nouveau Styrian cuisine – wine and the art of goulash. (p189)

Supersense Retro rocks at this born-again cafe, mixing coffee, vinyl and cult Polaroid cameras. (p107)

Burgenland wines Intimate, small-scale wine producers attracting global recognition. (p157)

South Styrian wine roads Cracking white wines with creative food to boot. (p195)

Viennese Beisln & Heurigen Seek out new-wave wine taverns and neo-*Beisln* with a modern spin. (p107)

Winter Sports

Major resorts Downhill skiing and snowboarding in Kitzbühel, St Anton am Arlberg and Mayrhofen. (p311)

Schladming Alpine skiing on pistes and on a glacier, plus gripping spectator events. (p203)

Epic descents Streif in Kitzbühel, Run of Fame in St Anton and Harakiri in Mayrhofen will test your mettle. (p311)

Après-ski Never hotter than in St Anton and Ischgl. (p328)

Low key Snowshoeing, sledding and cross-country skiing in Seefeld, even for nonskiers. (p316)

Lookouts & High Rides

Dachstein Eispalast and Skywalk Dangle precariously at the vertical rock face before reaching the viewing platform at the top. (p203)

Hintertuxer Gletscher A cable-car ride to the glacier with views to die for. (p308)

Riesenrad Vienna's iconic Ferris wheel combines a great ride with fantastic city views. (p83)

Festung Hohensalzburg Views over the spires, domes and rooftops of Salzburg. (p229)

Edelweiss Spitze On the Grossglockner Road; 360-degree views of more than 30 peaks over 3000m. (p266)

Balthazar im Rudolfsturm Fantastic views over the Hallstätter See and a great place to sip on a long drink. (p213)

Mountain Biking & Cycling

Danube Valley cycle path Pedal from the German border via the vine-clad Wachau and Vienna to Slovakia. (p47)

Schladming With 900km of bike trails and some challenging mountain-bike runs. (p203)

Bodensee Radweg Highly scenic trail looping around Lake Constance. (p333)

Tauernradweg A 310km monster of mountain landscapes in Hohe Tauern National Park. (p267)

Dachstein Tour Fab three-day mountain-bike trail. (p48)

Nordkette Singletrail Innsbruck's tough trail, one of the most exhilarating downhill rides in the country. (p296)

Top: MUMOK museum, Vienna (p80)
Bottom: Skywalk viewing platform, Dachstein (p214)

PLAN YOUR TRIP IF YOU LIKE...

Month by Month

TOP EVENTS

Salzburg Festival, July

Styriarte, June

Christmas markets, December

Spectaculum, July

Donauinselfest, June

January

The flakes are falling and the ski season is revving. One of the coldest months of the year in Austria, this is the right time to hit the peaks for downhill or cross-country skiing, or for snowshoe hikes.

☆ Mozartwoche

An ode to the city's most famous son, Mozart Week stages a series of concerts in Salzburg in late January. (p239)

☆ New Year Concerts

Vienna rings in the new year on 1 January with classical concerts. The Vienna Philharmonic's performance in Vienna's Staatsoper is a glittering affair. (p112)

🎭 Perchtenlaufen

Locals dress as *Perchten* (spirits crowned with elaborate headdresses) and parade through the streets across much of western Austria in a celebration to bring good fortune and bountiful harvests for the year.

February

The winter months are freezing, but in Vienna the museums and cultural scene are in full swing. Crowds are down. On the slopes the skiing is usually still excellent.

☆ Opernball

Of the 300 or so Vienna balls held in January and February, the lavish Opern-ball is the most illustrious. (p96)

March

The sun is thawing the public squares. Hiking and cycling are becoming possible from late March, but many sights outside Vienna are still dormant.

🎭 Easter

Easter is when families come together to celebrate. Salzburg celebrates with Osterfestspiele (p239), Vienna with OsterKlang Festival (p96).

April

Spring has properly sprung and city gardens are at their blooming best. Room rates and crowds remain low. Snow still polishes the highest peaks of the Alps.

May

Cities are a delight on bright spring days: uncrowded and often warm. A hike to a mountain *Alm* (meadow) becomes a romp through flowers, and from April onwards all sights and activities flick to summer schedules.

☆ Musikwochen Millstatt

In Millstatt in Carinthia, a string of concerts are held between May and September, mostly in the medieval abbey.

🎭 Wiener Festwochen

In Vienna, arts from around the world hit the stages until mid-June. (p96)

☆ Höhenrausch

Modern art in weird and wonderful places is what Höhenrausch is all about, with city tours, rooftop walks, art installations and entertainment drawing crowds to Linz. (p162)

June

The snow finally melts and hiking and kayaking are excellent, with near-empty trails and warm but not overly hot weather. Mountain lakes are slowly warming up. Big-hitting sights in Vienna and Salzburg start to get crowded.

☆ Donauinselfest

Vienna gets down for a three-day festival of rock, pop, hardcore, folk and country music on the Donauinsel. (p96)

☆ Tanzsommer

A selection of top international contemporary dance groups takes to the stage for a month during the Tanzsommer in June and July. (p297)

☆ SommerSzene

Salzburg's cutting-edge dance, theatre and music bash ignites from mid-June to mid-July. (p239)

☆ Styriarte

Graz' most important cultural festival offers almost continuous classical concerts in June and July. (p186)

July

School holidays begin in July, the time when families enjoy the warm weather on lakes and in the mountains. Cities can be sweltering and crowded, but restaurant dining is at its alfresco best.

☆ ImPulsTanz

Vienna's premier avant-garde dance festival takes place from mid-July to mid-August, with the participation of dancers, choreographers and teachers in this five-week event. (p96)

☆ Salzburger Festspiele

World-class opera, classical music and drama take the stage across Salzburg from late July to August. (p239)

☆ Spectaculum

On the last Saturday in July, electric lights are extinguished and the town of Friesach returns to the Middle Ages. (p280)

August

School holidays continue to propel families into the resorts, making things a bit crowded. Hit some isolated spots in the fine weather – seek out a *Heuriger* (wine tavern) or an alpine peak.

☆ Bregenzer Festspiele

Beginning in late July and continuing until late August, this is Vorarlberg's top-class cultural event, with classical music and performances on a floating, open-air stage. (p334)

☆ La Strada Graz

This upbeat summer arts festival brings street theatre, dance, puppet theatre and 'nouveau cirque' to the streets of Graz. (p186)

September

The temperatures are beginning a gradual descent and crowds are tailing off. Museums and most of the activities are still in season, however, and a couple of top-class festivals are revving into action.

☆ Brucknerfest

Linz stages its most celebrated festival, a series of classical concerts based on composer Anton Bruckner. (p163)

☆ Internationale Haydntage

International and Austrian performers take the audience through the range of works by Josef Haydn throughout much of September in his home town of Eisenstadt. (p149)

☆ Mountain Yoga Festival

St Anton practises tree pose for its Mountain Yoga Festival, giving the resort an added dose of Zen in early September. (p327)

October

Goldener Oktober – the light picks out the golds and russets of autumn, the mountains are growing chilly at night, the wine harvest is in and some museums are preparing to close for winter.

☆ Steirischer Herbst

Held in Graz each year, this avant-garde festival has a program of music, theatre, film and more. (p186)

☆ Viennale Film Festival

For two weeks from mid-October, city cinemas host screenings from fringe films through documentaries to short and feature films. (p96)

November

Many museums outside the capital have gone into winter hibernation, the days are getting short

and the weather can be poor. Cafes, pubs and restaurants become the focal point.

🏃 St Martin's Day

Around 11 November the new wine is released and St Martin's Day is marked with feasts of goose washed down by the nectar of the gods.

🎊 Wien Modern Festival

Contemporary music and pop culture take to the fore at this three-week festival, held at 16 venues across Vienna.

December

Snow! Ski resorts are gathering momentum and

in Vienna and other cities the theatres and classical-music venues are in full swing – often the best performances are during the coldest months.

🎊 Christmas Markets

Christkindlmärkte (Christmas markets) spring up around the country from early December until the 24th and Austrians sip mulled wine on public squares.

🎊 Silvester

Book early for the night of 31 December, celebrated with fireworks and a blaze of crackers and rockets on Vienna's crowded streets. (p97)

Itineraries

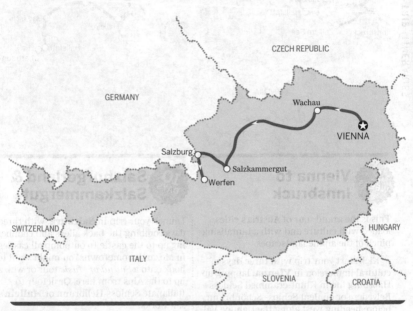

 Vienna to Salzburg

This itinerary is Austria in a nutshell, winging you from Vienna's opulent palaces and coffee houses to the vine-stitched Wachau Valley, and west to the Alps in Salzburgerland. Mozart, Maria and landscapes no well-orchestrated symphony or yodelling nun could ever quite capture – this one has the lot.

Devote a couple of cultural days to swanning around Habsburg palaces, world-class galleries hung with Klimts and sumptuous coffee houses in **Vienna**.

A breezy hour's train ride west and you're in the heart of wine country and on the Danube in the picture-book **Wachau**. Linger for a day or two to lap up the castles, abbeys and local rieslings.

Swing west now for two days to the **Salzkammergut**, where cinematic mountain backdrops rim lakes of bluest blue. Base yourself in ludicrously pretty Hallstatt for peak-gazing swims and a visit to Dachstein's astonishing ice caves. From here, head west to **Salzburg** for a feast of baroque art, prince-archbishop palaces, Mozart and more. After a couple of days, tag on a day in **Werfen** with its high-on-a-hill castle and extraordinary Eisriesenwelt – all backdropped by the Tennengebirge's jagged limestone peaks.

 ## Vienna to Innsbruck

2 WEEKS

This is the grand tour of Austria's cities, loaded with culture and with a tantalising pinch of the alpine landscapes.

Kick start your trip with three days of cultural immersion in **Vienna**, lapping up Habsburg life in Klimt-crammed Schloss Belvedere or opulent Schloss Schönbrunn, before heading west along the Danube Valley to **Krems an der Donau**. Pause here for cutting-edge galleries and wine tastings, factoring in a trip to the spirit-lifting Benedictine abbey-fortress in **Melk**, slung high above the Danube.

On day seven (a day or two earlier in winter), head on to **Linz**, an industrial city with edgy galleries like Lentos and Ars Electronica. The trail to mountain-rimmed **Hallstatt** and the lakes of the Salzkammergut are soothingly beautiful on day eight.

From Hallstatt, either venture to **Salzburg**, a pristine, castle-topped baroque city, for a Mozart and Maria fix, or stop off in lakeside **Zell am See**, where hiking trails thread among some of Austria's highest peaks, before continuing to **Innsbruck** for a dose of culture, hiking, skiing – whatever takes your fancy.

 ## Salzburgerland & Salzkammergut

10 DAYS

Launch your trip in **Salzburg**, with three days combing the back alleys and clambering up to the castle to outpomp all castles in Mozart's hometown. You might want to hook onto a *Sound of Music* tour or whizz up to the Alps from here. Or detour to Italianate Schloss Hellbrunn or **Hallein**'s salt works.

From Salzburg, the road dips south to the most gently picturesque of the lakes in the Salzkammergut, the **Wolfgangsee**, where summertime swimming, walking and cycling are splendid. Tick off some the lesser-known towns on hikes or rides over the next few days.

From lakeside St Wolfgang or St Gilgen, it's a short bus hop to **Bad Ischl**, a cracking base for exploring other lakes in the Salzkammergut over the next three days. The most dramatic of these is the Hallstätter See, with **Hallstatt** or more laid back (but less historic) **Obertraun** perfect for overnighting. Near Obertraun, take in Dachstein's surreal ice caves on a cable-car ride and tack on a hike in the area.

Top: View over St
Wolfgang (p223)

Bottom: Schloss
Belvedere, Vienna
(p83)

DZIEWUL/SHUTTERSTOCK ©

Styria & Carinthia

This spin of the south takes you to chilled-out, culture-packed Graz, the vineyards of Styria, the astonishingly turquoise Wörthersee and many other lakes, villages and little-known trails besides.

Factor in three or four days to slip under the surface of **Graz**, Austria's friendly, easygoing second city, where space-age galleries, Renaissance courtyards and a spirited food and nightlife scene rival for your attention. On the third day, venture out along the south Styrian **wine roads**, a Tuscan-like landscape hugging the Slovenian border with vineyards at every bend.

A train takes you to Klagenfurt via **Leoben** where you can break the journey for a few hours and check out its Museums-Centre Leoben. The remaining five days can be divided between **Klagenfurt** and **Wörthersee**, **Villach** or **Spittal an der Drau**, all towns with a sprinkling of sights and plenty of outdoor activities. Towns such as **Hermagor** in the Gail Valley have great cycling, hiking and (in winter) skiing possibilities at Nassfeld.

Tyrol

Wherever you go in Tyrol you'll be confronted by mountains. Grab your hiking boots or skis and dive into these incredible alpine valleys.

Start with a few days in laid-back **Innsbruck**. Stroll the historic Altstadt (old town), taking in its galleries, Habsburg treasures and upbeat nightlife, or take the futuristic funicular to the Nordkette. From Innsbruck, go south for scenic skiing in the **Stubai Glacier** or west to the exquisite baroque abbey in **Stams**.

On day five head to the spectacularly rugged **Ötztal**, where you can dip into pre-history at Ötzi Dorf and thermal waters at Aqua Dome spa. Spend the next couple of days rafting near **Landeck**, exploring the Rosengartenschlucht gorge at **Imst**, or hiking and skiing in **St Anton am Arlberg**.

In week two, return to Innsbruck and swing east. Factor in a day for the pristine medieval town of **Hall**, and the crystal-studded Swarovski Kristallwelten in **Wattens**. The alpine scenery of the **Zillertal** will have you itching to head outdoors. Round out at fortress-topped **Kufstein** and the legendary mountains of **Kitzbühel**.

Plan Your Trip
Skiing & Snowboarding

No matter whether you're a slalom expert, a fearless free rider or a beginner, there's a slope with your name on it in Austria. And, oh, what slopes! Granted, the Swiss and French Alps may have the height edge, but Austria remains Europe's best skiing all-rounder. This land is the origin of modern skiing (thanks to Hannes Schneider's dashing Arlberg technique), the birthplace of Olympic legends and the spiritual home of après-ski. Here you'll find intermediate cruising, knee-trembling black runs and summertime glacier skiing – in short, powdery perfection for every taste and ability.

Best Skiing Regions

Ski Amadé (p261) Salzburgerland's Ski Amadé is Austria's biggest ski area, covering a whopping 760km of pistes in 25 resorts divided into five snow-sure regions. Among them are low-key Radstadt and family-friendly Filzmoos. Such a vast area means that truly every level is catered for: from gentle cruising on tree-lined runs to off-piste touring.

Ski Arlberg (p325) As of winter 2016/2017, thanks to zippy new cable cars linking up Lech and St Anton am Arlberg, Ski Arlberg is Austria's largest interconnected area, with 305km of slopes to pound and 87 ski lifts. It's also one of the country's most famous skiing regions. After all, this is the home of St Anton am Arlberg, a Mecca to expert skiers and boarders, with its great snow record, challenging terrain and terrific off-piste; not to mention the most happening après-ski in Austria, if not Europe.

Kitzbühel (p311) The legendary Hahnenkamm, 170km of groomed slopes, a car-free medieval town centre and upbeat nightlife all make Kitzbühel one of Austria's most popular resorts. Critics may grumble about unreliable snow – with a base elevation of 762m, Kitzbühel is fairly low

Top Slopes

Cruise, carve, party and quake in your boots at some of these top spots:

Top descents The Streif, part of the epic Hahnenkamm, is Kitzbühel's king of scary skiing. Mayrhofen's Harakiri is Austria's steepest run, with a gradient of 78%. It's pitch-black and there's no turning baaaaaack...

Top family skiing Filzmoos for its uncrowded nursery slopes, chocolate-box charm and jagged Dachstein mountains. Heiligenblut is refreshingly low-key and has a ski kindergarten.

Top snowboarding Mayrhofen is a mecca to free riders, and some say it has Austria's most *awesome* terrain park, Vans Penken.

Top après-ski Join the singing, swinging, Jägermeister-fuelled fun in St Anton am Arlberg, Austria's après-ski king. Wild inebriation and all-night clubbing are the winter norm in raucous rival Ischgl.

Top glacier skiing The Stubai Glacier has snow-sure pistes within easy reach of Innsbruck. Head to the Kitzsteinhorn Glacier for pre- and post-season skiing at 3203m, with arresting views of the snowy Hohe Tauern range.

Austria Outdoors

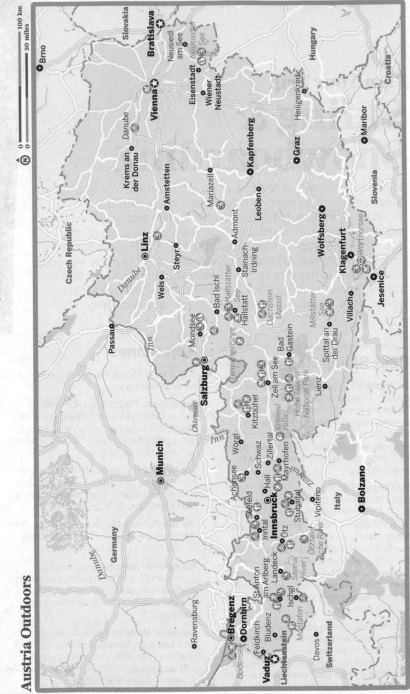

by alpine standards – but that doesn't stop skiers who come for the varied downhill, snowboarding and off-piste.

Zillertal Arena (p308) Mayrhofen is the showpiece of the Zillertal Arena, with 143km of slopes. As well as being intermediate heaven, Mayrhofen has Austria's steepest black run, the kamikaze-like Harakiri with a 78% gradient, and appeals to freestylers for its fantastic terrain park. Even if snow lies thin in the valley, it's guaranteed at the nearby Hintertux Glacier.

Zell am See–Kaprun (p257) The lakeside resort of Zell am See and its twin Kaprun share 138km of sunny slopes. Pistes tend to be more of the tree-lined and scenic kind, making this a sound choice for novices and families. Even if the snow coverage is thin on the lower slopes, there's fresh powder and a terrain park at the Kitzsteinhorn Glacier to play in. The après-ski in Zell am See's car-free old town is lively but not rowdy. The entire region affords gorgeous views of the glacier-capped Hohe Tauern range.

Silvretta-Montafon (http://winter.silvretta-montafon.at; Vorarlberg; 1-/2-day pass €39/78) The iconic arrow-shaped peak of Piz Buin (3312m) dominates the Silvretta-Montafon ski area. Tucked away in the southeast corner of Vorarlberg, this serene and beautiful valley's low-key resorts appeal to families, cruisers and ski tourers. Besides 246km of slopes to play on, there is off-piste fun from sledding to winter hiking.

Silvretta Arena (p323) Ischgl is the centrepiece of the Silvretta Arena, comprising 238km of prepared slopes and 71 ultramodern lifts. High slopes above 2000m mean guaranteed snow, mostly geared towards confident intermediates, off-piste fans and boarders. The resort has carved a name for itself as a party hot spot, with big-name season opening and closing concerts, and pumping (borderline sleazy) après-ski. For those seeking a quieter vibe, Galtür, Kappl and Samnaun (Switzerland) are nearby.

Sölden (p318) The Ötztal is defined by some of the wildest and highest mountains in Austria. Its main ski resort is snow-sure Sölden, with 145km of slopes between 1350m and 3340m, a state-of-the-art lift network and a crazy après-ski scene. The terrain is intermediate heaven, but presents more of a challenge on long runs such as the 50km Big 3 Rally and off-piste. A bonus to skiing here is the snow reliability on two glaciers – Rettenbach and Tiefenbach – making this a great pre- or late-season choice.

Ski-Run Classifications

Piste maps are available on most tourist office websites and at the valley stations of ski lifts; runs are colour-coded according to difficulty as follows:

➡ **Blue** Indicates easy, well-groomed runs that are suitable for beginners.

➡ **Red** Indicates intermediate runs, which are groomed but often steeper and narrower than blue runs. Skiers should have a medium level of ability.

➡ **Black** For expert skiers with polished technique and skills. The runs are mostly steep, not always groomed and may have moguls and steep vertical drops.

Lift Passes

Costing around €250 or thereabouts for a week, lift passes are a big chunk out of your budget. The passes give access to one or more ski sectors and nearly always include ski buses between the different areas. Lift passes for lesser-known places may be as little as half that charged in the jet-set resorts. Count on around €35 to €50 for a one-day ski pass, with substantial reductions for longer-term passes. Children usually pay half-price, while under-fives ski for free (bring a passport as proof of age).

Most lift passes are now 'hands-free', with a built-in chip that barriers detect automatically, and many can be prebooked online.

SLOPE SAVERS
· ·

It's worth checking websites such as www.igluski.com, www.skiingaustria.co.uk, www.ifyouski.com and www.j2ski.com for last-minute ski deals and packages. Local tourist offices and www.austria.info might also have offers.

You can save time and euros by prebooking ski and snowboard hire online at Snowbrainer (www.snowbrainer.com), which gives a discount of up to 50% on shop rental prices.

BORIS-B/SHUTTERSTOCK ©

Top: Skiing at St Anton am Arlberg (p324)

Bottom: Street scene, St Anton am Arlberg (p324)

Safety

➡ Avalanches are a serious danger in snowbound areas and can be fatal.

➡ If you're skiing off-piste, never go alone and take an avalanche pole (a collapsible pole used to determine the location of an avalanche victim), a transceiver and a shovel and – most importantly – a professional guide.

➡ See www.lawine.at (in German) for the avalanche risk and snow coverage by region.

➡ UV rays are stronger at high altitudes and intensified by snow glare; wear ski goggles and sunscreen.

➡ Get in good shape before hitting the slopes and build up gradually.

➡ Wear layers to adapt to the constant change in body temperature; make sure your head, wrists and knees are protected (preferably padded).

➡ Before you hurtle down that black run, make sure you're properly insured and read the small print: mountain-rescue costs, medical treatment and repatriation can soon amount to triple figures.

Resources

Books

Alpine Ski Mountaineering: Central and Eastern Alps (Bill O'Connor) Great guide detailing ski tours through the Silvretta, Ötztal, Stubai and Ortler ranges.

Where to Ski and Snowboard (Chris Gill and Dave Watts) Updated annually, this is an indispensable guide to the slopes, covering everything from terrain to lift passes.

Which Ski Resort – Europe: Our Top 50 Recommendations (Pat Sharples and Vanessa Webb) Written by a freestyle champ and a ski coach, this handy guide has tips on everything from off-piste to après-ski.

Websites

Bergfex (www.bergfex.com) A great website with piste maps, snow forecasts of the Alps and details of every ski resort in Austria.

If You Ski (www.ifyouski.com) Resort guides, ski deals and info on ski hire and schools.

MadDog Ski (www.maddogski.com) Entertaining ski guides and insider tips on everything from accommodation to après ski.

On the Snow (www.onthesnow.co.uk) Reviews of Austria's ski resorts, plus snow reports, webcams and lift pass details.

Where to Ski & Snowboard (www.wheretoski andsnowboard.com) Key facts on resorts, which are ranked according to their upsides and downsides, plus user reviews.

World Snowboard Guide (www.worldsnowboard guide.com) Snowboarder central, with comprehensive information on most Austrian resorts.

Equipment Hire & Tuition

Skis (downhill, cross-country, telemark), snowboards, boots, poles and helmets can be rented at sport shops like Intersport (www.intersport.at) in every resort. Ski, snowboard or cross-country ski rental costs around €28/127 per day/week, or €34/158 for top-of-the-range gear. Boot hire is around €16/61 per day/week. With Intersport, children 14 and under pay half-price, under-10s get free ski hire when both parents rent equipment, and you can ski seven days for the price of six.

Most ski resorts have one or more ski schools; for a list of regional ski schools, visit Snowsport Austria (www.snowsport austria.at). Group lessons for both adults and children typically cost €70 per day (two hours in the morning, two hours in the afternoon), €200 for four days and €260 for six days. The more days you take, the cheaper the per-day rate gets. Private instruction is available on request. Kids can start learning from the age of four.

Cross-Country Skiing & Snowshoeing

Cross-country skiing *(Langlauf)* in Austria is considerably greener and cheaper than downhill skiing – a day pass costs as little as €3 with a guest card. The two main techniques are the classic lift-and-glide method on prepared cross-country tracks *(Loipen)* and the more energetic 'skating' technique. The basics are easy to master at a cross-country school and tracks are graded from blue to black according to difficulty.

Seefeld features among Austria's top cross-country skiing destinations, with 279km of *Loipen* criss-crossing the region including a floodlit track. Zell am See is another hot spot, with 40km of groomed trails providing panoramic views of the Hohe Tauern mountains. Other great resorts to test your stamina and stride include the Bad Gastein region, with 90km of well-marked cross-country trails. To search for cross-country regions and packages, see www.langlauf-urlaub.at (in German).

Tired of the crowded slopes? Snowshoeing is a great alternative for nonskiers. On a sunny day, there's little that beats making enormous tracks through deep powder and twinkling forests in quiet exhilaration. If you imagine snowshoes as old-fashioned, tennis-racquet-like contraptions, think again: the new ones are lightweight and pretty easy to get the hang of. Many resorts in the Austrian Alps have marked trails and some offer guided tours for a small charge. It costs roughly €15 to €20 to hire a set of snowshoes and poles for the day.

Plan Your Trip
Hiking in Austria

Der Berg ruft (the mountain calls) is what Austrians say as they gallivant off to the hills at the weekend, and what shopkeepers post on closed doors in summer. And what more excuse do you need? For Austrians, Wandern (walking) is not a sport, it's second nature. Kids frolicking in alpine pastures, nuns Nordic-walking in the hills, super-fit 70-somethings trekking over windswept 2000m passes – such universal wanderlust is bound to rub off on you sooner or later. With its towering peaks, forest-cloaked slopes and luxuriantly green valleys, the country's landscapes are perfectly etched and the walking opportunities are endless. Strike into Austria's spectacularly rugged backyard, listen closely and you too will hear those mountains calling...

Walking Light

If you love long-distance hiking but find carrying a rucksack a drag, you might want to consider *Wandern ohne Gepäck* (literally 'walking without luggage'). Many regions in Austria now offer this clever scheme, where hotels transport your luggage to the next hotel for a small extra charge. Visit www.austria.info or www. wanderhotels.com for more details.

If you would prefer your Sherpa to be of the cute and woolly kind, llama trekking could be just the thing. Many towns, including Lienz in the **Dolomites** (☑0664 431 27 29; www.dolomitenlama.at; Oberlienz 36; one-day trek €60-125), now offer this family favourite. Nothing motivates kids to walk quite like these hikes, which reach from two-hour forest strolls to two-week treks on pilgrimage routes. The llamas carry your luggage and leave you free to enjoy the scenery. Contact local tourist offices for more options.

Walk Designations

Austria is criss-crossed with well-maintained *Wanderwege* (walking trails), which are waymarked with red-white-red stripes (often on a handy rock or tree) and yellow signposts. Bear in mind, though, that these are no substitute for a decent map and/or compass in the Alps. Like ski runs, trails are colour-coded according to difficulty:

Blue The blue routes (alternatively with no colour) are suitable for everyone; paths are well marked, mostly flat and easy to follow.

Red The red routes require a good level of fitness, surefootedness and basic mountain experience. They are sometimes steep and narrow, and may involve scrambling and/or short fixed-rope sections.

Black For experienced mountain hikers with a head for heights, black routes are mostly steep, require proper equipment and can be dangerous in bad weather.

HIKING EQUIPMENT CHECKLIST

Clothing
- ☐ windproof and waterproof jacket
- ☐ breathable fleece
- ☐ loose-fitting walking trousers, preferably with zip-off legs
- ☐ hiking shorts
- ☐ T-shirts or long-sleeved shirts
- ☐ socks (polypropylene)
- ☐ sun hat
- ☐ sunglasses
- ☐ swimwear (optional)

Footwear
- ☐ walking boots with a good grip
- ☐ trekking sandals or thongs
- ☐ socks

Other Equipment
- ☐ backpack or daypack
- ☐ sleeping bag
- ☐ water bottle
- ☐ map
- ☐ compass
- ☐ Swiss Army knife

For Emergencies
- ☐ emergency food rations
- ☐ first-aid kit
- ☐ torch (flashlight) with batteries and bulbs
- ☐ whistle
- ☐ mobile (cell) phone
- ☐ transceiver
- ☐ shovel
- ☐ avalanche pole

Miscellaneous Items
- ☐ camera and lenses
- ☐ umbrella
- ☐ insect repellent
- ☐ high-energy food (eg nuts, dried fruit, bread, cured meat)
- ☐ at least 1L of water per person, per day
- ☐ sunscreen (SPF30+)
- ☐ toiletries, toilet paper and towel
- ☐ stuff sacks

For Hikes above 2000m
- ☐ thermal underwear
- ☐ extra clothing
- ☐ gaiters
- ☐ gloves
- ☐ warm hat
- ☐ walking sticks

ÖAV Membership

Before you hit the trail in the Austrian Alps, you might want to consider becoming a member of the **Österreichischer Alpenverein** (ÖAV, Austrian Alpine Club; www.alpenverein.at). Adult membership costs €55.50 per year and there are significant discounts for students and people aged under 25 or over 61. Membership gets you discounts of up to 50% at Austrian (ÖAV) and German (DAV) alpine huts, plus other benefits including insurance, workshops, access to climbing walls countrywide and discounts on maps. The club also organises walks. There is an arm of the club in England, the Austrian Alpine Club (www.aacuk.org.uk). You should allow at least two months for your application to be processed.

Of the 1000-odd huts in the Austrian Alps, 241 are maintained by the ÖAV.

Weather

If there's one rule of thumb in the Austrian Alps, it's to never take the weather for granted. It may *look* sunny but conditions can change at the drop of a hat – hail, lightning, fog, torrential rain, you name it. Check the forecast before embarking on long hikes at high altitudes. Tourist offices also display and/or provide mountain-weather forecasts.

Österreichischer Alpenverein (www.alpenverein.at) A reliable web source for forecasts for the alpine regions.

Snow Forecast (www.snow-forecast.com) Up-to-date snow forecasts for major Austrian ski resorts.

Wetter Österreich (www.wetter.at) Day and three-day weather forecasts, plus up-to-date weather warnings.

Top: Hiking in the Hohe
Tauern National Park
(p256)

Bottom: Llama
trekking near Lienz
(p287)

NORBERT EISELE-HEIN/GETTY IMAGES ©

TOP FIVE LONG-DISTANCE HIKES

NAME	START	FINISH	DISTANCE	DURATION
Adlerweg	St Johann in Tyrol near Kitzbühel	St Anton am Arlberg	300km	3-4 weeks
Arnoweg	Salzburg	Salzburg	1200km	2 months
Berliner Höhenweg	Finkenberg near Mayrhofen	Mayrhofen	70km	8 days
Salzburger Almenweg	Pfarrwerfen near Werfen	Pfarrwerfen	350km	1 month
Stubai Höhenweg	Neustift im Stubaital	Neustift im Stubaital	120km	8 days

Safety

Most walker injuries are directly attributable to fatigue, heat exhaustion and inadequate clothing or footwear. Falling as a result of sliding on grass, scree or iced-over paths is a common hazard; watch out for black ice. On high-alpine routes, avalanches and rock falls can be a problem. A few common-sense rules will help you stay safe when walking:

➧ Always stick to the marked and/or signposted route, particularly in foggy conditions. With some care, most walking routes can be followed in fog, but otherwise wait by the path until visibility is clear enough to proceed.

➧ Study the weather forecast before you go and remember that weather patterns change suddenly in the mountains.

➧ Increase the length and elevation of your walks gradually, until you are acclimatised to the vast alpine scale; this will help prevent altitude sickness and fatigue.

➧ Where possible, don't walk in the mountains alone. Two is considered the minimum number for safe walking, and having at least one additional person in the party will mean someone can stay with an injured walker while the other seeks help.

➧ Inform a responsible person, such as a family member, hut warden or hotel receptionist, of your plans, and let them know when you return.

Resources

Books

Consider investing in a dedicated walking guide if you're planning on doing a lot of hiking. Here are a few to get you started:

100 Mountain Walks in Austria (Kev Reynolds, Cicerone) A useful guide, listing more than 100 walks in 10 regions (mostly in the Alps).

Alpine Flowers-Alpenblumen (NF 1300; Kompass) Become well-versed in the local flora with this handy pocket guide complete with colour illustrations.

Walking Austria's Alps Hut to Hut (Jonathan Hurdle) An informative and inspirational guide covering multiday routes and Austria's alpine huts.

Walking Easy in the Swiss & Austrian Alps (Chet Lipton) Covers gentle two- to six-hour hikes in the most popular areas.

Walking in Austria (Kev Reynolds, Cicerone) Gives the inside scoop on 102 routes, from day walks to multiday, hut-to-hut hikes.

LEVEL	HIGHLIGHTS	RESOURCES
moderate	Classic alpine landscapes from the Kaisergebirge's limestone peaks to the Arlberg region's rugged mountainscapes	See www.adlerweg.tirol.at for maps, brochures and route descriptions
demanding	Epic circular tour of the Austrian Alps, taking in gorges, valleys and Hohe Tauern National Park's glacial landscapes	Rother's walking guide to Arnoweg covers the trail in detail, or see www.arnoweg.com
demanding	High-alpine, hut-to-hut route taking in the beautiful lakes, glaciers and mountains of the Zillertal Alps	See www.naturpark-zillertal.at for a detailed route description in German; Alpenvereinskarte 1:25,000 map No 35 *Zillertaler Alpen* covers the route
moderate	A hut-to-hut route taking in Salzburgerland's fertile *Almen* (alpine pastures), karst scenery and the eternally ice-capped peaks of Hohe Tauern	See www.salzburger-almenweg.at for detailed route descriptions, maps and a virtual tour
moderate-demanding	A classic circular hut-to-hut route passing glaciers, rocky peaks and wild alpine lakes	Download maps and route descriptions at www.stubaier-hoehenweg.at; Cicerone's *Trekking in the Stubai Alps* is a reliable guide

Websites

Get planning with the routes, maps and GPS downloads on the following websites:

Bergfex (www.bergfex.com) Plan your dream hike with detailed route descriptions (many are in German) and maps, searchable by region, fitness level and length. Free GPS downloads.

Austria Info (www.austria.info) Excellent information on walking in Austria, from themed day hikes to long-distance treks. Also has details on national parks and nature reserves, hiking villages and special walking packages. Region-specific brochures are available for downloading.

Naturfreunde Österreich (NFÖ, Friends of Nature Austria; www.naturfreunde.at) Hundreds of walking routes, walk descriptions, maps and GPS downloads, including Nordic walking and snowshoeing routes. Also information on NFÖ huts, tips on mountain safety and up-to-date weather reports.

Österreichischer Alpenverein (www.alpenverein.at) Search for alpine huts and find information on events, tours, hiking villages and conservation. There's a section on the country's 10 *Weitwanderwege* (long-distance trails), which stretch from 430km to 1400km and showcase different areas of Austria's stunning landscape.

Maps

The best place to stock up on maps is a *Tabak* (tobacconist), newsagent or bookshop. Usually they only have local maps, although bookshops in the major cities offer a wider selection. Outdoor-activities shops usually sell a limited variety of walking maps. Many local tourist offices hand out basic maps that may be sufficient for short, easy walks.

A great overview map of Austria is Michelin's 1:400,000 national map No 730 *Austria*. Alternatively, the ANTO (www.austria.info) can send you a free copy of its 1:800,000 country map. Visit www.austrianmap.at for a zoomable topographic country map. The following high-quality walking maps can be purchased online:

Freytag & Berndt (www.freytagberndt.at) Publishes a wide selection of reliable 1:50,000-scale walking maps.

Kompass (www.kompass.at) Has a good series of 1:50,000 walking maps and includes a small booklet with contact details for mountain huts and background information on trails.

ÖAV (www.alpenverein.at) Produces large-scale (1:25,000) walking maps that are clear, detailed and accurate.

SOS SIX

The standard alpine distress signal is six whistles, six calls, six smoke puffs, six yodels – that is, six of whatever sign or sound you can make – repeated every 10 seconds for one minute. If you have a mobile phone, make sure you take it with you. Mountain rescue, reached by calling ☎140, in the Alps is very efficient but extremely expensive, so make sure you have adequate insurance (read the fine print).

Regions

In a land where even the tiniest of villages can have scores of fabulous walks, the question is not *where* you can walk in Austria, but *how*. For purists, that means the high-alpine trails which dominate in the mountainous west of the country, but lowland areas such as the vine-strewn Wachau can be just as atmospheric. Tourist offices are usually well armed with brochures, maps and information on local guides.

In summer, lots of places run themed guided hikes, which are sometimes free with a guest card; for instance in Innsbruck and Kitzbühel. Other regions such as Hohe Tauern National Park and Naturpark Zillertaler Alpen charge a small fee (usually around €5). The walks can range from herb trails to wildlife spotting, half-day hikes to photo excursions.

Accommodation

Hiking Hotels

Gone are the days when hiking meant a clammy tent and week-old socks. Austria has seriously upped the ante in comfort with its so-called *Wanderhotels* (hiking hotels). These hotels are run by walking specialists who offer guided walks from leisurely strolls to high-alpine hikes, help you map out your route and have equipment (eg poles, flasks and rucksacks) available

for hire. Most establishments are family-run, serve up regional cuisine and have a sauna or whirlpool where you can rest your weary feet. See www.wanderhotels.com for something to suit every taste and pocket, from farmstays to plush spa hotels.

Going a step further is Austria's Wanderdörfe (www.wanderdoerfer.at), a countrywide network of 44 hiker-friendly villages and regions. Here, you can expect well-marked short- and long-distance walks, beautiful scenery and alpine huts, good infrastructure (eg trains and/or hiking buses) and hosts geared up for walkers. You can order a free brochure online.

Hut-to-Hut Hiking

One of the joys of hiking in Austria is spending the night in a mountain hut. These trailside refuges give you the freedom to tackle multiday treks in the Alps with no more than a daypack. The highly evolved system means you're hardly ever further than a five- to six-hour walk from the next hut, so there's no need to lug a tent, camping stove and other gear that weighs hikers down. Huts generally open from mid-June to mid-September, when the trails are free of snow; the busiest months are July and August, when advance bookings are highly recommended. Consult the ÖAV (www.alpenverein.at) for hut contact details and opening times.

Accommodation is in multibed dorms called *Matratzenlager*, or in the *Notlager* (emergency shelter – wherever there's space) if all beds have been taken. Blankets and pillows are provided but you might need to bring your own sleeping sheet. In popular areas, huts are more like mountain inns, with drying rooms and even hot showers (normally at an extra charge).

Most huts have a convivial *Gaststube* (common room), where you can socialise and compare trekking tales over drinks and a bite to eat. ÖAV members can order the *Bergsteigeressen* – literally 'mountaineer's meal' – which is low in price but high in calories, though not necessarily a gastronomic treat! It's worth bringing your own tea or coffee, as *Teewasser* (boiled water) can be purchased from the hut warden.

Top Hikes

Grab your rucksack and get out and stride on the following trails:

➡ **Top day hikes** The Zillertal Circuit is especially beautiful in early summer, when the alpine roses are in bloom. A moderately challenging hike in the Silvretta Alps is the Radsattel Circuit, taking in glaciers, jewel-coloured lakes and the iconic peak of Piz Buin.

➡ **Top high-alpine hike** A classic high-level trail is the Pinzgauer Spaziergang, affording mesmerising views of the snowcapped Hohe Tauern and Kitzbühel Alps with little real effort.

➡ **Top short hike** Take a photogenic forest stroll for close-ups of the 380m-high Krimmler Wasserfälle (p267), Europe's highest waterfall. The Rosengartenschlucht Circuit is an easygoing hike through Imst's dramatic gorge.

➡ **Top kid-friendly hike** Kids in tow? Rent a gentle-natured llama for the day to explore the rugged splendour of the Dolomites near Lienz. Or skip up to a meadow hut from the shores of Weissensee in Carinthia.

For a map of top hiking regions, see p34.

WALK DESCRIPTIONS IN THIS GUIDE

➡ The times and distances for walks are provided only as a guide.

➡ Times are based on the actual walking time and do not include stops for snacks, taking photos, rests or side trips. Be sure to factor these in when planning your walk.

➡ Distances should be read in conjunction with altitudes – significant elevation can make a greater difference to your walking time than lateral distance.

Plan Your Trip
Cycling & Adventure Sports

Austria is one of Europe's most bike-friendly lands. It is interlaced with well-marked cycling trails that showcase the mountains, valleys and cities from their best angles. Whether you want to test your stamina on hairpin bends and leg-aching mountain passes, blaze downhill on a mountain bike in the Alps, or freewheel leisurely around the country's glorious lakes, Austria has routes that will take your breath away.

Transporting Bikes

Look for the bike symbol at the top of timetables or on the ÖBB website (www.oebb.at) to find trains where you can take your bike. Bike tickets within Austria cost 10% of the full ticket price, while for international routes they cost €12.

Many of Austria's leading resorts have cottoned onto the popularity of downhill mountain biking and now allow cyclists to take their bikes on the cable cars for free or for a nominal charge in summer, allowing you to enjoy the downhill rush without the uphill slog!

Accommodation

Throughout Austria you'll find hotels and pensions (guesthouses) geared up for cyclists, particularly in the Alps. So-called *Radhotels* go a step further with everything from storage facilities to bike repairs and staff well informed on local routes. You can browse for bike-friendly hotels by region on www.bike-holidays.com and www.radtouren.at. Local tourist offices can also point you in the right direction and sometimes offer special packages.

For a map of top cycling regions, see p34.

When to Go

Warmer temperatures from May to October beckon cyclists, while downhill mountain bikers head to the Alps from late June to mid-September. Snow rules out cycling at higher elevations in winter, but this can be a quiet time to explore Austria's low-lying valleys. Pedalling up alpine passes in July and August can be a hot, tiring, thirsty business; take ample sunscreen and water, and factor in time for breaks.

Cycling & Mountain Biking

Websites

Radtouren (www.radtouren.at) An excellent site listing Austria's major cycling routes and hotels.

Radfahren (www.radfahren.at) Easy-to-navigate website with descriptions on cycling trails (including long-distance routes), bike-friendly hotels, bike rental and transport throughout Austria. Has interactive maps.

Bike Holidays (www.bike-holidays.at) Search by region for mountain-bike (MTB) trails, cycling routes, free-ride parks and bike hotels in Austria.

Biken (http://bike-holidays.at) Handy source for information on cycling and mountain biking in Salzkammergut and Upper Austria. You can order free brochures including *Cycling Country Austria*.

Maps & Guides

Local tourist offices usually stock brochures and maps on cycling and mountain biking. Cycle clubs are another good source of information. For more detailed maps and guides try the following:

Kompass (www.kompass.at) For cycle tour maps at scales between 1:125,000 and 1:50,000. Covers long-distance routes well, including those along the Bodensee, Danube and Inntal.

Esterbauer (www.esterbauer.com) Produces the Bikeline series of cycling and mountain-biking maps and guides, which give comprehensive coverage of Austria's major trails.

Freytag & Berndt (www.freytagberndt.at) Stocks a good selection of cycling maps and produces the Austria Cycling Atlas detailing 160 day tours.

Rentals

City and mountain bikes are available for hire in most Austrian towns and resorts. Intersport (www.intersport.at) has a near monopoly on rental equipment, offering a selection of quality bikes in 260 stores throughout Austria. Day rates range from around €18 for standard bikes to €25 for e-bikes (electric bikes). All prices include bicycle helmets and there's a 50% reduction on children's bikes. Those who want to plan their route ahead can search by region and reserve a bike online.

Cycling Routes

There's more to cycling in Austria than the exhilarating extremes of the Alps, as you'll discover pedalling through little-explored countryside with the breeze in your hair and the chain singing. There are plenty of silky-smooth cycling trails that avoid the slog without sacrificing the grandeur; many of them circumnavigate lakes or shadow rivers.

Danube Cycle Path Shadowing the mighty Danube for 380km from Passau to Bratislava, this cycle route takes in some lyrical landscapes.

WESTEND61/GETTY IMAGES ©

Cycling in Tyrol (p302)

Wending its way through woodlands, deep valleys and orchards, the trail is marked by green-and-white signs on both sides of the river. Esterbauer's Bikeline *Danube Bike Trail* is useful for maps and route descriptions. See www.donauradweg.at (in German) for details on the route and an interactive map, and www.donau-radweg.info for tours.

Inn Trail Starting in Innsbruck and travelling 302km through Austria to Schärding, the Inn Trail (www.innregionen.com) sticks close to the turquoise Inn River. It's basically downhill all the way, passing through fertile farmland, alpine valleys and castle-topped towns in Tyrol, Bavaria and Upper Austria. The final stretch zips through bucolic villages and countryside to Schärding. The route is well marked, but signage varies between regions.

Bodensee Cycle Path Touching base with Bregenz in Vorarlberg, this 270km cycleway encircles the Bodensee (Lake Constance), Europe's third-largest lake. Marked with red-and-white signs, the mostly easygoing trail zips through Austria, Germany and Switzerland, passing through woodlands, marshes, orchards, vineyards and historic towns. Come in early autumn for fewer crowds, new wine and views of the Alps on clear days. Visit www.bodensee-radweg.com for details.

GPS FREEWHEELING

It's easier to navigate Austria's back-country and find little-known bike trails with a GPS tour. Check www.bike-gps.com for downloadable cycling and mountain-biking tours. Alternatively, head to www.gps-tour.info for hundreds of tours in Austria.

Salzkammergut Trail This 345km circular trail explores the pristine alpine lakes of the Salz-kammergut, including Hallstätter See, Attersee and Wolfgangsee. Though not exactly flat, the trail is well signposted (R2) and only moder-ate fitness is required. To explore in greater depth, pick up Esterbauer's Bikeline *Radatlas Salzkammergut*.

Tauern Trail Rolling through some of Austria's most spectacular alpine scenery on the fringes of the Hohe Tauern National Park, the 310km Tauern Trail is not technically difficult, but cycling at high altitude requires stamina. It begins at Krimml, then snakes along the Salzach River to Salzburg, then further onto the Saalach Valley and Passau. The trail is marked with green-and-white signs in both directions. For maps and GPS tracks, see www.tauernradweg.com.

Mountain Biking

The Austrian Alps are an MTB (mountain biking) Mecca, with hairpin bends, back-breaking inclines and heart-pumping descents. The country is crisscrossed with mountain-bike routes, with the most chal-lenging terrain in Tyrol, Salzburgerland, Vorarlberg and Carinthia. Following is a sample of the tours and regions that at-tract two-wheeled speed demons.

Dachstein Tour Hailed as one of the country's top mountain-bike routes, this three-day tour circles the rugged limestone pinnacles of the Dachstein massif and blazes through three provinces: Salzburgerland, Upper Austria and Styria. You'll need a good level of fitness to tackle the 182km trail that starts and finishes in Bad Goisern, paus-ing en route near Filzmoos. For details, see www.dachsteinrunde.at.

Salzburger Almentour On this 146km trail, bikers pedal through 30 *Almen* (mountain pastures) in three days. While the name conjures up visions of gentle meadows, the route involves some strenu-ous climbs up to tremendous viewpoints like Zwölferhorn peak. Green-and-white signs indicate the trail from Annaberg to Edtalm via Wolfgang-see. Route details and highlights are given online (www.almentour.com, in German).

Silvretta Mountain Bike Arena Sidling up to Switzerland, the Silvretta Mountain Bike Arena in the Patznauntal is among the biggest in the Alps, with 1000km of trails, some climbing to almost 3000m. Ischgl makes an excellent base, with a technique park and plenty of trail information available at the tourist office. The 15 free-ride trails for speed freaks include the Velill Trail, involving 1300m of descent. Tour details are available at www.silvretta-bikeacademy.at, in German.

Kitzbühel Covering 800km of mountain bike trails, the Kitzbühel region ranks as one of Austria's top freewheeling spots. Routes range from 700m to 2300m in elevation and encompass trial circuits, downhill runs and bike parks. The must-experience rides include the Hahnenkamm Bike Safari from Kitzbühel to Pass Thurn, affording far-reaching views of Grossglockner and Wilder Kaiser.

Stubaital & Zillertal These two broad valleys running south from the Inn River in Tyrol are flanked by high peaks crisscrossed with 800km of mountain bike trails. The terrain is varied and the landscape splendid, with gorges, waterfalls and glaciers constantly drifting into view. Highlights include the alpine route from Mayrhofen to Hin-tertux Glacier and the dizzying roads that twist up from Ginzling to the Schlegeisspeicher.

Adventure Sports
Rock Climbing & Via Ferrate

Synonymous with mountaineering legends like Peter Habeler and South Tyrolean Reinhold Messner, Austria is a summer-time paradise for ardent *Kletterer* (rock climbers). In the Alps there's a multitude of climbs ranking all grades of difficulty. Equipment rental (around €10) and guided tours are widely available.

If you are not quite ready to tackle the three-thousanders yet, nearly every major resort in the Austrian Alps now has a *Klettersteig* (via ferrata). These fixed-rope routes, often involving vertical ladders, ziplines and bridges, are great for getting a feel for climbing; all you'll need is a har-ness, helmet and a head for heights.

Top: Climbing in the Alps

Bottom: Kayaking in Salzburgerland (p250)

Resources

Bergsteigen (www.bergsteigen.at) Search by region or difficulty for climbing routes, via ferrate and ice-climbing walls.

ÖAV (www.alpenverein.at) Official website of the Austrian Alpine Club, with a dedicated page on climbing (in German).

Rock Climbing (www.rockclimbing.com) Gives details on more than 1000 climbing tours in Austria, many with climbing grades and photos.

Regions

For serious mountaineers, the ascent of Grossglockner (3798m), Austria's highest peak, is the climb of a lifetime. Professional guides can take you up into the wild heights of the Hohe Tauern National Park, a veritable climbing nirvana.

Sheer granite cliffs, bizarre rock formations and boulders make the Zillertal Alps another hot spot, particularly Ginzling and Mayrhofen.

Other climbing magnets include Pelstein in Lower Austria, the limestone peaks of the Dachstein and the Tennengebirge in Salzburgerland.

Water Sports

Austria may be landlocked but it offers plenty of watery action on its lakes and rivers in summer. You can windsurf on Neusiedler See, white-water raft in Tyrol or scuba dive in Wörthersee. Zipping across lakes by wind power is the most popular water sport in the country, and if Olympic medals are anything to go by, the locals aren't bad at it either.

Rafting & Canoeing

Rafting, canoeing or kayaking the swirling white waters of Austria's alpine rivers are much-loved summertime escapades. Big rivers that support these fast-paced sports include the Enns and Salza in Styria; the Inn, Sanna and Ötztaler Ache in Tyrol; and the Isel in East Tyrol. Tours start from around €30 and usually include transport and equipment.

Well-known rafting centres include Landeck, Innsbruck for adventures on the Inn, Zell am Ziller and St Anton am Arlberg.

Windsurfing & Sailing

Sailing, windsurfing and kitesurfing are all extremely popular pursuits on Austria's lakes.

Close to Vienna lies Neusiedler See, one of the few steppe lakes in Central Europe and the number-one place for windsurfing and kitesurfing thanks to its stiff winds. It hosts a heat of the Surf World Cup from late April to early May.

St Gilgen and Mondsee in Salzkammergut are highly scenic lakes for water sports; the latter harbours Austria's largest sailing school. Millstätter See in Carinthia, Achensee in Tyrol and the vast Bodensee in Vorarlberg are other popular spots to set sail.

Österreichischer Segelverband (Austrian Sailing Federation; www.segelverband.at) Can provide a list of clubs and locations in the country.

Kitesurfing (www.kitesurfing.at) For the lowdown on kitesurfing on Neusiedler See.

Swimming & Diving

Bath-warm or invigoratingly cold? Alpine or palm-fringed? Much of Austria is pristine lake country and there are scores to choose from. Carinthia is famed for its pure waters, which can heat up to a pleasantly warm 28°C in summer; Millstätter See and Wörthersee offer open-water swimming and scuba diving with great visibility. You can also make a splash in lakes such as Hallstätter See and Attersee in Salzkammergut, and Bodensee in Vorarlberg.

On the Beach

There's no sea for miles, but nearly all of Austria's major lakes are fringed with *Strandbäder* (lidos) for an invigorating dip, many of which have beaches, outdoor pools and barbecue areas. Some are free, while others charge a nominal fee of around €4 per day. If you dare to bare all, *FKK* (nudist) beaches, including those at Hard (p334) on Bodensee, Hallstätter See, Milstätter See and even the Donauinsel (p89) in Vienna, welcome skinny-dippers.

Paragliding

Wherever there's a mountain and a steady breeze, you'll find paragliding and hanggliding in Austria. On a bright day in the Alps, look up to see the sky dotted with people catching thermals to soar above peaks and forests. In many alpine resorts, you can hire the gear, get a lesson or go as a passenger on a tandem flight; prices for the latter start at around €100. Most people fly in summer, but a crystal-clear winter's day can be equally beautiful.

Tyrol is traditionally a centre for paragliding, with narrow valleys and plenty of cable cars. A good place to head is Zell am Ziller. Another scenic paragliding base is Zell am See in the rugged Hohe Tauern National Park.

Find the best place to spread your wings at www.flugschulen.at, which gives a regional rundown of flight schools offering paragliding and hang-gliding.

Canyoning

For a buzz, little beats scrambling down a ravine and abseiling down a waterfall while canyoning. This wet, wild sport has become one of the most popular activities in the Austrian Alps. Guided tours costing between €50 and €80 for half a day abound. Most companies provide all the gear you need, but you'll need to bring swimwear, sturdy shoes, a towel and a head for heights. A good level of fitness is also recommended.

Top locations for canyoning include Mayrhofen in the Zillertal, the Ötztal and Lienz.

Plan Your Trip
Eat & Drink Like a Local

Schnitzel with noodles may have been Maria's favourite, but there's way more to Austrian food nowadays thanks to a generation of new-wave chefs adding a pinch of imagination to seasonal, locally grown ingredients. Worldly markets, well-stocked wineries and a rising taste for organic, foraged flavours are all making Austria a culinary destination to watch.

The Year in Food

Spring (Mar–May)

Chefs add springtime oomph to dishes with *Spargel* (asparagus) and *Bärlauch* (wild garlic). *Maibock* (strong beer) is rolled out for beer festivals in May.

Summer (Jun–Aug)

It's time for *Marille* (apricot) madness in the Wachau, touring dairies in Tyrol and the Bregenzerwald and eating freshwater fish by lake shores. Bludenz reaches melting point in July with its Milka Chocolate Festival. Every village gets into the summer groove with beer festivals and thigh-slapping folk music.

Autumn (Sep–Nov)

Misty autumn days dish up a forest feast of mushrooms and game and *Sturm* (young wine) brings fizz to *Heuriger* (tavern) tables. Sip new *Most* (perry and cider) in the Mostviertel's orchards. Goose lands on tables for St Martin's Day (11 November).

Winter (Dec–Feb)

Try *Vanillekipferl* (crescent-shaped biscuits) and mulled wine at twinkling Christmas markets. Vienna's coffee houses are the perfect winter warmer.

Food Experiences

Though Austria can't be put on the same culinary pedestal as France or Italy, food is still likely to be integral to your travels here: whether you're sipping tangy cider in the apple orchards of the Mostviertel, sampling creamy alpine cheeses in the Bregenzerwald or eating local fish on the shores of the Salzkammergut's looking-glass lakes.

Meals of a Lifetime

➡ **Esszimmer** (p245) Andreas Kaiblinger works culinary magic with market-fresh ingredients at this Michelin-starred number in Salzburg.

➡ **Obauer** (p253) The Obauer brothers believe in careful sourcing at this address of foodist rigour in the Alps.

➡ **Mayer's** (p260) Michelin-starred dining with a dash of romance at this lakefront palace in Zell am See.

➡ **Die Wilderin** (p299) A welcome addition to Innsbruck with foraged flavours, occasional live jazz and a bistro buzz.

➡ **Waldgasthaus Triendlsäge** (p317) Hop in a horse-drawn sleigh to reach this woody winter wonderland of a restaurant, hidden in the forest above Seefeld.

➡ **Meierei im Stadtpark** (p105) Lots of style, a bright ambience and Vienna's finest goulash.

➡ **Schulhaus** (p306) Once a school house, now a hilltop restaurant in Tyrol's Zillertal, with farm-fresh ingredients and big Alpine views.

➡ **Hermagorer Bodenalm** (p286) Still a rustic hunger and thirst with a *Brettljause* (cold platter) at this alpine meadow hut above Weissensee.

➡ **Aiola Upstairs** (p188) Good food enjoyed with a sensational view over Graz's historic centre.

Cheap Treats

It's not all about fine dining: some of your most memorable food experiences are likely to be on the hoof. Vienna's *Würstelstände* (sausage stands) are the stuff of snack legend, but there's more to street food here. Falafel, bagels, organic burgers, healthy wraps, salads and sushi to-go – you'll find it all in the mix in Austria's worldly cities.

On almost every high street there is a *Bäckerei* (bakery), where you can grab a freshly made roll, and a *Konditorei* for a pastry or oven-fresh *Krapfen* (doughnut). Many *Metzgereien* (butchers) have stand-up counters where you can sink your teeth into a wurst, schnitzel or *Leberkässemmel* (meatloaf roll), often with change from €5.

Top Five Snack Spots

➡ **Bitzinger Würstelstand am Albertinaplatz** (p102) Join opera-goers and late-night nibblers to bite into a cheesy *Käsekrainer* or spicy *Bosna* bratwurst at the king of Vienna's sausage stands.

➡ **Kröll** (Map p298; Hofgasse 6; strudel slice €3.70; ⊗6am-9pm) Strudels sweet and savoury at this busy-as-a-beehive cafe in Innsbruck's Altstadt.

➡ **Yppenplatz 4** (p105) Does excellent organic *Würstel* produced by nearby Ottakringer brewery, along with freshly cooked crisps, right in the middle of the marketplace.

➡ **Cafesito** (p334) Pair deliciously chewy bagels with smoothies and fair-trade coffee at this boho cafe in Bregenz.

➡ **IceZeit** (p243) Salzburg's best ice cream. Enough said.

Dare to Try

➡ **Graukäse** The Zillertal's grey, mouldy, sour-milk cheese is tastier than it sounds, honest!

➡ **Käsekrainer** A fat cheese-filled sausage, way off the calorie-counting Richter scale. It's a popular wee-hour, beer-mopping snack at Vienna's sausage stands.

➡ **Leberknödelsuppe** Dig into liver dumpling soup, the starter that gets meals off to a hearty kick all over Austria.

➡ **Rindfleischsulz** Jellied beef brawn, often drizzled in pumpkin-seed oil vinaigrette.

➡ **Schnecken** *Escargots* to the French, snails to English speakers, these gastropods are slithering onto many of the top menus in the country.

➡ **Waldviertel Mohn** Poppy dumplings, desserts, strudels and noodles add a floral addition to menus in the Waldviertel.

➡ **Zillertaler Bauernschmaus** We dare you to try this farmer's feast of cold cuts, sauerkraut and dumplings. Not because of the ingredients, but because pronouncing it will surely get your tongue in a twist!

Local Specialities

Locavore is huge in Austria, where locals take genuine pride in their home-grown produce. Bright and early Saturday morning, you'll see them combing farmers markets, baskets and jute bags in hand, for whatever is seasonal. It's as much a matter of ethics as taste: Austrians believe firmly in supporting their farmers, cheese-makers and vintners, many going out of their way to buy organic, regionally sourced goods.

Chefs often make the most of seasonal, regional ingredients, too, and many have been quick to piggyback on the Slow Food trend (look for the snail symbol) in recent years. Piquant *Bergkäse* mountain cheese in Bregenzerwald, lake fish on the shores of Neusiedlersee, dark, nutty pumkin-seed oil in Styria and tangy Rieslings from the Wachau never taste better than at the source.

Vienna

Nothing says classic Austrian grub like the classic Wiener schnitzel, a breaded veal cutlet, often as big as a boot, which is fried to golden perfection. Imperial favourites with a Hungarian flavour – paprika-spiced *Fiakergulasch* and *Tafelspitz mit Kren* (boiled beef with horseradish) are big. Wines produced on the city's fringes are served at rustic *Heurigen* (wine taverns) with hunks of dark bread topped with creamy, spicy Liptauer fresh cheese. Regionally grown *Suppengemüse* (soup vegetables such as carrots, celery, radish and root vegetables) pop up at markets and on menus.

Vienna is naturally also king of Austria's *Kaffeehaus* (coffee house) scene.

Lower Austria

If one fruit could sum up this region, the Wachau's tiny, juicy *Marille* (apricot), made into jam, schnapps and desserts, would rise to the challenge. Spreading north of the Danube Valley, the rural Waldviertel peps up everything from pasta to desserts with poppy seeds, while the orchard-wealthy Mostviertel to the south is cider and perry country. Some of Austria's finest wines are produced in the vines that march up the hillsides here, including tangy Grüner Veltiner and riesling whites, fruity Zweigelt and medium-bodied *Blauburgunder* (Pinot noir) reds. Trout, carp and asparagus are also fished and grown locally.

Salzburg & Salzburgerland

Salzburg's *Mozartkugel* is a chocolate-coated pistachio marzipan and nougat confection that ungraciously translates as 'Mozart's Ball'. Like Upper Austrians, Salzburgers lean heavily towards noodle and dumpling dishes like cheese and onion-topped *Pinzgauer Kasnocken,* but this gives way to fish in the lakeside Salzkammergut. *Salzburger Nockerln*, the town's favourite desserts, are massive soufflé-like baked concoctions (don't even ask how many egg whites are in them!) sprinkled with icing sugar.

Burgenland

Like Lower Austria, Burgenland is one of Austria's premier wine regions, but it is also famous for its Neusiedlersee fish – species like perch-pike, pike, carp and catfish. Toss in nuts, orchard produce and ham from a species of woolly pig called the Mangalitza and the region makes for a mouth-watering trip.

Carinthia

Cheese, hams and salamis, game, lamb and beef count among the regional produce in mountainous Carinthia. Wherever there are lakes you'll also find trout and other freshwater fish on menus. On meat-free Fridays, some Carinthians dig into local pasta known as *Kärntner Nudel*, filled with potato, cheese, mint, wild parsley-like chervil, mushrooms and any number of combinations of these.

Styria

Styria is also a producer of Mangalitza ham, as well as beef locally produced from Almochsen cattle, raised in mountain meadows in the region about 30km northeast of Graz. What the visitor to Styria, however, will immediately notice is that pumpkin oil is used to dress everything from salads to meats. This healthy, dark oil has a nutty flavour and here it often stands on tables alongside the salt and pepper.

Tyrol & Vorarlberg

These two regions have one thing in common: cheese, most notably what is called locally *Heumilchkäse* (hay-milk cheese), which aficionados claim is the purest form of milk you can find. *Gröstl*, or *Gröstel* in some other regions, is a fry-up from leftovers, usually potato, pork and onions, topped with a fried egg, but there are sausage varieties and the *Innsbrucker Gröstl* or *Gröstl Kalb* has veal.

Upper Austria

With Bavaria in Germany and Bohemia in the Czech Republic just over the border, it's unsurprising that Upper Austria is one of the country's *Knödel* (dumpling) strongholds. Sweet tooth? Well, you won't want to miss *Linzer Torte*, a crumbly tart with a lattice pastry top, filled with almonds, spices and redcurrant jam.

How to Eat & Drink

When to Eat

➡ **Frühstuck (breakfast)** Austrians are the first to reel off the old adage about breakfast being the most important meal of the day. During the week, the locals may just grab a jam-spread *Semmel* (roll) and a coffee or a bowl of muesli, but at the weekend breakfast is often a leisurely, all-morning affair. A rising number of coffee houses and cafes have Sunday brunch buffets for around €15 to €20, with everything from sunny-side-up eggs to salmon, antipasti, cereals, fresh-pressed juices and *Sekt* (sparkling wine). You won't need to eat again until dinner.

➡ **Mittagessen (lunch)** Another meal locals rarely skip, lunch is often a soup or salad followed by a main course. Standard hours are 11.30am to 2.30pm.

➡ **Kaffee und Kuchen (coffee and cake)** The exception to not snacking between mealtimes is this three o'clock ritual. Indulge at a local *Konditorei* (confectioner's) or coffee house.

➡ **Apéritif** The trend for pre-dinner drinks is on the rise. The pavement terrace tipple of choice? Aperol spritz.

➡ **Abendessen (dinner)** Late-night city dining aside, Austrians tend to dine somewhat earlier than their European counterparts, with kitchens open from 7pm to 9pm or 9.30pm. Many places have a *Kleine Karte* (snack menu) outside of these hours.

Where to Eat

➡ **Beisln/Gasthäuser** Rural inns often with wood-panelled, homely interiors and menus packed with *gutbürgerliche Küche* (home cooking) – *Tafelspitz*, schnitzel, goulash and the like.

➡ **Brauereien** Many microbreweries and brewpubs serve meaty grub, too. Their beer gardens are popular gathering spots in summer.

➡ **Cafes** These can range from bakery-cafes for a quick coffee and sandwich to all-organic delis and Eiscafés, or ice-cream parlours.

➡ **Heurigen** Going strong since medieval times, Austria's cosy wine taverns are often identified by a *Busch'n* (green wreath or branch) hanging over the door.

➡ **Imbiss** Any kind of snack or takeaway joint, the most famous being the Würstelstand (sausage stand).

➡ **Kaffeehäuser** Vienna's 'living rooms' are not only famous for their delectable tortes, cakes and arm-long coffee menus. Many also serve inexpensive breakfasts, lunches and snacks around the clock.

➡ **Konditoreien** Traditional cake shop cafes; many do a sideline in confectionery.

➡ **Neo-Beisln** New-wave Beisln often with retro-cool decor and a creative, market-fresh take on Austrian classics. Typically found in the cities (especially Vienna).

➡ **Restaurants** Cover a broad spectrum, from pizzeria bites to Michelin-starred finery.

Menu Decoder

➡ **Degustationsmenü** Gourmet tasting menu

➡ **Hauptspeise** Main course or entree – fish, meat or vegetarisch (vegetarian)

➡ **Kindermenü** Two-or three-course kids' menu; sometimes includes a soft drink

➡ **Laktosefrei/Glutenfrei** Lactose-/gluten-free

➡ **Mittagstisch/Mittagsmenü** Fixed lunch menu; usually two courses, with a soup or salad followed by a main

➡ **Nachtisch** Dessert, sometimes followed by coffee or a glass of schnapps

➡ **Speisekarte** À la carte menu

➡ **Tagesteller** Good-value dish of the day; generally only served at lunchtime

➡ **Vorspeise** Starter, appetiser

➡ **Weinkarte** Wine list

Regions at a Glance

Vienna

Art & Architecture
Music
Drinking in Style

Peerless Palaces

Palaces, churches and art spaces such as the Hofburg, Schloss Schönbrunn, Schloss Belvedere, Stephansdom, the MuseumsQuartier and Albertina make it literally impossible to turn a corner in Austria's capital without bumping into an architectural or artistic masterpiece.

Classical Music Highs

Listen to the music of Mozart at palatial venues across town, visit Mozart's former home, embrace decadence and operatic greats at the Staatsoper or head to the Klangforum where the up-and-coming composers perform.

Coffee Houses & Classy Bars

Viennese coffee houses are legendary: sip, read, pause in palatial surrounds like Café Gloriette or at hip modern renditions such as Café Drechsler. Grab a cocktail in Secessionist architect Adolf Loos' minuscule bar or visit a *Heuriger* (wine tavern).

p60

Lower Austria & Burgenland

Food
Culture
Outdoor Activities

Local Produce

The Wachau region of the Danube Valley has top-class restaurants and local produce such as beef, cheeses and Waldviertel poppy seed. Burgenland around Neusiedler See is famous for its wines and *Heurigen* (wine taverns), where nothing beats a glass of Austria's finest to wash down a cold platter.

Cultural Highs

Stift Melk in the Wachau region is the monarch among abbeys, Schloss Grafenegg is a top-class venue for outdoor music and opera, Krems and Schloss Schallaburg host great exhibitions, and Eisenstadt has its splendid Schloss Esterházy.

Cycling & Water Sports

The most popular cycling path in Lower Austria is along the Danube River in the beautiful Wachau region. For lakeside cycling and watersports, don't miss the Neusiedler See in Burgenland.

p121

Upper Austria

Culture
Architecture
Rural Retreats

Avant-garde Arts

Linz' strikingly lit Ars Electronica Center propels visitors into the future with robotic wizardry and virtual voyages, while the rectangular Lentos gallery hosts cutting-edge art exhibitions. Modern art and sculpture also hang out in the Landesgalerie.

Historic Abbeys & Churches

Kremsmünster's Benedictine abbey and St Florian's baroque Augustinian abbey hide ecclesiastical treasures. Linz has neo-Gothic Neuer Dom and opulent Alter Dom, while Kefermarkt is known for the Gothic altar in its church.

Country Escapes

Rolling countryside is scattered with storybook towns like Steyr and spa retreats like Bad Hall. Farmstays in the Mühlviertel and Traunviertel offer total peace. Hike in the limestone wilderness of the Nationalpark Kalkalpen.

p158

Styria

Culture
Outdoor Pursuits
Wine

Cultural Graz

Famous for its festivals throughout the year, the capital, Graz, makes up for its small size with some big cultural hits and an ensemble of top-rate museums, including Schloss Eggenberg.

Hiking, Biking & Skiing

Hiking trails abound in Styria – some easy, others challenging – and some good hikes and mountainbike rides can be had in the cleaved valleys of the remote Nationalpark Gesäuse, or in the more popular Schladming area. Here, the mountains soar to dizzying heights and the pistes rev to life in winter.

Vineyards & Wine Roads

The wine at restaurant tables often hails from the vineyards hugging the slopes at the nearby Slovenian border. Tangy riesling whites and full-bodied Pinot reds are complemented by some cracking restaurants on the south Styrian wine roads.

p179

The Salzkammergut

Lakes
Outdoor Pursuits
Natural Highs

Lake Swimming

With its contrast of soaring mountains and deep lakes nestled in steeply walled valleys, the Salzkammergut is the best place to slip into lake waters. Some of these are cold – very cold – but others such as the Hallstätter See, the Wolfgangsee or Mondsee are perfect for challenging open-water swimming or quick dips.

Hiking, Cycling & Skiing

Hallstatt and Obertraun are terrific bases for lakeside hiking, forays into the heights of the Dachstein mountains – don't miss the 5Fingers – and winter ski rambles. The cycling is superb in the Salzkammergut, too – both the mountain variety and easier touring.

Salt Mines & Ice Caves

Go in search of the 'white gold' that gives the region its name at Hallstatt's showcase salt mines. Or delve into a subzero world of glittering ice at the Dachstein Caves.

p207

Salzburg & Salzburgerland

High Culture
Natural Wonders
Drinking in History

Palaces & Spas

Salzburg's regal Residenz, the magnificent baroque Altstadt, and the Festung Hohensalzburg are cultural highlights. Belle-époque Bad Gastein is famous for its radon-laced springs.

Ice Caves & Waterfalls

Hikers are captivated by the Tennengebirge's landscapes. Underground lies Eisriesenwelt, the world's largest accessible ice caves, near the precipitous Liechtensteinklamm gorge. Hohe Tauern National Park is a 'greatest hits' of alpine scenery, with wondrous glaciers, 3000m peaks and 380m-high Krimmler Wasserfälle.

Coffee Houses & Brewpubs

Cake comes with a dollop of history at grand coffee houses like Bazar and Sacher. Swing over to monastery-run brewery Augustiner Bräustübl or the cavernous StieglKeller for a 365-day taste of Oktoberfest.

p227

Carinthia

Lakes
Winter Sports
Cycling

Lake Swimming

The Wörthersee is a summer playground for the rich, the famous and the rest of us. This is warm in summer and convenient to Klagenfurt, but those who like their waters cooler can head for Weissensee, Austria's highest alpine swimming lake.

Top Slopes

At the far-flung but popular Nassfeld ski field near Hermagor, skiers take the 6km-long Millennium-Express cable car up to the slopes for some top skiing. Nordic skiing, ski hikes and ice skating are also excellent, especially in some of the province's rugged and remote regions.

Mountain Biking

Eleven kilometres downhill on one mighty run – mountain biking is a favourite pastime in Carinthia, but so too is touring on the trails and routes around Hermagor, Weissensee or outside Villach.

p269

Tyrol & Vorarlberg

Skiing
Outdoor Activities
History & Heritage

Star Slopes

Tyrol has Austria's finest slopes – quite some feat in this starkly mountainous country. Alpine resorts like St Anton am Arlberg, Kitzbühel, Mayrhofen and Ischgl excel in downhill, off-piste and upbeat après-ski. Seefeld has cross-country runs of Olympic fame.

Hiking & Cycling

Tyrol has some of the most scenic alpine hiking and cycling in Austria. Summer calls high-altitude walkers and mountain bikers to the valleys and peaks of the ruggedly beautiful Zillertal, Ötztal and Patznauntal. In Vorarlberg, cyclists and beach-goers descend on glittering Bodensee.

Palaces & Dairies

Palatial Hofburg, Renaissance Schloss Ambras and galleries of Old Masters beckon in Innsbruck. In Vorarlberg, soak up the back-to-nature feel in the rolling dairy country of the Bregenzerwald, sprinkled with farmstays and chocolate-box villages like Schwarzenberg.

p291

On the
Road

Vienna
p60

Upper Austria
p158

The Salzkammergut
p207

Lower Austria & Burgenland
p121

Salzburg & Salzburgerland
p227

Styria
p179

Tyrol & Vorarlberg
p291

Carinthia
p269

Vienna

POP 1,766,750 / ✎ 01

Best Places to Eat

➜ Steirereck im Stadtpark (p106)

➜ Punks (p103)

➜ Lingenhel (p103)

➜ Plachutta (p107)

➜ Blue Mustard (p104)

➜ Griechenbeisl (p103)

Best Places to Sleep

➜ Grand Ferdinand Hotel (p100)

➜ Magdas (p98)

➜ Grätzlhotel (p98)

➜ my MOjO vie (p97)

➜ DO & CO (p100)

Why Go?

Few cities in the world glide as effortlessly between the present and the past as Vienna. Its splendid historical face is easily recognised: grand imperial palaces and bombastic baroque interiors, museums flanking magnificent squares.

But Vienna is also one of Europe's most dynamic urban spaces. A stone's throw from Hofburg, the MuseumsQuartier houses some of the world's most provocative contemporary art behind a striking basalt facade. Outside, a courtyard buzzes on summer evenings with throngs of Viennese drinking and chatting.

The city of Mozart is also the Vienna of Falco (Hans Hölzel), who immortalised its urban textures in song. In this Vienna, it's OK to mention poetry slam and Stephansdom in one breath.Throw in an abundance of green space within the city limits and the 'blue' Danube cutting a path east of the historical centre and this is a capital that is distinctly Austrian.

When to Go

➜ Vienna has such a strong range of sights and activities that any time – summer or winter – is a good time to go.

➜ July, August and holidays such as Easter, Christmas and New Year are the most crowded.

➜ Crowds are down in spring and autumn, but weather can be changeable.

➜ In summer catch some rays on the Danube and loll about drinking made-on-the-premises wine in the outdoor gardens of the Heurigen (wine taverns).

➜ Hiking among the Vienna woods in October yields a spectacular autumn view of the capital.

➜ In December go ice skating in front of the Rathaus (town hall) or sip Glühwein (mulled wine) at one of the capital's atmospheric Christmas markets.

History

Vienna was probably an important trading post for the Celts when the Romans arrived around 15 BC. They set up camp and named the place Vindobona, after the Celtic tribe Vinid. The settlement blossomed into a town by the 3rd and 4th centuries, and vineyards were introduced to the surrounding area.

In AD 881 the town surfaced in official documents as Wenia. Over the ensuing centuries control of Vienna changed hands a number of times before the city fell under the rule of the Babenburgs. The Habsburgs inherited it, but none of them resided here permanently until Ferdinand in 1533. The city was besieged by Ottoman Turks in 1529.

Vienna was a hotbed of revolt and religious bickering during the Reformation and Counter-Reformation, and suffered terribly through plague and siege at the end of the 17th century. However, the beginning of the 18th century heralded a golden age for the city, with baroque architecture, civil reform and a classical-music revolution.

Things turned sour at the beginning of the 19th century – Napoleon occupied the city twice, in 1805 and 1809. His reign over Europe was brief, and in 1814–15 Vienna hosted the Congress of Vienna in celebration of his defeat. Vienna grew in post-Napoleonic Europe and in 1873 hosted its second international event, the World Fair. The advent of WWI stalled the city's architectural and cultural development and, by the end of the war, the monarchy had been consigned to the past.

The 1920s saw the rise of fascism, and in 1934 civil war broke out in the city streets. The socialists were defeated and Vienna's city council dissolved. On 15 March 1938 Hitler entered the city to the cries of 200,000 ecstatic Viennese.

Vienna suffered heavily under Allied bombing, and on 11 April 1945 advancing Russian troops liberated the city. The Allies joined them until Vienna became independent in 1955, and since then it has gone from the razor's edge of the Cold War to the focal point between new and old EU member nations.

◎ Sights

◎ Innere Stadt

★**Stephansdom** CATHEDRAL
(St Stephan's Cathedral; Map p66; ✆ tours 01-515 323 054; www.stephanskirche.at; 01, Stephansplatz; main nave adult & one child €6, addition-

al child €1.50; ☺ public visits 9am-11.30am & 1-4.30pm Mon-Sat, 1-4.30pm Sun; Ⓤ Stephansplatz) Vienna's Gothic masterpiece Stephansdom – or Steffl (Little Stephan), as it's ironically nicknamed – is Vienna's pride and joy. A church has stood here since the 12th century, and reminders of this are the Romanesque **Riesentor** (Giant Gate) and **Heidentürme**. From the exterior, the first thing that will strike you is the glorious tiled **roof**, with its dazzling row of chevrons and Austrian eagle. Inside, the magnificent Gothic stone **pulpit** presides over the main nave, fashioned in 1515 by Anton Pilgrim.

One often-overlooked detail is the pulpit's handrail, which has salamanders and toads fighting an eternal battle of good versus evil up and down its length. The baroque **high altar**, at the very far end of the main nave, shows the stoning of St Stephen. The chancel to its left has the winged **Wiener Neustadt altarpiece**, dating from 1447; the right chancel has the Renaissance red-marble **tomb of Friedrich III**. Under his guidance the city became a bishopric (and the church a cathedral) in 1469. Note that the main nave is closed during Mass (held up to eight times a day).

Tour options include self-guided **audio tours** (adult and one child €8, additional child €1.50) and **guided tours** (adult/child €5.50/2), which include entry to the nave.

★**Hofburg** PALACE
(Imperial Palace; Map p66; www.hofburg-wien.at; 01, Michaelerkuppel; ☐1A, 2A Michaelerplatz, ☐D, 1, 2, 46, 49, 71 Burgring, Ⓤ Herrengasse) FREE Nothing symbolises Austria's resplendent cultural heritage more than its Hofburg, home base of the Habsburgs from 1273 to 1918. The oldest section is the 13th-century **Schweizerhof** (Swiss Courtyard), named after the Swiss guards who used to protect its precincts. The Renaissance **Swiss gate** dates from 1553. The courtyard adjoins a larger courtyard, **In der Burg**, with a monument to Emperor Franz II adorning its centre. The palace now houses the Austrian president's offices and a raft of museums.

The Hofburg owes its size and architectural diversity to plain old one-upmanship; new sections were added by the new rulers, including the early baroque **Leopold Wing**, the 16th-century **Amalia Wing**, the 18th-century **Imperial Chancery Wing** and the Gothic **Burgkapelle** (Royal Chapel).

Vienna Highlights

1 Stephansdom
(p61) Scaling Vienna's glorious Gothic cathedral and beloved icon.

2 Schloss Schönbrunn (p87)
Savouring the bombastic pomp and the views from its gardens.

3 Museums-Quartier (p77)
Hanging out in this art space spiked with bars and alive with urban energy.

4 MUMOK (p80)
Being provoked by naked bodies smeared with salad (among other modern-art flourishes).

5 Café Sperl
(p108) Slowing down and indulging in cake and coffee at one of Vienna's legendary coffee houses.

6 Schank zum Reichsapfel (p102)
Immersing yourself in one of Vienna's *Heuriger* (wine taverns) on a ramble.

7 Riesenrad (p83)
Spinning around in the giant rectangles dangling off Vienna's oversized Ferris wheel, in the Prater outdoor area.

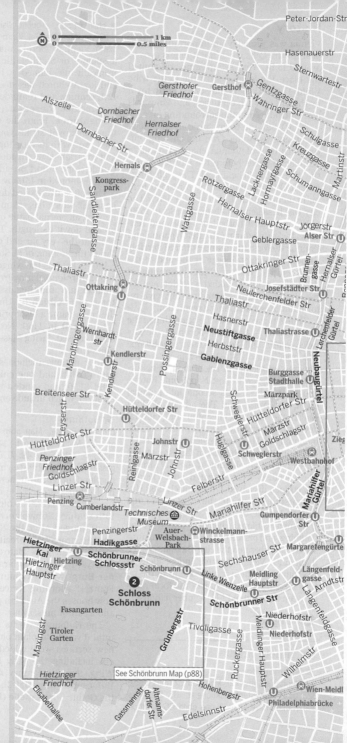

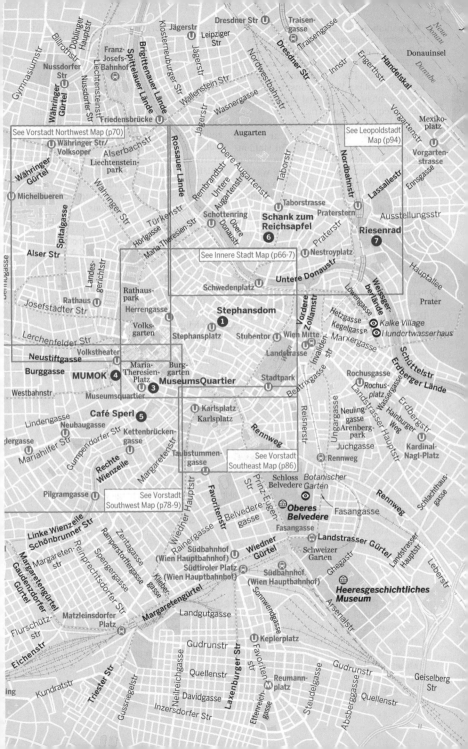

★ **Spanish Riding School**   PERFORMING ARTS
(Spanische Hofreitschule; Map p66; ☑ 01-533 90 31-0; www.srs.at; 01, Michaelerplatz 1; performances €25-217; ⊘ hours vary; ☑ 1A, 2A Michaelerplatz, ⓤ Herrengasse) The world-famous Spanish Riding School is a Viennese institution truly reminiscent of the imperial Habsburg era. This unequalled equestrian show is performed by Lipizzaner stallions formerly kept at an imperial stud established at Lipizza (hence the name). These graceful stallions perform an equine ballet to a program of classical music while the audience watches from pillared balconies – or from a cheaper standing-room area – and the chandeliers shimmer above.

There are many different ways to see the Lipizzaner. **Performances** are the top-shelf variant, and for seats at these you will need to book several months in advance. The website lists performance dates and you can order tickets online. As a rule of thumb, performances are at 11am on Sunday from mid-February to June and mid-August to December, with frequent additional performances on Saturday and occasionally other days of the week. For standing-room tickets, book at least one month in advance. During the summer break, it hosts special 'Piber meets Vienna' performances. Visi-

tors to the **Morgenarbeit** (morning training sessions; adult/child €15/7.50, 10am to noon Tuesday to Friday January to June and mid-August to December) can drop in for part of a session.

One-hour **guided tours** (adult/child €16/8; 2pm, 3pm and 4pm March to late January, 2pm, 3pm and 4pm Tuesday to Sunday late January and February), held in English and German, take you into the performance hall, stables and other facilities. A **combined morning training and tour** (adult/child €31/15) is another option. The visitor centre on Michaelerplatz sells all tickets. Morning training tickets can also be bought at the entrance during training sessions.

★ **Kaiserappartements**   PALACE
(Imperial Apartments; Map p66; www.hofburg-wien. at; 01, Michaelerplatz; adult/child €12.90/7.70, incl guided tour €15.90/9.20; ⊘ 9am-6pm Jul & Aug, to 5.30pm Sep-Jun; ⓤ Herrengasse) The Kaiserappartements (Imperial Apartments), once the official living quarters of Franz Josef I and Empress Elisabeth, are dazzling in their chandelier-lit opulence. The highlight is the Sisi Museum (p71), devoted to Austria's most beloved empress, which has a strong focus on the clothing and jewellery of Austria's monarch. Multilingual audio guides

VIENNA IN...

Two Days

Jump on tram 1 at Schwedenplatz and circle the **Ringstrasse** for a brief but rewarding informal tour of the boulevard's buildings. Get out at Kärntner Strasse and wander towards the heart of the city, where the glorious Gothic **Stephansdom** (p61) awaits.Make your way to the **Hofburg** (p61) before crossing the Ringstrasse to the **Kunsthistorisches Museum** (p73), home to a breathtaking art collection. Recharge your batteries at one of the many Innere Stadt restaurants before attending a performance atthe **Staatsoper** (p112). On day two visit imperial palace **Schönbrunn** (p87) before heading to the **Leopold Museum** (p77), a treasure chest of Austrian artists. Take an early dinner at Vienna's celebrated **Naschmarkt** (p101), then cross the city for a ride on the **Riesenrad** (p83) Ferris wheel. Finish the day with local food and a drink in a traditional *Beisl* (bistro pub).

Four Days

Start the third day with an exploration of the **Schloss Belvedere** (p83), an unequalled baroque palace. See Klimt's sumptuous Beethoven Frieze in the **Secession** (p81), then end the night in a bar like **Dachboden** (p99).The fourth day is best dedicated to your special interests. Read up on the sights and cobble together your itinerary. You might focus on music, dropping into the Sammlung Alter Musik Instrumente in the **Neue Burg Museums** (p68), taking in the other collection stoo, repose in a coffee house, then spend the afternoon visiting the **Haus der Musik** (p65) or **Mozarthaus** (p69). After that, cap off the visit with music in a club or in a classical venue like the **Musikverein** (p112) to experience the music of Beethoven or Mozart where it was originally played.

THE WHITE HORSE IN HISTORY

The Lipizzaner stallion breed dates back to the 1520s, when Ferdinand I imported the first horses from Spain for the imperial palace. His son Maximilian II imported new stock in the 1560s, and in 1580 Archduke Charles II established the imperial stud in Lipizza (Lipica, today in Slovenia), giving the horse its name. Austria's nobility had good reason for looking to Spain for its horses: the Spanish were considered the last word in equine breeding at the time, thanks to Moors from the 7th century who had brought their elegant horses to the Iberian Peninsula. Italian horses were added to the stock around the mid-1700s (these too had Spanish blood) and by the mid-18th century the Lipizzaner had a reputation for being Europe's finest horses.

Over the centuries, natural catastrophe, but more often war, caused the Lipizzaner to be evacuated from their original stud in Slovenia on numerous occasions. One of their periods of exile from the stud in Lipica was in 1915 due to the outbreak of WWI. Some of the horses went to Laxemburg (just outside Vienna), and others to Bohemia in today's Czech Republic (at the time part of the Austro-Hungarian Empire).

When the Austrian monarchy collapsed in 1918, Lipica passed into Italian hands and the horses were divided between Austria and Italy. The Italians ran the stud in Slovenia, while the Austrians transferred their horses to Piber, near Graz, which had been breeding military horses for the empire since 1798 – at that time stallions were mostly crossed with English breeds.

The fortunes of our pirouetting equine friends rose and fell with the collapse of the Habsburg empire and advent of two world wars. When WWII broke out, Hitler's cohorts goose-stepped in and requisitioned the Piber stud in Austria and started breeding military horses and pack mules there. They also decided to bring the different studs in their occupied regions together under one roof, and Piber's Lipizzaner wound up in Hostau, situated in Bohemia. Fearing the Lipizzaner would fall into the hands of the Russian army as it advanced towards the region in 1945, American forces seized the Lipizzaner and other horses in Hostau and transferred them back to Austria.

Today, Piber still supplies the Spanish Riding School with its white stallions.

are included in the admission price. Guided tours take in the Kaiserappartements, the Sisi Museum and the **Silberkammer** (Silver Depot; ⊘ 9am-6pm Jul & Aug, to 5.30pm Sep-Jun), whose largest silver service caters to 140 dinner guests.

★ **Kaiserliche Schatzkammer**   MUSEUM
(Imperial Treasury; Map p66; www.kaiserliche-schatzkammer.at; 01, Schweizerhof; adult/child €12/free; ⊘ 9am-5.30pm Wed-Mon; Ⓤ Herrengasse) The Kaiserliche Schatzkammer contains secular and ecclesiastical treasures, including devotional images and altars, particularly from the baroque era, of priceless value and splendour – the sheer wealth of this collection of crown jewels is staggering. As you walk through the rooms you see magnificent treasures such as a golden rose, diamond-studded Turkish sabres, a 2680-carat Colombian emerald and, the highlight of the treasury, the imperial crown.

The wood-panelled **Sacred Treasury** has a collection of rare religious relics: fragments of the True Cross, the Holy Lance that pierced Jesus on the Cross, one of the nails from the Crucifixion, a thorn from Christ's crown and a piece of tablecloth from the Last Supper.

Multilingual audio guides cost €4 (the shorter highlight audio tour is free) and are very worthwhile. A combined Schatz der Habsburger (Treasures of the Habsburgs) ticket, which includes the Kunsthistorisches Museum and Neue Burg, costs €20.

★ **Haus der Musik**   MUSEUM
(Map p66; www.hausdermusik.com; 01, Seilerstätte 30; adult/child €13/6, with Mozarthaus Vienna €18/8; ⊘ 10am-10pm; 🚊 D, 1, 2, 71, Ⓤ Karlsplatz) The Haus der Musik explains the world of sound and music to adults and children alike in an amusing and interactive way (in English and German). Exhibits are spread over four floors and cover everything from how sound is created, from Vienna's Philharmonic Orchestra to street noises. The staircase between floors acts as a piano; its glassed-in ground-floor courtyard hosts musical events. Admission

Innere Stadt

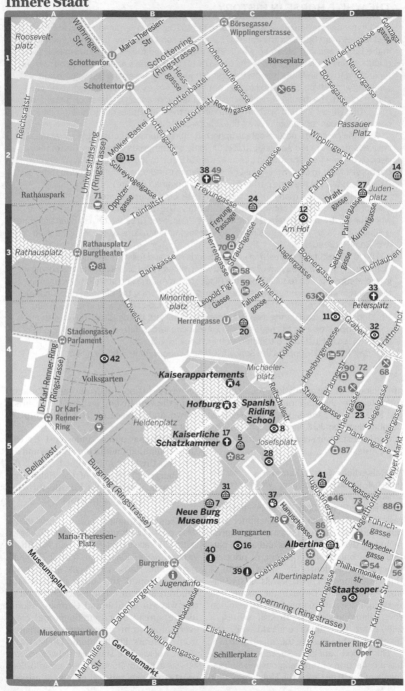

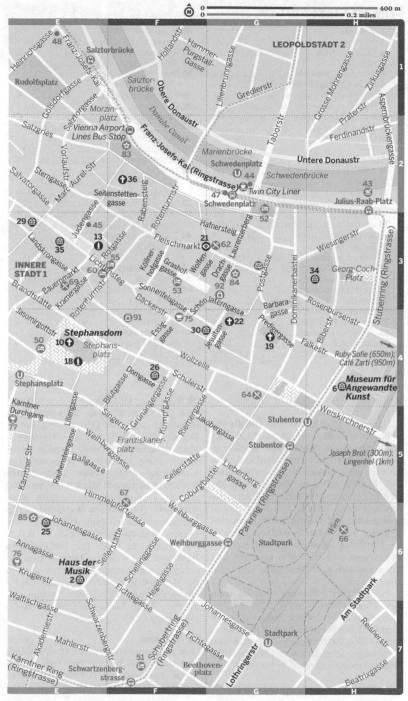

0   400 m
0   0.2 miles

LEOPOLDSTADT 2

Heinrichsgasse
48 Franz-Josefs-Kai
Salztorbrücke
Rudolfsplatz
Gölsdorfgasse
Sartorigasse
Morzin-
platz
Salzgries
St Vienna Airport
Lines Bus Stop
83
Vorlaufstr
Marc Aurel-Str
Salvatorgasse
Sterngasse
Landskrongasse
29
35
INNERE
STADT 1
Bauernmarkt
69
Brandstätte
Kramergasse
Jasomirgottstr
91
50
10
18
Stephansdom
Stephans-
platz
Stephansplatz
Kärntner
Durchgang
77
Seitenstetten-
gasse
Judengasse
45
13
Rotgasse
Lichtensteg
55
60
Rotenturmstr
Rabensteig
Rotenturmstr
Bäckerstr
Essig-
gasse
Jesuiten-
gasse
36
Hollandstr
Salztor-
brücke
Obere Donaustr
Danube Canal
Franz-Josefs-Kai
Hammer-
Purgstall-
Gasse
Lilienbrunngasse
Gredlerstr
Marienbrücke
Schwedenplatz
44
Schwedenbrücke
47
Schwedenplatz
52
Hafnersteig
Fleischmarkt
21
62
Köllner-
hofgasse
Grashof-
gasse
Sonnenfelsgasse
Wolfen-
gasse
Laurenzerberg
Drach-
gasse
92
84
Schönlaterngasse
75
30
22
19
Wollzeile
Taborstr
Grosse Mohrengasse
Praterstr
Ferdinandstr
Untere Donaustr
Twin City Liner
Julius-Raab-Platz
43
Wiesingerstr
Postgasse
Dominikanerbastei
34
Georg-Coch-
Platz
Barbara-
gasse
Predigergasse
Falkestr
Rosenbursenstr
Biberstr
Stubenring (Ringstrasse)
Ruby Sofie (650m);
Café Zartl (950m)
Museum für
6 Angewandte
Kunst
Zirkusgasse
Aspernbrückengasse

26
Domgasse
Schulerstr
64
Blugasse
Singerstr
Grünangergasse
Kumpfgasse
Riemergasse
Jakobergasse
Stubentor
Stubentor
Weiskirchnerstr
Kärntner Str
Lilliengasse
Rauhensteingasse
Weihburggasse
Ballgasse
Franziskaner-
platz
Sellerstätte
Liebenberg-
gasse
Coburgbastei
Parkring (Ringstrasse)
Joseph Brot (300m);
Lingenhel (1km)
67
Himmelpfortgasse
Weihburggasse
Weihburggasse
85
25
Johannesgasse
76
Annagasse
Krugerstr
Haus der
Musik
2
Sellerstätte
Schellinggasse
Hegelgasse
Fichtegasse
Johannesgasse
Stadtpark
Wien
66
Am Stadtpark
Walfischgasse
Akademiestr
Mahlerstr
Schwarzenbergstr
51
Schwartzenberg-
strasse
Schubertring
(Ringstrasse)
Beethoven-
platz
Fichtegasse
Lothringerstr
Stadtpark
Reisnerstr
Beatrixgasse
Kärntner Ring
(Ringstrasse)

VIENNA SIGHTS

Innere Stadt

is discounted after 8pm. The nearest tram stop is Kärntner Ring/Oper.

Floor 1 hosts the **Museum of the Vienna Philharmonic.** Find out about the history of the orchestra's famous New Year's concerts and listen to recent highlights. You can even compose your own waltz by rolling dice. Floor 2, called the **Sonosphere,** has plenty of engaging instruments, interactive toys and touch screens. Test the limits of your hearing and play around with sampled sounds to record your own CD (€7). One of the highlights for aficionados of everyday audioscapes is a collection of street and subway sounds from New York, Tokyo and other places.

Floor 3 covers Vienna's classical composers and is polished off with an amusing interactive video in which you conduct the Vienna Philharmonic Orchestra. Floor 4 has the so-called **Virtostage** in which your own body language and movements shape the music to create an opera.

★**Neue Burg Museums** MUSEUM
(Map p66; ☑01-525 240; www.khm.at; 01, Heldenplatz; adult/child €15/free; ☉10am-6pm Wed-Sun; ☒D, 1, 2, 71 Burgring, Ⓤ Herrengasse, Museumsquartier) The Neue Burg is home to the three Neue Burg Museums. The **Sammlung Alter Musik Instrumente** (Collection of Ancient Musical Instruments) contains a wonderfully diverse array of instruments. The **Ephesos Museum** features artefacts unearthed during Austrian archaeologists' excavations at Ephesus in Turkey between1895 to 1906. The **Hofjägd und Rüstkammer** (Arms and Armour) museum contains ancient armour dating mainly from the 15th and 16th centuries. Admission includes the Kunsthistorisches Museum and all three Neue Burg museums. An audio guide costs €4.

★**Albertina** GALLERY
(Map p66; www.albertina.at; 01, Albertinaplatz 3; adult/child €12.90/free; ☉10am-6pm Thu-Tue, to 9pm Wed; ☒D, 1, 2, 71 Kärntner Ring/Oper, Ⓤ Karlsplatz, Stephansplatz) Once used as the

Habsburg's imperial apartments for guests, the Albertina is now a repository for what's regularly touted as the greatest collection of graphic art in the world. The permanent Batliner Collection – with over 100 paintings covering the period from Monet to Picasso – and the high quality of changing exhibitions are what really make the Albertina worthwhile.

Multilingual audio guides (€4) cover all exhibition sections and tell the story behind the apartments and the works on display.

French impressionism and post-impressionism, as well as the works of the Swiss Alberto Giacometti, were the original focus of the Batliner Collection, but over time husband and wife benefactors Herbert and Rita Batliner added a substantial number of Russian avant-garde works to create a who's who of 20th-century and contemporary art: Monet, Picasso, Degas, Cézanne, Matisse, Chagal, Nolde, Jawlensky and many more.

Tickets (but not the audio guides) are valid for the whole day, so you can nip out for lunch and return later to finish off a visit.

A branch of the Österreichisches Filmmuseum (p115) is located here.

Mozarthaus Vienna MUSEUM
(Map p66; 🖉 01-512 17 91; www.mozarthausvienna.at; 01, Domgasse 5; adult/child €11/4.50, with Haus der Musik €18/8; ⏲ 10am-7pm; Ⓤ Stephansplatz) The great composer spent 2½ happy and productive years at this residence between 1784 and 1787. Exhibits include copies of music scores and paintings, while free audio guides recreate the story of his time here. Mozart spent a total of 11 years in Vienna, changing residences frequently and sometimes setting up his home outside the Ringstrasse in the cheaper Vorstädte (inner suburbs) when his finances were tight. Of these the Mozarthaus Vienna is the only one that survives.

The exhibition begins on the top floor, overlooking a narrow, closed-in inner courtyard, and covers the society of the late 18th century, providing asides into prominent figures in the court and Mozart's life, such as the Freemasons (to whom he dedicated a number

Vorstadt Northwest

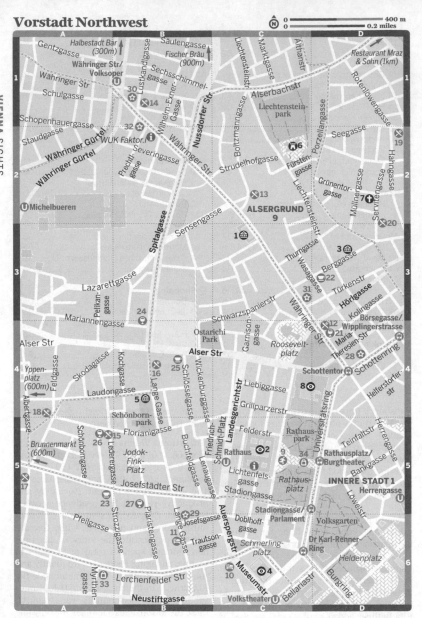

of pieces). Coverage of Mozart's vices – his womanising, gambling and ability to waste excessive amounts of money – gives it an edge.

Retaining its original stucco ceilings, the middle floor concentrates on Mozart's music and his musical influences. It was in this house that he penned *The Marriage of Figaro*. A surreal holographic performance of scenes from *The Magic Flute* is in another room. The final floor has Mozart's bedroom and a few pieces of period furniture in glass cases to give a feel for the era.

Vorstadt Northwest

Cathedral South Tower   TOWER
(Südturm; Map p66; www.stephanskirche.at; 01, Stephansplatz; adult/child €4.50/2; ⊙9am-5.30pm; Ⓤ Stephansplatz) In 1433 Stephansdom's south tower reached its final height of 136.7m, and today you can ascend the 343 steps to a small platform for one of Vienna's most spectacular views over the rooftops of the Innere Stadt (you don't need a ticket for the main nave). When the foundation stone for the south tower was laid in 1359, Rudolf IV is said to have used a trowel and spade made of silver.

Two towers were originally envisaged, but the Südturm grew so high that little space remained for the second.

Sisi Museum   MUSEUM
(Map p66; ☑01-533 75 70; 01, Michaelerkuppel; adult/child €12.90/7.70, incl guided tour €15.90/9.20; ⊙9am-6pm Jul & Aug, to 5.30pm Sep-Jun) Inside the Kaiserappartements, the Sisi Museum is devoted to Austria's Empress Elisabeth, affectionately known as Sisi. A partial reconstruction of her luxurious coach is a highlight, but it's the details that give a feel for the life of the empress: a reconstruction of the dress she wore on the eve of her wedding and her sunshade, fans and gloves. Multilingual audio guides are included in the admission price. Guided tours take in the Kaiserappartements and the adjoining Silberkammer. (p65)

Nationalbibliothek Prunksaal   LIBRARY
(Grand Hall; Map p66; ☑01-534 10; www.onb.ac.at; 01, Josefsplatz 1; adult/child €7/free; ⊙10am-6pm Tue, Wed & Fri-Sun, to 9pm Thu; 🚋D, 1, 2, 71 Burgring, Ⓤ Herrengasse) Austria's flagship library, the Nationalbibliothek contains an astounding collection of literature, maps, globes of the world and other cultural relics; its highlight, though, is the **Prunksaal** (Grand Hall), a majestic baroque hall built between 1723 and 1726, with a fresco by Daniel Gran. Commissioned by Karl VI (whose statue is under the central dome), the library holds some 200,000 leather-bound scholarly tomes. Audio guides cost €3.

Rare volumes, mostly from the 15th century, are stored within glass cabinets, opened to beautifully illustrated pages of text. The exquisite fresco by Gran depicts the emperor's apotheosis.

A combined ticket that includes the **Esperantomuseum** (Map p66; ☑01-534 10 730; www.onb.ac.at; 01, Herrengasse 9, ground fl; adult/child €4/free; ⊙10am-6pm Fri-Wed, to 9pm Thu Jun-Sep, 10am-6pm Tue, Wed & Fri-Sun, to 9pm Thu Oct-May; 🚋1A, 2A Michaelerplatz, Ⓤ Herrengasse), **Globenmuseum** (Map p66; ☑01-534 10 710; www.onb.ac.at; 01, Herrengasse 9, 1st fl; adult/child €4/free; ⊙10am-6pm Fri-Wed, to 9pm Thu Jun-Sep 10am-6pm Tue, Wed & Fri-Sun, to 9pm Thu Oct-May; 🚋1A, 2A Michaelerplatz, Ⓤ Herrengasse) and **Papyrusmuseum** (Map p66; ☑01-534 10 420;

www.onb.ac.at; 01, Heldenplatz; adult/free €4/free; ⊙10am-6pm Tue, Wed & Fri-Sun, to 9pm Thu; 🚌D, 1, 2, 71 Burgring, Ⓤ Herrengasse, Museumsquartier) as well as the new **Literaturmuseum** (Literature Museum; Map p66; www.onb.ac.at/literaturmuseum; 01, Grillparzerhaus, Johannesgasse 6; adult/child €7/free; ⊙10am-6pm Tue, Wed & Fri-Sun, to 9pm Thu; Ⓤ Stephansplatz) costs €15.

Kunstforum
GALLERY

(Map p66; www.bankaustria-kunstforum.at; 01, Freyungasse 8; adult/child €11/4; ⊙10am-7pm Sat-Thu, to 9pm Fri; Ⓤ Herrengasse) The private Kunstforum museum gets about 300,000 visitors each year, and for good reason – it stages an exciting program of changing exhibitions, usually highlighting crowd-pleasing Modernist or big-name contemporary artists. The work of Miquel Barceló, Botero, Frida Kahlo, Balthus and Martin Kippenberger have all had their turn in recent years.

Schottenkirche
CHURCH

(Map p66; www.schotten.wien; 01, Freyung; ⊙ museum 11am-5pm Tue-Sat, church shop 10am-6pm Mon-Fri, to 5pm Sat, closed Mon in high season; Ⓤ Herrengasse, Schottentor) 🆓 The Schottenkirche (Church of the Scots), at the northern end of Herrengasse, was founded by Benedictine monks probably originating from Scotia Maior (Ireland); the present facade dates from the 19th century. The interior has a beautifully frescoed ceiling and terracotta-red touches.

Although the main nave can only be entered during services at noon and 6pm daily, it's possible to peek through the gates. A small art and artefacts **museum** (adult/child €8/2) in the adjoining monastery displays religious pieces, but of more interest is the church **shop**, which stocks homemade schnapps, honey and jams.

Cathedral Pummerin
CATHEDRAL BELL

(Boomer Bell; Map p66; www.stephanskirche. at; Stephansplatz; adult/child €5.50/2; ⊙9am-5.30pm; Ⓤ Stephansplatz) Weighing 21 tonnes, the Pummerin is Austria's largest bell and was installed in the **north tower** of Stephansdom in 1957. While the rest of the cathedral was rising up in its new Gothic format, work was interrupted on this tower due to a lack of cash and the fading allure of Gothic architecture. It's accessible only by lift today (you don't need a ticket for the main nave).

Stephansdom Katakomben
HISTORIC SITE

(Catacombs; Map p66; 📞01-515 523 054; www. stephanskirche.at; 01, Stephansplatz; 30min tour

adult/child €5.50/2; ⊙tours 10-11.30am & 1.30-4.30pm Mon-Sat, 1.30-4.30pm Sun; Ⓤ Stephansplatz) The area on Stephansplatz around the cathedral was originally a graveyard – making it the dead centre of Vienna in a very literal sense. But with plague and influenza epidemics striking Europe in the 1730s, Karl VI ordered the graveyard to be closed and henceforth Vienna buried its dead beneath Stephansdom in the 'New Tombs', which in the 19th century became more wistfully known as *Katakomben* (catacombs). Entrance is allowed only on a tour.

Museum für Volkskunde
MUSEUM

(Map p70; www.volkskundemuseum.at; 08, Laudongasse 15-19; adult/child €8/free; ⊙10am-5pm Tue-Sun; 🚌5, 33, Ⓤ Rathaus) Housed in turn-of-the-18th-century **Palais Schönborn**, this folklore museum gives a taste of 18th- and 19th-century rural dwellings, and is stocked with handcrafted sculptures, paintings and furniture from throughout Austria and its neighbouring countries. Many of the pieces have a religious or rural theme, and telltale floral motifs are everywhere. Temporary exhibitions are regularly featured. Tram to Laudongasse.

Jüdisches Museum
MUSEUM

(Jewish Museum; Map p66; 📞01-535 04 31; www. jmw.at; 01, Dorotheergasse 11; adult/child incl Museum Judenplatz €10/free; ⊙10am-6pm Sun-Fri; Ⓤ Stephansplatz) Housed inside Palais Eskeles, Vienna's Jüdisches Museum showcases the history of Jews in Vienna, from the first settlements at Judenplatz in the 13th century to the present. Spaces devoted to changing exhibitions are complemented by its permanent exhibition covering 1945 to the present day; the highlight is the startling collection of ceremonial art on the top floor. Combined tickets to the Jüdisches Museum and Museum Judenplatz are valid for four days.

Museum Judenplatz
MUSEUM

(Map p66; 📞01-535 04 31; www.jmw.at; 01, Judenplatz 8; adult/child incl Jüdisches Museum €10/free; ⊙10am-6pm Sun-Thu, to 5pm Fri; Ⓤ Stephansplatz, Herrengasse) The main focus of Museum Judenplatz is on the excavated remains of a medieval synagogue that once stood on Judenplatz, with a film and numerous exhibits to elucidate Vienna's Jewish history. It was built in the Middle Ages, but Duke Albrecht V's 'hatred and misconception' led him to order its destruction in 1421. The basic outline of the synagogue can still be seen here. Combined tickets to the Museum Judenplatz and Jüdisches Museum (p72) are valid for four days.

After entering the museum you watch an informative 12-minute video (with English subtitles) on Judaism, the synagogue and the Jewish quarter. Next up are the excavations, after which you can search the databases for lost relatives or friends if you wish. Glass cases containing fragments, such as documents from Jewish history in Vienna, are dotted throughout the museum. An audio guide costs €2 (in German and English; there's a special children's version, too).

Neidhart-Fresken   MUSEUM
(Map p66; ☑ 01-535 90 65; www.wienmuseum.at; 01, Tuchlauben 19; adult/child €5/free; ☺10am-1pm & 2-6pm Tue-Sun; Ⓤ Stephansplatz) An unassuming house on Tuchlauben hides a remarkable decoration: the oldest extant secular frescoes in Vienna. The small frescoes, dating from 1407, tell the story of the minstrel Neidhart von Reuental (1180–1240), as well as life in the Middle Ages, in lively scenes. They were discovered when the house was set to be redeveloped into apartments in 1979. The artworks are in superb condition considering their age.

Ruprechtskirche   CHURCH
(St Rupert's Church; Map p66; ☑ 01-535 60 03; www.ruprechtskirche.at; 01, Ruprechtsplatz 1; ☺10am-noon Mon & Tue, 10am-noon & 3-5pm Wed, 10am-5pm Thu & Fri, 11.30am-3.30pm Sat; 🚊1, 2, Ⓤ Schwedenplatz) Vienna's oldest church is believed to date from 740. The lower levels of the tower date from the 12th century, the roof from the 15th century and the iron Renaissance door on the west side from the 1530s. In summer, its stone walls are clad in ivy. The interior is sleek and worth a quick viewing, with a Romanesque nave from the 12th century. Note that there are no public visiting hours on Sunday due to religious services.

Beethoven Pasqualatihaus   MUSEUM, HOUSE
(Map p66; www.wienmuseum.at; 01, Mölker Bastei 8; adult/child €5/free; ☺10am-1pm & 2-6pm Tue-Sun; 🚊D, 1, 2, Ⓤ Schottentor) Beethoven resided on the 4th floor of this house from 1804 to 1814 (he apparently lived in around 80 places in his 35 years in Vienna, but thankfully not all of them are museums). During that time he composed Symphonies 4, 5 and 7 and the opera *Fidelio*, among other works. His two rooms (plus another two from a neighbouring apartment) have been converted into this airy museum, which has a not-too-overwhelming collection of portraits, articles and personal belongings.

The house is named after its long-time owner, Josef Benedikt Freiherr von Pasqualati.

Ankeruhr   MONUMENT
(Anker Clock; Map p66; 01, Hoher Markt 10-11; Ⓤ Stephansplatz, Schwedenplatz) An art nouveau masterpiece created by Franz von Matsch in 1911, this mechanical clock was named after the Anker Insurance Co, which commissioned it. Over a 12-hour period, figures including Roman Emperor Marcus Aurelius (who died in Vienna in AD 180), Josef Haydn, Eugene of Savoy, Maria Theresia and others pass across the clock face, indicating the time against a static measure showing the minutes. At noon, all the figures trundle past in succession to the tune of organ music.

Once the centre of the Roman outpost, the **Hoher Markt** is Vienna's oldest square.

⊙ Ringstrasse

Emperor Franz Josef was largely responsible for the monumental architecture around the Ringstrasse, a wide, tree-lined boulevard encircling much of the Innere Stadt. In 1857 he decided to tear down the redundant military fortifications and exercise grounds and replace them with grandiose public buildings in a variety of historical styles. Work began the following year and reached a peak in the1870s. The stock-market crash in 1873 put a major dampener on plans, and other grand schemes were shelved due to lack of money and the outbreak of WWI. The Ring is easily explored on foot or bicycle; if you've not the time, jump on tram 1 or 2, both of which run sections of the boulevard and offer a snapshot of the impressive architecture.

★**Kunsthistorisches Museum**   MUSEUM
(KHM, Museum of Art History; Map p78; www.khm.at; 01, Maria-Theresien-Platz; adult/child incl Neue Burg museums €15/free; ☺10am-6pm Fri-Wed, to 9pm Thu Jun-Aug, closed Mon Sep-May; Ⓤ Museumsquartier, Volkstheater) One of the unforgettable experiences of any trip to Vienna is a visit to the Kunsthistorisches Museum, brimming with works by Europe's finest painters, sculptors and artisans. Occupying a neoclassical building as sumptuous as the art it contains, the museum takes you on a time-travel treasure hunt from Classical Rome to Egypt and

Kunsthistorisches Museum

HALF-DAY TOUR OF THE HIGHLIGHTS

The Kunsthistorisches Museum's scale can seem daunting; this half-day itinerary will help you make the most of your visit.

Ascend the grand marble staircase, marvelling at the impact of Antonio Canova's *Theseus Slaying the Centaur*. Turn right into the Egyptian and Near Eastern Collection, where you can decipher the reliefs of the **Offering**

Chapel of Ka-ni-nisut ❶ in room II. Skip through millennia to Ancient Rome, where the intricacy of the **Gemma Augustea Cameo** ❷ in room XVI is captivating. The other wing of this floor is devoted to the Kunstkammer Wien, hiding rarities such as Benvenuto Cellini's golden **Saliera** ❸ in room XXIX.

Head up a level to the Picture Gallery, a veritable orgy of Renaissance and baroque art. Bearing to the East Wing brings you to Dutch, Flemish and German Painting, which starts with Dürer's

Gemma Augustea Cameo
Greek & Roman Antiquities, Room XVI

Possibly the handiwork of imperial gem-cutter Dioscurides, this sardonyx cameo from the 1st century AD shows in exquisite bas-relief the deification of Augustus, in the guise of Jupiter, who sits next to Roma. The defeated barbarians occupy the lower tier.

LEEMAGE/GETTY IMAGES ©

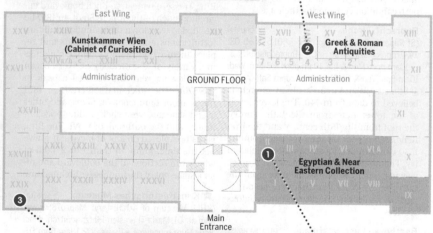

East Wing

West Wing

XXV XXIV XXII XX XIX XVII XV XIV XIII

Kunstkammer Wien (Cabinet of Curiosities)

XXIVa/b/c XXIII XXI 7 6 5 4 3 2 1 **Greek & Roman Antiquities** ❷

XXVI Administration **GROUND FLOOR** Administration

XXVII XII

XI

XXVIII XXXI XXXIII XXXV XXXVIII I III IV VI VIA X

XXIX ❸ XXXII XXXIV XXXVI ❶ **Egyptian & Near Eastern Collection**

V VII VIII IX

Main Entrance

Saliera
Kunstkammer Wien, Room XXIX

Benvenuto Cellini's hand-wrought gold salt cellar (1543) is a dazzling allegorical portrayal of Sea and Earth, personified by Tellus and trident-bearing Neptune. They recline on a base showing the four winds, times of day and human activities.

DIETER NAGL/AFP/GETTY IMAGES ©

Offering Chapel of Ka-ni-nisut
Egyptian & Near Eastern Collection, Room II

Reliefs and hieroglyphs depict the life of high-ranking 5th-dynasty official Ka-ni-nisut, together with his wife, children and entourage of mortuary priests and servants. This 4500-year-old tomb chamber is a spectacular leap into the afterlife.

spirit-lifting **Adoration of the Trinity** ❹ in room XV, takes in meaty Rubens and Rembrandt works en route, and climaxes with Pieter Bruegel the Elder's absorbingly detailed **The Tower of Babel** ❺ in room X. Allocate equal time to the Italian, Spanish and French masters in the halls opposite. Masterpieces including Raphael's **Madonna of the Meadow** ❻ in room 4, Caravaggio's merciful **Madonna of the Rosary** ❼ in room V and Giuseppe **Arcimboldo's Summer** ❽ in room 7 steal the show.

TOP TIPS

» Pick up an audio guide and a floor plan in the entrance hall to orientate yourself.

» Skip to the front of the queue by booking your ticket online.

» Visit between 6pm and 9pm on Thursday for fewer crowds.

» Flash photography is not permitted.

The Tower of Babel
Dutch, Flemish & German Painting, Room X

The futile attempts of industrial souls to reach godly heights are magnified in the painstaking detail of Bruegel's *The Tower of Babel* (1563). Rome's Colosseum provided inspiration.

ART MEDIA/PRINT COLLECTOR/GETTY IMAGES ©

Madonna of the Meadow
Italian, Spanish & French Painting, Room 4

The Virgin Mary, pictured with infants Christ and St John the Baptist, has an almost iridescent quality in Raphael's seminal High Renaissance 1506 masterpiece, set against the backdrop of a Tuscan meadow.

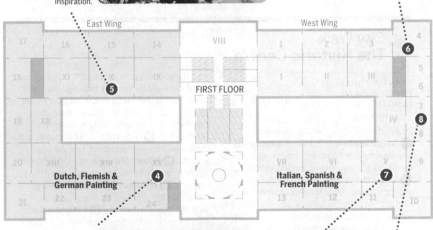

East Wing

West Wing

VIII

FIRST FLOOR

❺

❻

❽

Dutch, Flemish & German Painting ❹

Italian, Spanish & French Painting ❼

Adoration of the Trinity
Dutch, Flemish & German Painting, Room XV

Dürer's magnum opus altarpiece was commissioned by Nuremberg merchant Matthäus Landauer in 1511. Angels, saints and earthly believers surround the Holy Trinity, while Dürer hides in the bottom right-hand corner.

DEA PICTURE LIBRARY/GETTY IMAGES ©

Madonna of the Rosary
Italian, Spanish & French Painting, Room V

Caravaggio's trademark chiaroscuro style brings depth, richness and feeling to this 1607 masterpiece. Holding infant Jesus, the Madonna asks St Dominic to distribute rosaries to the barefooted poor who kneel before her.

Summer
Italian, Spanish & French Painting, Room 7

Italian court painter Giuseppe Arcimboldo's *Summer* (1563) was a hit with the Habsburgs. The most striking of his four seasons cycle, this masterwork celebrates seasonal abundance in the form of a portrait composed of fruit and vegetables.

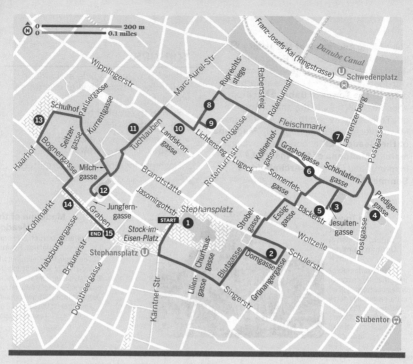

🏃 City Walk
The Historic Centre

START STEPHANSDOM
FINISH GRABEN
LENGTH 3KM; 1½ TO FIVE HOURS

Begin at Vienna's signature cathedral, ❶ **Stephansdom** (p61). After following a small section of Kärntner Strasse, you'll wind through the atmospheric backstreets to ❷ **Mozarthaus Vienna** (p69), where the great composer lived for almost three years.

A series of narrow lanes leads you down towards two fine baroque churches. The interior of the ❸ **Jesuitenkirche** is pure deception, with frescoes creating the illusion of a dome, while the 1634 ❹ **Dominikanerkirche** is Vienna's finest reminder of the early baroque period of church building. The Jesuitenkirche is opposite the ❺ **Austrian Academy of the Sciences**, housed in a university building dating from 1755.

During daylight hours, you can enter ❻ **Heiligenkreuzerhof** from the eastern side (at night time, enter it from Grasshofgasse). Busy ❼ **Fleischmarkt** is the heart of the

traditional Greek quarter. Climb the stairs and enter the lively bars on ❽ **Judengasse**, the centre of the traditional Jewish quarter. Hoher Markt – Vienna's oldest square – is a busy commercial street; highlights here are the art-nouveau ❾ **Ankeruhr** (p73), a mechanical clock with historic figures marking the time, and the ❿ **Römer Museum**, Roman ruins dating from the 1st to the 5th century. You'll then pass the ⓫ **Neidhart-Fresken** (p73) mural and reach the most impressive church this side of Stephansdom, the ⓬ **Peterskirche**, with a fresco on the dome painted by JM Rottmayr and a golden altar.

Northwest of here, ⓭ **Am Hof** is spiked by an impressive Mariensäule column. As you make your way along Graben back towards Stephansplatz, pop into ⓮ **Adolf Loos' Public Toilets**, replete with mahogany-panelled stalls with opaque glass doors and exquisite tiling, then admire the gilded baroque ⓯ **Pestsäule memorial** (1693) to Vienna's 75,000 plague victims on Graben.

the Renaissance. If your time's limited, skip straight to the **Picture Gallery**, where you'll want to dedicate at least an hour or two to Old Masters.

The huge range of art amassed by the Habsburgs is simply extraordinary. Keep an eye out for Picture Gallery highlights such as Pieter Bruegel the Elder's *Tower of Babel* (1563), Raphael's *Madonna of the Meadow* (1506) and Giuseppe Arcimboldo's *Summer* (1563).

★**Staatsoper**   NOTABLE BUILDING
(Map p66; www.wiener-staatsoper.at; 01, Opernring 2; 🚊 D, 1, 2, 71 Kärntner Ring/Oper, Ⓤ Karlsplatz) Few concert halls can hold a candle to the neo-Renaissance Staatsoper, Vienna's foremost opera and ballet venue. Even if you can't snag tickets to see a tenor hitting the high notes, you can get a taste of the architectural brilliance and musical genius that have shaped this cultural bastion by taking a 40-minute guided tour (adult/child €7.50/3.50). Tours (in English and German) generally depart on the hour between 10am and 4pm.

Built between 1861 and 1869 by August Siccardsburg and Eduard van der Nüll, the Staatsoper initially appalled the Viennese public and Habsburg royalty and quickly earned the nickname 'stone turtle'. Despite the frosty reception, it went on to house some of the most iconic directors in history, including Gustav Mahler, Richard Strauss and Herbert van Karajan.

The contents of its former Staatsopernmuseum, which closed in 2014, are now displayed in the **TheaterMuseum** (Map p66; 📞 01-525 24 3460; www.theatermuseum.at; 01, Lobkowitzplatz 2; adult/child incl all exhibitions €8/free; ⊙ 10am-6pm Wed-Mon; 🚊 D, 1, 2, 62, 71 Kärntner Ring/Oper, Ⓤ Stephansplatz) near the Hofburg.

Guided tours take in highlights such as the foyer, graced with busts of Beethoven, Schubert and Haydn and frescoes of celebrated operas, and the main staircase, watched over by marble allegorical statues embodying the liberal arts. The **Tea Salon** dazzles in 22-carat gold leaf, the **Schwind Foyer** captivates with 16 opera-themed oil paintings by Austrian artist Moritz von Schwind, while the **Gustav Mahler Hall** is hung with tapestries inspired by Mozart's 'The Magic Flute'. You'll also get a behind-the-scenes look at the stage, which raises the curtain on around 300 performances each year.

ⓘ **VIENNA CARD**

Vienna Card (Die Wien-Karte; 48/72 hours €21.90/24.90) allows unlimited travel on the public transport system (including night buses) and hundreds of discounts at selected museums, cafes, *Heurigen* (wine taverns), restaurants and shops across the city, and on guided tours and the City Airport Train (CAT). The discount usually amounts to 5% to 25% off the normal price. It can be purchased at Tourist Info Wien (p119), the city's main tourist office, the Airport Information Office (p119) and many concierge desks at the top hotels.

★**Leopold Museum**   MUSEUM
(Map p78; www.leopoldmuseum.org; 07, Museumsplatz 1; adult/child €13/8; ⊙ 10am-6pm Fri-Wed, to 9pm Thu Jun-Aug, 10am-6pm Wed & Fri-Mon, to 9pm Thu Sep-May; Ⓤ Volkstheater, Museumsquartier) Part of the **MuseumsQuartier** (Museum Quarter; MQ; Map p78; www.mqw.at; 07, Museumsplatz; ⊙ information & ticket centre 10am-7pm; Ⓤ Museumsquartier, Volkstheater), the Leopold Museum is named after ophthalmologist Rudolf Leopold, who, after buying his first Egon Schiele for a song as a young student in 1950, amassed a huge private collection of mainly 19th-century and modernist Austrian artworks. In 1994 he sold the lot – 5266 paintings – to the Austrian government for €160 million (individually, the paintings would have made him €574 million), and the Leopold Museum was born. **Café Leopold** (Map p78; www.cafe-leopold.at; 07, Museumsplatz 1; ⊙ 10am-midnight Sun-Wed, to 4am Thu, to 6am Fri & Sat; 🛜; Ⓤ Museumsquartier, Volkstheater) is located on the top floor.

The Leopold has a white, limestone exterior, open space (the 21m-high glass-covered atrium is lovely) and natural light flooding most rooms. Considering Rudolf Leopold's love of Schiele (1890–1918), it's no surprise the museum contains the world's largest collection of the painter's work: 41 paintings and 188 drawings and graphics. Among the standouts are the ghostly *Self Seer II Death and Man* (1911), the mournful *Mother with Two Children* (1915) and the caught-in-the-act *Cardinal and Nun* (1912).

Other artists well represented include Albin Egger-Lienz, with his unforgiving depictions of pastoral life, Richard Gerstl and

Vorstadt Southwest

A B C D

1

Lerchenfelder Str

Neustiftgasse

Halbgasse

Zieglergasse

Myrthengasse

Neubaugasse

Kirchengasse

12

16

Kaiserstr

Burggasse

2

Shottenfeldgasse

Stuckgasse

Kandlgasse

Bandgasse

Hermanngasse

Westbahnstr 24

Boutiquehotel
Stadthalle
(600m)

3

Zieglergasse

Mondscheingasse

Zollergasse

Kirchengasse

14

Lindengasse

Richtergasse

Neubaugasse

4

Andreasgasse

Neubaugasse

31

Schadekgasse

Apollogasse

Shottenfeldgasse

Zieglergasse

Ameringstr

Esterházy
Park

Kaiserstr

Zieglergasse

Neubaugürtel

Mariahilfer Str

Esterházygasse

Otto 39
Bauer-gasse

Brauergasse

Schmalzhofgasse

Köngasse
26

5

Fuger-
gasse

Mariahilfer Gürtel

Burgerspitalgasse

Millergasse

38

Haydngasse

Webgasse

Liniengasse

Gumpendorfer Str

Hofmühlgasse

6

Wallgasse

Stumpergasse

Mittelgasse

Sandwirtgasse

Liniengasse

Grabnergasse

7

A B C D

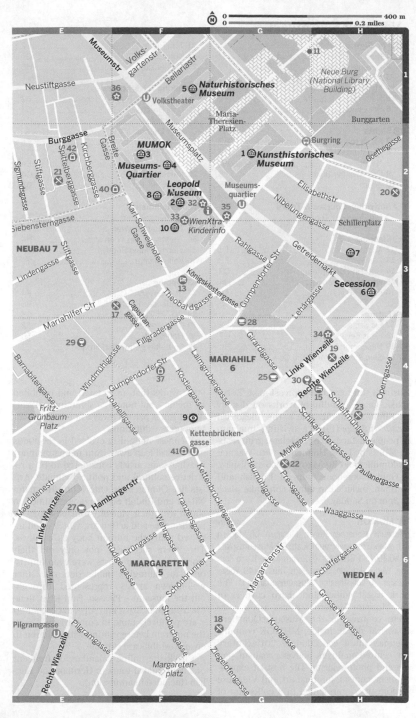

N

0 — 400 m
0 — 0.2 miles

11

Neue Burg
(National Library
Building)

Museumstr

Volks-
gartenstr

Bellariastr

Neustiftgasse

36

5 **Naturhistorisches
Museum**

Volkstheater

Maria-
Theresien-
Platz

Burggarten

Burgring

Goethegasse

Burggasse

Breite
Gasse

Kirchbergasse

42

Spittelberggasse

MUMOK
3

Museums-
Quartier

4

1 **Kunsthistorisches
Museum**

Museumsplatz

21

Stiftgasse

Sigmundsgasse

40

**Leopold
Museum**

8

2

32

35

Museums-
quartier

Elisabethstr

20

Schillerplatz

Nibelungengasse

Karl-Schweighofer-
Gasse

33

10

**WienXtra-
Kinderinfo**

Siebensterngasse

NEUBAU 7

Stiftgasse

Lindengasse

Rahlgasse Str

Getreidemarkt

7

Mariahilfer Ctr

Capistran
gasse

17

13

Königsklostergasse

Theobaldgasse

Gumpendorfer Str

Lehargasse

Secession
6

29

Fillgradergasse

Windmühlgasse

Gumpendorfer Str

28

Girardgasse

Laimgrubengasse

**MARIAHILF
6**

34

19

Linke Wienzeile

Opernasse

Barnabitengasse

37

Köstlergasse

25

30

Rechte Wienzeile

15

Schikanedergasse

23

Joanelligasse

Fritz-
Grünbaum
Platz

9

Kettenbrücken-
gasse

Mühlgasse

Schleifmühlgasse

Paulanergasse

41

22

Pressgasse

Linke Wienzeile

Magdalenestr

Hamburgerstr

27

Kettenbrückengasse

Franzensgasse

Heumühlgasse

Waaggasse

Grüngasse

Wehrgasse

Margaretenstr

Schäffergasse

Wien

Rüdiggasse

**MARGARETEN
5**

Schönbrunner Str

WIEDEN 4

Grosse Neugasse

Pilgramgasse

Pilgramgasse

18

Krongasse

Strobachgasse

Ziegelofengasse

Rechte Wienzeile

Margareten-
platz

Vorstadt Southwest

Austria's third-greatest expressionist, Kokoschka. Of the handful of works on display by Klimt, the unmissable is the allegorical *Death and Life* (1910), a swirling amalgam of people juxtaposed by a skeletal grim reaper. Works by Loos, Hoffmann, Otto Wagner, Waldmüller and Romako are also on display.

Guided one-hour tours in English and German, included in admission, take place at 3pm on Sunday.

★ **MUMOK**   GALLERY
(Museum Moderner Kunst; Museum of Modern Art; Map p78; www.mumok.at; 07, Museumsplatz 1; adult/child €11/free; ⊙ 2-7pm Mon, 10am-7pm Tue, Wed & Fri-Sun, 10am-9pm Thu; 📮 49 Volkstheater, Ⓤ Volkstheater, Museumsquartier) The dark basalt edifice and sharp corners of the Museum Moderner Kunst are a complete contrast to the MuseumsQuartier's historical sleeve. Inside, MUMOK contains Vienna's finest collection of 20th-century art, centred on fluxus, nouveau realism, pop art and photo-realism. The best of expressionism, cubism, minimal art and Viennese Actionism is represented in a collection of 9000 works that are rotated and exhibited by theme – but note that sometimes all this Actionism is packed away to make room for temporary exhibitions.

Viennese Actionism evolved in the 1960s as a radical leap away from mainstream art in what some artists considered to be a restrictive cultural and political climate. Artists like Günter Brus, Otto Mühl, Hermann Nitsch and Rudolf Schwarzkogler aimed to shock with their violent, stomach-churning performance and action art, which often involved using the human body as a canvas. They were successful: not only did their work shock, some artists were even imprisoned for outraging public decency. Other well-known artists represented throughout the museum – Picasso, Paul Klee, René Magritte, Max Ernst and Alberto Giacometti – are positively tame in comparison. Check the program before visiting with children to ensure exhibits are suitable.

Check the online calendar for frequent one-hour guided tours in German and English (included in admission).

★**Secession**   MUSEUM

(Map p78; www.secession.at; 01, Friedrichstrasse 12; adult/child €9/5.50; ⊙10am-6pm Tue-Sun; ⓤKarlsplatz) In 1897, 19 progressive artists swam away from the mainstream Künstlerhaus artistic establishment to form the Vienna Secession *(Sezession)*. Among their number were Klimt, Josef Hoffman, Kolo Moser and Joseph M Olbrich. Olbrich designed the new exhibition centre of the Secessionists, which combined sparse functionality with stylistic motifs. Its biggest draw is Klimt's exquisitely gilded *Beethoven Frieze*. Guided tours in English (€3) lasting one hour take place at 11am Saturday. An audio guide costs €3.

The 14th exhibition (1902) held in the building featured the 34m-long *Beethoven Frieze*. It was intended as a temporary display, little more than an elaborate poster for the main exhibit, Max Klinger's *Beethoven* monument. Since 1983 it has been on display in the basement. Multilingual brochures explain the various graphic elements, which are based on Richard Wagner's interpretation of Beethoven's ninth symphony. The small room you enter before viewing the frieze tells the story of the building. It served as a hospital during WWI and was torched by the retreating Germans during WWII (the gold dome survived the fire). The ground floor is still used as it was originally intended: presenting temporary exhibitions of contemporary art.

The building is certainly a move away from the Ringstrasse architectural throwbacks. Its most striking feature is the delicate **golden dome** rising from a turret on the roof that deserves better than the description 'golden cabbage' accorded it by some Viennese. Other features are the Medusa-like faces above the door with dangling serpents instead of earlobes, minimalist stone owls gazing down from the walls and vast ceramic pots supported by tortoises at the front.

★**Naturhistorisches Museum**   MUSEUM

(Museum of Natural History; Map p78; www.nhm-wien.ac.at; 01, Maria-Theresien-Platz; adult/child €10/free, rooftop tours €8; ⊙9am-6.30pm Thu-Mon, to 9pm Wed, rooftop tours in English 3pm Fri, Sat & Sun; ⓤMuseumsquartier, Volkstheater) Vienna's astounding Naturhistorisches Museum covers four billion years of natural history in a blink. With its exquisitely stuccoed, frescoed halls and eye-catching cupola, this late-19th-century building is the identical twin of the Kunsthistorisches Museum which sits opposite. Among its minerals, fossils and dinosaur bones are one-of-a-kind finds like the minuscule 25,000-year-old Venus von Willendorf and a peerless 1100-piece meteorite collection. Panoramic rooftop tours take you onto the building's roof to view the ornate architecture up-close; children under 12 aren't allowed.

★**Museum für Angewandte Kunst**   MUSEUM

(MAK, Museum of Applied Arts; Map p66; www.mak.at; 01, Stubenring 5; adult/under 19yr €9.90/free, 6-10pm Tue free, tours €2; ⊙10am-6pm Wed-Sun, to 10pm Tue, English tours noon Sun; ⓖ2 Stubentor; ⓤStubentor) MAK is devoted to craftsmanship and art forms in everyday life. Each exhibition room showcases a different style, which includes Renaissance, baroque, orientalism, historicism, empire, art deco and the distinctive metalwork of the Wiener Werkstätte. Contemporary artists were invited to present the rooms in ways they felt were appropriate, resulting in eye-catching and

HITLER IN VIENNA

Born in Braunau am Inn, Upper Austria, in 1889, with the name Adolf Schicklgruber (his father changed the family name when they moved to Germany in 1893), Adolf Hitler moved to Vienna when he was just 17. Six unsettled, unsuccessful, poverty-stricken years later he abandoned the city and moved to Munich to make a name for himself. He later wrote in *Mein Kampf* that his Vienna years were 'a time of the greatest transformation that I have ever been through. From a weak citizen of the world I became a fanatical anti-Semite'. Whether this had anything to do with being twice rejected by the Akademie der bildenden Künste (Academy of Fine Arts), who dismissed his work as 'inadequate', he did not say. Even though he was convinced that proper training would have made him into a very successful artist, these rejections caused Hitler to write to a friend that perhaps fate may have reserved for him 'some other purpose'. This 'purpose' became all too clear to everyone over time.

Hitler briefly returned to Vienna in 1938 at the head of the German army and was greeted by enthusiastic crowds on Heldenplatz. He left a day later.

unique displays. The 20th-century design and architecture room is one of the most fascinating, and Frank Gehry's cardboard chair is a gem.

The collection encompasses tapestries, lace, furniture, glassware and ornaments; Klimt's *Stoclet Frieze* is upstairs. The basement Study Collection has exhibits based on types of materials: glass and ceramics, metal, wood and textiles. Here you'll find anything from ancient oriental statues to unusual sofas (note the red-lips sofa).

★Rathaus   LANDMARK
(City Hall; Map p70; www.wien.gv.at; 01, Rathausplatz 1; ⊙tours 1pm Mon, Wed & Fri Sep-Jun, 1pm Mon-Fri Jul & Aug; 🚃D, 1, 2 Rathaus, ⓤRathaus) FREE The crowning glory of the Ringstrasse boulevard's 19th-century architectural ensemble, Vienna's neo-Gothic City Hall was completed in 1883 by Friedrich von Schmidt of Cologne Cathedral fame and modelled on Flemish city halls. From the fountain-filled **Rathauspark**, where Josef Lanner and Johann Strauss I, fathers of the Viennese waltz, are immortalised in bronze, you get the full effect of its facade of lacy stonework, pointed-arch windows and spindly turrets. One-hour guided tours are in German; multilingual audio guides are free.

The main spire is 102m high if you include the pennant held by the medieval knight, or Rathausmann, guarding its tip.

Guided tours lead through the **Arkadenhof**, one of Europe's biggest arcaded inner courtyards, and the barrel-vaulted **Festsaal** (Festival Hall), which hosts the **Concordia Ball** in June. Look for the reliefs of composers Mozart, Haydn, Gluck and Schubert in the orchestra niches. In the **Stadtsitzungsaal** (Council Chamber), a 3200kg, flower-shaped chandelier dangles from a coffered ceiling encrusted with gold-leaf rosettes and frescoes depicting historic events such as the foundation of the university in 1365. Other tour highlights include the **Stadtsenatssitzungssaal** (Senate Chamber), lavishly decorated in green damask, the **Wappensäle** (Coat of Arms Halls) and tapestry-adorned **Steinsäle** (Stone Halls).

Akademie der Bildenden Künste   MUSEUM
(Academy of Fine Arts; Map p78; www.akbild.ac.at; 01, Schillerplatz 3; adult/child €8/free; ⊙10am-6pm Tue-Sun; 🚃D, 1, 2 Kärntner Ring/Oper, ⓤMuseumsquartier, Karlsplatz) Founded in 1692, the Akademie der Bildenden Künste is an often underrated art space. Its gallery concentrates

on the classic Flemish, Dutch and German painters, and includes important figures such as Hieronymus Bosch, Rembrandt, Van Dyck, Rubens, Titian, Francesco Guardi and Cranach the Elder, to mention a handful. Hour-long tours (€3, in German only) take place at 10.30am every Sunday. Audio guides cost €2. The supreme highlight is Bosch's impressive and gruesome *Triptych of the Last Judgement* altarpiece (1504–08).

It depicts the banishment of Adam and Eve on the left panel and the horror of Hell in the middle and right panels. The building itself has an attractive facade and was designed by Theophil Hansen (1813–91), of Parlament fame. It still operates as an art school and is famous for turning down Adolf Hitler twice and accepting Egon Schiele (though the latter was happy to leave as quickly as possible). Directly in front of the academy is a **statue of Friedrich Schiller**, 18th-century German playwright.

Kunsthalle Wien   MUSEUM
(Arts Hall; Map p78; 🖉01-521 890; www.kunsthallewien.at; 07, Museumsplatz 1; both halls adult/child €12/free; ⊙11am-7pm Fri-Wed, to 9pm Thu; 🚃49 Volkstheater, ⓤMuseumsquartier, Volkstheater) The Kunsthalle is a collection of exhibition halls in the MuseumsQuartier used to showcase local and international contemporary art. Its high ceilings, open planning and functionality have helped the venue leapfrog into the ranks of the top exhibition spaces in Europe. Programs, which run for three to six months, rely heavily on photography, video, film, installations and new media. Weekend visits include one-hour guided tours in English and German.

The Saturday tours (Halle 1 at 3pm, Halle 2 at 4pm) focus on a theme, while Sunday tours (same locations and times) give an overview.

Volksgarten   GARDENS
(Map p66; www.bmlfuw.gv.at; 01, Dr-Karl-Renner-Ring; ⊙6am-10pm Apr-Oct, 6.30am-7pm Nov-Mar; 🚃D, 1, 2, 46, 49, 71 Dr-Karl-Renner-Ring, ⓤVolkstheater, Herrengasse) FREE Spreading out between the Burgtheater and Heldenplatz, the Volksgarten (People's Garden) is great for relaxing among dignified rose bushes and even more dignified statues. A **monument to Empress Elisabeth** is in the northeast corner, not far from the **Temple of Theseus**, an imitation of the one in Athens (commissioned by Napoleon), and the Volksgarten ClubDiskothek (p108).

Burggarten GARDENS
(Castle Garden; Map p66; www.bmlfuw.gv.at/ministerium/bundesgaerten; 01, Burgring; ◐6am-10pm Apr-Oct, 7.30am-5.30pm Nov-Mar; 🚊D, 1, 2, 46, 49, 71 Burgring, Ⓤ Museumsquartier) **FREE** Tucked behind the Hofburg, the Burggarten (Castle Garden) is a leafy oasis amid the hustle and bustle of the Ringstrasse and Innere Stadt. The marble **statue of Mozart** is the park's most famous tenant, but there's also a **statue of Franz Josef** in military garb. Lining the Innere Stadt side of the Burggarten is the **Schmetterlinghaus** (Butterfly House; Map p66; 🖉01-533 85 70; www.schmetterlinghaus.at; 01, Burggarten; adult/child €6.50/3.50; ◐10am-4.45pm Mon-Fri, to 6.15pm Sat & Sun Apr-Oct, 10am-3.45pm Nov-Mar; 🚊D, 1, 2, 71 Burgring, Ⓤ Karlsplatz) and the beautiful art nouveau Palmenhaus (p109) bar.

◉ Across the Danube Canal

The districts across the Danube Canal from the Innere Stadt are predominantly residential neighbourhoods, largely void of individual sights of interest to the average visitor. But this is Vienna's outdoor playground.

★ Riesenrad FERRIS WHEEL
(Map p94; www.wienerriesenrad.com; 02, Prater 90; adult/child €9.50/4; ◐9am-11.45pm, shorter hours in winter; ♿; Ⓤ Praterstern) Top of every Prater wish-list is the Riesenrad; at least for anyone of an age to recall Orson Welles' cuckoo clock speech in British film noir *The Third Man* (1949), set in a shadowy postwar Vienna. Built in 1897 by Englishman Walter B Basset, the ferris wheel rises to 65m and takes about 20 minutes to rotate its 430-tonne weight one complete circle – giving you ample time to snap some fantastic shots of the city spread out at your feet.

This unmissable icon also achieved celluloid fame in the James Bond flick *The Living Daylights,* and *Before Sunrise,* directed by Richard Linklater.

★ Prater PARK
(Map p94; www.wiener-prater.at; ♿; Ⓤ Praterstern) Spread across 60 sq km, central Vienna's biggest park comprises woodlands of poplar and chestnut, meadows and tree-lined boulevards, as well as children's playgrounds, a swimming pool, golf course and race track. Fringed by statuesque chestnut trees that are ablaze with russet and gold

in autumn and frilly with white blossom in spring, the central Hauptallee avenue is the main vein, running straight as a die from the Praterstern to the **Lusthaus** (🖉01-728 95 65; 02, Freudenau 254; mains €11-19; ◐noon-10pm Mon-Fri, to 6pm Sat & Sun, shorter hours winter; 🛜; 🚊77A).

Madame Tussauds Vienna MUSEUM
(Map p94; www.madametussauds.com/wien; 02, Riesenradplatz 1; adult/child €20.50/16.50; ◐10am-8pm, shorter hours in winter; Ⓤ Praterstern) This waxwork wonderland in the Würstelprater is a stage for a host of sculpted celebrities – Nicole Kidman, Michael Jackson and Johnny Depp star among them. Other figures such as Emperor Franz Joseph and his beloved Sisi, Klimt, Freud and Falco give the experience a distinctly Austrian edge.

There are hands-on exhibits that let you interact with the wax, from taking an IQ test with Albert Einstein to composing with Mozart and Beethoven.

Donauturm TOWER
(www.donauturm.at; 22, Donauturmstrasse 4; adult/child €7.90/5.70, combined ticket incl Riesenrad €13.50/7.40; ◐10am-midnight; Ⓤ Kaisermühlen Vienna International Centre) At 252m, the Danube Tower in Donaupark is Vienna's tallest structure. Its revolving restaurant at 170m allows fantastic panoramic views of the city and beyond – the food tends to be tried and trusted Viennese favourites. The adventurous can bungee jump off the side of the tower; see the website for details.

◉ Inside the Gürtel

The districts that lie inside the Gürtel area dense concentration of apartment blocks pocketed by leafy parks, with a couple of grand baroque palaces thrown in for good measure.

★ Schloss Belvedere PALACE
(Map p86; www.belvedere.at; adult/child Oberes Belvedere €14/free, Unteres Belvedere €12/free, combined ticket €20/free; ◐10am-6pm; 🚊D, 71 Schwarzenbergplatz, Ⓤ Taubstummengasse, Südtiroler Platz) A masterpiece of total art, Schloss Belvedere is one of the world's finest baroque palaces. Designed by Johann Lukas von Hildebrandt (1668–1745), it was built for the brilliant military strategist Prince Eugene of Savoy, conqueror of the Turks in 1718. What giddy romance is evoked in its sumptuously frescoed halls, replete with

artworks by Klimt, Schiele and Kokoschka; what stories are conjured in its landscaped gardens, which drop like the fall of a theatre curtain to reveal Vienna's skyline.

★ **Sigmund Freud Museum**   MUSEUM, HOUSE
(Map p70; www.freud-museum.at; 09, Berggasse 19; adult/child €10/4; ☺10am-6pm; ⊞D, ⓤSchottentor, Schottenring) Sigmund Freud is a bit like the telephone – once he happened, there was no going back. This is where Freud spent his most prolific years and developed the most significant of his groundbreaking theories; he moved here with his family in 1891 and stayed until forced into exile by the Nazis in 1938.

Freud's youngest daughter, Anna, helped to transform the apartment into this museum in 1971. A mirror she gave to her father, which hangs in his study window, is perhaps the most haunting artefact in the collection, along with the scarcely transformed waiting room area. Different thematic exhibits take over the former living areas each year and there a window-front installation space downstairs is given over to various contemporary artists. A contemporary art collection, in memory of Viennese artist Franz West, is also occasionally on show. Tram to Schlickgasse.

★ **Josephinum**   MUSEUM
(Map p70; www.josephinum.meduniwien.ac.at; 09, Währinger Strasse 25; adult/child €8/free, guided tours €4; ☺4pm-8pm Wed, 10am-6pm Fri-Sat, guided tour 11am Fri; ♿; ⓤWähringer Strasse/Volksoper) Architecture fans sometimes visit this Enlightenment-era complex for its superb 1785 neo-classical structures alone, although Joseph II's purpose-built medical academy for army surgeons does, in fact, house the city's most unusual museum. The highlight is its large collection of 200-year-old anatomical and obstetric models made of wax: while designed as visual aids for teaching, they were also intended for public viewing and to this day are exhibited in their original display cases, made of rosewood and Venetian glass.

Three rooms of this earnest gore can occasionally make you feel like you've wandered onto the set of a horror movie or some hitherto unexplored part of your psyche. If you are confident you can hold down your breakfast, don't forget to save enough time to also see the large collection of medical instruments – 'everything from tourniquets to cystoscopes', the website promises – death masks and an oddly compelling collection of oil paintings, watercolours and photographs depicting operations and medical conditions.

★ **Oberes Belvedere**   GALLERY
(Upper Belvedere; 03, Prinz-Eugen-Strasse 27; adult/child €14/free; ☺10am-6pm) Rising splendidly above the gardens and commanding sweeping views of Vienna's skyline, the Oberes Belvedere is one of Vienna's unmissable sights. Built between 1717 and 1723, its peerless art collection, showcased in rooms replete with marble, frescoes and stucco, attest to the unfathomable wealth and cultured tastes of the Habsburg Empire.

★ **Heeresgeschichtliches Museum**   MUSEUM
(Museum of Military History; www.hgm.or.at; 03, Arsenal; adult/under 19yr €6/free, 1st Sun of month free; ☺9am-5pm; ⓤSüdtiroler Platz) The superb Heeresgeschichtliches Museum is housed in the Arsenal, a large neo-Byzantine barracks and munitions depot. Spread over two floors, the museum works its way from the Thirty Years' War (1618–48) to WWII, taking in the Hungarian Uprising and the Austro-Prussian War (ending in 1866), the Napoleonic and Turkish Wars, and WWI. Highlights on the 1st floor include the Great Seal of Mustafa Pasha, which fell to Prince Eugene of Savoy in the Battle of Zenta in 1697.

On the ground floor, the room on the assassination of Archduke Franz Ferdinand in Sarajevo in 1914 – which set off a chain of events culminating in the start of WWI – steals the show. The car he was shot in (complete with bullet holes), the sofa he bled to death on and his rather grisly bloodstained coat are on show. The eastern wing covers the republic years after WWI up until the Anschluss in 1938; the excellent displays include propaganda posters and Nazi paraphernalia, plus video footage of Hitler hypnotising the masses.

★ **Wien Museum**   MUSEUM
(Map p86; www.wienmuseum.at; 04, Karlsplatz 8; adult/child €10/free, 1st Sun of month free; ☺10am-6pm Tue-Sun; ⓤKarlsplatz) Home to 150,000 artefacts, the Wien Museum provides a fascinating romp through Vienna's history, from Neolithic times to the mid-20th century, putting the city and its personalities in a meaningful context. Exhibits are spread over three floors, including spaces for two temporary exhibitions.

The **ground floor** gets off to an impressive start, tracing the history of the city from 5600 BC to the late Middle Ages. Standouts include medieval helms with bizarre ornamentations, Celtic gold coins and artefacts from the Roman military camp of Vindobona. The real attention-grabber, though, is the jewel-like stained glass and sculpture retrieved from Stephansdom post-WWII bombing. Of particular note are the 14th-century *Fürstenfiguren*, the princely figures salvaged from the cathedral's west facade.

The **1st floor** takes a brisk trot through the Renaissance and baroque eras and has a fascinating model of the city in its medieval heyday. Both Turkish sieges are well represented.

Top billing goes to the **2nd floor**, however, which zooms in on Vienna's fin-de-siécle artistic heyday. On show is the intact modernist living room Adolf Loos designed for his nearby apartment in 1903, replete with mahogany and marble, alongside stellar Secessionist works such as Klimt's mythology-inspired, gold-encrusted *Pallas Athene* (1898) and Egon Schiele's *Young Mother* (1914).

★**Karlskirche** CHURCH
(St Charles Church; Map p86; www.karlskirche.at; 04, Karlsplatz; adult/child €8/free; ◷9am-6pm Mon-Sat, noon-7pm Sun; ⓤKarlsplatz) Built between 1716 and 1739, after a vow by Karl VI at the end of the 1713 plague, Vienna's finest baroque church rises at the southeast corner of Resselpark. It was designed and commenced by Johann Bernhard Fischer von Erlach and completed by his son Joseph. The huge elliptical copper **dome** reaches 72m; the highlight is the lift (elevator) to the cupola (included in admission) for a close-up view of the intricate frescoes by Johann Michael Rottmayr. Audio guides cost €2.

The enormous twin columns at the front are modelled on Trajan's Column in Rome and show scenes from the life of St Charles Borromeo (who helped plague victims in Italy), to whom the church is dedicated. The admission price covers the **Museo Borromeo** chapel and a small museum with a handful of religious art and clothing purportedly from the saint. The high altar panel shows the ascension of St Charles Borromeo. In front of the church is a pond, replete with a Henry Moore sculpture from 1978.

Unteres Belvedere PALACE
(Lower Belvedere; Map p86; 03, Rennweg 6; adult/child €12/free; ◷10am-6pm Thu-Tue, to 9pm Wed;

🚋D) Built between 1714 and 1716, Lower Belvedere is a treat of baroque delights. Highlights include Prince Eugene's former residential apartment and ceremonial rooms, the **Groteskensaal** (Hall of the Grotesque; now the museum shop), a second **Marmorsaal** (Marble Hall), the **Marmorgalerie** (Marble Gallery) and the **Goldenes Zimmer** (Golden Room).

Temporary exhibitions are held in the **Orangery**, with a walkway gazing grandly over Prince Eugène's private garden. Attached to the Orangery is the **Prunkstall**, the former royal stables, where you can now trot through a 150-piece collection of Austrian medieval art, including religious scenes, altarpieces, sculpture and Gothic triptychs.

Belvedere Gardens GARDENS
(Map p86; 03, Rennweg/Prinz-Eugen-Strasse; ◷6.30am-8pm, shorter hours in winter; 🚋D) The three-tiered garden that unfurls between the two Belvederes was laid out in classical French style by Dominique Girard, a pupil of André le Nôtre of Versailles fame. Topiary fringes the ornamental parterres. Water nymphs frolic around the **Lower Cascade**, where you can also spy Greco-Roman statues of the eight muses and putti depicting the 12 months of the year.

Mythical beasties guard the **Upper Cascade**, which splashes down five steps into the basin below. As you approach the Oberes Belvedere (p84), note the winged sphinxes, symbols of power and wisdom, which seem poised to take flight.

Palais Liechtenstein PALACE
(Map p70; ☑01-319 57 67; www.liechtensteinmuseum.at; 09, Fürstengasse 1; tours €20; ◷guided tours 3pm 1st & 3rd Fri of the month; 🚋D, ⓤRossauer Lände) Once the architectural muse of Italian landscape painter Canaletto, Palais Liechtenstein is a sublime baroque palace that sits in beautifully landscaped, sculpture-dotted grounds. It also houses the private art collection of Prince Hans-Adam II of Liechtenstein (whose family resided in Vienna until the Nazi Anschluss in 1938), with around 200 paintings and 50 sculptures dating from 1500 to 1700. The palace can be visited twice monthly on hour-long guided tours (in German; English-language audio guide available). Book ahead.

On the ground floor, the unmissable **Gentlemen's Apartment Library** is a magnificent neoclassical hall containing about 100,000 books and frescoes by Johann

Vorstadt Southeast

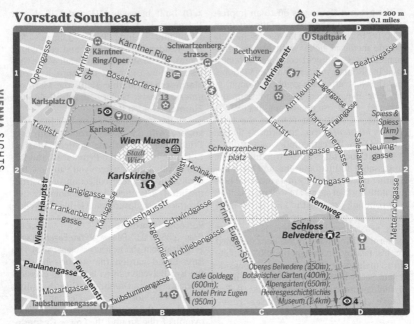

Vorstadt Southeast

Michael Rottmayr. Upstairs is the **Herkulessaal** (Hercules Hall) – so named for the Hercules motifs within its ceiling frescoes by renowned Roman painter Andrea Pozzo (1642–1709). Surrounding the hall are seven **art galleries** providing a trip through 200 years of art history, including such stunners as Raphael's *Portrait of a Man* (1503) and Rubens' intensely perceptive *Portrait of Clara Serena Rubens* (1616), alongside masterpieces of the Van Dyck and Frans Hals ilk. Keep an eye out for one of the world's most valuable pieces of furniture, the **Florentine Badminton Cabinet**, made for the British nobleman Henry Somerset, the 3rd Duke of Beaufort, in the 1720s.

To get here take tram D to Seegasse.

Stadtbahn Pavillons   NOTABLE BUILDING
(Map p86; www.wienmuseum.at; 04, Karlsplatz; adult/child €5/free; ⊙10am-6pm Tue-Sun Apr-Oct; ⓤKarlsplatz) Peeking above the Resselpark at Karlsplatz are two of Otto Wagner's finest designs, the Stadtbahn Pavillons. Built in 1898 at a time when Wagner was assembling Vienna's first public transport system (1893–1902), the pavilions are gorgeous examples of *Jugendstil*, with floral motifs and gold trim on a structure of steel and marble.

The west pavilion holds an exhibit on Wagner's most famous *Jugendstil* (art nouveau) works, the **Kirche am Steinhof** (☑910 60-11 204; 14, Baumgartner Höhe 1; tour €8, Art Nouveau tour, including church €12; ☺4-5pm Sat, noon-4pm Sun, tours 3-4pm Sat, 4-5pm Sun; ☐47A, 48A Baumgartner Höhe) and **Postsparkasse** (Map p66; www.ottowagner.com; 01, Georg-Coch-Platz 2; museum adult/child €8/free; ☺10am-5pm Mon-Fri; ☐1, 2, Ⓤ Schwedenplatz). The eastern pavilion is home to **Club U** (Map p86; www.club-u.at; 04, Künstlerhauspassage; ☺9pm-4am; Ⓤ Karlsplatz).

In 1977, the pavilions were dismantled to make room for the U-Bahn to run beneath them and were rebuilt 1.5m higher.

Hundertwasserhaus   LANDMARK
(03, cnr Löwengasse & Kegelgasse; ☐1 Hetzgasse) This residential block of flats bears all the wackily creative hallmarks of Hundertwasser, Vienna's radical architect and lover of uneven surfaces, with its curvy lines, crayon-bright colours and mosaic detail.

It's not possible to see inside, but you can cross the road to visit the **Kalke Village** (www.kalke-village.at; 03, Kegelgasse 37-39; ☺9am-6pm; ☐1 Hetzgasse) FREE, also the handiwork of Hundertwasser.

Botanischer Garten   GARDENS
(www.botanik.univie.ac.at; 03, Rennweg 14; ☺10am-1hr before dusk; ☐71, O) FREE These botanical gardens, belonging to the Vienna University, have tropical glasshouses and 11,500 species from six continents, including wonders such as Chinese dwarf bamboo, gingko biloba, tulip trees and Japanese plum yews.

◉ Outside the Gürtel

★ **Schloss Schönbrunn**   PALACE
(Map p88; www.schoenbrunn.at; 13, Schönbrunner Schlossstrasse 47; adult/child Imperial Tour €13.30/9.80, Grand Tour €16.40/10.80, Grand Tour with guide €19.40/12.30; ☺8.30am-6.30pm Jul & Aug, to 5.30pm Sep, Oct & Apr-Jun, to 5pm Nov-Mar; Ⓤ Hietzing) The Habsburgs' overwhelmingly opulent summer palace is now a Unesco World Heritage site. Of the palace's 1441 rooms, 40 are open to the public; the Imperial Tour takes you into 26 of these, including the private apartments of Franz Joseph and Sisi, while the Grand Tour covers all 40 and includes the precious 18th-century interiors from the time of Maria Theresia.

These mandatory tours are done with an audio guide or, for an additional charge, a tour guide.

Because of the popularity of the palace, tickets are stamped with a departure time and there may be a gap of an hour or more, so buy your ticket straight away and then explore the gardens, or book and buy for a specific time online.

Schloss Schönbrunn Gardens   GARDENS
(Map p88; www.schoenbrunn.at; 13, Schloss Schönbrunn; ☺6.30am-dusk; Ⓤ Hietzing) FREE The beautifully tended formal gardens of the palace, arranged in the French style, are a symphony of colour in summer and a combination of greys and browns in winter; all seasons are appealing in their own right. The grounds, which were opened to the public by Joseph II in 1779, hide a number of attractions in the tree-lined avenues (arranged according to a grid and star-shaped system between 1750 and 1755).

From 1772 to 1780 Ferdinand Hetzendorf added some of the final touches to the park under the instructions of Joseph II: fake **Roman ruins** (Map p88; adult/child €3.60/2.80; ☺8.30am-6.30pm Jul & Aug, to 5.30pm Apr-Jun, Sep & Oct, to 5pm Nov-Mar) in 1778; the **Neptunbrunnen** (Neptune Fountain; Map p88; adult/child €3.60/2.80; ☺8.30am-6.30pm Jul & Aug, to 5.30pm Apr-Jun, Sep & Oct, to 5pm Nov-Mar), a riotous ensemble from Greek mythology, in 1781; and the crowning glory, the **Gloriette** (Map p88; adult/child €3.60/2.80; ☺9am-6pm, closed early Nov–mid-Mar) in 1775.

The original **Schöner Brunnen** (Fountain; Map p88) fountain gushes near the Roman ruins while the baroque Irrgarten (p92) – a maze complex – is a late-20th-century re-creation with both classical labyrinthian hedges, a viewing platform, games, puzzles and a contemporary playground designed by famous designer Günter Beltzig.

To the east of the palace is the **Kronprinzengarten** (Privy Garden; Map p88; www.schoenbrunn.at; adult/student & child €3.60/2.80; ☺8.30am-6.30pm Jul & Aug, to 5.30pm Apr-June, Sep & Oct, to 5pm Nov-Mar), planted with citrus and flush with pergolas, a pond and a tripartite parterre based on embroidery patterns.

Klimt Villa   MUSEUM
(www.klimtvilla.at; 13, Feldmühlgasse 11; adult/child €10/5; ☺10am-6pm Thu-Sat Apr-Dec; ☐58) The Klimt Villa, which opened to the public in September 2012 following a complete

Schönbrunn

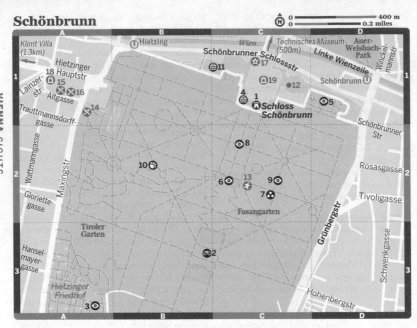

Schönbrunn

◎ Top Sights
1 Schloss Schönbrunn C1

◎ Sights
2 Gloriette B3
3 Hietzinger Friedhof A3
4 Kindermuseum C1
5 Kronprinzengarten D1
6 Neptunbrunnen C2
7 Roman Ruins C2
8 Schloss Schönbrunn Gardens C2
9 Schöner Brunnen C2
10 Tiergarten B2
11 Wagenburg C1

⊕ Activities, Courses & Tours
12 Hofbackstube Schönbrunn C1
13 Irrgarten C2

⊗ Eating
14 Maxing Stüberl A1
15 Pure Living Bakery A1
16 Waldemar A1

⊕ Entertainment
17 Marionetten Theater C1

⊕ Shopping
18 1130Wein A1
19 Schönbrunn Christmas Market C1

makeover, immerses you in the sensual world of Vienna's most famous Secessionist. Set in landscaped grounds in a leafy corner of Hietzing, the 1920s neo-baroque villa was built on and around the site of the original rustic studio, the artist's last, where he worked from 1911 to 1918.

Standouts include carefully reproduced furnishings and carpets, as well as Klimt's headily erotic sketches of his models. Just as special is the intimate atmosphere of strolling through the painter's one-time gardens, where two of his rose bushes still produce

blowsy, fragrant flowers. While it can take a little imagination to sense the studio, Moritz Nähr's original photos give a sense of life here, with Klimt and his entourage draped in flowing haute-bohemian robes, as depicted in portraits such as *Adele Bloch-Bauer II* and *Frederike Beer* (both of which Klimt painted here).

Wagenburg
MUSEUM

(Imperial Coach Collection; Map p88; www.kaiserli che-wagenburg.at; 13, Schloss Schönbrunn; adult/ child €8/free; ⊙9am-5pm mid-Mar–Nov, 10am-

4pm Dec–mid-Mar) The Wagenburg displays carriages ranging from tiny children's wagons up to sumptuous vehicles of state, but nothing can compete with Emperor Franz I Stephen's (1708–65) coronation carriage. Weighing in at 4000kg and dripping in ornate gold plating, it has Venetian glass panes and painted cherubs.

🏃 Activities

Oberlaa Therme Wien
SPA

(☑01-680 09; www.thermewien.at; 11, Kurbadstrasse 14; adult/child 3hr €18.50/12.50, full day €25.90/16; ☺9am-10pm Mon-Sat, 8am-10pm Sun; 🚼; 🚌67 Oberlaa-Therme Wien) If you want to rest museum-weary feet or escape the city for a day, Therme Wien might hit the mark. At Austria's largest thermal baths, the water bubbles at a pleasant 27° to 36°C, while jets, whirlpools, waterfalls and grotto-like pools pummel and swirl you into relaxation.

Besides a mosaic of indoor and outdoor baths, there are pools where kids can splash, dive and rocket down flumes to their hearts' content, a sauna complex where grown-ups can detox in herb-scented steam rooms with names like 'morning sun' and 'rainbow', and gardens where you can sunbathe or play volleyball and boules on warm days.

Citybike Wien
CYCLING

(Vienna City Bike; www.citybikewien.at; 1st/2nd/3rd hr free/€1/2, per hr thereafter €4) Over 120 Citybike Wien bike-share stands are located across the city. A credit card and €1 registration fee is required to hire bikes; just swipe your card in the machine and follow the multilingual instructions. The bikes are intended as an alternative to transport and can only be locked up at a bike station (unless you use your own lock).

A lost bike will set you back €600.

Wiener Eistraum
ICE SKATING

(Map p70; www.wienereistraum.at; 01, Rathausplatz; adult/child from €4, pre-heated skate hire €7.50/5.50; ☺9am-10pm late Jan-early Mar; 🚋D, 1, 2 Rathaus, ⓤRathaus) In the heart of winter, Rathausplatz transforms into two connected ice rinks covering a total of 8000 sq metres. It's a magnet for the city's ice-skaters, and the rinks are complemented by DJs, food stands, special events and *Glühwein* (mulled wine) bars. The skating path zigzags through the nearby park and around the entire square.

There's a free skating area and free equipment for beginners and children, open 9am to 4pm Monday to Friday, 8am to 10pm Saturday and Sunday. At 5pm Monday to Friday, eight curling lanes set up here.

★ Space and Place
WALKING TOUR

(http://spaceandplace.at) For the inside scoop on Vienna, join Eugene on one of his fun, quirky tours. The alternative line-up keeps growing: from Vienna Ugly tours, homing in on the capital's ugly side, to Smells Like Wien Spirit, a playful exploration of the city through smell, and the sociable Coffeehouse Conversations. See the website for dates and details

★ Donauinsel
OUTDOORS

(Danube Island; ⓤDonauinsel) The svelte Danube Island stretches some 21.5km from opposite Klosterneuburg in the north to the Nationalpark Donau-Auen in the south and splits the Danube in two, creating a separate arm known as the Neue Donau (New Danube). Created in 1970, it is Vienna's aquatic playground, with sections of beach (don't expect much sand) for swimming, boating and a little water skiing.

The tips of the island are designated FKK (*Freikörperkultur*; free body culture) zones reserved for nudist bathers, who also enjoy dining, drinking, walking, biking and in-line skating *au naturel* – it's quite a sight. Concrete paths run the entire length of the island, and there are bicycle and in-line-skate rental stores. Restaurants and snack bars are dotted along the paths, but the highest concentration of bars – collectively known as Sunken City and Copa Cagrana – is near Reichsbrücke and the U1 Donauinsel stop. In late June the island hosts the Donauinselfest (p96).

Pedal Power
CYCLING

(Map p94; ☑01-729 72 34; www.pedalpower.at; 02, Ausstellungsstrasse 3; bike rental per hr/half-/full day €6/19/30, guided bike tours €29-64, Segway tours €79; ☺8.30am-7pm Apr-Oct; ⓤPraterstern) Pick up city and mountain bikes here, or hook onto one of the Segway tours, covering the main city highlights including the Ringstrasse, the Rathaus, Hofburg and more, or guided bike tours ranging from a three-hour spin of the city's standout cities to an all-day pedal through the Wachau Valley vineyards. Visit the website for further details.

For an extra €6, you can arrange for the two wheels to be conveniently dropped off and picked up at your hotel. Child seats and helmets are an extra €5/3 respectively.

VIENNA FOR CHILDREN

Vienna is a wonderfully kid-friendly city. Children are welcomed in all aspects of everyday life, and many of the city's museums go out of their way to gear exhibitions towards children. Children's servings are typically available in restaurants, and, when kids need to burn off energy, playgrounds are plentiful.

Museums

Exhibits especially well suited to children include the following:

➡ The **Haus der Musik** (p65) has lots of practical exhibits for almost all ages to promote an understanding of music.

➡ The **Naturhistorisches Museum** (p81) has a superb anthropology section where you can have a photo of yourself taken as a prehistoric human and delve into forensics. Check for schedules for its *Nacht im Museum* (Night at the Museum) program, where kids (who must be accompanied by adults) can get a torch (flashlight) tour and bed down overnight (BYO sleeping bags).

➡ The **Technisches Museum** (www.technischesmuseum.at; 14, Mariahilfer Strasse 212; adult/under 19yr €12/free; ⊘ 9am-6pm Mon-Fri, 10am-6pm Sat & Sun; ⛟; ⎗ 52, 58 Winckelmannstrasse, Ⓤ Schönbrunn) has lots of hands-on exhibits to promote the understanding of science and technology.

The MuseumsQuartier has a couple of spaces created especially for kids:

➡ **Zoom** (Map p78; ☎ 01-524 79 08; www.kindermuseum.at; 07, Museumsplatz 1; exhibition adult/child €4/free, activities child €4-6, accompanying adult free; ⊘12.45-5pm Tue-Sun Jul & Aug, 8.30am-4pm Tue-Fri, 9.45am-4pm Sat & Sun Sep-Jun, activity times vary; Ⓤ Museumsquartier, Volkstheater) has exhibition sections and programs of hands-on arts and crafts (from eight months to 14 years old).

➡ **Dschungel Wien** (Map p78; ☎ 01-522 07 20; www.dschungelwien.at; 07, Museumsplatz 1; adult/child tickets from €6/4.50; ⊘ box office 2.30-6.30pm Mon-Fri, 4.30-6.30pm Sat & Sun; Ⓤ Museumsquartier, Volkstheater) is a children's theatre with dance and occasional English performances.

Playgrounds & Open Spaces

Playgrounds are everywhere, but the **Jesuitenwiese** in the Prater – along Hauptallee, about 1.5km east of Praterstern – has a good one with a Wild West theme, while on the

---

Nationalpark Donau-Auen   OUTDOORS

(☎01-400 04 9495; www.donauauen.at; 22, Dechantweg 8; ⊘national park house 10am-6pm Wed-Sun Mar-Oct; ⎗91A, 92A, 93A, ⎗S80) A vast ribbon of greenery looping along the Danube from the fringes of Vienna to the Slovakian border, the 9300-hectare Donau-Auen National Park is one of the last remaining major wetlands in Europe. Established in 1996, the park comprises around 65% forest, 20% lakes and waterways and 15% meadows, which nurture some 700 species of fern and flowering plants.

The park's quieter reaches attract abundant birdlife and wildlife, such as red deer, beavers, fire-bellied toads, eagles, kites and a high density of kingfishers. The wien-lobAU National Park House, located at the northern entrance to the park, offers a series of themed guided tours, ranging from winter walks to birdwatching rambles, most of which cost around €10/5 for adults/children. Boat tours into the national park leave from Salztorbrücke and last 4½ hours; booking is necessary. See the website for further details.

Alte Donau   WATER SPORTS

(22, Untere Alte Donau; Ⓤ Alte Donau) The Alte Donau, a landlocked arm of the Danube, is separated from the Neue Donau by a sliver of land. It carried the main flow of the river until 1875. Now the 160-hectare water expanse is a favourite of Viennese sailing and boating enthusiasts, and also attracts swimmers, walkers, fishermen and, in winter (if it's cold enough), ice skaters.

Strandbad Alte Donau   SWIMMING

(22, Arbeiterstrandbadstrasse 91; adult/child €5.50/3; ⊘9am-8pm Mon-Fri & 8am-8pm Sat &

Donauinsel (p89) there's the **Wasserspielplatz Donauinsel** where toddlers can paddle and kids can dart across water on flying foxes and cross suspension bridges. Take the U-Bahn to Donauinsel, then walk seven minutes downriver. Inside the **MuseumsQuartier** (p77) there's a sand pit from about May to September, as well as various events. Open-air winter ice rink **Wiener Eistraum** (p89) has a special area for children.

Schloss Schönbrunn

The splendid Schloss Schönbrunn palace will enchant children, who can dress up as princes and princesses at its **Kindermuseum** (Map p88; www.kaiserkinder.at/kindermuseum.html; 13, Schloss Schönbrunn; adult/child €8.80/6.70; ☺10am-5pm; ⛹) (Children's Museum), and check out exhibitions of natural science, archaeology and toys. Guided tours (in English by reservation) lasting 1½ hours let them discover the lives of the Habsburg children.

Performances of *The Magic Flute* (2½ hours) and *Aladdin* (1¼ hours) take place at the palace's puppet theatre, the **Marionetten Theater** (p115).

The **maze** at Schloss Schönbrunn is good fun for everyone, and the **Labyrinthikon** playground is designed for kids, with 14 playing stops for climbing, crawling and educational exploration.

Kids will also love visiting the world's oldest zoo, Schönbrunn **Tiergarten** (Map p88; www.zoovienna.at; adult/child €18.50/9; ☺9am-6.30pm high season, to 4.30pm low season; ⛹), which is home to some 750 animals including giant pandas and Siberian tigers.

Need to Know

➡ **Public Transport** Free for children under six years; half-price on single tickets under 15 years.

➡ **Restaurants** Nappy (diaper) changing facilities are rare. Dedicated kids' menus are also uncommon but children's servings are usually on offer.

➡ **Hotels** Cots (cribs) usually available. Children under 12 often stay free in their parents' room.

➡ **Breastfeeding in Public** Fine.

➡ **Babysitters** Best arranged through your hotel.

Sun May–mid-Sep; Ⓤ Alte Donau) This bathing area makes great use of the Alte Donau during the summer months. It's a favourite of Viennese locals and gets extremely crowded at weekends during summer. Facilities include a restaurant, beach-volleyball court, playing field, slides and plenty of tree shade.

Sailing School Hofbauer BOATING
(☎01-204 34 35; www.hofbauer.at; 22, An der Obere Alte Donau 191; ☺Apr-Oct; Ⓤ Alte Donau) Hofbauer rents sailing boats (€16.50 per hour) and row boats (€11 per hour) on the eastern bank of the Alte Donau and can provide lessons (in English) for those wishing to learn or brush up on their skills. Pedal boats (€14 per hour) and surf boards (€15.50) are also available for hire.

3 City Wave WATER SPORTS
(Map p86; www.3citywave.at; 03; Schwarzenbergplatz; ☺10am-10pm Sun-Thu, to 11pm Fri & Sat mid-Jun–Sep; Ⓤ Stadtpark; Karlsplatz) Surfing? In the heart of Vienna? Yep. This artificial wave in front of the Hochstrahlbrunnen fountain on Schwarzenbergplatz draws novices and pros alike. A 50-minute freesurfer session cost €39. Kids' surf camps are also available.

Wiener Eislaufverein SKATING
(Map p86; www.wev.or.at; 03, Lothringerstrasse 22; adult/child €7/6, boot hire €6.50; ☺9am-8pm Sat-Mon, to 9pm Tue-Fri; ⓓD Schwarzenbergplatz; Ⓤ Stadtpark) Fancy a twirl? At 6000 sq metres, the Wiener Eislaufverein is the world's largest open-air skating rink. It's close to the Ringstrasse and Stadtpark. Remember to bring mittens and a hat.

WHAT'S FREE

Vienna offers a wealth of opportunities to experience the city for free, from strolls through the city streets soaking up the spectacular architecture to a number of free museums, exhibitions, public buildings, parks and churches, as well as fabulous free entertainment, festivals and events.

Free Museums & Exhibitions

Some museums are free for those under 19 years, and permanent exhibitions at the municipal museums run by the City of Vienna are free on the first Sunday of the month. If you're interested in modern or contemporary art, drop into any of the free private art galleries scattered throughout the Innere Stadt. Most stock a program with a useful map with listings of exhibitions and gallery locations.

The following places are free:

➡ **Dorotheum** (Map p66; www.dorotheum.com; 01, Dorotheergasse 17; ◷10am-6pm Mon-Fri, 9am-5pm Sat; Ⓤ Stephansplatz) Sensational auction house packed with everything from paintings to furnishings and household objects.

➡ **Archiv des Österreichischen Widerstands** (Austrian Resistance Archive; Map p66; ✒ 01-228 94 69-319; www.doew.at; 01, Wipplingerstrasse 8; ◷9am-5pm Mon-Wed & Fri, to 7pm Thu; Ⓤ Stephansplatz) Exhibition documenting the antifascist resistance movement under Nazi rule.

➡ **Neidhart-Fresken** (p73) Frescoes surviving from the 14th century.

➡ **Schloss Belvedere Gardens** (p85) Exquisitely laid out gardens between Upper and Lower Belvedere palaces.

➡ **Schloss Schönbrunn Gardens** (p87) Expansive gardens, manicured and adorned in some parts, but also with pleasant wooded parkland.

➡ **Museum für Angewandte Kunst** (p81) Tuesday from 6pm to 10pm. Vienna's best collection of applied arts.

➡ **Hundertwasserhaus** (p87) A building designed by the eccentric architect Friedensreich Hundertwasser (the interior is closed to the public).

➡ **Otto Wagner Buildings** (Map p78; 06, Linke Wienzeile & Köstlergasse; Ⓤ Kettenbrückengasse) **& Naschmarkt** (p101) Also check out the Gürtel U-Bahn stations, designed by this architect who shaped so much of the city in the late 19th and early 20th centuries.

Free Public Buildings

The Ringstrasse is home to many spectacular buildings, including the **Hofburg** (p61) palace complex, which is free to wander (individual museums and attractions within the

---

Irrgarten OUTDOORS
(Maze; Map p88; adult/child €5.30/3; ◷8.30am-5.30pm) Schloss Schönbrunn palace garden's 630m-long Irrgarten is a classic hedge design based on the original maze that occupied its place from 1720 to 1892; adjoining this is the **Labyrinth**, a playground with games, climbing equipment and a giant mirror kaleidoscope.

Hofbackstube Schönbrunn FOOD & DRINK
(Court Bakery Schönbrunn; Map p88; ✒ 01-24 100-300; per person incl strudel/coffee & strudel €5/10; ◷10am-5pm Apr-Oct, to 4pm Nov-Mar, shows on the hour) It's a little touristy, but if you fan-

cy snagging some tips on how to knock up a perfectly crisp apple strudel, stop by this basement bakery, with live shows on the hour. Enjoy the result with a cup of coffee.

Badeschiff SWIMMING
(Map p66; www.badeschiff.at; 01, Danube Canal; adult/child €5/2.50; ◷8am-10pm May-Sep, bar 10am-1am year-round, kitchen 10am-10pm year-round; ᖡ1, Ⓤ Schwedenplatz) Swim on (not in!) the Danube. Floating on the bank of the Danube, between Schwedenplatz and Urania, this 28m-long lap pool has multiple decks with umbrella-shaded sun loungers and an open-air football pitch on the plat-

Hofburg incur admission fees). Other Ringstrasse highlights include the **University Main Building** (Map p70; ☑01-427 70, tours 01-427 71 7525; www.univie.ac.at; 01, Dr-Karl-Lueger-Ring 1; guided tours adult/child €5/3; ⊗7am-10pm Mon-Fri, to 7pm Sat, guided tours in English 11.30am Sat; ⊠D, 1, 2, ⓊSchottentor), and the **Justizpalast** (Supreme Court; Map p70; ☑01-521 52-0; www.ogh.gv.at; 01, Schmerlingplatz 11; ⊗7.30am-4.30pm Mon-Fri; ⊠D, 1, 2 Burgring, ⓊVolkstheater).

➡ **Stephansdom** (p61) The northern side-aisle is free to visit.

➡ **Rathaus** (p82) Vienna's splendid City Hall has free guided tours.

➡ **Zentralfriedhof** (www.friedhoefewien.at; 11, Simmeringer Hauptstrasse 232-244; ⊗7am-8pm, shorter hours in winter; ⊠6, 71 Zentralfriedhof) Beethoven, Brahms, Strauss and Schubert are among the luminaries buried at this cemetery.

➡ **Servitenkirche & Servitenviertel** (Map p70; www.rossau.at; 09, Servitengasse 9; ⊗Mass only; ⓊRossauer Lände) Wonderfully quiet church grounds and quarter around it.

➡ **Prater** (p83) Vienna's park and woodland across the Danube Canal.

➡ **Donauinsel** (p89) An island and recreation area in the middle of the Danube River.

➡ **Augarten** (Map p94; www.kultur.park.augarten.org; 03, Obere Augartenstrasse; ⊗6am-dusk; ⓊTaborstrasse) Eighteenth-century parkland with paths and meadows.

➡ **Hietzinger Friedhof** (Map p88; www.friedhoefewien.at; 13, Maxingstrasse 15; audio guide €7; ⊗7am-dusk; ⓊHietzing) Burial place of Gustav Klimt, Otto Wagner and other notable Viennese.

Free Entertainment

Free festivals and events abound during summer, including rock, pop, folk and country performances at the **Donauinselfest** (p96), opera, operettas and concerts at the **Musikfilm Festival** (p96), and films at outdoor cinemas including the **Kino Unter Sternen** (p97). The spectacle of Vienna's pride parade, the **Regenbogen Parade** (Rainbow Parade; www.hosiwien.at/regenbogenparade; ⊗mid-Jun), is also free.

In April, May, June and September and on Silvester (New Year's Eve), an open-air LED video wall sets up outside the **Staatsoper** (p112), screening operatic performances, with 180 chairs set up for each broadcast.

Winter freebies include wandering the city's enchanting **Christkindlmärkte** (Christmas markets; p95).

You can often hear DJs spinning for free in bars, and sometimes at open-air spaces such as the **MuseumsQuartier** (p77).

form suspended above. It doubles as a bar at night; in winter the pool closes and the ship is a bar and restaurant only.

The hold of the ship contains a bowling alley and dance floor where DJs spin regularly. Tram to Julius-Raab-Platz.

★ **Hot Rod City Tour**   DRIVING
(Map p66; ☑01-660 87 73; www.hotrod-city-tour-wien.com; 01, Judengasse 4; 2hr tour per person €99-119; ⊗10am-8pm Oct-May, 8am-10pm Jun-Sep; ⓊSchwedenplatz) If you've ever wanted to get behind the wheel of a mini hot rod, this is your chance. The low-to-the-ground one-person vehicles set off in convoy and

cover a circuit of the city in 1½ hours, with Vienna's landmarks as a backdrop. Helmets, walkie-talkies and insurance are included in the price; you'll need a valid driver's licence (foreign licences accepted).

Vienna Explorer   CYCLING, WALKING
(Map p66; ☑01-890 96 82; www.viennaexplorer.com; 01, Franz-Josefs-Kai 45; ⊗tours Easter-Oct, bike rental 8.30am-6pm year-round; ⊠1, ⓊSchwedenplatz) This long-standing outfit is excellent for bike tours in Vienna itself (three hours; adult/child $29/14.50) and further afield through the Wachau vineyards (10½ hours; €64/39), and it also has Vienna city walking tours (2½ hours;

Leopoldstadt

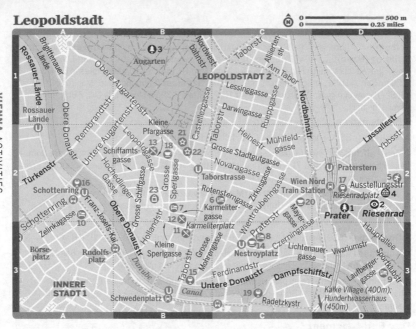

Leopoldstadt

€16/8). There's a bike rental service (per hour/day from €5/15) if you want to head out on your own. Tram to Salztorbrücke.

★**Wrenkh Cookery School**   COOKING
(Map p66; ☎01-533 15 26; www.wrenkh-wien.at; 01, Bauernmarkt 10; ☺per person from €48; Ⓤ Stephansplatz) This cookery school based in its eponymous restaurant (p104) has classes in English and German covering Austrian classics such as schnitzels, *Tafelspitz* (boiled beef), fresh-water fish, and apple strudel, along with international cuisines (Indian, Thai etc) and vegetarian and vegan cui-

sine. Look out for foraging expeditions, too. Courses start from €48 for 2½ hours to €130 for 6 hours. Check programs online.

☞ Tours

Fiaker Carriage Rides   TOURS
(20min/40min/1hr tour €55/80/110) One of the most romantic ways to see Vienna is aboard a *Fiaker*, a traditional-style open carriage (seating up to four passengers) drawn by a pair of horses. Drivers generally speak English and will point out places of interest en route. Lines of horses, carriages and bowler-hatted drivers can be found at Stephansplatz, Albertinaplatz and Heldenplatz at the Hofburg.

Short tours take you through the old town, while long tours include the Ringstrasse.

Vienna Walks & Talks   WALKING
(☑01-774 89 01; www.viennawalks.com) Vienna Walks & Talks offers the excellent 1½-hour Third Man Tour (adult/child €19/16.50), based on the 1949 film, as well as many other options in both English and German.

Vienna Tour Guides   WALKING
(www.wienguide.at; adult/child €16/8) Vienna Tour Guides is an organisation of highly knowledgeable guides who conduct over 60 different guided walking tours (some in English) covering everything from art-nouveau architecture to Jewish traditions in Vienna. Tours last roughly 1½ to two hours; some require a valid public transport pass and extra euros for entrance fees into sights.

The monthly *Wiener Spaziergänge* (Vienna's Walking Tours) leaflet from tourist offices details all tours, gives the various departure points and also indicates which tours are given in English.

Vienna Sightseeing Tours   BUS
(☑01-712 468 30; www.viennasightseeingtours.com; 04, Rainergasse 1; Hop On Hop Off tour €17-25, other tours €39-119; ⊙6.30am-6.30pm; 🚊D, Ⓤ Südtiroler Platz/Wien Hauptbahnhof) Vienna Sightseeing Tours runs the Hop On Hop Off city tour and the tours by the affiliated Cityrama. These take in Schönbrunn as well as some thematic (mostly music) tours in Vienna, but there are also tours to Bratislava, Budapest, Prague and Salzburg. The latter include hotel pick-ups and entrance fees.

DDSG Blue Danube   CRUISE
(Map p66; ☑01-588 80; www.ddsg-blue-danube.at; 01, Schwedenbrücke; 1½-hour tours adult/child €22/11; ⊙10.30am-6.20pm Easter-Oct; Ⓤ Schwe-

denplatz) DDSG Blue Danube's boats cover a variety of cruise routes; some of the most popular include circumnavigating Leopoldstadt and Brigittenau districts using the Danube Canal and the Danube as their thoroughfare. Select tours include passing through the Nussdorf locks (built by Otto Wagner around 1900) or continuing on to the Wachau.

Ring Tram   TOURS
(Map p66; ☑01-790 91 00; www.wienerlinien.at; 01, Schwedenplatz, Platform C; adult/child €9/4; ⊙10am-5.30pm; 🚊1, 2, Ⓤ Schwedenplatz) You can do a DIY tour of the Ringstrasse by public tram, but if you prefer a seamless tour with video screens and multilingual commentary, hop on the Ring Tram tour, which operates a continuous 30-minute loop around the Ringstrasse (no stops). Tour tickets are valid for one unbroken trip – meaning you can't hop on and off.

Oldtimer Bus Tours   BUS
(Map p78; ☑01-503 74 43 12; www.oldtimertours.at; 01, departure from Heldenplatz; tours adult/child €19/12; ⊙May–mid-Oct; 🚊D, 1, 2, 71 Burgring, Ⓤ Museumsquartier) Vintage open-top (closed if rainy) coaches trundle around the city centre and occasionally up to the Wienerwald (Vienna Woods). Tours last one hour and leave from in front of the Hofburg at Heldenplatz from Tuesday to Sunday at 11.15am, 12.45pm, 2.15pm and 4pm.

Redbus City Tours   BUS TOUR
(Map p66; ☑01-512 40 30; www.redbuscitytours.at; 01, Kärntner Strasse 25; 24hr adult/child €24/12, 48hr €30/15; ⊙9am-7pm; 🚊D, 1, 2 Kärntner Ring/Oper, Ⓤ Karlsplatz) These hop-on, hop-off tours include a 1½-hour route covering the main sights in and around the Innere Stadt and two-hour tours hitting all of the city's big sights. Buses leave from outside the Albertina.

✦✦ Festivals & Events

★**Christkindlmärkte**   CHRISTMAS MARKET
(www.wien.info/en/shopping-wining-dining/markets/christmas-markets; ⊙mid-Nov–25 Dec) Vienna's much-loved Christmas market season runs from around mid-November to Christmas Eve. Magical *Christkindlmärkte* set up in streets and squares, with stalls selling wooden toys, holiday decorations and traditional food such as *Wurst* (sausages) and *Glühwein* (mulled wine). The centrepiece is the **Rathausplatz Christkindlmarkt** (Map p70; www.christkindlmarkt.at; ⊙10am-10pm 13 Nov–26 Dec; 🚊D, 1, 2 Rathaus, Ⓤ Rathaus).

Opernball
CULTURAL

(www.wiener-staatsoper.at; ⊙ Jan/Feb; 🚇 D 1, 2, 71 Kärntner Ring/Oper, Ⓤ Karlsplatz) Of the 300 or so balls held in January and February, the Opernball (Opera Ball) is number one. Held in the Staatsoper (p112) on the Thursday preceding Ash Wednesday, it's a supremely lavish affair, with the men in tails and women in shining white gowns.

OsterKlang Festival
MUSIC

(Sound of Easter Festival; www.osterklang.at; ⊙ Mar or Apr) Orchestral and chamber music recitals fill some of Vienna's best music halls during this 'Sound of Easter' festival. The highlight is the opening concert, which features the Vienna Philharmonic.

Wiener Festwochen
ART

(Vienna Festival; www.festwochen.at; ⊙ mid-May–mid-Jun) A wide-ranging program of theatrical productions, concerts, dance performances and visual arts from around the world, the month-long Wiener Festwochen takes place from mid-May to mid-June at various venues city-wide.

Donauinselfest
MUSIC

(https://donauinselfest.at; ⊙ late Jun) FREE Held over three days on a weekend in late June, the Donauinselfest features a feast of rock, pop, folk and country performers, and attracts almost three million onlookers. Best of all, it's free!

Jazz Fest Wien
MUSIC

(www.viennajazz.org; ⊙ late Jun–mid-Jul) From the end of June to mid-July, Vienna swings to jazz, blues and soul flowing from the Staatsoper and a number of clubs across town.

Viennale Film Festival
FILM

(www.viennale.at; ⊙ late Oct–early Nov) The country's best film festival features fringe and independent films from around the world. Screenings take place at numerous locations around the city.

Musikfilm Festival
FILM

(http://filmfestival-rathausplatz.at; 01, Rathausplatz; ⊙ mid-Jul–early Sep; 🚇 D, 1, 2 Rathaus, Ⓤ Rathaus) Once the sun sets, the Rathausplatz is home to free screenings of operas, operettas and concerts. Turn up early for a good seat. Food stands and bars create a carnival-like atmosphere.

ImPulsTanz
DANCE

(www.impulstanz.com; ⊙ mid-Jul–mid-Aug) Vienna's premiere avant-garde dance festival attracts an array of internationally renowned troupes and newcomers between mid-July and mid-August. Performances are held in the MuseumsQuartier, Volkstheater and a number of small venues.

INTO THE WOODS: THE WIENERWALD

If you really want to get into the great outdoors, scamper across to the Wienerwald. The Austrian capital's rural escape vault, this 45km swath of forested hills, fringing the capital from the northwest to the southeast, was immortalised in 'Tales from the Vienna Woods,' the concert waltz by Johann Strauss Junior in 1868.

These woods are made for walking and the city council website (www.wien.gv.at/umwelt/wald/freizeit/wandern/wege) details nine walks, a couple of which take you into the forest. You'll need about three hours to complete the 7.2km trail No 4, which threads up to the **Jubiläumswarte**. Rising above the Wienerwald's green canopy, this lookout tower offers sweeping views from the uppermost platform that take in most of Vienna and reach as far as the 2076m hump of Schneeberg. The climb to the top is exhilarating. Grab some picnic supplies, jump on tram 49 to Bahnhofstrasse, and walk in the direction of the tram to Rosentalgasse, then follow the signs. From the Jubiläumswarte, the trail is mainly through suburbs, so it's nicer to return the way you came.

A slightly longer alternative is trail No 1, an 11km loop, which starts in Nussdorf (take tram D from the Ring) and climbs **Kahlenberg** (484m), a vine-streaked hill commanding fine city views. On your return to Nussdorf you can undo all that exercise by imbibing at a *Heuriger* (wine tavern). You can spare yourself the leg work by taking the Nussdorf-Kahlenberg 38A bus in one or both directions.

Another way of exploring the Wienerwald on your own is on one of the 46 marked mountain-bike trails. These are signposted and graded according to difficulty. The website www.wienerwald.info lists and maps the routes.

Lange Nacht der Museen
CULTURAL

(Long Night of Museums; http://langenacht.orf. at; ⊙1st Sat Oct) On the first Saturday of October, around 500 museums nationwide open their doors to visitors between 6pm and 1am. One ticket (adult/child €15/12; available at museums) allows entry to them all – including 80-plus in Vienna alone. The ticket price also includes public transport around town.

Kino Unter Sternen
FILM

(Cinema Under Stars; www.kinountersternen.at; ⊙late Jun–mid-Jul; Ⓤ Karlsplatz) A favourite Viennese summer activity, this open-air cinema is held over three weeks in the Resselpark on Karlsplatz. Admission is free; stalls sell food and drink.

Kino wie noch nie
FILM

(Map p94; www.kinowienochnie.at; 02, Augarten; tickets €8.50; Ⓤ Taborstrasse) Every summer the Augarten plays host to this two-month open-air cinema, which screens a mixed bag of arthouse, world, cult and classic films.

Silvester
NEW YEAR

(⊙31 Dec) The Innere Stadt becomes one big party zone for Silvester, which features outdoor concerts and loads of fireworks in the crowded streets.

🛏 Sleeping

From luxury establishments where chandeliers, antique furniture and original 19th-century oil paintings abound and statement-making design hotels at the cutting edge to inexpensive youth hostels, Vienna's lodgings cover it all. In between are homey, often family-run *Pensionen* (guesthouses), many traditional, and less ostentatious hotels, plus a smart range of apartments.

★ my MOjO vie
HOSTEL $

(Map p78; ☑0676-551 11 55; www.mymojovie. at; 07, Kaiserstrasse 77; dm €24-28, d/tr/q with private bathroom €80/120/160, s/d/tr/q with shared bathroom €40/60/90/116; @ ⌘; Ⓤ Burggasse-Stadthalle) An old-fashioned cage lift rattles up to these design-focused backpacker digs. Everything you could wish for is here – well-equipped dorms with two power points per bed, a self-catering kitchen, netbooks for surfing, guidebooks for browsing and musical instruments for your own jam session. There's no air-con but fans are available in summer.

THE VIENNALE

Vienna's annual international film festival, the 'fringe-like' **Viennale** (p96), is the highlight of the city's celluloid calendar. For two weeks from mid-October, public cinemas screen works ranging from documentaries to short and feature films.

Ticket sales commence on the Saturday before the festival begins. You can book by credit card, online or via a special hotline number that is published on the website once sales begin. Tickets can be picked up at any of the booths set up around town, such as the **Viennale main booth** (Map p78; www.viennale.at; 06, MuseumsQuartier, cnr Mariahilfer Strasse; ⊙10am-8pm; Ⓤ Museumsquartier).

Hotel am Brillantengrund
HOTEL $

(Map p78; ☑01-523 36 62; www.brillanten grund.com; 07, Bandgasse 4; s/d/tr/q from €69/79/99/119; @ ⌘; ☒49 Westbahnstrasse/ Zieglergasse, Ⓤ Zieglergasse) In a lemon-yellow building set around a sociable courtyard strewn with potted palms, this community linchpin works with local artists and hosts regular exhibitions, along with DJs, live music and other events such as pop-up markets and shops. Parquet-floored rooms are simple but decorated with vintage furniture, which variously incorporate local artworks, funky wallpapers and retro light fittings. Breakfast included.

Its cafe is also a favourite in the 'hood and cooks up Filipino cuisine alongside Austrian and Mediterranean dishes.

Gal Apartments
APARTMENT $

(Map p94; ☑0650 561 19 42; www.apartments vienna.net; 02, Grosse Mohrengasse 29; apt d/tr/q €89/99/152; @ ⌘; Ⓤ Nestroyplatz, Taborstrasse) For a superb home away from home, check into these roomy apartments smack in the action of up-and-coming Leopoldstadt. Occupying a renovated Biedermeier house, the apartments are dressed in modern furniture and *Jugendstil*-inspired paintings. It's a short walk to the Karmelitermarkt, the Prater and the Augarten, and the subway whips you to the centre of town in less than 10 minutes.

Angel's Place
GUESTHOUSE $

(☑01-89 20 432; www.angelsplace-vienna. eu; 15, Weiglgasse 1; d €60-76, ste €100; ⌘;

U Schönbrunn) A wine cellar has been converted into this cute guesthouse, in a workaday residential neighbourhood, a 10-minute stroll from Schloss Schönbrunn's gates. The warm-hued basement rooms are homey, with wood floors, bright textiles and original brick vaulting. There's a shared kitchen if you want to rustle up a snack; continental breakfast costs an extra €6.

Hotel Drei Kronen
PENSION $

(Map p78; ✆ 01-587 32 89; www.hotel3kronen.at; 04, Schleifmühlegasse 25; s/d from €69/92; @ ✆; U Kettenbrückengasse) Within stumbling distance of the Naschmarkt (some rooms overlook it), this family-owned abode is one of Vienna's best-kept secrets. Palatial touches (shiny marble, polished brass, white-and-gold wallpaper) are distinctly Viennese, but nonetheless a casual feel prevails. Rooms are fitted with *Jugendstil* furniture and art (including many prints by Klimt).

The breakfast buffet is huge, with pastries, cereals, bacon and free-range eggs, as well as *Sekt* (sparkling wine), an unheard-of luxury in a three-star pension.

★Magdas
BOUTIQUE HOTEL $$

(Map p94; ✆ 01-720 02 88; www.magdas-hotel.at; 02, Laufbergergasse 2; d €70-150) How clever: the Magdas is a hotel making a social difference as here the staff who welcome guests are refugees. The former retirement home turned boutique hotel opened its doors in 2016 and hit the ground running. The rooms are retro cool, with one-of-a-kind murals, knitted cushions and upcycling. The pick of them have balconies overlooking the Prater, just around the corner.

★Hotel Capricorno
HOTEL $$

(Map p66; ✆ 01-533 31 04-0; www.schick-hotels. com/hotel-capricorno; 01, Schwedenplatz 3-4; s/d incl breakfast from €118/146; P ✆; 🚌 1, 2, U Schwedenplatz) Set behind an unpromising mid-20th-century facade, Hotel Capricorno was stunningly made over in 2015 in lustrous velveteens in zesty lime, orange, lemon and aubergine shades. Most of its 42 rooms have balconies (front rooms overlook the Danube Canal; rear rooms are quieter). Onsite parking – rare for Vienna – is available for just €24 per day. It's a 10-minute walk from Stephansdom.

★Hotel Rathaus
Wein & Design
BOUTIQUE HOTEL $$

(Map p70; ✆ 01-400 11 22; www.hotel-rathaus-wien.at; 08, Lange Gasse 13; s/d/tr/ste from

€110/130/160/170/300; ❀ ✆; U Rathaus, Volkstheater) Each of the 39 open-plan, minimalist rooms at this boutique hotel is dedicated to an Austrian winemaker, and the minibars are stocked with premium wines from the growers themselves. With clever backlighting, rooms reveal a razor-sharp eye for design, especially the opalescent ones with hybrid beds and bathtubs. Some rooms overlook the inner courtyard space.

The hotel offers wine tastings in its chandelier-lit bar, and excursions to Austria's nearby wine-growing regions. Wine is also a theme at breakfast (guests/non-guests €18/24), with wine-based cheese, preserves and cakes alongside muesli, fruit, fish and cold cuts.

★Grätzlhotel
BOUTIQUE HOTEL $$

(Map p94; ✆ 01-208 39 04; www.graetzlhotel. com; 02, Grosse Sperlgasse 6; d €119-189) Where electricians, lamp makers and bakers once plied a trade, the Grätzlhotel has injected new life into Leopoldstadt with ultra-cool interiors courtesy of some of Vienna's top architects. Just around the corner from Karmelitermarkt, the suites are minimalist and streamlined, with vintage lights and homely touches – kitchens with Nespresso makers, retro radios and Viennese Saint Charles Apotheke toiletries.

Breakfast is served in **Zur Rezeption** (breakfast €6.80-8.90; ◷ 9am-6pm Sat-Tue, 9am-11pm Wed-Fri) cafe – the go-to place if you want any tips about the area, though the walking map in your room should get you off to a head-start. Check in is relaxed (you'll be given a code to enter), and free bikes are available for zipping around the sights or cruising on down to the nearby Danube

Hotel Capri
HOTEL $$

(Map p94; ✆ 01-214 84 04; www.hotelcapri.at; 02, Praterstrasse 44-46; s €75-105, d €109-149, tr €119-168, q €139-199; P ✆; U Nestroyplatz) This midranger looks nondescript on the face of things, but its merits are many: it's five minutes' walk from Prater, two U-Bahn stops from Stephansplatz, and staff bend over backwards to please. Done up in pastel colours, rooms are streamlined and immaculate, all with flat-screen TVs and kettles. Breakfast is a wholesome spread of fruit, cereals, cold cuts and eggs.

Spiess & Spiess
PENSION $$

(✆ 01-714 85 05; www.spiess-vienna.at; 03, Hainburger Strasse 19; s €105-145, d €140-180; ❀ @ ✆;

U Rochusgasse) The Spiess family goes out of its way to make you welcome at this elegant, well-positioned pension. The spacious, crisp white rooms have been designed with care and utmost taste; the pricier ones come with fireplaces and balconies. Breakfast is a tempting smorgasbord of fresh fruit salad, bacon and eggs, cereals and pastries.

Ruby Sofie   BOUTIQUE HOTEL $$

(✆ 01-361 96 60 60; www.ruby-hotels.com; 03; Marxergasse 17; d €74-119; U Wien Mitte) 'Lean luxury' is the ethos of this slick boutique hotel occupying the Sofiensäle, a grand former concert hall. Interiors are minimal-stylish, the vibe laid-back, and the pared-down rooms come with oak floors and vintage furnishings, docking stations, in-room tablets and rain-showers. There's also a library, a bar where you can loan out a guitar, a yoga terrace and free bikes.

Breakfast is worth the extra €12, placing the accent on regional and organic, with fresh fruits, breads, Viennese coffee and superfoods.

Hotel Kärntnerhof   HOTEL $$

(Map p66; ✆ 01-512 19 23; www.karntnerhof.com; 01, Grashofgasse 4; s €79-129, d €105-225, tr €175-259, ste €219-359; P @ ⎗; U Stephansplatz) Recent renovations have restored the Hotel Kärntnerhof's art-nouveau-era glory with *Jugenstil* colours (grey and sage), English wallpapers and Italian fabrics while retaining the period paintings lining the walls and wood- and frosted-glass–panelled lift to the roof terrace. On-site parking costs €20.

Opera Suites   PENSION $$

(Map p66; ✆ 01-512 93 10; www.operasuites.at; 01, Kärntner Strasse 47; d €155-170, apt from €168; ⎗; ⎘ D, 1, 2, 71, U Karlsplatz) Located directly across from the famous Café Sacher (p113) and close to the major sights, Opera Suites offers comfortable standard and superior rooms (all with Nespresso coffee machines and mini bars), as well as apartments in the surrounding streets with kitchenettes. Continental breakfast costs €10. Tram to Kärntner Ring/Oper.

Das Tyrol   HOTEL $$

(Map p78; ✆ 01-587 54 15; www.das-tyrol.at; 06, Mariahilfer Strasse 15; s €109-229, d €149-259, studios €149-299; ✳ @ ⎗; U Museumsquartier) Design is the word at Das Tyrol. Done out in zesty yellow and green hues, the spacious rooms feature original artworks, such as Dieter Koch's playful Donald and Daisy Duck paintings, and Nespresso machines. Corner rooms have small balconies overlooking Mariahilfer Strasse; studios have kitchenettes. Breakfast, with eggs cooked to order and Prosecco, will keep you going all morning.

The gold-tiled spa has a sauna and a 'light therapy' shower where you can watch fish swim in the aquarium.

Pertschy Palais Hotel   HOTEL $$

(Map p66; ✆ 01-534 49-9; www.pertschy.com; 01, Habsburgergasse 5; s €91-148, d €125-183, f €153-228; ⎗; U Herrengasse, Stephansplatz) The baroque, 18th-century-built Palais Cavriani's quiet yet central location, just off the Graben, is hard to beat. Staff are exceedingly friendly, and children are warmly welcomed (toys for toddlers and high chairs for tots are available). Decorated in creams, royal-reds and golds, its 55 spacious, antique-furnished rooms have parquet floors. Family rooms have period fireplaces (alas not in use).

25hours Hotel   DESIGN HOTEL $$

(Map p70; ✆ 01-521 51; www.25hours-hotels.com; 07, Lerchenfelder Strasse 1-3; d €160-190, ste €195-330; P ⎗; U Volkstheater) Decked out in bold colours, the 217 Dreimeta-designed rooms here include 34 suites with kitchenettes. Top-whack suites come with terraces commanding grandstand views of the Hofburg. The **Dachboden** (⊙ 3pm-1am) rooftop bar, Mermaid's Cave sauna area and free use of electro-bikes for whizzing about town make it a class act.

Steigenberger Hotel Herrenhof HOTEL $$

(Map p66; ✆ 01-534 040; www.steigenberger.com; 01, Herrengasse 10; d €160-213, ste €509-709; ✳ @ ⎗; U Herrengasse) Decorated throughout in subtle aubergine hues, the 196-room Steigenberger Hotel Herrenhof offers style at great value. The 24- to 28-sq-metre superior rooms and 35-sq-metre deluxe rooms are complemented by free use of the two-storey wellness area with a sauna, steam bath and fully equipped gym. Corner deluxe rooms have extra-large windows. Its restaurant is well regarded.

Hotel Prinz Eugen   HOTEL $$

(✆ 01-505 17 41; http://prinz-eugen-vienna.hotel-rv.com; 04, Wiedner Gürtel 14; s €55-72, d €67-88; ✳ @ ⎗; U Südtiroler Platz) Though not as flash as the chandelier-lit marble lobby might suggest, this is nevertheless a sound pick, bang opposite the Hauptbahnhof and five minutes' walk from Belvedere. Rooms are dressed in plush fabrics, wood furnishings and muted tones, and those on higher floors look out across Vienna's rooftops. The huge buffet breakfast will keep you going most of the day.

Benediktushaus
GUESTHOUSE **$$**

(Map p66; ☑ 01-534 989 00; www.benediktushaus. at; 01, Freyung 6a; s €80, d €125, tr €135, q €140; ☞; ⓤ Schottentor) Rest your weary head in a Benedictine monastery – you'd never guess you're in the heart of the action when you peer out your window into the tranquil, tree-filled courtyard. It's run by the Scottish Abbey next door. The tidy, TV-free rooms are simple and soothing, and a few period antiques add atmosphere around the halls.

Boutiquehotel Stadthalle
HOTEL **$$**

(☑ 01-982 42 72; www.hotelstadthalle.at; 15, Hackengasse 20; incl breakfast s €87-117, d €117-137, f €145-155; Ⓟ ☞; ⓤ Schweglerstrasse) ✈ The world's first urban hotel with a zero-energy balance makes the most of solar power, rainwater collection and LED lighting and has a roof planted with fragrant lavender. Vivid shades of purple, pink and peach enliven the 79 vintage-meets-modern rooms, which are split over two buildings divided by an ivy-draped courtyard where organic breakfast is served.

Altstadt
PENSION **$$**

(Map p78; ☑ 01-522 66 66; www.altstadt.at; 07, Kirchengasse 41; s €129-186, d €194-216, ste €199-427; ✷ ☞; ⓤ Volkstheater) Otto Ernst Wiesenthal has poured his passion and impeccable taste into creating one of Vienna's most outstanding guesthouses in Spittelberg. Design elements by Vitra and Philippe Starck merge seamlessly with original art from luminaries including Andy Warhol and Prachensky. The 45 individually decorated rooms have high ceilings, plenty of space and natural light. Children are charged by age (0-6/7-12/13-18 free/€20/40).

Free afternoon tea includes homemade cakes to the lavish breakfast with salmon, antipasti and *Sekt*; there's an open fire where you can nurse a glass of red.

★ Grand Ferdinand Hotel
DESIGN HOTEL **$$$**

(Map p66; ☑ 01-918 804 00; www.grandferdinand.com; 01, Schubertring 10-12; dm/d/ste from €30/180/500; ✷ ☞ ✷; ☐ 2, 71) An enormous taxidermied horse stands in the reception area of this ultrahip newcomer, which is shaking up Vienna's accommodation scene by offering parquet-floored dorms with mahogany bunks alongside richly coloured designer rooms with chaises longues and chandeliered suites with private champagne bars. Breakfast (€29) is served on the panoramic rooftop terrace, adjacent to the heated, open-air infinity pool.

There are three restaurants: one on the rooftop (for guests only), as well as a ground-floor modern European restaurant and a goulash and champagne bar (both open to non-guests). If you need to rent wheels, zoom off in one of the hotel's Maseratis (per day from €220). The nearest tram stop is Schwarzenbergplatz.

★ Hotel Sacher
HISTORIC HOTEL **$$$**

(Map p66; ☑ 01-514 56 780; www.sacher.com; 01, Philharmonikerstrasse 4; d from €398, ste from €745; ✷ @ ☞; ☐ D, 1, 2, 71 Kärntner Ring/Oper, ⓤ Karlsplatz) Stepping into Hotel Sacher is like turning back the clocks 100 years. The lobby's dark-wood panelling, original oil paintings and deep red shades and heavy gold chandelier, is reminiscent of a fin de siècle bordello. The smallest rooms are surprisingly large and suites are truly palatial. Extras include a taste of the cafe's (p113) famous *Sacher Torte* on arrival.

The state-of-the-art spa complex has a herbal sauna, an ice fountain and fitness room.

★ Hotel Imperial
HOTEL **$$$**

(Map p86; ☑ 01-501 100; www.grandluxuryhotels.com; 01, Kärntner Ring 16; d/ste from €425/525; @ ☞; ☐ D, 1, 71 Karlsplatz, ⓤ Karlsplatz) This rambling former palace, with all the marble and majesty of the Habsburg era, has service as polished as its crystal. Suites are filled with 19th-century paintings and genuine antique furniture (and come with butler service), while 4th- and 5th-floor rooms in Biedermeier style are far cosier and may come with a balcony. Breakfast costs €41.

★ DO & CO
DESIGN HOTEL **$$$**

(Map p66; ☑ 01-241 88; www.docohotel.com; 01, Stephansplatz 12; d €249-289, ste €960-1550; @ ☞; ⓤ Stephansplatz) Up-close views of Stephansdom extend from higher-priced rooms at this swanky hotel, and all 43 rooms come with state-of-the-art entertainment systems and multicountry power sockets. Some have in-room Jacuzzis, but be aware that bathrooms (not toilets) have transparent glass walls. Cathedral views also unfold from the 6th-floor bar and 7th-floor rooftop restaurant and terrace. The breakfast buffet costs €29.

Radisson Blu Style Hotel   DESIGN HOTEL $$$

(Map p66; ☑01-22 780 3214; www.radissonblu. com/stylehotel-vienna; 01, Herrengasse 12; d/ste from €170/290; ❉ ☎; ⓤ Herrengasse) Although part of a global chain, this glamorous hotel is a contender for the title of 'most fashionable hotel address' in Vienna, with overtones of art nouveau and art deco in its snazzy contemporary decor, and amenities including Nespresso machines in all rooms. Breakfast costs €23 per person.

Topazz Vienna   LUXURY HOTEL $$$

(Map p66; ☑01-153 222 40; www.hoteltopazz.com; 01, Lichtensteg 3; d €259-359; ❉ ☎; ⓤ Stephansplatz) Luxurious furnishings in subtle green and grey hues at the 32-room Topazz are inspired by the Wiener Werkstätte period around the turn of the 20th century. Most of the deluxe and prestige rooms have large, padded porthole window seats; superior rooms have small balconies. Its sister hotel, Lamée Vienna, is across the street.

Lamée Vienna   LUXURY HOTEL $$$

(Map p66; ☑01-153 222 40; www.hotellamee. com; 01, Rotenturmstrasse 15; d €259-379, ste €349-479; ☎; ⓤ Stephansplatz) Decorated in art deco and 1930s styles, this hotel has junior suites and suites complementing its superior, deluxe and prestige rooms. The minibar is restocked daily for free in the higher-category rooms. Its sister hotel, Topazz Vienna, is located directly across the road.

✗ Eating

Dining in Vienna gives you a taste of the city's history, at its street stands sizzling up sausages, candlelit vaulted-cellar wine bars and earthy, wood-panelled *Beisln* (bistro pubs) serving goulash and Wiener Schnitzel; its present, at hip cafes, multiethnic markets and international eateries; and its future, at innovative spaces with a wave of exciting chefs pushing in new directions.

★ Mamamon   THAI $

(Map p70; ☑01-942 31 55; www.mamamonthai-kitchen.com; 08, Albertgasse 15; mains €7-9.50; ☺11.30am-9.30pm Mon-Fri, noon-9.30pm Sat; ⓤ Josefstädter Strasse, Rathaus) Owner Piano, who named her restaurant for her mum Mon, has spiced up Vienna's burgeoning Southeast Asian food scene with a menu of southern Thai flavours, street-style decor and an indie soundtrack. On mild nights, a young, happy crowd spills out into the courtyard, while single diners pull up a stool at the large communal table or window seats within.

Piano's plump *tod mun* (fish cakes; €6) are some of the best outside of – or in – Thailand, and her herb-strewn papaya salad (€7.50), full-frontal pork *larb* (€6.50) and the addictive sticky-rice accompaniment have a cult-like following. There's an interesting list of other snacky starters, curries and stir-fries but it's hard to go past the daily curry and rice (€6 to €8.50), which often uses fresh, seasonal ingredients while still keeping it totally authentic (note that it's always fish on Fridays, but it often sells out by lunch).

★ Naschmarkt   MARKET $

(Map p78; 06, Linke & Rechte Wienzeile; ☺6am-7.30pm Mon-Fri, to 6pm Sat; ⓤ Karlsplatz, Kettenbrückengasse) Vienna's aromatic Naschmarkt unfurls over 500m along Linke Wienzeile between the U4 stops of Kettenbrückengasse and Karlsplatz. The western (Kettengasse) end has all sorts of meats, fruit and vegetables (including exotic varieties), spices, wines, cheeses, olives, Indian and Middle Eastern specialities and fabulous kebab and falafel stands. In all, there are 123 fixed stalls, including a slew of sit-down restaurants.

Another 35 places are allocated for temporary stalls such as farmers' stands. The market peters out at the eastern end to stalls selling Indian fabrics, jewellery and trashy trinkets. An adjoining Flohmarkt (flea market; p116) sets up on Saturdays.

★ Vollpension   CAFE $

(Map p78; www.vollpension.wien; 04, Schleifmühlgasse 16; dishes €2.80-7.90; ☺9am-10pm Tue-Sat, to 8pm Sun; ☑; ☒1, 62 Wien Paulanergasse) This white-painted brick space with mismatched vintage furniture, tasselled lampshades and portraits on the walls is run by 15 *omas* (grandmas) and *opas* (grandpas) along with their families, with more than 200 cakes in their collective repertoire. Breakfast, such as avocado and feta on pumpernickel bread, is served until 4pm; lunch dishes include a vegan goulash with potato and tofu.

Traditional red-wine organic goulash with bread dumplings and frankfurter sausages with fresh horseradish mustard are among the other specialities in store.

★ Bitzinger Würstelstand am Albertinaplatz
STREET FOOD $

(Map p66; www.bitzinger-wien.at; 01, Albertinaplatz; sausages €3.40-4.40; ⏰8am-4am; 🚇Kärntner Ring/Oper, ⓤKarlsplatz, Stephansplatz) Behind the Staatsoper, Vienna's best sausage stand has cult status. Bitzinger offers the contrasting spectacle of ladies and gents dressed to the nines, sipping beer, wine (from €2.30) or Joseph Perrier Champagne (€19.90 for 0.2L) while tucking into sausages at outdoor tables or the heated counter after performances. Mustard (€0.40) comes in *süss* (sweet, ie mild) or *scharf* (fiercely hot).

★ Eis Greissler
ICE CREAM $

(Map p78; www.eis-greissler.at; 06, Mariahilfer Strasse 33; 1/2/3/4/5 scoops €1.50/ 2.80/3.80/4.80/5.30; ⏰11am-10pm; ⓤMuseumsquartier) 🍦 The inevitable queue makes Eis Greissler easy to spot. Locals flock here whatever the weather for ice cream made from organic milk, yoghurt and cream from its own farm in Lower Austria, and vegans are well catered for with soy and oat milk varieties. All-natural flavours vary seasonally but might include cinnamon, pear, strawberry, raspberry, chocolate, hazelnut or butter caramel.

Waldemar
CAFE $

(Map p88; 📱0664 361 61 27; www.waldemar-tagesbar.at; 13, Altgasse 6; sandwiches €4.90-6, lunch mains €4.30-6.90; ⏰7.30am-8pm Mon-Fri, 9am-8pm Sat & Sun; ⓤHietzing) This stylish and airy breakfast-to-aperitif spot is unashamedly internationalist in both its menu and look. Join the casual-chic locals for baguettes and jam or a choice from the dedicated 'müsli & co' menu, or pop in for a groaning toasted sandwich or steaming bowl of Thai green curry or dahl at lunchtime. Sweet staff also turn out good coffee.

Schank zum Reichsapfel
AUSTRIAN $

(Map p94; 📱01-212 25 79; http://zumreichsapfel.at; 02, Karmeliterplatz 3; mains €7.50-14.20; ⏰4pm-midnight Mon-Sat; 🚇Karmeliterplatz (Taborstrasse), ⓤNestroyplatz) This is a delightfully warm, wooden *Heuriger* in the traditional mould, with dark wood panelling, a tiled oven and a jovial crowd of locals digging into platters of rustic bread, speck, ham, sausage and salami and sipping Austrian wines. More substantial mains hailing from Carinthia are of the *Schopfbratl* (pork roast) with dumplings, goulash and *Kasnudeln* (cheese noodles) ilk.

Trześniewski
SANDWICHES $

(Map p66; www.trzesniewski.at; 01, Dorotheergasse 1; sandwiches €1.20-3.60; ⏰8.30am-7.30pm Mon-Fri, 9am-6pm Sat, 10am-5pm Sun; ⓤStephansplatz) Trześniewski has been serving exquisite open-faced finger-style sandwiches for over 100 years. Choose from 22 delectable toppings incorporating primarily Austrian-sourced produce – chicken liver, smoked salmon and horseradish cream cheese and wild paprika and red pepper, egg and cucumber – on dark Viennese bread. This branch is the flagship of a now 10-strong chain in Vienna.

Pure Living Bakery
CAFE $

(Map p88; www.purelivingbakery.com; 13, Altgasse 12; cakes & snacks €4-10.50; ⏰9am-9pm; 🔌; ⓤHietzing) Inspired by her time in the USA, sweet-toothed traveller Kirsten has brought the laid-back mood and food of a US deli to Vienna. Decked out with surf boards and coffee sacks, wicker chairs and holiday snapshots, this living room of a cafe is the place to unwind over an organic quinoa salad, freshly toasted bagel with smoked salmon and avocado, or superfood smoothie.

Pot plants and pink and blue deckchairs lend a personal touch to the pretty garden, where you can easily while away a sunny afternoon reading a magazine, sipping a shake and nibbling on locally baked goodies such as deep-filled apple pie, warm cinnamon rolls and giant cookies. Gluten-free options are available.

Harvest
VEGAN $

(Map p94; 📱0676 492 77 90; http://harvest-bistrot.at; 02, Karmeliterplatz 1; mains €10-12, brunch €15.50, lunch €8.80; ⏰11am-11pm Mon, Tue, Thu & Fri, 10am-6pm Sat & Sun; 🔌; 🚇Karmeliterplatz (Taborstrasse), ⓤNestroyplatz) A bubble of bohemian warmth, Harvest swears by seasonality in its super-healthy vegetarian and vegan dishes, swinging from lentil, pear, walnut and smoked tofu salad to coconutty vegetable curries. Candles, soft lamp light and mismatched vintage furniture set the scene, and there's a terrace for summer dining. Alt Wien roasted coffee, homemade cakes and weekend brunches round out the picture.

Soupkultur
SOUP $

(Map p66; www.soupkultur.at; 01, Wipplingerstrasse 32; soups €2.40-4.90, salads €5-9; ⏰11.30am-3.30pm Mon-Thu, to 3pm Fri, closed Sat & Sun; 🔌; 🚇D, 1, ⓤSchottentor) Organic produce and aromatic spices are blended, sliced and chopped into an assortment of different soups and salads each week, ranging from red-lentil soup to traditional Hungarian goulash, Caesar salad to Thai papaya salad. There's token seating, but count on taking it away via cup or container – a leafy park is just around the corner. Tram to Wipplingerstrasse.

Leones Gelato
GELATERIA $

(Map p70; www.leones.at; 08, Langegasse 78; 1/2/3 scoops €1.80/3.30/4.50; ☺noon-10pm; ⓊAlser Strasse) This smart eat-in gelateria does everything right. Flavours keep it simple and veer towards the traditional, so there are no gaudy colours or chocolate-bar varieties. These are all kept fresh under the oh-so-Italian domed metal lids. Coffee is also the business here: as an added bonus, have it frappé style or as an *affogato*.

Keep an eye out for one of their summertime pop-ups in other neighbourhoods.

Café Goldegg
CAFE $

(www.cafegoldegg.at; 04, Argentinierstrasse 49; snacks €3.50-6, mains €10-13; ☺8am-8pm Mon-Fri, 9am-8pm Sat, 9am-7pm Sun; 🛜🖋; Ⓤ Südtiroler Platz) Goldegg is a coffee house in the classic Viennese mould, with its green velvet booths, wood panelling, billiard tables and art-nouveau sheen – but with a twist. Staff are refreshingly attentive, and alongside menu stalwarts such as goulash, you'll find lighter dishes like toasted paninis with homemade basil pesto and Ayurvedic vegetable curries.

Suppenwirtschaft
SOUP $

(Map p70; www.suppenwirtschaft.at; 09, Servitengasse 6; dishes €4.80-6.60; ☺11.30am-6pm Mon-Fri; 🖋; Ⓤ Rossauer Lände) 🍜 This chic little eat-in and takeaway kitchen focuses mainly on soups and a few curries and salads from a weekly menu; it fits in well with the genteel style of Servitengasse. All dishes are made fresh each day using ingredients foraged at the Naschmarkt. Everything is half-price from 5pm to 6pm.

★ Flein
AUSTRIAN $$

(Map p70; 🗹01-319 76 89; 09, Boltzmanngasse 2; mains €9.20-19.50; ☺11.30am-3pm & 5.30-11.30pm Mon-Fri; 🚌38, 41, ⓊSchottentor) Deep in the University district, rustic Flein is hidden behind high walls and an unassuming green door. Up the garden path is an exquisitely simple, ridiculously atmospheric room; for balmy nights, there are tables spaced here and there under the trees. Food combines traditional dishes with some lovely, Italian-influenced cooking, and surprises

with the occasional international twist (hello, kimchi!).

Staff are young and English-speaking, and will happily walk you through the daily handwritten German menu, be it a starter of Venetian-style eggplant, fat lamb sausages or seasonal fish mains. Wines are well chosen and prices reflect their pedigree. Tram to Sensengasse.

★ Lingenhel
MODERN EUROPEAN $$

(🗹01-710 15 66; www.lingenhel.com; 03, Landstrasser Hauptstrasse 74; mains €19-24; ☺shop 8am-8pm, restaurant 8am-10pm Mon-Sat; ⓊRochusgasse) One of Vienna's most exciting gastro newcomers, Lingenhel is an ultra-slick deli-shop-bar-restaurant, lodged in a 200-year-old house. Salamis, wines and own-dairy cheeses tempt in the shop, while much-lauded chef Daniel Hoffmeister helms the kitchen in the pared-back, whitewashed restaurant. The season-inflected food – simple as char with kohlrabi and pork belly with aubergines – tastes profoundly of what it ought to.

Be sure to sample, too, the cheeses made in its dairy – from creamy goat's cheese to buffalo mozzarella – or hook onto one of its cheese-making workshops (see website for details). The bar is a stylish spot to work up an appetite over the house vermouth and tonic.

★ Punks
MODERN EUROPEAN $$

(Map p70; 🗹0664 275 70 72; www.punks.wien; 08, Florianigasse 50; small plates €4.50) The name might be a giveaway, but this guerilla-style restaurant *is* indeed shaking up an otherwise genteel neighbourhood. Patrick Müller, Anna Schwab and René Steindachner have 'occupied' a former wine bar and eschewed the usual refit or any form of interior decoration; the focus is, quite literally, on the kitchen, with a menu of inventive small dishes prepared behind the bar.

Each of these are named for their primary ingredient, be that kohlrabi, *Käse* (cheese) or the freshwater-fish *wels*, although each involves a precise, if often fun, mix-and-match of flavours, textures and colours with beautiful, locally-sourced, seasonal produce. Order two or three per person, or just ask for the whole menu to be served if there's a few of you dining. Prosecco is worshipped here, so say yes to a glass, then follow with some excellent natural wines.

★ Griechenbeisl
BISTRO $$

(Map p66; 🗹01-533 19 77; www.griechenbeisl. at; 01, Fleischmarkt 11; mains €15-28; ☺11.30am

VIENNA EATING

11.30pm; ✂; 🚊1, 2, Ⓤ Schwedenplatz) Dating from 1447 and frequented by Beethoven, Brahms, Schubert and Strauss among other luminaries, Vienna's oldest restaurant has vaulted rooms, wood panelling and a figure of Augustin trapped at the bottom of a well inside the front door. Every classic Viennese dish is on the menu, along with three daily vegetarian options. In summer, head to the plant-fringed front garden.

Its warren of rooms include the oldest section, the Zither Stüberl, and the Mark Twain Zimmer (named for another former guest), inscribed with the autographs of Twain and others, which has been granted heritage status.

★ **Skopik & Lohn**   MODERN EUROPEAN **$$**
(Map p94; ✐ 01-219 89 77; www.skopikundlohn. at; 02, Leopoldsgasse 17; mains €13-27; ☺ 6pm-1am Tue-Sat; Ⓤ Taborstrasse) The spidery web of scrawl that creeps across the ceiling at Skopik & Lohn gives an avant-garde edge to an otherwise French-style brasserie – all wainscoting, globe lights, cheek-by-jowl tables and white-jacketed waiters. The menu is modern European, with a distinct Mediterranean slant, with spot-on dishes like slow-braised lamb with mint-pea puree, almonds and polenta, and pasta with summer truffle and monkfish.

★ **Said the Butcher to the Cow**   BURGERS, STEAK **$$**
(Map p78; ✐ 01-535 69 69; http://butcher-cow.at; 01, Opernring 11; mains €10.80-31.90; ☺ kitchen 5-11pm Tue-Sat, bar 5pm-1am Tue & Wed, 5pm-2am Thu-Sat; 🚊 D, 1, 2, 71 Kärnter Ring/Oper, Ⓤ Karlsplatz) Not only does this hip hangout have a brilliant name, it serves knock-out brioche-bun burgers (chicken teriyaki with wasabi mayo; black tiger prawns with bok choy; red wine vinegar-marinated halloumi with mango chutney; black bean and guacamole with boletus mushrooms), chargrilled steaks, and house-speciality cheesecakes. Better yet, it moonlights as a gin bar with 30 varieties and seven different tonics.

★ **Wrenkh**   BISTRO **$$**
(Map p66; ✐ 01-533 15 26; www.wrenkh-wien.at; 01, Bauernmarkt 10; mains €8-25; ☺ 11am-11pm Mon-Sat; ✂; Ⓤ Stephansplatz) Wrenkh specialises in vegetables (lentils in white-wine sauce with bread dumplings; paprika-marinated sweet potato with roasted goats cheese; creamed spinach-stuffed roast potatoes with apple and celery salad) but also creates some superb fish-based dishes (sautéed mountain-stream trout with with cherry-tomato potato salad) and meat options (dry-aged rib-eye with miso and aubergine crème). On weekdays, bargain-priced 2-/3-course lunch menus cost €9.50/10.50.

It also runs a cookery school (p94).

★ **Blue Mustard**   INTERNATIONAL **$$**
(Map p66; ✐ 01-934 67 05; www.bluemustard.at; 01, Dorotheergasse 6-8; 4-course menus €59-63, mains €15-25, street food €4.50-8.50; ☺ kitchen 5-10pm Mon-Sat, street-food truck 8am-5pm Mon-Sat, bar 5pm-2am Mon-Thu, 5pm-4am Fri & Sat; Ⓤ Stephansplatz) Backlit wood hand-carvings of Stephansdom's Gothic windows, a wall-to-wall neon-lit map of Vienna and a street-food truck parked in the foyer make this one of Vienna's hottest new openings. Alexander Mayer's 'Journey menus' might start in Vienna (*Beuschel* veal ragout) and end in Naples (*Torta Ricotta e Pera* – poached pear and ricotta in an almond-and-hazelnut biscotti) with spectacular cocktail pairings.

Street food from the retro gold truck spans Vietnamese spring rolls to fajitas and falafel. Or drop by the bar for sensational craft cocktail creations, such as El Cipote (tequila, aloe vera liqueur, jalapenos and pineapple juice). Infusions include bacon-infused vodka and sage-infused gin.

★ **Tian Bistro**   VEGETARIAN **$$**
(Map p78; ✐ 01-890 466 532; www.tian-bistro.com; 07, Schrankgasse 4; mains €10-18; ☺ 11.30am-10pm Mon-Fri, 9am-10pm Sat & Sun; ✂; 🚊 49 Siebensterngasse/Stiftgasse, Ⓤ Volkstheater) Colourful tables set up on the cobbled laneway outside Tian Bistro in summer, while indoors, a glass roof floods the atrium-style, greenery-filled dining room in light. It's the cheaper, more relaxed offspring of Michelin-starred vegetarian restaurant Tian (p107), and serves sublime vegetarian and vegan dishes such as black truffle risotto with Piedmont hazelnuts, as well as breakfast until 2pm on weekends.

Joseph Brot   BISTRO **$$**
(03, Landstrasser Hauptstrasse 4; breakfast €6.70-14.60, lunch mains €12.50-17.50; ☺ bakery 7.30am-9pm Mon-Fri, 8am-6pm Sat & Sun, bistro 8am-9pm Mon-Fri & 8am-6pm Sat & Sun; Ⓤ Wien Mitte) Purveyors of some of Vienna's finest bread, Joseph Brot's newest bakery, bistro and patisserie is a winner. Besides wonderfully fresh loaves – organic olive-tomato ciabatta and rye-honey-lavender, for instance – it

does wholesome breakfasts, speciality teas, healthy smoothies and utterly divine pastries. Season-driven specials such as sea-bream with tomatoes, artichokes and olives star on the lunch menu in the stripped-back bistro.

Meierei im Stadtpark
AUSTRIAN $$
(Map p66; ☑ 01-713 31 68; http://steirereck.at; 03, Am Heumarkt 2a; set breakfasts €20-24, mains €11.50-22; ☺ 8am-11pm Mon-Fri, 9am-7pm Sat & Sun; ☑; Ⓤ Stadtpark) In the green surrounds of Stadtpark, the Meierei is most famous for its goulash served with lemon, capers and creamy dumplings (€18), and its selection of 120 types of cheese. Served until noon, the bountiful breakfast features gastronomic showstoppers such as poached duck egg with sweet potato, cress and wild mushrooms, and warm curd-cheese strudel with elderberry compote.

It also rolls out Viennese classic fare with unusual twists, along the lines of veal with chive dumplings.

Ubl
AUSTRIAN $$
(Map p78; ☑ 01-587 64 37; 04, Pressgasse 26; mains €8.50-18; ☺ noon-2pm & 6pm-10pm Wed-Sun; Ⓤ Kettenbrückengasse) This much-loved *Beisl*'s menu is loaded with Viennese classics, such as *Schinkenfleckerl* (oven-baked ham and noodle casserole), *Schweinsbraten* (roast pork) and four types of schnitzel, and is enhanced with seasonal cuisine throughout the year. You could do worse than finish the hefty meal off with a stomach-settling plum schnapps. The tree-shaded garden is wonderful in summer.

Maxing Stüberl
AUSTRIAN $$
(Map p88; www.maxingstueberl.at; mains €9-18.50; ☺ 11am-2pm Mon-Sat; Ⓤ Hietzing) Once the favourite of Johann Strauss, this traditional wood-clad dining room serves up fabulously traditional dishes made with only the best produce from owner Christine Schenk's home region of Pielachtal in lower Austria. Music and candles only add to the atmosphere.

Starters include boiled beef aspic with onions and pumpkin seed oil or beef broth with liver dumplings; mains keep it just as real with fried black pudding (blood sausage) with sauerkraut and roasted potatoes or the speciality of chicken cooked on an iron griddle. The curd dumplings with stewed berries are also memorable.

Café Français
FRENCH $$
(Map p70; ☑ 01-319 09 03; www.cafe-francais.at; 09; Währingerstrasse 6-8; mains €8-19.50; ☺ 9am-midnight Mon-Sat) The Viennese flock to this big, bold and sexy French all-rounder. Big windows and park views make it a lovely morning spot and small dishes like Provençal-style sardines, fish soup or Moroccan *harira* soup make for a great lunch. Night-time brings the after-work, well-to-do *apero* crowd and dinner service with hearty (if not always entirely authentic) mains.

Yppenplatz 4
INTERNATIONAL $$
(www.yppenplatz4.at; 16, Yppenplatz 4; mains €9-12.80; ☺ 10am-11pm Mon-Sat; ☒ 2, Ⓤ Josefstädter Strasse) A reimagined *Würstelstand* fashioned from wood and glass from the office of local brewer Ottakringer, Yppenplatz 4 is the new fashionable face of this once edgy neighbourhood. While the menu spans global pub standards – risotto, pulled pork, burgers – it's the brewer's own handmade organic *Würstel* (sausages) that get rave reviews, along with freshly cooked potato crisps dusted with rosemary salt.

Brauwerk, Ottakringer's 'creative' brewery, showcase its excellent craft beers here too, and the young waiters are happy to help find your perfect sausage and *hausmarke* beer to match. Tram to Neulerchenfelder Strasse.

Wetter
ITALIAN $$
(☑ 01-406 07 75; www.wettercucina.at; 16, Payergasse 13/4; mains €9-20; ☺ 5pm-midnight Tue-Fri, 10am-10pm Sat; ☒ 4) Italian food is commonplace in Vienna, but it can get a bit samesame. With its pretty *platz*-side outlook, Wetter would be appealing whatever the menu, and it's great for a market pit-stop espresso. But its well-cooked regional specialities – from roast wild boar and Genovese-style tripe to flash-fried sardines and fat, house-made ravioli – that bring in the locals. Tram to Yppengasse.

La Salvia
ITALIAN $$
(www.lasalvia.at; 16, Yppenplatz; antipasta plates €7-10, pasta €9-12; ☺ 4-10pm Tue-Thu, 10am-10pm Fri, 9am-4pm Sat; ☒ 2, Ⓤ Josefstädter Strasse) Trieste in neighbouring Friuli-Venezia Giulia was once Vienna's seaside salon and La Salvia celebrates this long association through its Friulian and Istrian offerings. Locals love to come here for a mid-market shop platter of San Daniele prosciutto and Friulian mountain cheese – fresh from farmers just over the border – or a casual weeknight glass of *vino* and plate of pasta.

It's also one of the best places in town to stock up on a broad range of Italian deli goods, from Prosecco and *dolci* (sweets) to

VIENNESE SPECIALITIES

Vienna has a strong repertoire of traditional dishes. One or two are variations on dishes from other regions. Classics include:

➡ **Schnitzel** *Wiener Schnitzel* should always be crumbed veal, but pork is gaining ground in some places.

➡ **Goulash** *Rindsgulasch* (beef goulash) is everywhere in Vienna but attains exquisite heights at **Meierei im Stadtpark** (p105).

➡ **Tafelspitz** Traditionally this boiled prime beef swims in the juices of locally produced *Suppengrün* (fresh soup vegetables), before being served with *Kren* (horseradish) sauce.

➡ **Beuschel** Offal, usually sliced lung and heart with a slightly creamy sauce.

➡ **Backhendl** Fried, breaded chicken, often called *steirischer Backhendl* (Styrian fried chicken).

➡ **Zwiebelrostbraten** Slices of roast beef smothered in gravy and fried onions.

➡ **Schinkenfleckerln** Oven-baked ham and noodle casserole.

➡ **Bauernschmaus** Platter of cold meats.

The undeniable monarchs of all desserts are *Kaiserschmarrn* (sweet pancake with raisins) and *Apfelstrudel* (apple strudel), but also look out for *Marillenknödel* (apricot dumplings) in summer.

---

canned sustainably caught fish, pasta and pesto.

La Tavolozza
ITALIAN $$

(Map p70; ☑ 01-406 37 57; www.latavolozza.at; 08, Florianigasse 37; pizza €7-14.50, mains €14.50-22; ⊙ 5pm-midnight Mon-Fri, from noon Sat & Sun; 🚋 2, Ⓤ Rathaus) You'll feel part of the *famiglia* at this friendly neighbourhood Italian place, where tightly packed tables are lit by candlelight. The food is superb: crisp bread fresh from a wood oven is followed by generous, well-seasoned portions of grilled fish and meat, washed down with beefy Chianti reds. Seasonal specialities like truffles often star on the menu. Tram to Lederergasse.

Stomach
AUSTRIAN $$

(Map p70; ☑ 01-310 20 99; 09, Seegasse 26; mains €12-20; ⊙ 4pm-midnight Wed-Sat, 10am-10pm Sun; Ⓤ Rossauer Lände) Stomach has been serving seriously good food for years. The menu brims with carefully plated meat, fish and vegetable dishes, including Styrian roast beef, cream-of-pumpkin soup, and, when in season, wild boar and venison. The interior is authentically rural, and the overgrown garden pretty. 'Stomach', interestingly, comes from rearranging the word Tomaschek, the butcher's shop originally located here.

Haas Beisl
AUSTRIAN $$

(Map p78; ☑ 01-586 25 52; www.haasbeisl.at; 05, Margaretenstrasse 74; mains €10-19; ⊙ 11.30am-

10pm Mon-Sat, to 9pm Sun; Ⓤ Pilgramgasse) Warm and woody, this traditional Margareten *Beisl* is absolutely genuine and a great place to enjoy decent food in a very local atmosphere. Classics such as offal, sweetmeats, goulash and dumplings are prepared the way your grandmother might have done them. Two-course midweek lunch menus cost €7.90.

★ Steirereck im Stadtpark
GASTRONOMY $$$

(Map p66; ☑ 01-713 31 68; http://steirereck.at; 03, Am Heumarkt 2a; mains €48-52, 6-/7-course menus €142/152; ⊙ 11.30am-2.30pm & 6.30pm-midnight Mon-Fri; Ⓤ Stadtpark) Heinz Reitbauer is at the culinary helm of this two-starred Michelin restaurant, beautifully lodged in a 20th-century former dairy building in the leafy Stadtpark. His tasting menus are an exuberant feast, fizzing with natural, integral flavours that speak of a chef with exacting standards. Wine pairing is an additional €79/89 (six/seven courses).

The seasons play a definitive role, but you might begin, say, with young beets with wild lettuce, chia and eucalyptus, followed by milk-fed veal with melon, eggplant and sorrel. Be sure to save an inch for the legendary cheese trolley or delectable desserts such as milk and hay with raspberries. Service is predictably flawless, reservations are essential.

★**Plachutta** AUSTRIAN $$$
(Map p66; ☑01-512 15 77; www.plachutta.at; 01, Wollzeile 38; mains €16.50-27.20; ⊗11.30am-11.15pm; Ⓤ Stubentor) If you're keen to taste *Tafelspitz* (boiled beef), you can't beat this specialist wood-panelled, white-tableclothed restaurant. It serves no fewer than 13 varieties from different cuts of Austrian-reared beef, such as *Mageres Meisel* (lean, juicy shoulder meat), *Beinfleisch* (larded rib meat) and *Lueger Topf* (shoulder meat with beef tongue and calf's head). Save room for the Austrian cheese plate.

Its marquee-like outdoor terrace is heated in chilly weather.

★**Tian** VEGETARIAN $$$
(Map p66; ☑01-890 46 65-2; www.taste-tian.com; 01, Himmelpfortgasse 23; 2/3-course lunch menus €29/34, 4-/6-course dinner menus €93/108; ⊗noon-2pm & 5.45-9pm Tue-Sat; ☑; ☐2, Ⓤ Stephansplatz) ☞ Christian Holper's chandelier-lit, lounge-style restaurant takes vegetarian cuisine to Michelin-starred heights (tomato and white-raspberry soup, *porcini* risotto with spruce shoots, green-almond quinoa with broccoli), with regionally sourced produce – including from Tian's own garden. Wine-paired dinner menus cost €138/173 for four/six courses; on a languid afternoon, try the three-course lunch menu with free-flowing champagne or wine (€99). Tram to Weihburggasse.

★**Meinl's Restaurant** INTERNATIONAL $$$
(Map p66; ☑01-532 33 34 6000; www.meinlamgraben.at; 01, Graben 19; mains €16-39, 4-/5-course menus €67/85; ⊗noon-midnight Mon-Sat; ☎☑; Ⓤ Stephansplatz) Meinl's combines cuisine of superlative quality with an unrivalled wine list and views of Graben. Creations at its high-end restaurant span calamari and white-truffle risotto, apple schnapps-marinated pork fillet with green beans and chanterelles. Its on-site providore (p116) has a cafe and sushi bar, and its cellar wine bar (p108) serves great-value lunch menus.

Restaurant Mraz & Sohn INTERNATIONAL $$$
(☑01-330 45 94; www.mraz-sohn.at; 20, Wallenstein Strasse 59; 4-/6-/9-course menu €65/86/112; ⊗7pm-midnight Mon-Fri; ☐5 Rauscherstrasse, Ⓤ Jägerstrasse) Mraz & Sohn is not only a snappy name, it really is a family-owned-and-run restaurant. The highly esteemed *chef de cuisine*, Markus Mraz, is the creative force behind the two Michelin stars and other accolades awarded for dish-

es that shine with creative flair and taste profoundly of their main ingredients – be it succulent Wagyu beef or octopus.

Kim ASIAN $$$
(Map p70; ☑0664 425 88 66; www.kim.wien; 09, Währingerstrasse 46; lunch mains €10, 5-course dinner menu €75; ⊗noon-3pm & 6-11pm Wed-Fri; Ⓤ Währinger Strasse) ☞ Kim Kocht puts her own creative spin on Korean and Japanese cuisine at this understatedly stylish restaurant. Her menus are constantly changing but often feature fish dishes – such as lemongrass-chilli tuna with rice noodles – as the main course. The food is winningly fresh, making best use of organic produce. It's advisable to book well ahead. She also offers **cooking courses**.

🍷 **Drinking & Nightlife**

In this city where history often waltzes with the cutting edge, the drinking scene spans vaulted wine cellars here since Mozart's day to boisterous beer gardens, boho student dives and dressy cocktail bars, retro and rooftop bars. And with over 700 hectares of vineyards within its city limits, a visit to a *Heuriger* is a quintessential Viennese experience.

★**Das Loft** BAR
(Map p94; 02, Praterstrasse 1; ⊗10am-2am; ☐2 Gredlerstrasse, Ⓤ Schwedenplatz) Wow, what a view! Take the lift to Le Loft on the Sofitel's 18th floor to reduce Vienna to toy-town scale in an instant. From this slinky, glass-walled lounge, you can pick out landmarks such as the Stephansdom and the Hofburg over a pomegranate martini or mojito. By night, the backlit ceiling swirls with an impressionist painter's palette of colours.

★**Supersense** CAFE
(Map p94; 02, Praterstrasse 70; lunch special €5.50-6.50, breakfast €3.80-8; ⊗9am-7pm Mon-Fri, 10am-5pm Sat) Housed in an ornate Italianate mansion dating to 1898, this retro-grand cafe brings a breath of cool new air to the Prater area. The cafe at the front, which rolls out locally roasted coffee, great breakfasts and day specials, gives way to a store that trades in everything from vinyl to cult Polaroid cameras, calligraphy sets and hand-bound notebooks.

★**Botanical Gardens** COCKTAIL BAR
(Map p70; www.botanicalgarden.at; 09, Währinger Strasse 6-8; ⊗5pm-3am Tue-Sat) A subterranean

BEISLN

A Viennese tradition, a *Beisl* is akin to a bistro pub, dishing up heaping portions of goulash, Wiener schnitzel, *Tafelspitz* (prime boiled beef) and other favourites along with wine and/or beer on unadorned tables in wood-panelled surrounds. In the warmer months, many *Beisln* open onto terraces or lantern-lit cobbled courtyards. Linger over a drink, enjoy the classic Austrian fare and soak up the unique atmosphere at stalwarts such as **Griechenbeisl** (p103). These institutions have inspired a new breed of neo-*Beisln*, with a slightly upmarket edge and often organic produce.

mirror of Cafe Stein's sunny spaces above, Botanical Gardens makes for a cosy, magical retreat once Vienna's weather turns chilly. A dark nautical theme ticks all the cocktail-revival scene boxes, but with enough local eccentricity to keep things interesting.

But it's the cocktails (and their makers) that are the star here, with high-quality spirits, fresh juices and the intriguing use of herbs, spices and other botanicals like kaffir, tonka bean and rosemary.

★POC Cafe   COFFEE
(Map p70; www.poccafe.com; 08, Schlösselgasse 21; ◷8am-5pm Mon-Fri; 🚋5, 43, 44, Ⓤ Schottentor) Friendly Robert Gruber is one of Vienna's coffee legends and his infectious passion ripples through this beautifully rambling, lab-like space. POC stands for 'People on Caffeine'; while filter, espresso-style or a summertime iced cold-brew are definitely this place's raison d'etre, it's also known for moreish sweets like killer poppy-seed cake, cheesecake or seasonal fruit tarts. Tram to Lange Gasse.

★Meinl's Weinbar   WINE BAR
(Map p66; www.meinlamgraben.at; 01, Graben 19; ◷11am-midnight Mon-Sat; Ⓤ Stephansplatz) In the basement of food emporium Meinl am Graben (p116), this wine cellar stocks a vast selection of Austrian wines along with a smattering of international labels. Over 30 wines are available by the glass; between 11.30am and 2.30pm it also serves superb lunch menus (two-/three-course menus €10.50/13.50). For the full gourmet experience, book into the restaurant (p107).

★Loos American Bar   COCKTAIL BAR
(Map p66; www.loosbar.at; 01, Kärntner Durchgang 10; ◷noon-5am Thu-Sat, to 4am Sun-Wed; Ⓤ Stephansplatz) Loos is *the* spot in the Innere Stadt for a classic cocktail such as its signature dry Martini, expertly whipped up by talented mixologists. Designed by Adolf Loos in 1908, this tiny 27 sq metre box (seating just 20-or-so patrons) is bedecked from head to toe in onyx and polished brass, with mirrored walls that make it appear far larger.

★Strandbar Herrmann   BAR
(Map p94; www.strandbarherrmann.at; 03, Herrmannpark; ◷10am-2am Apr-early Oct; 🛜; 🚋0 Hintere Zollamtstrasse, Ⓤ Schwedenplatz) You'd swear you're by the sea at this hopping canalside beach bar, with beach chairs, sand, DJ beats and hordes of Viennese livin' it up on summer evenings. Cocktails are two for the price of one during happy hour (6pm to 7pm). Cool trivia: it's located on Herrmannpark, named after picture-postcard inventor Emanuel Herrmann (1839–1902).

★Café Sperl   COFFEE
(Map p78; www.cafesperl.at; 06, Gumpendorfer Strasse 11; ◷7am-11pm Mon-Sat, 11am-8pm Sun; 🛜; Ⓤ Museumsquartier, Kettenbrückengasse) With its gorgeous *Jugendstil* fittings, grand dimensions, cosy booths and unhurried air, 1880-opened Sperl is one of the finest coffee houses in Vienna. The must-try is *Sperl Torte*, an almond-and-chocolate-cream dream. Grab a slice and a newspaper (over 10 daily in English, French and German), order a coffee (34 kinds), and join the rest of the people-watching patrons.

A live pianist plays from 3.30pm to 5.30pm on Sunday.

★Café Leopold Hawelka   COFFEE
(Map p66; www.hawelka.at; 01, Dorotheergasse 6; ◷8am-midnight Mon-Wed, to 1am Thu-Sat, 10am-midnight Sun; Ⓤ Stephansplatz) Opened in 1939 by Leopold and Josefine Hawelka, whose son Günter still bakes the house speciality *Buchtein* (sweet jam-filled, sugar-dusted yeast rolls) to Josefine's secret recipe today, this low-lit, picture-plastered coffee house is a living slice of Viennese history. It was once the hangout of artists and writers – Friedensreich Hundertwasser, Elias Canetti, Arthur Miller and Andy Warhol included.

★Volksgarten ClubDiskothek   CLUB
(Map p66; http://volksgarten.at; 01, Burgring 1; ◷Apr–mid-Sep; 🚋D, 1, 2, 71 Dr-Karl-Renner-

Ring, ⓤMuseumsquartier, Volkstheater) Spilling onto the Volksgarten's lawns, these early 19th-century premises are split into three areas: the Wintergarten lounge bar with vintage 1950s furnishings and palms, Cortic Säulenhalle ('column hall'), hosting live music and theme nights, and hugely popular ClubDiskothek (cover charge from €3). Hours vary; check the program online.

★ Brickmakers Pub & Kitchen CRAFT BEER

(Map p78; ✍01-997 44 14; www.brickmakers.at; 07, Zieglergasse 42; ⊘4pm-2am Mon-Fri, 10am-2am Sat, 10am-1am Sun; ⓤZieglergasse) British racing-green metro tiles, a mosaic floor and a soundtrack of disco, hip-hop, funk, and soul set the scene for brilliant craft beers and ciders: there are 30 on tap at any one time and over 150 by the bottle. Pop-ups take over the kitchen, and at lunch and dinner guest chefs cook anything from gourmet fish and chips to BBQ-smoked beef brisket.

Demel COFFEE

(Map p66; www.demel.at; 01, Kohlmarkt 14; ⊘9am-7pm; ◪1A, 2A Michaelerplatz, ⓤHerrengasse, Stephansplatz) Within sight of the Hofburg, this elegant and regal cafe has a gorgeous rococo period salon. Demel's speciality is the *Ana Demel Torte*, a calorie-bomb of chocolate and nougat, as well as the Eduard-Sacher-Torte. The window displays an ever-changing array of edible art pieces (ballerinas and manicured bonsai, for example).

Fluc CLUB

(Map p94; www.fluc.at; 02, Praterstern 5; ⊘6pm-4am; ⓤPraterstern) Located on the wrong side of the tracks (Praterstern can be rough around the edges at times) and housed in a converted pedestrian passage, Fluc is the closest that Vienna's nightlife scene comes to anarchy – without the fear of physical violence.

Black-clad students, alcoholics and the occasional TV celebrity all share the stripped-back venue without any hassle, and DJs or live acts play every night (techno and electro feature heavily).

Balthasar CAFE

(Map p94; ✍0664 381 68 55; http://balthasar.at; 02, Praterstrasse 38; ⊘7.30am-7pm Mon-Fri, 9am-5pm Sat; ⓤNestroyplatz) With pops of bold colour and lampshades that look like deflated golden helium balloons, this quirky cafe brews some of Vienna's best coffee – including a feisty espresso. The pastries, baguettes and brownies are good, too.

Palmenhaus BAR

(Map p66; ✍01-533 10 33; www.palmenhaus.at; 01, Burggarten; ⊘10am-midnight Mon-Fri, 9am-midnight Sat, 9am-11pm Sun; ◪D, 1, 2, 71 Burgring, ⓤKarlsplatz, Museumsquartier) Housed in a beautifully restored *Jungendstil* palm house with high arched ceilings, glass walls and steel beams, looking through into the adjacent *Schmetterlinghaus* (butterfly house), the Palmenhouse opens onto a glorious covered summer terrace facing the Burggarten. The relaxed, welcoming ambience makes it ideal for a glass of wine or coffee. DJs occasionally spin on weekend evenings.

Classic Austrian dishes (mains €16.80 to €32) such as schnitzel are excellent; reserve ahead if you plan on dining.

Café Landtmann CAFE

(Map p66; www.landtmann.at; 10, Universitätsring 4; ⊘7.30am-midnight; 🛜; ◪D, 1, 2, ⓤRathaus) Freud, Mahler and Marlene Dietrich all had a soft spot for this coffee house, which opened its doors in 1873. Today, it attracts politicians and theatre-goers with its elegant interior and close proximity to the Burgtheater, Rathaus and Parliament. The list of traditional coffee specialities is formidable and the dessert menu features *Sacher Torte* (chocolate cake) and *Apfelstrudel* (apple strudel).

There's free live piano music from 8pm to 11pm, Sunday to Tuesday. Take a tram to Rathausplatz.

Café CI CAFE

(www.ci.or.at; 16, Payergasse 14; mains €7-11, snacks €4.50-7.50; ⊘8am-2am Mon-Sat, from 10am Sun; ◪2, ⓤJosefstädter Strasse) Something's always happening at this cafe founded to support new immigrants 30 years ago, be it a reading, an exhibition or language or dance classes. Come summer, its terrace throngs with Ottakringer locals sipping organic beers; in winter they retreat inside to browse the daily papers and dig into heart-warming goulash or *ćevapčići* (spicy Serbian sausages). Tram to Neulerchenfelder Strasse/Brunnengasse.

Flex CLUB

(Map p94; www.flex.at; 01, Augartenbrücke; ⊘9pm-6am Tue-Sat, club from 11pm; ◪1, 2, ⓤSchottenring) Down by a graffiti-strewn stretch of the Danube, Flex might attract a very young and mainstream crowd these days but still manages a semblance of its one-time edginess. The sound system is rumoured to be one of Europe's best, entry prices are usually reasonable and dress code unheard of. Local and international DJs are joined by occasional live acts.

Nights vary wildly from hardcore drum and bass to indie or electronic (for which the club is best known). In summer, the **Flex Cafe** (no cover charge) has picnic tables lining the canal, which overflow with happy drinkers, and its own, slightly more subdued, dance floor.

Café Rüdigerhof
CAFE

(Map p78; 05, Hamburgerstrasse 20; ☺9am-2am; ⓤKettenbrückengasse, Pilgramgasse) Rüdigerhof's facade is a glorious example of *Jugendstil* architecture, and the '50s furniture and fittings inside could be straight out of an *I Love Lucy* set. The atmosphere is homey and familiar and the wraparound garden huge and shaded. Hearty Austrian fare (huge schnitzels, spinach *Spätzle*, goat's cheese strudel) is way above average. On Saturday mornings it fills with Naschmarkt shoppers.

Lane & Merriman's
IRISH PUB

(Map p70; ☏01-402 47 64; www.laneandmerrimans.net; 09, Spitalgasse 3; ☺4pm-midnight Mon, Tue & Thu, 11am-midnight Wed, Fri & Sat; ⓤAlser Strasse) Yes, it's an Irish pub – there's that iconic Jane Bown portrait of Samuel Beckett in the window. But forget your preconceptions: David Gannon's contemporary take on the much-maligned institution is a delight. David will probably steer you towards an Austrian bio beer over Guinness; you're equally welcome in for a pot of tea and a slice of chocolate cake.

The drinks list and food are far from bog standard. Pub classics – fish and chips, burgers, soup and soda bread, UK-style chicken tikka – are made with locally sourced and organic produce where possible; there's a nightly special for €9.99. The breakfast menu ranges from a full Irish (€12) to organic porridge with stewed apples (€3.95), and tasty canapes (€3.50) to accompany the weekday happy hour cocktails (themselves a big draw at €5 a pop).

Tunnel
BAR, CAFE

(Map p70; www.tunnel-vienna-live.at; 08, Florianigasse 39; ☺9am-2am Mon-Sat, to midnight Sun; ⓘⓗ; ⓖ2, ⓤRathaus) This laid-back, endearingly boho cafe attracts students and all comers. By day it's a relaxed spot to grab an ancient wooden table and flick through a communal book or magazine with coffee or opt for lunchtime beers and Latin American snacks. The mood cranks up a notch with (mostly free) gigs at 9pm, from folk to indie, Latin to jazz.

The full line-up is posted online and includes pub quizzes in German, occasional English-speaking standup comedy and a big screen for big football matches. Tram to Lederergasse.

Weinstube Josefstadt
WINE BAR

(Map p70; 08, Piaristengasse 27; ☺4pm-midnight Apr-Dec, closed Jan-Mar; ⓤRathaus) Weinstube Josefstadt is one of the loveliest *Stadtheurigen* (city wine taverns) in Vienna. A leafy green oasis spliced between towering residential blocks, its tables of friendly, well-liquored locals are squeezed in between the trees and shrubs looking onto a pretty, painted *salettl*, or wooden summerhouse. Wine is local and cheap, food is typical, with a buffet-style meat and fritter selection.

Note that the location is not well signposted – the only indication of its existence is a metal *Busch'n* (green wreath) hanging from a doorway.

Kruger's American Bar
BAR

(Map p66; www.krugers.at; 01, Krugerstrasse 5; ☺6pm-4am Mon-Sat, 7pm-4am Sun; ⓖD, 1, 2, 71, ⓤStephansplatz) Retaining some of its original decor from the 1920s and 30s, this dimly lit, wood-panelled American-style bar is a legend in Vienna, furnished with leather Chesterfield sofas and playing a soundtrack of Frank Sinatra, Dean Martin and the like. The drinks list runs to 71 pages; there's a separate cigar and smoker's lounge. Tram to Kärntner Ring/Oper.

Salm Bräu
MICROBREWERY

(Map p86; www.salmbraeu.com; 03, Rennweg 8; ☺11am-midnight; ⓖ71 Unteres Belvedere, ⓤKarlsplatz) Salm Bräu brews its own *Helles, Pils* (pilsner), *Märzen* (red-coloured beer with a strong malt taste), *G'mischt* (half *Helles* and half *Dunkel* – dark) and *Weizen* (full-bodied wheat beer, slightly sweet in taste). Smack next to Schloss Belvedere and hugely popular, with a happy hour from 3pm to 5pm Monday to Friday and noon to 4pm Saturday.

Sperlhof
COFFEE

(Map p94; 02, Grosse Sperlgasse 41; ☺4pm-1.30am; ⓤTaborstrasse) Every Viennese coffee house ought to be just like the wood-panelled, poster-plastered, fantastically eccentric Sperlhof, which opened in 1923. It still attracts a motley crowd of coffee sippers, daydreamers, billiard and ping-pong players and chess whizzes today. If you're looking for a novel, check out the table of secondhand books.

Café Berg
CAFE

(Map p70; www.cafe-berg.at; 09, Berggasse 8; ☺10am-midnight Mon-Sat, to 11pm Sun; 🛜; 🚇 D, 1, Ⓤ Schottentor) Café Berg is Vienna's leading gay bar, although it's welcoming to all walks of life. Its staff are some of the nicest in town, the layout sleek and smart, and the vibe chilled. It's a brilliant all-rounder too, with breakfast and lunch served during the day and events and wine in the evening.

KaffeeModul
COFFEE

(Map p70; www.kaffeemodul.at; 08, Josefstädterstrasse 35; ☺7.30am-5.30pm Mon-Fri, 10am-2pm Sat) Can't take another milky *melange*? Head here for espressos, flat whites and cold brew. Billed as 'Vienna's smallest coffee shop', happy conversation bats from one side to the other of the tiny, bench-lined space, and from the stools streetside. There's nothing but coffee, apart from cookies, but what's on offer is direct-trade, small-batch roasted and expertly made.

Halbestadt Bar
COCKTAIL BAR

(www.halbestadt.at; 09, Stadtbogen 155; ☺7pm-2am Mon-Thu, to 3am Fri & Sat; Ⓤ Nussdorferstrasse) The impeccable hospitality starts when you can't open the glass door. The host swings it forth, escorts you in and offers to advise you on your order. More than 500 bottles grace the walls of the tiny, atmospheric space under the *Bogen* (railway arch) and mixologists hold court creating enticing cocktails. Note there's no bookings; it fills up fast.

Rafael's Vinothek
WINE BAR

(Map p78; 06, Naschmarkt stand 121; ☺10am-7.30pm Mon-Fri, to 6pm Sat; Ⓤ Kettenbrückengasse) Over 450 different wines from all over Austria are stocked at this Naschmarkt *Vinothek* (wine shop). Many are available to drink at its wine-barrel tables by the glass or bottle, accompanied by cheese and charcuterie platters in a chaotically sociable atmosphere – it's a favourite spot for a tipple for stallholders from the entire market.

Juice Deli
JUICE BAR

(Map p78; www.juicedeli.at; 06, Mariahilfer Strasse 45, shop 20, Raimundhof; ☺9.30am-7pm Mon-Fri, 11am-6pm Sat; Ⓤ Neubaugasse) 🌿 Tucked in a courtyard reached via a narrow alleyway leading off Mariahilfer Strasse, this one-off locavore spot uses regionally sourced, seasonal organic fruit, vegetables and herbs in its cold-pressed juices and smoothies such as mango and banana with handmade almond milk. It also has detox water varieties (lemongrass and mint; ginseng). Plastic packaging is shunned in favour of glass bottles.

A handful of tables set up on the tiny terrace out the front in warm weather.

Fischer Bräu
MICROBREWERY

(📋01-369 59 49; www.fischerbraeu.at; 19, Billrothstrasse 17; ☺4pm-12.30am; Ⓤ Nussdorfer Strasse) Fischer Bräu brews a new beer every four to six weeks, and a *Helles* (light) lager all year round. Live music often plays on Sunday afternoons in the rollicking, table-packed beer garden in summer. Cash only.

Café Tirolerhof
COFFEE

(Map p66; 📋01-512 78 33; 01, Führichgasse 8; ☺7am-10pm Mon-Sat, 9.30am-8pm Sun; 🛜; 🚇 D, 1, 2, 71 Kärntner Ring/Oper, Ⓤ Stephansplatz, Karlsplatz) Lovingly renovated *Jugendstil* decor from the 1920s, giant arched windows and homemade *Apfelstrudel* make Tirolerhof an inviting choice in the Innere Stadt.

Heuriger Huber
WINERY

(📋01-485 81 80; www.sissi-huber.at; 16, Roterdstrasse 5; ☺3pm-midnight Tue-Sat, hours can vary; 🚇10, 44) Riesling and Weissburgunder (Pinot blanc) are the main wines produced by this charming *Heuriger* (wine tavern), which has a sprawling Mediterranean garden surrounded by olive groves, citrus orchards and drifts of lavender. Seafood, salads, pastas and grilled meats appear on its select menu. Confirm opening hours before you visit. Take tram 10 or 44 to Dornbach/Güpferlingstrasse.

Café Drechsler
COFFEE

(Map p78; www.cafedrechsler.at; Linke Wienzeile 22; ☺8am-midnight Sun-Thu, to 2am Fri & Sat; 🛜; Ⓤ Kettenbrückengasse) Sir Terence Conran worked his magic with polished marble bar and table tops, Bauhaus light fixtures and whitewashed timber panels at Drechsler, one of the liveliest coffee houses in town. Food includes its legendary *Gulasch* (goulash). DJs spin in the evening, keeping the vibe upbeat and hip.

Café Jelinek
COFFEE

(Map p78; www.sternan.at; 06, Otto-Bauer-Gasse 5; ⊙9am-9pm; Ⓤ Zieglergasse) With none of the polish or airs and graces of some other coffee houses, this shabbily grand cafe is Viennese through and through. The wood-burning stove, picture-plastered walls and faded velvet armchairs draw people from all walks of life with their cocoon-like warmth. Join locals lingering over freshly roasted coffee, cake and the daily newspapers.

Tanzcafé Jenseits
BAR, CLUB

(Map p78; www.tanzcafe-jenseits.com; 06, Nelken-gasse 3; ⊙8pm-4am Tue-Sat; Ⓤ Neubaugasse) Bordello meets bohemian at this brothel turned bar, where soft lighting, red velvet and gilt mirrors keep the mood intimate. Jenseits has left its insalubrious past behind and today packs in a creative crowd who jostle for space on its tiny dance floor. The mercurial DJs flick from soul to trashy pop tunes in the blink of an eye.

Café Zartl
COFFEE

(03, Rasumofskygasse 7; ⊙7am-11pm; 🕿; 🚍1 Rasumofskygasse, Ⓤ Rochusgasse) A withered beauty of a coffee house, Zartl pings you back to when it opened in 1883, with its striped banquettes, cocoon-like warmth and, at times, somnambulant staff. Come for lazy breakfasts, people-watching and coffee with delightfully flaky strudel. You'll be mostly among regulars.

Café am Heumarkt
COFFEE

(Map p86; 03, Am Heumarkt 15; ⊙9am-11pm Mon-Fri; Ⓤ Stadtpark) Look for the house number, not the name, as there's no sign at this old-school charmer of a coffee house. Inside it's a 1950s time-warp – all shiny parquet, leather banquettes and marble tables. Do as the locals do: grab a newspaper, play billiards and unwind over coffee and no-nonsense Viennese grub.

Kaffee Alt Wien
CAFE

(Map p66; ☑01-512 52 22; www.kaffeealtwien.at; 01, Bäckerstrasse 9; ⊙10am-2am Sun-Thu, to 3am Fri & Sat; 🕿; Ⓤ Stephansplatz) Low-lit and full of character, bohemian Alt Wien is a classic dive attracting students and arty types. It's a one-stop shop for a lowdown on events in the city – every available wall space is plastered with posters advertising shows, concerts and exhibitions. The goulash is legendary and perfectly complemented by dark bread and beer.

☆ Entertainment

From opera, classical music and theatre to live rock or jazz, Vienna offers a wealth of entertainment opportunities. The capital is home to the German-speaking world's oldest theatre, the Burgtheater, as well as the famous Wiener Sängerknaben (Vienna Boys' Choir) and the Vienna Philharmonic Orchestra, which performs in the acoustically superb Musikverein.

★Staatsoper
OPERA

(Map p66; ☑01-514 44 7880; www.wiener-staatsoper.at; 01, Opernring 2; tickets €10-208, standing room €3-4; 🚍D 1, 2, 71 Kärntner Ring/Oper, Ⓤ Karlsplatz) The glorious Staatsoper is Vienna's premiere opera and classical-music venue. Productions are lavish, formal affairs, where people dress up accordingly. In the interval, wander the foyer and refreshment rooms to fully appreciate the gold-and-crystal interior. Opera is not performed here in July and August (tours still take place). **Tickets** (Map p66; ☑01-514 44 7810; www.bundestheater.at; 01, Operngasse 2; ⊙8am-6pm Mon-Fri, 9am-noon Sat & Sun; Ⓤ Stephansplatz) can be purchased up to two months in advance.

Tickets to the annual Opernball (p96) range from €490 to an eye-watering €21,000 and sell out years in advance.

★Burgtheater
THEATRE

(National Theatre; Map p66; ☑01-514 44 4440; www.burgtheater.at; 01, Universitätsring 2; seats €7.50-61, standing room €3.50, students €9; ⊙box office 9am-5pm Mon-Fri; 🚍D, 1, 2 Rathaus, Ⓤ Rathaus) The Burgtheater hasn't lost its touch over the years – this is one of the foremost theatres in the German-speaking world, staging some 800 performances a year, which reach from Shakespeare to Woody Allen plays. The theatre also runs the 500-seater Akademietheater, which was built between 1911 and 1913.

Tickets at the Burgtheater and Akademietheater sell for 75% of their face value an hour before performances. Advance bookings are recommended, although, depending on the performance, some last-minute tickets may be available.

★Musikverein
CONCERT VENUE

(Map p86; ☑01-505 81 90; www.musikverein.at; 01, Musikvereinsplatz 1; tickets €24-95, standing room €4-6; ⊙box office 9am-8pm Mon-Fri, to 1pm Sat Sep-Jun, 9am-noon Mon-Fri Jul & Aug; Ⓤ Karlsplatz) The opulent Musikverein holds the proud title of the best acoustics of any concert hall in Austria, which the Vienna Philharmonic Orchestra embraces. The lavish interior can be visited by 45-minute guided tour (in English and German; adult/child €6.50/4) at 10am, 11am and noon Monday to Saturday. Smaller-scale performances are held in the Brahms Saal. There are no student tickets.

Tickets for the famous New Year's Eve concert cost anything from €25 (standing room) to €800; due to high demand, a ballot takes place in January or February – register at www.wienerphilharmoniker.at. Standing-room tickets are available up to seven weeks in advance.

★ **MuTh**   CONCERT VENUE
(Map p94; ☑ 01-347 80 80; www.muth.at; 02, Obere Augartenstrasse 1e; Vienna Boys' Choir Fri performance €39-89; ☺ 4-6pm Mon-Fri & 1 hour before performances; ⓤ Taborstrasse) Opened to much acclaim in December 2012, this striking baroque meets contemporary concert hall is the new home of the Wiener Sängerknaben, or Vienna Boys' Choir, who previously only performed at the Hofburg. Besides Friday afternoon choral sessions with the angelic-voiced lads, the venue also stages a top-drawer roster of dance, drama, opera, classical, rock and jazz performances.

The acoustics are second to none in the 400-seat auditorium and there's a cafe where you can grab a drink before or after a show.

Theater an der Wien   THEATRE
(Map p78; ☑ 01-588 85; www.theater-wien.at; 06, Linke Wienzeile 6; tickets €10-160, standing room €7, student tickets €10-15; ☺ box office 10am-6pm Mon-Sat, 2-6pm Sun; ⓤ Karlsplatz) The Theater an der Wien has hosted some monumental premiere performances, including Beethoven's *Fidelo*, Mozart's *Die Zauberflöte* and Strauss Jnr's *Die Fledermaus*. These days, besides staging musicals, dance and concerts, it's re-established its reputation for high-quality opera, with one premiere each month.

Student tickets go on sale 30 minutes before shows; standing-room tickets are available one hour prior to performances.

Volksoper   OPERA, DANCE
(People's Opera; Map p70; ☑ 01-514 44 3670; www. volksoper.at; 09, Währinger Strasse 78; ☺ Sep-Jun; ⓤ Währinger Strasse) Offering a more intimate experience than the Staatsoper, the Volksoper specialises in operettas, dance performances, musicals and a handful of standard, heavier operas. Standing and im-

VIENNA'S COFFEE HOUSES

Great works of art have been created in these 'living rooms' of the Viennese. Patronised by luminaries such as Mahler, Klimt, Freud, Trotsky and Otto Wagner in their day, Vienna's *Kaffeehäuser* (coffee houses) were added to the Unesco list of Intangible Cultural Heritage in 2011. Many retain their opulent original decor, and often specialise in a particular cake, such as the *Sacher Torte*, an iced-chocolate cake with apricot jam once favoured by Emperor Franz Josef, at **Café Sacher** (Map p66; www.sacher.com; 01, Philharmonikerstrasse 4; ☺ 8am-midnight; ☑ D, 1, 2, 71 Kärntner Ring/Oper, ⓤ Karlsplatz). New-wave coffee houses are putting their own twist on the tradition.

paired-view tickets go for between €3 to €10 and, like many venues, there is a plethora of discounts and reduced tickets for sale 30 minutes before performances. The Volksoper closes for July and August.

Metro Kinokulturhaus   CINEMA
(Map p66; ☑ 01-512 18 03; www.filmarchiv. at; 01, Johannesgasse 4; film tickets adult/child €8.50/7; ☺ 2-9pm Mon-Fri, 11am-9pm Sat & Sun; ⓤ Stephansplatz) Part of the Austrian Film Archive, the Metro Kinokulturhaus opened in 2015 and is now a showcase for exhibitions (most are free, though some incur an admission charge). The restored **cinema** here was first converted for screenings in 1924 and retains its wood panelling and red-velvet interior; it shows historic and art-house Austrian films (in German).

Hofburg Concert Halls   CLASSICAL MUSIC
(Map p66; ☑ 01-587 25 52; www.hofburgorchester. at; 01, Heldenplatz; tickets €42-55; ☑ D, 1, 2, 71 Burgring, ⓤ Herrengasse) The Neue Hofburg's concert halls, the sumptuous Festsaal and Redoutensaal, are regularly used for Strauss and Mozart concerts, featuring the Hofburg Orchestra and soloists from the Staatsoper and Volksoper. Performances start at 8.30pm and tickets are available online and from travel agents and hotels. Seating is not allocated, so get in early to secure a good seat.

Jazzland   LIVE MUSIC
(Map p66; ☑ 01-533 25 75; www.jazzland.at; 01, Franz-Josefs-Kai 29; cover €11-20; ☺ 7pm-2am

Mon-Sat mid-Aug–mid-Jul, live music from 9pm; 1, 2, U Schwedenplatz) Buried in a former wine cellar beneath Ruprechtskirche, Jazzland is Vienna's oldest jazz club, dating back nearly 50 years. The music covers the whole jazz spectrum, and features both local and international acts. Past performers have included Ray Brown, Teddy Wilson, Big Joe Williams and Max Kaminsky.

B72
LIVE MUSIC

(www.b72.at; 08, Hernalser Gürtel 72; ⊘8pm-4am Sun-Thu, to 6am Fri & Sat; 44, U Alser Strasse) Fringe live acts, alternative beats and album launches are the mainstay of B72's entertainment line-up, which all attract a predictably youthful crowd. Its tall glass walls and arched brick interior are typical of most bars along the Gürtel, as is the happy grunginess. Its name comes from its location, *Bogen* (railway arch) 72. Tram to Hernalser Gürtel.

De France
CINEMA

(Map p70; ⊘01-317 52 36; www.defrance.at; 01, Schottenring 5; D, 1, 2, U Schottentor) De France screens films in their original language, with subtitles, in its two small cinemas. The schedule includes a healthy dose of English-language films.

Votivkino
CINEMA

(Map p70; ⊘01-317 35 71; www.votivkino.at; 09, Währinger Strasse 12; ; U Schottentor) Built in 1912, the Votiv is one of the oldest cinemas in Vienna. It's been extensively updated since then and is now among the best cinemas in the city. Its three screens feature a mix of Hollywood's more quirky ventures and art-house films in their original language.

The 11am Tuesday screening is reserved for parents with babies, and weekend afternoons feature special matinées for kids.

VIENNA BOYS' CHOIR

Founded by Maximilian I in 1498 as the imperial choir, the Wiener Sängerknaben (Vienna Boys' Choir) is the most famous of its type in the world. The experience will be very different depending on where you see the performance. The most formal occasions are held in the Burgkapelle, where the focus is obviously on sacral music. Performances at other venues might range from pop through to world music. Regardless of the setting and style of the performance, the beauty and choral harmony of the voices remains the same.

The choir sings during Sunday mass in the **Burgkapelle** (Royal Chapel; Map p66; ⊘01-533 99 27; www.hofmusikkapelle.gv.at; 01, Schweizer Hof; ⊘10am-2pm Mon & Tue, 11am-1pm Fri; 2A Heldenplatz, D, 1, 2, 71 Burgring, U Herrengasse) in the Hofburg, but occasional concerts are also given during the week at other venues in Vienna and elsewhere. Sunday performances in the Burgkapelle are held from mid-September to June at 9.15am. Other venues where you can hear the choir include **MuTh** (p113), the choir's dedicated hall in Augarten, which hosts regular Friday afternoon performances.

The Vienna Boys' Choir website (www.wienersaengerknaben.at) has links to the venues alongside each performance date.

Book tickets through the individual venue. Tickets for the Sunday performances at Burgkapelle cost €10 to €36 and can be booked through the **booking office** (Map p66; ⊘01-533 99 27; www.hofmusikkapelle.gv.at; 01, Schweizerhof; tickets €10-36; U Herrengasse) by sending an email or fax. It's best to book about six weeks in advance.

For orders under €60, you pay cash when you pick up your tickets, which can be done from 11am to 1pm and 3pm to 5pm at the booking office of the chapel in the Schweizerhof of the Hofburg on the Friday before the performance. You can also pick them up between 8.15am and 8.45am on the Sunday, but this is less advisable as queues are long. If your order amounts to €60 or more, you will be sent the bank details for transferring the money. Credit cards and cheques aren't accepted. Seats costing €10 do not afford a view of the choir itself.

Tickets for a free *Stehplatz* (standing-room space) are available from 8.30am. Uncollected tickets are also resold on the day from 8am. The queues for these and for standing-room tickets are long, so arrive very early – around 7am – and be prepared to wait.

WUK
ARTS CENTRE

(Workshop & Culture House; Map p70; ☑ 01-40 12 10; www.wuk.at; 09, Währinger Strasse 59; ☺ information 9am-8pm Mon-Fri, 3pm-8pm Sat & Sun; Ⓤ Währinger Strasse) WUK is many things to many people. It hosts a number of events in its concert hall: mid-size international and local rock acts vie with clubbing nights, classical concerts, film evenings, theatre and children's shows. Women's groups, temporary exhibitions and practical skills workshops are also on-site, along with a cafe with a fabulous cobbled courtyard.

Konzerthaus
CONCERT VENUE

(Map p86; ☑ 01-242 002; www.konzerthaus.at; 03, Lothringerstrasse 20; ☺ box office 9am-7.45pm Mon-Fri, to 1pm Sat, plus 45min before performance; ◙ D Gusshausstrasse, Ⓤ Stadtpark) The Konzerthaus is a major venue in classical-music circles, but throughout the year ethnic music, rock, pop or jazz can also be heard in its hallowed halls. Up to three simultaneous performances, in the Grosser Saal, the Mozart Saal and the Schubert Saal, can be staged; this massive complex also features another four concert halls.

Students can pick up €16 tickets 30 minutes before performances; children receive 50% discount.

Radiokulturhaus
CONCERT VENUE

(Map p86; ☑ 01-501 70 377; http://radiokulturhaus.orf.at; 04, Argentinierstrasse 30a; tickets €7-27; ☺ box office 4-7pm Mon-Fri; ◙ D Plösslgasse, Ⓤ Taubstummengasse) Expect anything from odes to Sinatra and R.E.M. or an evening dedicated to Beethoven and Mozart at the Radiokulturhaus. Housed in several performance venues including the Grosser Sendesaal – home to the Vienna Radio Symphony Orchestra and the Klangtheater (used primarily for radio plays) – this is one of Vienna's cultural hot spots.

The venue also presents dance, lectures and literary readings as well as low-key performances in its cafe.

Marionetten Theater
PUPPET THEATRE

(Map p88; ☑ 01-817 32 47; www.marionettentheater.at; 13, Schloss Schönbrunn; tickets full performances adult €11-39, child €9-25; ☺ box office on performance days from 11am; Ⓤ Schönbrunn) This small theatre in Schloss Schönbrunn puts on performances of the much-loved productions *The Magic Flute* (2½ hours) and *Aladdin* (1¼ hours). They're a delight for kids young, old and in between. The puppet costumes are exceptionally ornate and eye-catching.

Kammeroper
THEATRE

(Map p66; ☑ Wien Ticket 01-588 85; www.theaterwien.at; 01, Fleischmarkt 24; tickets €6-156; ◙ 1, 2, Ⓤ Schwedenplatz) The Kammeroper ranks as Vienna's third opera house after the Staatsoper (p112) and Volksoper (p113), and the small venue is perfect for unusual and quirky opera productions. In summer the entire company is transported to the Schlosstheater Schönbrunn to continue performances in more opulent surroundings.

Österreichisches Filmmuseum
CINEMA

(Austrian Film Museum; Map p66; ☑ 01-533 70 54; www.filmmuseum.at; 01, Auginerstrasse 1; adult/child €10.50/6; ◙ D, 1, 2, 71 Kärntner Ring/Oper, Ⓤ Karlsplatz) Situated inside the Albertina (p68), the Austrian Film Museum shows a range of films with and without subtitles in the original language, featuring a director, group of directors or a certain theme from around the world in programs generally lasting a couple of weeks. Screenings are generally at 6.45pm; check the website for other times.

Vienna's English Theatre
THEATRE

(Map p70; ☑ 01-402 12 60; www.englishtheatre.at; 08, Josefsgasse 12; tickets €24-47; ☺ box office 10am-7.30pm Mon-Fri, 5-7.30pm Sat performance days mid-Aug–Jun, closed Jul–mid-Aug; ◙ 2 Rathaus, Josefstädter Strasse, Ⓤ Rathaus) Founded in 1963, Vienna's English Theatre is the oldest foreign-language theatre in Vienna (with the occasional show in French or Italian). Productions range from timeless pieces, such as Shakespeare, to contemporary works and comedies. Students receive a 20% discount. Standby tickets for €10 go on sale 15 minutes before showtime.

Volkstheater
THEATRE

(Map p78; ☑ 01-521 11-400; www.volkstheater.at; 07, Neustiftgasse 1; tickets €11-53; ☺ box office 10am-7.30pm Mon-Sat; Ⓤ Volkstheater) With a seating capacity close to 1000, the Volkstheater is one of Vienna's largest theatres. Built in 1889, the interior is suitably grand. While most performances are translations (anything from Woody Allen to Ingmar Bergman to Molière), only German-language shows are staged. Students can buy unsold tickets for €5 one hour before performances start. Advanced bookings are necessary.

Tanzquartier Wien
DANCE

(Map p78; ☑ 01-581 35 91; www.tqw.at; 07, Museumsplatz 1; tickets €10-57; ☺ box office 10am-4.30pm mid-Jul–Aug, 9am-7.30pm Mon-Fri, 10am-

7.30pm Sat Sep–mid-Jul; Ⓤ Museumsquartier, Volkstheater) Tanzquartier Wien, located in the MuseumsQuartier, is Vienna's first dance institution. It hosts an array of local and international performances with a strong experimental nature. Students receive advance tickets at 30% discount. Unsold tickets (€8) go on sale 15 minutes before showtime.

🏠 Shopping

With a long-standing history of craftsmanship, in recent years this elegant city has spread its creative wings in the fashion and design world. Whether you're browsing for hand-painted porcelain in the Innere Stadt, new-wave streetwear in Neubau or epicurean treats in the Freihausviertel, you'll find inspiration, a passion for quality and an attentive eye for detail.

1130 Wein
FOOD & DRINKS

(Map p88; www.1130wein.at; Lainzerstrasse 1; ⊘10am-7pm Mon-Fri, to 3pm Sat; Ⓤ Hietzing) Pop into this neighbourhood *Vinothek* for tastings with the delightful Robert Sponer-Triulzi, who stocks a huge range of interesting, top-quality (though not always expensive) wines from all over Austria. He'll challenge you with a new varietal or two and make sure you come away with a drop you'll love. There's chilled whites if you're picnicking.

★ Flohmarkt
MARKET

(Flea Market; Map p78; 05, Linke Wienzeile; ⊘6.30am-6pm Sat; Ⓤ Kettenbrückengasse) One of the best flea markets in Europe, this Vienna institution adjoining the **Naschmarkt**'s (Map p78; www.wienernaschmarkt.eu; 06, Linke & Rechte Wienzeile; ⊘6am-7.30pm Mon-Fri, to 6pm Sat; Ⓤ Kettenbrückengasse) southwestern end brims with antiques and *Altwaren* (old wares). Stalls hawking books, clothes, records, ancient electrical goods, old postcards, ornaments, carpets, you name it, stretch for several blocks. Arrive early, as it gets increasingly crammed as the morning wears on, and be prepared to haggle.

It's very atmospheric – more like the markets of Eastern Europe – with goods piled up in apparent chaos on the pavement.

★ Meinl am Graben
FOOD & DRINKS

(Map p66; www.meinlamgraben.at; 01, Graben 19; ⊘8am-7.30pm Mon-Fri, 9am-6pm Sat; Ⓤ Stephansplatz) Vienna's most prestigious providore brims with quality European foodstuffs. Chocolate and confectionery dominate the ground floor, and impressive cheese and cold meats are tantalisingly displayed upstairs. The basement stocks European and Austrian wine and fruit liqueurs and has a classy on-site wine bar (p108); there's also an exceptional on-site restaurant (p107).

★ Steiff
TOYS

(Map p66; www.steiff-galerie-wien.at; 01, Bräunerstrasse 3; ⊘10am-12.30pm & 1.30-6pm Mon-Fri, 10am-12.30 & 1.30-5pm Sat; Ⓤ Stephansplatz) Founded in Germany in the late 19th century, Steiff is widely regarded as the original creator of the teddy bear, which it presented at the Leipzig Toy Fair in 1903: an American businessman bought 3000 and sold them under the name 'teddy bear' after US president Theodore ('Teddy') Roosevelt. Today its flagship Austrian shop is filled with adorable bears, along with other premium quality cuddly toys.

★ Beer Lovers
DRINKS

(Map p78; http://beerlovers.at; 06, Gumpendorfer Strasse 35; ⊘11am-8pm Mon-Fri, 10am-5pm Sat; Ⓤ Kettenbrückengasse) A wonderland of craft beers, this emporium stocks over 1000 labels from over 125 different breweries in over 70 styles, with more being sourced every day. Tastings are offered regularly, and cold beers are available in the walk-in glass fridge and in refillable growlers. It also stocks craft ciders, small-batch liqueurs and boutique nonalcoholic drinks such as ginger beers.

★ Die Werkbank
DESIGN

(Map p78; www.werkbank.cc; 07, Breite Gasse 1; ⊘noon-6.30pm Tue-Fri, 11am-5pm Sat; Ⓤ Volkstheater) Furniture, lamps, rugs, vases, jewellery, watches, graphic art, bags, even bicycles are among the creations you might find on display at 'The Workbench', an all-white space that operates as a design collective, where some of Vienna's most innovative designers showcase their works.

★ Dirndlherz
CLOTHING

(Map p70; http://dirndlherz.at; 07, Lerchenfelder Strasse 50; ⊘11am-6pm Thu & Fri, to 4pm Sat; Ⓤ Volkstheater) Putting her own spin on Alpine fashion, Austrian designer Gabriela Urabl creates one-of-a-kind, high-fashion *Dirndls*, from sassy purple-velvet bosomlifters to 1950s-style gingham numbers and *Dirndls* emblazoned with quirky motifs like pop-art, and punk-like conical metal studs. T-shirts with tag-lines like '*Mei Dirndl is in da Wäsch*' ('My *Dirndl* is in the wash') are also available.

SHOPPING STREETS

Kärntner Strasse The Innere Stadt's main shopping street and a real crowd-puller.

Kohlmarkt A river of high-end glitz.

Neubau The city's hottest designers along boutique-clogged streets like Kirchengasse,Lindengasse and Neubaugasse.

Mariahilfer Strasse Vienna's mile of high-street style, with big names and even bigger crowds.

Freihausviertel Lanes packed with home-grown fashion, design and speciality food stores, south of Naschmarkt around Schleifmühlgasse.

Theobaldgasse Just off Mariahilfer Strasse, Theobaldgasse's hole-in-the-wall shops purvey everything from fair-trade fashion to organic food.

Gumpendorferstrasse Retro fashion, up-market cosmetics, designer lighting – it's all on this funky 6th-district street.

Josefstädter Strasse An old-fashioned shopping street filled with idiosyncratic shops selling anything from *Altwaren* (old wares) to gemstones.

★**Wald & Wiese**   FOOD, COSMETICS
(Map p66; www.waldundwiese.at; 01, Wollzeile 19; ⊙9.30am-6.30pm Mon-Fri, 9am-5pm Sat; Ⓤ Stephansplatz) 🌿 Some 5000 bee colonies and 600 bee-keepers harvest honey within Vienna's city limits, including on the rooftops of the Rathaus, Staatsoper, Kunsthistorisches Museum, Secession and several hotels. The fruits of their labour are sold at this specialist honey boutique, which also sells honey-based beverages including mead, honey-and-whisky liqueur and grappa, along with beeswax candles, hand creams, toothpaste, royal jelly...

During the truffle season, it sells locally harvested truffles and related products (including truffle honey), too.

★**Wiener Rosenmanufaktur**   FOOD, COSMETICS
(Map p66; www.wienerrosenmanufaktur.at; 01, Schönlaterngasse 7; ⊙3-7pm Mon-Fri, 11am-5pm Sat Jul & Aug, 1-6.30pm Mon-Fri, 11am-6.30pm Sat, 2-5pm Sun Sep-Jun; Ⓤ Schwedenplatz) Roses grown by Ingrid Maria Heldstab in her garden in Vienna's 23rd district are used in an incredible array of products, from jams (including spicy versions with ginger), jellies and liqueurs – which you can taste in store – to soaps, aromatic oils and other cosmetics. The tiny shop occupies one of Vienna's oldest buildings, the Basiliskenhaus, which dates from 1212.

★**J&L Lobmeyr Vienna**   HOMEWARES
(Map p66; www.lobmeyr.at; 01, Kärntner Strasse 26; ⊙10am-7pm Mon-Fri, to 6pm Sat; Ⓤ Stephansplatz) Reached by a beautifully ornate wrought-iron staircase, this is one of Vienna's most lavish retail experiences. The collection of Biedermeier pieces, Loos-designed sets, fine/arty glassware and porcelain on display here glitters from the lights of the chandelier-festooned atrium. Lobmeyr has been in business since 1823, when it exclusively supplied the imperial court.

Today production is more focused towards pieces inspired by the Wiener Werkstätte artists from the early 20th century. This movement sought to bring a philosophy of artistic craftsmanship into functional design, later helping pave the way for art deco.

Karmelitermarkt   MARKET
(Map p94; 02, Karmelitermarkt; ⊙6am-7.30pm Mon-Fri, to 5pm Sat; 🚊2 Karmeliterplatz, Ⓤ Taborstrasse) A market with a long tradition, the Karmelitermarkt reflects the ethnic diversity of its neighbourhood; you're sure to see Hasidic Jews on bikes or scooters shopping for kosher goods here. Set in an architecturally picturesque square, the market springs to life when the midday lunching locals descend on its terrific array of places to eat.

Fruit and vegetable stalls share the marketplace with butchers selling kosher and halal meats. On Saturday, the square features a Bauernmarkt, where farmers set up stalls brimming with seasonal goods, freshly baked bread, specialty salamis and organic herbs. The Viennese fill their bags here in the morning before doing brunch or lunch in one of the delis, many with outdoor seating, such as **Kaas am Markt** (Map p94; www.

kaasammarkt.at; 02, Karmelitermarkt 33-36; light meals & mains €5-9; ⏰9am-6pm Tue-Fri, 8am-2pm Sat; 🥗; 🚇2 Karmeliterplatz, Ⓤ Taborstrasse) 🍴 and **Tewa** (Map p94; ☎0676 84 77 41 211; http://tewa-karmelitermarkt.at; 02, Karmelitermarkt 26-32; breakfast €5.50-9.80, lunch €6.90-7.90; ⏰7am-11pm Mon-Sat; 🚇2 Karmeliterplatz, Ⓤ Taborstrasse).

Bauernmarkt Yppenplatz MARKET

(16, Yppenplatz; ⏰9am-1pm Sat; 🚇2, Ⓤ Josefstädter Strasse) *Bauern* (farmers) stalls join the usual market traders of the Brunnenmarkt and Yppenplatz every Saturday morning, when local farmers come to town to sell their meats, dairy, fruit and vegetables; as do artisan producers from around Vienna and occasionally as far afield as Styria, Carinthia and Slovenia. Tram to Neulerchenfelder Strasse.

Brunnenmarkt MARKET

(16, Brunnengasse; ⏰6am-6.30pm Mon-Fri, to 2pm Sat; 🚇2, Ⓤ Josefstädter Strasse) Over 170 stalls fill the area between Thaliastrasse and Ottakringer Strasse every Saturday in what is Vienna's largest street market. It's an enthralling sprawl of Turkish grocers, fruit and vegetable producers and tack which gradually and almost imperceptibly flows into the happily hipster Yppenmarkt.

About a quarter of the traders are here on weekdays – far less busy but less of a buzz, too. Tram to Neulerchenfelder Strasse.

Palais Ferstel SHOPPING CENTRE

(Map p66; 01, Strauchgasse 4; ⏰10am-6.30pm Mon-Fri, to 6pm Sat; Ⓤ Herrengasse) With its hexagonal skylight, allegorical sculptures and beautifully lit arcades in Italian Renaissance style, Palais Ferstel hearkens back to a more glamorous age of consumption. Opened in 1860, it sidles up to the ever-grand **Café Central** (Map p66; www.palaisevents.at; 01, Herrengasse 14; ⏰7.30am-10pm Mon-Sat, 10am-10pm Sun; 🍴; Ⓤ Herrengasse) and likewise bears the hallmark of architect Heinrich von Ferstel, the Habsburgs' blue-eyed boy in the mid-19th century.

Today, it shelters upmarket delis, jewellers and chocolatiers; pop in for a mosey through even if you have no intention of buying.

Staud's FOOD

(www.stauds.com; 16, Yppenplatz; ⏰8am-12.30pm Tue-Sat, 3.30-6pm Fri; 🚇2, Ⓤ Josefstädter Strasse) 🍴 Ask the Viennese who makes Austria's best jam and you'll invariably hear 'Staud's'. Hans Staud is rigorous about sourcing the finest ingredients for his sweet and savoury preserves. This pavilion shop stocks vegetables with pickled oomph, chutneys, wine jellies, horseradishes, jams and compotes like tangy greengage, apricot and wild lingonberry, all of which make unique gifts. Tram to Neulerchenfelder Strasse.

Die Schwalbe FASHION & ACCESSORIES

(Map p78; www.die-schwalbe.at; 06, Otto-Bauer-Gasse 24; ⏰11.30am-6.30pm Mon-Sat; Ⓤ Neubaugasse) 'Eco-urban steetwear' here spans hoodies and pullovers to T-shirts, jackets, shorts and pants, plus accessories such as beanies, caps and scarves from small-scale

---

CHRISTMAS MARKETS

From around mid-November to late December, *Christkindlmärkte* (Christmas markets) bring festive cheer into the city's squares, courtyards and cobbled lanes. Each has its own flair but all have *Glühwein* (mulled wine), *Maroni* (chestnuts) and twinkling trees. Annual dates and times are listed on www.wien.info.

Favourites include the following:

Rathausplatz (p95) A whopper of a tree, 150 stalls and kid-pleasing activities from cookie-baking workshops to pony rides, all set against the atmospheric backdrop of the neo-Gothic Rathaus.

Schönbrunn (Map p88; ⏰10am-9pm daily 3rd week Nov-26 Dec; 🚇1A, Ⓤ Schönbrunn) Shop for nutcrackers, crib figurines and puppets at this handicraft market in the palace courtyard, with loads of events for the kids, and daily classical concerts at 6pm weekdays and 2pm weekends.

Spittelberg (Map p78; www.spittelberg.at; 07, Spittelberggasse; ⏰2-9pm Mon-Thu, 2-9.30pm Fri, 10am-9.30pm Sat, 10am-9pm Sun 13 Nov-23 Dec; Ⓤ Volkstheater, Museumsquartier) The cobbled lanes of this Biedermeier quarter set the scene for this market, beloved of the Viennese, where stalls sell quality arts and crafts.

labels including Blueberry Rockster, Habu San, Hemp Hoodlamb and Plasma Lab. Its piercing lounge is open from 1pm to 6.30pm Tuesday to Friday and 1pm to 5pm on Saturdays.

Blühendes Konfekt FOOD
(Map p78; www.bluehendes-konfekt.com; 06, Schmalzhofgasse 19; ⊙10am-6.30pm Wed-Fri; Ⓤ Zieglergasse, Westbahnhof) 🍴 Violets, forest strawberries and cherry blossom, mint and oregano – Michael Diewald makes the most of what grows wild and in his garden to create confectionery that fizzes with seasonal flavour. Peek through to the workshop to see flowers and herbs being deftly transformed into one-of-a-kind bonbons and mini bouquets that are edible works of art.

ℹ Information

EMERGENCY
Police Station (☑01-31 31 00; www.polizei. gv.at/wien; 01, Deutschmeisterplatz 3; ⊙24hr)
Women's Emergency Line (Frauennotruf; ☑01-717 19; www.frauennotruf.wien.at; ⊙24hr) Counselling and emergency services hotline for women.

MEDICAL SERVICES
Allgemeines Krankenhaus (☑01-40 40 00; www.akhwien.at; 09, Währinger Gürtel 18-20) Has an emergency room.

MONEY
ATMs are widely available. Credit cards are not always accepted in budget hotels or budget to midrange restaurants. Bars and cafes usually only accept cash.

POST
Main Post Office (Map p66; www.post.at; 01, Fleischmarkt 19; ⊙7am-10pm Mon-Fri, 9am-10pm Sat & Sun; 🚊1, 2, Ⓤ Schwedenplatz)

TOURIST INFORMATION
Airport Information Office (⊙7am-10pm) Full services, with maps, Vienna Card and walk-in hotel booking. Located in the **Vienna International Airport** arrival hall.
Die Villa (☑01-586 8150; http://dievilla.at; 06, Linke Wienzeile 102; ⊙hours vary; Ⓤ Pilgramgasse) Vienna's main point for gay and lesbian information, Die Villa has advice and information on what's on offer in the city.
Jugendinfo (Vienna Youth Information; Map p66; ☑01-4000 84 100; www.wienxtra.at/jugendinfo; 01, Babenbergerstrasse 1; ⊙2-7pm Mon-Wed, 1-6pm Thu-Sat; 🚊D, 1, 2, 71 Burgring, Ⓤ Museumsquartier) Jugendinfo offers various reduced-priced event tickets for 14 to 26 year olds. Staff can tell you about events around town.

Rathaus Information Office (Map p70; ☑01-525 50; www.wien.gv.at; 01, Rathaus; ⊙8am-6pm Mon-Fri; 🚊D, 1, 2 Rathaus, Ⓤ Rathaus) City Hall provides information on social, cultural and practical matters, and is geared as much to residents as to tourists. There's a useful info-screen.
Tourist Info Wien (Map p66; ☑01-245 55; www.wien.info; 01, Albertinaplatz; ⊙9am-7pm; 🕿; 🚊D, 1, 2, 71 Kärntner Ring/Oper, Ⓤ Stephansplatz) Vienna's main tourist office has free maps and racks of brochures.
WienXtra-Kinderinfo (Map p78; ☑01-4000 84 400; www.wienxtra.at/kinderaktiv; 07, Museumsplatz 1; ⊙2-6pm Tue-Fri, 10am-5pm Sat & Sun; Ⓤ Museumsquartier) Marketed primarily at children (check out the knee-high display cases), this tourist office has loads of information on activities for kids and a small indoor playground. It's located inside the MuseumsQuartier courtyard, near the Mariahilfer Strasse entrance.

ℹ Getting There & Away

AIR
Located 19km southwest of the city centre, **Vienna International Airport** (VIE; ☑01-700 722 233; www.viennaairport.com; 🕿) operates services worldwide. Facilities include restaurants and bars, banks and ATMs, money-exchange counters, supermarkets, a post office, car-hire agencies and two left-luggage counters open 5.30am to 11pm (per 24 hours €4 to €8; maximum six-month storage). Bike boxes (€35) and baggage wrapping (per item €12) are available.

Bratislava, Slovakia's capital, is only 60km east of Vienna, and **Airport Bratislava** (BTS; ☑02-3303 3353; www.bts.aero; Ivanská cesta), serving Bratislava, makes a feasible alternative to flying into Austria

BOAT
The Danube is a traffic-free access route for arrivals and departures from Vienna. Eastern Europe is the main destination; **Twin City Liner** (Map p66; ☑01-904 88 80; www.twincityliner. com; 01, Schwedenplatz; one-way adult €20-35; 🚊1, 2, Ⓤ Schwedenplatz) connects Vienna with Bratislava in 1½ hours, while its sister company **DDSG Blue Danube Schiffahrt** (☑01-588 80; www.ddsg-blue-danube.at; 02, Handelskai 265, Reichsbrücke; one-way €99-109, return €125; ⊙9am-5pm Mon-Fri, 10am-4pm Sat & Sun, closed Sat & Sun Nov-Feb) links Budapest with Vienna from mid-May to September, departing Vienna Wednesday, Friday and Sunday, departing Budapest Tuesday, Thursday and Saturday. DDSG tickets may also be obtained or picked up at Twin City Liner.

Slovakian ferry company **LOD** (✉ in Slovakia 421 2 529 32 226; www.lod.sk; Schiffstation Reichsbrücke, Handelskai 265 (Vienna departure point); one-way/return €20/29; ☺ late Apr-early Oct) runs hydrofoils between Bratislava and Vienna (1½ hours) five to seven days per week from late April to early October. The season can vary depending on weather conditions.

BUS

Eurolines (✉ 0900 128 712; www.eurolines.at; 03, Erdbergstrasse 200; ☺ office 8am-6pm; ⓤ Erdberg) has basically tied up the bus routes connecting Austria with the rest of Europe. Its main terminal is at the U3 U-Bahn station Erdberg but some buses stop at the U6 and U1 U-Bahn and train station Praterstern, and at Südtiroler Platz by Vienna's Hauptbahnhof.

TRAIN

Austria's train network is a dense web reaching the country's far-flung corners. The system is fast, efficient, frequent and well used. **Österreiche Bundesbahn** (ÖBB; www.oebb.at) is the main operator, and has information offices at all of Vienna's main train stations. Tickets can be purchased online, at ticket offices or train-station ticket machines. Long-distance train tickets can be purchased onboard but incur a €3 service charge. Tickets for local, regional and intercity trains must be purchased before boarding.

❶ Getting Around

TO/FROM THE AIRPORT

Vienna Airport Lines (✉ 01-700 732 300; www.postbus.at; ☺ 8am-7.30pm Mon-Sat) has three services connecting different parts of Vienna with the airport. The most central is the **Vienna Airport Lines bus stop** (Map p66) at Morzinplatz/Schwedenplatz (bus 1185; one way/return €8/13, 20 minutes), running via the Wien-Mitte train station.

A taxi to/from the airport costs between €25 and €50. The yellow **Taxi 40100** (p120) in the arrival hall (near the bookshop) has a fixed airport rate of €36. **C&K Airport Service** (✉ 01-444 44; www.cundk.at) has rates starting at €33.

Slovaklines (www.slovaklines.sk) in conjunction with Eurolines (www.eurolines.com) runs buses between Airport Bratislava and Vienna International Airport and on to Südtiroler Platz at Vienna's Hauptbahnhof (one way/return €7.50/13, one hour, up to two per hour).

Buses leave outside the Airport Bratislava arrival hall between 8.30am and 9.35pm daily, and

from Südtiroler Platz at Vienna's Hauptbahnhof from 8.30am and 9.35pm daily.

You can also take bus 61 to the centre of Bratislava and pick up a frequent train from Bratislava train station to Vienna.

BICYCLE

Vienna is a fabulous place to get around by bike. Bicycles can be carried free of charge on carriages marked with a bike symbol on the S-Bahn and U-Bahn from 9am to 3pm and after 6.30pm Monday to Friday, after 9am Saturday and all day Sunday. It's not possible to take bikes on trams or buses. The city also runs the **Citybike Wien** (p89) shared-bike program, with bike stands scattered throughout the city.

CAR & MOTORCYCLE

You may consider hiring a car to see some of the outer sights but in Vienna itself it's best to stick with the excellent public transport system.

PUBLIC TRANSPORT

Vienna's comprehensive and unified public transport network is one of the most efficient in Europe. Flat-fare tickets are valid for trains, trams, buses, the underground (U-Bahn) and the S-Bahn regional trains. Services are frequent and you rarely have to wait more than 10 minutes.

Transport maps are posted in all U-Bahn stations and at many bus and tram stops. Free maps are available from **Wiener Linien** (✉ 01-7909-100; www.wienerlinien.at), located in nine U-Bahn stations. The Karlsplatz, Stephansplatz and Westbahnhof information offices are open 6.30am to 6.30pm Monday to Friday and 8.30am to 4pm Saturday and Sunday. Those at Schottentor, Praterstern, Floridsdorf, Philadelphiabrücke and Erdberg are closed at weekends.

TAXI

Taxis are reliable and relatively cheap by Western European standards. City journeys are metered; the minimum charge is roughly €3.80 from 6am to 11pm Monday to Saturday and €4.30 any other time, plus a per kilometre fee of €1.42. A telephone reservation costs an additional €2.80. A tip of 10% is expected. Taxis are easily found at train stations and taxi stands all over the city. To order one, contact **Taxi 40100** (✉ 01-401 00; www.taxi40100.at) or **Willkommen Taxi** (✉ 01-60 160; www.taxi60160.at). These accept common credit and debit cards (check before hopping in, though).

Lower Austria & Burgenland

Best Places to Eat

➡ Gut Drauf at Gut Oggau (p154)

➡ Weingut Gabriel (p153)

➡ Zur Dankbarkeit (p156)

➡ Zum Kaiser von Österreich (p127)

Best Places to Sleep

➡ Gut Purbach (p155)

➡ Burg Bernstein (p152)

➡ Schloss Starrein (p137)

➡ Restaurant & Hotel Schloss Grafenegg (p131)

➡ St Martins Therme & Lodge (p156)

➡ Raffelsberger Hof (p130)

Why Go?

Surrounding Vienna on all sides, Lower Austria is a cradle of Austrian civilisation and a region offering visitors one of the country's most lively cultural landscapes. Outdoor activities, some great museums, wine, food and a glimpse into the age of the Romans at Carnuntum make leaving the capital for a day or longer an attractive prospect.

And naturally everyone's heard of the Danube River, which cuts a picturesque valley, the Wachau, through the region's northwest. A place of magnificent natural beauty, this is truly a European highlight for its vineyards, castles, abbeys and medieval villages.

To the south of the capital, under-visited Burgenland is all but the typical Austria of the holiday brochures; you won't find soaring mountains, glacial lakes and bombastic architecture here, just bucolic flatlands spread like a well-tenderised schnitzel around the jewel in its crown – Neusiedler See – a shallow Mecca for extreme water-sports fans and paddling toddlers alike.

When to Go

➡ Visit Burgenland, especially the Neusiedler See region in the north, between April and October.

➡ From November to March, Burgenland goes into low-season hibernation and its prime attraction – the outdoors – becomes cold, grey and windswept.

➡ Visit Lower Austria during the April to October warm season, when the Wachau is often bathed in a soft light and you can make the most of the Danube River and its sights and activities.

➡ Autumn is the best time to enjoy wine in the Wachau, and from 11 November (St Martin's Day) each year young wine is sold.

Lower Austria & Burgenland Highlights

1 Danube Valley (p124) Wandering the cultural landscape of the Wachau.

2 Rust (p153) Sipping wines in one of the pretty *Heurigen* (wine taverns).

3 Stift Melk (p131) Going baroque at Melk's magnificent monastery on the banks of the Danube.

4 Neusiedler See (p152) Making a splash in Austria's slurping steppe lake.

5 Semmeringbahn (p147) Riding the footplate of this remarkable engineering feat in Semmering.

6 Neusiedler See-Seewinkel National Park (p156) Twitching at your leisure in Seewinkel's haven for bird life.

7 St Martins Therme & Lodge (p156) Taking to the thermal waters in Frauenkirchen.

8 Krems an der Donau (p124) Scrambling through the cobbled streets.

9 Schneeberg (p145) Hiking or catching the train up Lower Austria's highest peak.

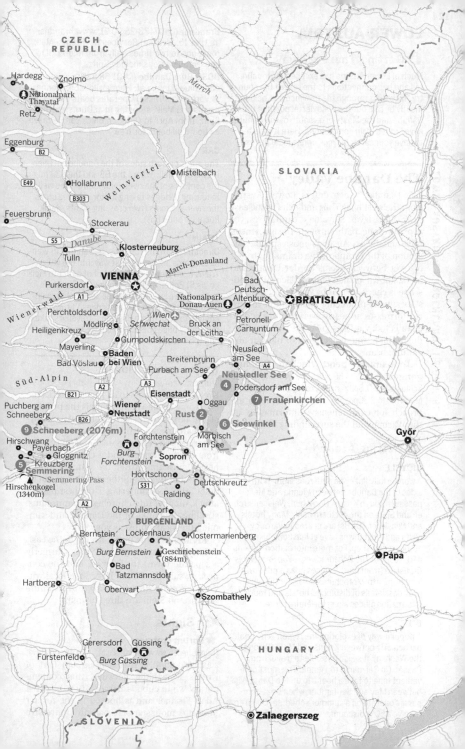

LOWER AUSTRIA

❶ Getting There & Away

Much of Lower Austria has excellent autobahn, rail and bus connections to the rest of the country. Travelling through the province can be done mostly by rail, but the Waldviertel north of the Danube and the Mostviertel south of the Danube have limited train connections. Here it's better to have your car or bicycle, or use local buses.

The Danube Valley

The Danube, which enters Lower Austria from the west near Ybbs and exits in the east near Bratislava, Slovakia's capital, carves a picturesque path through the province's hills and fields. Austria's most spectacular section of the Danube is the dramatic stretch of river between Krems an der Donau and Melk, known as the **Wachau**. Here the landscape is characterised by vineyards, forested slopes, wine-producing villages and imposing fortresses at nearly every bend. The Wachau is today a Unesco World Heritage site, due to its harmonious blend of natural and cultural beauty.

Tourismusverband Wachau Nibelungengau (☑02713-300 60 60; www.wachau.at; Schlossgasse 3, Spitz an der Donau; ⊙9am-4.30pm Mon-Thu, to 2.30pm Fri) are the people to approach for comprehensive information on the Wachau and the surrounding area.

❶ Getting Around

BICYCLE

A wonderfully flat cycle path runs along both sides of the Danube between Vienna and Melk, passing through Krems, Dürnstein, Weissenkirchen and Spitz on the northern bank. Many hotels and *Pensionen* (B&Bs) are geared towards cyclists and most towns have at least one bike-rental and -repair shop. For more information, pick up a free copy of *The Donauradweg – Von Passau bis Bratislava* (from tourist offices or as a pdf download from http://brochures.austria.info), which provides details of distances, hotels and tourist information offices along the entire route.

BOAT

A popular way of exploring the region is by boat, particularly between Krems and Melk (through the Wachau); it's also possible to travel from Passau (in Germany) to Vienna. The most convenient time to take a boat trip on the Danube is between May and September, when boat companies operate on a summer schedule. Children receive a 50% discount.

Brandner (☑07433-25 90 21; www.brandner. at; Ufer 15, Wallsee) Services the Krems–Melk route one to two times daily from mid-April to late October; stops include Spitz.

DDSG Blue Danube (☑01-58 880; www. ddsg-blue-danube.at; Handelskai 265, Vienna; Ⓜ Vorgartenstrasse) Operates boats between Krems and Melk, stopping in at Dürnstein and Spitz, from April to October. Bikes can be taken on board all boats for free.

CAR

The roads on both sides of the Danube between Krems and Melk, where the B3 and the B33 hug the contours of the river, lend themselves well to touring. Bridges taking motor vehicles cross the river at Krems (two crossing points), Melk, Pöchlarn and Ybbs.

TRAIN

Direct trains from Franz-Josefs-Bahnhof in Vienna to Krems are the easiest way into the valley. Trains from Vienna's Westbahnhof direct to Melk go via St Pölten and don't follow the Danube Valley. There is a seasonal rail service between Krems and Dürnstein but this doesn't run often enough to be of much use. Most travellers take the hourly buses between the two towns that hug the Danube all the way.

Krems an der Donau

☑02732 / POP 23,900

Krems, as it's known to its friends, marks the beginning of the Wachau and is the prettiest of the larger towns on the Danube. Enjoyable eating and drinking, an atmospheric historical centre, rivers of top-quality wine from local vineyards and a couple of unexpected museums attract the summer tourist crowds, but the rest of the year things can be quiet. Aimless wandering is the best plan of attack, dipping into churches and museums, strolling the banks of the Danube and sampling the local whites as you go.

Krems has three parts: Krems to the east, the smaller settlement of Stein (formerly a separate town) to the west, and the connecting suburb of Und. Hence the local witticism: *Krems und Stein sind drei Städte* (Krems and Stein are three towns).

◉ Sights

★**Forum Frohner**   GALLERY
(Kunstmeile; www.kunsthalle.at; Minoritenplatz 4; adult/child €5/4; ⊙11am-7pm Tue-Sun) Part of Krem's Kunsthalle network, this contemporary white cube is named after the artist Adolf Frohner and is housed in the former Minorite monastery. It has an impressive

calendar of conceptual work, both international and Austrian.

Stift Göttweig
ABBEY

(Göttweig Abbey; ☑02732-855 81-0; www.stiftgoettweig.at; Furth bei Göttweig; adult/child €8.50/5; ☻9am-6pm Jun-Sep, 10am-6pm Mar-May, Oct & Nov) Founded in 1083, the abbey was devastated by fire in the early 18th century and so sports an impressive baroque interior. Still a working monastery today, aside from the sublime view back across the Danube Valley from its garden terrace and restaurant, the abbey's highlights include the Imperial Staircase with a heavenly ceiling fresco painted by Paul Troger in 1739, and the over-the-top baroque interior of the Stiftskirche, which has a Kremser Schmidt work in the crypt.

Fully guided tours take in the abbey's Imperial Wing, church and summer vestry; shorter tours explore either the Imperial Wing or the church and vestry.

The best way to reach Göttweig is by train from Krems (€2.20, 10 minutes, every two hours), though it's a steep walk uphill from the Klein Wien station .

Pfarrkirche St Veit
CHURCH

(Pfarrplatz 5; ☻dawn-dusk) Known as the 'Cathedral of the Wachau', the large baroque parish church boasts colourful frescoes by Martin Johann Schmidt, an 18th-century local artist who was also known as Kremser Schmidt and occupied a house from 1756 near the Linzer Tor in Stein. The baroque building is the work of Cipriano Biasino, who worked on several churches in the Wachau, including the abbey church at Stift Göttweig.

Kunsthalle Krems
GALLERY

(www.kunsthalle.at; Franz-Zeller-Platz 3; €10; ☻10am-5pm Tue-Sun) The flagship of Krems' Kunstmeile, an eclectic collection of galleries and museums, the Kunsthalle has a program of changing exhibitions. These might be mid-19th-century landscapes or hardcore conceptual works, but are always well curated. Guided tours (€3) run on Sundays at 2pm.

Piaristenkirche
CHURCH

(Frauenbergplatz; ☻dawn-dusk) Reached by a covered stairway from the Pfarrkirche, Krems' most impressive church has a wonderful webbed Gothic ceiling and huge, austerely plain windows. It's most atmospheric after dark when you can best imagine the spectacle of the massive baroque altar for the 18th-century parishioners.

Karikaturmuseum
MUSEUM

(www.karikaturmuseum.at; Steiner Landstrasse 3a; adult/child €10/3.50; ☻10am-6pm) Austria's only caricature museum occupies a suitably tongue-in-cheek chunk of purpose-built architecture opposite the Kunsthalle. Changing exhibitions and a large permanent collection of caricatures of prominent Austrian and international figures make for a fun diversion.

Museum Krems
MUSEUM

(www.museumkrems.at; Körnermarkt 14; admission €5; ☻11am-6pm Wed-Sun Apr & May, daily Jun-Oct) Housed in a former Dominican monastery, the town's museum has collections of religious and modern art, including works by Kremser Schmidt, who painted the frescoes in Pfarrkirche St Veit, as well as winemaking artefacts and a section on the famous Krems mustard.

🏃 Activities

Weingut der Stadt Krems
WINE

(www.weingutstadtkrems.at; Stadtgraben 11; ☻9am-noon & 1-5pm Mon-Fri, 9am-noon Sat) This city-owned vineyard yielding 200,000 bottles per year, with almost all Grüner Veltliner and riesling, offers a variety of wine for tasting and purchase.

🛏 Sleeping

Hotel Alte Poste
HOTEL $

(☑02732-822 76; www.altepost-krems.at; Obere Landstrasse 32; s €36-52, d €66-90; ℙ) This medium-sized guesthouse located in a historic 500-year-old house has an enchanting courtyard and basic but rather sweet rooms.

ÖAMTC Donaupark Camping
CAMPGROUND $

(☑02732-844 55; www.donauparkcamping-krems.at; Yachthafenstrasse 19; camp sites per adult/child/car €5.50/3, per tent €4-9; ☻Easter–mid-Oct; ℙ) Well-maintained camp site alongside the Danube with cycle hire and a snack bar.

Hotel-Garni Schauhuber
HOTEL $

(☑0660 4003 412; Steiner Landstrasse 16; s/d €40/72; ☻🛜) The Schauhuber is charmingly old-fashioned, with sparkling tiled surfaces, whitewashed walls and large rooms. Breakfast is hearty.

Kolpinghaus
DORMITORY $

(☑02732-835 41; www.kolpingkrems.at; Alauntalstrasse 95 & 97; s/d €40/75; ☻reception 8am-5pm Mon-Fri, to noon Sat & Sun; ℙ🛜) These super student quarters are available to travellers any time of year: a great deal if you don't

Krems an der Donau

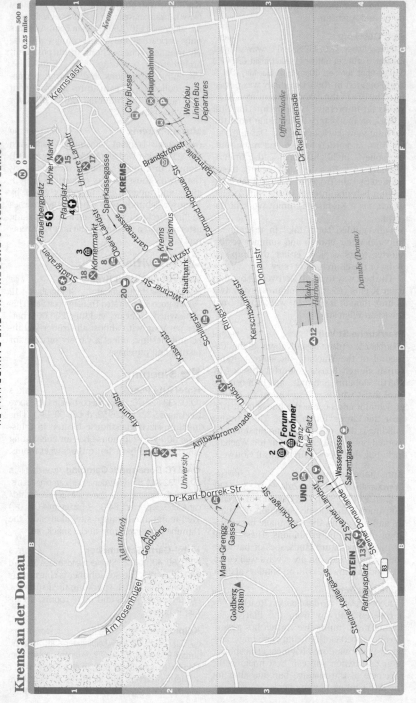

500 m
0.25 miles

Krems

KREMS

Kremstalstr
Kremstalstr

City Buses
Hauptbahnhof
Wachau
Linien Bus
Departures

Hoher Markt 15
Untere Landstr 17
Frauenbergplatz
5
Pfarrplatz 4
Brandströmstr
Bahnzeile
Edmund-Hofbauer-Str

Körnermarktstr
Sparkassegasse
8
Gartengasse
3
Obere Landstr
Krems
Tourismus
Utzstr
18
6
Stadtgraben
20
Stadtpark
J Wichner Str
Ringstr
Donaustr
Schillerstr
9

Kasernstr
Kerschbaumerstr

Offizierslacke
Dr-Riel-Promenade

16
Undstr
Alauntalstr

Yacht
Harbour

12

Anibaspromenade

Danube (Donau)

1 Forum
Frohner
Franz-
Zeller-Platz
2

University
11
14

Dr-Karl-Dorrek-Str

Anibaspromenade

Wassergasse
Salzamtgasse
10
UND
19
7
Plöckinger Str
Maria-Grengg-
Gasse

Am
Goldberg

Am Rosenhügel

Alaunbach

Goldberg
(318m)

STEIN
13
21
Steiner Landstr
Donaulände
Steinertor
Steiner-Kellergasse
Rathausplatz
B3

Krems an der Donau

LOWER AUSTRIA & BURGENLAND THE DANUBE VALLEY

mind the trek up to the university. Some of the basic but comfortable rooms are huge, with bathrooms the size of some hotel singles, as well as their own kitchens. Only con is the institutional checkout time of 10am.

Hotel Unter den Linden   HOTEL $$
(☑ 02732-821 15; www.udl.at; Schillerstrasse 5; s €62-82, d €86-112; 🛜) This big, family-run hotel has knowledgeable and helpful owners, bright, welcoming rooms and a convenient location in Krems itself. Its mix of historic and streamlined modern works well throughout and breakfast is taken in the folksy dining room. Book ahead.

Arte Hotel Krems   DESIGN HOTEL $$
(☑ 02732-71 123; www.arte-hotel.at; Dr-Karl-Dorrek-Strasse 23; s/d €100/145; 🅿🛜) The art of the title might be a stretch but what you do get here are large, well-designed rooms with open plan bathrooms, all scattered with '60s-tilting furniture and big, bright patterns.

There's a separately owned wellness studio in the building, and a decent grill restaurant in the same complex.

✖ Eating

Filmbar im Kesselhaus   INTERNATIONAL $
(www.filmbar-kulinarium.at; Dr-Karl-Dorreck-Strasse 30; mains €6-12; ⊙ 10am-midnight Wed-Sun; 🛜) This stylish student restaurant and bar injects a bit of life into the otherwise very quiet university campus and has become *the* place in the area to meet up for a drink (and an art-house film), even if your student days

are long gone. The organic menu's a mix of snacky, international things such as burritos, pasta and vegetable skewers.

Schwarze Kuchl   AUSTRIAN $
(www.schwarze-kuchl.at; Untere Landstrasse 8; mains €8-13; ⊙ 8.30am-7.30pm Mon-Fri, to 5pm Sat) For some good, honest local grub, head to this daytime tavern on the main drag through town where you can enjoy veal goulash, apricot-filled pancakes and Waldviertel potato-and-beef hotpot *(Gröstl)* while warming your toes on the huge tiled oven.

Blauenstein   AUSTRIAN $$
(☑ 0699 1930 788; www.blauenstein.at; Donaulände 56, Stein; mains €16.50-19.50, 4-course menu €42; ⊙ 5-11pm Thu-Mon, 11am-3pm Fri-Sun) Upstairs in the regional government building, this bright dining room does nicely modernised Austrian dishes with a sweet view over the Danube. There's also a regionally focused wine bar downstairs for a pre- or post-stroll glass.

Jell   AUSTRIAN $$
(www.amon-jell.at; Hoher Markt 8-9; mains €13-23; ⊙ 10am-10.30pm Tue-Fri, to 2pm Sat & Sun) Occupying a gorgeous stone house, Jell is hard to beat for a rustic atmosphere and fine wine from its own vineyard. Its friendly staff also adds to a great regional experience; located just east of Pfarrkirche St Veit.

★ **Zum Kaiser von Österreich**   AUSTRIAN $$$
(☑ 0800 400 171 052; www.kaiser-von-oesterreich.at; Körnermarkt 9; 3-/4-/5-/6-course menu €45.50/49.50/59.50/69.50; ⊙ 6-11pm Tue-Sat)

The 'Emperor of Austria' is one of Krems' most well loved upmarket restaurants. Interiors recall a hunting lodge which sets the scene for menus that are built around the region's bounty of game, from deer to pheasant to rabbit.

Late Kloster Und   AUSTRIAN $$$
(02732-70 493; www.late.at; Undstrasse 6; 3-/4-/5-/10-course menu €50/60/65/85; ☺5-10pm Tue-Sat) A rather over-the-top interior gives you a clue that this is fine dining territory. Well-known chef Charly Teuschl does deconstructed dishes that impress. A lovely yard in the old monastery space and an impressive wine selection round off one of the best restaurants in the Wachau.

🍷 Drinking & Nightlife

Weinstein   WINE BAR
(0664 1300 331; www.weinstein.at; Donaulände 56, Stein) A Danube-facing wine bar that has a very comprehensive line-up of local wines by the glass. The kitchen turns out good drinking food, say carpaccio in summer or chilli con carne in winter.

Piano   BAR
(www.piano-krems.at; Steiner Landstrasse 21; ☺5pm-2am Mon-Thu, to 3am Fri & Sat, to midnight Sun) A crossover crowd of students, young workers and mellow jazz types pack in tightly at this lively and off-beat pub. It does a couple of local sausage snacks and sandwiches to go with its expertly assembled selection of beers.

Stadtcafe Ulrich   CAFE
(www.stadtcafe-ulrich.at; Südtirolerplatz 7; ☺7am-11pm Mon-Thu, to midnight Sat, 9am-11pm Sun) Krems' busiest cafe is this elegantly high-ceilinged Viennese job next to the Steinertor (the medieval gateway into the Old Town).

🛍 Shopping

Galerie der Regionen   GIFTS & SOUVENIRS
(02732-850 15 15; www.volkskultureuropa.org; Donaulände 56, Haus der Regionen; ☺10am-noon & 1-6pm Mon-Sat) A kitsch-free showcase of Austrian craftsmanship, spanning traditional clothing, scarves, jewellery and homewares. Look out for the iconic Reiss enamelware with folk patterns.

❶ Information

Krems Tourismus (02732-82 676; www.krems.info; Utzstrasse 1; ☺9am-6pm Mon-Fri, 11am-6pm Sat, 11am-4pm Sun, shorter hours

in winter) Helpful office well stocked with info and maps.
Main Post Office (Brandströmstrasse 4-6)

Getting There & Away

For boats, the **river station** is near Donaustrasse, about 1.5km west of the train station.
Autovermietung Becker (02732-82433; www.rent.becker.at; Wachauer Strasse 30) rents cars from €65 per day.

Frequent daily trains connect Krems with Vienna (€17.60, one hour). **Wachau Linien** (0810 222 324; www.vor.at) runs buses along the Danube Valley as far as Melk (hourly, one hour). The Wachau Ticket (€10) is available from the driver and gives one day's unlimited travel on all buses – including Krems **city buses** – and the Danube ferries.

Dürnstein

 02711 / POP 875
The pretty town of Dürnstein, on an impossibly photogenic curve in the Danube, is not only known for its beautiful buildings but also for the castle above the town where Richard I of England, yes, the Lionheart, was once imprisoned.

Busy with visitors in summer, Dürnstein completely shuts up shop over the winter.

◉ Sights

Kuenringerburg   CASTLE
FREE Kuenringerburg, the castle high on the hill above the town, is where Richard the Lionheart was incarcerated from 1192 to 1193. His crime was insulting Leopold V; his misfortune was to be recognised despite his disguise when journeying through Austria on his way home from the Holy Lands. His liberty was granted only upon payment of an enormous ransom of 35,000kg of silver (this sum partly funded the building of Wiener Neustadt).

Chorherrenstift   MONASTERY
(www.stiftduernstein.at; Stiftshof; adult/child €3/1.50; ☺9am-6pm Mon-Sat, 10am-6pm Sun Apr-Oct) Of the picturesque 16th-century houses and other prominent buildings lining Dürnstein's streets, the meticulously restored Chorherrenstift is the most impressive. It's all that remains of the former Augustinian monastery originally founded in 1410; it received its baroque facelift in the 18th century (overseen by Josef Munggenast, among others). Kremser Schmidt did many of the ceiling and altar paintings. En-

try includes access to the porch overlooking the Danube and an exhibition on the Augustinian monks who lived here until 1788.

🏃 Activities

Domäne Wachau
WINE

(☑02711-371 15; www.domaene-wachau.at; ⏱10am-5pm Mon-Sat Apr-Oct, closed Sat Nov-Mar) If you're intent on tasting the best of what the Wachau has to offer, it's a good idea to do a broad range of vineyards, from the innovative family-run operations to the big boys like Domäne Wachau, one of the region's most well known producers internationally. A large modern tasting room is set back just from the river and staffed by an army of keen young assistants. It also stocks some nice local food products if wine's not your thing.

🛏 Sleeping

Pension Böhmer
GUESTHOUSE $

(☑02711-239; Hauptstrasse 22; s €45, d €55-68; 🅿) This small pension in the heart of town has comfortable rooms that overlook the main street. Downstairs there's a couple of atmospheric rooms and a cobbled entrance which is perfect for a leisurely wine. The Böhmer can also sort you out for the best local apricot schnapps and jams.

Hotel Sänger Blondel
HOTEL $$

(☑02711-253; www.saengerblondel.at; Klosterplatz/Dürnstein 64; s €79-89, d €119-139; 🅿🛜) One of the best-value options in town, this hotel has generously sized rooms furnished in light woods, some with sofas. A couple have views to the Danube and others look out onto the castle or garden.

Hotel Schloss Dürnstein
HOTEL $$$

(☑02711-212; www.schloss.at; Dürnstein 2; s €159-189, d €209-318; ⏱Apr–mid-Oct; 🅿@🛜🏊) This castle does over-the-top old-fashioned luxury. Rooms are furnished in antiques and overstuffed sofas, a massage can be arranged for your arrival, and there's a sauna and steam bath. The terrace restaurant enjoys staggering views over the river. Closed over the winter.

🍴 Eating

Weinschenke Altes Presshaus
CAFE $

(Dürnstein 10; snacks & mains €3.50-9.50; ⏱2pm-late Tue-Sat, from 11am Sun Apr-Oct) Centrally located *Heuriger*-style place selling local wine – lots of Veltliner – and a long menu of snacks and hearty meals such as goulash,

---

A HIKE FROM DÜRNSTEIN

After visiting the **Kuenringerburg** (p128), where Richard the Lionheart was incarcerated, hike the Schlossbergweg (marked green) from there to **Fesselhütte**, about one hour by foot from the castle, to enjoy sausage, soup or wine at this forest tavern. A road also leads up here from Weissenkirchen.

---

schnitzel and wild boar steaks. Very popular among visitors and locals alike. The snacks here are totally authentic with old favourites such as black pudding, pork fat and crackling or liver pâté on brown bread.

Fesselhütte
AUSTRIAN $

(www.fesslhuette.at; Dürsteiner Waldhütten 23; mains €8-12; ⏱9.30am-6pm Wed-Sun Apr-Oct) This lovely old forest dining room serves up a selection of platters, a hot lunch dish and homemade cakes and pastries. Sit out in the garden with a glass of wine from a Wachau vineyard too.

★ Restaurant Loibnerhof
AUSTRIAN $$

(☑02732-828 90; www.loibnerhof.at; Unterloiben 7; mains €16-26; ⏱11.30am-midnight Wed-Sun) Situated 1.5km east of Dürnstein's centre, this family-run restaurant inside a Biedermeiered 400-year-old vaulted cellar serves up creative takes on Waldviertel cooking. In summer, there are tables out in the family's orchard. Take away the house nut schnapps, apricot jam or foie gras parfait.

ℹ Information

High visitor numbers didn't stop Dürnstein scrapping its tourist office in 2013 – try the **rathaus** (Town Hall; ☑02711-219; www.duernstein.at; Hauptstrasse 25; ⏱8am-noon Mon-Fri, plus 1-4pm Mon, 1-7pm Tue), which also has some information.

ℹ Getting There & Away

Brandner (www.brandner.at; landing station near Chorherrenstift) boats connect Dürnstein with Krems (20 to 30 minutes) once or twice daily from mid-April to late October.

Dürnstein is linked to Melk (45 minutes, hourly) and Krems (25 minutes, 18 daily) by bus. This is by far the most convenient way to travel.

Dürnstein's train station is called Dürnstein-Oberloiben, with connections to Krems (17 minutes, three daily) and Weissenkirchen (seven minutes, three daily).

LOWER AUSTRIA & BURGENLAND THE DANUBE VALLEY

Weissenkirchen

☑ 02715 / POP 1445

Weissenkirchen, 12km from Krems, has a laid-back elegance as well as historic cache, but somehow eludes the crowds. The main attraction is the fortified Gothic parish church, and below it, the charming **Teisenhoferhof** arcaded courtyard, with a covered gallery and lashings of flowers and dried corn.

◉ Sights

Wachau Museum   MUSEUM
(☑ 02715-22 68; Weissenkirchen 32; adult/child €6/2.50; ⊙ 10am-5pm Tue-Sun Apr-Oct) Directly below the church, the tiny, pretty Wachau Museum showcases artists of the Danube School.

Weissenkirchen Parish Church   CHURCH
This 15th-century Gothic church sits on a hilltop overlooking the town; its front doors are approached along a labyrinth of covered pathways. Look out for the baroque altar (you can't miss it) and loll about on its garden terrace with lovely Danube views.

⊨ Sleeping

★ **Raffelsberger Hof**   HOTEL $$$
(☑ 02715-22 01; www.raffelsbergerhof.at; Freisingerplatz 54; s/d €150/230; ⊙ mid-Apr–Nov; P 🌊) This is an exceptionally atmospheric hotel, set in a small, gently modernised Renaissance castle. Rooms aren't large but are fabulously comfortable and the opposite of stuffy. Apart from charming public areas and garden, the hotel has a natural and beautifully landscaped 'pond' swimming pool.

❶ Getting There & Away

Weissenkirchen has boat and train connections to Dürnstein, but the easiest way to reach the village from there is by local bus (eight minutes, 18 daily).

Spitz

☑ 02713 / POP 1700

Situated 17km west of Krems on the north bank of the Danube, Spitz is a pleasant town that doesn't get as clogged with visitors as Dürnstein. It has a picturesque old town centre, and offers some good hiking in the surrounding forests and vineyards. To reach the old town, turn left after leaving the station then head right up Marktstrasse to Kirchenplatz.

Six kilometres west of Spitz, Mühldorf is home to the castle and hotel Burg Oberranna.

🏃 Activities

Spitz hiking   HIKING
Pick up some maps from the tourist office and hike up to the castle ruin Burgruine Hinterhaus on the bluff for fantastic views of the valley. Other trails run through the forests of the Jauerling Naturpark (Jauerling Nature Reserve) behind here. Hikes offering picturesque views also begin from Rotes Tor (Red Gate, 15 minutes' walk from the parish church on Marktstrasse).

⊨ Sleeping

Hotel Wachauer Hof   HOTEL $
(☑ 02713-23 03; www.wachauerhof-spitz.at; Hauptstrasse 15; s €47-53, d €78-90; P ⊙) This centrally located hotel has comfortable rooms and a restaurant with outside seating in summer.

★ **Burg Oberranna**   HISTORIC HOTEL $$
(☑ 02713-8221; www.burg-oberranna.at; s/d €88/148; P ⊙) Surrounded by woods and overlooking the valley, this rather special hotel occupies a medieval *Schloss*. It's been sensitively restored and retains much of the original structure, including an ancient Romanesque chapel crypt. Furnished with antiques, it's very atmospheric. The hotel is about 6km from Spitz; if you're not driving, you'll need to catch a taxi.

❶ Information

Tourist Office (☑ 02713-23 63; www.spitz-wachau.com; Mittergasse 3a; ⊙ 9am-1pm & 2-6pm Mon-Sat Apr-Oct) The tourist office, situated 400m west of the station, has excellent free maps of the town with hiking trails marked and maintains a comprehensive *Heuriger* calendar. Note it has unspecified and irregular hours in low season.

❶ Getting There & Away

Trains connect Spitz and Krems (35 minutes, three daily) but the bus (35 minutes, 20 daily) is a better option. A taxi to Burg Oberanna costs about €17.

Maria Taferl & Artstetten

☑ 07413 / POP 850

Located off the river on the northern side of the Danube in the Waldviertel, the small town of Maria Taferl is famous for its **Pfarr-und Wallfahrtskirche Maria Taferl** (Parish

& Pilgrimage Church; www.basilika.at; Maria Taferl 1; ⊙7am-8pm) high above the Danube Valley. Created by Jakob Prandtauer (of Melk fame), this baroque church has two onion domes and dark dome-frescoes. Its altar is a complex array of figures in gold. You'll find lots of hotels and B&Bs if you decide to stay in town, and some of the most spectacular views across the Danube are provided by the village's location.

About 6km east of Maria Taferl and about the same distance off the Danube is Artstetten, where there's also a castle. This was created out of a 13th-century medieval castle and has seen modifications over the past 700 years, including Renaissance features. It gained fame and glory after passing into the hands of the Habsburgs in the early 19th century, winding up in the possession of Archduke Franz Ferdinand. Inside is a **museum** (www.schloss-artstetten.at; Artstetten 1, Artstetten; adult/child €8/5; ⊙9am-5.30pm Apr-Oct; P) devoted to the luckless heir, displaying photos and stories of his and his wife's time at the castle and their fateful trip to Sarajevo where his murder kicked off WWI. Their tomb is in the church.

Feuersbrunn

About 10km east of Krems near the road to Tulln stands Schloss Grafenegg, a mid-19th century historicist fantasy that's now a venue for exhibitions and concerts as well as a museum. Two kilometres away, the hamlet of Feuersbrunn is home to a couple of the region's best eating and sleeping options.

⊙ Sights

Schloss Grafenegg　　　　　　　CASTLE
(www.grafenegg.com; Grafenegg 10; adult/child €6/4; ⊙10am-5pm Tue-Sun mid-Apr–Oct; P) About 6km south of Diendorf is this historicist castle with the look and feel of an ornate Tudor mansion set in English woods, although look a little closer and you'll spot faux Gothic, baroque and Biedermeier elements. The castle's manicured 19th-century gardens are perfect for a picnic.

🛏 Sleeping

Hotel Villa Katharina　　　　　HOTEL $$
(☑02738-229 80; www.moerwald.at; Kleine Zeile 10; s €82-98, d €120-140; P👤🐾🛜) This small, pretty country hotel has simple, light and stylish rooms set among the vines, each spritzed with colours that reflect the wine-growing region. Its attached Restaurant Zur Traube is something of a destination in itself.

✕ Eating

Restaurant & Hotel
Schloss Grafenegg　　　RESTAURANT $$
(☑02735-2616-0; www.moerwald.at; Grafenegg 12; mains €16.80-29.80; ⊙10am-10pm Wed-Sun Easter-Dec; P👤) This traditional hotel restaurant, with an atmospherically retro interior, is owned by celebrity chef and winemaker Toni Mörwald and is known for its attention to detail.

Restaurant Zur Traube　　　AUSTRIAN $$
(☑02738-229 80; www.moerwald.at/restaurant-zur-traube; Kleine Zeile 13-17; mains €16.50-24.50; ⊙noon-3pm & 6-10pm, closed Mon-Wed Jul & Aug; P👤) This upmarket place retains the charm of its past life as a village inn. Fittingly Austrian classics are served here, but updated with a contemporary eye and freshness. There's a particularly impressive cellar to choose a glass or a bottle from (as it should with the restaurant called 'the grape').

ⓘ Getting There & Away

To reach Schloss Grafenegg from Vienna, take the train to nearby Wagram-Grafenegg (€3.80, 20 minutes, around nine daily) and walk 2km northeast to the castle or grab a taxi. It's about a 40- to 50-minute drive from Vienna.

Melk

📞 02752 / POP 5260

With its blockbuster abbey-fortress set high above the valley, Melk is a high point of any visit to the Danube Valley. Separated from the river by a stretch of woodland, this pretty town makes for an easy and rewarding day trip from Krems or even Vienna. Combine a visit with nearby renaissance-era Schloss Schallaburg, 6km south of town, and you have yourself a day packed with architectural interest.

Melk is one of the most popular destinations in Austria so you certainly won't be alone on its cobbled streets. It's also one of the few places in the Wachau that has a pulse in winter, making it a year-round option.

⊙ Sights

Stift Melk　　　　　　　　　ABBEY
(Benedictine Abbey of Melk; www.stiftmelk.at; Abt Berthold Dietmayr Strasse 1; adult/child €11/6, with guided tour €13/8; ⊙9am-5.30pm, tours 10.55am

LOWER AUSTRIA & BURGENLAND THE DANUBE VALLEY

& 2.55pm May-Sep, tours only 11am and 2pm Nov-Mar) Of the many abbeys in Austria, Stift Melk is the most famous. Possibly Lower Austria's finest, the monastery church dominates the complex with its twin spires and high octagonal dome. The interior is baroque gone barmy, with regiments of smirking cherubs, gilt twirls and polished faux marble. The theatrical high-altar scene, depicting St Peter and St Paul (the church's two patron saints), is by Peter Widerin. Johann Michael Rottmayr created most of the ceiling paintings, including those in the dome.

Historically, Melk was of great importance to the Romans and later to the Babenbergs, who built a castle here. In 1089, the Babenberg margrave Leopold II donated the castle to Benedictine monks, who converted it into a fortified abbey. Fire destroyed the original edifice, which was completely baroque-ified between 1702 and 1738 according to plans by Jakob Prandtauer and his disciple, Josef Munggenast. It's claimed nine million bricks were used to create the 500 rooms – don't worry though, you don't have to visit them all! (Most of the complex is taken up by a school, monks' quarters and offices.)

Besides the monastery church, highlights include the Bibliothek (library) and the Marmorsaal (Marble Hall); both have amazing trompe l'oeil–painted tiers on the ceiling (by Paul Troger) to give the illusion of greater height, and ceilings are slightly curved to aid the effect. Eleven of the imperial rooms, where dignitaries (including Napoleon) stayed, are now used as a somewhat overcooked concept museum.

Before or after a tour of the main complex, take a spin around the Nordbastei where you'll discover some quirky temporary exhibitions, a viewing terrace and the Stift's gift shop.

A combined ticket with Schloss Schallaburg is €18. From around November to March, the monastery can only be visited by guided tour (11am and 2pm daily). Always phone or email ahead, even in summer, to ensure you get an English-language tour.

Schloss Schallaburg
PALACE

(☑ 02754-6317; www.schallaburg.at; Schallaburg 1; adult/child €11/3.50; ☺ 9am-5pm Mon-Fri, to 6pm Sat & Sun Apr-early Nov) This palace is famous not only for its stunning architecture but also for the innovative exhibitions it houses, along with its stunning gardens. A wonderful curio are the 400 terracotta sculptures, completed between 1572 and 1573, the larg-

Driving & Cycling Tour
The Danube Valley

START KREMS
FINISH KREMS
LENGTH 150KM; ONE DAY

From the Krems-Stein roundabout in **❶ Krems an der Donau** take the B3 southwest towards Spitz. About 3km from Krems-Stein you approach the small settlement of Unterloiben, where on the right you can see the **❷ Franzosendenkmal** (French Monument), erected in 1805 to celebrate the victory of Austrian and Russian troops here over Napoleon. Shortly afterwards the lovely town of **❸ Dürnstein**, 6km from Krems, comes into view with its blue-towered Chorherrenstift backed by Kuenringerburg, the castle where Richard the Lionheart was imprisoned in 1192.

The valley is punctuated by picturesque terraced vineyards as you enter the heart of the Wachau. In **❹ Weissenkirchen**, 12km from Krems, you'll find a pretty fortified parish church on the hilltop. The Wachau Museum here houses work by artists of the Danube school.

A couple of kilometres on, just after Wösendorf, you find the church of **❺ St Michael**, in a hamlet with 13 houses. If the kids are along for this ride, now's the time to ask them to count the terracotta hares on the roof of the church (seven, in case they're not reading this!).

Some 17km from Krems, the pretty town of **❻ Spitz** swings into view, surrounded by vineyards and lined with quiet, cobblestone streets. Some good trails lead across hills and to *Heurigen* (wine taverns) here (start from the church).

Turn right at Spitz onto the B217 (Ottenschläger Strasse). The terraced hill on your right is **❼ 1000-Eimer-Berg**, so-named for its reputed ability to yield 1000 buckets of wine each season. On your left, high above the valley opening, is the castle ruin **❽ Burgruine Hinterhaus**. Continue along the B217 to the mill wheel and turn right towards **❾ Burg Oberranna** (p130), 6km west of Spitz in Mühldorf. Surrounded by woods, this castle and hotel overlooking the valley is furnished with period pieces and has a refreshing old-world feel.

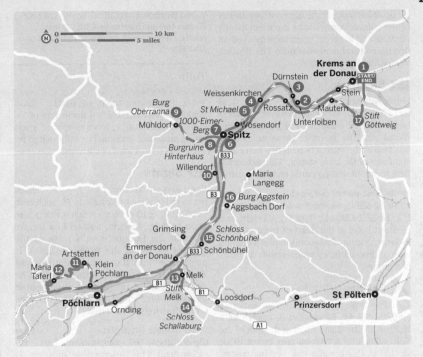

From here, backtrack down to the B3 and continue the circuit. The valley opens up and on the left, across the Danube, you glimpse the ruins of Burg Aggstein.

⑩ Willendorf, located 21km from Krems, is where a 25,000-year-old figurine of Venus was discovered. The original is today housed in the Naturhistorisches Museum in Vienna. Continuing along the B3, the majestic Stift Melk rises up across the river. There's some decent swimming in the backwaters here if you're game to dip into the Danube.

At Klein Pöchlarn, a sign indicates a turn-off on Artstettner Strasse (L7255): follow it for 5km to **⑪ Artstetten**, unusual for its many onion domes. From here, the minor road L7257 winds 6.5km through a sweeping green landscape to **⑫ Maria Taferl** high above the Danube Valley.

Head 6km down towards the B3. Turn left at the B3 towards Krems and follow the ramp veering off to the left and across the river at the Klein Pöchlarn bridge. Follow the road straight ahead to the B1 (Austria's longest road) and turn left onto this towards Melk.

This first section along the south bank is uninteresting, but it soon improves. Unless the weather isn't playing along, across the river you can make out Artstetten in the distance, and shortly **⑬ Stift Melk** (p131) will rise up ahead in a golden shimmering heap.

From Stift Melk, a 7km detour leads south to the splendid Renaissance castle of **⑭ Schloss Schallaburg** (p132). To reach the castle from the abbey in Melk, follow the signs to the *Bahnhof* (train station) and Lindestrasse east, turn right into Hummel-strasse/Kirschengraben (L5340) and follow the signs to the castle.

Backtrack to the B33. Be careful to stay on the south side of the river. When you reach the corner of Abt-Karl-Strasse and Bahnhof-strasse, go right and right again at the river. Follow the B1 for 4km to **⑮ Schloss Schön-bühel**, a 12th-century castle standing high on a rock some 5km northeast of Melk. Continue along this lovely stretch of the B33 in the direction of Krems. About 10km from Schloss Schönbühel the ruins of **⑯ Burg Aggstein** swing into view. This 12th-century hilltop castle was built by the Kuenringer family and now offers a grand vista of the Danube.

About 27km from Melk some pretty cliffs rise up above the road. From Mautern it's a detour of about 6km to **⑰ Stift Göttweig** (p125).

est of which support the upper-storey arches of the palace. Yearly shows are thematically curated, and in recent years have focused on diverse cultural moments from The Beatles, Venice and Byzantium.

🛏 Sleeping

Hotel Wachau   HOTEL **$$**
(🗷 02752-525-31; www.hotel-wachau.at; Am Wachberg 3; s €62-82, d €95-135; P🛜) Bright, clean rooms run the gauntlet between modern business and Austrian twee at this hotel 2km southeast of the train station. The restaurant here turns out well-prepared regional cuisine.

Hotel Restaurant zur Post   HOTEL **$$**
(🗷 02752-523 45; www.post-melk.at; Linzer Strasse 1; s €66-82, d €130-142; P@🛜) A bright and pleasant hotel in the heart of town offering 25 large, comfortable rooms in plush colours with additional fancy touches such as brass bed lamps.

🍴 Eating

Zum Fürsten   INTERNATIONAL **$**
(🗷 02752-523 43; Rathausplatz 3; mains €4.50-10.50; ⊙ 10.30am-11pm) Right at the foot of the Stift, relax after a tour on faux velvet 1970s seating at this popular cafe serving pastas, strudel, chilli con carne and other international dishes.

Zur Post   AUSTRIAN **$$**
(🗷 02752-523 45; Linzer Strasse 1; mains €7.90-20; ⊙ 11.30am-10pm Mon-Sat; 🗷) This traditional and understated restaurant is in the hotel of the same name on Melk's main drag. Waldviertel carp, Wiener Schnitzel, Danube catfish and organic lamb grace the menu, which also features several vegetarian options.

ℹ Information

Melk Tourist Office (🗷 02752-511 60; www.stadt-melk.at; Kremser Strasse 5; ⊙ 9.30am-6pm Mon-Sat, to 4pm Sun Apr-Oct, 9am-5pm Mon-Thu, to 2.30pm Fri Nov-Mar)

ℹ Getting There & Away

Boats leave from the canal by Pionierstrasse, 400m north of the abbey. **Wachau Linien** (p128) runs buses along the Danube valley between Melk and Krems (hourly, one hour).

   Wachau Touristik Bernhardt (🗷 02713-022 22; www.wachau-touristik.at; per day €12) rents out bicycles from the ferry station in Melk and from the train station in Spitz.

   There are regular train services to Melk from St Pölten (€6.20, at least hourly, 20 minutes),

Vienna Westbahnhof (€16.50, hourly, one hour 20 minutes) and Salzburg €43.10, at least hourly, 2½ hours with a change in St Pölten or Amstetten).

Tulln

🗷 02272 / POP 14,510

Tulln, the home town of painter Egon Schiele and situated 30km northwest of Vienna on the Danube, has a couple of interesting museums and can be easily visited on a day trip from Vienna or Krems.

◉ Sights

Egon Schiele Museum   MUSEUM
(www.egon-schiele.eu; Donaulände 28; adult/child €5.50/3.50; ⊙ 10am-5pm Tue-Sun Apr-Oct) The Egon Schiele Museum, housed in a former jail near the Danube, vividly presents the story of the life of the Tulln-born artist. It presents around 100 of his paintings and sketches, and a mock-up of the cell where he was briefly imprisoned, when he fell foul of the law in 1912 when over a hundred of his erotic drawings were seized.

Egon Schiele Birthplace   MUSEUM
(Bahnhofstrasse 69, Hauptbahnhof Tulln; €2; ⊙ 9am-8pm) This interpretive museum is based in a touching re-creation of Egon Schiele's actual birthplace and family home. The son of the railway station inspector Adolf Schiele, Egon Schiele spent the first 11 years of his life, from 1890, in the apartment at the train station that formed part of his father's employment.

Minoritenkirche   CHURCH
(Minoritenplatz 1; ⊙ 8am-7pm) Alongside the tourist office, the rococo Minorite church from 1739 is decorated with magnificent ceiling frescoes dedicated to St Johannes Nepomuk.

Museum im Minoritenkloster   MUSEUM
(Minoritenplatz 1) This city-promoted museum space features some excellent changing exhibitions based around mostly Austrian artists. Recent shows have featured Schiele (surprise, surprise), Wilhelm Kaufmann and Paschek. Admission prices vary with the exhibition. It adjoins the Minorite church.

Pfarrkirche St Stephan   CHURCH
(Wiener Strasse 20; ⊙ 7.30am-7.30pm) This parish church combines Gothic and baroque elements, along with the wonderful 13th-century frescoed Romanesque funerary chapel.

🛏 Sleeping & Eating

Donaupark Camping   CAMPGROUND $
(☑ 02272-652   00; www.campingtulln.at;
Donaulände 76; camp sites per adult/tent & car
€8.50/6; ☺ Apr-Oct; 🛜) Campground located
just east of the centre on the river and alongside a pretty forest.

Junges Hotel Tulln   HOSTEL $
(☑ 02272-651 65 10; www.tulln.noejhw.at; Marc-
Aurel-Park 1; dm/s/d €23.50/34/54; Ⓟ ☺) Youth
hostel near the Danube catering for seminar
guests as well as tourists. Dorms sleep between four and eight guests.

Hotel Nibelungenhof   HOTEL $$
(☑ 02272-626   58; www.nibelungenhof.info;
Donaulände 34; s €48-69, d €98; 🛜) Situated
along the Danube River with a lovely terrace
garden and cafe-restaurant downstairs, this
hotel has individually furnished rooms in
bright and attractive colours. The lounge has
a large library of books and a proper open fire.

Gasthaus zur Sonne   AUSTRIAN $$
(☑ 02272-646 16; Bahnhofstrasse 48; mains €9-25;
☺ 11.30am-1.30pm & 6-9pm Tue-Sat) This traditional restaurant serves excellent versions
of trad dishes such as goulash and veal liver
in a balsamic vinegar. Reserve ahead – it's
popular.

ℹ Information

Tourist Office (☑ 02272-675 660; www.
tullner-donauraum.at; Minoritenplatz 2; ☺ 9am-
7pm Mon-Fri, 10am-7pm Sat & Sun, closed Sat
& Sun Oct-Apr) One block north of Hauptplatz
from the fountain end.

ℹ Getting There & Away

Several regional and S-Bahn trains each hour
connect Tulln with Vienna's Franz-Josefs-
Bahnhof (€7.80, 30 to 45 minutes) and hourly
trains go to Krems (€10, 35 minutes).

Waldviertel & Weinviertel

Forming a broad swath across Lower Austria north of the Danube, the undervisited
Waldviertel (Woods Quarter) begins near
Krems and the Kamptal in the east (the latter borders the largely agricultural and winemaking region, the Weinviertel or 'Wine
Quarter') and ends at the Czech border in the
north and west. The Waldviertel is a hugely
underrated and highly picturesque region
of rolling hills and rural villages, and while
there isn't actually much forest to speak of,

there are a number of fine attractions and
retreats. The Kamptal in particular is a great
place for escaping the tourist crowds.

Drosendorf
☑ 02915 / POP 1200

Situated on the extreme northern fringe of
the Waldviertel, hard on the Czech border,
the lovely fortressed town of Drosendorf
is often overlooked by the Viennese – it's
simply too far-flung. Yet, with a completely
intact town wall, it is a unique and beautiful town and one well worth the trouble
it takes to reach it. A fortress walk begins
at the Information Service; it passes the
castle, a mostly baroque structure on top
of Romanesque foundations, and exits
through the Hornertor, the main gate in
the southeast dating from the 13th to 15th
centuries. Cross the moat and follow the
wall clockwise.

🛏 Sleeping & Eating

Schloss Drosendorf   HOTEL $
(☑ 02915-232   10; www.schloss-drosendorf.at;
Schlossplatz 1; s/d €48/70; Ⓟ ☺ ☎) If you're
staying overnight in town, there are several
good options, but this is the most atmospheric, if slightly tizzied up, choice. Plus it's great
value.

MOKA   CAFE
(☑ 02915-22 27; www.moka.at; Hauptplatz 5; ☺ 9am-
6pm Thu-Mon Apr-Oct) The rather knowingly
nostalgic MOKA just doesn't do poppy-seed
cake, but a whole range of poppy-seed cakes.
These include white poppy-seed, poppy-seed
with almond or chocolate-topped versions
alongside the traditional darkly fragrant one.
The coffee here is also spot on, plus there's a
spritz menu and a terrace for summer days.
And yes, this is cake that's worth a detour.

ℹ Information

Information Service (☑ 02915-232 10;
Schlossplatz 1; ☺ 8am-4.30pm Mon-Thu, to
12.30pm Fri) This information service is located
inside the castle. An information stand with a
useful walk-by-numbers brochure (in German)
as well as an accommodation list is situated on
Hauptplatz, inside the walls.

ℹ Getting There & Away

To reach Drosendorf from Vienna (Praterstern
station), take the train leaving every two hours
to Retz (€15.80, 70 minutes), making sure it
connects with one of several buses on weekdays

(€6.80, one hour). The only way into the Czech Republic from here is to backtrack to Retz, from where there are trains to Znojmo, or hike (or take a taxi) 6km to the first village (Vratěnín) on the other side of the border, from where there are buses further into Moravia.

Langenlois

02734 / POP 7235

The pretty but hard-working town of Langenlois is at the centre of the winegrowing Kamptal. Lush lowlands meet gently rolling hills and vines stretch in rows as far as the eye can see. White wines – Grüner Veltliner, riesling, Welschriesling and Weissburgunder in particular – reach stellar heights here and the town square is full of *Vinothek* (wine merchants) and seemingly every lane and road is lined with *Heuriger* – rustic wine taverns – or cellar doors.

🏃 Activities

Loisium Weinwelt   WINE
(www.loisium.at; Loisium Allee 1; 90min audio tour adult/child €11.50/6.30; ⊙10am-7pm) Across the vines from the Loisium Hotel is the Loisium Weinwelt, a paean to Langenlois' long history of wine growing as well as its present and future. It's something of an architectural statement too, set within an aluminium cube designed by New York architect Steven Holl. Multilingual audio tours here set off every 30 minutes and lead you through a 1.5km network of ancient and very deep tunnels.

🛏 Sleeping

Loisium Hotel   HOTEL $$$
(02734-77 100-0; www.loisiumhotel.at; Loisium Allee 2; d €175-220; P🐕@🛜🏊) This contemporary hotel set among the vines has large, light and modern rooms. Bathrooms have a pared back glamour and all rooms have balconies. There's a great restaurant and bar on site but the highlight is the spa, with large sauna and steam room area and a very pleasant 20m heated outdoor pool (it's open all year too).

🍸 Drinking & Nightlife

★**Weingut Hirsch**   WINERY
(02735-24 60; www.weingut-hirsch.at; Hauptstrasse 76, Kammern) Johannes Hirsch and his family make some of Austria's most elegant and uncompromising wines. Grapes are grown using biodynamic farming methods, picked by hand and, uniquely for this region, soft pruned; wine is a fruitful combination of modern and traditional 'slow' practices in the cellar. The winery concentrates on Grüner Veltliner and riesling only, and each of the wines comes from a single vineyard.

ℹ Information

Ursin Haus Tourist Service (02734-20 00; www.langenlois.at; Kamptalstrasse; ⊙10am-6pm) This wine emporium also does double duty as the town's tourism information service. It has comprehensive lists of all the town's wine offerings including seasonal *Heurigers*, cellar doors and restaurants. The main tourist website also lists these and has a downloadable map of the Langenlois Wine Route.

ℹ Getting There & Away

Langenlois is best experienced with your own car, but there are regular buses from Vienna (1¼ hours, €14.90), St Pölten (one hour, €8.60) and Krems (30 minutes, €3.30)

Nationalpark Thayatal

Tight against the border of Austria and the Czech Republic (a stretch of the old Iron Curtain) in the northwestern reaches of the Weinviertel is Austria's smallest national park, the Thayatal. This unique piece of landscape is one of Central Europe's last natural valleys and is actually two parks; its other half, Podyjí National Park, is located across the border. Of the 3000 plant species found in Austria, about 1300 occur in Thayatal. The landscape consists of a deep canyon cut by the Thaya river (the Dyje in Czech), numerous rock formations, steep slopes, some dry grassland and meadows and large stretches of gnarled primeval forest. Walking is by far the most popular activity here, with trails sometimes crossing from one country into the next and back again.

⊙ Sights

Nationalparkhaus   EXHIBIT
(Nationalpark Thayatal; 02949-700 50; www.np-thayatal.at; exhibition adult/child €4/2.50; ⊙9am-4pm mid-Mar–Sep, from 10am Oct) The Nationalparkhaus, near Hardegg, has loads of information and an exhibition on the park's various ecosystems and animal residents, including wildcats, storks and lizards. Hardegg, the natural jump-off point for the park, is not easy to get to without your own transport.

🛏 Sleeping

⭐ **Schloss Starrein**　　　APARTMENT $
(☑ 0664 13 12 333; www.gutstarrein.org; Starrein 1; apt €75; 🅿 🛜) A short drive from the national park, in the heart of Waldviertel farmland, young owners Peter and Sabine have one guest apartment in the family *Schloss*, with more to come. On the top floor of a semi-restored and extremely atmospheric 12th-century and Renaissance castle, it's a beautiful, airy and generous space, simply and stylishly decorated with a well-equipped kitchen and super comfortable bed. One 'window' looks over the castle's exquisite original chapel, others the fields beyond.

🛍 Shopping

Gut Starrein　　　FOOD & DRINKS
(☑ 0664 350 2084; www.gutstarrein.org; Starrein 1; ⊙ 9am-noon Sat, or call ahead to arrange a time) A small but very beautiful *Hofladen* (farm shop) sits off the courtyard in this beautiful *Schloss*. Some produce comes from owner Peter and Sabine Eichinger's surrounding farm, the rest from like-minded locals. This includes several potato and onion varieties, fresh herbs, heritage grains like einkorn, and oats, oils, local beef and sausages, vodka and artisanal cow hides.

❶ Getting There & Away

Without your own wheels, it's best approached by train from Vienna to Retz (€15.80, one hour), from where you take a bus to Pleising, then another to Hardegg. It's far easier with a car.

Wienerwald

The Wienerwald encompasses gentle wooded hills to the west and southwest of Vienna, and the wine-growing region directly south of the capital. For the Viennese, it's a place for walking, climbing and mountain biking. Numerous walking and cycling trails in the area are covered in the *Wienerwald Wander-und Radkarte,* available free from local tourist offices and the region's main office, Wienerwald Tourismus.

Attractive settlements, such as the grape-growing towns of **Perchtoldsdorf** and **Gumpoldskirchen**, speckle the Wienerwald. Picturesque **Mödling**, only 15km south of Vienna, was once favoured by the artistically inclined: Beethoven's itchy feet took him to Hauptstrasse 79 from 1818 to 1820, and Austrian composer Arnold Schön-

berg stayed at Bernhardgasse 6 from 1918 to 1925. More information is available from the Tourismus Information Mödling.

About 20km from Mödling is **Heiligenkreuz** and the 12th-century Cistercian abbey **Stift Heiligenkreuz** (☑ 02258-8703; www.stift-heiligenkreuz.at; Heiligenkreuz 1; adult/child €7.50/3.80; ⊙ tours 10am, 11am, 2pm, 3pm & 4pm Mon-Sat, 11am, 2pm, 3pm & 4pm Sun). The chapter house is the final resting place of most of the Babenberg dynasty, which ruled Austria until 1246. The abbey museum contains 150 clay models by Giovanni Giuliani (1663–1744), a Venetian sculptor who also created the Trinity column in the courtyard. Note that tours in English are by advance request only.

Mayerling, which lies 6km southwest of Heiligenkreuz, is unremarkable now, but the tragic royal murder-suicide that occurred here in 1889 still draws visitors to the site. The **Carmelite convent** (☑ 02258-22 75; karmel-mayerling.org; Mayerling 1; adult/child €6.70/4; ⊙ 9am-6pm) can be visited although it post-dates the event and there is nothing to see beyond a few mementos. Rather creepily, the altar in the chapel was built exactly where the bodies of Archduke Rudolf and Maria were found.

Between Mayerling and Weissenbach-Neuhaus, situated about 5km from both on the L4004 and accessible from the Schwarzensee parking area and bus stop, is **Peilstein** (716m), with rock climbing on the **Peilstein Klettersteig**. This is one of the most picturesque climbs in the region and a favourite among the Viennese. Peilsteinhaus, a hut and restaurant with a kids' playground, can be reached by hiking trails (01/06) via Mayerling from Heiligenkreuz (16km, 4½ hours to Peilstein). From the Schwarzensee/Peilstein bus stop, it's a half-hour hike and from Weisenbach it takes 1½ hours.

🏃 Activities

Peilstein Klettersteig　　　CLIMBING
This little mountain is one of Vienna's favourite easy weekend climbs with a via ferrata and ropes that make it suitable for beginners and children. Hiking trails also lead to Peilsteinhaus, a hut and restaurant with a kids' playground.

❶ Information

Tourismus Information Mödling (☑ 02236-267 27; www.moedling.at; Kaiserin

Elisabeth-Strasse 2; ⊙9am-12.30pm & 1.30-5pm Mon-Fri)

Wienerwald Tourismus (☑02231-621 76; www.wienerwald.info; Hauptplatz 11, Purkersdorf; ⊙9am-5pm Mon-Fri) Numerous walking and cycling trails in the area are covered in the *Wienerwald Wander und Radkarte*.

ℹ Getting There & Away

To really get under the skin of this region, it's best to have your own bicycle or car, but trains and buses will carry you to the main centres. The main road through the area is the A21 that loops down from Vienna, passes by Heiligenkreuz, then curves north to join the A1 just east of Altlengbach.

Bus connections are from Baden bei Wien to Heiligenkreuz (€2, 20 to 30 minutes, seven daily on weekdays) or from Baden to Schwarzensee (€5.70, one hour, six daily Monday to Saturday).

To get here by train, take the S1 or S2 from Wien-Meidling via Perchtoldsdorf (€2.20, 11 minutes, four hourly) to Gumpoldskirchen (€3.80, 27 minutes, hourly) and the S50 from Wien-Meidling (or S60 from the Westbahnhof) to Purkersdorf (€3.80, 20 minutes, hourly). Indirect trains from Baden bei Wien to Weissenbach-Neuhaus (€5.80, 50 minutes, seven daily Monday to Saturday) require a change in Leobersdorf.

Baden bei Wien

☑02252 / POP 25,100

With its sulphurous mineral springs and lush green parks, gardens and woods, this spa town on the eastern fringes of the Wienerwald is a picturesque anachronism. Baden has a long history of receiving notable visitors; the Romans came here to wallow in the medicinal waters, Beethoven blew into town in the hope of a cure for his deafness, and in the early 19th century it flourished as the favourite summer retreat of the Habsburgs. Much of the town centre is in the 19th-century Biedermeier style. Note that Baden goes into virtual hibernation between October and March.

The centre is about 15 minutes by foot from the train station. Follow Kaiser-Franz-Joseph-Ring west and turn right into Wassergasse.

◉ Sights

★**Arnulf Rainer Museum** MUSEUM
(www.arnulf-rainer-museum.at; Josefsplatz 5; adult/child €6/4; ⊙10am-5pm) Located inside the former Frauenbad (Women's Bathhouse) near the tram terminus, this interesting museum showcases the work of its namesake

Arnulf Rainer, who was born in Baden in 1929. A recalcitrant art school dropout, he began painting in a surrealist style before developing his idiosyncratic multimedia and performance works.

This includes the infamous painting with chimpanzees episode where Rainer attempted to mimic the work of a number of painting apes only to be chased by one of his unwilling collaborators. The museum has retained the delightful marble features of the Biedermeier bathhouse from 1815, making it all the more worth a visit. Exhibitions change twice a year.

Dreifaltigkeitssäule MONUMENT
This monument on Hauptplatz to the Holy Trinity, dating from 1714, is one of Austria's wierdest (with a very dribbly someone-left-my-cake-out-in-the-rain meets baroque styling).

Kurpark PARK
The *Kurpark* is a magnificent setting for a stroll or as a place to repose on the benches in front of the bandstand, where free concerts are held from May to September. Attractive flower beds complement monuments to famous artists (Mozart, Beethoven, Strauss, Grillparzer etc). Near the southern entrance to the park, the Undine-Brunnen (fountain) is a fine amalgam of human and fish images.

Rollett Museum MUSEUM
(Weikersdorfer Platz 1; adult/child €3.50/2; ⊙3-6pm Wed-Mon) The Rollett Museum, southwest of the town centre and just off Weilburgstrasse (a five-minute walk southeast of the Thermalstrandbad), covers important aspects of the town's history. The most unusual exhibit is the collection of skulls, busts and death masks amassed by the founder of phrenology, Josef Gall (1752–1828), who sparked the craze of inferring criminal characteristics from the shape of one's cranium. Not pleasant.

🏃 Activities

Thermalstrandbad SWIMMING
(Helenenstrasse 19-21; all-day adult/child €7.80/3.90; ⊙8.30am-7.30pm May-Sep) A purpose-built functionalist building from 1926 houses this pool complex and includes a strip of precious shipped-in sand. The building itself is worth a peek, but it's also a pleasant place to while away an afternoon on the grass or having a splash. At times you do get a fair whiff of Baden's signature 'poached egg' smell – from

the sulphur contained in its healing waters – but it's not always that obvious.

Kronprinz-Rudolf-Weg
CYCLING

Cycling or hiking the 12-km long Kronprinz-Rudolf-Weg along the Schwechat River to Mayerling is a good summer alternative to museums or the baths. The tourist office has a free trail description (in German) and bikes can be hired in town. The trail can be combined with a 6km return northern branch trail to Heiligenkreuz.

Römertherme
SPA

(Roman Baths; ☑ 02252-450 30; www.roemertherme.at; Brusattiplatz 4; 3hr/all-day €15.30/18.90; ⊙ 10am-10pm) The Römertherme is a modern wellness-focused baths with a number of therapeutic pools and a large range of treatments. Admission weekdays is slightly cheaper.

🛏 Sleeping

Villa Inge
PENSION $

(☑ 02252-431 71; Weilburgstrasse 24-26; s/d from €45/68; ⊙ Apr-Oct; 🅿 ❋ @) This large villa is set alongside the river close to the Thermalstrandbad. Rooms are spacious and the breakfast room is lovely and bright, looking out to the garden. It offers good value for Baden, especially for its family apartment (from €120).

★ Hotel Schloss Weikersdorf
HOTEL $$

(☑ 02252-48 301 0; www.hotelschlossweikersdorf.at; Schlossgasse 9-11; s €85-140, d €125-185; 🅿 @ 🛜 ❋) For the total Baden experience, look no further than this ultra-padded hotel set in beautiful gardens. Rooms are smart and some have balconies and there are massage services, relaxation coves, lounges and other wellness facilities. It also has three places to eat, including the Rosenkavalier restaurant, one of Baden's best.

Hotel Herzoghof
HOTEL $$

(☑ 02252-872 97; www.hotel-herzoghof.at; Kaiser-Franz-Ring 10; s/d €100/149; 🅿 🛜) This central hotel opposite the *Kurpark* offers simple, modern rooms and good value for money. There's a sauna and steam bath on-site.

🍷 Drinking & Nightlife

Cafe Central
CAFE

(Hauptplatz 19; ⊙ 7am-8pm Tue-Sat, 8am-8pm Sun) The town's Hauptplatz standard is a delightful old dame with a gem of a mid-20th-century interior and formal waiters.

Weinkult
WINE BAR

(www.weinkult.at; Pfarrgasse 7; ⊙ 11.30am-8pm Tue-Fri, 10.30am-5pm Sat) This wine shop sells almost 150 Austrian wines and serves a dozen by the glass, rotating the selection on a weekly basis.

ℹ Information

Baden Tourismus (☑ 226 00-600; www.baden.at; Brusattiplatz 3; ⊙ 9am-6pm Mon-Sat, to 4pm Sun May-Sep, to 5pm Mon-Fri Oct-Apr)

ℹ Getting There & Away

Bus 360 departs every 30 to 60 minutes (€6, 40 minutes) from the Oper in Vienna. In Baden, bus 362 runs between the Thermalstrandbad and Bahnhof via the centre.

Regional and S-Bahn trains connect Baden with Wien-Meidling (€4, 20 minutes, three times hourly) and with Wiener Neustadt (€5.30, 20 minutes).

A *Lokalbahn* tram (€6.50, one hour, every 15 minutes, 40 minutes) connects the Oper in Vienna with Josefsplatz in Baden.

March-Donauland

The March-Donauland, stretching from the eastern border of Vienna to the Slovakian border, is dominated by the Danube and its natural flood plains, an area dotted with industry throughout the pretty, if not particularly inspiring, countryside. Carnuntum, an important Roman camp during the days of the Roman Empire, and the Nationalpark Donau-Auen are found here and make for an interesting day trip.

ℹ Information

Nationalparkhaus Wien-lobAU (☑ 01-4000-49495; www.donauauen.at; Dechantweg 8, Vienna; ⊙ 10am-6pm Wed-Sun Mar-Oct)

ℹ Getting There & Away

Vienna's backyard is serviced by regular trains and buses and is criss-crossed with cycle paths. You're also only a quick hop from the Slovakian capital of Bratislava here.

Petronell-Carnuntum

☑ 02165 / POP 1240

The Roman town of Carnuntum was the most important political and military centre in the empire's northeast, once known as Upper Pannonia; with a population of 50,000 people at its peak, it made Vienna look like a village in comparison. The town developed around AD 40 but was abandoned some 400 years later. The main sights are spread between the modern-day settlement Petronell-Carnuntum, the larger spa town of Bad Deutsch-Altenburg about 4km away, and Hainburg, another 4km east of this.

Sights

Museum Carnuntinum   MUSEUM
(Badgasse 40-46, Bad Deutsch-Altenburg; ⊙9am-5pm mid-Mar–Nov) This museum of archaeological finds is the largest of its kind in Austria, having amassed over 3300 Roman treasures in its 100-year existence. The museum's highlight, *Tanzende Mänade* (Dancing Maenad), a marble figure with a most perfect bum, is usually displayed here. While in Bad Deutsch-Altenburg, take a stroll around the *Kurpark* (spa gardens), situated alongside the Danube.

Freilichtmuseum Petronell   RUINS
(www.carnuntum.at; Hauptstrasse 1a, Petronell-Carnuntum; adult/child €11/9; ⊙9am-5pm mid-Mar–mid-Nov) The open-air museum is the major attraction in Petronell-Carnuntum itself and lies on the site of the old civilian town. It includes ruins of the public baths and a totally reconstructed temple of Diana. Strapping young actors lead happily kitsch tours in tunics and togas, and you can buy replicas of Roman sandals and clothing here for your next toga party. The museum is very touristy, but nevertheless interesting and fun; descriptions everywhere are in *Lingua Anglica*.

Sleeping

Hotel-Gasthof Stöckl   HOTEL $
(☑02165-623 37; www.gasthof-stoeckl.at; Hauptplatz 3, Bad Deutsch-Altenburg; s/d €48/72; P❋🛜🏊) Comfortable, centrally located hotel with a solar-heated outdoor pool, and a sauna and steam bath.

★**Hotel Altes Kloster**   HOTEL $$
(www.alteskloster.at; Fabriksplatz 1, Hainburg an der Donau; s/d €85/140; P🛜) A modern and cleanly stylish hotel has taken over this 17th-century monastery in the historic Old Town of Hainburg. Rooms are large and soothing and there's a spa area for guests with sauna, steam bath, and infrared cabin. The half-board option (room rate plus €21, full-board room rate plus €28) is good value; the hotel's restaurant is one of the better ones around here.

ℹ Information

Bad Deutsch-Altenburg Tourist Office
(☑02165-629 00; www.bad-deutsch-altenburg.gv.at; Erhardgasse 2; ⊙8am-noon & 1-7pm Mon, to 4pm Tue-Thu, 8am-1pm Fri)
Petronell-Carnuntum Tourist Office
(☑02163-337 70; www.carnuntum.co.at; Hauptstrasse 1a; ⊙9am-5pm mid-Mar–mid-Nov) At the open-air museum.

ℹ Getting There & Away

There are hourly S-Bahn departures from Wien-Mitte for Petronell-Carnuntum, Bad Deutsch-Altenburg (both €7.50, 50 minutes) and Hainburg (€9.20, one hour).

The cycle path from Vienna goes along the north bank of the Danube, crosses to the south near Bad Deutsch-Altenburg, and continues into Slovakia.

St Pölten

☑02742 / POP 51,920
A destination few may even notice as they scream through on their way from Vienna to Salzburg, St Pölten may be Lower Austria's capital but it retains a very drowsy atmosphere. Though no beauty, it has a quaint-ish *Altstadt* (old town) contrasted by the new, oh-so-21st-century Landhausviertel (Landhaus Quarter).

History

The borders of Lower Austria were drawn by the Babenberg rulers in the 13th century, but in 1278 the region and empire-to-be fell to the Habsburgs. In a strange twist of fate – an ailing economy in the 1920s stalled the decision to give Lower Austria its own capital, and later the Nazis favoured making Krems the capital – St Pölten became capital of Lower Austria only in 1986, ending a long-running situation in which Lower Austria was administered geographically from Vienna, but was in fact a separate province. Ironically, it happens to have the oldest known municipal charter – granted in 1159. The *Altstadt* is noted for its baroque buildings: baroque master Jakob Prandtauer lived and died in the city.

Sights

Dom   CATHEDRAL
(Domplatz 1; ⊙dawn-dusk) Jakob Prandtauer was one of the most important architects of the baroque epoch, and the cathedral, his masterpiece of baroque rebuilding in St

St Pölten

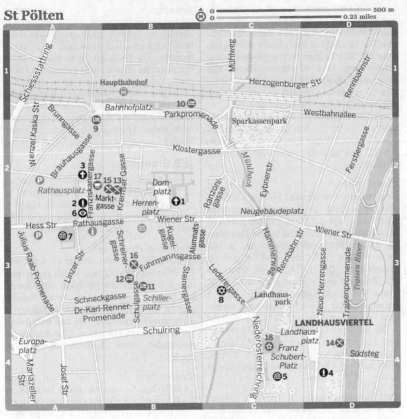

St Pölten

◎ Sights

🛏 Sleeping

✖ Eating

🍷 Drinking & Nightlife

✹ Entertainment

Pölten, has an impressive interior with lashings of fake marble and gold, augmented by frescoes by Daniel Gran. While exploring the cathedral, be sure to visit the cloister with its old gravestones.

Landesmuseum MUSEUM
(☎ 02742-90 80 90; www.landesmuseum.net; Franz-Schubert-Platz 5; adult/child/family €5.50/3.50/11; ⊕ 9am-5pm Tue-Sun) The Lower Austria State Museum houses an interesting collection on the history, art and environment of the

region. A wave made from glass, frozen in movement above the entrance, sets the mood, and indeed water is a theme throughout. The highlight of the art collection spanning the Middle Ages to the present is the 13th-century Lion of Schöngrabern. The museum is situated in the Landhausviertel (State Parliament Quarter) of town, a modern conflux of state buildings alongside the river. For a bird's-eye view of the quarter take the lift to the top of the **Klangturm** (Landhausplatz; ⊙8am-6pm Mon-Sat, 9am-5pm Sun) FREE, which often stages temporary art exhibitions.

Rathausplatz
SQUARE

Situated in the heart of St Pölten, Rathausplatz is a pretty town square lined with cafes and eye-catching pastel-coloured buildings. It is dominated by the **Rathaus** on its southern side, which has a baroque facade (1727) designed by Joseph Munggenast. On the northern fringe is the **Franziskanerkirche** (Rathausplatz 12; ⊙dawn-dusk), completed in 1770 with a grandiose altar offset by side altar paintings by Kremser Schmidt. Between the two is the tall **Dreifaltigkeitssäule** (Trinity Column; Rathausplatz), dating from 1782, a captivating white, oversized swirl of motifs, built partly as a religious vow following the passing of the plague.

Stift Herzogenburg
ABBEY

(☑02782-83112 13; www.stift-herzogenburg.at; Herzogenburg; adult/child €9/7; ⊙tours 9.30am, 11am, 1.30pm, 3pm & 4.30pm Apr-Oct) A short drive or train ride from town, Stift Herzogenburg is one of the Danube's baroque gems. You'll need to take a tour (book in advance for an English-speaking guide), which takes in the Stiftskirche and a painting collection which includes local Gothic panel works, stained glass and some surprisingly non-religious baroque paintings.

Stadtmuseum
MUSEUM

(www.stadtmuseum-stpoelten.at; Prandtauerstrasse 2; adult/child €5/2; ⊙10am-5pm Wed-Sun) Although it obviously can't compete with the best of the bunch in Vienna, the City Museum is excellent and well worth a visit. Its permanent collection focusing on art nouveau in St Pölten is on the 1st floor, and a section on the ground floor is devoted to local archaeological treasures. Admission includes usually worthwhile temporary exhibitions.

Synagoge
SYNAGOGUE

(Dr-Karl-Renner-Promenade 22; ⊙9am-3pm Mon-Fri) St Pölten's main synagogue dates from 1912 and has attractive art-nouveau features. The Nazis laid it to waste during the pogroms of 1938, and during the Hitler years, the building wound up in the hands of the city council, which used it as a camp for Russian forced labour victims before the Red Army arrived and turned it into a grain store. Today, it houses an institute for Jewish history.

🛏 Sleeping

Jugendherberge St Pölten
HOSTEL $

(☑02742-321 96; www.oejhv.at; Bahnhofplatz 1a; dm/s/d €25/32/48; @🛜) The youth hostel is about as convenient to the train station as it gets – it's all but in the same building.

Stadthotel Hauser Eck
HOTEL $$

(☑02742-733 36; www.hausereck.at; Schulgasse 2; s €43-55, d €120-140; ⊜🛜) This newly renovated hotel inside a rambling art-nouveau building offers excellent value in the historic part of town. Rooms are well appointed if sometimes on the snug side and bathrooms are kept sparklingly clean. The restaurant downstairs offers Austrian and Italian staples.

Gasthof Graf
HOTEL $$

(☑02742-35 27 57; www.hotel-graf.at; Bahnhofplatz 7; s/d from €75/110; P🅿🛜) Opposite the train station, this 30-room hotel has no-frills rooms with cheapo furniture and brightly coloured walls as well as more expensive quarters with a touch trendier retro-design feel. The downstairs restaurant has affordable mains served with second-hand cigarette smoke.

Metropol
HOTEL $$$

(☑02742-707 00; www.hotel-metropol.at; Schillerplatz 1; s €92-108, d €142-158; P⊜🛜) Cosy, upmarket and aimed at a business and culture clientele, the Metropol is not cheap (low season prices are 20% less), but for these prices you do get free use of the sauna, steam bath and infrared lamps. Its restaurant serves up steak and good business-type meals.

🍴 Eating

Lilli's Gastwirtschaft
AUSTRIAN $

(Rathausplatz 15; mains €7-13; ⊙10am-8pm Mon-Fri, to 2pm Sat; ☑) ⌇ This homely restaurant does a lunch menu for €6.30 and often uses organic beef from the Waldviertel region. Expect to find classics well prepared, including *Tafelspitz* (boiled beef in broth with apples) and apricot-filled dumplings.

Landhaus Stüberl
AUSTRIAN $

(www.landhausstueberl.at; Landhausboulevard 27; breakfast €4-6, lunch menu €7, mains €8.50-12; ☺ 7am-7pm Mon-Thu, to 5pm Fri) The name suggests a traditional tavern, but this post-millenium eatery in the Landhausviertel is anything but, and is aimed firmly at bureaucrats from the nearby Landtag and culture managers who come here to finger their devices and 'touch base'. The food is Italo-Austrian and can be picked at indoors or on the terrace overlooking the Traisen River.

Backwerk
BAKERY $

(Kremser Gasse 19; snacks €0.79-2.50; ☺ 7am-6pm Mon-Fri, 8am-3pm Sat) The St Pölten branch of this German budget bakery is the place to put together a euro-watching lunch on the run.

Restaurant Galerie
AUSTRIAN $$

(☑ 02742-351 305; www.restaurantgalerie.at; Fuhrmannsgasse 1; mains €18.50-28.50, 4-course menu €35.50-57.50; ☺ 11.30am-2pm & 6-9.30pm Mon Fri) Galerie serves delicious, if pricey, Viennese cuisine and has a great wine list, especially for Italian and French vintages. Although Wiener schnitzel isn't on the menu, it's always available if you ask nicely.

🍷 Drinking & Nightlife

Cinema Paradiso
CAFE

(☑ 02742-214 00; Rathausplatz 14; ☺ 9am-1am) Super-central trendoid spot for mulling over a paper or something heart-pumping. True to its name, it's also an art-house cinema.

☆ Entertainment

FestSpielHaus
PERFORMING ARTS

(☑ 02742-90 808 0222; www.festspielhaus.at; Kulturbezirk 2) FestSpielHaus is a modern theatre which features an impressive array of music, theatre and dance performances from both Austria and abroad.

ℹ Information

Post Office (Wiener Strasse 12)

Tourist Office (☑ 02742-33 30; www.st-poelten.gv.at; Rathausplatz 1; ☺ 8am-5pm Mon-Fri, 9am-5pm Sat, 10am-5pm Sun, closed Sat & Sun Nov-Mar)

ℹ Getting There & Away

St Pölten has good road connections: the east–west A1/E60 passes a few kilometres south of the city and the S33 branches north from there, bypassing St Pölten to the east, and continuing to Krems.

Trains run around three times an hour from Vienna Westbahnhof to St Pölten (€10.10, 30 minutes). There are also hourly direct trains to Krems (€6.60, 45 minutes), twice hourly departures for Melk (€6.20, 20 minutes) and at least four a day to Mariazell (€17, 2½ hours).

Süd-Alpin

This southern corner of Lower Austria, known as the Süd-Alpin (Southern Alps), has some of the province's most spectacular landscapes. Here the hills rise to meet the Alps, peaking at Schneeberg (2076m), a mountain popular among the Viennese for its skiing and hiking possibilities. Nearby Semmering has long been a favourite of the capital's burghers, due mainly to its crisp alpine air. One of the greatest highlights of the area though is the journey there; the winding railway over the Semmering Pass has been designated a Unesco World Heritage site.

Wiener Neustadt

☑ 02622 / POP 41,640

Wiener Neustadt used to be known simply as Neustadt (New Town) or Nova Civitas and was built by the Babenbergs in 1194 with the help of King Richard the Lionheart's ransom payment (so if you're English, those town walls, by rights, belong to you!). It became a Habsburg residence in the 15th century during the reign of Friedrich III. His famous AEIOU (*Alles Erdreich Ist Österreich Untertan;* Everything in the world is subservient to Austria) engraving can be found throughout the city. The town was severely damaged in WWII (only 18 homes were left unscathed), so what you see today is mainly a post-war rebuild.

◉ Sights

Dom
CATHEDRAL

(Domplatz; ☺ dawn-dusk) This cathedral runs an architectural gauntlet from the Romanesque (it dates from the late 13th century) to the Gothic and beyond to the baroque. The simplicity of the facade and clear lines are striking from the outside, but inside it will drive those who love the symmetry of the Romanesque style to despair as the nave is noticeably out of kilter with the sanctuary.

LANDHAUSVIERTEL

The Landhausviertel (State Parliament Quarter), to the southeast of the historical core of St Pölten, is a contemporary conflux of state buildings and cultural institutions strung out in a statement-making jumble of glass and steel alongside the river. To get your bearings, first head to the **Klangturm** (p142) from the top of which (reached by lift) there are 360-degree views not just of the neighbourhood but of almost all of St Pölten. There's a small gallery at the base of the tower and an information centre. A few steps from the tower stands the **Landesmuseum** (p141), housing an engaging collection on the history, art and environment of the region. The new-millenium feel of the quarter is reflected in the program of the nearby **FestSpielHaus** (p143), which attracts an impressive list of musicians, orchestras, theatre companies and dance ensembles from Austria and beyond.

Hauptplatz SQUARE

The town's main piazza is closed off on one side by the **Rathaus**, which is something of a hybrid of styles. It began life as a Gothic building, was given some Renaissance flourishes from the late 16th century, and then when imitations came into vogue from the early 19th century a neo-Gothic spire was tacked onto it. In the centre of the square is the **Mariensäule** (Column of Mary) from 1678, flanked by a group of woe-begotten saints.

Neukloster CHURCH

(Ungargasse; ⊙dawn-dusk) This church's claim to fame is as the venue for the very first performance of Mozart's Requiem in 1793. Architecturally, the 14th-century church is fairly straight up and down Gothic, with a vaulted ceiling and high windows, but the interior has had a major baroque do-over. The clash of styles leaves a little to be desired; the most attractive features are the tranquil cloisters, reached by an unmarked door on the right and sporting a Renaissance-era well.

Stadtmuseum MUSEUM

(☑02622-373 951; www.stadtmuseum.wiener-neu stadt.at; Petergasse 2a; adult/child €6/2; ⊙10am-

4pm Wed-Sun, to 8pm Thu) Partly housed in the former St Peter's monastery, the city museum has artefacts from the Dom and other displays on town history. Its prize item is the 15th-century Corvinus Chalice that, according to legend, was a present from the Hungarian king Matthias Corvinus. Note the tower is only open until 2.30pm.

Militärakademie CASTLE

(Military Academy; Burgplatz 1) FREE Dating from the 13th century, this former castle was turned into a military academy in the mid-18th century (founded by Empress Maria Theresia) and was even commanded by the young Rommel in his pre-'desert fox' days. The academy had to be completely rebuilt after WWII, and its real highlight is St-Georgs-Kathedrale, with a fine late-Gothic interior. Maximilian I, who was born in the castle, is buried under the altar.

🛏 Sleeping & Eating

Jugendhotel Europahaus HOSTEL $

(☑02622-296 95; www.hostel.or.at; Promenade 1; dm/s/d €17/20.50/41; ⊙reception 7-10am & 5-8pm; 🅿⊝) This HI hostel occupying a prime piece of real estate in the *Stadtpark*, near the *Wasserturm*, is often full so call or book ahead.

Hotel Corvinus HOTEL $$

(☑02622-24 134; www.hotel-corvinus.at; Bahngasse 29-33; s/d €85/120; 🅿🛜) The cube-like exterior may not appeal, but this four-star hotel is comfortable inside. It mainly caters to business and seminar guests with 68 bright rooms sweetened with extras such as a wellness area, a bar and a leafy terrace.

Cafe Bernhart CAFE $

(Hauptplatz 20; mains €9-12; ⊙8am-6pm Mon-Fri, to 5pm Sat) This cafe done out in delightfully 1980s meets old-Vienna style is where locals linger longer over a Melange and the day's news. It's strangely captivating.

Hartig's AUSTRIAN $

(Domplatz 2; mains €9-15; ⊙11.30am-midnight) In the shadow of the Dom, this *Gasthof* (restaurant) serves a range of Austrian classics in a *Beisl* (bistro pub) atmosphere. The beer garden out the back is one of the most pleasant in town.

Zum Weissen Rössl BISTRO $

(Hauptplatz 3; mains €7-12; ⊙7am-8pm Mon-Sat) This cosily curtained eatery, tucked away beneath the arcading of the Rathaus, serves affordable Austrian classics, including a choice of a small or large goulash. There's outdoor seating on Hauptplatz.

ℹ Information

Tourist Office (☑ 02622-373; www.wiener-neustadt.gv.at; Hauptplatz 3; ⊙ 8am-5pm Mon-Fri, to noon Sat) Stocks a free English-language booklet, *Cultural Promenade*, describing the central sights and giving their locations on a map.

ℹ Getting There & Away

Several trains each hour connect Wiener Neustadt with Wien-Meidling (€10.70, 30 to 40 minutes). Postbus services depart from the northern end of Wiener Neustadt train station.

Schneeberg, Raxalpe & Höllental

To the north of Semmering are two of Lower Austria's highest peaks, Schneeberg (2076m) and the Raxalpe (2007m). The area is easily reached by train from Vienna, making it popular for hiking.

The trailhead for hiking or taking the cogwheel railway is Puchberg am Schneeberg, where the tourist office can tell you about hiking conditions on Schneeberg.

On the southern side of Schneeberg is the scenic Höllental (Hell's Valley), a deep, narrow gorge created by the Schwarza River. Rising to the south of Höllental is the Raxalpe, another place for walkers.

🏃 Activities

Schneebergbahn　　　　　　　　RAIL
(☑ 02636-3661 20; www.schneebergbahn.at; Bahnhofplatz 1, Puchberg am Schneeberg; Salamander 1 way/return €26.10/36; ⊙ late Apr-late Oct) The Schneebergbahn leaves from Puchberg am Schneeberg and takes about an hour on the Salamander and around 1¼ hours on the steam train (plus an €8 surcharge); check the website for the timetable.

Raxseilbahn　　　　　　　CABLE CAR
(☑ 02666-524 97; www.raxseilbahn.at; 1 way/return €15/26) From Hirschwang, a small village in Höllental, the Raxseilbahn cable car ascends to 1547m and a wealth of hiking trails. Although long updated, this was Austria's first cable car, built in 1926.

🛏 Sleeping & Eating

Dambóckhaus　　　　　　　　HUT $
(☑ 02636-22 59; www.damboeckhaus.at; Hochschneeberg 8; tw €66; ⊙ May-Oct) Up on the plateau, this super homey hut is tended to with love by hosts Willi and Gisi. Rooms are basic but comfortable and there are good meaty mains and homemade sweets for mountain appetites.

★**Hotel Looshaus**　　　　HISTORIC HOTEL $$
(☑ 02666-529 11; www.looshaus.at; Kreuzberg 60, Payerbach; s/d €60/104, without bathroom €53/90) Although most of the guests here are Viennese on a quick mountain break, this hotel is also something of an architectural pilgrimage site for those with a fascination for 20th-century design. The hotel was a late work of Alfred Loos, a private country home that was completed in 1930. It's been a hotel and run by the same family since 1959.

While it's spotless and very well maintained, little has changed and herein lies the charm. It's a fabulous time capsule of early-Modernist design. Each room is different, but all feature beautiful built-in furniture and interesting use of colour. The front rooms have lovely views of the valley and to the Alps beyond, but you can't really go wrong here. You can eat hearty Austrian standards in the central double height dining room or out on the terrace in summer. It's a few minutes up the hill from Reichenau an der Rax.

Gasthof Pension Schmirl　　GUESTHOUSE $$
(☑ 02636-2277; www.schmirl.at; Muthenhofer Strasse 8; s/d €33/66; P ⊝) Gasthof Pension Schmirl has comfortable rooms on the edge of town near the railway. Some have balconies, in others you can psyche yourself for the stiff climb ahead with window views of Schneeberg.

Hotel Marienhof　　　　　　HOTEL $$
(☑ 02666-529 95; www.marienhof.at; Hauptstrasse 71-73, Reichenau; s €90, d €160-210; P ☒) The Hotel Marienhof is a rambling grand old dame with a huge old-world restaurant, clubby bars and a lovely garden terrace. Rooms have high ceilings, lots of upholstery and swaggy curtains. The deluxe rooms are worth the extra.

Berghaus Hochschneeberg　　HUT $$
(☑ 02636-22 57; www.berghaushochschneeberg.at; Hochschneeberg 6; s/d €42/84) Berghaus Hochschneeberg is at the mountain railway station and has lovely old-fashioned rooms, as well as a restaurant. Half-board can be had for another €10 per night.

Baumgartenhütte HUT

(☏072099 1234; www.schneebergbahn.at; Hoch-schneeberg 5; ⊗daily when train runs) A cosy mountain hut along the rail line; known for its good home cooking.

Hengsthütte AUSTRIAN

(☏02636-21 03; www.hengsthuette.at; Hochsch-neeberg 1; ⊗8am-8pm Tue-Sun Apr-Oct, Sat & Sun Nov-Mar) This hut, along the rail line, serves up mountain favourites like pork and dump-lings and apple cake, along with wines and organic juices. No overnights.

ℹ Information

Tourist Office (☏02636-22 56; www.puch berg.at/tourismus; Sticklergasse 3; ⊗9am-noon & 2-4.30pm Mon-Thu, 9am-noon Fri) The tourist office can tell you about hiking condi-tions on Schneeberg. From May to October, it also operates a window at the train station from 8am to 4pm.

ℹ Getting There & Away

This region is an easy drive from Vienna and all the larger towns are well serviced by rail from Vienna and Graz.

Semmering

☏02664 / POP 600

With its clean air and grandiose peaks ris-ing out of deeply folded valleys, Semmering is a popular alpine resort for the Viennese, especially among an older audience who come to this spa town in summer for peace-ful walks or to ride the dramatic railway (it gets younger when it's time to hit the ski pistes). There's no real centre to this gently melancholy resort: it's mostly ranged along Hochstrasse, which forms an arc behind the train station.

☊ Activities

This is good hiking country, and there's a nice alpine golf course. It's an easy if not particularly hard-core ski destination for the Viennese too.

Hiking

Towering over Semmering to the south is the **Hirschenkogel** ('Zauberberg'; 1340m), where a modern cable car whisks walkers (one way/return €10/14) or skiers to the top. The tourist office and Infostelle have maps and brochures on walks.

Two fairly easy trails follow the scenic route of the Semmeringbahn, starting be-hind the train station. One follows the line for 17km to Mürzzuschlag in Styria, where frequent trains chug you back to Semmer-ing, and a second leads to Breitenstein and Klamm (Lower Austria), 9.5km and 15km respectively from the start. At Klamm, the trail divides and one route leads to Payer-bach (21km from the start) and another to Gloggnitz (23km from the start).

Skiing

The tourist office can provide information on ski schools. A winter skiing day pass for the Hirschenkogel cable car costs €31.50. Regional skiing day passes are also available for €34.50.

Cycling

If the hills don't kill you, they'll make you stronger. The tourist office rents bicycles (per 24 hours €12).

☵ Sleeping & Eating

Hotel-Restaurant Belvedere HOTEL $

(☏02664-22 70; www.belvedere-semmering.at; Hochstrasse 6; s from €45, d €70-80; P ☀) The family-run Belvedere has simple alpine de-cor, rooms with balconies and features such as a small swimming pool, a sauna and a large garden and patio area. Doubles with connecting doors are suitable for families. It's close to some good hiking paths.

Pension Löffler GUESTHOUSE $

(☏02664-23 04; www.pension-loeffler.at; s/d €45/80; ☎) A good choice if you're here for the skiing, with just a short walk to the runs and Semmering's apres-ski action. Rooms are simple but comfortable; there's a good restaurant and cafe downstairs.

★ Panorama Hotel Wagner HOTEL $$

(☏02664-25 12; www.panoramahotel-wagner.at; Hochstrasse 267; s/d from €74/118; P @ ☎) The Wagner family look after body and mind at this seriously ecofriendly hotel: rooms have untreated wood furniture, natural cotton bedding and grand views of the valley. Felt slippers are provided so you leave the ener-gy and the grime of the street behind you. A pretty garden, a well-stocked library with hammocks, a sauna, a spa and massage fa-cilities make chilling out easy.

Grand Hotel Panhans HOTEL $$

(☏02664-818 10; www.panhans.at; Hochstrasse 36; s €70-90, d €140-210; ☎ ☀) The four-star Grand Hotel Panhans feels like it's from a different era, although rooms are crisply modern. The resort facilities here include a swimming pool and wellness area (nonguests are welcome too). Rooms and apartments have a choice of either forest or mountain views. The Wintergarten restaurant is Semmering's most upmarket place to eat.

ℹ️ Information

Infostelle Bahnhof (www.semmeringbahn. at; ⏱9-11.30am & 2-5pm May-Oct) Run by railway enthusiasts – stocks material on the Semmeringbahn and the town itself. Ask for the brochure for an interesting rail-enthusiast's walking route.

Tourismusbüro Semmering (📞02664-200 25; www.semmering.at; Semmering 248; ⏱9am-5pm) A good tourist office with comprehensive listings of hotels and restaurants.

ℹ️ Getting There & Away

If you're driving, consider taking the small back road northwest of Semmering to Höllental via Breitenstein; the road winds its way down the mountain, passing under the railway line a number of times and taking in the spectacular scenery you see on the train trip.

Semmering has train connections with Breitenstein (€2.20, eight minutes), Klamm (€3.70, 15 minutes), Payerbach (€3.30, 30 minutes) and Gloggnitz (change in Payerbach; €5.90, 40 minutes). At least five direct EC/IC trains between Graz (€19.30, one hour 20 minutes) and Vienna (€21.20, 1¼ hours) stop at Semmering.

BURGENLAND

Burgenland is the youngest of Austria's provinces, arising after the collapse of the Austrian empire at the end of WWI.

History

In the 10th century the area fell into the hands of Hungary, but German-speaking peasants gradually settled land between the Hungarian villages. The arrival of the Turks in the 16th century quashed both the Hungarians and the Austrian-Germans, and devastated the local population. Landlords, without anyone to tend their farms, invited substantial numbers of Croats to settle, laying the foundations for the area's Hungarian and Croatian influences today – around 10% of the population is Croatian, and Croatian, along with Hungarian, is a recognised local

SEMMERING PASS BY TRAIN

For its time, it was an incredible feat of engineering and it took more than 20,000 workers' years to complete. Even today, it never fails to impress with its switchbacks, 15 tunnels and 16 viaducts. This is the **Semmeringbahn** (Semmering Railway; www.semmeringbahn. at), a 42km stretch of track that begins at Gloggnitz and rises 455m to its highest point of 896m at Semmering Bahnhof.

Completed in 1854 by Karl Ritter von Ghega, the Semmering line was Europe's first alpine railway; due to its engineering genius, it gained Unesco World Heritage status in 1998. It passes through some impressive scenery of precipitous cliffs and forested hills en route; the most scenic section is the 30-minute stretch between Semmering and Payerbach.

From Vienna, most express services heading to Graz stop at Mürzzuschlag, from where you take a regional train to Semmering (€21.50, 1¾ hours).

language; a few small towns in middle Burgenland bear Croatian signage.

With the demise of the Habsburg empire after WWI, Austria lost control of Hungary, but it eventually managed to retain the German-speaking western region of Hungary under the Treaty of St Germain. The new province of Burgenland was born, named for the 'burg' suffix of the four western Hungarian district names at that time – Pressburg (Bratislava), Wieselburg (Moson), Ödenburg (Sopron) and Eisenburg (Vasvär). As Hungary was loathe to lose Ödenburg (Sopron), a controversial plebiscite held in December 1921 resulted in Sopron remaining Hungarian. Burgenland lost its natural capital, and Eisenstadt became the new *Hauptstadt*.

ℹ️ Getting There & Around

The A2 autobahn, heading south from Vienna towards Graz and Carinthia, runs parallel to the western border of Burgenland. Its many exits provide quick, easy access to much of the province. The A4 leads to Neusiedl am See. Eisenstadt and the northern extension of Neusiedler See are easily reached by train from Vienna and Lower Austria.

Burgenland is a cyclist's dream. Much of the landscape is flat or has gently rolling hills and is criss-crossed with well-marked cycle paths. Local tourist offices can supply cycle maps. From Neusiedl am See, the 135-km Neusiedler See bike trail leads south, crossing into Hungary (bring your passport) for 38km before the path re-emerges in Austria, just south of Mörbisch am See on the western side of the lake.

Fahrräder Bucsis (☑ 02167-207 90; www. fahrraeder-bucsis.at; train station, Neusiedl am See; per day €15; ⊙ 8.30am-7pm Mar–mid-Oct) The bike path begins at its door.

Nextbike (☑ 02742-229 901; www.nextbike. at; per hour €1, 24hr €8) Has over 16 stations around the Neusiedler See and in Eisenstadt where you can hire and drop off a rented bicycle. The website explains the steps and how to register (which you need to do in advance on the website).

Eisenstadt

☑ 02682 / POP 13,350

The small, elegant capital of Burgenland is best known for its most famous former resident, 18th-century musician and composer Joseph Haydn. Watched over by a wonderful palace, there are a couple of good museums and some pretty streets to wander. It's an easy day trip from Vienna or a more affordable base than the Neusiedler See towns for touring the vineyards.

◎ Sights

★**Schloss Esterházy**   PALACE
(www.esterhazy.at; Esterházyplatz 1; all museums adult/child €36/18; ⊙ 10am-5pm mid-Mar–Apr & Oct, 10am-6pm May-Sep, 10am-5pm Fri-Sun Nov–mid-Mar) Schloss Esterházy, a giant, Schönbrunn-yellow castle-palace that dominates Esterházyplatz, is Eisenstadt's most compelling attraction. Dating from the 14th century, the *Schloss* (castle) received a baroque makeover and a later one in neoclassical style. Many of the 256 rooms are occupied by the provincial government, but 25 can be viewed on tours. The regular tour covers about seven rooms, giving you an insight into the history of the palace and the lives of the people who inhabited it.

A highlight is the frescoed **Haydn Hall**, where during Haydn's employment by the Esterházys from 1761 to 1790, the composer conducted an orchestra on a near-nightly basis.

The **Haydn Explosive** exhibition across the palace courtyard offers an interesting conflux of history and the new: Haydn's music accompanies you as you walk past exhibitions on the life and work of the great composer, a holograph depicts a string quartet, period furniture is projected onto the ceiling and a minuscule hole in the floor has an odd projection of a bare-breasted woman shouting abuse while burning in hell. To get the most out of the palace and Haydn, do the tour, then the Haydn exhibition.

Österreichisches
Jüdisches Museum   MUSEUM
(Jewish Museum of Austria; ☑ 02682-651 45; www.ojm.at; Unterbergstrasse 6; adult/child €5/3; ⊙ 10am-5pm Tue-Sun May-Oct) Situated in the former Judengasse – a street where Eisenstadt's Jewish population lived in the Middle Ages – this museum has a permanent exhibition illustrating the rituals and lifestyle of Eisenstadt's Jews. Descriptions are in German and Hebrew. Part of the museum is the historic private synagogue of Samson Wertheimer, who was born in Worms in Germany in 1658 and rose to the position of rabbi in Hungary. He financed the synagogue, and it was one of the few to survive after 1938.

Bergkirche   CHURCH
(☑ 02682-626 38; www.haydnkirche.at; Haydnplatz 1; ⊙ 9am-5pm Apr-Oct) This unusual church contains the white-marble tomb with Haydn's remains. It began life as a small chapel and in 1701 was transformed into a bizarre representation of Calvary, the mountain outside Jerusalem upon which Christ is thought to have been crucified. Manage all the dungeon-like rooms and you'll be feeling the Stations of the Cross in your feet; get to the top of the 'mountain', though, and awaiting you is not a gaggle of stone-throwing sinners but a fantastic view over town.

Haydn-Haus   MUSEUM
(www.haydnhaus.at; Josef-Haydn-Gasse 21; adult/child €5/4.50; ⊙ 9am-5pm Mon-Sat, from 10am Sun Jun–mid-Nov, 9am-5pm Tue-Sat, from 10am Sun mid-Mar–May) Situated in a house dating from the early 18th century, this museum dedicated to Haydn was where the great composer lived from 1766 to 1778. One more for the Haydn fans, the collection offers an insight into his private life and has reconstructed rooms with furniture from the era. Original portraits cover the walls, and there are some rare exhibits such as a fortepiano that was made in Eisenstadt, along with a

letter from Haydn's lover to the son that he is generally believed to have fathered.

Landesmuseum
MUSEUM

(www.landesmuseum-burgenland.at; Museumgasse 1-5; adult/child €6/5; ⊙9am-5pm Tue-Sat, from 10am Sun) The Landesmuseum plunges you deep into the local history of the region, seemingly all at once, including a collection of Roman mosaics, ancient artefacts, winemaking equipment and some interesting propaganda posters from the 1920s. There's also a room devoted to Franz Liszt, replete with a warty death mask of the Hungarian composer.

Activities

Weingut Esterházy
WINE

(www.esterhazywein.at; Trausdorf 1, Trausdorf; ⊙10am-6pm Apr-Oct, closed Sat & Sun Nov-Mar) Located 10 minutes' drive out into the countryside from the centre of Eisenstadt, this large-scale cellar door is a gateway to the Neidlersee wine district. One of the region's largest producers, Esterházy wines are still made by the ancient once-noble local family. These are beautiful wines, that despite their reach and stylish contemporary labels, are far from commercial or bland.

Festivals & Events

Internationale Haydntage
MUSIC

(www.haydnfestival.at; ⊙Sep) A two-week series of concerts attracting excellent local acts and top international performers. It features everything from chamber pieces to full-scale orchestral performances. Most events take place in the Haydn Hall or the Bergkirche.

Sleeping

Hotel-Pension Vicedom
PENSION $$

(☑02682-642 22; www.vicedom.at; Vicedom 5; s €65 d €105-125; ♨️🐕) While this might sound like a downtown hipster bolthole, it's in fact a three-star guesthouse with basic but contemporary rooms in a 21st-century building in an epicentral location. Ask for a room with floorboards; breakfasts are good.

Hotel Ohr
HOTEL $$

(☑02682-624 60; www.hotelohr.at; Rusterstrasse 51; s €69-105 d €95-179; P♨️🐕) The Ohr is a family-run hotel with nicely styled modern rooms and within walking distance of the centre. There's two distinct classes of room with quite a price hike for the admittedly better four-star section. Its rustic-styled restaurant is one of the best in town.

Eating

Haydnbräu
AUSTRIAN $

(www.haydnbraeu.at; Pfarrgasse 22; mains €10.40-17.50; ⊙9am-11pm; 🔌) Duck into this microbrewery and restaurant for some of the best-value eating in town: culinary classics such as schnitzel and goulash are complemented by seasonal dishes. The generous lunch menu is a steal at €7.40 and the snack menu has small portions suitable for kids.

Restaurant Henrici
AUSTRIAN $$

(Esterhazyplatz 5; mains €16.50-23; ⊙10am-11pm Mon-Fri, from 9am Sat & Sun) This smart restaurant shares the former gatehouse of Schloss Esterházy with its sister wine bar Selektion (p150). It's an atmospheric space to graze or dine, with a crowd-pleasing menu of burgers, pasta, Mediterranean-style

THE WINES OF BURGENLAND

The wine produced throughout this province is some of the best in Austria, due in no small part to the 300 days of sunshine per year, rich soil and excellent drainage. Although classic white varieties have a higher profile, the area's reds are more unusual, and the finest of the local wines is arguably the red Blaufränkisch, whose 18th-century pedigree here predates its arrival in the Danube region and Germany.

Middle Burgenland, especially around the villages of Horitschon and Deutschkreutz, has a long tradition of Blaufränkisch, which is also at home in southern Burgenland.

Sweet wines are also produced here. One of the best is **Weingut Gerhard Nekowitsch** (p157).

Austria's smallest wine region, the Neusiedler See, is also known for its innovative and pioneering wine producers, many of them opting to create biodynamic, natural or minimum intervention wines. This booming and often youthful scene makes for some great, and far more local and laid-back, wine experiences than those along the Danube. One of the best ways to go tasting here is to hire a bicycle in Neusiedl am See and pedal south through the vineyards towards the national park.

Eisenstadt

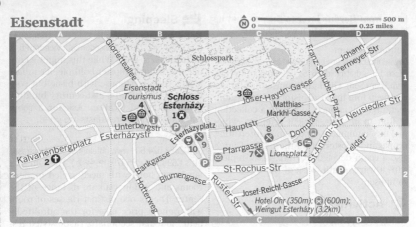

fish dishes or local specialities such as the Esterházy-Rostbraten – roast beef with potato spatzle – and the Esterházy-Cream Cake.

As you might imagine, there's a very comprehensive regional wine list too.

Kredenz CAFE **$$**
(www.kredenz.at; Pfarrgasse 33; mains €9-17; ⊙10am-10pm Mon-Thu, to midnight Fri & Sat) This small cafe and bistro-style eatery serves a small range of dishes but it does them well. The lunch menu (€8.90) might include offerings like carrot and ginger soup with chicken breast and herb-scented risotto.

🍷 Drinking & Nightlife

★ Selektion Vinothek
Burgenland WINE BAR
(☑02682-633 45; www.selektion-burgenland. at; Esterhazyplatz 4; ⊙11am-10pm Mon-Wed, to midnight Thu-Sat, 3-8pm Sun) Set in the one-time gatehouse of Schloss Esterházy, with a summer terrace that has a fabulous outlook across to its buttercup yellow loveliness, this wine emporium is a very pleasurable way to get to know Burgenland's wines. You can do a themed tasting flight or just buy a bottle.

ℹ Information

Eisenstadt Tourismus (☑02682-673 90; www.eisenstadt.at; Glorietteallee 1; ⊙9am-5pm Mon-Fri, 9am-1pm Sat Apr-Sep, 9am-5pm Mon-Thu, to 3pm Fri Oct)
Main Post Office (Ignaz-P-Semmelweis-Gasse 7)

ℹ Getting There & Away

Hourly direct **buses** (Domplatz) leave from Vienna's Hauptbahnhof Vorplex (€16.30, one hour 20 minutes). Direct trains also leave hourly from the Hauptbahnhof (€23.10, one hour 10 minutes).

Güssing

☑03322 / POP 3820
If you haven't developed castle fatigue by this stage, head 40km south of Bad Tatzmannsdorf to Güssing, a peaceful town on the banks of the Strembach River. Here the arresting **Burg Güssing** (☑03322-434 00; www.burgguessing.info; Batthyanystrasse 10; adult/child €6/4; ⊙9am-5pm Tue-Sun Easter-Oct;

P) rises dramatically over the river and town. The castle, a mix of ruin and renovation, contains plenty of weapons from the Turks and Hungarians, striking portraits from the 16th century and a tower with 360-degree views of the surrounding countryside. A modern 100m **funicular railway** (Schrägaufzug; 1-way/return €1/2; ⊙10am-5pm Tue-Sun Easter-Oct) helps those with weary legs reach the castle. The castle's restaurant has a terrace with extensive views over the countryside.

If you missed the open-air museum in Bad Tatzmannsdorf, head 5km west of Güssing to the **Freilichtmuseum** (www.freilicht-museum-gerersdorf.at; Gerersdorf bei Güssing 66; adult/child €5.50/3; ⊙9am-5pm Mon-Fri, 10am-6pm Apr–mid-Nov; P) at **Gerersdorf**. An hour or two could easily slip by while you explore the 30-odd buildings and their traditional furniture and fittings, which capture the rural culture of Burgenland in the 18th and 19th centuries.

✖ Eating

Burg Güssing   AUSTRIAN **$$**
(✆ 03322-425 79; www.burgrestaurant.net; Batthyanystrasse 10; mains €11-24; ⊙10am-10pm Tue-Sun Mar-Dec) Enjoy a menu of traditional dishes as well as burgers from the castle terrace.

❶ Information

Tourist Office (✆ 03322-440 03; www.sued burgenland.info; Hauptplatz 7; ⊙9am-noon Mon-Fri) The tourist office in Güssing can help with private rooms.

❶ Getting There & Away

Every one to two hours daily direct buses connect Güssing (€7.50, 45 to 70 minutes) with Oberwart. On weekdays and Saturday, several direct buses connect Güssing and Geresdorf (€2, 10 minutes).

Lockenhaus

Lockenhaus, in the centre of Burgenland, is famous for its castle, or more accurately, for its former resident Elizabeth Báthory. Better known as the 'Blood Countess', she has gone down in history for her reign of terror early in the 17th century, when she reputedly tortured and murdered over 600 mainly peasant women for her own sadistic pleasure. The castle has long been cleansed of such gruesome horrors but still contains an im-

pressive torture chamber, complete with an iron maiden.

If you want to sleep here, the Burghotel Lockenhaus has rooms and a sauna.

Some 13km east of Lockenhaus is the tiny village of Klostermarienberg, home to a now-defunct monastery housing what must be the only dog museum in Europe, the **Europäisches Hundemuseum** (www.kul turimkloster.at; Klostermarienberg; €5; ⊙2-5pm Sun May-Aug; P). The odd collection of dog paraphernalia includes paintings, statues and intriguing photos of dogs dressed for war during WWI and WWII, complete with gas masks. Take a few minutes to visit the monastery's crypt, a chamber containing archaeological finds dating from the 13th and 14th centuries.

Bernstein, 15km west of Lockenhaus, is dominated by the impressive Burg Bernstein, now a hotel.

Each is furnished with a fabulous array of antiques from the Almásy family collection and are truly special. Andrea and Alexander are welcoming and down-to-earth hosts; Alexander will be happy to show you around and Andrea's wonderful cooking makes breakfast and dinner a treat. For those who have read Michael Ondaatje's The English Patient, there's an extra frisson to it all; this was the childhood home of the fictionalised László Almásy.

In the town centre is a small **Felsenmuseum** (✆ 03354-66 20; www.felsenmuseum.at; Hauptplatz 5; €6; ⊙9am-6pm Mar-Oct, to 5pm Nov & Dec, closed Jan & Feb), which focuses on the gemstone serpentine and local mining (it was first mined in the town in the mid-19th century). You'll also find a cool little all day cafe down by the lake where you can have lunch or dinner.

You can visit the **Südburgenländisches Freilichtmuseum** (www.freilichtmuseum-badtatzmannsdorf.at; Josef Hölzel-Allee; €1; ⊙9am-6pm; P), a small but rewarding open-air museum filled with thatched buildings from 19th-century Burgenland. The local tourist office helps with accommodation.

☂ Activities

Burgenland Therme   SPA
(✆ 03353-89 90; www.burgenlandtherme.at; Am Thermenplatz 1, Bad Tatzmannsdorf; day card adult/child €24/14.50; ⊙9am-10pm Sun-Thu, to 12.30am Fri, to 11pm Sat) If your body needs some TLC, stop in at the spa-town of Bad Tatzmannsdorf, 15km south of Bernstein, and take the

ℹ NEUSIEDLER SEE CARD

If you are staying overnight in Eisenstadt or in towns on the Neusiedler See, make sure you get the Neusiedler See Card (www.neusiedler-see.at), which gives you free transport on buses and trains around the lake and on town buses, as well as free or discount admission to many sights. Take the registration form given to you by your hotel to an issuing office (tourist offices are the easiest) and you'll be given the card free for the duration of your stay. Available between late March and late October only.

waters at this large modern spa complex, currently operated by Aviva. In summer the natural swimming pond is the best spot.

🛏 Sleeping & Eating

Burghotel Lockenhaus   HISTORIC HOTEL **$$**
(📞 02616-23 94; www.ritterburg.at; s/d €98/136; **P**) Burghotel Lockenhaus has antique furnished rooms, and a sauna. Breakfast costs €8; there's an extra €15 supplement for heating from October to March. Apartments with kitchenettes attached to the castle wall are also available (€161, including breakfast).

★ Burg Bernstein   HOTEL **$$$**
(Bernstein Castle; 📞 03354-63 82; www.burg-bernstein.at; Schlossweg 1, Berstein; s €117-177, d €170-347; ⊙ late Apr–mid-Oct; **P** 🛜) This ancient *Schloss* is everything you could want in a destination hotel. The building's foundations date from 1199, and it retains much of its pre-modern atmosphere, with a beautiful internal courtyard and a tumbling, artfully wild garden and moat beyond. Thirteen bedrooms are available for guests; all have evocative if totally modern bathrooms but beyond that have been minimally renovated.

Kantine 48   INTERNATIONAL **$**
(📞 03354-200 23; Badgasse 48, Bernstein; mains €7-11; ⊙ 10am-10pm Mon-Sat, to 5pm Sun) This cool little all-day cafe by the lake has a warm kitchen going at lunchtime and in the evenings from 6pm. Whether you're swimming or not, it's a perfect stop for a burrata and salad plate, a green chicken curry or a fresh pasta with rocket and ricotta.

ℹ Information

Tourist Office (📞 03353-70 15; www.bad.tatzmannsdorf.at; Joseph-Haydn-Platz 3, Bad Tatzmannsdorf; ⊙ 8am-5.30pm Mon-Fri, 9.30am-2.30pm Sat, 9.30-11.30am Sun, closed Sun Nov-Mar) The local tourist office helps with accommodation.

ℹ Getting There & Away

You're better off with your own transport in this region as bus connections can be thin. Three direct weekday buses connect Lockenhaus and Eisenstadt (€14, 1½ hours). On weekdays hourly and on Saturday two-hourly direct buses go north from Oberwart (where there's a train station) to Bad Tatzmannsdorf (€2.50, five minutes); from Oberwart to Bernstein (€5, 30 minutes, every one to three hours) or Lockenhaus (€6.80, one hour, twice each weekday) is also manageable.

Neusiedler See

Neusiedler See, Europe's second-largest steppe lake, is the lowest point in Austria. The lake's average depth is 1.5m, which means the water warms quickly in summer. Add to this the prevailing warm winds from the northwest and you have a landlocked Austrian's dream come true. Thousands of tourists flock to the lake for windsurfing and sailing during the summer months. The best swimming beaches (and OK, they're not that flash) are on the eastern side of the lake; the western shore is thick with reed beds. These reedy stretches are, however, ideal breeding grounds for nearly 300 bird species – around Seewinkel is a favourite for birdwatching.

But best of all, there are acres of vineyards, making some of Austria's most sought-after and innovative wines. Rust, on the western shore of the lake, is a perfect place to sample wine in a *Heuriger* (wine tavern), as is Oggau.

The area is also perfect for cycling: a flat cycle track winds all the way round the reed beds, the ferries scuttling across the lake carry bikes, and most hotels and pensions cater well to cyclists. It's possible to do a full circuit of the lake with a short foray into Hungarian territory.

ℹ Information

Neusiedler See Tourismus (📞 02167-86 00; www.neusiedlersee.com; Obere Hauptstrasse 24, Neusiedl am See; ⊙ 8am-5pm Mon-Fri) The main information centre for the entire lake region.

ℹ️ Getting There & Away

There are hourly trains from Vienna Südbahnhof to Neusiedl am See and from there bus or regional rail connections to all of the larger towns. You can also arrange car and driver day trips from Vienna via the Neusiedlersee tourist office.

ℹ️ Getting Around

From late spring to early autumn, ferries connect Illmitz with Mörbisch, Rust and Fertörákos in Hungary; Rust with Podersdorf, Breitenbrunn and Fertörákos; and Breitenbrunn with Podersdorf. See www.neusiedlersee.com for current schedules and prices.

Bus connections are frequent.

Rust

📞 02685 / POP 1900

Rust, 14km east of Eisenstadt, is one of the most agreeable towns that cluster around the Neusiedler See. Its reed shoreline and hidden boatsheds give it a sleepy, swampy feel on a steamy day, and in the summer months storks glide lazily overhead, make out with each other, and clack their beaks from rooftop roosts. Dozens of storks make their homes on chimneys in town, although it's wine, not storks, that has made Rust prosperous. In 1524 the emperor granted local vintners the right to display the letter 'R' (a distinctive insignia as a mark of origin from Rust) on their wine barrels and today the corks still bear this mark. It's best to sample this history in one of the town's many *Heurigen*.

⊙ Sights

Katholische Kirche   CHURCH
(Haydengasse; ⊙10.30am–noon & 2.30–5pm Mon–Sat, 3–5pm Sun) The church's tower is a good vantage point for observing storks and the priest doesn't seem to mind. It's at the southern end of Rathausplatz.

Fischerkirche   CHURCH
(Rathausplatz 16; ⊙dawn–dusk Apr–Oct) At the opposite end of Rathausplatz from the Katholische Kirche, this is the oldest church for miles around, built between the 12th and 16th centuries.

🏃 Activities

Seebad Rust   SWIMMING
(www.seebadrust.at; Ruster Bucht 2; adult/child €4.50/2.50; ⊙9am–7pm May–mid-Sep) Access to the lake and bathing facilities is 1km down the reed-fringed Seepromenade. The swimming here is an acquired taste, very

reedy but ultimately refreshing. There are slides, grassy areas and a number of bars, cafes and restaurants too.

🛏️ Sleeping & Eating

Storchencamp Rust   HOSTEL, CAMPGROUND $
(📞 02685-595; www.gmeiner.co.at; Ruster Bucht 2; dm €31-42, s/d €37/54, camp sites per adult/child/tent/car €6.50/4/4.50/4.50; ⊕🐾) This friendly hostel right on the harbour forms part of the bathing complex and has modern, clean rooms. You can also stay in a teepee for €12 per night. It also operates a popular, friendly 200-pitch campground, which has a large children's playground, cheap bike rental, close proximity to the lake and free access to the bathing area. The campground is only open April to October.

Hotel Sifkovits   HOTEL $$
(📞 02685-276; www.sifkovits.at; Am Seekanal 8; s/d €85/135; ⊙high season only; 🅿️⊕🐾) Close to the centre of town, Sifkovits is a fine, family-run hotel with 34 large, simply done rooms, a lift and extras like its downstairs lounge with a bowl of fruit and a refrigerator stocked with free mineral water. It also has a good restaurant and a soothing garden. Cots and extra beds for kids are available.

TiMiMoo Boutique Hotel Bürgerhaus   BOUTIQUE HOTEL $$$
(📞 02685-6162; www.hotelbuergerhaus-rust.at; Hauptstrasse 1; ste €255; 🅿️🐾) With spiral staircases inside a 1537 former bakery and Biedermeier-style rooms with vaulted ceilings and drapes around the beds, this sweetly nostalgic hotel may be a little pretty for some tastes. Service is great and it caters superbly for children, with cots on hand, and the option of an extra bed at a discount.

Peter Schandl   AUSTRIAN $
(www.buschenschankschandl.at; Hauptstrasse 20; mains €7-14; ⊙4pm–midnight Mon & Wed-Fri, from 11am Sat & Sun mid-Mar–mid-Nov) Set in an 18th-century townhouse, and with a shaded courtyard, noted winemaker Peter Schandl serves up a menu that's beyond usual cellar door fare. Seasonal offerings might include a cream soup of pumpkin with ginger and roasted pumpkin seeds, a peppery, coarse liver sausage and cucumber-mustard relish or a meatloaf with cabbage. Just off Rathausplatz.

Weingut Gabriel   WINE TAVERN $$
(www.weingut-gabriel.at; Hauptstrasse 25; cold platters €13; ⊙from 4pm Thu & Fri, from 2pm Sat

ℹ️ STAYING IN SOPRON

Staying just over the border in Hungary and 'commuting' to the Neusiedler See is both a sensible budget hack and a really fun thing to do. Accommodation in Sopron, just 14km from Mörbisch, can work out far cheaper than on the Austrian side of the border, either by reserving through popular booking websites or going for a private rental. Not only that, food and some decent local wines are considerably cheaper (wine ridiculously so). Do check how much your hire car will charge you extra to cross borders – it should only be a token charge.

& Sun Apr-Oct; 🐾) Don't miss this rustic wine spot on the main drag. Not only is the pay-by-weight buffet brimming with delicious sausage and cold cuts, the wine is good, and in season, the idyllic cobblestone courtyard is a wonderful vantage point to observe the local storks.

🍷 Drinking & Nightlife

⭐ Gut Drauf at Gut Oggau WINERY
(☎ 0664 2069 298; www.gutoggau.com; Hauptstrasse 31, Oggau; ⊙ noon-10pm Thu-Sun May-Aug, 4-10pm Fri, noon-10pm Sat & Sun Feb-Apr & Sep) It's worth planning ahead to visit this wonderful cellar door, a few kilometres north of Rust, in the hamlet of Oggau. Young winemakers Eduard Tscheppe and Stephanie Tscheppe-Eselböck create highly individual, biodynamic and minimal intervention wines for their gorgeous new-school *Heuriger*. Apart from their own wines, they also offer a selection of reasonably priced drops from like-minded Austrian and Italian producers.

ℹ️ Information

Tourist Office (☎ 02685-502; www.rust.at; Conradplatz 1, Rathaus; ⊙ 9am-noon & 1-4pm Mon-Fri, 9am-6pm Sat, to noon Sun) Has a list of wine growers offering tastings, plus hotels and private rooms in the town.

ℹ️ Getting There & away

Hourly buses connect Eisenstadt and Rust (€3.80, 25 minutes). For Neusiedl am See (€3.80, 40 minutes, every one to two hours), change to the train at Schützen am Gebirge train station. Ferries cross the lake to Podersdorf, Breitenbrunn and Fertörákos.

Mörbisch am See

☑ 02685 / POP 2300

Mörbisch am See is a sleepy community 6km south of Rust and only a couple of kilometres shy of the Hungarian border. Soaking up the relaxed atmosphere and taking in quaint whitewashed houses with hanging corn and flower-strewn balconies is the order of the day here.

The town's tranquil mood changes dramatically during summer evenings with the **Seefestspiele** (www.seefestspiele-moerbisch.at; ⊙ mid-July–Aug), a summer operetta festival that attracts some 200,000 people each year. Then there's **Opern Festspiele** (www.ofs.at; ⊙ early Jul-late Aug), an opera festival held in an old Roman quarry near St Margareten, around 7km northwest.

ℹ️ Information

Tourist Office (☎ 02685-8430; www.moerbisch.com; Hauptstrasse 23; ⊙ 9am-5pm Mon-Fri, to noon Sat & Sun) The local tourist office can advise on accommodation and what's available, the festivals, lakeside facilities and give you a list of *Heurigen*.

ℹ️ Getting There & Away

Frequent buses go to Mörbisch via Rust from Eisenstadt (€4.30, 40 minutes). A foot- and cycle-only border crossing into Hungary, 2km south of Mörbisch, is handy for those circumnavigating the lake. There are no border controls, but you do need to be able to show your passport on demand. Alternatively, jump on the ferry across the lake to stay within Austria.

Purbach am See

☑ 02683 / POP 2835

Purbach am See, 17km north of Rust, is one of the prettiest towns along the lake. Its small, compact centre is filled with squat houses and it is still protected by bastions and three gates – reminders of the Turkish wars. While there isn't a lot to see in the town – nor has it direct access to Neusiedler See – it's nice to soak up the slow pace of life and wander from one wine cellar to the next along historic Kellergasse and Kellerplatz, both outside the town's walls.

🛏️ Sleeping

Gasthof zum Türkentor GUESTHOUSE $
(☎ 02683-34 00; www.foltin.at; Hauptgasse 2; s/d €40/65; 🅿️ 🛜) A sweet old-fashioned guest-

house, situated within the old city wall, at the entrance to the historic part of town.

Storchencamp Camping Purbach & Jugendherberge CAMPGROUND $

(☑02683-55 38; www.gmeiner.co.at; Türkenstrasse 13; camp sites per adult/child/tent/car €5/3.50/2.90/3, dm €22; ☺Apr-Oct; @🛜🛉) This camping ground and dorm-only hostel is on the edge of the reed beds and has loads of sporting facilities.

Weingut & Weingasthof Kloster am Spitz HOTEL $$

(☑02683-5519; www.klosteramspitz.at; Waldsiedlung 2; s €75, d €120-150; P🛜) Weingut & Weingasthof Kloster am Spitz, on the northwestern fringe of town among vineyards (follow Fellnergasse), is a small former monastery with a modern hotel. Rooms are simple but have great views.

★ Gut Purbach HOTEL $$$

(☑02683-560 86; www.gutpurbach.at; Hauptgasse 64; r/ste €176/265) This is the 'See's most stylish sleeping choice. Five rooms, including one suite, mix beautiful old bones with rustic antiques and contemporary design pieces. No two rooms are the same but they all have large, incredibly comfortable beds.

✖ Eating

★ Kloster Am Spitz AUSTRIAN $$$

(www.hotel-restaurant.klosteramspitz.at; mains €17-26, 5-/6-course set menu €50/60) A deceptively rustic dining room is the scene for smart, contemporary dining at this lovely central winery restaurant. Freshwater fish and eels, local lamb and curd cheeses feature on both the experimental and the old favourites menu. During summer you can eat in a trellised courtyard with views back down to the town and lake beyond.

ⓘ Information

Tourist Office (☑02683-5920; www.purbach.at; Am Kellerplatz 1; ☺9am-7pm) The tourist office has information on accommodation and wine.

ⓘ Getting There & Away

Purbach has direct train connections with Neusiedl am See (€3.70, 12 minutes, hourly), Eisenstadt (€3.80, 15 minutes, hourly) and Vienna Hauptbahnhof (€13.50, one hour, hourly), and direct bus connections with Eisenstadt (€3.80, 20 minutes, at least one every two hours). From Rust, get off in Schützen am Gebirge (centre)

and walk 300m to the train station to change to a regional train.

Podersdorf am See

☑02177 / POP 2075

Podersdorf am See, on the eastern shore, is the only town which can truly claim to be totally *Am See* (on the lake). This fact, combined with a reed-free location, are the possible reasons it's become the most popular holiday destination in the Neusiedler See region and Burgenland.

🏃 Activities

St Martins Therme & Lodge Spa Resort SPA

(☑02172-20 500 600; www.stmartins.at; Im Seewinkel 1, Frauenkirchen; day tickets adult/child €26/13.50; ☺9am-10pm) In Frauenkirchen, 8km southeast from Podersdorf, you can take the cure at this modern spa resort fed by hot springs. Set in an interesting wetlands landscape, you can also swim outdoors in the lake fed by mineral springs. Nonguests are welcome to visit the extensive spa facilities.

Book ahead at the hotel for free pick-up from Frauenkirchen train station if arriving by rail or bus. St Martins can also be easily reached by bike on a detour from the main bike path (there's a Nextbike station at the spa and others at the train station and the basilica in Frauenkirchen).

Surf & Segelschule Nordstrand WATER SPORTS

(☑0664-277 6140; www.nordstrand.at; Seeufergasse 17) Surf & Segelschule Nordstrand rents out sailing boats and holds weekday sailing courses.

Mission To Surf WATER SPORTS

(☑0680-234 6529; www.surf-schule.at) Has equipment for hire and offers kite-surfing courses.

🛏 Sleeping & Eating

Book ahead for July and August and on spring weekends. Seestrasse, the street leading from the tourist office to the lake, has many small places to stay.

Hotels and resorts have the best upmarket dining; there's no shortage of fast-food places and cafes along the lakeshore.

Strandcamping CAMPGROUND $

(☑02177-22 79; www.podersdorfamsee.at; Strandplatz 19; camp site per adult/child/tent/car

REED EXPLORATIONS

Although Purbach isn't located directly on the lake shore, it's inside a nature reserve and has reed banks that invite exploration on a bicycle ride or an easy walk. Kirchengasse/Gartengasse, one block north of the tourist office, leads down to the reeds, and from there a 2.5km path follows a canal out to the lake. An alternative ride or walk is to follow the Kirschblutenradweg (B12) north along the reeds to Breitenbrunn (about 4.5km), turn right onto the Schilflehrpfad (Reed Educational Path) and follow that out to the lake (about 3km), where there's lake swimming. Hire bikes from the camping ground or ask at the tourist office. **Canoe Excursions** (☑ 0664 382 8540; www.natur-neusiedlersee.com; 2hr adult/child €22/16; 🖈) takes you out into the reeds and is also suitable for kids. Book at least one day ahead.

€7.80/5/5.50/5.50; ☉ late-Mar–Oct) Right by the beach, this popular camping ground is one of the largest around and has plenty of shade from the sweltering heat in high summer.

Steiner B&B $
(☑ 02177-2790; www.steinergg.at; Seestrasse 33; s/d €40/80; 🅿 😊) This central *Gästehaus* (guesthouse) has welcoming staff, a tranquil, homey atmosphere and spartanly clean rooms with updated bathrooms and balconies.

★**Seewirt** HOTEL $$
(☑ 02177-24 15; www.seewirtkarner.at; Strandplatz 1; s €62-95, d €111-201; 🅿 😊 🛜) Having bagged a prime spot right next to the ferry terminal and beach, the four-star Seewirt fills up quickly. Rooms are crisp, fuss-free and full of sea-refracted light, and the restaurant serves no-nonsense Austrian fare.

Hotel-Restaurant Pannonia HOTEL $$
(☑ 02177-22 45; www.pannonia-hotel.at; Seezeile 20; s €50-68, d €95-130; 🅿 😊 🛜 🏊) A little way back from the waterfront, this smartly renovated hotel has modern furnishings and a large grassy area where children can go bananas. The owners run a second hotel across the road with family rooms. The restaurant has a wine list the size of a short novel and serves seasonal dishes such as venison carpaccio on wild-garlic pesto with tomatoes.

St Martins Therme & Lodge SPA $$$
(☑ 02172-205 00; www.stmartins.at; Im Seewinkel 1, Frauenkirchen; d per person €175-230; 🅿 😊 @ 🛜) In Frauenkirchen, 8km inland from Podersdorf, this large modern resort has luxurious rooms with views over the wetlands. It's a large place and occasionally can be full of conference-goers. Book ahead at the hotel for free pick-up from Frauekirchen train station if arriving by rail or bus.

★**Zur Dankbarkeit** AUSTRIAN $$
(☑ 02177-22 23; www.dankbarkeit.at; Hauptstrasse 39, Podersdorf; mains €9-19; ☉ 11am-9pm Fri-Tue Apr-Nov, Fri-Sun Jan-Mar, closed Dec) This lovely old restaurant serves some of the best regional cooking around. The inner garden, with its trees and country ambience, is the ideal spot to knock back some local wine.

Drinking & Nightlife

Weinklub 21 WINE BAR
(www.weinclub21.at; Seestrasse 37; tastings €5-12; ☉ 9am-noon & 4-9pm May-Sep) This excellent *Vinothek* represents 21 wine producers in the town and region; it holds regular tastings and events.

ℹ Information

Tourist Office (☑ 02177-2227; www.podersdorfamsee.at; Hauptstrasse 2; ☉ 8am-4.30pm Mon-Fri, 9am-4.30pm Sat, 9am-noon Sun Mar-Oct)

ℹ Getting There & Away

Buses leave hourly or two-hourly connecting Neusiedl and Podersdorf (€3.80, 16 minutes). Ferries connect Podersdorf with Rust and Breitenbrunn on the western shore.

Seewinkel
☑ 02175

Seewinkel is the heart of the **Neusiedler See-Seewinkel National Park**, and a grassland and wetland of immense importance to birds and other wildlife. The vineyards, reed beds, shimmering waters and constant birdsong make this an enchanting region for an excursion. This is an excellent area for birdwatching and explorations on foot or by bicycle.

The protected areas cannot be directly accessed by visitors, so to really get into the birdwatching you need a pair of binoculars. There are viewing stands along the way.

The park has its own information centre on the northern fringes of Illmitz, the Nationalparkhaus. It has a small display on the ecology and staff can tell you the best places to spot local wildlife.

The town of **Illmitz**, 4km from the lake, is surrounded by the national park and makes for a good base. Staff at its tourist office can provide information on the region. Arkadenweingut-Gästehaus is a lovely arcaded homestead in the centre of Illmitz.

🏃 Activities

Weingut Gerhard Nekowitsch   WINE
(📞 02175-20 39; www.nekowitsch.at; Urbanusgasse 2, Illmitz) Sweet dessert wines are currently enjoying a renaissance in Austria. *Eiswein* (wine made from grapes picked late and shrivelled by frost) and selected late-picking for sweet or dessert wines are being complemented by *Schilfwein*, made by placing the grapes on reed (*Schilf*) matting so they shrivel in the heat. The guru of *Schilfwein* is Gerhard Nekowitsch from Weingut Gerhard Nekowitsch.

🛏 Sleeping

Arkadenweingut-Gästehaus   GUESTHOUSE $
(📞 02175-33 45; www.arkadenweingut-heiss.at; Obere Hauptstrasse 20, Illmitz; s/d €43/66; 🅿😊) This simple guesthouse is set in a lovely arcaded homestead in the centre of Illmitz. Rooms aren't fancy but are comfortable and spotless.

ℹ Information

Nationalparkhaus (www.nationalpark-neus iedlersee-seewinkel.at; 🕑 8am-5pm Mon-Fri, 10am-5pm Sat & Sun, closed Sat & Sun Nov-Mar)

Tourist Office (📞 02175-2383; www.illmitz. co.at; Obere Hauptstrasse 2-4; 🕑 8am-noon & 1-5pm Mon-Fri, 9am-noon & 1-5pm Sat, 9am-noon Sun, closed Sat & Sun Nov-Jun) Staff at

the tourist office can provide information on the region and help with accommodation.

ℹ Getting There & Away

Illmitz is connected with Möbisch, Rust, and Fertörákos in Hungary by ferry and Neusiedl am See by hourly buses (€6.80, 30 minutes).

Wiesen

During summer the small town of Wiesen, about 5km north of Forchtenstein, morphs into Austria's version of Glastonbury. The series of summer **festivals** hosted here is the biggest in the country and ranges across the musical spectrum. See www.wiesen.at for details.

Straddling a dolomite spur some 20km southwest of Eisenstadt, **Burg Forchtenstein** (www.esterhazy.at; Melinda Esterházy-Platz 1; each attraction adult/child €9/7, two attractions €13/6.50, Esterházy complete €36/18; 🕑 10am-6pm late Mar-Oct) is one of Burgenland's most imposing castles. Built in the 14th century and enlarged by the Esterházys (still owners today) in 1635, the castle's highlights include an impressive collection of armour and weapons, portraits of regal Esterházys in the Ahnengalerie and spoils from the Turkish wars (the castle curators will proudly tell you Forchtenstein was the only castle in the area not to fall to the Turks), along with a grand view from its ramparts. Its Schatzkammer contains a rich collection of jewellery and porcelain. Combination tickets (adult/child €13/6.50) for two of the attractions are available.

ℹ Getting There & Away

Trains to Wiesen leave Vienna's Wien-Meidling station at least every two hours (€11, 50 to 80 minutes).

Upper Austria

Best Places to Eat

➡ Cafe Jindrak (p164)

➡ Freistadt Brauhaus (p176)

➡ Paul's (p164)

➡ Knapp am Eck (p171)

➡ Löwenkeller (p174)

Best Places to Sleep

➡ Hotel am Domplatz (p163)

➡ Hotel Christkindlwirt (p170)

➡ Minichmayr (p171)

➡ Hotel Goldener Adler (p175)

Why Go?

Unfolding across the gently undulating countryside, this under-the-radar region has a taste of all that is great about Austria. For starters, there's the mighty Danube and a rich musical heritage, old-world coffee houses and castle-topped medieval towns, and resplendent Augustinian abbeys and spas.

Beyond the high-tech museums and avant-garde galleries of Linz lies a land in miniature filled with surprises: from rustic farmhouses serving home-grown *Most* (cider) to the limestone pinnacles of the Kalkalpen, where the elusive lynx roams and picturesque towns such as Steyr and Schärding are painted in a palette of ice cream–coloured hues. Whether you're among the mist-enshrouded hills rippling towards the Czech Republic or wheat fields fading into a watercolour distance at dusk, you'll find these landscapes have a quiet, lingering beauty of their own.

When to Go

➡ Summer is a fine time to cycle along the Danube and through the countryside. Come in September for cutting-edge technology festivals and free riverside concerts in Linz. Rooms are at a premium from June to September, so book ahead.

➡ Autumn is perfect for crisp walks through the forests. Room rates fall from October, along with visitor numbers.

➡ Winter brings glittering Christmas markets galore. From early December to mid-April, cross-country skiers glide through the Nationalpark Kalkalpen, while downhill skiers carve up the slopes at Wurzeralm and Hinter Stoder.

➡ The spring shoulder season from March to May is a great time to see the orchards in blossom and to celebrate Schubert in Steyr.

ℹ️ Getting There & Around

AIR

Austrian Airlines, Lufthansa, Ryanair and Air Berlin are the main airlines servicing **Blue Danube Airport Linz** (LNZ; ☎ 07221-60 00; www.linz-airport.at; Flughafenstrasse 1, Hörsching). There are flights to Vienna, Salzburg and Graz, as well as Berlin, Frankfurt, Düsseldorf, Stuttgart and Zürich. Ryanair serves London Stansted.

CAR & MOTORCYCLE

The A1 autobahn runs east–west to Vienna and Salzburg; the A8 heads north to Passau and the rest of Germany; and the A9 runs south into Styria.

PUBLIC TRANSPORT

Upper Austria's bus and train services are covered by the **Oberösterreichischer Verkehrsverbund** (www.ooevv.at). Prices depend on the number of zones you travel (one zone costs €2.20). As well as single tickets, daily, weekly, monthly and yearly passes are available. Express trains between Vienna and Salzburg pass through Linz and much of southern Upper Austria, and there are also express trains heading south from Linz to St Michael in Styria, from where connections to Klagenfurt and Graz are possible.

LINZ

☎ 0732 / POP 197,500

'In Linz beginnt's' (it begins in Linz) goes the Austrian saying, and it's spot on. This is a city on the move, with its finger on the pulse of the country's technology industry. Daring public art installations, a burgeoning cultural scene, a cyber centre and a cutting-edge gallery that look freshly minted for a sci-fi movie all signal tomorrow's Austria.

Linz seized the reins as European Capital of Culture in 2009, and in 2014 Austria's third-largest city became a Unesco City of Media Arts. Sitting astride the Danube, Linz is not only a contemporary hub but also harbours a charming Altstadt filled with historic baroque architecture.

History

Linz was a fortified Celtic village when the Romans took over and named it Lentia. By the 8th century, when the town came under Bavaria's rule, its name had changed to Linze, and by the 13th century it was an important trading town for raw materials out of Styria. In 1489 Linz became the imperial capital under Friedrich III until his death in 1493.

Like much of Upper Austria, Linz was at the forefront of the Protestant movement in the 16th and 17th centuries. With the Counter-Reformation, however, Catholicism made a spectacular comeback. The city's resurgence in the 19th century was largely due to the development of the railway, when Linz became an important junction.

Adolf Hitler was born in nearby Braunau am Inn and spent his school days here. His Nazi movement built massive iron and steel works, which still employ many locals. After WWII Linz was at the border between the Soviet- and US-administered zones. Since 1955, Linz has flourished into an important industrial city, port and provincial capital.

⊙ Sights

★**Ars Electronica Center** MUSEUM
(www.aec.at; Ars-Electronica-Strasse 1; adult/child €9.50/7.50; ⊙ 9am-5pm Tue, Wed & Fri, 9am-9pm Thu, 10am-6pm Sat & Sun) The technology, science and digital media of the future are in the spotlight at Linz' biggest crowd-puller. In the labs you can interact with robots, animate digital objects, print 3D structures, turn your body into musical instruments, and (virtually) travel to outer space. Kids love it. Designed by Vienna-based architectural firm Treusch, the centre resembles a futuristic ship by the Danube after dark, when its LED glass skin kaleidoscopically changes colour.

★**Mariendom** CATHEDRAL
(Neuer Dom; Herrenstrasse 26; ⊙ 7.30am-7pm Mon-Sat, 8am-7.15pm Sun) Also known as the Neuer Dom, this neo-Gothic giant of a cathedral lifts your gaze to its riot of pinnacles, flying buttresses and filigree traceried windows. Designed in the mid-19th century by Vinzenz Statz of Cologne Dom fame, the cathedral sports a tower whose height was restricted to 134m, so as not to outshine Stephansdom in Vienna. The interior is lit by a veritable curtain of stained glass, including the Linzer Fenster, depicting scenes from Linz' history.

★**Lentos** GALLERY
(www.lentos.at; Ernst-Koref-Promenade 1; adult/child €8/4.50, guided tours €3; ⊙ 10am-6pm Tue, Wed & Fri-Sun, 10am-9pm Thu) Overlooking the Danube, the rectangular glass-and-steel Lentos is strikingly illuminated by night. The gallery guards one of Austria's finest modern-art collections, including works by Warhol, Schiele, Klimt, Kokoschka and

Lovis Corinth, which sometimes feature in the large-scale exhibitions. There are regular guided tours in German and 30-minute tours in English at 4pm on the first Saturday of the month. Alternatively, download Lentos' app from the website.

Landesgalerie
GALLERY

(www.landesgalerie.at; Museumstrasse 14; adult/child €6.50/4.50; ⊘9am-6pm Tue, Wed & Fri, 9am-9pm Thu, 10am-5pm Sat & Sun) Housed in a sumptuous late-19th-century building, the Landesgalerie focuses on 20th- and 21st-century paintings, photography and installations. The rotating exhibitions often zoom in on works by Upper Austrian artists, such as Alfred Kubin's expressionist fantasies and Valie Export's shocking Viennese Actionist–inspired pieces. The open-air **sculpture park** contrasts modern sculpture with the gallery's neoclassical architecture.

Schlossmuseum
CASTLE, MUSEUM

(www.landesmuseum.at; Schlossberg 1; adult/child €6.50/4.50; ⊘9am-6pm Tue, Wed & Fri, 9am-9pm Thu, 10am-5pm Sat & Sun) Romans, Habsburg emperors, fire – Linz' castle has seen the lot. Enjoy the panoramic city views before delving into this museum's trove of treasures, gathered from abbeys and palaces over the centuries. The collection skips through art, archaeology, historical weapons and instruments, technology and folklore. The Gothic ecclesiastical paintings are a real highlight.

Hauptplatz
SQUARE

Street performers entertain the crowds, trams rumble past and locals relax in pavement cafes on the city's centrepiece square, framed by ornate baroque and pastel-coloured Renaissance houses. The square's **Dreifaltigkeitssäule** (trinity column) – a 20m pillar of Salzburg marble carved in 1723 to commemorate the town's deliverance from war, fire and plague – glints when it catches the sunlight.

Kepler Salon
CULTURAL CENTRE

(www.kepler-salon.at; Rathausgasse 5) FREE The great astronomer, mathematician and astrologer Johannes Kepler lived here while he completed the groundbreaking Rudolphine Tables. The house now harbours the Kepler Salon, which opens to the public when it hosts science-themed events. The genius is also commemorated by the Planet Fountain at the Landhaus, and by the university named after him, where he taught from 1612 to 1626.

Alter Dom
CATHEDRAL

(www.dioezese-linz.at; Domgasse 3; ⊘7am-7pm) The twin towers of this late-17th-century cathedral dominate Linz' skyline. With its stucco-work, pink-marble altar and gilt pillars, the interior is remarkably ornate. Famous local lad Anton Bruckner served as organist here from 1856 to 1868.

Martinskirche
CHURCH

(☑guided tours 0732-77 74 54; Römerstrasse; guided tours by donation; ⊘admission by guided tour only) One of Austria's oldest churches, Martinskirche was first mentioned in 799. Inside are Roman inscriptions and a kiln, and a painting believed to date from the early 13th century of the famous *Volto Santo* sculpture in Lucca, Italy.

Landhaus
HISTORIC BUILDING

(Landhausplatz 1) This striking Renaissance former convent, with a trio of interlinking courtyards, is now the seat of Upper Austrian parliament and government. The bronze **Planet Fountain** dates from 1582.

Bischofshof
HISTORIC BUILDING

(Bischofstrasse) This ornate baroque bishop's residence was built by Michael Pruckmayer following designs by Jakob Prandtauer, who also made his mark on the abbeys in St Florian and Melk. The interior is closed to the public.

Donaupark
PARK

(Ernst-Koref-Promenade; ⊘24hr) Next to Lentos on the southern bank of the Danube is the Donaupark, the city's green escape vault. Modern sculptures rise above the bushes in the well-tended gardens, which are a magnet for walkers, joggers, skaters, picnickers and city workers seeking fresh air in summer.

Botanischer Garten
GARDENS

(Roseggerstrasse 20; adult/child €3/2; ⊘7.30am-7.30pm May-Aug, shorter hours rest of year) These peaceful botanical gardens, 1.7km southwest of the centre, nurture 10,000 species, from native alpine plants to orchids, rhododendrons, tropical palms and one of Europe's largest cacti collections.

🏃 Activities

Pöstlingbergbahn
HERITAGE RAILWAY

(www.linzag.at; Hauptplatz; adult/child return €6.10/3.10; ⊘6am-10.30pm Mon-Sat, 7.30am-10pm Sun Apr-Oct, 6am-8.30pm Mon-Sat, 7.30am-8.30pm Sun Nov-Mar) It's a gentle hike to the top of **Pöstlingberg**, or a precipitous

Upper Austria Highlights

1 **Ars Electronica Center** (p159) Playing with pixels at Linz' cutting-edge technology and science centre.

2 **Steyr** (p170) Falling for the storybook lanes and fast-flowing rivers of Steyr.

3 **Baumkronenweg** (p176) Walking high above the treetops in Kopfing.

4 **Nationalpark Kalkalpen** (p172) Hiking through the wilderness of Austria's second-biggest national park.

5 **Therme Geinberg** (p178) Drifting away at one of Austria's top spas.

6 **Augustiner Chorherrenstift** (p167) Catching an organ concert

at St Florian's monumental Augustinian abbey.

7 **Mauthausen Memorial** (p168) Journeying to Austria's past at the KZ Mauthausen concentration camp.

8 **Stift Engelszell** (p177) Sampling the beers, liqueurs and cheeses at Austria's only Trappist brewery.

Linz

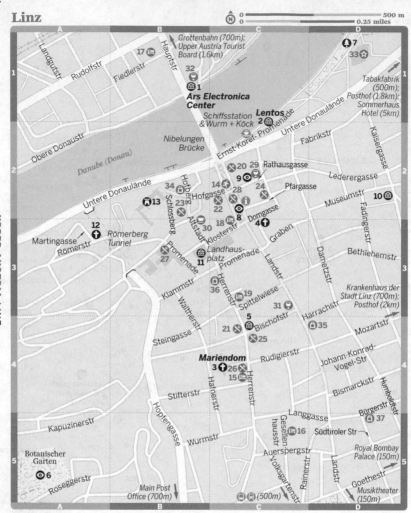

15-minute ride aboard the narrow-gauge Pöstlingbergbahn. It's Austria's steepest adhesion railway (running on electricity alone, rather than cables and pulleys), and indeed one of the world's steepest, which is quite some feat for such a low-lying city.

At the summit is the turn-of-the-century **Grottenbahn** (Am Pöstlingberg 16; adult/child €5/3; ⊙10am-6pm Jun-Aug, 10am-5pm Mar-May, Sep & Oct, closed Nov-Feb), where families – and anyone who loves a bit of cult kitsch – can board the dragon train to trundle past gnomes, glittering stalactites and scenes from Grimms' fairy tales.

✸ Festivals & Events

Höhenrausch ART
(www.hoehenrausch.at; ⊙mid-May–mid-Oct) Every year during the warmer months, central Linz' rooftops come alive during this festival featuring interactive Austrian and international art projects. The theme changes each year; 2016, for instance, celebrated 'Different Angels', with highlights including a rooftop mirror maze, an open-air cinema, a 20m-high flying fox, and a rooftop soundgarden with piano strings and organ pipes operated by the wind.

Linz

Linz Fest MUSIC
(www.linzfest.at; Donaupark; ⊙mid-May) This huge shindig on the third weekend in May brings free rock, jazz and folk concerts to the riverside Donaupark (p160).

Pflasterspektakel CARNIVAL
(www.pflasterspektakel.at; ⊙late Jul) Musicians, jugglers, actors, poets, fire-breathers and acrobats from across Europe descend on Linz for this three-day street festival held throughout the city.

Ars Electronica Festival CULTURAL
(www.aec.at; ⊙early Sep) This boundary-crossing five-day event showcases cyber-art, music written and performed by computers, and other marriages of technology and art at various venues across town.

Brucknerfest MUSIC
(www.brucknerhaus.at; ⊙mid-Sep–late Oct) Linz pays homage to native son Anton Bruckner with classical music during this six-week festival held at the Brucknerhaus (p166).

🛏 Sleeping

★Hotel am Domplatz DESIGN HOTEL **$$**
(☑0732-77 30 00; www.hotelamdomplatz.at; Stifterstrasse 4; d €111-175, ste €280-340; ❋🖭) 🐾 Adjacent to the neo-Gothic Mariendom (ask for a room overlooking the cathedral), this glass-and-concrete cube filled with striking metal sculptures has streamlined, Nordic-style pristine-white and blonde-wood rooms with semi-open bathrooms. Wind down with a view at the rooftop spa. In fine weather, the cathedral-facing terrace is a prime spot for breakfast (€18), which includes a glass of bubbly.

Spitz Hotel DESIGN HOTEL **$$**
(☑0732-73 37 33; www.spitzhotel.at; Fiedlerstrasse 6; s/d/apt from €99/119/149; 🅿❋@🖭) 🐾 Austrian architect Isa Stein has left her avant-garde imprint on the Spitz, from the lobby's moulded furnishings to UFO-style lighting. Each of the hotel's minimalist rooms spotlights an aspect of Linz' arts scene, and features clean lines, hardwood floors, coffee-making facilities and bespoke pieces by local creatives; there's a choice

of open-plan or enclosed bathrooms. Some rooms have balconies.

Hotel Kolping
HOTEL $$

(☑0732-66 16 90; www.hotel-kolping.at; Gesellenhausstrasse 5; s €72-94, d €96-122; P ❋ 🛜) Hidden down a backstreet in central Linz, Kolping has bright, spotless pine-furnished rooms and attentive service. The breakfast buffet (included in the rate) is among the best in town with locally sourced organic produce including farmyard eggs, regional cheeses and fresh seasonal fruit. Packed lunches can be arranged by request.

Zum Schwarzen Bären
HISTORIC HOTEL $$

(☑0732-77 24 77; www.linz-hotel.com; Herrenstrasse 11; s €92-105, d €129-140, f €148-160, ste €190; P ❋ 🛜) The birthplace of acclaimed tenor Richard Tauber, this 15th-century hotel is run by the friendly Nell family. Overlooking a courtyard, the rooms have been made-over in monochrome hues and parquet; some even sport waterbeds. The wood-panelled restaurant dishes up Austrian classics.

Wolfinger
HISTORIC HOTEL $$

(☑0732-77 32 910; www.hotelwolfinger.at; Hauptplatz 19; s €82-102, d €102-143, tr €127-163, q €153-183; P @ 🛜) This 500-year-old hotel on the main square has an air of old-world grandeur. Archways, stucco and period furniture lend rooms character; those at the back are quieter and some have balconies.

🍴 Eating

★ Cafe Jindrak
CAFE $

(www.jindrak.at; Herrenstrasse 22; dishes €3-8.80; ⊗8am-6pm Mon-Sat, 8.30am-6pm Sun; 🚼) Join the cake-loving locals at this celebrated cafe – the original shop (1929) of a now nine-strong chain that produces over 100,000 of its famous *Linzer Torte* each year made to its family recipe. You'd need a huge fork (and appetite) to tackle the torte that set a Guinness World Record in 1999, measuring 4m high and weighing 650kg.

Non Solo Vino
DELI, ITALIAN $

(☑0732-79 77 88; www.nonsolovino.at; Bischofstrasse 15; mains €8-18.50, antipasti €5.50-8; ⊗10am-6pm Mon-Fri, 9am-1pm Sat; 🍴) A combined deli and restaurant, Non Solo Vino believes in careful sourcing; its *Formaggi* (cheeses), *Salumi* (cold meats), antipasti and pastas are top quality. It knocks super-fresh ingredients into lunch dishes such as beef carpaccio with rocket and homemade ra-

violi. Arrive early to nab a seat in the tiny courtyard when the weather's fine.

k.u.k. Hofbäckerei
CAFE $

(Pfarrgasse 17; dishes €3-6; ⊗6.30am-6.30pm Mon-Fri, 7am-12.30pm Sat) The Empire lives on at this gloriously stuck-in-time cafe in a timber-framed building dating from 1371. Here Fritz Rath bakes some of the best *Linzer Torte* in town – rich, spicy and with a wonderful crumbly lattice pastry. In summer, the best seats are in the shady courtyard.

Promenadenhof
AUSTRIAN $

(☑0732-77 76 61; www.promenadenhof.at; Promenade 39; mains €8-19.50; ⊗kitchen 10am-1am Mon-Sat, bar 5pm-2am Mon-Sat) Promenadenhof enjoys a loyal following for spot-on Austrian fare such as *Tafelspitz* (prime boiled beef) and Styrian-style chicken salad, served in vaulted *Stuben* (parlours) and a beer garden, as well as over 100 different mostly Austrian wines.

Gragger
BAKERY $

(www.gragger.at; Hofgasse 3; dishes €3-6; ⊗7.30am-6pm Mon-Fri, 8am-5pm Sat; 🍴) 🍃 Breakfast (until 11am) and a daily changing menu of wholesome soups, salads and delicious organic breads are served on wooden tables in this vaulted cafe.

Stadtmarkt
MARKET $

(Hauptplatz; ⊗9am-2pm Tue & Fri) 🍃 Pick up a picnic from the 25-plus stalls at Linz' twice-weekly farmers market.

★ Paul's
BURGERS $$

(☑0732-783 38; www.pauls-linz.at; Herrenstrasse 36; mains €12.50-29.50; ⊗kitchen 11.30am-10.30pm Mon-Fri, 2-10.30pm Sat, bar 10.30am-1am Mon-Fri, 2pm-3am Sat) Facing the monumental Mariendom cathedral, this A-line building's facade is split down the middle: half is stone, the other half is fronted by floor-to-ceiling glass that's lit up in vivid red at night. Flame-grilled burgers on brioche buns are the house speciality, including a Wagyu burger with whisky sauce and a blackened lobster burger; it also grills superb steaks.

Royal Bombay Palace
INDIAN $$

(☑0732-65 86 05; www.bombaypalace.at; Goethestrasse 34; mains €12.60-18.40; ⊗6-11pm Tue-Sat, 11.30am-2.30pm & 6-10pm Sun) The heavenly aromas at this elegant, authentic restaurant emanate from the 150kg stone mortar, where the chefs pound herbs and spices, and from the hand-built Tandoor oven. Organic *palak paneer* (spinach and homemade cottage cheese), *masala gosht* (lamb in sesame and cashew nut sauce), butter chicken, and pike perch in lovage seed and yoghurt sauce are all menu highlights.

Verdi Restaurant & Einkehr AUSTRIAN $$
(☑ 0732-73 30 05; www.verdi.at; Pachmayrstrasse 137; mains €10-32; ☺ 5pm-midnight Tue-Sat) Linz spreads out picturesquely before you from this gastro duo 5km north of the city centre. At ultra-chic Verdi, Erich Lukas prepares seasonal dishes with panache and precision, such as quail breast with herby risotto and plump free-range chicken with truffle gnocchi. Wood-beamed Einkehr, in the same building, is an altogether cosier affair and serves Austrian comfort food.

Cubus FUSION $$
(☑ 0732-94 41 49; http://cubus.at; Ars-Electronica-Strasse 1; mains €12.50-30; ☺ 9am-10.30pm Mon-Sat, to 5pm Sun; ☜) On the 3rd floor of the Ars Electronica Center (p159), this glass cube has stellar views over the Danube to the south bank and glows purple after dark. The menu is seasonally inspired, fresh and contemporary, along the lines of poached salmon with herb risotto and orange-fennel salad. The two-course weekday-only lunch is a snip at €8.50.

Alte Welt AUSTRIAN $$
(☑ 0732-77 00 53; www.altewelt.at; Hauptplatz 4; mains €9-18; ☺ 11.30am-2.30pm & 5.30pm-midnight Mon-Fri, noon-2.30pm & 5.30pm-midnight Sat, 5.30pm-midnight Sun) Set around an arcaded inner courtyard, Alte Welt serves hearty fare, such as roast pork and beef ragout, and a good-value two-course midweek lunch (€7.50). By night the cellar hosts jam sessions, live jazz and plays that attract students and arty types.

Herberstein ITALIAN, JAPANESE $$$
(☑ 0732-78 61 61; www.herberstein-linz.at; Altstadt 10; sushi €5-13, mains €21.50-37; ☺ kitchen 4pm-11.30pm Mon-Sat, bar 4pm-4am) Chic Herberstein comprises a Japanese-style lounge with a sushi bar, an ivy-draped garden and a glamorous Italian restaurant. Brick vaults and clever backlighting set the scene for Björn Laubner's pared-down Italian dishes, such as beef fillet with tagliatelle, pan-seared cod with broccoli and cauliflower, and pumpkin ravioli with spinach and parmesan – all beautifully cooked and presented.

🍷 Drinking & Nightlife

★Bar Neuf COCKTAIL BAR
(www.barneuf.com; Rathausgasse 9; ☺ 7pm-2am Thu-Sat) Linz' best cocktails are swizzled up at this intimate bar decorated in glossy white metro tiles beneath an exposed-brick arched ceiling. Alongside classic and custom creations, nine different cocktails appear each season: apples, dried fruit and nuts feature in winter, summer sees sun-ripened fruits and fresh herbs, while spring introduces floral infusions and autumn brings grapes, blackberries and pears.

Madame Wu TEAHOUSE
(www.madamewu.net; Altstadt 13; ☺ 10am-9pm Mon-Wed, to midnight Thu-Sat, 1-8pm Sun) Full of cosy nooks, this Asian-style tearoom has a terrific tea selection (over 200 varieties) and an open fireplace. Afternoon tea (€15; with Prosecco €18) is served daily at 3pm and includes dainty cucumber and salmon sandwiches, and scones with clotted cream and homemade strawberry jam. On Saturdays at 5pm it hosts a Chinese tea ceremony (€15).

Stiegelbräu zum Klosterhof MICROBREWERY
(www.klosterhof-linz.at; Landstrasse 30; ☺ 9am-midnight) Pass on the mediocre food and go straight for the freshly tapped Stiegl beer at the cavernous Klosterhof. Centred on a huge fountain, the chestnut tree–shaded beer garden has space for 1350 thirsty punters. Catch live music every night in summer and most weekends in winter.

Cubus Terrace COCKTAIL BAR
(Ars-Electronica-Strasse 1; ☺ 9am-1am Mon-Sat, to 6pm Sun; ☜) There's no finer spot to see Linz light up than this glass-walled cafe on the top floor of the Ars Electronica Center. Pick out the landmarks over a sunset cocktail. Live music plays on Thursdays in summer.

LINZER TORTE

Old-style cafes such as **Cafe Jindrak** and **k.u.k. Hofbäckerei** are the place to try the classic *Linzer Torte*. Made to a 17th-century recipe with hazelnuts, spices and tangy redcurrant jam, the multilayered cake is the greatest rival to Vienna's *Sacher Torte*.

UPPER AUSTRIA LINZ

Strom
BAR

(www.stwst.at; Kirchengasse 4; ⊙2pm-1am Tue-Thu, to 4am Fri & Sat) DJs spin hip-hop, electro and funk at this upbeat bar, where party-goers spill out onto Kirchengasse in summer. Upstairs is rough 'n' ready Stadtwerk, which hosts clubbing events, gigs and party nights.

☆ Entertainment

Tabakfabrik
CULTURAL CENTRE

(https://tabakfabrik-linz.at; Peter-Behrens-Platz 11) A shining example of Linz' cultural renaissance is this cultural centre, lodged in a former tobacco factory. Check the website program for details of upcoming events from exhibitions to readings, film screenings, concerts and party nights.

Musiktheater
THEATRE

(☑0732-761 10; www.landestheater-linz.at; Am Volksgarten 1) Designed by London-based architect Terry Pawson, Linz' Musiktheater, a strikingly geometric opera house, opened in April 2013. It's the city's main stage for operas, operettas, ballets, musicals and children's productions.

Posthof
MUSIC, THEATRE

(☑0732-77 05 48-0; www.posthof.at; Posthofstrasse 43) Dockside Posthof covers everything from blues, funk and rock gigs to cutting-edge theatre and dance. Festivals are occasionally held here. Take bus 27 or 270 to Hafen/Posthofstrasse.

Brucknerhaus
LIVE MUSIC

(☑0732-76 12-0; www.brucknerhaus.at; Untere Donaulände 7) Linz' premier music venue stages top-drawer classical and jazz concerts. There is a dedicated program for kids of different ages ('mini' and 'midi' music).

ⓘ LINZ CARD

The Linz Card (one day adult/child €18/15, three days adult/child €30/25) grants unlimited use of public transport; entry to major museums including the Ars Electronica Center, Schlossmuseum, Lentos and the Landesgalerie; plus discounts on other sights, city tours and river cruises. The three-day card also includes a round-trip on the Pöstlingbergbahn. Buy the Linz Card at the tourist office, airport, museums and some hotels.

🛍 Shopping

A/T Store
DESIGN

(Hofburg 10; ⊙10am-6pm Mon-Fri, to 3pm Sat) Most of the products at this hip little concept store are made by Austrian designers, while a handful of others from Scandinavia and the Netherlands share the same minimalist aesthetic. Fashion (women's and men's), shoes, watches and jewellery sit alongside perfumes, hand and body lotions, and gourmet items such as ice creams, preserves and alpine herb and spice packs.

Vinyl Corner
MUSIC

(www.vinylcorner.at; Bürgerstrasse 14; ⊙11am-6pm Mon-Fri, 9am-3pm Sat) Traditional Austrian folk, French *chansons* à la Édith Piaf, funk, jazz, rock, reggae, metal, rap, classical, cabaret...you name it, this collector's dream has it on vinyl. It also sells posters, turntables and cleaning kits.

Confiserie Isabella
FOOD

(www.confiserie-isabella.at; Landstrasse 33; ⊙8.30am-7.30pm Mon-Sat) Pralines, bonbons, jellies and marshmallows are among the delights at this nostalgic sweet shop.

Göttin des Glücks
FASHION & ACCESSORIES

(www.goettindesgluecks.com; Herrenstrasse 2; ⊙10am-1pm & 1.30-6pm Mon-Fri, 10am-1pm & 1.30-5pm Sat) 🌿 Wear it with a conscience is the maxim at fair-trade and sustainable-fashion-focused Göttin des Glücks, which has a delightfully casual array of supple cotton jerseys, shirts, skirts and shorts. It has sister boutiques in Vienna, Innsbruck, St Pölten and Graz.

Imkerhof
FOOD

(www.imkereizentrum.at; Altstadt 15; ⊙9am-1pm & 1.30-6pm Mon-Fri, 9am-noon Sat) Honey you can eat, drink and bathe in (including chestnut and acacia varieties) fills the shelves here.

ⓘ Information

Krankenhaus der Stadt Linz (☑0732-78 06; Krankenhausstrasse 9) The main hospital is located 1km east of the centre.

Tourist Information Linz (☑0732-7070 2009; www.linztourismus.at; Hauptplatz 1; ⊙9am-7pm Mon-Sat, 10am-7pm Sun May-Sep, 9am-5pm Mon-Sat, 10am-5pm Sun Oct-Apr) Upper Austria information as well as brochures and accommodation listings.

Upper Austria Tourist Board (☑0732-22 10 22; Freistaedter Strasse 119) This overarching tourist board has the lowdown on activities, accommodation and eating in the region.

ℹ Getting There & Away

The **Schiffsstation** (Untere Donaulände 1) is on the south bank next to the Lentos Kunstmuseum. From May to early October, **Wurm + Köck** (🗹 0732-78 36 07; www.donauschiffahrt.de; Untere Donaulände 1) sends boats westwards to Passau, Germany (one way €26, 6½ hours, 2.20pm Tuesday to Thursday, Saturday and Sunday; 2.20pm Saturday early October) and east to Vienna (€59, 11½ hours, 9am Saturday).

Regional buses depart from stands at the main bus station adjacent to the Hauptbahnhof.

Linz is on the main rail route between Vienna (€18.90, 1½ hours) and Salzburg (€12.80, 1¼ hours); express trains run twice hourly in both directions. Buy tickets at www.westbahn.at.

Up to six trains depart daily for Prague (€48.80, 4¾ hours). Tickets are sold at www.oebb.at.

ℹ Getting Around

TO/FROM THE AIRPORT

Blue Danube Airport Linz (p159) is 13km southwest of town. A direct shuttle bus service, bus 601, connects the Hauptbahnhof (€3.10, 20 minutes) with the airport hourly from 5am to 8.30pm Monday to Saturday, every two hours Sunday. Alternatively, there are hourly train connections between Linz and Hörsching (nine minutes, €2.20), a three-minute ride from the airport by free shuttle bus. Use the free phone at the station to dial 🗹 0800 206 600 for a pick-up. The service is very reliable and runs daily from 5am to 10pm.

PUBLIC TRANSPORT

Linz AG (www.linzag.at) has an extensive bus and tram network, but by early evening services become infrequent. Single tickets (€1.10), day passes (€4.40) and weekly passes (€13.10) are available from pavement dispensers, *Tabakladen* (tobacconist) shops and the Hauptbahnhof. Drivers don't sell tickets – buy and validate your tickets before you board.

AROUND LINZ

St Florian

🗹 07224 / POP 5769

Unassuming St Florian, a market town 18km southeast of Linz, hides one of Austria's finest Augustinian abbeys. Supposedly buried under the abbey, St Florian was a Roman officer who converted to Christianity and was subsequently tortured and drowned in the Enns River in the year 304 for his beliefs. Legend has it that Florian, the patron saint of firefighters and of Upper Austria, saved a burning village with a single water-filled bucket. In many Austrian churches, he's depicted as a Roman warrior dousing flames with a bucket of water.

◉ Sights

★**Augustiner Chorherrenstift**   ABBEY
(www.stift-st-florian.at; Stiftstrasse 1; tours adult/child €8.50/3.50; ☉ tours 11am, 1pm & 3pm May–mid-Oct) Rising like a vision above St Florian, this abbey dates at least to 819 and has been occupied by the Canons Regular, living under Augustinian rule, since 1071. Today its imposing yellow-and-white facade is overwhelmingly baroque.

You can only visit the abbey's interior by guided tour, which takes in the resplendent apartments adorned with rich stuccowork and frescoes. They include 16 emperors' rooms (once occupied by visiting popes and royalty) and a galleried library housing 150,000 volumes.

The opulent **Marble Hall** pays homage to Prince Eugene of Savoy, a Frenchman who frequently led the Habsburg army to victory over the Turks. Prince Eugene's Room contains an amusing bed featuring carved Turks, which gives a whole new meaning to the idea of sleeping with the enemy!

A high point of the tour is the **Altdorfer Gallery**, displaying 14 paintings by Albrecht Altdorfer (1480–1538) of the Danube School. The sombre and dramatic scenes of Christ and St Sebastian reveal a skilful use of chiaroscuro. Altdorfer cleverly tapped into contemporary issues to depict his biblical scenes (for example, one of Christ's tormentors is clearly a Turk).

The **Stiftsbasilika** (open 6.30am to dusk) is an exuberant affair: its altar is carved from 700 tonnes of pink Salzburg marble and the huge 18th-century organ, which is literally dripping with gold, was Europe's largest at the time it was built. To hear the organ in full swing, time your visit to see one of the 20-minute concerts (p168).

Alongside Anton Bruckner's simple tomb in the **crypt** are the remains of some 6000 people believed to be Roman, which were unearthed in the 13th century. Stacked in neat rows behind a wrought-iron gate, their bones and skulls create a spine-tingling work of art.

ST FLORIAN'S HEAVENLY MUSIC

Famous Austrian Romantic composer Anton Bruckner was born 8km from St Florian in the village of Ansfelden in 1824. A choirboy in St Florian and church organist from 1850 to 1855, he was buried in the crypt below his beloved organ in 1896. Indeed the Augustiner Chorherrenstift abbey has a long musical tradition, associated with names such as Schubert and Michael Haydn, and is world famous for its resident boys' choir, the St Florianer Sängerknaben; see www.florianer.at for concert dates.

🛏 Sleeping & Eating

Gästehaus Stift St Florian   GUESTHOUSE **$$**
(☑ 07224-89 02 13; www.stift-st-florian.at; Stiftstrasse 1; s/d incl breakfast €54/86) It's oh-so-quiet at this guesthouse within the abbey's walls, overlooking the cloisters and manicured gardens. Antique furniture, solid wood floors and candles add character to the fittingly spartan rooms, which are flooded with natural light.

Landgasthof zur Kanne   GUESTHOUSE **$$**
(☑ 07224-42 88; www.gasthof-koppler.at; Marktplatz 7; s/d €56/90; P) 🍴 This yellow-fronted 14th-century guesthouse on the main square scores points for its clean, snug rooms and its restaurant (open Tuesday to Saturday), which serves fresh produce from the Koppler family's farm.

Zum Goldenen Löwe   AUSTRIAN **$$**
(☑ 07224-89 30; www.goldenerloewe-wimhofer.at; Speiserberg 9; mains €7-15; ⊘11.30am-10pm Thu-Mon, 11.30am-2pm Tue) The sound of the chef pounding humongous schnitzels welcomes you to this wood-panelled restaurant opposite the abbey gates. The sunny beer garden out back overlooks rolling countryside. Weekday lunch specials go for €6.70.

☆ Entertainment

Augustiner Chorherrenstift Concerts   CLASSICAL MUSIC
(tickets €4.50, incl guided abbey tour €11; ⊘2.30pm Mon, Wed-Fri & Sun late May-early Oct) To hear the organ of the Stiftsbasilika (p167) in full swing, time your visit to see one of the 20-minute concerts.

ℹ Information

The small **tourist office** (☑ 07224-56 90; www.st-florian.at; Marktplatz 2; ⊘1-5pm Tue-Thu, 12.30-5pm Fri May-Oct) is in the centre of town on Marktplatz.

ℹ Getting There & Away

St Florian (officially Markt St Florian) is not accessible by train. Buses depart frequently from the main bus station at Linz' Hauptbahnhof (€3.10, 25 minutes, up to three per hour Monday to Saturday, fewer Sunday).

Mauthausen

Mauthausen's status as a quarrying centre prompted the Nazis to site KZ Mauthausen concentration camp here. Prisoners were forced into slave labour in the granite quarry and many died on the *Todesstiege* (stairway of death) leading from the quarry to the camp. Some 100,000 prisoners died or were executed on site between 1938 and 1945. It has been turned into the emotive **Mauthausen Memorial** (www.mauthausen-memorial.at; Erinnerungsstrasse 1; adult/child €5/3, audioguide €3; ⊘9am-5.30pm Mar-Oct, 9am-3pm Tue-Sun Nov-Feb), which tells its history, and that of other camps such as those at Ebensee and Melk.

Visitors can walk through the remaining living quarters (each designed for 200, but housing up to 500) and see the disturbing gas chambers. The former Sick Quarters now shelters most of the camp's harrowing material – charts, artefacts and many photos of both prisoners and their SS guards. It is a stark and incredibly moving reminder of human cruelty.

Guided tours (included in admission) take place in German year-round; English tours are only available in July and August.

Bus 360 from Linz (€5.20, 40 minutes, hourly) drops you 1.5km from the Mauthausen Memorial at the Mauthausen OÖ Linzer Strasse/Hauptschule stop, from where it's a steep walk uphill to the memorial.

Trains link Linz with Mauthausen (€5.20, 25 minutes, hourly), most requiring a change in St Valentin. Mauthausen Memorial is 4km northwest of the train station (follow the KZ Mauthausen signs), around an hour's walk, of which the final 1.5km is uphill.

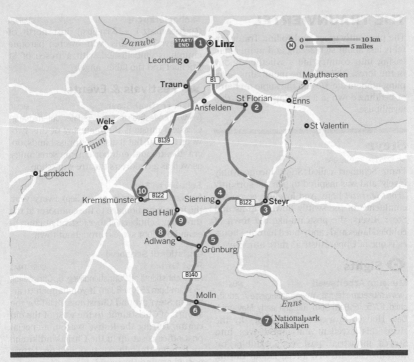

Driving Tour
Upper Austria Highlights

START LINZ
END LINZ
LENGTH 160KM; ONE DAY

This off-the-beaten-track drive meanders through Upper Austria's bucolic landscapes to resplendent abbeys, rustic villages, spa towns and limestone mountains.

After you've checked out high-tech developments and magnificent historic architecture in innovative ① **Linz**, head south along the B1. Stop off in ② **St Florian** to explore its majestic Augustinian abbey, a masterpiece of baroque art and the final resting place of Romantic composer Anton Bruckner.

Continue south on minor roads through patchwork fields studded with *Vierkanthof*, huge square farmhouses with inner courtyards. The rolling countryside brings you to riverside ③ **Steyr**, the picture-book town that inspired Schubert's *Trout Quintet* and a relaxed place for lunch. Atmospheric Bräuhof, on the main street, has a lantern-lit vaulted dining room, a buzzing pavement terrace

and fantastic mid-week lunch specials. Afterwards, take a stroll through Steyr's photogenic, pastel-shaded streets.

Follow the emerald-tinted Steyr River west along the B122 to ④ **Sierning**, dominated by its Renaissance *Schloss*. From here, the B140 shadows the river south to the pretty church-topped town of ⑤ **Grünburg**. It's just a 15-minute drive south to ⑥ **Molln**, the northern gateway to the spectacular limestone peaks, waterfalls and wilderness of ⑦ **Nationalpark Kalkalpen**. Get information at Molln's national park visitor centre.

Refreshed by the mountain air, head north, passing Grünburg and swinging west along a country road to tiny ⑧ **Adlwang**. Here Gangl farmhouse is a good stop for home-grown apple juice and *Most* (cider). Five minutes north sits the spa town of ⑨ **Bad Hall**, where you can bathe at Mediterrana Therme. A short drive west along the B122 leads to ⑩ **Kremsmünster**, whose opulent Benedictine abbey harbours an incredible library and observatory. Drive back to Linz via the scenic church-dotted villages lining the B139.

THE TRAUNVIERTEL

The pleasantly green and rolling Traunviertel is less about sightseeing and more about easing into country life – whether hiking in the forest, skiing in the mountains, sampling homemade *Most* in the apple orchards or bedding down in a rambling *Vierkanthof* farmhouse.

Steyr

📞 07252 / POP 38,395

Franz Schubert called Steyr 'inconceivably lovely' and was inspired to pen the sprightly *Trout Quintet* here. And lovely it is: on the confluence of the swiftly flowing Enns and Steyr Rivers, the postcard-like old town of cobbled lanes and candy-hued baroque houses is one of Upper Austria's most attractive.

◉ Sights

Museum Arbeitswelt MUSEUM
(www.museum-steyr.at; Wehrgrabengasse 7; adult/child €7/5; ⊙9am-5pm Tue-Sun early May–mid-Dec) Housed in a converted factory by the river, this excellent museum delves into Steyr's industrial past with exhibits on working-class history, forced labour during WWII and the rise of the Socialist Party.

Stadtmuseum MUSEUM
(Grünmarkt 26; ⊙10am-4pm Tue-Sun Apr-Oct, 10am-4pm Wed-Sun Nov-Mar) FREE Set in an early-17th-century granary with an eye-catching sgraffito mural facade, this museum showcases Steyr's culture and folklore through its artefacts. The baroque and Biedermeier nativity figurines are the highlight of the permanent collection.

Schlosspark PARK
(Blumauergasse; ⊙24hr) Footpaths through this quiet park lead to baroque **Schloss Lamberg**, sitting pretty between the confluence of the Enns and Steyr Rivers. A steep passageway next to the **Bummerlhaus** (Stadtplatz 32), with overhanging arches, squeezes through the old city walls and climbs up to cobbled Berggasse and the park.

Stadtpfarrkirche CHURCH
(www.dioezese-linz.at; Brucknerplatz 4; ⊙8am-6pm) The spire of this Gothic church is one of Steyr's most visible landmarks. The church shares features with Stephansdom in Vienna and the same architect, Hans Puchsbaum.

Michaelerkirche CHURCH
(Michaelerplatz 1; ⊙8am-6pm) Just north of the Steyr River, this twin-towered baroque church is embellished with a fresco of St Michael and the fallen angels.

☆ Festivals & Events

Musik Festival Steyr MUSIC
(www.musikfestivalsteyr.at; ⊙late Jul–mid-Aug) Classical music is the mainstay of this two-week festival, but it also sees brass bands, opera, theatre and outdoor cinema screenings, as well as a children's theatre workshop.

Schubert@Steyr MUSIC
(www.schubertatsteyr.at; ⊙late Sep) Every year, the town pays homage to the composer at the three-day Schubert@Steyr festival at churches and outdoor stages throughout town.

Christkindl Seasonal Post Office CHRISTMAS
(www.christkindl.at; Christkindlweg 6, Christkindl; ⊙10am-5pm 25 Nov-6 Jan) If you happen to arrive in Steyr around Christmas, head for the suburb of Christkindl, to the west of the old centre. During the festive season, a special post office is set up in the Christkindlkirche to handle the almost two million letters posted around the world.

🛏 Sleeping

Gasthof Bauer PENSION $
(📞07252-544 41; www.bauer-gasthof.at; Josefgasse 7; s/d €45/76; 🅿🛜) Run by the same family since 1880, this cosy 14-room pension sits on a little island in the Steyr River. The rooms are simple but comfy, and there's a leafy chestnut tree–shaded garden and a restaurant (mains €7.50 to €11.50) serving fresh, local fare and good-value lunch menus (€7.80). It's a 1km walk northwest of Stadtplatz. Cash only.

Campingplatz Forelle CAMPGROUND $
(📞07252-780 08; www.forellesteyr.at; Kematmüllerstrasse 1a; camp sites per adult/child/tent €5.50/2.40/2; ⊙Apr-Oct) Open during the warmer months, this tree-shaded campground on the banks of the Enns is 3.3km northeast of the centre. It has a playground, activities such as canoeing and tennis, plus repair facilities and bike storage for cyclists. Take bus 1 from the centre.

★Hotel Christkindlwirt HOTEL $$
(📞07252-521 84; www.christkindlwirt.at; Christkindlweg 6, Christkindl; s €82-89, d €22-142; @🛜)

Slip down the laneway behind the pilgrimage church in Christkindl to find this boutique haven. Many of the contemporary, warm-coloured rooms have balconies with river views. Candles create a restful feel in the grotto-like spa, which has a sauna, a steam room and treatments such as shiatsu massage. The panoramic terrace of its restaurant (mains €9.90 to €31.90) overlooks the valley below.

Minichmayr HOTEL $$
(☑07252-534 10; www.hotel-minichmayr.at; Haratzmüllerstrasse 1-3; s €84-105, d €125-175; ☎) At the confluence of the Steyr and Enns Rivers, this 500-year-old property has fresh, modernised rooms with light cream tones that are elegant in their simplicity, and a superb Austrian restaurant with intricately carved honey-coloured wood panelling and stupendous views of the rivers and town beyond. Views also extend from the upstairs spa sheltering a Jacuzzi and steam room.

Stadthotel Styria HISTORIC HOTEL $$
(☑07252-515 51; www.stadthotel.at; Stadtplatz 40; s/d/tr €102/160/205; ▣☎) Steyr's most historic hotel occupies a 400-year-old townhouse right on the Stadtplatz. Many of the rooms have original features, from period furnishings to beams; a frescoed breakfast room overlooks the rooftops. Rooms at the rear of the building are more modern but two have large private terraces. There's a sauna and hammam for guests' use.

✖ Eating

★ Knapp am Eck EUROPEAN $$
(☑07252-762 69; http://knappameck.at; Wehrgrabengasse 15; mains €11-23; ☺11am-2pm & 6pm-midnight Tue-Sat) ☞ A cobbled lane shadows the Steyr River to this locavore bistro, which utilises organic, seasonal produce to create dishes such as tender lamb with polenta and sage-stuffed pork. By night, candles and lanterns illuminate the ivy-covered walls, trailing roses and chestnut trees in the garden. Its three-course lunch (midweek only) costs €19.

Orangerie im Schlosspark EUROPEAN $$
(☑07252-740 74; www.orangerie-steyr.at; Blumauergasse 1; mains €12.80-24.80; ☺11.30am-10.15pm Thu-Mon May-Sep, 11.30am-10.15pm daily Dec, shorter hours rest of year; ☑) This beautifully converted 18th-century orangery opens onto a leafy terrace facing the Schlosspark. The chef cooks fresh, seasonal dishes ranging from chanterelle tagliatelle to hearty beef

broth with homemade dumplings. During the week, its two-course lunch menus (€7.80 to €9.80) always offer a vegetarian option.

Bräuhof AUSTRIAN $$
(☑07252-420 00; www.braeuhof.at; Stadtplatz 35; mains €9.50-24.50; ☺10am-11pm) Dine by lantern light under 300-year-old vaults or on the pavement terrace at the atmospheric Bräuhof. Meaty numbers such as pork medallions wrapped in ham and served with a mushroom cream sauce are matched with full-bodied Austrian wines. During the week, the three-course lunch menu is a bargain at €8.50.

Gasthof Mader AUSTRIAN $$
(☑07252-533 58; www.mader.at; Stadtplatz 36; mains €8.50-19, 3-/4-/5-course dinner menus €32/39/48; ☺kitchen 11am-10pm Mon-Sat, bar 8am-1am Mon-Sat) With its Gothic vaults, frescoed *Schubertstüberl* (parlour) and arcaded inner courtyard, Mader is historic dining at its best. Specialities such as crisp roast pork with dumplings or trout served with parsley potatoes figure on the thoroughly Austrian menu. Upstairs are a dozen comfortable rooms (single/double/family €95/138/158).

☕ Drinking & Nightlife

★ Yovela COFFEE
(☑0676-694 02 46; www.yovelacoffee.com; Kirchengasse 1; ☺8.30am-6pm Mon-Fri, to 5pm Sat Sep–mid-Jul) ☞ The aroma of freshly roasting coffee wafts out of this cafe, which is filled with hessian sacks of organic beans. The owners set up shop here in 2002 and now supply some of Vienna's leading coffee houses. On the last Saturday of the month they also run three-hour courses (in English and German; €54) covering roasting, brewing and cupping. Cash only.

ℹ Information

Tourist Office (☑07252-532 29-0; www.steyr.info; Stadtplatz 27; ☺9am-6pm Mon-Fri, to noon Sat) On the main square in the Rathaus.

ℹ Getting There & Away

BUS
Regional buses depart from the Hauptbahnhof; city buses leave from outside the Hauptbahnhof to the north.

TRAIN
Some trains from Linz (€8.20, 50 minutes, hourly Monday to Saturday, fewer Sunday) require a change at St Valentin. Most trains

for Wels (€13.20, 1¼ hours, hourly Monday to Saturday, fewer Sunday) also require a change in St Valentin.

Bad Hall

☑ 07258 / POP 4812

A sleepy spa town 18km west of Steyr, Bad Hall's big draw is the Mediterrana Therme.

◉ Sights

Kurpark   PARK

(☺ dawn-dusk) Opposite the Mediterrana Therme, this 34-hectare park features exotic and native woodlands, aromatic gardens, blooming flower beds and regularly changing art installations, as well as playgrounds for the kids. To inhale the spa's iodised salt for free, head for the central pavilion, where 1000L of the stuff filters through twig walls every hour.

🏃 Activities

Mediterrana Therme   SPA

(www.eurothermen.at; Kurhausstrasse 10; day ticket adult/child €20/14.50; ☺ 9am-midnight) The iodine-rich, 40°C waters that gush from Bad Hall's thermal springs are hailed for their therapeutic properties. Outside there are massage jets and mountain views, while inside an iodine steam room, a columned Roman bath and whirlpools pummel you into a blissfully relaxed state. A splash pool keeps tots amused.

ℹ Information

Tourist Office (☑ 07258-72 00-0; www.badhall.at; Kurpromenade 1; ☺ 8am-5.30pm Mon-Fri, 9am-noon & 1.30-5.30pm Sat, 1.30-5.30pm Sun Apr-Oct, shorter hours Nov-Mar) Located 200m southeast of the spa.

ℹ Getting There & Away

From Steyr, there are frequent buses to Bad Hall (€5.20, 35 minutes, hourly Monday to Saturday, every two hours Sunday).

Nationalpark Kalkalpen

This little-known, almost untouched wilderness of rugged limestone mountains, high moors and mixed forest is home to the elusive golden eagle and lynx. Bordering Styria, this is Austria's second-largest national park after Hohe Tauern. Its valleys and gorges cut through classic alpine landscapes, dominated by **Hoher Nock** (1963m).

🏃 Activities

Nationalpark Kalkalpen is a paradise for hikers, cyclists and rock climbers in summer and cross-country skiers in winter. Kompass map 70 (1:50,000) covers the park and its trails in detail. Other activities in the park's vicinity include paragliding, white-water rafting and caving.

Pro Adventures   ADVENTURE SPORTS

(☑ 0664 4412 111; www.pro-adventures.com; Gaisriegl 8, Vorderstoder; ☺ by reservation) Pro Adventures runs a diverse range of guided activities, among them white-water rafting (per day €75), river snorkelling (per half-day €49), via ferrata (per day €75) and caving (per half-day from €39), and offers canoe rental (per day €49). Multiday courses include igloo building (per two days €150) and hiking/cross-country skiing tours (from €250). Confirm meeting points when booking.

Mountain-hut accommodation can be arranged; ask for seasonal prices.

Flugschule   ADVENTURE SPORTS

(☑ 07562-56 00; www.fliegmit.at; Dambach 144, Windischgarsten; 20min tandem flight €130, 2-day training course €600; ☺ by reservation) This flying school runs paragliding and hang-gliding tandem flights and intensive instruction courses (in English and German) so you can fly solo. Flights mostly take place in the Hinterstoder ski resort area but also go to Nationalpark Kalkalpen; confirm the meeting point when you book.

Wurzeralm   SKIING, HIKING

(http://hiwu.at; Pyhrn 33, Wurzeralm; day pass winter/summer €39.50/15; ☺ lifts 9am-4.30pm early Dec-late Mar, 8.30am-12.15pm & 1-4.30pm late Jun-Oct) Europe's fastest cable car whisks you from Wurzeralm's car park to the ski area where 22km of slopes are serviced by seven ski lifts.

Hinterstoder   SKIING, HIKING

(www.hiwu.at; Hinterstoder 21, Hinterstoder; day pass adult/child €42.50/15; ☺ 8.30am-4.30pm Dec–mid-Apr, 8.45am-4.30pm mid-Jun–mid-Sep) Against a spectacular backdrop of rugged peaks, Hinterstoder offers 40km of ski slopes served by 14 lifts.

🛏 Sleeping & Eating

Hotel Freunde der Natur   HOTEL $$

(☑ 07563-681; www.naturfreundehotel.at; Wiesenweg 7, Spital am Pyhrn; s/d incl breakfast from €63/102; P 🛜) Handily positioned for Wurzeralm and the Nationalpark Kalkalpen, this 70-room chalet-style property overlooking the mountains offers great facilities including bike rental (per day from €8), a drying room and ski storage, as well as family-friendly amenities such as a playground, a kids' menu at the traditional Austrian restaurant, and interconnecting rooms.

Das Rössl　　　　　　　AUSTRIAN $$
(📋07562-205 55; www.dasroessl.at; Hauptstrasse 9, Windischgarsten; mains €9.40-24.80; ⊘ kitchen 11am-2pm & 5-10pm Mon, Tue & Thu-Sat, 11am-8pm Sun, bar 11am-midnight Mon, Tue & Thu-Sat, 11am-11pm Sun; 👶) The pick of places to dine in charming Windischgarsten, this oyster-grey guesthouse cooks up hearty dishes including rib-eye steak, Riesling-marinated pork and river trout. Carb-loading for outdoor adventures isn't a problem – every main comes with potato salad. Upstairs are 26 simple but comfortable rooms (doubles from €76); breakfast is available every day for overnight guests and included in the rate.

ℹ Information

Nationalpark Zentrum Molln (📋07584-36 51; www.kalkalpen.at; Nationalparkallee 1, Molln; ⊘9am-4pm Mon-Fri, to 2pm Sat & Sun May-Oct, shorter hours rest of year) Ultramodern, ecofriendly centre near the northern entrance to the park.

Tourismusverband Pyhrn-Priel (📋07562-52 66 00; www.urlaubsregion-pyhrn-priel.at; Hauptstrasse 28, Windischgarsten; ⊘8am-5pm Mon-Fri, 9am-noon Sat & Sun) Situated south of the park's boundary.

ℹ Getting There & Away

Direct buses run from Steyr to Molln (€6.20, 45 minutes, hourly Monday to Saturday, fewer services Sunday) and on to Windischgarsten (€6.80, one hour). From Windischgarsten local buses run to Hinterstoder and Wurzeralm during the skiing and hiking seasons.

To really get out and explore the area, however, you'll need your own wheels.

Wels

📋07242 / POP 58,664

Settled since the Neolithic era and a strategic Roman stronghold, Wels is the largest town in the Traunviertel. While there are few real sights, this is a handy base for exploring rural Upper Austria. The centre is a pleasure to stroll through, with a clutch of

Renaissance and baroque townhouses hiding inner courtyards and walled gardens. In summer the town springs to life with markets and open-air concerts.

⊙ Sights

Stadtplatz　　　　　　　HISTORIC SITE
Wels' main square is framed by slender townhouses, many of which conceal arcaded inner courtyards. Particularly attractive is the ivy-clad courtyard at No 18, nurturing palms, rhododendrons and Japanese umbrella trees. At the front, glance up to spy the 2000-year-old **Römermedaillon** (Roman medallion) relief.

Nearby at No 24, the Renaissance **Haus der Salome Alt** sports a *trompe l'oeil* facade and takes its name from one-time occupant Salome Alt, mistress of Salzburg's most famous prince-archbishop, Wolf Dietrich von Raitenau.

Burg Wels　　　　　　　CASTLE
(Burggasse 13; adult/child €4.50/2; ⊘10am-5pm Tue-Fri, 2-5pm Sat, 10am-4pm Sun) Set around a quiet, geranium-filled garden, this castle is where Emperor Maximilian I drew his last breath in 1519. The folksy museum contains everything from cannon balls to Biedermeier costumes. Must-sees include the horse-drawn cider press and the circular room that's a shrine to baking, with walls smothered in animal-shaped pastries and gigantic pretzels.

Stadtpfarrkirche　　　　　　　CHURCH
(www.stadtpfarre-wels.at; Pfarrgasse 27; ⊘8am-6pm) Built in the 14th century on the site of a wooden chapel first mentioned in 888, the refreshingly simple Stadtpfarrkirche is noteworthy for its Gothic stained glass.

🛏 Sleeping

Boutique Hotel Hauser　　　BOUTIQUE HOTEL $$
(📋07242-454 09; www.hotelhauser.com; Bäckergasse 7; s €94-125, d €125-160; ❋ 🛜 🏊) With its polished service, clean-lined contemporary rooms and seasonal rooftop pool, sauna and terrace, this epicentral boutique hotel outshines most of Wels' midrangers. Organic and regional produce, homemade cakes and jams spice up the breakfast buffet, and guests can refresh with free tea and fruit throughout the day.

Hotel Ploberger　　　　　　HOTEL $$
(📋07242-629 41; www.hotel-ploberger.at; Kaiser-Josef-Platz 21; s €99-119, d €131-151; P ❋ @ 🛜)

In the heart of town, this Best Western has fresh, contemporary rooms in monochrome hues, some with comforts such as Nespresso coffee-makers and DVD players. The sauna and open fire keep things cosy in winter.

✖ Eating

★ **Löwenkeller** INTERNATIONAL $$
(📞07242-797 85; www.loewenkeller.at; Hafergasse 1; 2-/3-course lunch menus €9.90/13.90, 3-/4-/5-course dinner menus €38/45/53, mains €16-28; ⏰11.30am-2pm & 6-10pm Tue-Fri, 6-10pm Sat) With its exposed stone, starchy white linen and polished service, Löwenkeller is by far the most sophisticated restaurant in town. Dishes such as poached trout served on spinach with dill oil, roast guinea fowl with locally picked forest mushroom sauce, and herb-crusted Upper Austrian lamb with parmesan risotto are presented with flair, and paired with Austrian wines from the cellar.

Gasthaus zur Linde AUSTRIAN $$
(📞07242-460 23; www.gasthaus-zur-linde.at; Ringstrasse 45; mains €9-18; ⏰11.30am-2pm & 5.30-9.30pm Tue-Sat; 🔉) Sizzling and stirring for the past 200 years, this family-run place radiates old-fashioned warmth. It dishes up Austrian classics alongside seasonal treats such as asparagus in spring and game in autumn. The weekday two-course lunch menu is great value at €8.60.

ℹ Information

Information, maps and audioguides (€4) of the city are available from the **tourist office** (📞07242-677 22-22; www.wels-info.at; Stadtplatz 44; ⏰9am-12.30pm & 1-6pm Mon-Sat) on the Stadtplatz.

ℹ Getting There & Away

Trains and buses arrive at the Hauptbahnhof, 1.25km north of Stadtplatz. The town is on the InterCity (IC) and EuroCity (EC) express rail route between Linz (€3.30, 15 minutes, up to three hourly) and Salzburg (€10.40, one hour, half-hourly). Other regular services include Passau (Germany; €16, one hour, hourly or better) and Vienna (€20.50, 1¾ hours, half-hourly).

Kremsmünster

📞07583 / POP 6435

Kremsmünster would be just another working Austrian town were it not for its majestic Benedictine abbey, looming large above the fertile Krems Valley.

◉ Sights

Stift Kremsmünster ABBEY
(📞07583-52 75-150; www.stift-kremsmuenster.at; Stift 1; tours adult/child €8/3; ⏰tours by reservation 10am, 11am, 2pm, 3.30pm & 4pm May-Oct, 11am, 2pm & 3.30pm Nov-Apr) Kremsmünster's enormous Benedictine abbey dates from 777, but was given a baroque facelift in the 18th century. Elaborate stucco and frescoes shape the long, low **Bibliothek** (library), where shelves creak under 160,000 volumes, and the **Kaisersaal** (Emperor's Hall). The most prized piece in the **Schatzkammer** (treasury) is the gold Tassilo Chalice, which the Duke of Bavaria donated to the monks in about 780. You can visit all three on a one-hour guided tour (available in several languages, including English).

Stiftskirche CHURCH
(Stift 1; ⏰8am-6pm) You don't have to tour the Stift Kremsmünster to enter its Stiftskirche. The marvellously over-the-top baroque church is criss-crossed with white stuccowork, draped in Flemish tapestries and festooned with dark, brooding paintings.

Sternwarte TOWER
(Observatory Tower; 📞07583-52 75-150; www.stift-kremsmuenster.at; Stift 1; adult/child €9/3; ⏰tours by reservation 10am, 2pm & 4pm May-Oct) Part of the Stift Kremsmünster complex, the 50m-high Sternwarte is dedicated to numerous schools of natural history. Spanning seven floors, the mind-boggling collection steps from fossilised starfish to the skeleton of an Ice Age cave bear. It's a giddy climb up a spiral staircase to the top floor, which displays the Keppler sextant and affords a bird's-eye perspective of the town and gently rolling countryside beyond. Guided tours in English and other languages.

Fischbehälter HISTORIC SITE
(Fish Basin; ⏰10am-4pm) The 17th-century cloisters of the Stift Kremsmünster comprise five fish ponds, each centred on a mythological statue. The trickle of water is calming and you can feed the carp for €1.

ℹ Getting There & Away

Trains link Kremsmünster with Linz (€7, 40 minutes, hourly or better).

Buses serve Wels (€4.20, 30 minutes, half-hourly Monday to Saturday).

THE MÜHLVIERTEL

The Mühlviertel is a remote, beautiful region of mist-enshrouded granite hills, thick woodlands and valleys speckled with chalk-white *Steinbloass* farmhouses. The scenery is redolent of the not-so-distant Czech Republic. This corner of Upper Austria is well worth a visit for its Gothic architecture, warm-hearted locals and total peace and quiet.

Freistadt

📞 07942 / POP 7502

Just 10km from the Czech border as the crow flies, Freistadt has some of the best-preserved medieval fortifications in Austria. Stroll through the town's narrow streets to gate towers and the gardens that have taken root in the original moat.

🅾 Sights

Schlossmuseum   MUSEUM

(www.museum-freistadt.at; Schlosshof 2; adult/child €6/1; ⊙ 9am-noon & 2-5pm Mon-Fri, 2-5pm Sat & Sun) The city's 14th-century castle, with a square tower topped by a tapering red-tiled roof, harbours this museum, exhibiting 600 works of engraved painted glass. Climb the 50m Bergfried tower for far-reaching views over Freistadt.

Stadtmauern   HISTORIC SITE

Freistadt's Altstadt sits within its sturdy 14th-century city walls complete with gate towers such as the medieval **Linzertor** and skeletal **Böhmertor**, which reflect its past need for strong defences as an important staging point on the salt route to Bohemia.

The moat encircling the town is now given over to gardens and allotments.

Hauptplatz   SQUARE

Freistadt's focal point is the elongated Hauptplatz, jammed between the old city walls. The square has some ornate buildings and a Gothic **Stadtpfarrkirche** (Parish Church; www.dioezese-linz.at; Hauptplatz; ⊙ 8am-6pm) capped with a baroque tower. Some of the houses along Waaggasse, just west of the Hauptplatz, are embellished with sgraffito mural designs.

🛏 Sleeping

Pension Pirklbauer   PENSION $

(📞 07942-724 40; www.pension-pirklbauer.at; Höllgasse 2-4; s €28-33, d €46-54) Nudging up against medieval Linzertor is this charming pension. Christine is a dab hand at making her guests feel at home, whether on the rooftop terrace overlooking the town's garden-filled moat or in the country-cottage rooms with pine wood, floral fabrics and squeaky-clean bathrooms.

Hotel Goldener Adler   HISTORIC HOTEL $$

(📞 07942-20 79 90; www.hotels-freistadt.at; Salzgasse 1; s/d/tr €59/98/125; P 🛜) Polished stone slabs, wrought-iron banisters and vaulted passages crammed with antique wagons and spinning wheels hint at this hotel's 700-year history (it's the 1841 birthplace of artist Karl Kronberger). Some of the 30 rooms have four-poster beds. Unwind in the sauna and whirlpool, or tuck into the famous beer-marinated Bohemian pork shoulder in the beer garden (mains €8 to €16).

UPPER AUSTRIA FREISTADT

BUYING INTO YOUR FAVOURITE BEER

Freistadt is a *Braucommune*, a town where the citizens actually own their brewery – when you buy a house, you automatically buy a share of your favourite tipple. Ownership is limited to the 149 households within the town walls, but if you have the spare change and *really* like your beer, properties sell for upwards of €400,000. Realistically, the brewery cannot be taken over, as the business would have to buy the whole town in order to take control.

The arrangement started way back in 1777 when the brewery opened. In the ensuing centuries the lucky owners would receive their share of the profits in liquid form, which would be distributed in *Eimer Bier* containers holding 56L. Each owner might get up to 130 containers! Nowadays, for better or worse, owners get a cash payment of equivalent value (which, on Friday and Saturday nights, often goes straight back to the brewery).

Practically every bar in town serves the local brew, including the **Freistadt Brauhaus** (p176), so it's not hard to see why the brewery remains a profitable business. If you'd like to learn more about Freistadt beer and stock up, nip into the **brewery shop** (www.freistaedter-bier.at; Brauhausstrasse 2; ⊙ 8am-5pm Mon-Fri, 9am-midnight Sat & Sun).

HIGH ABOVE THE TREETOPS

Tarzan wannabes can take a head-spinning walk above the treetops at **Baumkronenweg** (www.baumkronen weg.at; Knechtelsdorf 1, Kopfing; adult/child €9.50/6.50; ⊙10am-6pm mid-Mar–early Nov), a canopy boardwalk in Kopfing, 21km east of Schärding. Stretching 2.5km, the 45m-high trail snakes above misty spruce trees and passes lookout towers, hanging bridges and platforms that afford bird's-eye perspectives over the forest. You can sleep among the trees at the **Baumhotel** (☑07763-228 90; www.baumkronenweg.at; per adult/child €66/55; ⊙mid-Mar–early Nov).

✖ Eating

★**Freistadt Brauhaus**   AUSTRIAN $
(☑07942-727 72; www.freistaedter-bier.at; Brauhausstrasse 2; mains €8-14; ⊙kitchen 9am-11pm, bar to midnight) To sample Freistadt's hoppy brews, head to the town's brewery restaurant, which has a sprawling vaulted interior and beer garden. Meaty Austrian faves include roast pork drizzled with dark beer sauce and served with lashings of sauerkraut; the midweek two-course lunch menu costs a bargain €7.50. A keg is tapped at 6pm daily. There's a playground for the kids.

Gasthaus Ratsherrnstube   AUSTRIAN $$
(☑07942-724 39; http://ratsherrnstube-freistadt. stadtausstellung.at; Hauptplatz 1; mains €7.90-13.90; ⊙kitchen 8am-11pm Tue-Sun, bar to midnight) Right on Freistadt's main square, with terrace tables in summer, this large, traditional guesthouse turns out hearty Austrian fare including five different schnitzels, paprika-spiced *Müllerwurst* sausage with sauerkraut, pan-fried zander with parsley potatoes and *Käsenocken* (cheese dumplings). Children can order smaller versions of adults' dishes.

🍷 Drinking & Nightlife

Owning their own town brewery (p175) makes locals so passionate about *Freistädter* brews that they avoid places where it isn't on tap.

★**Suchan**   COFFEE
(www.suchankaffee.at; Pfarrplatz 3; ⊙8am-3pm Thu & Fri, to 2pm Sat & Sun) 🍃 Opening hours

are short as Suchan's coffee has become so popular throughout Austria and even Berlin that it spends the rest of the week roasting, using unmixed (single-origin), slow-drum and air-cooling techniques. All beans are organic and sourced from small-scale fair-trade farms. Bonus: it also operates two coffee carts around town, so look out for them if it's closed.

ℹ Information

The **Mühlviertler Kernland Tourist Office** (☑07942-757 00; www.muehlviertel.at/wo/region-freistadt.com; Waaggasse 6; ⊙8.30am-12.30pm & 1-5pm Mon-Fri) provides information on the town and its surrounds.

ℹ Getting There & Away

Freistadt is on a direct rail route from Linz (€9.10, one hour, every two hours). This line then wriggles its way to Prague, 205km north; Czech rail fares are lower than those in Austria, so you can save money by waiting and buying (in Czech currency) your onward tickets once you've crossed the border.

Frequent trains travel between Freistadt and Kefermarkt (€2.30, 10 minutes, hourly).

The B310, which connects to the A7 motorway to Linz, runs adjacent to the walled centre and then continues its way northwards towards Prague.

THE INNVIERTEL

Ping-ponged between Bavaria and Austria over the centuries, the Innviertel is a fertile farming region sliced in two by the Inn River, whose banks are a drawcard for cyclists in summer. There's beautiful baroque and Gothic architecture, most notably in Schärding.

Braunau am Inn

☑07722 / POP 16,351
Directly across the Inn from Germany, the working riverside town of Braunau am Inn is home to Austria's largest aluminium smelter and many other industrial plants, and serves as a pit stop for cyclists pedalling the Inn Radweg trail to or from Innsbruck. This border town has achieved unwanted attention as the birthplace of Hitler, though it would prefer to be described as *die gotische Stadt* (the Gothic city) in reference to its architecture from the era.

⊙ Sights

Stadtpfarrkirche St Stephan · CHURCH
(www.dioezese-linz.at; Kirchenplatz; ⊙8am-6pm)
To the west of Stadtplatz rises the spire of
late-Gothic Stadtpfarrkirche St Stephan.
Due to a calculation error made in 1893 that
measured it at some 100m, it was long believed to be the third-tallest spire in Austria,
but in 1952 it was discovered to measure
only 87m, relegating it to the sixth-highest
in the country.

Stadtplatz · SQUARE
This long main square is lined with elegant
pastel-hued townhouses; its southern end
narrows to the **Torturm**, a 16th-century gate
tower.

🛏 Sleeping & Eating

Hotel am Theaterpark · HOTEL $
(☑07722-634 71; www.hotelamtheaterpark-neussl.
at; Linzer Strasse 21; s/d/tr €50/73/87; 🅿🖥)
One of the best deals in town, this hotel has
28 bright, well-kept rooms, bike storage and
a little fitness room. You can wind down
over a glass of wine in the Gothic cellar or in
the tree-shaded garden.

Hotel Mayrbräu · HOTEL $$
(☑07722-633 87; www.mayrbraeu.at; Linzer
Strasse 13; s €57-82, d €92-112, tr €145; 🅿🖥)
This four-star hotel's large, warm rooms
make it a decent pick; the superior rooms
are the most spacious. A vaulted gallery full
of contemporary art and a vine-clad inner
courtyard lend character to the place. Breakfast included.

Brauhaus Bogner · AUSTRIAN $
(☑07722-223 58; www.hausbrauerei-bogner.
at; Haselbach 26; mains €7-11; ⊙kitchen 4-11pm
Tue-Sun, bar to 1am) One of Austria's smallest
breweries, Bogner is a rustic pub-restaurant
with solid Austrian fare – such as schnitzel
and *Spinat-Käsespätzle* (spinach handroll-
ed noodles with cheese sauce) – several
home-brewed beers and, often, live music.

ℹ Information

The **tourist office** (☑07722-626 44; www.
tourismus-braunau.at; Stadtplatz 2; ⊙9am-
6pm Mon-Fri, to noon Sat) is at the northern end
of the Stadtplatz.

ℹ Getting There & Away

By train, at least one change is normally required
from either Linz (€18.20, 1¾ hours, hourly) or

Salzburg (€13.40, 1¼ hours, hourly). From Wels,
there are several daily direct trains (€16.30, 1½
hours).

Schärding
☑07712 / POP 4954
Schärding is a storybook-pretty town on
the Inn, with peaceful riverfront walks and
a baroque centre studded with merchants'
houses in myriad sugared-almond shades,
including the identically gabled properties
lined up along the Silberzeile (Silver Row).

🛏 Sleeping & Eating

Hotel Stiegenwirt · HOTEL $
(☑07712-30 70-0; www.stiegenwirt-schaerding.at;
Schlossgasse 2-6; s €45-48, d €61-70; 🖥) Run by
the same family since 1910, Hotel Stiegen-
wirt offers simple but spotless rooms with
frosted-glass-fronted bathrooms (some with
balconies). It's situated right on Schärding's
picturesque main square and a stone's throw
from the Donauradweg and Inn-Radweg cycle paths. Bike rental is available (per day
from €10) along with bike storage. Rejuve-
nate post-ride in the sauna.

Hotel Forstinger · HOTEL $$
(☑07712-23 02-0; www.hotelforstinger.at; Unterer Stadtplatz 3; s €97-118, d €163-173, apt €198;
🅿✳🖥) Standing head and shoulders
above most places in town is antique-meets-
modern Hotel Forstinger, with a choice of
tastefully appointed rooms with either a
contemporary aesthetic or period features.
Apartments sleeping up to four people come

TRAPPIST BREW

The little riverside village of Engelhartszell an der Donau is home to one
of only eight licensed Trappist breweries
outside Belgium, and the only one in
Austria. At the abbey **Stift Engelszell**
(www.stift-engelszell.at; Stiftstrasse 6,
Engelhartszell an der Donau; ⊙church
8am-7pm Apr-Oct, to 5pm Nov-Mar, shop
9am-5pm Apr-Oct, shorter hours rest of
year), founded 1293, you can purchase
monk-made brews (dark Gregorius,
amber Benno, and blond Nivard); the
shop also sells liqueurs and cheeses
produced here by the monks. Adjoining
the shop is the abbey's gorgeous rococo
church, completed in 1764.

with kitchenettes. Organic breakfasts include vegetarian and vegan options and are served in the glass conservatory or in the flower-filled garden in fine weather.

Seven INTERNATIONAL **$$**
(☑ 07712-361 35; www.seven.or.at; Silberzeile 7; mains €6.50-19.50; ⊗ kitchen 11am-2pm & 6-10pm Wed-Sat & Mon, noon-9pm Sun, bar 10am-midnight Wed-Mon) A fine pick for a bite to eat is slick bistro Seven, with a people-watching terrace on the Silberzeile and a large, elongated dining room where you can dine on Austrian favourites, burgers and pastas. Top-notch coffee too.

❶ Information

The **tourist office** (☑ 07712-43 00-0; www.schaerding.at; Innbruckstrasse 29; ⊗ 9am-6pm Mon-Fri, 11am-3pm Sat & Sun Jun-Sep, shorter hours rest of year), near the bridge spanning the river into Germany, has a bike service point with pumps and repair kits.

❶ Getting There & Away

If you have your own transport, the approach to Schärding from Linz, via Engelhartszell along the Danube, is beautiful and certainly off the beaten track.

From April to October, an even more leisurely alternative is a one-hour **boat trip** (www.inn-schifffahrt.at; Leonhard-Kaiser-Weg 1; 1 way adult/child €10/5, return €14/7; ⊗ 11am & 2pm Tue-Sun Apr-Oct) between Ingling (across the river from Passau, Germany) and Schärding. Bikes are transported for free.

Trains connect Linz with Schärding (€15.20, 1¼ hours, up to two per hour Monday to Saturday, fewer services Sunday).

Geinberg

In the heart of rural Upper Austria, it's a surreal experience to soak in a bath-warm Caribbean saltwater lagoon, as underwater music plays and palms sway at **Therme Geinberg** (☑ 07723-85 01; www.therme-geinberg.at; Thermenplatz 1, Geinberg; 4hr ticket adult/child €18.10/13.20, day ticket €25.10/18.70; ⊗ 9am-10pm Sat-Thu, to 11pm Fri; ⊞), one of Austria's top spas. Saunas imitate a starry sky or smell deliciously of coconuts. After a steam, the icy sleet shower is an abrupt shock. Luxury accommodation is available (doubles from €256).

There are also several restaurants and cafes on-site (though none serve Caribbean food).

Trains link Geinberg with Braunau am Inn (€5.20, 25 minutes, hourly Monday to Friday, reduced services Saturday and Sunday), and with Schärding (€9.10, one hour, hourly Monday to Friday, reduced services Saturday and Sunday), which requires a change in Neumarkt-Kallham.

Styria

Best Places to Eat

➡ Aiola Upstairs (p188)

➡ Der Steirer (p189)

➡ Santa Clara (p189)

➡ T.O.M R (p196)

Best Places to Sleep

➡ Hotel Wiesler (p187)

➡ Schlossberg Hotel (p187)

➡ Loisium Südsteiermark (p194)

➡ Stadthotel Brunner (p204)

➡ Gasthof Kölblwirt (p203)

Why Go?

Austria's second-largest province is a picturesque combination of culture, architecture, rolling hills, vine-covered slopes and mountains. Graz, Austria's second-largest city, is Styria's photogenic and fabulously relaxed capital. Head south from Graz and you're in wine country, dubbed 'Styrian Tuscany'. This is also the land of *Kürbiskernöl* – the strong, dark pumpkin-seed oil ubiquitous in Styrian cooking.

The eastern stretch of Styria is dotted with rejuvenating thermal spas and centuries-old castles. If you're a fan of the former, Bad Blumau is a mandatory stop, not only to take the waters but also to appreciate its unusual architecture, designed by Friedensreich Hundertwasser. If you prefer castles, Schloss Riegersburg is one of Austria's best.

In the north and west, Styria's landscape changes to cold, fast-flowing alpine rivers, towering mountains and carved valleys. Highlights are Admont Abbey, charming Murau and Erzberg's open-cast mine. The very northwestern reaches of Styria stretch into Salzkammergut.

When to Go

➡ Unless you are here for the skiing, the best time to visit is during the main season from April to October.

➡ The wine roads of southern Styria peak in September, when there are festivals; in October, when the vineyards turn golden brown; and around St Martin's Day (11 November), when the young wine is released.

➡ From November many of the sights and cultural events – such as Graz's best sight, Schloss Eggenberg – close or end for the season.

➡ Skiers usually hit Schladming from mid-December (or year round on the Dachstein Glacier).

Styria Highlights

1 Graz (p189) Exploring the smart restaurants, lively bars and late night caverns of Styria's capital.

2 Schloss Eggenberg (p185) Amazing yourself at the capital's stunning Renaissance palace and museum.

3 Benedictine Abbey (p201) Wandering Admont's spectacular baroque abbey

and its library – the largest in the world.

4 Erzberg Ironworks & Mine (p200) Tripping underground, or overground, at Eisenerz.

5 Schladming (p203) Hiking the trails or glacier gazing around this laid-back Alpine resort.

6 Wine Roads (p195) Tasting your way through

'Styrian Tuscany', the vineyards of southern Styria.

7 Genuss Regal Vinofaktur (p194) Sampling local produce and getting to know your Grauburgunder from your Grüner.

8 Johnsbach (p202) Discovering the strange and touching beauty of one of Austria's earliest mountain climbing centres.

ℹ Getting There & Away

BUS

Postbus departures to Mariazell, which isn't on the train line, are integrated with train arrivals at Bruck an der Mur. To Eisenerz, integrated bus services leave from Leoben. For Admont and the

Gesäuse, the towns of Liezen and Hieflau form the main bus-transfer points.

CAR & MOTORCYCLE

The A2, from Vienna to Villach in Carinthia, runs through southern Styria, passing just below Graz, while the A9 runs an almost north–south course through the middle of Styria, making it straightforward to travel from Linz and Salzburg to Graz. The A9 also connects Graz with Slovenia, 40km to the south.

TRAIN

Styria's train lines are relatively sparse; the main line between Carinthia and Vienna passes well north of Graz through the region's main railhead, Bruck an der Mur. For Linz and Salzburg, a change is usually required at St Michael, 25km southwest of Bruck.

ⓘ Getting Around

Regional and city transport (☑ 050 678 910; www.verbundlinie.at) is based on a system of zones and time tickets. Tickets can be bought from machines for one to 22 zones; the price rises from a single trip in one zone (€2.20, valid for one hour) to 24-hour passes for one (€5) or multiple zones (eg €17 for four zones to Bärnbach). Weekly and monthly passes are also available.

In Graz, **Mobilzentral** (☑ 050 678 910; www. mobilzentral.at; Jakoministrasse 1; ⊙ 8am-6pm Mon-Fri, 9am-1pm Sat) is a useful store of information on Styrian regional buses. It also sells international train tickets.

GRAZ

☑ 0316 / POP 265,780

Austria's second-largest city is its most relaxed. Graz is an appealing place dotted with leafy green parkland, a sea of red rooftops and a narrow but fast-flowing river loudly gushing through its centre. A very beautiful bluff – connected to the centre by steps, a funicular and a glass lift – is the city's signature attribute. Architecturally, Graz hints at nearby Italy with its Renaissance courtyards and baroque palaces. That said, there's a youthful energy here too, with a handful of edgily modern buildings, a vibrant arts scene and great nightlife (thanks in part to its large student population (some 50,000 in four universities). This extends to both sides of the Mur, although the Lend district, across from the historic centre, skews young and edgy.

◉ Sights

⊙ Hauptplatz & Around

Domkirche   CHURCH
(www.domgraz.at; Burggasse 3; ⊙ dawn-dusk; ⬚ 1, 3, 4, 5, 6, 7 Hauptplatz) The Domkirche dates from the 15th century, and became a cathedral in 1786. The interior combines Gothic

and baroque elements, with reticulated vaulting on the ceiling; its highlights are Conrad Laib's panel painting *Crucifixion in the Throng* (1457) and the faded *Gottesplagenbild* fresco on the cathedral's exterior, which dates from 1485.

The fresco depicts life in the early 1480s, when Graz was besieged by its triple tragedy of Turkish invasion, the plague and locusts.

Stadtpfarrkirche   CHURCH
(Herrengasse 23; ⊙ dawn-dusk; ⬚ 1, 3, 4, 5, 6, 7 Hauptplatz) Rising up on Herrengasse between the main square and Jakominiplatz, the town parish church has an attractive baroque exterior. Inside, the post-WWII stained-glass window by Salzburg artist Albert Birkle has a controversial anomaly: the fourth panel from the bottom on the right (left of the high altar) clearly shows Hitler and Mussolini looking on as Christ is scourged.

Atelier Jungwirth   GALLERY
(☑ 0316-81 55 05; www.atelierjungwirth.com; Opernring 12; ⊙ 11am-5pm Tue-Fri, to 4pm Sat) Graz's most compelling contemporary art space specialises in photography. A calendar of shows spans reportage, fashion and more conceptual work and features some stellar international names like Paolo Roversi.

Neue Galerie Graz   GALLERY
(www.museum-joanneum.at; Joanneumsviertel; adult/child €9/3; ⊙ 10am-5pm Tue-Sun; ⬚ 1, 3, 4, 5, 6, 7 Hauptplatz) The Neue Galerie is the crowning glory of the three museums inside the Joanneumsviertel complex. The stunning collection on level 0 is the highlight. Though not enormous, it showcases vibrant works by painters such as Ernst Christian Moser, Ferdinand Georg Waldmüller and Johann Nepomuk Passini. Egon Schiele is also represented here.

Franziskaner Kirche   CHURCH
(☑ 0316-82 71 72; www.franziskaner-graz.at; Franziskanerplatz 14; ⊙ 8am-5pm) This church and monastery was founded by the Franciscan order in 1239. Its 14th-century chancel was rebuilt in a contemporary style after being gutted by an Allied bomb during WWII. The main reason to visit is, however, the serene, silent, rose-filled monastery garden, still surrounded by its original Gothic cloisters.

Graz

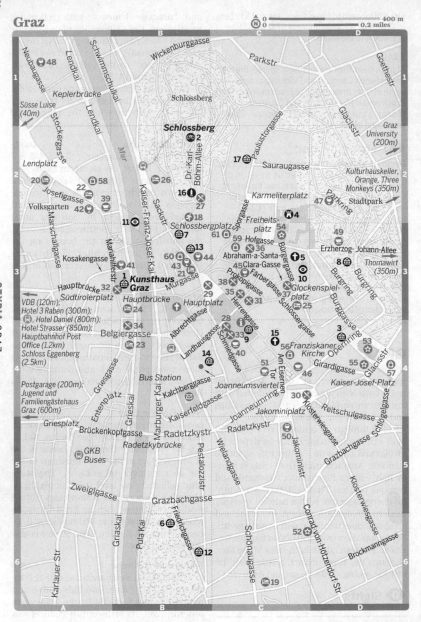

Naturkundemuseum   MUSEUM
(Museum of Natural History; www.museum-joan neum.at; Joanneumsviertel; adult/child €9/3; ⊙10am-5pm Tue-Sun; ▥; ▣1,3, 4, 5, 6, 7 Hauptplatz) Located inside the Joanneumsviertel complex of museums, the Museum of Nat- ural History has an excellent section on geology, with an interesting collection of stone slabs from different parts of the world. Butterfly buffs will find more than enough Lepidoptera pinned to the boards here.

Graz

Landeszeughaus MUSEUM
(Styrian Armoury; www.museum-joanneum.at; Herrengasse 16; adult/child €9/3; ◉10am-5pm Mon & Wed-Sun; ☐1, 3, 4, 5, 6, 7 Hauptplatz) If you have a passion for armour and weapons, you'll enjoy the Landeszeughaus, where more than 30,000 pieces of glistening weaponry are housed. The exhibition is one of Graz' most interesting and the largest of its kind in Austria.

Künstlerhaus Graz GALLERY
(☑0316-74 00 84; www.km-k.at; Burgring 2; adult/child €4/2; ◉10am-6pm Tue-Sun, to 8pm Thu) The city's edgiest contemporary art institution presents a program of installation, performance and video from international names and emerging Styrian artists. Set in the green of the Stadtpark, it's also an impressive piece of modernist architecture – a 1952 Leo Scheu – that was given a contemporary renovation in 2013. Look out for launches, films and performances on Thursday nights from 6pm.

Burg CASTLE, PARK
(Hofgasse; ☐30 Schauspielhaus, ☐1, 3, 4, 5, 6, 7 Hauptplatz) **FREE** Graz' 15th-century Burg today houses government offices. At the far end of the courtyard, on the left under the arch, is an ingenious double staircase (1499) – the steps diverge and converge as they spiral. It adjoins the city's green space, Stadtpark.

Mausoleum of Ferdinand II MAUSOLEUM
(www.domgraz.at; Burggasse 2; adult/child €6/2; ☉10.30am-12.30pm & 1.30-4pm Tue & Fri Jan-Apr, daily May-Dec; 🚊1, 3, 4, 5, 6, 7 Hauptplatz) The mannerist-baroque Mausoleum of Ferdinand II was designed by Italian architect Pietro de Pomis and begun in 1614; after Pomis' death the mausoleum was completed by Pietro Valnegro, while Johann Bernhard Fischer von Erlach chipped in with the exuberant stuccowork and frescoes inside. Ferdinand (1578–1637), his wife and his son are interred in the crypt.

Museum im Palais MUSEUM
(www.museum-joanneum.at; Sackstrasse 16; adult/child €9/3; ☉10am-5pm Wed-Sun; 🚊1, 3, 4, 5, 6 ,7 Hauptplatz) The revamped Museum im Palais is housed inside the baroque Palais Herberstein, which has an elegant staircase dating from 1757 and rooms that more than do justice to the exhibits on the theme of 'status symbols'. This takes in a permanent exhibition of treasures, including a carriage used by Friedrich III, dating from the mid-15th century, and special exhibitions.

Grazmuseum MUSEUM
(www.grazmuseum.at; Sackstrasse 18; adult/child €5/free; ☉10am-5pm Wed-Mon; 🚊1, 3, 4, 5, 6, 7 Hauptplatz) This small museum has a permanent collection featuring objects from city history, complemented by changing exhibitions. The main exhibition floors were closed for renovation at time of writing.

Museum der Wahrnehmung MUSEUM
(Museum of Perception; www.muwa.at; Friedrichgasse 41; adult/child €3.50/2, samadhi bath €45.60; ☉1-6pm Wed-Mon; 🚊34, 34E Museum der Wahrnehmung) Exploring sensory illusions, the Museum of Perception features a small changing exhibition of art works that have a close (or sometimes distant) relationship to perception, as well as gadgets that help you explore illusion for yourself. The samadhi, or meditative bath, is a therapeutic bath that deprives the body of all sensory input (book at least a week ahead, 16-year-olds and over only).

Joanneumsviertel NOTABLE BUILDING
(www.museum-joanneum.at) This historic building contains a number of museums, including the Neue Galerie Graz and the Naturkundemuseum, along with a couple of recently redesigned public spaces that are used for summer events.

Mur River & Around

★**Kunsthaus Graz** GALLERY
(www.kunsthausgraz.at; Lendkai 1; adult/child €9/3; ☉10am-5pm Tue-Sun; 🚊1, 3, 6, 7 Südtiroler Platz) Designed by British architects Peter Cook and Colin Fournier, this world-class contemporary-art space is known as the 'friendly alien' by locals. The building is signature Cook, a photovoltaic-skinned sexy biomorphic blob that is at once completely at odds with its pristine historic surroundings but sits rather lyrically within in it as well. Exhibitions change every three to four months.

Murinsel BRIDGE
(🚻; 🚊4, 5 Schlossplatz/Murinsel, 🚊1, 3, 6, 7 Südtiroler Platz) Murinsel is a constructed island-cum-bridge of metal and plastic in the middle of the Mur. This modern floating landmark contains a cafe, a kids' playground and a small stage. Even if you don't stop in, it's a great little detour that brings you up close to the fast-flowing river.

Schlossberg

★**Schlossberg** VIEWPOINT
(1hr ticket for lift or funicular €2.10, lift adult/child €1.40/0.90; 🚊4, 5 Schlossbergplatz) **FREE** Rising to 473m, Schlossberg is the site of the original fortress where Graz was founded and is marked by the city's most visible icon – the Uhrturm. Its wooded slopes can be reached by a number of bucolic and strenuous paths, but also by lift or Schlossbergbahn funicular. It's a brief walk or take tram 4 or 5 to Schlossplatz/Murinsel for the lift.

Uhrturm TOWER
(Clock Tower; 🚊4, 5 Schlossplatz/Murinsel (for lift)) **FREE** Perched on the southern edge of Schlossberg is the city's emblem, the Uhrturm. So beloved is the clock tower (which in its present form dates back to the 1560s), the townsfolk paid Napoleon a ransom of 2987 florins and 11 farthings to spare it during his 1809 invasion.

Volkskundemuseum MUSEUM
(www.museum-joanneum.at; Paulustorgasse 13a; adult/child €7/2.50; ☉2-6pm Wed-Sun late-Mar–Dec; 🚊30 Paulustor, 🚊1, 3, 4, 5, 6, 7 Hauptplatz) The Folk Life Museum is devoted to folk art and social history. Highlights include 2000 years of traditional clothing in an exhibition that brings together ways of life with clothing and belief.

⊙ Eggenberg

Schloss Eggenberg
PALACE

(www.museum-joanneum.at; Eggenberger Allee 90; adult/child €11.50/5.50; ☺ tours hourly 10am-4pm, apart from 1pm Tue-Sun late Mar-Oct, exhibitions 10am-5pm Wed-Sun; ☒1 Schloss Eggenberg) Graz' elegant palace was created for the Eggenberg dynasty in 1625 by Giovanni Pietro de Pomis (1565–1633) at the request of Johann Ulrich (1568–1634). Admission is on a highly worthwhile guided tour during which you learn about the idiosyncrasies of each room, the stories told by the frescoes and about the Eggenberg family itself.

Johann Ulrich rose from ordinariness to become governor of Inner Austria in 1625, at a time when Inner Austria was a powerful province that included Styria, Carinthia, and parts of Slovenia and northern Italy. His baroque palace was built on a Gothic predecessor (which explains an interesting Gothic chapel in one section of the palace, viewed from a glass cube) and has numerous features of the Italian Renaissance, such as the magnificent courtyard arcades.

The guided tour (available in English or German) takes you through the 24 *Prunkräume* (staterooms), which, like everything else in the palace and gardens, are based on astronomy, the zodiac, and classical or religious mythology. The tour ends at Planet Hall, which is a riot of white stuccowork and baroque frescoes. You'll need to buy a Joanneum ticket if you also want to visit the museums.

Schloss Eggenberg Museums
MUSEUM

(Alte Galerie & Museums; ☏ 0316-8017 9560; www.museum-joanneum.at/alte-galerie; Eggenberger Allee 90; adult/child €9/3; ☺ 10am-5pm Wed-Sun Apr-Oct, to 4pm Wed-Sun Nov-Dec, closed Jan-Mar; ☒1 Schloss Eggenberg) Graz' Schloss Eggenberg and park grounds are home to an ensemble of excellent museums, including the **Alte Galerie** (Old Gallery), with its outstanding collection of paintings from the Middle Ages to the baroque. Also very worthwhile are the **Archaeological Museum** housing relics from pre-history to classical times, and the **Coin Collection**.

Just a few of the highlights in the Alte Galerie are works by Lucas Cranach der Ältere, Martin Johann Schmidt and Pieter Brueghel the Younger. In a clever touch, each room has been individually coloured to highlight and complement the dominant

ⓘ GRAZ' MUSEUMS

Most of Graz' museums are under the umbrella of the Universalmuseum Joanneum with almost 20 locations throughout the city. Three museums are located inside the Joanneumviertel complex, an interesting and eye-catching building that is partially below ground.

Admission with a **24-hour ticket** (adult/child/family €13/4.50/26) allows you to visit the entire museum ensemble over two days (but within 24 hours). The major sites are **Schloss Eggenberg** (p185), **Kunsthaus Graz** (p184), **Landeszeughaus** (p183), **Museum im Palais** (p184), and **Naturkundemuseum** (p182) and the **Neue Galerie Graz** (p181), the latter two both in the Joanneumsviertel.

An alternative is the **48-hour ticket** (adult/child/family €19/7/38), available from any of the museums. Family tickets, valid for two adults and children under 14, also offer significant discounts.

tones of the paintings displayed in them. While the Coin Collection is more of eclectic interest (magnifying glasses on the case help to see the coins close up), the Archaeology Museum houses the exceptional Strettweg Chariot and a bronze mask, both dating from the 7th century BC, as well as a collection of Roman finds in the province.

Schloss Eggenberg Parkland
GARDENS

(www.museum-joanneum.at; Eggenberger Allee 90, Schloss Eggenberg; adult/child €2/free; ☺ 8am-7pm Apr-Oct, to 5pm Nov-Mar; ☒1 Schloss Eggenberg) Lending Graz' Schloss Eggenberg broad splashes of green, these palace gardens are a relaxing place for whiling away the time amid squawking peacocks and deer that roam among Roman stone reliefs. The Planetengarten is based on the same Renaissance theme of planets you find inside the palace itself.

Planetengarten
GARDENS

(Planet Garden; www.museum-joanneum.at; Eggenberger Allee 90, Schloss Eggenberg; ☺ 8am-7pm Apr-Oct, to 5pm Nov-Mar) The Planetengarten is a contemporary realisation of a Renaissance astronomical garden by artist Helga Tornquist. It's located within the Schloss Eggenberg Parkland.

STYRIA GRAZ

GUIDED TOURS

Graz Tourismus (p192) offers a number of walking tours (€10.50/6 per adult/child) in German and English at 2.30pm daily from May to October and at 2.30pm Saturdays from November to April. Also ask about its weekend day trips around Graz, or pick up its multilingual audio guide, using a handheld computer (€7.50/8.50 for two/four hours).

◉ Outside the City Centre

Bundesgestüt Piber　　　　HORSE STUD
(Piber Stud Farm; www.piber.com; Piber 1, Köflach; tours adult/child €12/7.50; ⊙tours 10am, 11am & hourly 1-4pm Apr-Oct, 11am & 2pm Nov-Mar; P ♿) West of Graz is the village of Piber, home to the world-famous Lipizzaner stallion stud farm. Originally the farm was based in Lipica (Slovenia), but was moved here when Slovenia was annexed after WWI. About 40 to 50 foals are born at the farm every year, but of these only about five stallions have the right stuff to be sent for training to the Spanische Hofreitschule (Spanish Riding School) in Vienna.

In summer, you have the choice of a do-it-yourself tour using a sheet map, using the free multilingual audioguide (deposit €10) or taking a fully fledged tour (tours only in winter).

To get to Piber from Graz, the most convenient weekday option is to catch the GKB (p192) morning bus No 700 at 8am from Graz' Griesplatz, arriving in Piber at 9.15am (you have to change to connecting bus 705 at Voitsberg Hauptplatz). The last bus leaves Piber at 4.57pm. Frequent trains also go to Köflach (€10.20, one hour), from where it's a 3.5km walk or taxi ride from Hauptplatz along Piberstrasse (follow the signs).

Österreichisches
Freilichtmuseum　　　　MUSEUM
(Austrian Open-Air Museum; www.freilichtmuseum. at; adult/child/family €10/5/28; ⊙9am-5pm Tue-Sun Apr-Oct) Located some 15km northeast of Graz and consisting of about 100 Austrian farmstead buildings, the Austrian Open-Air Museum in Stübing is ideal for a family outing. The museum is about a 20-minute walk from the Stübing train station; turn left out of the train station and pass over the tracks, then under them before reaching the entrance. Hourly trains make the journey from Graz (€4.30, 15 minutes).

FRida & FreD　　　　MUSEUM
(www.fridaundfred.at; Friedrichgasse 34; one exhibition adult/child/family €5/5/14.50; ⊙9am-5pm Mon, Wed & Thu, to 7pm Fri, 10am-5pm Sat & Sun; ♿; 🚋 34, 34E Museum der Wahrnehmung) This small but fun-packed museum is aimed at kids aged three to 12, and hosts two exhibitions, one for children from three to seven years, and a second for children from eight years and older. Both focus educationally and interactively on how animals and humans create their homes and houses. It also has some great workshops and theatre.

🏃 Activities

Fairytale Express　　　　RAIL
(Schlossberg Cave Railway; www.grazermaerchenbahn.at; Schlossbergplatz; adult/child €8.50/6.50; ⊙10am-5pm, closed first Mon of the month; ♿; 🚋 4, 5 Schlossbergplatz/Murinsel) The Fairytale Express is the longest grotto railway in Europe. The trip, taking around 35 minutes, winds its way around fairy-tale scenes through tunnels once used as a safe haven from the allied bombings during WWII. Recommended for children four and over; the temperature within the hill is between 8°C and 12°C, so make sure you wear suitable clothing.

★★ Festivals & Events

Graz has a very lively cultural life with a number of festivals throughout the year.

La Strada Graz　　　　CULTURAL
(www.lastrada.at; ⊙late Jul–early Aug) An outdoor summer arts festival with street theatre, dance, puppet theatre and 'nouveau cirque'.

Stadtfest　　　　MUSIC
(www.grazerstadtfest.at; ⊙early Jul) Renaissance courtyards are transformed into raucous stages for rock and classical music for the weekend.

Styriarte　　　　MUSIC
(📞0316-82 50 00; www.styriarte.com; ⊙Jun & Jul) Classical festival featuring almost continuous concerts. Some concerts are held in Renaissance courtyards and are free.

Steirischer Herbst CLASSICAL MUSIC, PERFORMANCE
(www.steirischerbst.at; ⊙Oct) An ambitious, sometimes edgy festival of new music, theatre and film, plus exhibitions and art installations.

📖 Sleeping

Hotel Daniel
HOTEL $

(📞0316-71 10 80; www.hoteldaniel.com; Europaplatz 1; d €65-350; P❄@🛜; 🚍1, 3, 6, 7 Hauptbahnhof) The Daniel's rooms are well designed and super simple, and while its small 'smart' rooms scrape into budget territory, it also now offers the super exclusive loft cube on the roof if you're looking for something out of the ordinary. The lobby area is a lot of fun, a great space to work or just hang out.

Hotel Strasser
HOTEL $

(📞0316-71 39 77; www.hotelstrasser.at; Eggenberger Gürtel 11; s/d €65/75; P@🛜; 🚍1, 3, 6, 7 Hauptbahnhof) Hotel Strasser's well-priced rooms have parquetry floors and high ceilings; some, including the single, are cosily wood-lined. Breakfast is not usually included in the quoted price and costs €9.

★Hotel Wiesler
HOTEL $$

(📞0316-70 66-0; www.hotelwiesler.com; Grieskai 4; d €155-210; P@; 🚍1, 3, 6, 7 Südtiroler Platz) The riverside Wiesler, a *Jugenstil* (art nouveau) gem from 1901, has been recently transformed into Graz' most glamorous hotel. Hotelier Florian Weltzer has shaken up everything, including the notion of room categories, and ensured that this is a luxury experience that is far from stuffy.

Rooms may have a wall left stripped bare, offset by a dramatic black chandelier, a freestanding bath nestled in a bay window, or a bedhead bookshelf complete with classic typewriter. Breakfast is still served under the *Spring* mosaic by Leopold Forstner – a scholar of Koloman Moser and friend of Gustav Klimt – while next door, in the Speisesaal restaurant, young street artist Josef Wurm's mural graces the 4.3-meter-high hall. Special.

★Schlossberg Hotel
HOTEL $$

(📞0316-80 70-0; www.schlossberg-hotel.at; Kaiser-Franz-Josef-Kai 30; s €140, d €155-185; P@🛜❄; 🚍4, 5 Schlossbergbahn) Central but just removed from the action, four-star Schlossberg is blessed with a prime location tucked below its namesake. Rooms are well sized, individually decorated and have an eccentric elegance. The hotel brings together three historic buildings so even the architecture is gently idiosyncratic. A small rooftop pool and vertiginous terraced garden make a stay here completely memorable.

Augarten Hotel
HOTEL $$

(📞0316-20 800; www.augartenhotel.at; Schönaugasse 53; s €125-165, d €155-200; P❄🛜❄; 🚍4, 5 Finanzamt) Augarten is decorated with the owner's private art collection, which includes works by Maria Lassnig, Franz West and Martin Kippenberger. All rooms are bright and modern, and have something of a masculine edge, though not overbearingly so. The larger rooms are worth it, with windows on two walls in some and a luxurious spaciousness.

Hotel Weitzer
HOTEL $$

(📞0316-70 30; www.hotelweitzer.com; Grieskai 12; d €115-165; P@🛜; 🚍1, 3, 6, 7 Südtiroler Platz) A big, busy but friendly hotel that retains its family-run origins, rooms here are decorated in a crisp, smart style. The hotel's lovely old bones banish the bland. There are good eating options on site, and there are sauna and fitness facilities.

Hotel Erzherzog Johann
HOTEL $$

(📞0316-81 16 16; www.erzherzog-johann.com; Sackstrasse 3-5; s €134, d €169-189; P⊖🛜; 🚍1, 3, 6, 7 Hauptplatz) A fabulously old-fashioned hotel, with swaggy curtains, parquet floors and loyal repeat visitors. Weekend deals and lower-demand periods are especially good value.

The hotel has a handful of curious theme rooms. These include the Wanda-Sacher-Masoch-Suite – named for the wife of writer Leopold von Sacher-Masoch, from whom we get the term *masochism* – a quaintly traditional room with no furs or whips in sight,

---

GRAZ FOR CHILDREN

With its green spaces, playgrounds and relaxed atmosphere, Graz is made for children. The creation of **FRida & FreD** (p186), Graz's first museum devoted to children, makes it even better. This small but fun-packed museum is aimed at kids up to the age of 12, and hosts workshops, exhibitions and theatre. It has loads of hands-on tasks and interactive displays.

The **Schlossberg Cave Railway** (p186), the longest grotto railway in Europe, is another highlight for the little 'uns. The 20-minute-long railway ride takes you past fairy-tale scenes in tunnels once used as refuge from Allied bombings during WWII.

or the Kaiser Maximilian Room where you can sleep in the ill-fated Habsburg's own made-in-Mexico bed.

Gasthof-Pension zur Steirer-Stub'n
GUESTHOUSE $$

(☎0316-71 68 55; www.pension-graz.at; Lendplatz 8; s €59-89, d €104-164; P 🛜; 🚌58, 58E, 63 Lendplatz, 🚊1, 3, 6, 7 Südtiroler Platz) This laid-back inn combines the best of a traditional atmosphere with a fresh, bright feel, complemented by features such as tiled floors in the corridors, indoor plants and lots of pine. There are patios outside many of the good-sized rooms overlooking Lendplatz.

Hotel zum Dom
HOTEL $$

(☎0316-82 48 00; www.domhotel.co.at; Bürgergasse 14; s €80-125, d €115-145; P ❄🛜🚗; 🚊30 Palais Trauttmansdorff/Urania, 🚊1, 3, 4, 5, 6, 7 Hauptplatz) Ceramics and other objects feature throughout the Hotel zum Dom, whose individually furnished rooms are traditional but far from bland. Bonus: they come either with steam/power showers or whirlpools; one even has a terrace whirlpool.

Hotel 3 Raben
HOTEL $$

(☎0316-71 26 86; www.dreiraben.at; Annenstrasse 43; s €80-90, d €105-125; P ❄🛜; 🚊1, 3, 6, 7 Esperantoplatz/Arbeiterkammer) This business hotel is conveniently located near the main train station and is easy if you're arriving by train. Rooms are nicely sized and comfortable, and can be discounted generously.

JUFA Graz
HOSTEL $$

(☎0316-70 83 210; www.jufa.eu/jufa-graz-city; Idlhofgasse 74; s €60, d €85; P ❄@🛜; 🚊31, 32, 33 Lissagasse) This clean and comfortable HI hostel is located about 800m south of the main train station and can be easily reached by bus from Jakominiplatz. No dorms, but there are 4-person rooms that make the rates more affordable.

Hotel Feichtinger Graz
HOTEL $$

(☎0316-72 41 00; www.hotel-feichtinger.at; Lendplatz 1a; s €61-75, d €108-145; P ⊖🛜; 🚊1, 3, 6, 7 Südtiroler Platz) This Graz business hotel offers some of the best-value beds in town. Rooms are spacious and simple and the suites and apartments are a particularly good deal.

✖ Eating

Given the official title of Genuss Haupstadt or 'capital of culinary delight' in 2008, Graz has a wonderful culinary scene with some great upmarket choices doing modern regional

cooking. Its hungry student population also means there's some great international and Asian cheapies and a vibrant coffee scene. Hofgasse's Italian quarter, with its terrace seating, serves up both good Italian cooking and a Mediterranean conviviality.

Mau Shi
ASIAN $

(☎0660 696 24 17; Herrengasse 7; mains €5.50-12; ⊙11.30am-midnight Mon-Sat, to 10pm Sun; 🛜) A fascinating series of interconnecting rooms decorated like your favourite share house makes up this friendly place, with tables spilling out into the pretty alleyway in summer. Young Graz comes here to feast on spring rolls, green curry and Indonesian salads along with big fruity cocktails and organic beer. Spice levels are authentic and there's a generous use of fresh herbs.

Kunsthauscafé
INTERNATIONAL $

(☎0316-71 49 57; www.kunsthauscafe.co.at; Südtirolerplatz 2; mains €6-16.50; ⊙9am-11pm Sun-Thu, to 1am Fri & Sat) A happy, young crowd fills the long tables here for a menu that incorporates burgers (from big beef to goat cheese), vaguely Mexican dishes, main-sized salads and the house special 'Styrian Sandwich', a combination of crispy pork belly, creamy sauerkraut and horseradish. It's very, very loud, but fun if you're in the mood.

Ginko Green Høuse
HEALTH FOOD $

(Herrengasse 7; daily meal €5.80, soup €4; ⊙8.30am-7pm Mon-Sat) The best spot in Graz if you're in need of a non-pastry breakfast (hello chia bowl!), a smoothie or bowl of soup. You can sit in or takeaway. And yes, they actually do pastries too, including a few gluten-free options.

Mangolds
VEGETARIAN $

(www.mangolds.at; Griesgasse 11; meals €6-12; ⊙11am-7pm Mon-Fri, to 4pm Sat; 🍴♿; 🚊1, 3, 6, 7 Südtiroler Platz) 🌿 Tasty vegetarian patties, rice dishes and more than 40 different salads are served at this pay-by-weight vegetarian cafeteria. It's an appealing place to while away a few hours over coffee and cake too.

★Aiola Upstairs
INTERNATIONAL $$

(www.aiola.at; Schlossberg 2; pasta €14.50-16.50, mains €19.50-27.50; ⊙9am-midnight Mon-Sat; 🛜; 🚊4, 5 Schlossbergplatz/Murinsel (for lift)) Ask locals for the best outdoor dining experience in Graz, and they'll direct you to Aiola. This wonderful restaurant on Schlossberg has great views from both its glass box interior and its beautiful summer terrace. Even better, the cooking up here is some of the city's best, with interesting international flavours and seasonal ingredients.

★ Der Steirer
AUSTRIAN, TAPAS $$

(✍0316-70 36 54; www.dersteirer.at; Belgiergasse 1; weekday lunch menu €8.90, mains €10.90-22; ☉11am-midnight; ✍; ⊠1, 3, 6, 7 Südtiroler Platz) This neo-*Beisl* (bistro pub) and wine bar has a beautiful selection of Styrian dishes, including a great goulash, lamb cutlets and stuffed peppers, all done in a simple, contemporary style. Its Styrian tapas concept works, and is a nice way to sample local flavours if you just feel like nibbling.

★ Santa Clara
ITALIAN $$

(✍0316-81 18 22; Bürgerasse 6; dinner €12-18; ☉5-10pm Tue-Fri) Santa Clara, an under-the-radar but long-beloved Graz favourite set in an ancient vaulted space, has loosened things up. Eschewing a regular menu structure, there's simply a nightly buffet of Italian-style antipasti. Teamed with a bowl of soup and a glass of wine, it makes for a satisfying dinner without the schnitzel bloat.

Thomawirt
BISTRO PUB $$

(✍0316-32 86 37; www.thomawirt.at; Leonhardstrasse 40-42; lunch menu €7 & €8, mains €9.20-13; ☉9am-1am; ✍❀; ⊠7 Merangasse) This neo-*Beisl* and pub in the uni quarter serves a lunch special weekdays from 11am, and other excellent lunch and dinner dishes ranging from Styrian classics to (expensive) steaks and vegetarian mains until 1am. Chill out with occasional music in the bar; the place is divided up into cafe, restaurant and lounge-bar areas.

Peppino im Hofkeller
ITALIAN $$

(✍0316-69 75 11; www.peppino-hofkeller.at; Hofgasse 8; mains €11-23; ☉noon-2.30pm & 5-11pm Tue-Sat; ⊠1, 3, 4, 5, 6, 7 Hauptplatz) This wine bar and restaurant is the perfect place for sipping from a large selection of Italian wines. Choose an authentic pasta or main dish from the blackboard; expect anything from octopus salad to porcini ravioli and venison from a small, changing menu. The owner-chef's roots in Lago Gardo show with some particularly lovely freshwater fish dishes.

Yamamoto
JAPANESE $$

(www.yamamoto-sushibar.at; Prokopigasse 4; mains €9-18; ☉noon-10pm Wed-Sat; ⊠1, 3, 4, 5, 6, 7 Hauptplatz) Yamamoto is a refreshingly authentic Japanese-owned restaurant. The sushi and sashimi are fresh and the noodles pull in a crowd.

★ Landhauskeller
AUSTRIAN $$$

(✍0316 83 02 76; www.landhaus-keller.at; Schmiedgasse 9; mains €17-34; ☉noon-1am Mon-Wed, to 2am Thu-Sat; ⊠1, 3 ,4, 5, 6, 7 Hauptplatz) What started as a spit-and-sawdust pub in the 16th century has evolved into a darkly atmospheric, super-stylish restaurant serving modern takes on Styrian specialities. Expect such creations as four different sorts of *Tafelspitz* (prime broiled beef), a simple grilled lake fish with chard, or an intriguing and delicious local take on tiramisu, using pumpkin seeds, pumpkin seed oil and macerated cherries.

Prato im Palais
AUSTRIAN $$$

(✍0316-23 20 98; www.prato.at; Sackstrasse 16; small/large degustation €69/98; ☉11am-midnight Mon-Sat; ⊠1, 3, 4, 5, 6, 7 Hauptplatz) Located inside Palais Herberstein, Prato combines a front bar and pretty courtyard for natural wines with fine dining restaurant. Prato's dishes are inspired by 19th-century chef Katharina Prato via her classic *Die Süddeutsche Küche* (The Southern German Kitchen). You can choose from a gourmet degustation or the 'home cooking' menu with Styrian dishes such as roast pork or trout.

El Gaucho
STEAK $$$

(✍0316-830 083; www.elgaucho.at/graz; Landhausgasse 1; mains €16-36; ☉5pm-11pm Mon-Fri, 11.30am-11pm Sat & Sun; ⊠1, 3 ,4, 5, 6, 7 Hauptplatz) Set inside the evocative Renaissance Landhaus building, El Gaucho seems like an unlikely place to feast on succulent Argentine and local steaks (with sides like truffle gnocchi that can be ordered as mains). The scene is lit in relaxing crimson and decorated with hanging glass bubbles, but in summer the best seats are in the buzzing courtyard.

🍷 Drinking & Nightlife

The cafe and bar scene in Graz is propelled by a healthy student crowd. Some cafes serve food and also change into bars as the night wears on. Most bars are concentrated in three areas: around the university, on Mehlplatz and Prokopigasse (dubbed the 'Bermuda Triangle'), and a third area stretching down to the market in Lend.

★ Promenade
CAFE

(www.promenade.aiola.at; Erzherzog-Johann-Allee 1; ☉9am-1am Mon-Thu, to 2am Fri & Sat, to midnight Sun; ⊠30 Schauspielhaus) Delightful Promenade is a Graz institution. Recently refurbished by the people behind the legendary

STYRIA GRAZ

FARMERS MARKETS & FOOD STANDS

➜ There are plenty of cheap eateries to be found near Graz University (trams 1 and 7), particularly on Halbärthgasse, Zinzendorfgasse and Harrachgasse.

➜ The freshest fruit and vegetables are at the farmers markets on **Kaiser-Josef-Platz** (⊘ 6am-noon Mon-Sat; 🚆 1, 7 Kaiser-Josef-Platz) and **Lendplatz** (⊘ 6am-1pm Mon-Sat; 🚆 1, 3, 6, 7 Südtiroler Platz), which also have brilliant little food stands every day.

➜ For fast-food stands, head for **Hauptplatz** (🚆 1, 3, 4, 5, 6, 7 Hauptplatz) and **Jakominiplatz** (🚆 1, 3, 4, 5, 6, 7, 13 Jakominiplatz).

Aiola, it's a pretty, modern take on the traditional coffee house. On a tree-lined avenue in the Stadtpark, it's the perfect place for weekend breakfasts – eggs or savoury plates – or for an afternoon spritz and a few of the smart little tapas-style dishes.

Freiblick Tagescafe ROOFTOP BAR
(📞 0316-83 53 02; freiblick.co.at; Sackstrasse 7-11, Kastner & Öhler; ⊘ 9.30am-7pm Mon-Fri, to 6pm Sat) This huge terrace cafe-bar tops the Kastner & Öhler department store and has the best view in the city. Enjoy the clouds and rooftops over breakfast platter and coffee or a lunchtime soup or salad. Or stop by in the afternoon for something from the Prosecco spritz menu or a Hugo Royal – Moët Chandon splashed with elderflower (€15).

Blendend COFFEE
(www.blendend.at; Mariahliferstrasse 24; ⊘ 4pm-2am Mon-Fri, from 9am Sat & Sun) A rambling, warm and endearingly boho addition to Lend's usual lineup of grungy bars, Blendend is a great drinking and snacking spot during the week and then turns all day cafe on weekends with beautiful homemade cakes and desserts competing with the spritzs and excellent local beers. In warmer weather all the action happens at the courtyard tables.

Buna COFFEE
(📞 0316-22 86 83; Schmiedgasse 11; ⊘ 8.30am-6.30pm Mon-Sat) Buna is one of Graz's upcoming independent coffee roasteries; this is its city centre cafe. Come for coffee chat and

expertly done flat whites, espressos and cold drip. You can takeaway or pull up a stool in the front window of this one-time shop.

Parkhouse BAR
(www.parkhouse.at; Stadtpark 2; ⊘ 10am-2am Mar-Oct, 9pm-2am Fri & Sat Nov-Feb) A super laid-back bar in a lovely rotunda-style building in the park, perfect for an early or late drink. Check the website for details of DJs or live music.

Operncafé CAFE
(www.operncafe.at; Opernring 22; coffee & cake €7; ⊘ 7.30am-11pm; 📞; 🚆 1, 3, 4, 5, 6, 7, 13 Jakominiplatz) This traditional cafe does old school beautifully with homemade pastries, lots of things to read and pleasant, suited waiters who have found a calling in life.

Tribeka COFFEE
(📞 0316-26 97 64; www.tribeka.at; Kaiserfeldgasse 6; ⊘ 7am-8pm Mon-Fri, from 8am Sat & Sun) This branch of the popular Graz chain is an early-morning coffee must if you're in need of 'good' coffee in the centre. Big windows and a raised streetside terrace fill up with freelancers and there's a good range of brownies, cheesecake and pastries for sustenance.

Süsse Luise CAFE
(Stand 9, Lendplatz; ⊘ 8am-11.30pm Mon-Sat) Farmers market Lendplatz does double duty in the the afternoons and evenings as one of Graz' most laid-back enclaves. This stall, with its tablecloths and charming staff, is a favourite for a spritz or local beer; it also does beautiful home-made cakes.

Postgarage CLUB
(www.postgarage.at; Dreihackengasse 42; ⊘ from 10pm Fri & Sat; 🚌 32, 33, 40 Griesplatz; 🚆 1, 3, 6, 7 Südtiroler Platz) Student-friendly retro theme nights and the occasional serious electronic night for happy 20-somethings. See the website for events and prices.

La Enoteca dei Ciclopi WINE BAR
(www.lenotecadeiciclopi.at; Sackstrasse 14; ⊘ 5-11pm Mon, 11.30am-11pm Tue-Fri, 10am-11pm Sat; 🚆 1, 3, 4, 5, 6, 7 Hauptplatz) This small wine bar with lovely courtyard tables is like stepping into a Sicilian home, with welcoming service and a range of excellent southern Italian wines. Stay for pasta or a plate of Sicilian antipasti.

Stockwerk Jazz JAZZ
(📞 0676 315 95 51; http://stockwerkjazz.mur.at; Jakominiplatz 18; concerts €12-18; ⊘ 4pm-1am Mon-Sat, to midnight Sun; 🚆 1, 3, 4, 5, 6, 7, 13 Jakominiplatz) In addition to being Graz' pre-

mier jazz bar-cum-pub for home-grown artists and international acts, this is also a great place to have a drink. It has rustic wooden features and a summer rooftop terrace.

Dom im Berg
CLUB

(www.spielstaetten.at; Schlossbergplatz; 🚋4, 5 Schlossplatz/Murinsel) The tunnels under Schlossberg were once used as air-raid shelters. Today, some of them have been refashioned into a large arts-clubbing venue. See the website for opening times and prices.

Exil
BAR

(Josefigasse 1; ⊙ 7.30pm-4am Tue-Sat; 🚋1, 3, 6, 7 Südtiroler Platz) Exil is a smoky indie bar with outdoor seating and a couple of turntables for Friday and Saturday nights. On busy nights, it's all taken onto the street.

Cafe Centraal
PUB

(www.centraal.at; Mariahilferstrasse 10; ⊙ 8am-2am; 🛜; 🚋1, 3, 6, 7 Südtiroler Platz) This traditional bar and *Beisl* with a dark-wood interior and outside seating has an alternative feel and super cheap eats from breakfast on.

p.p.c.
CLUB

(⌨ 0316-8141 4133; www.popculture.at; Neubaugasse 6; admission €8-10; ⊙ from 10pm Wed-Sat; 🚋4, 5 Kepplerbrücke) One of Graz' most popular dance places with a wide range of different nights each week.

Orange
BAR, CLUB

(www.cbo.at; Elisabethstrasse 30; ⊙ 9am-5am Wed-Sat, to 3am Mon & Tue, to 6pm Sun; 🚋7 Lichtenfelsgasse) A young, fashionable student crowd loves this place, which has a patio perfect for warm summer evenings. There's a small admission of around €5 from Wednesday to Saturday after 11pm, when there are DJs.

Insel Café
CAFE

(Murinsel; ⊙ 10am-midnight Mon-Fri, from 9.30am Sat & Sun; 🛜; 🚋4, 5 Schlossplatz/Murinsel) Grab a coffee or a spritz as the Mur splashes below your feet. Kids can entertain themselves in the play area while you kick back.

M1
COCKTAIL BAR

(www.m1-bar.at; Färberplatz 1, 3rd fl; ⊙ 4pm-2am Mon-Fri, from 9am Sat, to 11pm Sun; 🚋1, 3, 4, 5, 6, 7 Hauptplatz) M1 is a modern three-storey cafe-bar replete with rooftop terrace. Its spiral staircase can cause a few problems after a couple of the 200 or so cocktails on offer.

Kulturhauskeller
BAR, CLUB

(Elisabethstrasse 30; ⊙ 9pm-5am Tue-Sat; 🚋7 Lichtenfelsgasse) The brassy Kulturhauskeller

is a popular student hangout with a great cellar-pub feel and Wednesday karaoke night.

☆ Entertainment

To find out what's on where in the city, pick up a copy of the monthly *Megaphon* (€2.50, in German). For cinema listings, see www.uncut.at/graz.

Graz is an important cultural centre, hosting musical events throughout the year. **Theaterservice Graz** (⌨ 0316-80 00; www.theater-graz.com; Kaiser-Josef-Platz 10; ⊙ 9am-6pm Mon-Fri, to 1pm Sat, closed mid-Jul–mid-Aug; 🚋1, 7 Kaiser-Josef-Platz) is the ticket office for the Opernhaus and Schauspielhaus. It's also known for jazz: see Grazjazz (www.grazjazz.at) for upcoming events.

Opernhaus
OPERA

(www.theater-graz.com/oper; Kaiser-Josef-Platz 10; ⊙ closed early Jul–late Aug; 🚋1, 7 Kaiser-Josef-Platz) Graz' gold, white and red opera house. See website for performances and prices.

Schauspielhaus
THEATRE

(www.schauspielhaus-graz.com; Hofgasse 11; ⊙ closed early Jul–late Aug; 🚋30 Schauspielhaus, 🚋1, 3, 4, 5, 6, 7 Hauptplatz) Graz' main venue for theatre. See the website for dates and prices.

KIZ RoyalKino
CINEMA

(Conrad-von-Hötzendorf-Strasse 10; 🚋4, 5 Finanzamt) Screens English-language films.

🛍 Shopping

Hofbäckerei Edegger-Tax
FOOD

(www.hofbaeckerei.at; Hofgasse 6; ⊙ 7am-6pm Mon-Sat) The extravagantly carved neo-baroque oak facade of this historic bakery comes complete with a gold-plated double eagle above the entrance, testament to its one-time imperial patronage. Inside you'll find bread, the Styrian nutty-filled pastry *Panthertatzen* (panther's claw), as well as pumpkin seed and vanilla croissants and a cornucopia of sweet nutty biscuits. Everything is beautifully packaged.

VDB
SPICES, FOOD & DRINK

(www.vdb.co.at; Annenstrasse 25; ⊙ 10am-6pm Mon-Fri, 9am-1pm Sat) Manfred van den Berg has collected a wonderful assortment of spices as well as producing a couple of house-blend gins. Stock up on olive oils, chocolates, jams and pumpkin seed products.

Kastner & Öhler
DEPARTMENT STORE

(Sackstrasse 7-11; ⊙ 9.30am-7pm Mon-Fri, to 6pm Sat) Graz' main department store is the

STYRIA GRAZ

glamorous Kastner & Öhler, just north of Hauptplatz. There's a dedicated hiking and climbing section, with its own alpine cafe.

Buchhandlung Moser
BOOKS

(www.morawa-buch.at; Am Eisernen Tor 1; ⊙9am-6.30pm Mon-Fri, to 6pm Sat; 🚊1, 3, 4, 5, 6, 7, 13 Jakominiplatz) The main bookshop in town.

Steirisches Heimatwerk
CLOTHING

(🚩0316-82 71 06; www.heimatwerk.steiermark. at; Sporgasse 23; ⊙9.30am-6pm Mon-Fri, to 4pm Sat; 🚊1, 3, 4, 5, 6, 7 Hauptplatz) Austrians take their national dress very seriously and this is a well-respected supplier of beautifully crafted traditional kit, from *Dirndls* to alpine jumpers.

ℹ Information

Graz Airport Information Desk (🚩0316-29 02-172; www.flughafen-graz.at; ⊙5am-10pm) Facilities at the airport include an information desk, free internet terminals, and a bank with an ATM in arrivals.

Graz Tourismus (🚩0316-807 50; www.graz tourismus.at; Herrengasse 16; ⊙10am-7pm Apr-Oct & Dec, to 6pm Nov & Jan-Mar; phone line 10am-5pm; 🚩; 🚊1, 3, 4, 5, 6, 7 Hauptplatz) Graz' main tourist office, with loads of free information on the city and helpful and knowledgeable staff.

Hauptbahnhof Post Office (Hauptbahnhof; ⊙7am-8pm Mon-Fri, 8am-6pm Sat, 1-8pm Sun; 🚊1, 3, 6, 7 Hauptbahnhof) Located inside the main train station.

Main Post Office (Neutorgasse 46; ⊙8am-7pm Mon-Fri, 9am-noon Sat; 🚊1, 3, 4, 5, 6, 7, 13 Jakominiplatz)

ℹ Getting There & Away

AIR

Graz Airport (GRZ; 🚩0316-290 20; www. flughafen-graz.at) is 10km south of the town centre, just beyond the A2 and connected by train and bus with the Hauptbahnhof. Direct connections with Graz include to/from Berlin Tegel with **Air Berlin** (www.airberlin.com), Frankfurt am Main with **Lufthansa** (🚩0810 1025 8080; www.lufthansa.com), Zürich with **InterSky** (www.flyintersky.com), Rome with **Alitalia** (www.alitalia.com), Glasgow and Exeter in the UK with **Niki** (www.flyniki.com), inland flights to Vienna with **Austrian Airlines** (🚩05 1766 1000; www.austrian.com) and Niki, and with many other German cities on Austrian Airlines.

Facilities at the airport include an **information desk**, free internet terminals and wi-fi inside the security zone, and a bank with an ATM in arrivals on the ground floor.

BUS

Postbus (🚩05 17 17, 050 678 910; www. postbus.at) services depart from outside the Hauptbahnhof and from **Andreas-Hofer-Platz** (Andreas-Hofer-Platz) to all parts of Styria. Frequent direct **GKB buses** (🚩0316-59 87-0; www.gkb.at) run to Bärnbach (€8.60, 50 minutes) daily, and indirect buses to Piber (€9.20, 80 minutes) several times each day from Monday to Friday. All leave from Griesplatz. Six direct ÖBB buses daily (€28.60, two hours) leave for Klagenfurt from the Hauptbahnhof.

CAR RENTAL

Companies include **Avis** (🚩0316-81 29 20; www.avis.com; Reinighausstrasse 66), **Hertz** (🚩0316-82 50 07; www.hertz.com; Andreas-Hofer-Platz 1), which also has an office at the airport, and **MegaDrive** (🚩050 105 4130; www. megadrive.at).

Note that much of Graz is a *Kurzparkzone* (short-term parking zone); tickets are available from parking machines (€0.60 per 30 minutes, maximum three hours).

TRAIN

Trains to Vienna depart hourly (€37.30, 2½ hours), and five daily go to Salzburg (€48, four hours). All trains running north or west go via Bruck an der Mur (€12, 45 minutes, every 20 minutes), a main railway junction with more frequent services. Trains to Klagenfurt (€39, 2¾ to 3½ hours, seven daily) require a change in Leoben, or in Bruck an der Mur and again in Friesach (check with the conductor).

International direct train connections from Graz include Zagreb (€38, four hours), Ljubljana (€41, 3½ hours), Szentgotthárd (€14, 1½ hours) and Budapest (€70, 5½ hours).

ℹ Getting Around

BICYCLE

Rental is available from **Bicycle** (🚩0316-82 13 57; www.bicycle.at; Körösistrasse 5; per 24hr €10, Fri-Mon €16, per week €49; ⊙7am-1pm & 2-6pm Mon-Fri). **Mobilzentral** (p181) has city rental bicycles for €10 per day or €40 per week; **Radstation am Hauptbahnhof** (http://grazbike. at; Europaplatz 4; per ½day €5-10, 24hr €10-22, week €39-55; ⊙8am-11.45am & 12.45-5pm) has bike hire outside the main train station.

PUBLIC TRANSPORT

Graz has one zone (zone 101). Single tickets (€2.10) for buses and trams are valid for one hour, but you're usually better off buying a 24-hour pass (€4.70). Ten one-zone tickets cost €19.20, and weekly/monthly passes cost €12.70/42.60. Hourly and 24-hour tickets can be purchased from the driver; other passes can be purchased from *Tabak* (tobacconist) shops, pavement ticket machines or the tourist office.

TRAM

Trams 1, 3, 6 and 7 connect Jakominiplatz with the Hauptbahnhof every five to 20 minutes from around 4.45am to early evening Monday to Saturday. After that trams 1 and 7 do the run alone until services end just before midnight.

AROUND GRAZ

Bärnbach

📞 03142 / POP 5250

Otherwise unremarkable, Bärnbach is famous for its St Barbara Kirche, a church redesigned by Friedensreich Hundertwasser.

⊙ Sights

St Barbara Kirche   CHURCH
(Piberstrasse; ⊙ dawn-dusk) **FREE** Despite its post-war origin, St Barbara Kirche was in need of renovating in the late 1980s. Local citizens voted to commission the maverick Viennese artist Friedensreich Hundertwasser to undertake the redesign; work began in 1987 and was completed in 1988. It is a visual treat of bright colours and glistening copper dome. Leave a donation and pick up the explanation card in English, which reveals the rich symbolism behind the architectural features.

ℹ Information

Bärnbach Information (📞 03142-615 50; www.baernbach.at; Hauptplatz 1; ⊙ 8-11.30am Tue, Wed & Fri, 8-11.30am & 2-4.30pm Mon & Thu) Tourist information is available from the glass-making centre and Bärnbach Information inside the town hall.

ℹ Getting There & Away

Hourly trains run from Graz (€7.60, 50 minutes). The train station is 2.5km south of the church. Follow Bahnhofweg and Neue Landstrasse (turn right) to Piberstrasse. A **taxi** (📞 0664 340 22 47) to the centre of town costs about €7.

SOUTHERN STYRIA

Southern Styria is known as *Steirische Toskana* (Styrian Tuscany), and for good reason. Not only is this wine country, but the landscape is reminiscent of Chianti; gentle rolling hills cultivated with vineyards or patchwork farmland, dotted with small forests where deer roam. It's also famous for *Kürbiskernöl*, the rich pumpkin-seed oil generously used in Styrian cooking.

Deutschlandsberg

📞 03462 / POP 8200

In the heart of the Schilcher wine region, Deutschlandsberg is a bustling little town dominated by a well-restored castle, some 25 minutes' walk uphill from the town centre. Inside the castle is a **museum** (www.burgmuseum.at; Burgplatz 2; adult/child €9/4; ⊙ 10am-6pm Tue-Sun Apr-Oct) with exhibits on ancient history, the Celts, historical weapons and antique jewellery. The extensive collection, whose highlights include a delicate gold necklace from the 5th century BC, takes about 1½ hours to see. As with any good castle, there's a torture chamber in the underground vaults.

⊨ Sleeping

Burg Hotel   HOTEL $$
(📞 03462-56 56-0; www.burghotel-dl.at; Burgplatz 1; s €68, d €128-142; P 🅟 🛜) For sleeping arrangements, look no further than the Burg Hotel, which is located in the castle. Its crowning glory is the tower suite (€250 per night), which comes with complimentary champagne; rooms aren't exactly stylish but are sweetly fancy, large, peaceful and have views of the woods.

JUFA Hotel Deutschlandsberg   HOSTEL $$
(📞 05 7083-260; www.jufa.eu/jufa-deutschlandsberg-sport-resort; Burgstrasse 5, Deutschlandsberg; s/d €53/87; P 🅟 🛜) If you're on a budget, this hostel is a good option. It's set in a vineyard at the foot of the castle.

ℹ Information

Region Süd und West Steiermark (📞 03462-431 52; www.sws.st; Hauptplatz 36, Deutschlandsberg) Region Süd und West Steiermark handles telephone, email and postal enquiries for western and southern Styria.

Tourist Office (📞 03462-75 20; www.schilcherland-deutschlandsberg.at; Hauptplatz 34; ⊙ 9am-4pm Mon-Fri, 9am-noon Sat Mar-Oct, 9am-1pm Mon-Fri Nov-Feb) A good source of information on the town and environs.

ℹ Getting There & Away

Hourly trains (€10.20, one hour) connect Graz and Deutschlandsberg.

STYRIA BÄRNBACH

Ehrenhausen

📞 03453 / POP 1060

The picturesque town of Ehrenhausen, near the A9 connecting Graz with the Slovenian border, makes a fine base for exploring the vineyards of southern Styria.

The town is little more than one street of pastel-coloured houses dominated by the baroque **Pfarrkirche** (Hauptplatz; ☉ dawn-dusk). Before setting off for the wine country, you can follow the path (about three minutes' walk) on the right of the *Rathaus* up to the yellow and white **mausoleum** of Ruprecht von Eggenberg (1546–1611), hero of the Battle of Sisak against the Turks.

🛏 Sleeping

⭐ **Loisium Südsteiermark**   HOTEL, SPA $$$
(📞 03453-288 00; www.loisium-suedsteiermark.at; Am Schlossberg 1a, Ehrenhausen; r €215-270; P 🛜 🏊) A sister hotel to the original Loisium resort in the Kamptal, Loisium Südsteiermark ups the luxury ante in the south. Contemporary architecture, simple and stylish rooms, vineyard views and a seriously relaxing Aveda spa make this a hard place to leave but a delicious place to come back to after a hard day of wine tasting.

🛍 Shopping

Genuss Regal Vinofaktur   WINE
(📞 03453-406 77-0; www.genussregal.at; An der Mur 13, Vogau; ☉ 9am-7pm) While the Weinstrasse can seem impossibly rustic in places, this gourmet superstore is symbolic of Styria's rising status as a food and wine mecca. With its collection of precariously stacked shipping containers, it's certainly hard to miss. If you're short on time for cellar door

---

ℹ CYCLING THE WINE ROADS

Velovital (Gut Pössnitzberg; 📞 03454-205; www.velovital.com; Hauptplatz 2; from €19.50 per day; ☉ 9am-6pm) has an e-bike hire point in Leutschach at the tourist office. Pick-up is from 9am to noon and return between 5pm and 6pm daily. Other local pick-up points include **Gut Pössnitzberg** (p194). Reserve using online or by telephone. For touring bikes, you're better off hiring from **Bicycle** (p192) in Graz, taking the train to Ehrenhausen and setting out from there.

---

visits, you can stock up on most of the local producers here.

ℹ Information

Tourist Office (📞 0664 857 04 08; www.ehrenhausen.at; ☉ 9am-6pm Thu-Fri, 9am-1pm Sat) Ask for its list of *Buschenschenken* and the opening times. It also has very comprehensive accommodation lists.

ℹ Getting There & Away

Hourly trains (€10.20, 45 minutes) run from Graz to Ehrenhausen. The train station is about four minutes' walk east of Hauptplatz.

Leutschach

📞 03454 / POP 580

Leutschach is home to some of Syria's best-known wine producers. It's less a village than a cluster of vineyards and cellar doors set among rolling hills and winding roads.

🛏 Sleeping

This little rural town and the surrounding countryside have a number of places to stay from upmarket resort style places to family-run guesthouses.

Gut Pössnitzberg   HOTEL $$
(📞 03454-205; www.poessnitzberg.at; Pössnitz 168; s €80.50-99.50, d €140-198; P 🏊 🏊) Set on a particularly fetching bend of the road, this 'weinhotel' mixes contemporary architecture with Styrian style and hospitality. Rooms are designed for maximum relaxation with large bathrooms and the occasional in-room Jacuzzi; there's a beautiful elevated pool area.

Tscheppes Lang-Gasthof   HOTEL $$
(📞 03454-246; www.langgasthof-tscheppe.at; Hauptplatz 6; s €64-67, d €94-106; P 🏊 🛜) A popular four-star hotel with spa facilities, known for its herbal bath filled with hops (this is also a big hop-growing district). The restaurant (mains €9.80 to €21.50) is well-regarded.

🍷 Drinking

⭐ **Weingut Muster**   WINERY
(📞 03454-700 53; www.weingutmuster.com; Schlossberg 38) Despite having something of a cultish international following for their biodynamic, natural wines, Maria and Sepp Muster have one of the friendliest tasting rooms in the region. Come and talk terroir with Sepp in the pretty whitewashed cellar

STYRIAN WINE ROADS

The *Weinstrassen* (wine roads) of southern Styria comprise an idyllic bundle of winding roads crisscrossing a picturesque landscape that is reminiscent of Tuscany. The region is at its best about two weeks after the grape harvest (usually September), when *Sturm* (young wine) is sold. The **Weinlesefest** (Wine Harvest Festival; ☑ 03454-70 70 10; www. rebenland.at; tickets €12; ☉ late Sep–early Oct) takes place in Leutschach on the last week-end in September, with lots of wine and song.

The main towns in the region are Ehrenhausen, Gamlitz and Berghausen in the north, and the town of Leutschach in the west, less than 20km away but best reached via a serpentine route partly along the Slovenian border. Villages and clusters of vineyards rather than fully fledged towns dot the region, some of these offering picturesque and romantic places to stay overnight. Less rural accommodation is available in the Ehrenhausen. On weekends in September and October accommodation is usually booked out. During the week and at other times it's usually fine if you're flexible.

To explore further, from Leutschach a road veers left at the top of the main street. This leads to Eichberg-Trautenburg, a pretty region with numerous *Buschenschenken* (wine taverns) and narrow sealed roads. A walking trail (560) goes through forest, across meadows and partly alongside the road.

Regions along and south of the Alte Weinstrasse are more remote, while to the north the slopes of the Sausal range make for a very pretty patchwork of vines and small forests. Here too are a growing number of *Buschenschänke*, but often without the crowds.

and go for a walk through his vintage, and you'll feel better about the world.

ℹ Information

Tourist Office (☑ 03454-70 70 10; www.reben land.at; Hauptplatz 2, Leutschach; ☉ 9am-noon & 1-4pm Mon-Fri, 9am-noon Sat) Leutschach's tourist office has a free Freizeitkarte with hiking trails and *Buschenschenken* marked (opening times included). There are brochures and maps on racks outside when the office is closed.

ℹ Getting There & Away

You can take the train from Graz to Leibnitz (€6.50, 40 minutes), then bus it to Leutschach (€8.50, 45 minutes).

Riegersburg

☑ 03153 / POP 2490

Located 50km southeast of Graz at Riegersburg and perched on a 200m-high rocky outcrop, **Schloss Riegersburg** (☑ 03153-82 131; www.veste-riegersburg.at; Riegersburg 1; adult/child €12.50/7.50; ☉ 9am-6pm May-Sep, 10am-6pm Apr & Oct) is a hugely impressive 13th-century castle built for protection from invading Hungarians and Turks. Today it houses a **Hexenmuseum** on witchcraft, a **Burgmuseum** featuring the history of the Liechtenstein family, who acquired it in 1822, and an impressive collection of weapons. A **war memorial** is a reminder

of fierce fighting in 1945, when Germans occupying the castle were attacked by Russian troops.

A cable car on the north side whisks you up in 90 seconds (one-way €2.50).

🛏 Sleeping

Schloss Kapfenstein　　　HOTEL $$
(☑ 03157-300 30-0; www.schloss-kapfenstein. at; Kapfenstein 1; s €105-127, d €144-201; ℗ @) If you have your own transport, consider stopping in at the beautifully sited Schloss Kapfenstein, a hotel-restaurant 17km south of Riegersburg. Weekdays are least expensive; on weekends only Friday-to-Sunday packages are possible. The restaurant serves delightful Styrian cuisine in its outer courtyard overlooking the valley.

ℹ Information

Tourist Office (☑ 03153-86 70; www.riegers burg.com; Riegersburg 26; ☉ 8.30am-3pm Mon & Wed-Sat May-Oct, 8am-noon Mon & Wed-Fri Nov-Apr) For more information on the Schloss and other activities.

ℹ Getting There & Away

Frequent trains run from Graz to nearby Feldbach, and from there six weekday buses head for Riegersburg (€2.40, 20 minutes). The last bus back is at around 6pm; check before setting out.

The Sausal

This hilly region to the northwest of Ehrenhausen is a quieter and gentler alternative to the well-trodden wine routes. Its cellar doors often look over terraced vineyards from the top of a ridge, making for some beautifully elevated settings and tastings with a view.

✖ Eating

Gasthaus zum Schmeh   AUSTRIAN **$$**
(✆ 03456-220 33; www.gasthaus-zum-schmeh. at; Sausal 17, Pistorf; mains €15-22; ☺ 10am-10pm Wed-Fri, to 11pm Sat, to 6pm Sun) This welcoming, relaxed place has beautiful views from the terrace and windows. The cooking is less rustic than the surrounds, however, prepared with well-sourced local ingredients and with a lightness of touch, even traditionally rich dishes like calf's liver or sliced veal. Wines are well chosen and there are local beers for sunny afternoons.

★ T.O.M R   INTERNATIONAL **$$$**
(✆ 0660 400 87 34; tomr.at; Sankt Andrä im Sausal 1; 5-course lunch €68, 9-course lunch or dinner €99, Sunday brunch €45; ☺ 6.30-11pm Wed-Sat, 12.30-3pm Sat, 11am-3pm Sun) Celebrity chef Tom Reiderer's Leutschach restaurant was long South Styria's dining hotspot. He and wife Katrina have opened their new venture in a former rectory – a light, elegant fine dining room with a few upstairs rooms for overnight stays. Reiderer's cooking is exacting and highly visual, but there's a Styrian warmth and easiness here, along with beautiful local produce.

☗ Drinking

Almost everyone is here to drink wine, but wine appreciation aside, there's little to do at night.

Felber Jörgl   WINERY
(✆ 03456-3189; www.felberjoergl.at; Höch 47, Kitzeck im Sausal; ☺ 10am-6pm Thu-Mon) Half of the fun in the Sausal is driving the scenic roads and trying whichever places take your fancy. This beautifully sited cellar door is a good place to start with a range of mostly white wines and excellent meat and cheese plates.

❶ Getting There & Away

A lack of public transport and the spread out nature of the vineyards make this a destination best done by car or on bicycle.

NORTHERN STYRIA

Heading north from Graz the landscape of Styria begins to change; gentle hills and flat pastures are replaced by jagged mountains, virgin forests, deep valleys and cold, clear mountain streams. This is also the region's industrial heartland, home to the *Steirische Eisenstrasse* (Styrian Iron Road), where for centuries iron mining was the backbone of the economy. Two cultural highlights are the pilgrimage church of Mariazell and the abbey of Admont.

Mariazell

✆ 03882 / POP 1550

Mariazell, situated on the lower reaches of the eastern Alps, is one of Austria's icons. It offers opportunities for hiking, mountain biking and skiing, but what makes Mariazell so well known is its status as Austria's most important pilgrimage site. Its basilica, founded in 1157, holds a sacred statue of the Virgin, and busloads of Austrians flock to the site on weekends, 15 August (Assumption) and 8 September (Mary's name day). The mountain above town, **Bürgeralpe** (1270m), has a couple of restaurants and a small museum.

◉ Sights

★ Basilika   CHURCH
(Kardinal Eugen Tisserant Platz 1; ☺ 7am-8pm) Originally Romanesque, Mariazell's basilica underwent a Gothic conversion in the 14th century, followed by a massive baroque facelift in the 17th century. The result is a strange clash of styles, with the original Gothic steeple bursting like a wayward skeletal limb from between two baroque onion domes. Inside, Gothic ribbing combines with baroque frescoes and lavish stuccowork, while in the upper galleries there's a quite interesting **Schatzkammer** (Treasury; adult/child €4/1; ☺ 10am-3pm Tue-Sat, 11am-3pm Sun May-Oct), which contains votive offerings spanning six centuries, mainly naive-style paintings.

Unusually, the church is centred on a small but exquisite chapel, known as the **Gnadenkapelle** (Chapel of Grace). This gold and silver edifice houses the Romanesque statue of the Madonna, whose healing powers reputedly helped King Louis of Hungary defeat the Turks in 1377. Except for two days each year, she's dressed up rather doll-like in her *Liebfrauenkleid* (dress of Our Lady). Both Johann Bernhard Fischer von Erlach and his son Josef

Emmanuel had a hand in the baroque interior features; the crucifixion group sculpture (1715) on the high altar is by Lorenzo Mattielli.

Erlebniswelt Holzknechtland
MUSEUM
(entry & cable car adult/child €17.20/9.90; ⊙ 9am–5pm Apr–Oct) A small museum on Bürgeralpe devoted to wood and all its wonderful uses.

🏃 Activities

Erlaufsee
WATER SPORTS, WALKING
This small lake a few kilometres northwest of the town reaches about 22°C in summer and, apart from swimming, it offers good opportunities for windsurfing and scuba diving; contact addresses for water sports are listed in the booklet *Mariazellerland von A-Z*, available at the tourist office.

An easy four-hour *Rundwanderweg* (circuit trail) runs past the lake and south through forest back into Mariazell; alternatively, you can take the steam **Museumstramway** (museumstramway.at; one-way/return €7/10), which runs at weekends and holidays in July and August. It leaves from the Museumstramway Bahnhof.

Hotel Schwarzer Adler
CYCLING
(☑ 03882-286 30; www.hotelschwarzeradler.at; Hauptplatz 1; bicycles per day €14-18) Hires out trekking and mountain bikes.

Bürgeralpe
HIKING, SKIING
(www.buergeralpe.at) This mountain is a great starting or finishing point for hiking in the summer months, and also has skiing in winter. The **cable car** (☑ 03882-25 55; www.buergeralpe.at; adult/child return €18.80/11) operates year-round. The resort has an artificial lake used as a setting for special events. During winter, adult ski passes cost around €31 (daily) and €162 (weekly).

🛏 Sleeping

The only time finding a room in Mariazell can be problematic is around the pilgrim days. Aside from hotels and pensions, there is a smattering of private rooms.

Goldene Krone
HOTEL $
(☑ 03882-25 83; www.mariazell.at/krone; Grazer Strasse 1; s/d €48/96; @ 🛜) Goldene Krone's big and bright rooms have a homely feel, which is complemented by a Finnish sauna and billiard room (also with table football). The ground floor has an excellent restaurant (mains €9 to €16), featuring traditional Austrian cuisine and street-side seating.

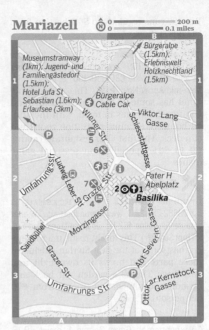

Mariazell

◉ Top Sights
1 Basilika B2

◎ Sights
2 Schatzkammer B2

◉ Activities, Courses & Tours
3 Hotel Schwarzer Adler A2

🛏 Sleeping
4 Goldene Krone A2
5 Hotel Drei Hasen A2

✕ Eating
6 Brauhaus Mariazell A2
7 Questers A2

Hotel Jufa St Sebastian
HOSTEL $
(☑ 05 7083 390; www.jufa.eu/jufa-erlaufsee-sport-resort; Erlaufseestrasse 49; s/d €47/74; P ⊝ @ 🛜 ⏚) Located halfway between Mariazell and Erlaufsee, this hostel has a sauna, solarium and fitness room.

Campingplatz Erlaufsee
CAMPGROUND $
(☑ 03882-49 37; www.st-sebastian.at; camp sites per adult/child/tent/car €5/2.5/4/3; ⊙ May–mid-Sep; P) A small camping ground in St Sebastian on the Erlaufsee, flanked by pine trees.

Bus 197 runs regularly to St Sebastian from the bus station.

★ **Hotel Drei Hasen** HOTEL **$$**
(☑ 03882-24 10; www.dreihasen.at; Wiener Strasse 11; s/d/ste €80/130/180; ⊘ closed mid-Mar–mid-Apr & Nov; P �@) This comfortable hotel has some of the most pleasant and comfortable rooms in town, with the added bonus of a sauna, relaxation room and sun deck. The first-class restaurant (mains €9 to €24) specialises in seasonal game dishes.

✗ Eating

Brauhaus Mariazell MICROBREWERY **$$**
(☑ 03882-25 23; www.bierundbett.at; Wiener Strasse 5; mains €12-18; ⊘ 10am-11pm Wed-Sat, 2-11pm Sun; @) This lovely, rustic microbrewery has some of the best Styrian cuisine in these parts and brews its own light and dark beer. There's a garden out back and upstairs accommodation (rooms from €70 per person).

Questers SEAFOOD **$$**
(www.questers.at; Grazer Strasse 4; mains €9-16, soup €3.50-6; ⊘ 10am-5pm, to 6pm Fri & Sat, to 4pm Sun) This gourmet shop serves sit-down meals and snacks but also has lots of tasty fish dishes and delicacies for a picnic, including mouthwatering *Krainer* sausage made from game.

ⓘ Information

Tourist Office (☑ 03882-23 66; www.mariazell-info.at; Hauptplatz 13; ⊘ 9am-5.30pm Mon-Fri, to 4pm Sat, to 12.30pm Sun, closed Sat & Sun Nov-Apr) Has a town map and brochure with walking trails marked; doesn't book rooms but has accommodation listings.

ⓘ Getting There & Away

A narrow-gauge train departs from St Pölten, 84km to the north, every two to three hours. It's a slow trip (€16, 2½ hours), but the scenery is good for the last hour approaching Mariazell. Bus is the only option for further travel from Mariazell into Styria; four direct buses run daily to/from Bruck an der Mur (€11.60, 1½ hours), with train connections to/from Graz (€24, 2¼ hours). There is also one early morning and one afternoon direct bus each way daily between Vienna (Südtiroler Platz) and Mariazell (€20, three hours).

Bruck an der Mur

☑ 03862 / POP 12,960

Bruck, at the confluence of the Mur and Mürz Rivers, is the Mur Valley's first real town and an important railway junction for Styria. Attractions are limited, but if you're breaking a journey here there are a few interesting things to see.

◉ Sights

Koloman-Wallisch-Platz SQUARE
The town square, with a food and flower market on Wednesday and Saturday, is graced by the Rathaus, with an attractive arcaded courtyard; Kornmesserhaus (1499) brings together Gothic and some Renaissance features and was based on the design of a Venetian palace. Other historic highlights include the art-nouveau facade at No 10 and the fine Renaissance-style wrought-iron well created by Hans Prasser in 1626.

Twice weekly, a food and flower market takes place on the main square.

Schloss Landskron RUINS
Several paths wind up to this castle, where local nobility held court until fire ravaged it along with the rest of the town in 1792. The population helped itself to the stone to rebuild their houses, and today all that remains is a clock tower and a couple of canons captured from the French.

Pfarrkirche CHURCH
(Kirchplatz; ⊘ dawn-dusk) This 15th-century Gothic church is on the way up to the castle.

ⓘ Information

Tourist Office (☑ 03862-890 12 10; www.tourismus-bruckmur.at; Koloman-Wallisch-Platz 1; ⊘ 8am-4.30pm Mon-Thu, to noon Fri) Reached by taking Bahnhofstrasse to the town's main square.

ⓘ Getting There & Away

Along with Leoben, Bruck is the region's main rail hub; all fast trains to Graz (€13, 45 minutes, hourly) pass through here. Other direct trains go hourly to Klagenfurt (€31.90, two hours) and hourly to Wien (€29.30, 1¾ hours). By road, the main autobahn intersect southeast of town. If you're planning to cycle in the region, the tourist office has useful maps. Postbus services arrive and depart next to the train station.

Leoben

📞 03842 / POP 24,850

Unprepossessing Leoben reveals a few surprises once you dig down into its modest urban soul. A revamped museum quarter is one very good reason to prolong a visit here between trains. The town is also a centre for metallurgical industries and home to Gösser beer, and achieved ultimate fame with the peace treaty signed here in 1797 by Napoleon and Emperor Franz II.

◎ Sights

Hauptplatz
SQUARE

Dating from the 13th century, this long, rectangular square has an attractive **Pestsäule** (Plague Column; 1717). Many of the elegant facades lining the square were created in the 17th century, including the baroque Hacklhaus from 1660. Leoben's connection with the iron industry is seen in the curious town motif displayed on the Altes Rathaus facade, which shows an ostrich eating horseshoes.

At the northern end you find a fountain from 1794 with an angel holding the town's heraldic shield, and at the opposite end is a fountain dedicated to miners (1799).

Kunsthalle
MUSEUM

(www.museumscenter-leoben.at; Kirchgasse 6; ⊙10am-5pm Mon-Sat) This museum complex stages some of Austria's best temporary exhibitions found outside the capital. Its permanent *Schienen der Vergangenheit* (Tracks of the Past) in the MuseumsCenter Leoben tells the history of Leoben and the town's industries. Check the website for information on prices and temporary exhibitions, which are staged for seven to eight months every second year. Combined tickets are available.

MuseumsCenter Leoben
MUSEUM

(www.museumscenter-leoben.at; Kirchgasse 6; adult/child/family €5/3.50/11; ⊙10am-5pm Tue-Sat, longer hours during Kunsthalle exhibitions) This is the cultural heart of Leoben, with an interesting *Schienen der Vergangenheit* (Tracks of the Past) section telling the history of Leoben and its industries, starting with the present and working back in time, and a large section with changing exhibitions. The standard is very high, so check the town's website for information on current exhibitions.

Pfarrkirche St Xaver
CHURCH

(Kirchplatz 1; ⊙8am-7pm) The simple exterior of this early baroque edifice, built in 1665

as a Jesuit church, belies a complex interior of white walls and black-and-gold baroque altars.

Altes Rathaus
HISTORIC BUILDING

(Hauptplatz 1) Leoben's connection with the iron industry is seen in the curious town motif displayed on the Altes Rathaus facade, which shows an ostrich eating horseshoes.

Hacklhaus
HISTORIC BUILDING

(Hauptplatz 9) Hauptplatz is lined with elegant 17th-century facades, including the baroque Hacklhaus.

🏃 Activities

Tourismusverband Leoben (p200) can help arrange tours into an early-Romanesque crypt of the **Stiftkirche** (foundation church) or visits to the local **Gösser Brewery**, both about 4km south of the centre in the suburb of Göss.

Asia Spa
SPA

(📞 03842-245 00; www.asiaspa.at; In der Au 3; 4hr spa adult/child €9/5, 4hr sauna adult €21.50) Leoben's spa centre offers massages and treatments. Note that children under 16 may not enter the sauna.

🛏 Sleeping

Pension Jahrbacher
PENSION $

(📞 03842-436 00; www.jahrbacher.at; Kirchgasse 14; s/d €39/69; 🛜) This small, centrally located *Pension* has comfortable rooms and is associated with Cafe am Schwammerlturm, a tiny cafe with wonderful outdoor seating on top of the circular city tower. From here you have breathtaking views over the town and countryside. Book ahead for the *Pension,* and if no one answers the door, drop by the antique shop next door or the cafe.

Falkensteiner Hotel
HOTEL $$

(📞 03842-405; www.leoben.falkensteiner.com; In der Au 1-3; s €100-230, d €110-240; 🅿 @ 🛜 🏊) This seminar and business hotel is part of the Asia Spa complex and offers quality, stylish rooms. Tones are warm and attractive, and one wall of the shower cubicle is glass and fronts the double bed (but has a curtain for the discreet). A night here includes use of the Asia Spa.

Hotel Kindler
HOTEL $$

(📞 03842-43 20 20; www.kindler.at; Straussgasse 7-11; s €56, d €100; 🛜) This clean, renovated hotel in the centre offers excellent value and is comfortable; its only drawback is that wooden-tiled floors cause sound to travel between rooms.

X Eating

This is home to Austrian favourite Gösser beer, so you'll find plenty of that on tap. There are a number of wine bars and taverns here which get lively with the local engineering crowd, but it's still a small town.

Cafe am Schwammerlturm CAFE $
(☎ 03842-436 00; www.jahrbacher.at; Homanngasse 11; ⊙ 11am-6pm Tue-Sun) This tiny cafe is a visual treat: it has wonderful outdoor seating on top of the circular city tower and breathtaking views over the town and countryside. The stairs are not for the fainthearted, but it has a (glass) lift.

★ Stadt Meierei AUSTRIAN, INTERNATIONAL $$
(☎ 03842-446 03; www.stadt-meierei.at; Homanngasse 1; lunch menu €8.90, mains €17-27; ⊙ 10am-11pm Tue-Sat) Run by chef Martin Neuretter and *chef de rang* and sommelier Isabella Pichler, this restaurant offers quality cuisine from a menu featuring lamb, beef, poultry and fish specialities.

ⓘ Information

Stadt Information Leoben (☎ 03842-440 18; www.leoben.at; Hauptplatz 12; ⊙ 8am-5pm Mon-Fri, 9am-noon Sat) Community and tourist-information centre with brochures.
Tourismusverband Leoben (☎ 03842-481 48; www.tourismus-leoben.at; Peter Tunner-Strasse 2; ⊙ 9am-5pm Mon-Fri) Main information centre for Leoben; stocks a *Bei uns zu Gast* booklet with useful listings. Its Leoben map also includes a great environs map with hiking trails.

ⓘ Getting There & Away

Leoben is 16km west of Bruck an der Mur (€4.40, 15 minutes, hourly) and is on the main rail route from there to Klagenfurt or Linz. The town centre is a 10-minute walk from Leoben Hauptbahnhof: cross the Mur and bear right.

Eisenerz

☎ 03848 / POP 4330

Eisenerz, nestled at the foot of the extraordinary Erzberg (Iron Mountain), is one of the important stops along the **Steirische Eisenstrasse** (Styrian Iron Road). This unusual peak has been completely denuded by open-cast stope mining and resembles a step pyramid. The outcome is eerie and surprisingly beautiful, with its orange and purple shades contrasting with the lush greenery and grey crags of surrounding mountains.

⊙ Sights

Erzberg INDUSTRIAL MUSEUM
(☎ 03848-32 00; www.abenteuer-erzberg.at; Erzberg 1; tours adult/child €17/7.50, combined tours €30/13.50, Hauly explosion tour €23/14.50; ⊙ tours 10am-3pm May-Oct, advance booking required; P ♿) Eisenerz' main attraction is its Erzberg ironworks, which can be seen up close on underground *Schaubergwerk* tours of the mine, abandoned in 1986, or alternatively on overground tours in a 'Hauly' truck along roads cut into the mountain. Both tours are usually in German, with English-language notes available. Each Thursday at 9am you can also ride up in a Hauly and watch the rock being blown up. The departure point is a 10-minutes walk from the centre, following the river's course.

Dress warmly for the 90-minute *Schaubergwerk* tours. There are fine views along the way of the 60-minute *Hauly Abenteuerfahrt* tours.

Wehrkirche St Oswald CHURCH
(Kirchenstiege 4; ⊙ 9am-7pm Apr-Oct) More a fortress than a Gothic church, this soaring bastion gained its heavy walls in 1532 as protection against the Turks.

🕴 Activities

Eisenerz is surrounded by lots of trails. The tourist office has a free town map with trails marked, including to the idyllic Leopoldsteiner See, only 3km north on the road towards Admont. This small lake has a wall of granite rising to 1649m as a backdrop; you can hire boats in summer – it's a very chilly swim, though.

🛏 Sleeping

Gästehaus Weninger GUESTHOUSE $
(☎ 03848-225 80; www.gaestehaus-weninger.at; Krumpentalerstrasse 8; s/d €49/76; P ☎) A very decent guesthouse with a fitness room and sauna, Weninger aims at those staying for a few days, but does take guests for one night at very short notice. Some bathrooms are cramped, but rooms are a good size.

JUFA Hotel Eisenerz-Almerlebnis HOSTEL $
(☎ 05 7083 340; www.jufa.eu/jufa-eisenerzer-ramsau-almerlebnisdorf; Ramsau 1; s/d €48/72; P @ ☎) This lovely HI hostel is 5km south of Eisenerz. It's situated at an altitude of

1000m, and has a sauna and indoor and outdoor climbing walls, as well as hiking trails going off into the mountains. There's a restaurant on-site. You will need a car to get here (a taxi costs about €13).

Gästehaus Tegelhofer   GUESTHOUSE $
(☑03848-20 86; www.gaestehaus-tegelhofer. at; Lindmoserstrasse 8; s/d €31/62; P ☎) This modern guesthouse offers great value, coming with spacious and clean rooms, and a free sauna and fitness room. There's also an inexpensive family apartment for two to six people.

✖ Eating

Gasthof zur Post   AUSTRIAN $
(Lindmoserstr 10; mains €8-12; ⊘11.30am-2.30pm Tue-Sun, 6-9.30pm Tue-Sat; P) The traditional Gasthof zur Post prides itself on local classics such as *Beuschel* (lung and heart) or inexpensive goulash and venison ragout.

Barbarastub'n   CAFE $
(Bergmannplatz 2; ⊘8.30am-7pm Mon-Sat, 2-6pm Sun) Drop by for delicious apple strudel or to relax on the comfy chairs out back over a tea or coffee. Has brochures and maps of the town, which are useful when the tourist office is closed.

ⓘ Information

Tourist Office (☑03848-25 11 81; www. eisenerz-heute.at; Dr Theodor Körner Platz 1; ⊘10am-noon & 3-5pm Mon-Fri) Helpful staff in the centre of the town. Good maps for hiking.

ⓘ Getting There & Away

Direct buses run hourly from Leoben to Eisenerz (€8.60, one hour), less frequently on Sundays. Several daily connect Eisenerz and Hieflau (€4.40, 25 minutes), where you can pick up buses and the occasional train to Selzthal and Liezen.

Trains no longer operate to Eisenerz, and at the time of research landslides had halted the special Vordernberg–Eisenerz **Nostalgie** (Nostalgic Train; ☑03849-832; www.erzbergbahn. at; adult/child €16/7.50) train. See the website for the latest on whether the service has resumed. For a taxi, call ☑4636.

Nationalpark Gesäuse

Established in 2003, Gesäuse is Austria's newest national park, set in a pristine region of jagged mountain ridges, rock towers, deep valleys, alpine pastures and dense spruce forests. It is washed by the Enns River, which is a favourite of rafting connoisseurs, and a number of companies offer rafting trips during the summer months. Hiking and mountain climbing, and to a lesser extent mountain biking, also feature among the park's outdoor activities; of the six peaks over 2000m within the park, **Hocktor** (2369m) is the highest and is popular among hikers.

Apart from a few mountain huts, you'll need to sleep in Admont or Johnsbach.

ⓘ Information

The staffed **national park pavilion** (☑03611-21 101-20; Gstatterboden 25; ⊘10am-6pm May-Oct) is a useful source of information; the tourist office in Admont also has information on accommodation and activities in the park.

ⓘ Getting There & Away

The park is best reached by the daily train to Gstatterboden (€6, 30 minutes) and Johnsbach im Nationalpark (€6, 30 minutes)

Buses connect the park with Admont (bus 912; €4.30, 22 minutes, four to seven daily), via Bachbrücke/Weidendom (€4.40, 12 minutes).

Admont

☑03613 / POP 2530

Admont, nestled in a broad section of the Enns Valley, is a low-key town that revs up during the day when groups arrive in buses to see its spectacular abbey. Each night it sinks back into pleasant oblivion. The town makes a good base for kicking off deeper into the region.

⦿ Sights

Benedictine Abbey   ABBEY
(☑03613-231 20; www.stiftadmont.at; Admont 1; adult/child/family €10/5.80/24; ⊘10am-5pm late-Mar–early Nov, to 2pm early Nov–late Dec, by arrangement late Dec–late Mar) Arguably Austria's most elegant and exciting baroque abbey, it brings together museums, religion, and modern art and architecture into an award-winning cultural ensemble.

The centrepiece of the abbey is its **Stiftsbibliothek**, the largest abbey library in the world. Survivor of a fire in 1865 that severely damaged the rest of the abbey, it displays about 70,000 volumes of the abbey's 200,000-strong collection, and is decorated with heavenly ceiling frescoes by Bartolomeo Altomonte (1694–1783) and statues (in wood, but painted to look like bronze) by Josef Stammel (1695–1765).

The abbey is also home to the **Kunsthistorisches Museum** (Art History Museum), featuring rare pieces such as its tiny portable altar from 1375, made from amethyst quartz and edged with gilt-silver plates; some Gerhard Mercator globes from 1541 and 1551; and monstrances from the 15th and 16th centuries. Each year innovative temporary exhibitions complement the permanent ones.

Another museum, the **Museum für Gegenwartskunst** (Museum for Contemporary Art), contains works by about 100 mainly Austrian artists, and has pieces you can explore with your hands. The **Naturhistorisches Museum** (Natural History Museum) began in 1674 with a small collection and today includes rooms devoted to flying insects (one of the largest collections in the world), butterflies, stuffed animals, wax fruit and reptiles. From the glass stairway and herb garden there are views to Gesäuse National Park.

📐 Sleeping

There are several good traditional guesthouses in town as well as in the surrounding countryside, along with a couple of modern places.

⭐ **JUFA Schloss Röthelstein** HOSTEL, HOTEL **$$**
(☑ 057 083 320; www.jufa.eu/hotel/roethelstein; Aigen 32; s/d/tr/q €65/105/135/207; 🅿 📶) The monks from the abbey once used to spend the summer in this baroque castle from the 17th century, about 5km southwest of the centre off Aignerstrasse. The renovated palace is flanked by carefully manicured lawns, has an elegant glass-roofed, arcaded inner courtyard and tastefully decorated rooms with wooden floors. Some of its 40 rooms are located in towers.

Hotel Spirodom Admont HOTEL **$$**
(☑ 03613-366 00; www.spirodom.at; Eichenweg 616; s/d €105/172; 🅿 📧 📶 ➳) Admont's fresh four-star hotel is located about 600m north of the abbey and lures guests with a pool, wellness facilities and views to either the abbey or parkland.

Hotel Gastof Traube HOTEL **$$**
(☑ 0660 658 67 77; www.hotel-die-traube.at; Hauptstrasse 3; s €51-62, d €110-129; 🅿 📶) One of the best places to stay in the centre of town, with modern rooms that are a notch above the others on Hauptstrasse.

ℹ️ Information

Tourist Office (☑ 03613-211 60 10; www.gesaeuse.at; Hauptstrasse 35; ⊙ 9am-5pm Mon-Fri, 10am-6pm Sat mid-May–mid-Oct) The tourist office is opposite the *Rathaus* and near the abbey church. It doubles as a national park office.

ℹ️ Getting There & Away

Admont is 15km to the east of Selzthal, but has very limited train services. Buses departing from Hieflau (€4.40, 30 minutes, three to nine daily) and Liezen (€4.40, 30 minutes, 7 to 15 daily) are the two main approaches to Admont. Buses connect Admont with the national park office in Gstatterboden (€4.40, 22 minutes, four to seven daily), via Bachbrücke/Weidendom (€4.40, 12 minutes). **Gasthaus Kamper** (☑ 03613-36 88; www.gh-kamper.at; Hauptstrasse 19; per hr €2, per day €7; 🚲) hires out trekking and mountain bikes as well as a couple of children's bikes.

Johnsbach
☑ 03611 / POP 150

Situated 17km southeast of Admont, the tiny settlement of Johnsbach is the focal point for hiking, climbing and water sports in the region. It is wedged on the bucolic stream, with rugged mountains rising up on all sides.

This is one of Austria's earliest mountain climbing centres; testimony to this is the poignant **Bergsteiger-Friedhof** (Mountain Climber Cemetery; www.johnsbach.at; Johnsbach; ⊙ dawn-dusk) **FREE**, where buried alongside local citizens are mountain climbers who have come to grief in the Gesäuse over the centuries. With its pretty whitewashed church, this is a beautiful and strangely touching place.

🏃 Activities

AOS Adventures KAYAKING, RAFTING
(☑ 03612-253 43; www.rafting.at; 3-4hr Enns rafting tours €54; ⊙ 8.30am-5pm Mon-Fri, tours 9am & 2pm, Gesäuse camp closed mid-Oct–Apr) Offers rafting, canoeing, stand-up paddleboarding on the Salza River, along with canyoning and zip-lines.

Haindlkarhütte HIKING
(☑ 0664 1140 046; www.haindlkar-huette.at; Johnsbach; ⊙ Sep–mid-Oct) This alpine club provides information, hut hire, guides and mountaineering courses.

📐 Sleeping & Eating

There are several good guesthouses offering food and a bed in the settlement.

★ **Gasthof Kölblwirt** PENSION **$**
(☑ 03611-216; www.koelblwirt.at; Johnsbach 65; s €45, d €66-72) Has it all: a pension, a restaurant specialising in Styrian beef, yodelling courses and Nordic ski hire. Pine-clad rooms are sweetly simple and the welcome is warm.

Gasthof zum Donner PENSION **$**
(☑ 03611-218; www.donnerwirt.at; Johnsbach 5, Johnsbach; s/d €45/75) This traditional alpine hotel has bright, comfortable rooms, a bustling restaurant (mains €9 to €13.50) with nice terrace seating and a sauna for post-hike steams.

❶ Getting There & Away

With your own wheels, take the B146 east and the signposted turn-off to Johnsbach. By bus, call about two hours ahead for the **Rufbus** (Taxi bus; ☑ 03613-4170, 03613-2406), which runs out four to five times daily from Admont Bahnhof (€5). Regular buses also run from Admont to the turn-off at Bachbrücke/ Weidendom (€5, 12 minutes), from where it's a 5km walk.

WESTERN STYRIA

Like northern Styria, western Styria is a mountainous region divided by jagged ranges and alpine streams. Murau is a picturesque town well placed for hikes and cycle trips into the surrounding forests. If you're heading this way from Graz, consider a detour to Seckau or Oberzeiring. The former is famous for its **Benedictine Abbey** (www.abtei-seckau.at; Seckau 1; tours adult/ child €5/3.50; ⊙ 8am-8pm year-round, tours 11am & 2pm May–late Oct), a stunning Romanesque basilica and the mausoleum of Karl II, while the latter is known for its **silver mine** (www.silbergruben.at; adult/child/ family €11.50/5/24; ⊙ tours 10.30am, 1.30pm & 3pm daily May-Oct, 3pm Wed Nov-Apr), now resurrected as an exhibition mine and small health resort for sufferers of respiratory diseases.

Schladming

☑ 03687 / POP 6785
Situated deep in the Ennstal (Enns Valley) in western Styria at the foot of the glacial Dachsteingebirge (Dachstein Mountains), Schladming is an easygoing ski resort that in summer also offers glacier skiing and snowboarding, easy access to hiking trails, white-water rafting on the Enns River and excellent mountain biking. On Hoher Dachstein (2995m), don't miss the opportunity to walk through a glacier crevice in the Eispalast or to admire views over the Ennstal from the Skywalk high-altitude panorama platform.

⊙ Sights

Dachstein Eispalast GLACIER
(www.dachsteingletscher.at; Ramsau am Dachstein; adult/child €10/5.50, gondola return adult/child €36/18.50; ⊙ 8.30am-4.30pm, gondola every 20min 7.50am-5.30pm) Situated in a crevice of the Dachstein Glacier along a sheer cliff face, the Eispalast creates the strange effect of walking through an enormous, hollow ice cube. A gondola, one of the world's most spectacular, whisks you up and terminates with a vertical thrust at the Skywalk viewing platform. About 10 buses daily (€8.90, 45 minutes) leave Planet Planai in Schladming for the base station near Ramsau.

🏃 Activities

The area around Schladming has more than 900km of mountain-bike trails, divided among 20 routes shown on the excellent, free mountain-bike map from the tourist office. Hiking trails begin almost from the centre of town – the tourist office's town map has trails marked.

Schladming Ski Fields SNOW SPORTS
(www.schladming-dachstein.at; day pass adult/ child from €46.50/23.50) From December to March the area's 223km of downhill ski pistes and 86 ski lifts rev into action. Skiing and snowboarding on the Dachstein Glacier can be done year-round but not all lifts are open in summer.

Most of the cross-country skiing is done across the valley in Ramsau (about €18 for ski hire). A medium-quality snowboard for the pistes costs €23 and snow-hiking shoes €18. Prices on the glacier are similar.

Riesachfälle Waterfalls HIKING
You can begin this popular walk from Talbachgasse in Schladming. Follow the stream for about 40 minutes along a mountain bike and walking trail to Untertal. From there it's about another 3½ hours to the waterfalls.

An alternative is to take the bus to the popular valley restaurant Gasthof zu Riesachfall (p205) and walk the forest trail (1½ hours, good shoes and head for heights required) or the gravel forestry road (two

STYRIA SCHLADMING

hours) to the falls and beyond to the Riesachsee (Lake Riesach).

[pi:tu] Bikecenter CYCLING
(☎0680 320 78 62; www.bikeparkplanai.at; Coburgstrasse 52; per day €20-80) This pro mountain-bike rental place is located at the Planai Stadium; offers discounts on e-mountain bikes with the Sommercard.

Trittscher BICYCLE, SKI RENTAL
(☎03687-226 47-11; www.tritscher.at; Salzburgerstrasse 24) In summer Trittscher rents mountain bikes for €15 per day and e-bikes for €25 per day. In winter it hires out ski equipment; see website for full price list as rates vary depending on equipment level.

🛏 Sleeping

New well-designed places keep popping up in Schladming. In summer the considerable number of hotels means you can often get a good deal. But book well ahead during the ski season and be prepared for high prices. The tourist office can help place you in smaller B&Bs and private rooms.

★ Stadthotel Brunner SPA HOTEL $$
(☎03687-225 13-0; www.stadthotel-brunner.at; Hauptplatz 14; d €148-168) This new hotel on the Hauptplaz is a delight. Petra Brunner and Thomas Radzik, a chef and musician respectively, are working some fresh ideas at this super stylish but friendly and relaxed place. Spacious, sexy rooms are complemented with a beautiful rooftop sauna and tea lounge; the brimming breakfast buffet has Ayurvedic elements as well as top-quality traditional dishes.

Post Hotel HOTEL $$
(☎03687-225 71; www.posthotel-schladming.at; Hauptplatz 10; r €100-150, apt €120-180; P☻@☎) The four-star Post Hotel has spacious, modern rooms decorated in tasteful tones. Some of its doubles have connecting doors for families, and its family apartment has a separate living room. It also has a sauna and a good half-board deal is available.

Jugendgästehaus Schladming HOSTEL $$
(☎05 708 33 30; www.jufa.at/schladming; Coburgstrasse 253; s/d €60/80; ☻☎) Situated in the pedestrian zone close to the Planai base station, this excellent hostel has maisonette rooms with upstairs and downstairs beds, doubles with beds you can shift together, as well as standard and family rooms, all neat, bright and with floor boards.

Hotel Landgraf HOTEL $$
(☎03687-223 95; www.landgraf.cc; Hauptplatz 37; s €75-95, d €120-150; P) Hotel Landgraf is a comfortable, functional B&B style place situated right in the centre of Schladming, upstairs from the popular *konditorei* (bakery cafe) of the same name. There are spacious apartments suitable for families. Note it doesn't issue the Sommercard and books out months ahead in winter.

🍴 Eating

A huge number of eating options fill the pretty old town streets, from traditional alpine comfort food to the ubiquitous ski-town favourites of pizza and Tex-Mex.

Bio Chi HEALTH FOOD $
(www.biochi.at; Martin Luther-Strasse 32; mains €9, salads €4.20-5.90; ☺8am-6pm Mon-Fri, to 2pm Sat; ☑) ♪ This welcoming and well-stocked health-food shop is a local institution and whips up leafy salads, vegetarian mains like chanterelle goulash with bread dumplings, and tempting sweets using organic ingredients, which you can wash down with freshly squeezed juices. It also does fresh, healthy breakfasts. The gluten-free cakes are excellent.

Stadtbräu AUSTRIAN $
(☎0664 517 96 20; www.kulinarwerk-schladming.com; mains €11.90-15.90; ☺10am-11pm Tue-Sun) A totally traditional vaulted dining room with an extensive menu and brisk service, what emerges from the kitchen will surprise. Styrian dishes – say, boiled beef with roast potatoes and horseradish, or the fleshtastic mixed grill of pork, chicken and steak – use excellent produce and are executed with a light touch.

Johann AUSTRIAN $$
(☎03687-225 71; www.posthotel-schladming.at; Hauptplatz 10; mains €13.50-27.50; ☺11.30am-1.30pm & 5.30-9.30pm) The Post Hotel's Johann restaurant mixes cosy pine and fresh green-and-white textiles in a sweetly upmarket dining room. There's an excellent selection of rather pricey wines to go with its carefully cooked Styrian and Austrian dishes.

Julius ITALIAN $$
(☎0664 251 33 99; www.julius-kitchen.com; Martin-Luther-Strasse 31; mains €13.90-16.90; ☺5-11pm Sun & Mon, 11am-2.30pm & 5-11pm Tue-Sat) A smart wine bar that also does good contemporary Italian dishes, this is a local favourite. There's a three-course fish menu that includes the tasty lobster ravioli with Croatian scampi and there are a number of

good meat-free pastas. The kitchen is happy to do vegan dishes on request too.

Gasthof zu Riesachfall
RESTAURANT **$$**
(📞03687-616 78; www.gasthaus-riesachfall.at; Untertalstrasse 66, Untertal; mains €9-16; ⊗10am-9pm late Apr–late Oct) A friendly alpine hut in Untertal with a nice weather terrace.

Die Tischlerei
INTERNATIONAL **$$$**
(📞03687-221 92; www.dietischlerei.co.at; set menus €31-45; ⊗11am-2pm & 5pm-midnight Tue-Sat, daily in high season) On a corner just a short walk beyond the centre, this big, modern restaurant serves up a number of set menus that span Mediterranean and Asian flavours, despite the bright Dirndls of the waitresses. Lunch menus, with a mostly Italian slant, are a bargain at two courses for €12.50 or three for €15.50.

Drinking & Nightlife

A laid-back après scene can be found in town and up the mountain, as well as some cosy pubs and elegant wine bars.

Hohenhaus Tenne
BAR
(www.tenne.com/schladming; Coburgstrasse 512; ⊗11am-4am Nov-Mar) Finding après-ski in Schladming in the ski season is as easy as falling down an icy hill. The Hohenhaus Tenne is a reliable place to tumble.

🛍 Shopping

Heimatgold
FOOD & DRINKS
(📞03687-2250 5350; www.heimatgold.at; Coburgstrasse 49; ⊗9am-6pm Mon-Fri, to 5pm Sat) A wonderful place to stock up on picnic supplies, self-catering needs or take-home gourmet gifts, Heimatgold champions the products of local farmers, from chocolate to pickles to raw milk and freshly prepared Styrian stews in jars.

ⓘ Information

Tourismusverband Schladming-Rohrmoos (📞03687-227 77 22; www.schladming.at; Rohrmoosstrasse 234; ⊗9am-6pm Mon-Sat, closed Sat Apr & Nov) Stocks mountain bike and hiking trail maps, has lots of tips on the region and will organise accommodation if you call ahead. A useful accommodation board and free telephone are situated outside.

ⓘ Getting There & Away

Every two hours trains pass through on their way to Graz (€37.30, 2½ hours) and at least five times daily to Salzburg (€19.10, 1½ hours). The

Dachsteinstrasse toll road to the gondola costs €6/2.80 per adult/child.

In summer five buses daily leave from Rathausplatz and Lendplatz to Riesachfall Wilde Wasser (€6.10, 35 minutes), the access point for the Riesachfälle waterfalls and the lake.

Murau

📞03532 / POP 2120

Murau, in the western reaches of the Murtal (Mur Valley) on the banks of the river, is an attractive town filled with pastel-coloured houses. Surrounded by forested hills and alpine meadows, its close proximity to Stolzalpe to the north and the Metnitzer mountains to the south makes it an excellent base for hiking and cycling in summer.

⊙ Sights

Schloss Murau
CASTLE
(📞03532-23 02 58; Schlossberg 1; tours adult/child €6/3; ⊗tours 2pm Wed & Fri Jun–late-Sep) Built in 1250 by the Liechtenstein family, who once ruled the region, Schloss Murau was transformed into its present late-Renaissance form in the 17th century. Tours take you through seven rooms, including the chapel and the Rittersaal (Knight's Room), where concerts are often held. The altar in the chapel dates from 1655 and was created by masters from the town of Judenberg. See the website for dates of special summertime children's tours.

Stadtpfarrkirche St Matthäus
CHURCH
(Schlossberg 8; ⊗dawn-dusk) Situated just below the castle, this restored church has Gothic and baroque elements that work surprisingly well together, especially in the combination of the Gothic crucifixion group (1500) and the baroque high altar (1655). The beautiful frescoes date from the 14th to the 16th centuries.

STYRIA MURAU

CYCLING & HIKING AROUND MURAU

Almost a dozen cycling tracks and mountain-bike trails can be accessed from Murau. The granddaddy of them all is the 450km-long Murradweg, which follows the course of the Mur River. Trails are numbered and routes marked on the Murau tourist office's useful *Rad & Mountainbike* booklet, also in English.

Hiking trails also branch out into the region from here, some beginning from the train station and others from the *Bundesstrasse* around Billa supermarket. A strenuous five-hour return hike to the Stolzalpen peak (1817m) begins at Billa. The tourist office has a useful *Wandern* booklet on hikes.

Intersport Pintar (p206), about 500m past the Billa supermarket, rents trekking and e-bikes.

Brewery Museum   MUSEUM
(☑ 03532-32 66 58; www.murauerbier.at; Raffaltplatz 19-23) 🖉 Murau is famous in Austria for its Brauerei Murau, which has a museum on beer making. Entry includes a glass of the local brew or a soft drink. Closed at time of writing; due to reopen mid-2017.

🏃 Activities

Intersport Pintar   CYCLING
(☑ 03532-23 97; www.sportpintar.at; Bundesstrasse 7a; per day bike €15, e-bike €25; ⊙ 8.30am-6pm Mon-Fri, to 12.30pm Sat) Bike rental is available here, about 500m past the Billa supermarket.

🛏 Sleeping & Eating

This laid-back part of Styria has some good little hotels along with guesthouses and private apartment rental.

Hotel Gasthof Lercher   HOTEL, PENSION $
(☑ 03532-24 31; www.hotel-restaurant-lercher.at; Schwarzenbergstrasse 10; s €45-80, d €74-163; Ⓟ@ 🛜) Hotel Lercher is two places in one: a three-star Gasthof with inexpensive rooms and – still excellent value – a four-star hotel. Many of the rooms have views

to the Stolzalpe, and even the cheapest are comfortably furnished. There's a sauna and steam bath. The restaurant serves delicious seasonal Styrian and Austrian classics (mains €12 to €18).

Jufa Murau   HOSTEL $
(☑ 05 7083 280; alt.jufa.eu/en/jufa-murau; St Leonhard Platz 4; s/d €51/70; Ⓟ 🛜) This HI hostel is situated in four buildings near the train station, and has a sauna and a peaceful inner courtyard. Call ahead in early autumn, when it closes for at least one month.

★**Hotel Ferner's Rosenhof**   HOTEL $$
(☑ 03532-23 18; www.hotel-ferner.at; Rosseggerstr 9; s €73-89, d €126-180; Ⓟ@ 🛜) With paredback, light wood rooms, a sauna and herbal steam bath, and an attractive restaurant terrace (mains €11 to €26), Hotel Ferner's Rosenhof has style and rustic cosiness. The more expensive larger rooms have balconies, and some have connecting doors for families.

Pizzeria Restaurant Platzhirsch   ITALIAN, AUSTRIAN $
(☑ 03532-33 39; Schillerplatz 10; pizza €7.20-10.90, mains €9.90-17.20; ⊙ 11am-11pm) Serves great eat-in and takeaway pizza, delicious pasta dishes and Austrian classics.

ℹ Information

Tourist Office (☑ 03532-27 20-0; www.murau-kreischberg.at; Liechtensteinstrasse 3-5; ⊙ 9am-5pm Mon-Fri year-round, 9am-noon Sat Jun-Sep) Has loads of brochures on the town and its surrounds, including hiking trails and bicycle ways.

ℹ Getting There & Away

If you're coming from Salzburgerland, the most pleasant mode of transport is the **Murtalbahn** (☑ 03532-22 33; www.stlb.at; one way/return €13.60/19), a steam train that chugs its way between Tamsweg and Murau once every Tuesday and Thursday from mid-June to mid-September on a narrow-gauge line.

Every two hours direct ÖBB trains connect Murau with Tamsweg (€8.40, one hour). Trains to Leoben (€15.10, 1½ hours, every two hours) require a change in Unzmarkt, also the junction for trains from Murau to Klagenfurt (€18.60, 2¼ hours, every two hours).

The Salzkammergut

Best Places to Eat

➡ Brot & Wein (p218)

➡ Holzingerbauer (p226)

➡ Restaurant zum Salzbaron (p213)

➡ Restaurant-Pizzeria Simmer (p214)

Best Places to Sleep

➡ Heritage Hotel Hallstatt (p213)

➡ Hotel Stroblerhof (p225)

➡ Im Weissen Rössl (p224)

➡ Halstätt Hideaway (p212)

Why Go?

The Salzkammergut is a spectacular region of alpine and subalpine lakes, picturesque valleys, rolling hills and rugged, steep mountain ranges rising to almost 3000m. Much of the region is remote wilderness, and even in the heavily visited parts, such as the Wolfgangsee and Mondsee, you'll always find isolated areas where peaceful, glassy waters provide limitless opportunities for boating, swimming, fishing or just sitting on the shore and chucking stones into the water. The popular Hallstätter See, flanked by soaring mountains that offer great hiking, is arguably the most spectacular of the lakes.

Salt was once the 'white gold' of the Salzkammergut, and the mines that made it famous now provide an interesting journey back in time to the settlers of the Iron Age Hallstatt culture, and to the Celts and Romans.

When to Go

➡ Head to the mountain lakes from July to early September for lake swimming. Lakes can be chilly or cold outside these months; the Wolfgangsee and Mondsee are warmest.

➡ The shoulder season (spring and autumn) has changeable weather, and in mid-summer short, sudden rain showers are not unusual.

➡ There's good skiing on the Dachstein mountains once the snow settles, from December to March. With the right experience, equipment and maps you can ski to the Schladming side of the range on a cross-country trail.

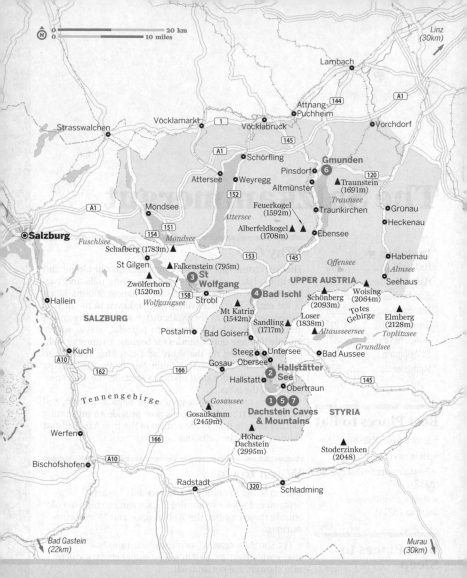

The Salzkammergut Highlights

1 **5Fingers Viewing Platform** (p214) Reeling from views high up in the Dachstein Mountains.

2 **Hallstätter See** (p211) Hiking lakes-edge from Obertraun to Hallstatt and cooling off in the crystal waters between trails.

3 **St Wolfgang** (p223)

Discovering Wolfgangsee's remarkable pilgrimage church, filled with priceless works of art.

4 **Kaiservilla** (p209) Strolling through Franz Josef's summer residence in Bad Ischl.

5 **Dachstein Caves** (p213) Plunging into the chilling

depths to marvel at masterfully illuminated towers of ice.

6 **Gmunden** (p217) Hunting for vintage ceramics in the backstreets and market squares of this charming town.

7 **Krippenstein** (p215) Winter skiing on the 11km downhill piste in the Dachstein Mountains.

❶ Getting There & Away

CAR & MOTORCYCLE
To reach the Salzkammergut from Salzburg by car or motorcycle, take the A1 to reach the north of the region, or Hwy 158 to Bad Ischl. Travelling north–south, the main road is Hwy 145 (the Salzkammergut Bundesstrasse), which follows the train line for most of its length.

TRAIN
By rail, the main routes into the province are from Salzburg or Linz, with a change at Attnang-Puchheim onto the regional north–south railway line. From Styria, change at Stainach-Irdning.

❶ Getting Around

BOAT
Numerous operators ply the waters between towns on the Attersee, Traunsee, Mondsee, Hallstätter See and Wolfgangsee.

BUS
Regular bus services connect all towns and villages in the area; services on weekends are less frequent or not at all. Hourly buses depart Salzburg for various towns in the region, including Bad Ischl, Mondsee and St Wolfgang; for services from Styria, see www.busbahnbim.at.

TRAIN
The Salzkammergut is crossed by regional trains on a north–south route, passing through Attnang-Puchheim on the Salzburg–Linz line and Stainach-Irdning on the Bischofshofen–Graz line. Hourly trains take 2½ hours to complete the journey. Attersee is also accessible by rail.

Small stations are not staffed; at an *unbesetzter Bahnhof* (unattended train station), use a platform ticket machine or pay on the train.

BAD ISCHL

✒ 06132 / POP 13,760

This spa town's reputation snowballed after the Habsburg Princess Sophie took a treatment here to cure her infertility in 1828. Within two years she had given birth to Emperor Franz Josef I; two other sons followed and were nicknamed the Salzprinzen (Salt Princes). Rather in the manner of a salmon returning to its place of birth, Franz Josef made an annual pilgrimage to Bad Ischl, making it his summer home for the next 60 years and hauling much of the European aristocracy in his wake. The fateful letter he signed declaring war on Serbia and sparking off WWI bore a Bad Ischl postmark.

Today's Bad Ischl is a handsome, if occasionally overrun, town that makes a handy base for visiting the region's five main lakes.

⊙ Sights

Kaiservilla PALACE
(www.kaiservilla.at; Jainzen 38; adult/child €14.50/7.50, grounds only €4.60/3.60; ⊙9.30am-5pm Apr-Sep, 10am-4pm Oct, 10am-4pm Sat & Sun Dec, 10am-4pm Wed Jan-Mar) Franz Josef's sprawling summer residence, the Italianate-style Kaiservilla, was an engagement present for him and his princess-to-be, Elisabeth of Bavaria, from his mother Princess Sophie. Elisabeth, who loathed the villa and her mother-in-law in equal measure, spent little time here, but the emperor came to love it and it became his permanent summer residence for more than 60 years. His mistress, Katharina Schratt, lived nearby in a house chosen for her by the empress.

Stadtmuseum MUSEUM
(www.stadtmuseum.at; Esplanade 10; adult/child €5.40/2.70; ⊙2-7pm Wed, 10am-5pm Thu-Sun Apr-Oct & Dec, 10am-5pm Fri-Sun Jan-Mar, closed Nov) The City Museum showcases the long history of Bad Ischl and stages changing exhibitions. This also happens to be the building where Franz Josef and Elisabeth were engaged, the day after they were formally introduced at a ball. You can also organise a tour of the historic Lehàr Villa (p209) here (adult/child €9.30/€5.40 for combined entrance).

Lehár Villa HOUSE
(Lehárkai 8; adult/child €5.70/2.70; ⊙10am-5pm Wed-Sun May-Sep) This pink villa was the home of opera composer Franz Lehár is a picture of late Imperial-era Austria in all its stuffy glory. Left exactly as Lehár left it, it's filled with period furniture, personal ephemera and a painting collection. It can only be visited on a tour – organise these at the Stadtmuseum. You can also buy a combined ticket for (adult/child €9.30/€5.40).

⋆ Activities

Salzkammergut Therme SPA
(www.eurothermen.at; Voglhuberstrasse 10; 4hr/day ticket adult €18/20.50 child €13/15; ⊙9am-midnight) If you'd like to follow in Princess Sophie's footsteps, check out treatments at this historic spa. Today it's a thoroughly modern operation, with the usual range of thermal pools and European spa treatments, as well

as local specialities like the 'brine' pool and a salt crystal room.

Festivals & Events

Lehár Festival
MUSIC
(www.leharfestival.at; tickets €26-80; ☉ Jul & Aug) The home of operetta composer Franz Lehár, Bad Ischl hosts the Lehár Festival, which stages musical works by Lehár and other composers.

▶️ Sleeping

Jugendgästehaus
HOSTEL $
(📞 06132-265 77; www.jugendherbergsverband.at; Am Rechensteg 5; dm/s/d €23/37/60; ☉ reception closed from 1pm Mon-Fri; ☺ @) The characterless but clean and light HI guesthouse is in the town centre behind Kreuzplatz. Prices are cheaper for stays of three or more nights.

Goldenes Schiff
HOTEL $$
(📞 06132-242 41; www.goldenes-schiff.at; Adalbert-Stifter-Kai 3; s €87-117, d €136-184, apt €184-198, junior ste €184-198; P@☎) Most doubles in this four-star hotel have bath tubs, and the best rooms (junior suites) have a touch of glamour, with large windows that overlook the river. Some rooms can be very plain but there's also a **wellness centre** with solarium and sauna, and a good **restaurant** (closed Tuesdays) serving classic Austrian cuisine (mains €15 to €30).

Hotel Garni Sonnhof
HOTEL $$
(📞 06132-230 78; www.sonnhof.at; Bahnhofstrasse 4; s €70-95, d €90-150; P☎) Nestled in a leafy glade of maple trees next to the station, this lovely hotel has cosy, traditional decor, a beautiful garden complete with a pond and a sunny conservatory. Large bedrooms mix interesting old furniture, rag rugs and wooden floors but are far from fussy. Use of the sauna and steam bath is included. Book well ahead.

Landhotel Hubertushof
HOTEL $$
(📞 06132-244 45; www.hubertushof.co.at; Götzstrasse 1; s €80-92, d €110-190; P@☎☜) This modern hotel has neat, bright rooms that manage to evoke rustic comfort without the heavy stuffiness. The open bathrooms in some rooms remind you you're in a spa town, and of course there's a sauna and infrared on-site. The tranquil swimming pool has an outdoor section.

Hotel Stadt Salzburg
HOTEL $$
(📞 06132-23 56 40; www.stadtsalzburg.at; Salzburger Strasse 25; s €51-62, d €88-104; ☎) Atmospheric public spaces, efficient staff and budget prices make this a good choice, despite the sometimes gently fading rooms. A bonus: the bus to St Gilgen and Salzburg stops at the door.

🍴 Eating

Cafe Zauner
CAFE $
(www.zauner.at; Pfarrgasse 7; pastries €3.80-6; ☉ 8.30am-6pm) Little has changed in grand Cafe Zauner since it opened in 1882. Its elegant interior with antique furnishings makes it the perfect place to relax over a luscious traditional pastry and black coffee.

Heurigen-Stöckl
PIZZA $
(www.heli-pizza.at; Kurpark, Kurhausstrasse; pizza €7-9.60; ☉ from 4pm Wed-Sun) Set among trees within the Kurpark, with plenty of outside tables for eating and drinking, this *Heuriger* (wine tavern) crosses the culinary line to serve pizza as well as light traditional tavern meals. Both can be washed down with carafes of wine or jugs of beer.

Restaurant Esplanade
AUSTRIAN $$
(www.zauner.at; Hasner Allee 2; mains €13.50-21; ☉ 10am-9pm May-Oct) This offshoot of the famous pastry shop Cafe Zauner serves quite decent Austrian staples – some using organic local meats – in a fabulously pleasant location beside the river. Given Zauner's pedigree, desserts are a big draw, too.

🍷 Drinking & Nightlife

Café Sissy
AUSTRIAN
(www.cafe-sissy.at; Pfarrgasse 2; ☉ 8am-midnight) Yet another Sissy (or Sisi, Sissi or Princess Elisabeth) pilgrimage site, with reproductions of her covering the walls of this popular riverside bar/cafe. You can breakfast here, lunch or dine on a Wiener schnitzel and other simple fare, or simply nighthawk at the front-room bar till the midnight hour. Somewhat lost in time but oddly appealing for it.

K.u.K. Hofbeisl
PUB
(www.kukhofbeisl.com; Wirerstrasse 4; ☉ 8-4am Mon-Sat, from 9am Sun) This rambling place has a *Beisl* (bistro pub; mains €11 to €22) open for lunch and dinner in one building, connected with a bar in the other, which is the liveliest late-night party place in town – DJs do their thing most Friday and Saturday nights. The cocktail list, though far from hipster-pleasing – is impressively ambitious, with about 150 cocktails in all.

❶ Information

Salzkammergut Touristik (☏ 06132-24 00 00; www.salzkammergut.co.at; Götzstrasse 12; ☺9am-7pm summer, 9am-6pm Mon-Fri, to 5am Sat rest of year) A helpful private regional agency that rents trekking and mountain bikes (per half-/full day €20/25) as well as Movelo electric bikes (e-bikes; per half-/full day €23/28). Internet service available (per 15 minutes €1).

Tourist Office (☏ 06132-27 75 70; www.badischl.at; Auböckplatz 5; ☺9am-6pm Mon-Sat, 10am-6pm Sun high season, 10am-6pm Mon-Sat, to 2pm Sun low season) This office runs a handy after-hours telephone service until 10pm for rooms and information.

❶ Getting There & Away

BUS

Postbus (☏ 05 17 17; www.postbus.at) services depart from outside the **train station** (Bahnhofstrasse 8), with hourly buses to Salzburg (€10.60, 1½ hours) via St Gilgen (€5.70, 40 minutes). Buses to St Wolfgang (€4.20, 36 minutes) go via Strobl.

TRAIN

Hourly trains to Hallstatt (€4.40, 25 minutes) go via Steeg/Hallstätter See or continue on to Obertraun (€4.90, 30 minutes). There are also hourly trains to Gmunden (€7.80, 40 minutes), as well as to Salzburg (€24.20, two hours) with various changes.

SOUTHERN SALZKAMMERGUT

Hallstätter See

The Hallstätter See, set among sharply rising mountains at an altitude of 508m, is one of the prettiest and most accessible lakes in the region. It offers some of the best hiking and swimming in summer, good skiing in winter, and a fascinating insight into the cultural history of the region any time of year. Just 5km around the lake lies Obertraun, the closest resort to the Dachstein ice caves.

The whole Hallstatt-Dachstein region became a Unesco World Heritage site in 1997.

Hallstatt

☏ 06134 / POP 790

With pastel-coloured houses that cast shimmering reflections onto the glassy waters of the lake and with towering mountains

---

❶ SALZKAMMERGUT ERLEBNIS CARD

The nontransferable Salzkammergut Erlebnis Card, available from tourist offices and hotels in the region, costs €4.90 and offers significant discounts for 21 days between 1 May and 31 October.

---

on all sides, Hallstatt's beauty alone would be enough to guarantee it fame. Boats chug tranquilly across the lake from the train station to the village, situated precariously on a narrow stretch of land between mountain and shore. (So small is the patch of land occupied by the village that its annual Corpus Christi procession takes place largely in small boats on the lake.) The sheer volume of visitors here can be nerve-fraying, especially in summer, with a sea of cars, buses and tour groups descending.

The centre of Hallstatt is at Hallstatt Markt, and Hallstatt Lahn is on the edge of town near the funicular to the Salzbergwerk. The train station is across the lake from Hallstatt; to get into town you have to take the ferry.

◉ Sights

Salzwelten MINE
(☏ 06134-200 24 00; www.salzwelten.at; Salzbergstrasse 21; return funicular plus tour adult/child/family €30/10/75; ☺9.30am-4.30pm Apr-Sep, to 3pm Oct, to 2.30pm Nov) The fascinating *Salzbergwerk* (salt mine) is situated high above Hallstatt on **Salzberg** (Salt Mountain) and is the lake's major cultural attraction. The bilingual German-English tour details how salt is formed and the history of mining, and takes visitors down into the depths on miners' slides – the largest is 60m (on which you can get your photo taken).

The **Hallstätter Hochtal** (Hallstatt High Valley) near the mine was also an Iron Age burial ground. An audioguide, available from the base station of the funicular, takes you through the numbered stations and explains the site and rituals of burial.

The funicular (p213) is the easiest way up to the mountain station, from where the mine is 15 minutes' walk; a switchback trail takes about 40 minutes to walk. Another option is to take the steps behind the Beinhaus and follow the trail until it joins the picturesque **Soleleitungsweg**; go left and follow the very steep trail past the waterfall and up steps. It's a tough climb, and not really for children.

THE SALZKAMMERGUT HALLSTÄTTER SEE

WORTH A TRIP

GOSAUSEE

This small lake is flanked by the impressively precipitous peaks of the Gosaukamm range (2459m). The view is good from the shoreline, and it takes a little over an hour to walk around the entire lake. The **Gosaukammbahn** (www.dachstein.at; return adult/child €14.30/8.60; ⌚8.15am-5pm May-Oct) cable car goes up to 1475m, where there are spectacular views and walking trails. One- to two-hourly Postbus services run to the lake from Bad Ischl (€6.10, one hour) via Steeg.

Before reaching the lake you pass through the village of Gosau, which has its own **tourist office** (☎06136 8295; www.dachstein-salzkammergut.at; Gosauseestrasse 5, Gosau; ⌚8am-6pm Mon-Fri, to 1pm Sat & Sun, closed Sat Sep-Jun) with an accommodation board outside. Gosau is at the junction of the only road to the lake and can be reached by Hwy 166 from Hallstätter See.

Weltkulturerbe Museum MUSEUM
(☎06134-82 06; www.museum-hallstatt.at; Seestrasse 56; adult/child/family €7.50/4/18; ⌚10am-6pm Apr-Oct, closed Mon & Tue Nov-Mar) This multimedia museum covers the region's history of Iron Age/Celtic occupation and salt mining. All explanations are in German and English. Its Celtic and Roman excavations are still going on beneath sports shop Dachsteinsport Janu, around the corner.

Beinhaus CHURCH
(Bone House; Kirchenweg 40; €1.50; ⌚10am-6pm May-Oct) This small ossuary contains rows of neatly stacked skulls, painted with decorative designs and the names of their former owners. Bones have been exhumed from the overcrowded graveyard since 1600, and although the practice waned in the 20th century, the last joined the collection in 1995. It stands in the grounds of the 15th-century Catholic **Pfarrkirche** (parish church), which has some attractive Gothic frescoes and three winged altars inside.

Dachsteinsport Janu MUSEUM
(Seestrasse 50; ⌚8am-6pm) FREE The Weltkulturerbe Museum's Celtic and Roman excavation work can be peeked at downstairs in Dachsteinsport Janu, a shop opposite the tourist office. There's an exhibition grave but it's an ongoing project, so there's often not that much else to see.

Activities

Tauchclub Dachstein DIVING
(☎0664 886 004 81; www.dive-adventures.at; courses from €35) Offers a full range of scuba dives, from the 'Try Dive' introductory course to night-time dives and professional training.

Sleeping

Campingplatz Klausner-Höll CAMPGROUND $
(☎06134-83 22; www.camping.hallstatt.net; Lahnstrasse 7; camp sites per adult/child/tent/car €9.30/5.20/5.70/4.70; ⌚mid-Apr–mid-Oct; P📶) Located on a grassy meadow in Hallstatt Lahn, conveniently close to the centre and almost right on the lake, this camping ground has a small kiosk, a common room for camping guests and an on-site laundry.

Seehotel Grüner Baum HOTEL $$
(☎06134-82 63; www.gruenerbaum.cc; Marktplatz 104; s €120, d €170-230; P📶) Rooms in the four-star Grüner Baum are tastefully furnished without going overboard. Three suites have enormous patios with beautiful views every which way, and doubles have smaller balconies large enough for seating, lending themselves to romantic lakeside sojourns.

Gasthof Zauner GUESTHOUSE $$
(☎06134-82 46; www.zauner.hallstatt.net; Marktplatz 51; s/d €150/180; ⌚closed Nov; P⊖📶) This quaint, ivy-covered guesthouse has super-tasteful, pine-embellished rooms, some with balconies and lake views. The restaurant (mains €12 to €25) is excellent, and not just for its fish.

Pension Sarstein GUESTHOUSE $$
(☎06134-82 17; Gosaumühlstrasse 83; d €81-101, apt for 2/3/4 people excl breakfast €100/130/150; 📶) The affable Fischer family take pride in their little guesthouse, a few minutes' walk along the lakefront from central Hallstatt. The old-fashioned rooms are not flash, but they are neat, cosy and have balconies with dreamy lake and mountain views. Family-sized apartments come with kitchenettes.

★**Halstätt Hideaway** BOUTIQUE HOTEL $$$
(☎0677 617 105 18; www.hallstatt-hideaway.com; Dr Mortonweg 24; ste €270-450; P📶) Six splendidly modern, beautifully textured private suites make up what is the region's most

stylish accommodation choice. While prices reflect the varying sizes and facilities of each of the suites, they all have their own particular appeal – be that alpine charm, a stuccoed ceiling or contemporary design pieces and killer terraces with hot tub in the penthouse.

Heritage Hotel Hallstatt　　　HOTEL **$$$**
(☑ 06134-20 03 60; www.heritagehotel.at; Landungsplatz 102; s €145, d €200-335; ☏) Rooms in this luxury hotel are spread across three buildings. The main building may claim the town's prime position at the landing stage on the lake, but 500-year-old Stocker House, a greystone beauty up the hill, is by far the most atmospheric. Rooms across all three buildings offer stunning views and have modern, rather reserved, decor.

✗ Eating

Balthazar im Rudolfsturm　　AUSTRIAN **$$**
(Rudolfsturm; mains €10.50-20; ☉9am-5pm May-Oct) Balthazar is situated 855m above Hallstatt and has the most spectacular terrace in the region. The menu is Austrian comfort food and the service is charming, but you're here for the gobsmacking views. It's best accessed by the funicular.

★Restaurant zum Salzbaron EUROPEAN **$$$**
(☑ 06134-82 63; www.gruenerbaum.cc; Marktplatz 104; mains €17-28; ☉11.30am-10pm; ☏☑) One of the best gourmet acts in town, the Salzbaron is perched alongside the lake inside the Seehotel Grüner Baum (p212) and serves a seasonal pan-European menu – the wonderful local trout features strongly in summer.

ⓘ Information

Tourist Office (☑ 06134-82 08; www. dachstein-salzkammergut.at; Seestrasse 99; ☉9am-5pm Mon-Fri, to 1pm Sat) Turn left from the ferry to reach this office. It stocks a free leisure map of lakeside towns, and hiking and cycling trails.

ⓘ Getting There & Around

BOAT
Hemetsberger Hallstättersee Schifffahrt (☑ 06134-82 28; www.hallstattschifffahrt. at; Am Hof 126) This family-run company does scheduled crossings between Obertraun and Hallstatt-Markt (€6, 25 minutes, four or five daily) from June to September, as well as the all-important year-round service between Hallstatt-Markt and Hallstatt train station (€2.50, 10 minutes, 15 times daily), connecting with trains in both directions on the main railway line. See website for prices.

It also does the circuit to Hallstatt Lahn via Hallstatt Markt, Obersee, Untersee and Steeg (€10, 90 minutes, three daily) from mid-July to August.

BUS
At least nine daily buses connect Hallstatt (Lahn) town with the cable car at Obertraun-Dachsteinseilbahn (€2.20, nine to 16 minutes).

CAR
Access into the village is restricted: electronic gates are activated during the day. Staying overnight in the centre gives you a discounted parking rate of €9 per 24 hours in the P1 parking zone (follow the signs, press 'Hotel Ticket' when entering and contact the attendant); you also get use of the special shuttle bus. See www. hallstatt.net/parking-in-hallstatt/cars for more. The rate otherwise is €12 per 24 hours.

FUNICULAR
You can ride the **funicular** (www.salzwelten. at; 1 way/return adult €9/16, child €4.50/8; ☉9am-6pm Apr-Sep, to 4pm Oct & Nov) without visiting the salt mine; runs from early April to late November.

TRAIN
Trains connect Hallstatt and Bad Ischl (€3.80, 25 minutes, hourly), and Hallstatt with Bad Aussee (€3.80, 15 minutes) every two hours. Hallstatt *Bahnhof* (train station) is across the lake from the village, and boat services coincide with train arrivals (€2.40, 10 minutes, last ferry to Hallstatt Markt 6.50pm).

Obertraun
☑ 06131 / POP 730

More low-key than Hallstatt, Obertraun is a sprawling, rather workaday village that offers great access to the Dachstein caves. It's also a good starting point for hikes around the lake, or more strenuous treks up to the caves themselves and beyond through alpine meadows.

⊙ Sights

★Dachstein Caves　　　　　　CAVE
(www.dachstein-salzkammergut.com; tour packages adult €12.30-37.40, child €10.80-20.60; ☉9am-4pm May-Sep) Climb to the Dachstein caves (Dachsteinhöhlen) and you'll find yourself in a strange world of ice and subterranean hollows, extending 80km in some places. The two caves, the **Dachstein Eishöhle** and the **Mammuthöhle**, take about 15 minutes to reach by foot, each in different directions from the Schönbergalm (p214) cable-car station at 1350m. Tours of each cave last an hour.

The ice in the Dachstein Eishöhle is no more than 500 years old, and forms an 'ice mountain' up to 8m high – twice as high now as it was when the caves were first explored in 1910. The formations here are illuminated with coloured light and the shapes they take are eerie and surreal. This cave can only be seen on a **guided tour**; if you ask the tour guides they will offer the tour with English commentary as well as German.

The ice-free Mammuthöhle is among the 30 or so deepest and longest caves in the world. Tours offer insight into the formation of the cave, which also has installations and artworks based on light and shadow to heighten the experience.

Krippenstein VIEWPOINT
(www.dachstein-salzkammergut.com; cable car return adult/child €29.30/16.10; ☺ mid-Jun–Oct) From Obertraun you can catch a cable car to Krippenstein (2109m), where you'll find the **5Fingers viewing platform**, which protrudes over a sheer cliff face in five differently shaped platforms (one is reminiscent of a diving board). On a clear day the views from here down across the lake are little short of magnificent; a glass floor allows you to peer directly down beyond your feet into a gaping void. It's definitely not for anyone who suffers vertigo.

🏃 Activities

Cable Car CABLE CAR
(www.dachstein-salzkammergut.com; adult/child return €29.30/16.10; ☺ May-Oct & Dec-Easter) A highlight in itself, the cable car departs about every 15 minutes from the valley station and has several stages, becoming more remote the further you go. After the middle station, Schönbergalm – where you alight for the caves – it continues to the highest point (2109m) of Krippenstein, where the eerie 5Fingers viewing platform dangles over the precipice, offering magnificent views.

The final stretch is to **Gjaid Alm**, taking you away from the crowds to an area where walking trails wind across the rocky meadows or lead higher into the mountains. Some of these trails begin at the simple and sought-after Gjaid Alm guesthouse (also a working organic farm), which is situated 10 minutes by foot from the cable car station.

🛏 Sleeping & Eating

Campingplatz Hinterer CAMPGROUND $
(☑ 06131-265; www.camping-am-see.at; Winkl 77; camp sites per adult/child/tent/car €10.80/8/3/5;

☺ May-Sep; 🅿 🛜) This eco-sensitive, pleasantly leafy campground is by the lake south of the river and has a bar. There are a few 'gypsy-style' caravans (€135 per night) for hire, too.

⭐ Gjaid Alm HUT $$
(☑ 06131-596; www.gjaid.at; Winkl 31; dm/s/d incl half-board €42/99/110; ☺ closed May & Nov; 🛜) This delightfully remote place is set in a rocky hollow replete with grazing cattle, sheep and horses, an easy 10-minute walk from the cable-car station. Rooms are bright, heated and very comfortable, all furnished in light woods and with views to the meadow. Remove your shoes before climbing the stairs. All dishes in the restaurant are prepared with organic ingredients.

Hotel Haus am See HOTEL $$
(☑ 06131-267 77; www.hotel-hausamsee.at; Obertraun 169; s/d €55/99; 🅿 🛜) Situated conveniently alongside the boat station and swimming area, this no-frills hotel has lots of comfortable rooms with balconies and views over the lake.

⭐ Restaurant-Pizzeria Simmer AUSTRIAN, ITALIAN $
(Seestrasse 178; mains €9.90-16, pizza €7.20-9.50; ☺ 10am-midnight Wed-Sun) Easily the most atmospheric of all the budget restaurants in the region, this Italo-Austrian place has cosy indoor seating and outdoor tables alongside a gurgling brook. The pizza is great, and there's ten-pin bowling out the back.

ℹ Information

The very helpful **tourist office** (☑ 06131-351; www.dachstein-salzkammergut.at; Obertraun 180; ☺ 8am-noon & 1-5pm Mon-Fri, 9am-noon Sat, closed Sat Sep-Jun) has a free lake and hiking trail map. It's on the way to the Dachstein cable car from the train station.

ℹ Getting There & Away

A **ferry** (p213) runs from Hallstatt Markt via Hallstatt Lahn to Obertraun (€5.50, 25 minutes, five daily).

At least nine daily buses connect Hallstatt (Lahn) town with the cable car at Obertraun-Dachsteinseilbahn (€2.20, nine to 16 minutes).

Obertraun-Dachsteinhöhlen is the train station for Obertraun settlement. There are trains to Bad Ischl (€5.90, 30 minutes, 12 daily) via Hallstatt (€2.60, three minutes).

ℹ Getting Around

Mountain and trekking bikes can be hired from **Seecafe Obertraun** (☏ 0650 617 71 65; Strandbad Obertraun; bicycle rental per day €15; ☺ May-Sep) and from **Sportshop Feuerer** (☏ 06131-267 60; Seestrasse 59; bicycle/e-bike rental per day €15/20).

A **taxi** (☏ 06131-542) to the cable-car valley station or between Hallstatt and Obertraun costs about €14.

Bad Aussee

☏ 03622 / POP 4880

Quiet, staid Bad Aussee is the largest Styrian town in the southern Salzkammergut. It is close to two lakes, and convenient by rail and a walking trail to a third, the Hallstätter See.

⊙ Sights

Altaussee Salzbergwerk   MUSEUM

(www.salzwelten.at; adult/child/family €22/11/46; ☺ tours hourly 9am-4pm Apr-Sep, 9am, 11am, 1pm & 3pm Oct, 7pm Wed year-round; 🅿🚻) Situated near the Altaussee about 6km north of

Bad Aussee, this working salt mine was the secret hiding place for art treasures stolen by the Nazis during WWII. All tours are bilingual (in German and English). Bus 955 (€2, 10 minutes) runs a few times each day from the Bad Aussee post office to the nearby stop 'Altaussee Scheiben' (though bike is a better option as the bus is infrequent).

Kammerhof Museum   MUSEUM

(☏ 03622-537 25 11; www.badaussee.at/kammerhofmuseum; Chlumeckyplatz 1; adult/child/family €5/3/8; ☺ hours vary) Kammerhof Museum, housed in a beautiful 17th-century building, covers local history and salt production. It also has some portraits of Anna Plöchl, the local postmaster's daughter who scandalously married a Habsburg prince. All explanations are in German but there's an English sheet available.

🏃 Activities

Schifffahrt Grundlsee   CRUISE

(☏ 03622-860 443 33; www.schifffahrt-grundlsee.at; adult/child €24/14; ☺ May-Oct) Offers three-hour boat tours of Grundlsee, Toplitzsee and Kammersee, the three lakes 5km to the

---

GETTING THE MOST OUT OF THE DACHSTEIN CAVES & MOUNTAINS

Planning the Day

To view one or both caves and the **5Fingers viewing platform** – about 15 minutes by foot from the **Krippenstein** (p214) station – allow a whole day, setting off from the valley cable car station around 10am. Take the cable car up to the first stop (Schönbergalm) by noon or earlier, and register at the information desk for the cave tours. Do the **Mammuthöhle** first, and allow 30 to 45 minutes to reach the **Rieseneishöhle** from there afterwards. If you only have time to see one cave, we recommend the Rieseneishöhle.

Over two days you can view one or both of the caves and the 5Fingers viewing platform; you can also take the final section of the cable car to **Gjaid Alm** station, drop by the Gjaid Alm meadow hut, and explore the area on walks or hike back down to the valley.

Discounts

There are various combined tickets and deals, including a ticket for all sections of the cable car and the caves in summer (return adult/child €43.40/23.90). Check them out at the valley station.

Winter Skiing

In winter Krippenstein is a ski and snowboard free-riding area (day pass €34). The cable car begins service in December, depending on completion of maintenance and snow conditions; it usually ends around Easter. Advanced cross-country ski hiking is also possible on the mountain.

For downhill skiers, the best piste is an 11km downhill run beginning at Krippenstein and going via Gjaid Alm station to the valley station. Hold onto your hat!

Sleeping & Eating on the Peaks

Gjaid Alm (p214) has a delightful setting and bright rooms. Regular meditation, climbing and Qi Gong courses are held here.

northeast of Bad Aussee. Bus 956 departs almost hourly from the post office to Grundlsee Seeklause (€2.20, 10 minutes) weekdays, or every two hours at weekends.

🛏 Sleeping

Pension Stocker   PENSION $
(📞 03622-524 84; www.zimmer-ausseerland.at/stocker; Altausseerstrasse 245; s/d €35/66; P 🛜)
Located 500m northwest of Kurhausplatz, this pretty pension has balconies, flower-filled window boxes and a large garden.

Josefinum   HOSTEL $
(📞 03622-521 24; Gartengasse 13; s/d €39/78; P ☺ 🛜) Peaceful retreat with basic rooms in the centre, run by nuns; meals are included. Telephone ahead for evening arrival.

★ Erzherzog Johann   HOTEL $$
(📞 03622-52 50 70; www.erzherzogjohann.at; Kurhausplatz 62; r per person €103-143; P @ 🛜 ☒) Bad Aussee's four-star hotel has rooms with comforts, but the facilities are what really catapult you into relaxation heaven: a wonderfully large sauna and wellness area, a 10m private swimming pool, and excellent bikes that are free for guests (or e-bikes for €20 per day). The hotel also caters to kids with a program of special activities.

Gasthof Blaue Traube   GUESTHOUSE $$
(📞 03622-523 63; www.blauetraube.at; Kirchengasse 165; s/d €50/90; 🛜) Historic guesthouse in the centre with modern and well-sized but somewhat bland rooms. There's wi-fi in the hall.

🍴 Eating

Konditerei Lewandofsky-Temmel   CAFE $
(Kurhausplatz 144; apple strudel €3.10; ☺ 8am-10pm Mon-Sat, from 9am Sun) Drop in for coffee and a slice of delicious apple strudel with crispy pastry, best enjoyed on the terrace alongside the Kurpark.

Restaurant Erzherzog Johann   AUSTRIAN $$
(📞 03622-52 50 70; www.erzherzogjohann.at; Kurhausplatz 62; mains €14-24, lunch buffet €15; ☺ noon-2pm & 6.30-9pm, lunch buffet Mon-Fri) The restaurant at the Hotel Erzherzog Johann has a very strong wine list, some good dishes and service with character.

ℹ Information

Tourist Office (📞 03622-523 23; www.ausseerland.at; Bahnhofstrasse 132; ☺ 9am-6pm Mon-Fri, to noon Sat) Excellent tourist office with helpful staff, located in the post office building. Pick up the town map, which has hiking trails marked for the region.

ℹ Getting There & Away

Bad Aussee is on the rail route between Bad Ischl (€7.90, 35 minutes) and Stainach-Irdning (€5.90, 35 minutes); trains run hourly in both directions. Buses arrive and depart from the tourist office/post office.

The train station is 1.5km south of the town centre – after getting off the train, dash to the bus stop out front for the connecting bus.

NORTHERN SALZKAMMERGUT

Traunsee

Traunsee is the deepest lake in Austria, going down to a cool 192m. The eastern flank is dominated by rocky crags, the tallest of which is the imposing Traunstein (1691m).

🏃 Activities

Traunsee Schiffahrt offers round-trip cruises of the lake. To explore the lake under your own steam you can rent pedal boats and electric boats from Schifffahrt Loidl (p220).

ℹ Getting There & Away

The Traunsee resorts are strung along the western shore and are connected by rail to each other and then to Bad Ischl.

ℹ Getting Around

BOAT

Traunsee Schiffahrt (📞 07612-667 00; www.traunseeschiffahrt.at; Rathausplatz) vessels tour the shoreline between mid-May and early October. There are connections from Gmunden's Rathausplatz to Landhotel Grünberg am See (adult/child €3/2.50, seven minutes, three daily), Traunkirchen (adult/child €8/6, 45 minutes, four daily) and Ebensee (adult/child €11/7.50, 70 minutes, four daily). Some boats do round-trip cruises of the lake (adult/child €19/13, 125 minutes, four daily).

BUS

The touristy **Bummelzug** (📞 0676-501 69 18; www.bummelzug-gmunden.at; adult/child return €5/3; ⊙10am-5pm May-Sep) runs to Seeschloss Ort (in Gmunden) on the western shore. **Panorama Shuttle** (www.feuerkogel.net; adult/child 1 way €3.50/2; ⊙8.50am-6.40pm May-Sep) runs seven trips daily to the end of the road on the eastern shore.

TRAIN

The Traunsee resorts are strung along the western shore and are connected by rail. Trains run between Gmunden and Traunkirchen (€3.10, 10 minutes, hourly) and Ebensee (€4.10, 20 minutes, hourly), continuing on to Bad Ischl (€8.10, 40 minutes).

Gmunden

📞07612 / POP 13,080

With its yacht marina, lakeside square and promenades, pretty, historic Gmunden exudes a breezy, riviera feel. It was known primarily for its large ceramics works and as a centre for the salt trade. While ceramics are still produced here, today it's mainly a weekend escape for fashionable Salzburgers.

⊙ Sights

★**Seeschloss Ort**   CASTLE
(www.schloss-ort.at; Orth 1; adult/child €4/free; ⊙10am-5pm May-Oct) This castle, set just beyond the lake's edge and reached by a cause-way, is believed to have been built on the ruins of a Roman fortress. It dates from 909 or earlier (although it was rebuilt in the 17th century after a fire) and has a picturesque courtyard, a late-Gothic external staircase and sgraffito from 1578. Flanking the lake on the eastern side and forming a backdrop for the castle is a pretty nature reserve known as **Toscana Park**.

★**K-Hof**   MUSEUM
(📞07612-79 44 23; www.k-hof.at; Kammerhofgasse 8; adult/child €6/2; ⊙1-5pm Wed-Fri, 10am-5pm Sat & Sun) A double act that combines with one of Austria's most unusual and refreshing museums, the **Museum for Sanitary Objects**, the K-Hof museum complex gives a fascinating insight into the history of the region. Exhibits cover ceramics manufacture (for which Gmunden is still famous), salt, fossils and the life of the 15th-century astronomer Johannes von Gmunden, whose theories influenced Copernicus.

Pfarrkirche   CHURCH
(Kirchplatz) [FREE] North of the Rathausplatz lies the 12th-century Pfarrkirche, a Gothic church later remodelled in baroque style. The altar, by the sculptor Thomas Schwanthaler (1634–1707), dates from 1678.

OUT & ABOUT AROUND BAD AUSSEE

Boat Trips

Five kilometres northeast of Bad Aussee, **Grundlsee** is a longer, thinner lake, with a good viewpoint at its western end, as well as watersports (including a sailing school) and walking trails. Extending from the eastern tip of the lake are two smaller lakes, **Toplitzsee** and **Kammersee**. Between May and October, three-hour **boat tours** (p215) take you through all three.

Hiking

The **Koppentalweg** is a picturesque 10km hiking and cycling trail that runs west through the lush Traun River valley; it connects via the Koppenbrüllerhöhlen (caves) with the Ostuferwanderweg running along the Hallstätter See. The trail begins at the Bad Aussee train station.

A map marked with hiking trails for the region can be obtained from the **tourist office** (p216).

Mountain Biking

Bike trails lead off from Bad Aussee to all the major lakes, including the Hallstätter See, and where there aren't trails the roads are generally suitable for riding. **Zweirad Friedl** (📞03622-529 18; www.zweiradfriedl.at; Meranplatz 38; mountain bike rental per day €15; ⊙9am-noon & 1pm-6pm Mon-Fri, 9am-noon Sat) hires out mountain bikes, and **Sport Käfmüller** (📞03622-549 11; www.sport-kaefmueller.at; Ischlerstrasse 121; mountain bike/e-bike rental per day €16/20; ⊙8.30am-12.30pm & 3-6pm Mon-Fri, 8.30am-12.30pmSat) does the same, as well as e-bikes.

Schloss Weyer PALACE

(Freygasse 27; adult/child €12/free; ⊙10am-noon & 2-5.30pm Tue-Fri, 10am-1pm Sat Jun-Sep) This palace contains a good collection of Meissen porcelain, silver and jewellery and has specialised temporary exhibitions dedicated to the same.

🕴 Activities

Grünberg Seilbahn CABLE CAR

(www.gruenberg.info; return adult/child €16.90/9.30; ⊙9am-6pm high season, to 5pm May-Jun & Sep–mid-Nov) A flash new cable car, leaving every 30 minutes, whisks visitors 984m up to the local mountain, **Grünberg**, where you'll find a lookout and numerous hiking and mountain bike trails, including a particularly pretty one down to the **Laudachsee**.

Kajak & Kanu Salzkammergut CANOEING

(☑07612-624 96; www.kajak-kanu.at; Traunsteinstrasse 13; kayaks & canoe rental per day €40-50, SUP €30; ⊙9.30am-1pm & 3pm-6.30pm Tue-Fri, 9.30am-1pm Sat high season, 3-6.30pm Tue-Thu, 9am-1pm & 3-6.30pm Fri, 9.30am-1pm Sat low season, closed Oct-Apr) Kayaks, Canadian canoes and stand-up paddle boards (SUP) can be hired here for paddling along the isolated eastern shore. From November to April you can call ahead to arrange hire.

🛏 Sleeping & Eating

★Seehotel Schwan HOTEL $$

(☑07612-63 39 10; www.seehotel-schwan.at; Rathausplatz 8; s €85-100, d €130-170; P ⊛) Some rooms at Gmunden's most luxurious hotel are more traditional than others, but all have a lightness of touch and there's a contemporary sensibility at work throughout. Despite its midtown locale, views are still dreamy; if you request a steam-shower room, you can even get some in-room wellness going on. The pretty restaurant specialises in – you guessed it – fish.

★Landhotel Grünberg am See GUESTHOUSE $$

(☑07612-777 00; www.gruenberg.at; Traunsteinstrasse 109; s €85-105, d €130-180; P ⊛ @ ⊛) Situated right on the lakeshore, a 10-minute drive from the town centre, this sweet, family-run hotel offers bright, spacious (if rather predictably furnished) rooms. It's definitely worth opting for those with lake views and balconies. Lake fish is served in the dining room, which also shares the

views, while the book-lined breakfast room is a cosy treat. Half-board is available.

Hotel Magerl HOTEL $$

(☑07612-636 75; www.pension-magerl.at; Ackerweg 18; s €59-68, d €104-119; P @ ⊛) This rambling pension is spread over three buildings near the cable-car station. From the outside the main building looks very drab, but rooms are clean and motel-style. It's worth asking for a room with floorboards – apart from the floorboards themselves, these are better furnished.

Keramikhotel Goldener Brunnen HOTEL $$

(☑07612-64 43 10; www.goldenerbrunnen.at; Traungasse 10; s €110, d €125-160; P ⊛) This smallish hotel in the centre has fresh, comfortable, corporate-style rooms. Public spaces are more atmospheric, with ceramics adding a decorative touch and a well-liked Austrian comfort food **restaurant** (mains €9 to €15).

Konditorei Grellinger BAKERY $

(www.konditorei-grellinger.at; Franz-Josef-Platz 6; cakes & pastries €1.50-5; ⊙9am-6.30pm Thu-Tue) While the lakeside places overflow with visitors, this historic *Konditorei* (bakery) attracts a decidedly more local crowd. The beautifully evocative interior of original fittings brightened via a clever contemporary eye would be worth the price of a (very good) coffee alone, but the pastries here are also praise-worthy, from the simple nut or poppy-seed-stuffed *Kipferl* to elaborate tortes.

🍷 Drinking & Nightlife

★Brot & Wein WINE BAR

(☑07612-703 56; www.brot-und-wein.at; Marktplatz 20; ⊙10am-2pm & 5pm-10pm Tue, 5pm-10pm Wed-Fri, 12.30-10pm Sat) The owner's astonishing collection of contemporary art posters dating back a couple of decades wallpaper this brilliant basement wine bar. During the week, head here in the evening for good-quality wine by the glass and cold platters. Or, if you're in town on a Saturday, join locals and market traders for a beautifully prepared hot lunch (€16 to €22).

Shopping

Wolfgang Leimer VINTAGE, CERAMICS

(Kirchengasse 5; ⊙11am-12.30pm Mon & Thu, 11am-6pm Tue & Fri, 11am-5pm Sat, closed Wed & Sun) A super-stuffed – but far from stuffy – vintage emporium, with a range of housewares,

Gmunden

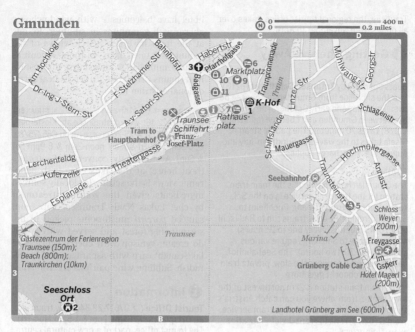

Gästezentrum der Ferienregion
Traunsee (150m);
Beach (800m);
Traunkirchen (10km)

Seeschloss Ort ②2

Traunsee

Marina

Freygasse ④4

Grünberg Cable Car

Landhotel Grünberg am See (600m)

Hotel Magerl (200m)

---

ephemera, furniture and clothes spread over several rooms and lined up in glass windows along a side arcade. This is the place to snare yourself some of the town's signature green-on-white glazed ceramics.

Der Kleine Laden CLOTHING
(📞0664 456 83 81; www.ingridthallinger.at; ⏰10am-12.30pm & 2.30-6pm Fri, 10am-1pm Sat) Ingrid Thallinger's beautiful textile pieces are sold at this stylish little shop and include hats, scarves and jersey tops and bottoms made by hand and from sustainable materials. A long-time local, Thallinger also displays works from other Gmunden makers and the street itself has a rather convivial vibe during the weekend opening.

ⓘ Information

Gästezentrum der Ferienregion Traunsee
(📞07612-643 05; www.traunsee.at; Toscana-park 1; ⏰8am-8pm Mon-Fri, 10am-7pm Sat & Sun high season, 8am-6pm Mon-Fri, 10am-4pm Sat & Sun May, Jun & Sep–mid-Oct, 9am-5pm Mon-Fri, 9am-1pm Sat, mid-Oct–Apr) Regional tourist office for the lake, with accommodation booking service and Movelo e-bike station. Also handles tourist service for the town from November to April.

Tourist Office (📞07612-65 75 20; www.traun see.at/gmunden; Rathausplatz 1; ⏰9am-5pm

Gmunden

◎ Top Sights
1 K-Hof C1
2 Seeschloss Ort A3

◎ Sights
3 Pfarrkirche B1

◉ Activities, Courses & Tours
4 Grünberg Seilbahn D3
5 Kajak & Kanu Salzkammergut D2

◉ Sleeping
6 Keramikhotel Goldener
  Brunnen C1
7 Seehotel Schwan C1

◉ Eating
8 Konditorei Grellinger B1

◉ Drinking & Nightlife
9 Brot & Wein C1

◉ Shopping
10 Der Kleine Laden C1
11 Wolfgang Leimer C1

Mon-Fri May-Oct) Has information and maps of town and the lake, as well as seasonal walking tours of the town. Helps with accommodation bookings. Gästezentrum der Ferienregion

Traunsee, the regional tourist office, takes over all duties from November to April.

ℹ️ Getting There & Away

BOAT

Boats operated by **Traunsee Schiffahrt** (p216) tour the shoreline from Gmunden to Ebensee between mid-May and early October. The one-way trip between Gmunden and Ebensee (adult/child €11/8) takes 70 minutes. The paddle steamer Gisela takes to the waves on Sunday in July and August (a €3 surcharge applies).

TRAIN

The Gmunden *Hauptbahnhof* is the main train station for the town; rail service is on the Salzkammergut line from Attnang-Puchheim to Stainach-Irdning. Regular trains run to Bad Ischl (€17.70, 45 minutes, every one to 1½ hours) although those to Salzburg require various changes (€17.70, two hours). The Seebahnhof, near the marina, services the slow, private train line from Vorchdorf-Eggenburg.

The main train station is 2km northwest of the town centre, from where you can catch Austria's shortest (and its longest-running) tram service. Tram G (€2.10) runs to Franz-Josef-Platz after every train arrival.

Traunkirchen

📞 07617 / POP 1643

The attractive hamlet of Traunkirchen sits on a spit of land about halfway along the western shore of the Traunsee. It's chiefly famous for the wooden **Fischerkanzel** (Fisherman's Pulpit; Klosterplatz 1; ☺8am-5pm) in the Pfarrkirche. This was carved in 1753 and depicts the miracle of the fishes, with the Apostles standing in a tub-shaped boat and hauling in fish-laden nets. The composition, colours (mostly silver and gold) and detail (even down to wriggling, bug-eyed fish) create a vivid impression.

🏃 Activities

Schifffahrt Loidl   BOATING

(📞 0664 371 56 46; www.schifffahrt-traunsee. at; Ortsplatz; pedal/electric boat rental per hour €10/15; ☺8am-5pm May–Sep) This operator rents out both pedal and electric boats, perfect for exploring the Traunsee on your own.

🛏️ Sleeping & Eating

Hotel Post   HOTEL $$

(📞 07617-230 70; www.hotel-post-traunkirchen.at; Ortsplatz 5; s/d from €103/166; 🅿🛜) All 55 of the spacious, contemporary and supremely comfortable rooms at this chalet-style

hotel have balconies – with windowboxes ablaze with geraniums in summer. Rooms at the front have dress-circle views of the mountain-framed lake. In-room amenities include mini bars; downstairs, the restaurant (mains €11.80 to €23) serves hearty traditional Austrian fare.

Restaurant Bootshaus   AUSTRIAN $$$

(📞 07617-22 16; www.dastraunsee.at; Klosterplatz 4; mains €31-37, 4-/5-/6-course menu €65/75/85; ☺6-9pm Thu, Fri & Mon, noon-2pm & 6-9pm Sat & Sun) A stunningly converted *Bootshaus* (boat house) at the lake's edge with panoramic views is the setting for locally sourced ingredients given the gourmet treatment by chef Lukas Nagl: Traunsee crab soup; sautéed *porcini* mushrooms picked in the surrounding forest and served with avocado cream; venison with cherry sauce; and lake-caught carp with asparagus and horseradish. Sublime wine pairings are available.

ℹ️ Information

Tourist Office (📞 07617-22 34; www.traunsee. at; Ortsplatz 1; ☺8am-12pm & 1-5pm Mon-Fri) The tourist office, part of a new cultural centre, can help with accommodation and information.

ℹ️ Getting There & Away

Trains run hourly to Traunkirchen from Gmunden (€2.40, 15 minutes).

Ebensee

📞 06133 / POP 7706

Ebensee lies on the southern shore of the turquoise waters of Traunsee and is a charming, if unassuming, market town. It's surrounded by spectacular peaks and offers access to the low-key skiing of Feuerkogel.

Ebensee was the site of a WWII concentration camp, part of the Mauthausen network. It was considered one of the worst of the SS's forced labour camps, but there is little commemoration of this horrific past.

🏃 Activities

A **cable car** (return adult/child €21.50/€10.70; ☺hourly) runs up to **Feuerkogel** (1592m), where you'll find walking trails leading across a flattish plateau. Within an hour's walk is **Alberfeldkogel** (1708m), a nature reserve popular for **hiking** in summer and for **cross-country skiing** in winter; it has an excellent view over the two Langbath lakes. Feuerkogel also provides access to winter skiing (www.feuerkogel.net; day pass adult/child €34/14.40; [⛷]), with easy-to-medium slopes.

✿ Festivals & Events

Glöcklerlauf   CULTURAL
(☉5 Jan) On Epiphany eve each year, the men of Ebensee don giant illuminated headdresses crafted from tissue paper for this pagan-inflected but now Christianised ritual. The 'Glöckler' – some 300 of them – roam through the streets when it gets dark, hoping to drive out evil spirits and win the favour of benevolent ones.

❶ Information

Tourist Office (☑ 06133-80 16; www.ebensee. com; Hauptstrasse 34; ☉9am-noon & 1-5pm Mon-Fri) Helpful for details on accommodation, and especially for activities such as hiking and mountain biking (bike hire and trails). Located by the Landungsplatz train station.

❶ Getting There & Away

Trains from Salzburg run to Ebensee-Landungsplatz (rather than the larger Ebensee station) hourly to half-hourly.

Attersee
☑ 07666 / POP 1590

The largest lake in the Salzkammergut is flanked by hills that gradually turn into mountains the further south you go. Also known as Kammersee, from its main town's lakeside neighbourhood, it's one of the less scenic and also less visited of the Salzkammergut's lakes. That said, its winds and clear waters attract local sailors and, in high summer, lake swimmers. Its waters are also home to many fish, which you'll be able to sample in area restaurants.

◉ Sights

Gustav Klimt Zentrum   MUSEUM
(www.klimt-am-attersee.at; Hauptstrasse 30, Kammer; adult/child €6/3; ☉9am-4pm Jul & Aug, 10am-3pm Wed-Sun Apr-Jun, Sep & Oct) High-tech multimedia exhibits provide an overview of symbolist painter Gustav Klimt's life and works on the Attersee, which for Klimt fans is comparable to Claude Monet's Giverny. There's also a cinema screening informative films with English subtitles. There's often an original work on loan displayed here. You can rent an audioguide (€3) for the lakeside Gustav Klimt-Themenweg trail.

Gustav Klimt-Themenweg   PUBLIC ART
(Gustav Klimt Artist Trail; Kammer) [FREE] This 2km-long lakeside trail has information boards with prints of works by Gustav Klimt. The Vienna Secessionist painter spent regular spells on the Attersee's shores at the turn of the 20th century, painting many of his renowned landscapes here; the trail passes his summer residences. .

🏃 Activities

SUP Attersee   WATER SPORTS
(www.sup-attersee.at; Strandbad Badgasse, Unterach am Attersee; equipment rental per hour/day €12/50; ☉11am-7pm Jul & Aug, noon-6pm Sat & Sun Apr-Jun & Sep) SUP Attersee rents stand-up paddle boards so you can get out on the lake's 26°C-warm waters.

Attersee-Schifffahrt   BOATING
(www.atterseeschifffahrt.at; ☉May–mid-Sep) Offers mostly alternating boat circuits of the northern (adult/child €12/6, 1¼ hours) and southern (€18/9, 2¼ hours) regions of the lake several times most days from early May to late September, and a full circuit (€21/10.50, 3¾ hours) in July and August.

❶ Information

Tourist Office (☑ 07666-77 19; www.attersee. at; Nussdorferstrasse 15; ☉9am-noon & 2-5pm Mon-Fri, 9am-noon Sat & Sun, closed weekends Sep-Jun) Can help with hotel bookings, along with addresses for aquatic sports equipment hire.

❶ Getting There & Away

The two lakeside towns of Attersee and Schörfling are each connected to the rail network by a line branching from the main Linz–Salzburg route (only regional trains stop); for Kammer-Schörfling change at Vöcklabruck, and for Attersee change at Vöcklamarkt.

Wolfgangsee

Named after a local saint, this lake has two very popular resorts, St Wolfgang and St Gilgen (of which St Wolfgang is the most appealing). The third town on the lake, Strobl, is a less remarkable but pleasant place at the start of a scenic toll road (per car and per person €3) to **Postalm** (1400m).

The Wolfgangsee is dominated by the 1783m **Schafberg** mountain on its northern shore. At the summit you'll find Austria's oldest mountain inn, a restaurant and phenomenal views over mountains and Mondsee, Attersee and, of course, Wolfgangsee. A cute historic steam train plies its way to the summit in summer, over lush fields and through dark forests.

ⓘ Getting There & Away

The only road to St Wolfgang approaches from Strobl in the east. A **Postbus** (p211) service runs between St Wolfgang and St Gilgen (€5.70, 50 minutes) with a connecting transfer in Strobl. For buses to Salzburg (€9.10, 1¾ hours) you need to connect in St Gilgen or Strobl (€2.40, 12 minutes).

ⓘ Getting Around

A **ferry service** (www.wolfgangseeschifffahrt. at; ☺ May-Oct) operates late March to October, running from Strobl to St Gilgen (adult/child €9.80/4.90, 75 minutes) and stopping at points en route. Services are most frequent from late June to early September. Boats run from St Wolfgang to St Gilgen (€7.40/3.70, 35 minutes) half-hourly during the day in high season, from late June to early September, tailing off to four to five in spring and autumn.

St Gilgen

📞 06227 / POP 3675

The ease of access to St Gilgen, 29km from Salzburg, makes this town very popular for day trippers, but it has also become popular in recent years because of its very scenic setting. Along with quieter Strobl, it's a good base for water sports on the lake, and is not quite as crowded as St Wolfgang.

◉ Sights

Mozarthaus   MUSEUM
(📞06227-202 42; www.mozarthaus.info; Ischlerstrasse 15; adult/child €4/2.50; ☺10am-noon Sat & Sun May-Oct) There are five houses worldwide dedicated to Mozart, but this one takes the interesting approach of focusing mostly on the family, especially his sister 'Nannerl' (Maria Anna), an accomplished composer and musician in her own right. Multilingual films tell the story, and there's a small exhibition.

**Muzikinstumente-Museum
der Völker**   MUSEUM
(Folk Music Instrument Museum; www.hoerant.at; Aberseestrasse 11; adult/child €4/2.50; ☺9-11am & 3-7pm Tue-Sun Jun–mid-Oct, 9-11am & 3-6pm Mon-Thu, 9-11am Fri, 3-6pm Sun Nov-May) This cosy little museum is home to 1500 musical

instruments from all over the world, all of them collected by one family of music teachers. The son of the family, Askold zum Eck, can play them all and will happily demonstrate for hours. Visitors are sometimes allowed to play, too.

Heimatkundliches Museum   MUSEUM
(www.heimatkundliches-museum-sankt-gilgen.at; Pichlerplatz 6; adult/child €4/2.50; ☺10am-noon & 3-6pm Tue-Sun Jun-Sep) The town museum has an eclectic collection ranging from embroidery – originally manufactured in the building – to religious objects and thousands of animal specimens.

🏃 Activities

Watersports such as **windsurfing, waterskiing** and **sailing** are popular activities in St Gilgen. There's a town swimming pool and a small beach (free) with a grassy area beyond the yacht marina.

The mountain rising over the resort is 1520m **Zwölferhorn** (www.12erhorn.at; cable car adult/child return €24.50/15), from where there are good views and **hiking trails** (two to 2½ hours) leading back to St Gilgen. In winter there's downhill **skiing**.

St Gilgen has one of the lake's best **playgrounds**, situated at the shore near the ferry landing. As well as swings, there's a nifty flying fox and slides, and things to climb or hang around on. It's partly shaded.

🛏 Sleeping & Eating

⭐**Jugendgästehaus
Schafbergblick**   HOSTEL $
(📞06227-23 65; www.jugendherbergsverband.at; Mondseer Strasse 7; dm/s/d €30/37/60; ☺reception 8am-1pm & 5-7pm Mon-Fri, 5-7pm Sat & Sun; 🅿@🛜) A pretty hostel with neat, bright rooms, grassy grounds and a fabulous lakeside location. It does, however, get a lot of school groups during term time.

⭐**Gasthof Zur Post**   GUESTHOUSE $$
(📞06227-21 57; www.gasthofzurpost.at; Mozartplatz 8; s €115-150, d €152-190, f €225; 🅿@🛜) This old inn's rooms are beautifully designed – some of the most stylish in the region. Some combine antique pieces set against a simple contemporary base, while others have a cosily modern-rustic style with bright felts and pale wood. The **restaurant** (mains €15 to €20) serves regional specialities in a low-ceilinged, whitewashed dining room, or outside on the elegant terrace.

Pension Falkensteiner PENSION $$
(✆06227-23 95; www.pension-falkensteiner.at; Salzburgerstrasse 13; s/d €59/118; P ⊜ @) A no-frills but spotless pension that has helpful management. All of the rooms are large, and some have balconies.

★ **M.** STEAK, PIZZA $$
(www.mwolfgangsee.at; Ischlerstrasse 18; steaks €13.90-23,90, pasta €9.20-14.40, pizza €7.20-11.20; ⊙5-10pm Mon-Fri, 11am-10.30pm Sat & Sun) This relaxed 'Mediterranean' restaurant by the lake has a modern dining room and tables out in the garden. You can also order pizza to take away – they're nicely authentic – and there's a small, well done (if somewhat predictable) menu of pastas, risottos and salads.

Fischer-Wirt Restaurant AUSTRIAN, SEAFOOD $$
(www.fischer-wirt.at; Ischlerstrasse 21; mains €9.50-18.50; ⊙8am-2pm & 6-9pm) Situated on the water's edge, this popular seafood restaurant does lake-fish three ways: fried with parsley potatoes, salmon steak with risotto or as part of a seafood dinner platter that includes both, as well as mussels and prawns.

🍸 **Drinking & Nightlife**

12AlmBar BAR
(www.12eralm.at; ⊙6pm-1am Thu-Sun) An archetypal resort bar, the Zwolfer Alm Bar is a loud, colourful basement party zone that goes from drinking spot to disco after 9pm. Check the website for events and parties.

ℹ **Information**

Tourist Office (✆06227-23 48; www.wolf gangsee.at; Mondsee Bundesstrasse 1a; ⊙9am-7pm Mon-Fri, to 5pm Sat, 10am-5pm Sun; 🛜) Helps find rooms and is a wi-fi hotspot. Brochures are also available inside the *Rathaus* (town hall) on Mozartplatz.

ℹ **Getting There & Away**

St Gilgen is 50 minutes from Salzburg by Postbus (p211), with hourly departures (€6.70) until early evening; buses continue on to Stobl and Bad Ischl (€5.70, 40 minutes). The bus station is near the base station of the cable car.

Boats (p222) run to St Wolfgang (adult/child €7.40/3.70, 45 minutes) roughly hourly from May to early September, tailing off to a few per day in shoulder seasons (May, September and October).

Hwy 154 provides a scenic route north to Mondsee.

St Wolfgang

✆06138 / POP 2820
St Wolfgang is a charming town situated on the steep banks of the Wolfgangsee. Although its streets can get clogged with visitors during the day, things usually settle down by early evening, which is the best time for a tranquil stroll along the forested lakeshore, past the gently creaking wooden boathouses.

The village's main fame arose as a place of pilgrimage, and today's visitors still come to see the same 14th-century church, packed with art treasures.

◉ **Sights**

Wallfahrtskirche CHURCH
(Pilgrimage Church; www.pfarre-sankt-wolfgang.at; Markt; €1; ⊙8am-6pm May-Sep, to 4pm Oct-Apr) St Wolfgang's impressive Wallfahrtskirche is a spectacular gallery of religious art, with glittering altars (from Gothic to baroque), an extravagant pulpit, a fine organ and countless statues and paintings. The most impressive piece is the winged **high altar**, created by celebrated religious artist Michael Pacher between 1471 and 1481 – it's a perfect example of the German Gothic style, enhanced with the technical achievements of Renaissance Italy.

🏃 **Activities**

A number of hotels have jetties for swimming, and a tourist office booklet details the many water sports on offer here. You can spend a lovely afternoon with a walk or cycle to Strobl, 6km away (around 1½ hours on foot), ending the excursion with a swim

Schafbergbahn RAIL
(www.wolfgangseeschifffahrt.at; Schafbergbahnstrasse; adult/child 1 way €24/12, return €34/17; ⊙May-Oct) If you don't fancy the four-hour walk from St Wolfgang to the 1783m summit of Schafberg, ride this historic steam train, the steepest cogwheel railway in Austria. Featured in *The Sound of Music,* it's a cute, local icon, but also passes through some beautiful alpine scenery.

Departures are approximately hourly between 9.15am and 3pm (the last trip down is 5.15pm). That said, the trip is so popular that you probably won't be able to get on the next train. Queue early, purchase a ticket for a specific service and then go for a wander along the lake or around St Wolfgang until your departure time. Apart from its summer season the train also does an Advent run, with weekend trips from mid-November to mid-December.

🛌 Sleeping

★ Hotel Cortisen am See   BOUTIQUE HOTEL $$

(☑06138-237 60; www.cortisen.at; Pilgerstrasse 15; d €125-195) Hotelier Roland Ballner goes all out to make guests feel at home at this lakeside retreat, which may seem all Austrian tradition on the outside but is a riot of colour and individual style within. Apart from the charming interior spaces there are beautiful lakeside lounging areas and a pretty restaurant. Note: this is a child-free hotel.

Hotel Peter   HOTEL $$

(☑06138-230 40; www.hotelpeter.at; Markt 54; s/d €100/150, ste €185; P@🛜) The generous-sized rooms at this four-star hotel have balconies looking onto the lake, as well as large bathrooms and old-fashioned, though far from faded, decor. The restaurant (mains €15 to €21), which has a terrace overlooking the lake, serves pasta and a good fish platter filled with poached, fried and baked local fish. There's also wi-fi.

Seehof Pension Apartments   APARTMENT $$

(☑06138-23 08; www.pension-seehof.com; Markt 68; 2-person/family/4-6–person apt €200/€185/€235; P🛜) These bright and very comfortable apartments all have terraces with lake views; the larger ones can work out to be good value if you're sharing. Some of the spotless modern kitchens have dishwashers and microwaves though others are a little less well-equipped. All are also wheelchair-accessible (with lift access).

★ Im Weissen Rössl   LUXURY HOTEL $$$

(☑06138-23 06; www.weissesroessl.at; Markt 74; s €165-195, d €240-410; P@🛜🏊) St Wolfgang's most famous hotel was the setting for Ralph Benatzky's operetta *The White Horse*. Rooms are somewhat idiosyncratic, and a little tired for the price, but the more expensive ones have a balcony and view over the lake. In any case, everyone's here for the wellness area and the impeccable haute-European service.

🍴 Eating

See Eck   AUSTRIAN $$

(☑0699 109 164 81; www.see-eck.at; Markt 92; mains €8-15; ⊙3.30pm-midnight Tue-Sun) A perfect match for St Wolfgang's older and well-to-do visitors, this smart, friendly wine

bar does a small and very interesting dinner menu each night. Italian-influenced dishes such as fish fillets with *fregola* (Sardinian pasta) or saffron-and-fennel beef tartare with tomato foam make a nice, light alternative to the usual Austrian fare.

Im Weissen Rössl   AUSTRIAN $$$

(www.weissesroessl.at; Markt 74; mains €12.50-33.50) There are two restaurants and a lovely wine cellar in this highly respected, fabulously traditional hotel. The Seerestaurant (mains €12.50 to €19), which is open all day, keeps it more casual with regional and international dishes, while the Romantik has a formal six-course menu for €65 as well as an à la carte menu (dinner only; mains €29 to €33.50).

ℹ Information

Tourist Office (☑06138-80 03; www.wolfgangsee.at; Au 140; ⊙9am-7pm Mon-Fri, to 6pm Sat, 10am-5pm Sun; 🛜) Helpful staff, at the eastern tunnel entrance; a wi-fi hot spot.
Tourist Office (Michael-Pacher-Haus; www.wolfgangsee.at; Pilgerstrasse; ⊙9am-noon & 2-5pm Jun-Sep) One of two tourist office branches in town, this second branch is smaller and located near the northwest end of the road tunnel.

ℹ Getting There & Away

The only road to St Wolfgang approaches from Strobl in the east.

Boats (p222) run to St Gilgen roughly half-hourly May to early September (adult/child €7.40/3.70, 45 minutes), tailing off to every couple of hours in shoulder seasons (May, September and October). Paddle-wheel and vintage boats complement these (€1 surcharge). Wolfgangsee ferries stop at the village centre (Markt stop) and at the Schafberg railway (p223).

A Postbus (p211) service runs between St Wolfgang and St Gilgen (€5.70, 50 minutes) with a connecting transfer in Strobl. For buses to Salzburg (€9.10, 1¾ hours) you need to connect in St Gilgen or Strobl (€2.40, 12 minutes).

ℹ Getting Around

Pro Travel (☑06138-25 25; www.protravel.at; Markt 152; per day mountain bike rental €25, e-bike/e-mountain bike rental €20/37; ⊙9am-6.30pm) has a large range of bikes for hire, including electric bikes (e-bikes). They're happy to suggest walking and cycling itineraries; you can prebook the night before for their Schwarzensee (p225) shuttle service.

Strobl

📞 06137 / POP 2750

While high-profile Wolfgangsee towns such as St Wolfgang and St Gilgen justifiably attract large numbers of visitors, the lesser-known and more low-key Strobl, at the eastern end of the lake, is well worth a visit for its friendly, low-key ambience and access to good hiking and cycling trails.

🏃 Activities

Schwarzensee   MOUNTAIN BIKING, HIKING

Situated 9km from Strobl at an altitude of 715m, Schwarzensee makes for a perfect day outing – either hiking or with conventional or e-bikes, which can be rented from **Sport Girbl** (📞 06137-74 84; www.sport-girbl.at; Bahnstrasse 300; bicycle rental per day €10-28; ⊙ 8am-noon & 2.30-6pm). This picturesque and isolated swimming lake has a few small restaurants, including Alm-Stadl Schwarzensee, which serves delicious smoked lake trout (and has a Movelo e-bike battery exchange station).

🛏 Sleeping & Eating

⭐**Hotel Stroblerhof**   HOTEL $$

(📞 06137-73 08; www.stroblerhof.at; Ischlerstrasse 16; s/d €80/160; 🅿 ❄ @ 🛜) This stylish hotel is the best place to stay and eat in Strobl. Combining a cosy chalet style with clean contemporary lines, and a very relaxing pool area, it's something of a surprise in this region.

Alm-Stadl Schwarzensee   AUSTRIAN, SEAFOOD $

(📞 0664 266 44 98; Schwarzensee; mains €9-15.50; ⊙ 10am-midnight April-early Nov) Alm-Stadl Schwarzensee, one of a couple of restaurants located by the remote and picturesque Schwarzensee, serves delicious smoked lake trout. (It also has a battery exchange station for Movelo e-bikes.)

ℹ Getting There & Away

Postbus (p211) line 150 runs to St Gilgen and St Wolfgang, where you can connect to transport to Salzburg.

Mondsee

📞 06232 / POP 3305

The town of Mondsee extends along the northern tip of this crescent-shaped lake, noted for its warm water. Coupled with its closeness to Salzburg (30km away), this makes it a highly popular lake for weekending Salzburgers, with the accompanying urban comforts.

⊙ Sights

Basilica Minor St Michael   CHURCH

(www.pfarre-mondsee.com; Kirchengasse 1; by donation; ⊙ 9am-7pm) If you're allergic to the film *The Sound of Music,* there's just one piece of advice: get out of town. Even the lemon-yellow baroque facade (added in 1740, incidentally) of the 15th-century parish church achieved notoriety by featuring in those highly emotional Von Trapp wedding scenes in the film.

Museum Mondseeland und Pfahlbaumuseum   MUSEUM

(www.mondseeland.org/museen.html; Marschal-Wrede-Platz; adult/child €3/1.50; ⊙ 10am-6pm Tue-Sun Jul & Aug, to 5pm Tue-Sun May, Jun & Sep, 10am-5pm Sat & Sun Oct) Next door to the parish church, this museum has displays on Stone Age finds and the monastic culture of the region (as Mondsee is a very old monastery site).

🏃 Activities

Segelschule Mondsee   WATER SPORTS

(📞 06232-354 82 00; www.segelschule-mondsee.at; Robert Baum Promenade 3; windsurf/kayak/SUP rental per half-day €35, sailboat rental per hour/day from €18/60; ⊙ 9am-6pm May-Sep) This large outfit offers sailing, kayaking, windsurfing and stand-up paddleboard (SUP) courses, as well as equipment hire.

🛏 Sleeping

Jugendgästehaus   HOSTEL $

(📞 06232-24 18; www.jugendherbergsverband.at; Krankenhausstrasse 9; dm/s/d €27/37/60; 🅿 🛜) This modern HI hostel is a few minutes' walk up the hill from the centre of town. Its usual range of rooms are simple and streamlined.

Hotel Krone   HOTEL $$

(📞 06232-22 36; www.hotelkrone.org; Rainerstrasse 1; s €75, d €104-144; 🅿 🛜) This attractive, comfortable, centrally located three-star has neat if unremarkable rooms, some with balconies. There are doubles that have a connecting door that families will find useful. The **restaurant** (mains €11.50 to €16.20) is open for lunch and dinner from Wednesday to Monday.

★ **Seegasthof-Hotel Lackner** HOTEL $$$
(☑ 06232-23 59; www.seehotel-lackner.at; Mond-seestrasse 1; r €230-260, junior ste €290-320; P ⊜)
Set on the shore of the Mondsee, the Lackner offers elegant, contemporary rooms with balconies and lovely lake views. A private beach is set among the reeds and the excellent terrace **restaurant** (closed Tuesdays; mains €17 to €28, six-course menu €75) serves venison and lamb dishes as well as fish, complemented by a *Vinothek* (wine bar).

Iris Porsche Hotel & Restaurant HOTEL $$$
(☑ 06232-22 37; www.irisporsche.at; Marktplatz 1; s €160-190, d €200-260; P ✻ ☎) Rooms in this modern, upmarket business hotel have lovely wooden floors and, in some, little roof terraces. There's a lift, a wellness area, bathtubs and steam showers in the spa. The **restaurant** (lunch mains €10 to €16, dinner mains €18 to €28) serves well-prepared fish and Austrian dishes. Good discounts offered in low season.

 **Eating**

★ **Holzingerbauer** AUSTRIAN $
(☑ 06232-38 41; www.holzingerbauer.at; Oberbur-gau 12; plates €6-15; ⊙ 3-11pm Mon, Tue, Thu & Fri) This farm table a short drive from Mond-see proper serves *Jause* (snack platters) in a fabulously bucolic setting. As hearty and homemade as the spread is, the appeal for Austrian holidaymakers is Holzingerbauer's own *Most*, the famous local cider.

★ **Schlossbräu Mondsee** AUSTRIAN $$
(☑ 06232-50 01; www.schlossbraeu-mondsee.at; Schlosshof 1a; mains €15-22; ⊙ 10.30am-midnight Tue-Fri, 9am-4pm Sat & Sun) This sprawling tavern somehow manages to be so much more than a hotel restaurant. Overlooking the main square and the Basilica of St Michael, there's a summer terrace outside and miles of woody tables under vaulted ceilings inside. Grab a bratwurst or grilled lake-fresh fish; young staff are friendly and happy to find you a beer you'll like.

ℹ Information

The **tourist office** (☑ 06232-22 70; www.mond see.at; Dr Franz Müller Strasse 3; ⊙ 8am-7pm Mon-Fri, 9am-7pm Sat & Sun, closed Sat & Sun Oct-May) can help with accommodation and hiking maps.

ℹ Getting There & Away

Hourly **Postbus** (p211) services connect Mond-see with Salzburg (€10.15, 45 minutes); five direct buses run weekdays to St Gilgen (€4.60, 20 minutes).

Expect to pay up to €30 for a ride to St Gilgen by **taxi** (☑ 0664 220 00 22).

Salzburg & Salzburgerland

Best Places to Eat

➜ Magazin (p245)

➜ Esszimmer (p245)

➜ Obauer (p253)

➜ Steinerwirt (p260)

➜ Ginger & Gin (p264)

Best Places to Sleep

➜ Haus Ballwein (p239)

➜ Villa Trapp (p242)

➜ Bio-Hotel Hammerhof (p254)

➜ Pension Hubertus (p258)

➜ Alpenblick (p262)

Why Go?

One of Austria's smallest provinces, Salzburgerland is proof that size really doesn't matter. Well, not when you have Mozart, Maria von Trapp and the 600-year legacy of the prince-archbishops behind you. This is the land that grabbed the world spotlight and shouted 'visit Austria!' with Julie Andrews skipping joyously down the mountainsides. This is indeed the land of crisp apple strudel, dancing marionettes and high-on-a-hilltop castles. This is the Austria of your wildest childhood dreams.

Salzburg is every bit as grand as you imagine it: a baroque masterpiece, a classical music legend and Austria's spiritual heartland. But it is just the prelude to the region's sensational natural beauty. Just outside the city, the landscape is etched with deep ravines, glinting ice caves, karst plateaux and mountains of myth – in short, the kind of alpine gorgeousness that no well-orchestrated symphony or yodelling nun could ever quite capture.

When to Go

➜ Prices peak in family-friendly Alpine resorts during winter, from December to early April. Salzburg twinkles at its Christmas markets. In January orchestras strike up at Mozartwoche, while hot-air balloons glide above Filzmoos' summits.

➜ Summer sees room prices soar in Salzburg and nosedive in Alpine resorts from June to September. Book months ahead for the colossal feast of opera, classical music and drama that is the Salzburg Festival, held from late July through August. Head for high-altitude hiking in the limestone Tennengebirge and Dachstein ranges and the glacier-capped Hohe Tauern National Park, or chill lakeside in Zell am See.

➜ Shoulder season months April, May, October and November bring few crowds and low room rates. Salzburg hosts Easter classical-music festivals.

Salzburg & Salzburgerland Highlights

1 **Festung Hohensalzburg** (p229) Surveying Salzburg from atop its clifftop fortress.

2 **Eisriesenwelt** (p252) Going subzero in the world's largest ice cave in Werfen.

3 **Schloss Hellbrunn** (p250) Getting drenched by fountains at this opulent palace.

4 **Schloss Mirabell** (p231)

Singing 'Do-Re-Mi' in these exquisite gardens.

5 **Salzwelten** (p251) Delving into the depths of a salt mine in Bad Dürrnberg.

6 **Grossglockner Road** (p265) Driving helter-skelter on this high-alpine road.

7 **Felsentherme** (p261) Bathing in the healing waters.

8 **Krimmler Wasserfälle** (p267) Hearing the thunder of Europe's highest waterfall.

9 **Kitzsteinhorn Glacier** (p257) Hiking and snowball fighting on this 3029m glacier.

10 **Pinzgauer Spaziergang** (p263) Coming face-to-face with Austria's Alpine giants.

History

Salzburg had a tight grip on the region as far back as 15 BC, when the Roman town Iuvavum stood on the site of the present-day city. This Roman stronghold came under constant attack from warlike Celtic tribes and was ultimately destroyed or abandoned due to disease.

St Rupert established the first Christian kingdom and founded St Peter's church and monastery in around AD 700. As centuries passed, the successive archbishops of Salzburg gradually increased their power and eventually were given the grandiose titles of Princes of the Holy Roman Empire.

Wolf Dietrich von Raitenau, Salzburg's most influential prince-archbishop from 1587 to 1612, spearheaded the total baroque makeover of the city, commissioning many of its most beautiful churches, palaces and gardens. He fell from power after losing a fierce dispute over the salt trade with the powerful rulers of Bavaria, and died a prisoner.

Another of the city's archbishops, Paris Lodron (1619–53), managed to keep the principality out of the Europe-wide Thirty Years' War. Salzburg also remained neutral during the War of the Austrian Succession a century later, but bit-by-bit the province's power waned and Salzburg came under the thumb of France and Bavaria during the Napoleonic Wars. In 1816 Salzburg became part of the Austrian Empire and was on the gradual road to economic recovery.

The early 20th century saw population growth and the founding of the prestigious Salzburg Festival in 1920. Austria was annexed to Nazi Germany in 1938 and during WWII some 40% of the city's buildings were destroyed by Allied bombings. These were restored to their former glory, and in 1997 Salzburg's historic *Altstadt* (old town) became a Unesco World Heritage site.

ⓘ Getting There & Around

AIR

Both scheduled and no-frills flights from Europe and the USA serve **Salzburg airport** (✆ 0662-858 00; www.salzburg-airport.com; Innsbrucker Bundesstrasse 95; ☎), a 20-minute bus ride from the city.

BUS

Salzburg's efficient bus network, run by **Salzburger Verkehrsverbund** (SVV; www.salzburg-verkehr.at), makes it easy to reach the province's smaller villages.

TRAIN

Salzburg is well connected to the rest of Austria by public transport, with excellent rail connections to Hohe Tauern National Park and neighbouring Salzkammergut. Salzburg's *Hauptbahnhof* (main train station) has good services to Germany, Italy and the Czech Republic.

SALZBURG

✆ 0662 / POP 146,631

The joke 'If it's baroque, don't fix it' is a perfect maxim for Salzburg: the storybook Old Town burrowed below steep hills looks much as it did when Mozart lived here 250 years ago. Standing beside the fast-flowing Salzach River, your gaze is raised inch by inch to graceful domes and spires, the formidable clifftop fortress and the mountains beyond. It's a backdrop that did the lordly prince-archbishops and Maria proud.

Beyond Salzburg's two biggest money-spinners – Mozart and *The Sound of Music* – hides a city with a burgeoning arts scene, wonderful food, manicured parks, quiet side streets where classical music wafts from open windows, and concert halls that uphold musical tradition 365 days a year. Everywhere you go, the scenery, the skyline, the music and the history send your spirits soaring higher than Julie Andrews' octave-leaping vocals.

◉ Sights

Salzburg's trophy sights huddle in the pedestrianised **Altstadt**, which straddles both banks of the Salzach River but centres largely on the left bank. Here the tangled lanes make for a serendipitous wander, leading to hidden courtyards and medieval squares framed by burgher houses and baroque fountains.

Many places close slightly earlier in winter and open longer – usually an hour or two – during the Salzburg Festival.

★ **Festung Hohensalzburg** FORT
(www.salzburg-burgen.at; Mönchsberg 34; adult/child/family €12/6.80/26.20, incl funicular €15.20/8.70/33.70; ⊙9am-7pm) Salzburg's most visible icon is this mighty, 900-year-old cliff-top fortress, one of the biggest and best preserved in Europe. It's easy to spend half a day up here, roaming the ramparts for far-reaching views over the city's spires, the Salzach River and the mountains. The fortress is a steep 15-minute jaunt from the

centre or a speedy ride up in the glass Festungsbahn funicular (p236).

The fortress began life as a humble bailey, built in 1077 by Gebhard von Helffenstein at a time when the Holy Roman Empire was at loggerheads with the papacy. The present structure, however, owes its grandeur to spendthrift Leonard von Keutschach, prince-archbishop of Salzburg from 1495 to 1519 and the city's last feudal ruler.

Highlights of a visit include the **Golden Hall** – where lavish banquets were once held – with a gold-studded ceiling imitating a starry night sky. Your ticket also gets you into the **Marionette Museum**, where skeleton-in-a-box Archbishop Wolf Dietrich steals the (puppet) show, as well as the **Fortress Museum**, which showcases a 1612 model of Salzburg, medieval instruments, armour and some pretty gruesome torture devices.

The Golden Hall is the backdrop for year-round **Festungskonzerte** (fortress concerts), which often focus on Mozart's works. See www.mozartfestival.at for times and prices.

★ Salzburg Museum   MUSEUM
(www.salzburgmuseum.at; Mozartplatz 1; adult/child €8.50/3; ⊙9am-5pm Tue-Sun, to 8pm Thu; 🖑) Housed in the baroque Neue Residenz palace, this flagship museum takes you on a fascinating romp through Salzburg past and present. Ornate rooms showcase everything from Roman excavations to royal portraits. There are free **guided tours** at 6pm every Thursday.

A visit starts beneath the courtyard in the strikingly illuminated **Kunsthalle**, presenting rotating exhibitions of art. Upstairs, prince-archbishops glower down from the walls at **Mythos Salzburg**, which celebrates the city as a source of artistic and poetic inspiration. Showstoppers include Carl Spitzweg's renowned painting *Sonntagsspaziergang* (Sunday Stroll; 1841), the portrait-lined **prince-archbishop's room** and the **Ständesaal** (Sovereign Chamber), an opulent vision of polychrome stucco curling around frescoes depicting the history of Rome according to Titus Livius. The early 16th-century Millefiori tapestry, Archbishop Wolf Dietrich's gold-embroidered pontifical shoe, and Flemish tapestries are among other attention-grabbers.

The **Panorama Passage** also provides some insight into Salzburg's past, with its Roman walls and potter's kiln and models of the city at different points in history.

Salzburg's famous 35-bell **glockenspiel**, which chimes daily at 7am, 11am and 6pm, is on the western flank of the Neue Residenz.

★ Residenz   PALACE
(www.domquartier.at; Residenzplatz 1; DomQuartier ticket adult/child €12/5; ⊙10am-5pm Wed-Mon) The crowning glory of Salzburg's new DomQuartier, the Residenz is where the prince-archbishops held court until Salzburg became part of the Habsburg Empire in the 19th century. An audioguide tour takes in the exuberant **state rooms**, lavishly adorned with tapestries, stucco and frescoes by Johann Michael Rottmayr. The 3rd floor is given over to the **Residenzgalerie**, where the focus is on Flemish and Dutch masters. Must-sees include Rubens' *Allegory on Emperor Charles V* and Rembrandt's chiaroscuro *Old Woman Praying*.

★ Museum der Moderne   GALLERY
(www.museumdermoderne.at; Mönchsberg 32; adult/child €8/6; ⊙10am-6pm Tue-Sun, to 8pm Wed) Straddling Mönchsberg's cliffs, this contemporary glass-and-marble oblong of a gallery stands in stark contrast to the fortress, and shows first-rate temporary exhibitions of 20th- and 21st-century art. The works of Alberto Giacometti, Dieter Roth, Emil Nolde and John Cage have previously been featured. There's a free **guided tour** of the gallery at 6.30pm every Wednesday. The Mönchsberg Lift whizzes up to the gallery year-round.

Dom   CATHEDRAL
(Cathedral; www.salzburger-dom.at; Domplatz; ⊙8am-7pm Mon-Sat, 1-7pm Sun May-Sep, shorter hours rest of year) FREE Gracefully crowned by a bulbous copper dome and twin spires, the Dom stands out as a masterpiece of baroque art. Bronze portals symbolising faith, hope and charity lead into the cathedral. In the nave, both the intricate stucco and Arsenio Mascagni's ceiling frescoes recounting the Passion of Christ guide the eye to the polychrome dome.

Residenzplatz   SQUARE
With its horse-drawn carriages, palace and street entertainers, this stately baroque square is the Salzburg of a thousand postcards. Its centrepiece is the **Residenzbrunnen**, an enormous marble fountain. The plaza is the late-16th-century vision of Prince-Archbishop Wolf Dietrich von Raitenau who, inspired by Rome, enlisted Italian architect Vincenzo Scamozzi to design it.

Mozarts Geburtshaus
MUSEUM

(Mozart's Birthplace; www.mozarteum.at; Getreide-gasse 9; adult/child €10/3.50; ⊗ 8.30am-7pm Jul & Aug, 9am-5.30pm Sep-Jun) Wolfgang Amadeus Mozart, Salzburg's most famous son, was born in this bright yellow townhouse in 1756 and spent the first 17 years of his life here. Today's museum harbours a collection of instruments, documents and portraits. Highlights include the mini-violin he played as a toddler, plus a lock of his hair and buttons from his jacket. In one room, Mozart is shown as a holy babe beneath a neon-blue halo – we'll leave you to draw your own analogies.

Mozart-Wohnhaus
MUSEUM

(Mozart's Residence; www.mozarteum.at; Makart-platz 8; adult/child €10/3.50; ⊗ 8.30am-7pm Jul & Aug, 9am-5.30pm Sep-Jun) Tired of the cramped living conditions on Getreidegasse, the Mozart family moved to this more spacious abode in 1773, where a prolific Wolfgang composed works such as the *Shepherd King* (K208) and *Idomeneo* (K366). Emanuel Schikaneder, a close friend of Mozart and the librettist of *The Magic Flute*, was a regular guest here. An audio guide accompanies your visit, serenading you with opera excerpts. Alongside family portraits and documents, you'll find Mozart's original fortepiano.

Untersberg
MOUNTAIN, VIEWPOINT

(www.untersbergbahn.at; cable car up/down/return €15/13.50/23.50, free with Salzburg Card; ⊗ 8.30-5.30pm Jul-Sep, shorter hours rest of year, closed Nov–mid-Dec) Rising above Salzburg and straddling the German border is the rugged 1853m peak of Untersberg. Spectacular views of the city, the Rositten Valley and the Tyrolean, Salzburg and Bavarian alpine ranges unfold from the summit. The mountain is a magnet to local skiers in winter, and hikers, climbers and paragliders in summer. From the cable car top station, short, easy trails lead to nearby viewpoints at **Geiereck** (1805m) and **Salzburg Hochthron**, while others take you much deeper into the Alps.

Stift Nonnberg
CONVENT

(Nonnberg Convent; Nonnberggasse 2; ⊗ 7am-dusk) FREE A short climb up the Nonnbergstiege staircase from Kaigasse or along Festungsgasse brings you to this Benedictine convent, founded 1300 years ago and made famous as the nunnery in *The Sound of Music*. You can visit the beautiful rib-vaulted **church**, but the rest of the convent is off-limits. Take €0.50 to switch on the light that illuminates the beautiful **Romanesque frescoes**.

ⓘ SALZBURGERLAND CARD

Available online and at tourist offices in the province, the Salzburgerland Card (www.salzburgerlandcard.com) provides discounts on 190 attractions throughout the province. A six-day card costs €62/31 for an adult/child.

Schloss Mirabell
PALACE

(Mirabellplatz 4; ⊗ Marble Hall 8am-4pm Mon, Wed & Thu, 1-4pm Tue & Fri, gardens 6am-dusk) FREE Prince-Archbishop Wolf Dietrich built this splendid palace in 1606 to impress his beloved mistress Salome Alt. It must have done the trick because she went on to bear the archbishop some 15 children (sources disagree on the exact number – poor Wolf was presumably too distracted by spiritual matters to keep count). Johann Lukas von Hildebrandt, of Schloss Belvedere fame, remodelled the palace in baroque style in 1721. The lavish interior, replete with stucco, marble and frescoes, is free to visit.

Erzabtei St Peter
ABBEY

(St Peter's Abbey; www.stift-stpeter.at; St Peter Bezirk 1-2; catacombs adult/child €2/1.50; ⊗ church 8am-noon & 2.30-6.30pm, cemetery 6.30am-7pm, catacombs 10am-6pm) A Frankish missionary named Rupert founded this abbey church and monastery in around 700, making it the oldest in the German-speaking world. Though a vaulted Romanesque portal remains, today's church is overwhelmingly baroque, with rococo stucco, statues – including one of archangel Michael shoving a crucifix through the throat of a goaty demon – and striking altar paintings by Martin Johann Schmidt.

Christmas Museum
MUSEUM

(Mozartplatz 2; adult/child €6/3; ⊗ 10am-6pm Wed-Sun) If you wish it could be Christmas every day, swing on over to this recently opened museum. The private collection brings festive sparkle in the form of advent calendars, hand-carved cribs, baubles and nutcrackers.

Schloss Leopoldskron
PALACE, NOTABLE BUILDING

(www.schloss-leopoldskron.com; Leopoldskronstrasse 56-58) The grand rococo palace of Schloss Leopoldskron, a 15-minute walk from Festung Hohensalzburg, is where the lake scene was filmed in *The Sound of Music*. Its Venetian Room was the blueprint for

Salzburg

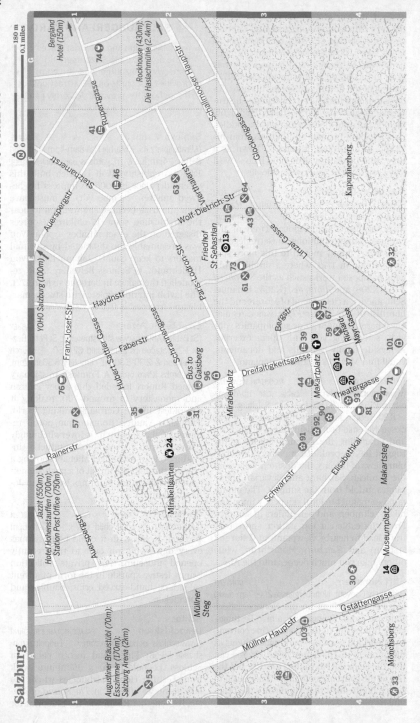

180 m
0.1 miles

Bergland
Hotel (150m)

Rockhouse (430m);
Die Haslachmühle (2.4km)

Bus to
Gaisberg

YOHO Salzburg (100m)

Jazzit (550m);
Hotel Hohenstauffen (700m);
Station Post Office (750m)

Augustiner Bräustübl (70m);
Esszimmer (170m);
Salzburg Arena (2km)

Mirabellgarten

Mirabellplatz

Müllner
Steg

Mönchsberg

Friedhof
St Sebastian

Kapuzinerberg

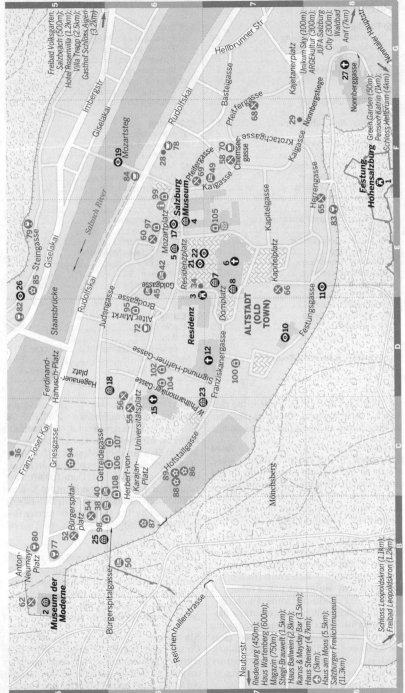

Salzburg

the Trapp's lavish ballroom, where the children bid their farewells. It's now a plush hotel, but you can admire it from the outside.

Mozartplatz
SQUARE
(Mozartplatz) On this stately baroque square, Mozart is literally and metaphorically put on a pedestal. The square hums with street entertainers and the clip-clop of horse-drawn carriages. It's flanked on one side by the Salzburg Museum (p230).

Dommuseum
MUSEUM
(www.domquartier.at; Kapitelplatz 6; DomQuartier ticket adult/child €12/5; ⊙10am-5pm Wed-Mon) The Dommuseum is a treasure trove of sacred art. A visit whisks you past a cabinet of Renaissance curiosities crammed with crystals, coral and oddities such as armadillos and pufferfish, through rooms showcasing gem-encrusted monstrances, stained glass and altarpieces, and into the **Long Gallery**, which is graced with 17th- and 18th-century paintings, including Paul Troger's chiaroscuro *Christ and Nicodemus* (1739).

Domgrabungsmuseum
MUSEUM
(Cathedral Excavations Museum; ☑0662-62 08 08 131; www.salzburgmuseum.at; Residenzplatz; adult/child €3/1; ⊙9am-5pm Jul & Aug, by request Sep-Jun) Map out the city's past with a romp of the rocks at this subterranean archaeology museum beside the Dom (p230). Particularly of interest are fragments of Roman mosaics, a milestone hewn from Untersberg marble and the brickwork of the former Romanesque cathedral.

Dreifältigkeitskirche
CHURCH
(Church of the Holy Trinity; Dreifaltigkeitsgasse 14; ⊙6.30am-6.30pm) Baroque master Johann Bernhard Fischer von Erlach designed this graceful church on the city's right bank. It's famous for Johann Michael Rottmayr's dome **fresco of the Holy Trinity**.

Steingasse
HISTORIC SITE
On the right bank of the Salzach River, this narrow, cobbled lane was, incredibly, the main trade route to Italy in medieval times. Look out for the 13th-century **Steintor** gate and the

house of **Joseph Mohr**, who wrote the lyrics to the all-time classic Christmas carol 'Silent Night'. The street is at its most photogenic in the late morning, when sunlight illuminates its pastel-coloured townhouses.

Friedhof St Sebastian
CEMETERY

(Linzer Gasse 41; ◎9am-6.30pm) Tucked behind the baroque Sebastianskirche (St Sebastian's Church), this peaceful cemetery and its cloisters were designed by Andrea Berteleto in Italianate style in 1600. Mozart family members and well-known 16th-century physician Paracelsus are buried here, but out-pomping them all is Prince-Archbishop Wolf Dietrich von Raitenau's mosaic-tiled mausoleum, an elaborate memorial to himself.

Spielzeugmuseum
MUSEUM

(Toy Museum; www.spielzeugmuseum.at; Bürgerspitalgasse 2; adult/child/family €4.50/2/9; ◎9am-5pm Tue-Sun; ♟) On the arcaded Bürgerspitalplatz, the Spielzeugmuseum takes a nostalgic look at toys, with its collection of dolls' houses and Steiff teddies. There's

also dress-up fun, marble games and a little builder's dream of a Bosch workshop. Parents can hang out in the 'adult parking areas' and at the free tea bar while the little ones let off excess energy.

Haus der Natur
MUSEUM

(www.hausdernatur.at; Museumsplatz 5; adult/child/family €8/5.50/20; ◎9am-5pm; ♟) Here kids can bone up on dinosaurs and alpine crystals in the natural history rooms, gawp at snakes and crocs in the reptile enclosure, and spot piranhas and coral reefs in the aquarium; blink-and-you'll-miss-them baby clownfish splash around in the 'Kinderstube'. Shark-feeding time is 10.15am on Mondays and Thursdays. There's also a science museum where budding scientists can race rowboats, take a biological tour of the human body and – literally – feel Mozart's music by stepping into a giant violin case.

Freilichtmuseum
MUSEUM

(www.freilichtmuseum.com; Hasenweg 1, Grossgmain; adult/child/family €11/5.50/22; ◎9am-6pm

ⓘ SALZBURG CARD

If you're planning on doing lots of sightseeing, save by buying the Salzburg Card (1-/2-/3-day card €27/36/42). The card gets you entry to all of the major sights and attractions, unlimited use of public transport (including cable cars) and numerous discounts on tours and events. The card is half-price for children and €3 cheaper in the low season.

Tue-Sun mid-Mar–Oct; ⓐ) Outside Salzburg, near Untersberg, the open-air Freilichtmuseum harbours around 100 archetypal Austrian farmhouses, evoking the crafts and trades of yore. It has tractors to clamber over, goats to feed, a butterfly watching area and a huge adventure playground. It's 21km southwest of Salzburg via the A1. Bus 180 comes here, running every two hours from Salzburg Hauptbahnhof (€3.50, 31 minutes).

Rupertinum GALLERY
(www.museumdermoderne.at; Wiener-Philharmoniker-Gasse 9; adult/child/family €6/4/8; ⊙10am-6pm Tue & Thu-Sun, to 8pm Wed) In the heart of the Altstadt, the Rupertinum is the sister gallery of the Museum der Moderne and is devoted to rotating exhibitions of modern art. There is a strong emphasis on graphic works and photography.

Franziskanerkirche CHURCH
(Franziskanergasse 5; ⊙6.30am-7.30pm) A real architectural hotchpotch, Salzburg's Franciscan church has a Romanesque nave, a Gothic choir with rib vaulting and a baroque marble altar (one of Fischer von Erlach's creations).

Festungsbahn Funicular CABLE CAR
(Festungsgasse 4; 1 way/return adult €6.80/8.40, child €3.70/4.60; ⊙9am-8pm, shorter hours in winter) The fast route to the fortress, the Festungsbahn whisks you up to the hilltop castle (p229) in a matter of minutes, saving you the legwork on the stiff uphill walking track that leads to the top.

Mozart Ton-und Filmsammlung MUSEUM
(www.mozarteum.at; Makartplatz 8; ⊙9am-1pm Mon, Tue & Fri, 1-5pm Wed & Thu) FREE Under the same roof as the Mozart-Wohnhaus (but accessed separately) is the Mozart Ton-und Filmsammlung, a film and music archive of interest to the ultra-enthusiast, with some 25,000 audiovisual recordings.

⚉ Activities

Salzburg's rival mountains are 540m Mönchsberg and 640m Kapuzinerberg – Julie Andrews and locals who are used to bigger things call them 'hills'. Both are thickly wooded and criss-crossed by walking trails, with photogenic views of the Altstadt's right bank and left bank, respectively.

There's also an extensive network of cycling routes, from a gentle 20-minute trundle along the Salzach River to Hellbrunn, to the highly scenic 450km Mozart Radweg through Salzburgerland and Bavaria.

Mönchsberg WALKING, HIKING
Rising sheer and rugged above the city, Mönchsberg commands photogenic views over the domes and spires of the Altstadt on one side and of the fortress perched high on the hill on the other. Trails head out in all directions.

Arguably the most scenic trail is the 4km panoramic walking track from Stift Nonnberg (p231) to Augustiner Bräustübl (p245), taking in Festung Hohensalzburg (p229) and Museum der Moderne (p230) en route and affording views deep into the Austrian and Bavarian Alps.

To get to the top, take the Mönchsberg Lift (Gstättengasse 13; 1 way/return €2.30/3.60, incl gallery entry €9.10/6.50; ⊙8am-7pm Mon, to 9pm Tue-Sun).

Gaisberg HIKING
(www.gaisberg.at) A road snakes up to 1287m Gaisberg, where stellar views of the Salzburg Valley, Salzkammergut lakes, the limestone Tennengebirge range and neighbouring Bavaria await. The best way to appreciate all this is on the 5km around-the-mountain circuit trail. Salzburgers also head up here for outdoor pursuits from mountain biking to cross-country skiing.

Bus 151 (€4.20, 40 minutes) runs at least every two hours from Mirabellplatz to Gaisberg in summer. From November to March the bus only goes as far as Zistelalpe, 1.5km short of the summit.

Rikscha Tours TOURS
(☑0662-634 02 40; www.rikschatours.at; Residenzplatz; ⊙May–Sep) Whizzing around Salzburg by rickshaw is the latest thing – the clued-up guides fill you in on anecdotes as they pedal. Tours range from a 40-minute spin of the historic centre (€36) to a 75-minute 'Round of Music' tour taking in the film locations of...you guessed it.

Stiegl-Brauwelt
BREWERY

(www.brauwelt.at; Bräuhausstrasse 9; adult/child €11.50/6.50; ☺10am-5pm) Brewing and bottling since 1492, Stiegl is Austria's largest private brewery. A tour takes in the different stages of the brewing process and (woo-hoo!) the world's tallest beer tower. A Stiegl beer and small gift are thrown in for the price of a ticket. The brewery is 1.5km southwest of the *Altstadt;* take bus 1 or 10 to Bräuhausstrasse.

Fräulein Maria's Bicycle Tours
CYCLING

(www.mariasbicycletours.com; Mirabellplatz 4; adult/child €30/18; ☺9.30am Apr-Oct, plus 4.30pm Jun-Aug) Belt out *The Sound of Music* faves as you pedal on one of these jolly 3½-hour bike tours, taking in locations from the film including the Mirabellgarten, Stift Nonnberg, Schloss Leopoldskron and Hellbrunn. No advance booking is necessary; just turn up at the meeting point on Mirabellplatz.

Cook & Wine
COOKING

(☑0662-23 16 06; www.cookandwine.at; Kaigasse 43) Italian restaurant Cook & Wine (p243) is a fun place to give cooking a whirl or master new skills. The cookery classes are themed: from five-course gourmet menus to spotlights on homemade pasta, fish and vegetarian food. Check the website for details of times and prices.

Salzburg Schifffahrt
CRUISE

(Makartsteg; adult/child €15/7.50; ☺mid-Mar–Oct) A boat ride along the Salzach is a leisurely way to pick out Salzburg's sights. Hour-long cruises depart from Makartsteg bridge, with some of them chugging on to Schloss Hellbrunn (adult/child €18/10, not including entry to the palace).

Kapuzinerberg
WALKING

Presiding over the city, the serene, thickly wooded 640m peak of Kapuzinerberg is criss-crossed by walking trails up to a *viewpoint* that gazes across the river to the castle-topped *Altstadt*. Note the six baroque Way of the Cross chapels as you make the short trek uphill.

Freibad Leopoldskron
SWIMMING

(Leopoldskronstrasse 50; adult/child €4.80/2.70; ☺9am-7pm May–mid-Sep; ▣) Salzburg's biggest outdoor pool, with laps for swimmers, kids' splash pools, diving boards, waterslides, table tennis, mini golf and volleyball. Bus 22 to Wartbergweg stops close by.

Bob's Special Tours
BUS

(☑0662-84 95 11; www.bobstours.com; Rudolfskai 38; ☺office 8.30am-5pm Mon-Fri, 1-2pm Sat & Sun) Minibus tours to *Sound of Music* locations (€48), the Bavarian Alps (€48) and Grossglockner (€96). Prices include a free hotel

---

SALZBURG IN...

Two Days

Get up early to see **Mozarts Geburtshaus** (p231) and boutique-dotted **Getreide-gasse** before the crowds. Take in the baroque grandeur of **Residenzplatz** (p230) and the stately **Residenz** (p230) palace. Coffee and cake in the decadent **Café Tomaselli** (p246) fuels an afternoon absorbing history at the hands-on **Salzburg Museum** (p230) or monastic heritage at **Stiftskirche St Peter** (p231). Toast your first day with homebrews in the beer garden at **Augustiner Bräustübl** (p245).

Begin day two with postcard views from the ramparts of **Festung Hohensalzburg** (p229), or absorbing cutting-edge art at **Museum der Moderne** (p230). Have lunch at **M32** (p244) or bag goodies at the **Grünmarkt** (p243) for a picnic in the gardens of **Schloss Mirabell** (p231). Chamber music in its sublime **Marble Hall** or enchanting puppetry at **Salzburger Marionettentheater** (p247) rounds out the day nicely.

Four Days

On day three, you can join a Mozart or *Sound of Music* tour. Hire a bike to pedal along the Salzach's villa-studded banks to summer palace **Schloss Hellbrunn** (p250). Dine in old-world Austrian style at **Bärenwirt** (p243) before testing the **right-bank nightlife**.

The fun-packed salt mines of **Hallein** and the Goliath of ice caves, **Eisriesenwelt** (p252) in Werfen, both make terrific day trips for day four. Or grab your walking boots or skis to head up to Salzburg's twin peaks: **Untersberg** (p231) and **Gaisberg** (p236).

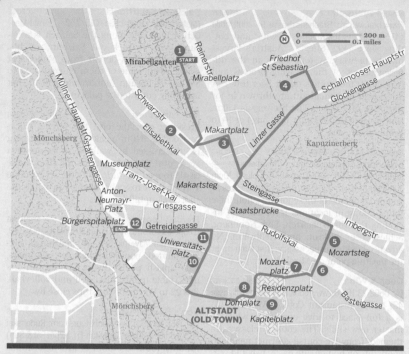

City Walk
In Mozart's Footsteps

START SCHLOSS MIRABELL
FINISH FÜRST
LENGTH 3KM; 1½ HOURS

Mozart was the ultimate musical prodigy: he identified a pig's squeal as G-sharp when he was two years old, began to compose when he was five and first performed for Empress Maria Theresia at the age of six. Follow in his footsteps on this classic walking tour.

Begin at baroque ❶ **Schloss Mirabell** (p231), where the resplendent Marmorsaal is often the backdrop for chamber concerts of Mozart's music. Stroll south through the fountain-dotted gardens, passing the ❷ **Mozarteum** (p248), a foundation honouring Mozart's life and works, and host of the renowned Mozartwoche festival. Around the corner on Makartplatz is the 17th-century ❸ **Mozart-Wohnhaus** (p231), where you can see how the Mozart family lived and listen to rare recordings of Mozart's symphonies. Amble north along Linzer Gasse to ❹ **Friedhof St Sebastian** (p235), the cemetery

where Wolfgang's father Leopold and his wife Constanze lie buried. Now retrace your steps towards the Salzach River, turning left onto medieval Steingasse and crossing the Art Nouveau ❺ **Mozartsteg** (Mozart Bridge). Look out for the ❻ **memorial plaque** at No 8, the house where Mozart's beloved Constanze died, as you approach ❼ **Mozart-platz** (p234), with its statue of the great man. Across the way is the ❽ **Residenz** (p230) palace where Mozart gave his first court concert at the ripe old age of six. Beside it rests the baroque ❾ **Dom** (p230), where Mozart's parents were married in 1747 and where little Wolfgang was baptised in 1756; Mozart later composed sacred music here and was cathedral organist. Follow Franziskanergasse to reach the ❿ **Kollegienkirche** on Universitätsplatz, where Mozart's D Minor Mass, K65, premiered in 1769. On Getreidegasse, stop to contemplate the birthplace of a genius at ⓫ **Mozarts Geburtshaus** (p231) and buy some famous chocolate Mozartkugeln (Mozart balls) at ⓬ **Fürst** (p248).

pick-up for morning tours starting at 9am. Reservations essential.

Salzburg Panorama Tours   BUS
(☑ 0662-883 21 10; www.panoramatours.com; Mirabellplatz; ☺ office 8am-6pm) Boasts the 'original *Sound of Music* Tour' (€42) as well as a huge range of others, including *Altstadt* walking tours (€18), Mozart tours (€51) and Bavarian Alps excursions (€42).

🎪 Festivals & Events

Salzburg Festival   ART
(Salzburger Festspiele; www.salzburgerfestspiele. at; ☺ Jul & Aug) The absolute highlight of the city's events calendar is the Salzburg Festival (p241). It's a grand affair, with some 200 productions – including theatre, classical music and opera – staged in the impressive surrounds of the Grosses Festspielhaus (p247), **Haus für Mozart** (House for Mozart; ☑ 0662-804 55 00; www.salzburgerfestspiele.at; Hofstallgasse 1) and the baroque **Felsenreitschule** (Hofstallgasse 1). Tickets vary in price between €11 and €430; book well in ahead.

Mozartwoche   MUSIC
(Mozart Week; www.mozarteum.at; ☺ Jan) World-renowned orchestras, conductors and soloists celebrate Mozart's birthday with a feast of his music in late January.

Christkindlmarkt   CHRISTMAS MARKET
(www.christkindlmarkt.co.at; ☺ Nov–26 Dec) Salzburg is at its storybook best during Advent, when Christmas markets bring festive sparkle and choirs to Domplatz and Residenzplatz, starting in late November.

Osterfestspiele   MUSIC
(Easter Festival; www.osterfestspiele-salzburg.at; ☺ Mar-Apr) This springtime shindig brings orchestral highlights, under Christian Thielemann's sprightly baton, to the Festspielhaus.

SommerSzene   CULTURAL
(www.sommerszene.net; ☺ Jun-Jul) Boundary-crossing performing arts are the focus of this event held from late June to early July.

🛏 Sleeping

Salzburg is pricey, but you can get deals if you're willing to go the extra mile. Ask the tourist office for a list of private rooms and pensions. Medieval guesthouses, avant-garde design hotels and chilled-out hostels all huddle in the *Altstadt*. (Note that high-season prices jack up another 10% to 20% during the Salzburg Festival.)

If Salzburg is booked solid, consider staying in Hallein or across the border in Bavaria.

★ Haus Ballwein   GUESTHOUSE $
(☑ 0662-82 40 29; www.haus-ballwein.at; Moosstrasse 69a; s €55-59, d €69-83, tr €85-90, q €90-98; P �🛜) With its bright, pine-filled rooms, mountain views, free bike hire and garden, this place is big on charm. The largest, quietest rooms face the back and have balconies and kitchenettes. It's a 10-minute trundle from the *Altstadt;* take bus 21 to Gsengerweg. Breakfast is a wholesome spread of fresh rolls, eggs, fruit, muesli and cold cuts.

Haus Steiner   GUESTHOUSE $
(☑ 0662-83 00 31; www.haussteiner.com; Moosstrasse 156; s/d €38/64; P 🛜) Good-natured Rosemarie runs a tight ship at this sunny yellow chalet-style guesthouse that's ablaze with flowers in summer. The pick of the petite rooms, furnished in natural wood, come with fridges, balconies and mood-lifting mountain views; family-sized apartments have kitchenettes. Breakfast is copious and it's just a 15-minute ride away from the *Altstadt* on bus 21 (get off at Hammerauerstrasse).

Haus am Moos   GUESTHOUSE $
(☑ 0662-82 49 21; www.ammoos.at; Moosstrasse 186a; s/d €30/60; P 🛜🏊) A slice of rural calm just a 15-minute ride from town on bus 21, this alpine-style chalet is a find. Many of the rooms have balconies with gorgeous mountain views and some come with canopy beds. A breakfast of muesli, cold cuts, eggs and fresh breads gears you up for the day, and there's an outdoor pool for an afternoon dip.

YOHO Salzburg   HOSTEL $
(☑ 0662-87 96 49; www.yoho.at; Paracelsusstrasse 9; dm €19-23, d €72-93; @ 🛜) Free wi-fi, secure lockers, comfy bunks, plenty of cheap beer and good-value schnitzels – what more could a backpacker ask for? Except, perhaps, a merry sing-along with *The Sound of Music* screened daily (yes, *every* day) at 7pm. The friendly crew can arrange tours, adventure sports such as rafting and canyoning, and bike hire.

Stadtalm   HOSTEL $
(☑ 0662-84 17 29; www.stadtalm.at; Mönchsberg 19c; dm €20) This turreted hostel plopped on top of Mönchsberg takes in the entire Salzburg panorama, from the city's spires and fortress to Kapuzinerberg. Digs are simple

but you won't find them cheaper elsewhere. There's a good-value restaurant on-site.

★ Gästehaus im Priesterseminar
GUESTHOUSE $$

(☑ 0662-877 495 10; www.gaestehaus-priesterse-minar-salzburg.at; Dreifaltigkeitsgasse 14; s €65-85, d €116-130) Ah, the peace is heavenly at this one-time seminary tucked behind the Drei-fältigkeitskirche. Its bright, parquet-floored rooms were recently given a total make-over, but the place still brims with old-world charm thanks to its marble staircase, antique furnishings and fountain-dotted court-yard. It's still something of a secret, though, so whisper about it quietly...

Die Haslachmühle
GUESTHOUSE $$

(☑ 0664 179 90 60; www.haslachmuehle.at; Mühl-strasse 18, Gnigl; d €119-179; P ☎) Sitting be-low Gaisberg and surrounded by attractive gardens and countryside, this charismatic B&B is lodged in a historic 16th-century flour mill. The family go out of their way to please, and the incredibly spacious, sunny,

wood-floored rooms feature touches like ce-ramic ovens, mountain views and Nespres-so machines. It's a 15-minute ride from the *Hauptbahnhof* on bus 155 (Salzburg Küh-berg stop).

Hotel Am Dom
BOUTIQUE HOTEL $$

(☑ 0662-84 27 65; www.hotelamdom.at; Goldgasse 17; s €109-219, d €119-349; ❄ ☎) Antique meets boutique at this *Altstadt* hotel, where the original vaults and beams of the 800-year-old building contrast with razor-sharp design features. Artworks inspired by the musical legends of the Salzburg Festival grace the rooms, which sport caramel-champagne colour schemes, funky lighting, velvet throws and ultra-glam bathrooms.

Hotel Rosenvilla
GUESTHOUSE $$

(☑ 0662-62 17 65; www.rosenvilla.com; Höfelgasse 4; s €70-120, d €120-180, ste €170-260; P ☎) This guesthouse goes the extra mile with its sharp-styled contemporary rooms, fault-less service and incredible breakfasts (€13) with spreads, breads, cereals, eggs and fruit

---

DIY SOUND OF MUSIC TOUR

Do a Julie and sing as you stroll on a self-guided tour of *The Sound of Music* film loca-tions. Let's start at the very beginning:

➡ **The Hills Are Alive** Cut! Make that *proper* mountains. The opening scenes were filmed around the jewel-coloured Salzkammergut lakes. Maria makes her twirling entrance on alpine pastures just across the border in Bavaria.

➡ **A Problem Like Maria** Nuns waltzing on their way to mass at Benedictine **Stift Nonnberg** (p231) is fiction, but it's fact that the real Maria von Trapp intended to become a nun here before romance struck.

➡ **Have Confidence** Residenzplatz (p230) is where Maria belts out 'I Have Confidence' and playfully splashes the spouting horses of the Residenzbrunnen fountain.

➡ **So Long, Farewell** The grand rococo palace of **Schloss Leopoldskron** (p231), a 15-minute walk from Festung Hohensalzburg, is where the lake scene was filmed. Its Venetian Room was the blueprint for the Trapp's lavish ballroom, where the children bid their farewells.

➡ **Do-Re-Mi** The Pegasus fountain, the steps with fortress views, the gnomes...the Mirabellgarten at **Schloss Mirabell** (p231) might inspire a rendition of 'Do-Re-Mi' – especially if there's a drop of golden sun.

➡ **Sixteen Going on Seventeen** The loved-up pavilion of the century hides out in **Hellbrunn Park** (p250), where you can act out those 'Oh, Liesl'/'Oh, Rolf' fantasies.

➡ **Edelweiss & Adieu** The **Felsenreitschule** (p239; Summer Riding School) is the dramatic backdrop for the Salzburg Festival in the movie, where the Trapp Family Singers win the audience over with 'Edelweiss' and give the Nazis the slip with 'So Long, Farewell'.

➡ **Climb Every Mountain** To Switzerland, that is. Or content yourself with alpine views from **Untersberg** (p231), which appears briefly at the end of the movie when the family flees the country.

FESTIVAL TIME

In 1920 dream trio Hugo von Hofmannsthal, Max Reinhardt and Richard Strauss combined their creative forces and the **Salzburg Festival** (p239) was born. Now, as then, one of the highlights is the staging of Hofmannsthal's morality play *Jedermann* (Everyman) on Domplatz. A trilogy of opera, drama and classical concerts of the highest calibre have since propelled the five-week summer festival to international renown, attracting some of the world's best conductors, directors, orchestras and singers.

Come festival time, Salzburg crackles with excitement, as a quarter of a million visitors descend on the city for some 200 productions. Theatre premieres, avant-garde works and the summer-resident **Vienna Philharmonic** performing works by Mozart are all in the mix. The Festival District on Hofstallgasse has a spectacular backdrop, framed by Mönchsberg's cliffs. Most performances are held in the cavernous **Grosses Festspielhaus** (p247), which accommodates 2179 theatregoers; the **Haus für Mozart** (p239) in the former royal stables; and the baroque **Felsenreitschule** (p239).

If you're planning to visit during the festival, don't leave *anything* to chance – book your flights, hotel and tickets months in advance. Sometimes last-minute tickets are available at the **ticket office** (p248), but they're like gold dust. Ticket prices range from €11 to €430.

to jump-start your day. Take bus 7 to Finanzamt or walk 15 minutes along the tree-lined riverfront into the centre.

Pension Katrin
PENSION **$$**

(☑ 0662 83 08 60; www.pensionkatrin.at; Nonntaler Hauptstrasse 49b; s €66-69, d €115-122, tr €159-165, q €179-186; P ☎) With its flowery garden, bright and cheerful rooms and excellent breakfasts, this pension is one of the homiest in Salzburg. The affable Terler family keeps everything spick and span, and nothing is too much trouble for them. They'll even help you with upstairs with your luggage. Take bus 5 from the *Hauptbahnhof* to Wäschergasse.

Arte Vida
GUESTHOUSE **$$**

(☑ 0662-87 31 85; www.artevida.at; Dreifaltigkeitsgasse 9; s €69-129, d €89-145, apt €160-220; ☎) Arte Vida has the boho-chic feel of a Marrakech *riad*, with its lantern-lit salon, communal kitchen and serene garden. Asia and Africa have provided the inspiration for the rich colours and fabrics that dress the individually designed rooms. Your affable hosts Herbert and Karoline happily give tips on Salzburg and its surrounds, and can arrange massages and private yoga sessions.

Haus Wartenberg
GUESTHOUSE **$$**

(☑ 0662-84 84 00; www.hauswartenberg.com; Riedenburgerstrasse 2; d €89-121, f €198-250; P @ ☎) This welcoming, family-run pension is just a 15-minute stroll southwest of the *Altstadt*. It's set in vine-strewn gardens

and housed in a gorgeous 17th-century chalet full of creaky floors and family heirlooms. The chunky pinewood and florals in the country-style rooms are in keeping with the character of the place. Take bus 1, 4 or 5 to Moosstrasse.

Weisse Taube
HISTORIC HOTEL **$$**

(☑ 0662-84 24 04; www.weissetaube.at; Kaigasse 9; s/d/tr/q €143/155/281/324; ☎) Housed in a listed 14th-century building in a quiet corner of the *Altstadt*, the 'white dove' is a solid choice. Staff go out of their way to help and the warm-coloured rooms are well kept (some have fortress views). Breakfast is a generous spread.

Hotel Mozart
HISTORIC HOTEL **$$**

(☑ 0662-87 22 74; www.hotel-mozart.at; Franz-Josef-Strasse 27; s €80-110, d €120-190, tr €150-220; P ☎) An antique-filled lobby gives way to spotless rooms with comfy beds and sizeable bathrooms at the Mozart. You'll have to fork out an extra €12 for breakfast, but it's a good spread, with fresh fruit, boiled eggs, cold cuts and pastries.

Hotel Amadeus
HISTORIC HOTEL **$$**

(☑ 0662-87 14 01; www.hotelamadeus.at; Linzer Gasse 43-45; s €76-137, d €135-231, q €192-391; ☎) Centrally situated on the right bank, this 500-year-old hotel has a boutique feel, with bespoke touches such as chandeliers and four-poster beds in the vibrantly coloured rooms. Guests are treated to free tea or coffee in the afternoon.

★Villa Trapp HOTEL $$$
(☎0662-63 08 60; www.villa-trapp.com; Traunstrasse 34; s €65-130, d €114-280, ste €290-580; P 📶) Marianne and Christopher have transformed the original von Trapp family home into a beautiful guesthouse (for guests only, we might add). The 19th-century villa is elegant, if not *quite* as palatial as in the movie, with tasteful wood-floored rooms and a balustrade for sweeping down à la Baroness Schräder.

★Hotel Schloss Mönchstein HERITAGE HOTEL $$$
(☎0662-848 55 50; www.monchstein.at; Mönchsberg Park 26; d €350-650, ste €695-1900; P ❄ 📶) On a fairy-tale perch atop Mönchsberg and set in hectares of wooded grounds, this 16th-century castle is honeymoon (and second mortgage) material. Persian rugs, oil paintings and Calcutta marble finish the rooms to beautiful effect. A massage in the spa, a candlelit tower dinner for two with Salzburg views, a helicopter ride – just say the word.

Hotel Sacher HERITAGE HOTEL $$$
(☎0662-88 97 70; www.sacher.com; Schwarzstrasse 5-7; s €226-336, d €267-651, ste €502-3898; P ❄ @ 📶) Tom Hanks, the Dalai Lama and Julie Andrews have all stayed at this 19th-century pile on the banks of the Salzach. Scattered with oil paintings and antiques, the rooms have gleaming marble bathrooms, and fortress or river views. Compensate for indulging on chocolate *Sacher Torte* in the health club.

Goldener Hirsch LUXURY HOTEL $$$
(☎0662-808 40; www.goldenerhirschsalzburg.com; Getreidegasse 37; r €195-813; P ❄ @ 📶) A skylight illuminates the arcaded inner courtyard of this 600-year-old *Altstadt* pile, where famous past guests include Queen Elizabeth II and Pavarotti. Countess Harriet Walderdorff tastefully scattered the opulent rooms with objets d'art and hand-printed fabrics. Downstairs are two restaurants: wood-beamed s'Herzl and vaulted Restaurant Goldener Hirsch.

Hotel Bristol LUXURY HOTEL $$$
(☎0662-87 35 57; www.bristol-salzburg.at; Makartplatz 4; s €185-275, d €260-300, ste €390-560; P ❄ 📶) The Bristol transports you back to a more decadent era. Chandelier-lit salons, champagne at breakfast, exquisitely crafted furniture, service as polished as the marble – this is pure class. Even Emperor Franz Josef and Sigmund Freud felt at home here.

Arthotel Blaue Gans BOUTIQUE HOTEL $$$
(☎0662-84 24 91; www.hotel-blaue-gans-salzburg.at; Getreidegasse 41-43; s €189-219, d €229-335, ste €449-519; ❄ 📶) Contemporary design blends harmoniously with the original vaulting and beams of this 660-year-old hotel. Rooms are pure and simple, with clean lines, lots of white and streamlined furnishings. The restaurant is well worth a visit.

Hotel Goldgasse HISTORIC HOTEL $$$
(☎0662-84 56 22; www.hotelgoldgasse.at; Goldgasse 10; s €130-180, d €220-260, ste €350-480, q €450-580; ❄ @ 📶) Bang in the heart of the *Altstadt*, this 700-year-old townhouse has oodles of charm – some rooms have four-poster beds, while paintings of Emperor Franz Josef hang guard over others. The sunny terrace overlooks the rooftops of the old town.

Hotel & Villa Auersperg BOUTIQUE HOTEL $$$
(☎0662-88 94 40; www.auersperg.at; Auerspergstrasse 61; s €129-180, d €155-295, ste €235-335; P @ 📶) 🍃 This charismatic villa and hotel duo fuse late-19th-century flair with contemporary design. Guests can relax by the lily pond in the vine-strewn garden or in the rooftop wellness area with its sauna, tea bar and mountain views. Free bike hire is a bonus. Local organic produce features at breakfast.

Wolf Dietrich HISTORIC HOTEL $$$
(☎0662-87 12 75; www.salzburg-hotel.at; Wolf-Dietrich-Strasse 7; s €90-148, d €140-262, ste €200-348; P 📶 🏊) Central Wolf Dietrich exudes old-fashioned elegance, with rooms dressed in polished wood furnishings and floral fabrics. There's even a suite based on Mozart's *Magic Flute*, with a star-studded ceiling and freestanding bath. By contrast, the spa and indoor pool are ultramodern. Organic produce is served at breakfast.

Hotel Wolf HISTORIC HOTEL $$$
(☎0662-843 45 30; www.hotelwolf.com; Kaigasse 7; s €108-138, d €198-238, ste €218-258; 📶) Tucked in a quiet corner of the *Altstadt*, Hotel Wolf occupies a lovingly converted 15th-century building. Uneven stone staircases and antique furnishings are a nod to its past, while the light, parquet-floored rooms range from modern to rustic.

✖ Eating

Salzburg's eclectic dining scene skips from the traditional to the supertrendy to the downright touristy. This is a city where schnitzel is served with a slice of history in vaulted taverns; where you can dine in

Michelin-starred finery or be serenaded by a warbling Maria wannabe. Save euros by taking advantage of the lunchtime *Tagesmenü* (fixed menu) served at most places.

Ludwig
BURGERS $

(📞0662-87 25 00; www.ludwig-burger.at; Linzer Gasse 39; burgers €6.90-10.80; ⏰11am-10pm; 🚲) Gourmet burger joints are all the rage in Austria at the moment and this hip newcomer fits the bill nicely, with its burgers made from organic, regional ingredients, which go well with hand-cut fries and homemade lemonade and shakes. It also rustles up superfood salads and vegan nut-mushroom-herb burgers. An open kitchen is the centrepiece of the slick, monochrome interior.

Heart of Joy
CAFE $

(📞0662-89 07 73; www.heartofjoy.at; Franz-Josef-Strasse 3; lunch €9.40-11.80, snacks & light meals €4.90-9.90; ⏰8am-7pm; 🛜🚲) This Ayurveda-inspired cafe has an all-vegetarian, part-vegan and mostly organic menu. It does great bagels, salads, homemade cakes (including gluten-free ones) and juices and creative breakfasts, plus day specials like homemade pumpkin risotto with parmesan and quinoa-filled aubergines with cashew-coriander dip.

Stiftsbäckerei St Peter
BAKERY $

(Kapitelplatz 8; ⏰7am-5pm Mon-Tue & Thu-Fri, to 1pm Sat) Next to the monastery, where the watermill turns, this 700-year-old bakery turns out Salzburg's best sourdough loaves from a wood-fired oven.

Grünmarkt
MARKET $

(Green Market; Universitätsplatz; ⏰7am-7pm Mon-Fri, to 3pm Sat) A one-stop picnic shop on one of Salzburg's grandest squares, for regional cheese, ham, fruit, bread and gigantic pretzels.

Organic Pizza Salzburg
PIZZA $

(📞0664 597 44 70; Franz-Josef-Strasse 24a; pizza €8.50-13.20; ⏰5-10pm Tue-Thu, 2-10pm Fri & Sat) Good-natured staff, groovy music and awesome pizzas whipped up with super-fresh, organic ingredients make this a terrific choice. It's a tiny place so be prepared to wait at busy times – it's worth it.

Spicy Spices
INDIAN $

(📞0662-87 07 12; Wolf-Dietrich-Strasse 1; day special €8, with soup €9.50; ⏰noon-9pm; 🚲) 'Healthy heart, lovely soul' is the mantra of this all-organic, all-vegetarian haunt. Service is slow but friendly. It's worth the wait for

the good-value *thali* (appetisers) and curries mopped up with *paratha* (flat bread).

IceZeit
ICE CREAM $

(Chiemseegasse 1; scoop €1.40; ⏰11am-8pm) Grab a cone at Salzburg's best ice-cream parlour, with flavours from salted peanut and caramel to passionfruit.

Bärenwirt
AUSTRIAN $$

(📞0662-42 24 04; www.baerenwirt-salzburg.at; Müllner Hauptstrasse 8; mains €9-19; ⏰11am-11pm) Sizzling and stirring since 1663, Bärenwirt is Austrian through and through. Go for hearty *Bierbraten* (beer roast) with dumplings, locally caught trout or organic wild-boar bratwurst. A tiled oven warms the woody, hunting-lodge-style interior in winter, while the river-facing terrace is a summer crowd-puller. The restaurant is 500m north of Museumplatz.

Johanneskeller im Priesterhaus
AUSTRIAN $$

(📞0662-26 55 36; www.johanneskeller.at; Richard-Mayr-Gasse 1; mains €10-20; ⏰5pm-midnight Tue-Sat) Full of cosy nooks and crannies, this brick-vaulted cellar is reached via a steep flight of stairs. The menu is succinct but well thought-out, with mains swinging from classic Austrian – Styrian pork roast with dumplings and sauerkraut, say – to Mediterranean numbers like gyros (rotisserie meat) with tzatziki. It's all bang on the money.

Cook & Wine
ITALIAN $$

(📞0662-23 16 06; www.cookandwine.at; Kaigasse 43; mains €15-26.50; ⏰11.30am-11pm Tue-Sat) Highly regarded chef and food and wine connoisseur Günther Grahammer is the brains behind this slick new operation. It combines a wine bar, a cookery school and a smart, bistro-style restaurant serving Italian-inflected dishes along the lines of antipasti, meltingly tender veal cheeks, trilogy of regional fish cooked a hot stone.

Zum Zirkelwirt
AUSTRIAN $$

(📞0662-84 27 96; www.zumzirkelwirt.at; Pfeifergasse 14; ⏰11am-midnight) A jovial inn serving good old-fashioned Austrian grub is what you get at Zum Zirkelwirt, which has a cracking beer garden on a tucked-away square and a cosy, wood-panelled interior for winter imbibing. Go straight for classics like *Kaspressknödelsuppe* (cheese dumpling soup) and *Schweinsbraten im Weissbier-Kümmelsafterl* (pork roast in wheat beer and cumin sauce).

SALZBURG & SALZBURGERLAND SALZBURG

K+K

AUSTRIAN $$

(☎0662-84 21 56; Waagplatz 2; mains €17-35; ⏱11am-2pm & 6pm-midnight; 🍴) This buzzy restaurant on the square is a warren of vaulted and wood-panelled rooms, with a lovely terrace great for people-watching to boot. Whether you go for Alpine salmon on a bed of spinach, saddle of venison in morel sauce or good old bratwurst with lashings of potatoes and cabbage, the food here hits the mark.

Green Garden

VEGETARIAN $$

(☎0662-84 12 01; www.thegreengarden.at; Nonntaler Hauptstrasse 16; mains €9.50-15; ⏱noon-2pm & 5.30-9pm Tue-Sat; 🍴) 🌱 The Green Garden is a breath of fresh air for vegetarians and vegans. Locavore is the word at this bright, modern cottage-style restaurant, pairing dishes like wild herb salad, lemon-goats-cheese tortellini with asparagus and vegan burgers with organic wines in a totally relaxed setting.

Zwettler's

AUSTRIAN $$

(☎0662-84 41 99; www.zwettlers.com; Kaigasse 3; mains €9.50-21; ⏱11.30am-1am Tue-Sat, to midnight Sun) This gastro-pub has a lively buzz on its pavement terrace. Local grub such as schnitzel with parsley potatoes and venison ragout goes well with a cold, foamy Kaiser Karl wheat beer. The two-course lunch is a snip at €7.90.

Afro Café

INTERNATIONAL $$

(www.afrocafe.at; Bürgerspitalplatz 5; lunch €8.70, mains €12-17; ⏱9am-midnight Mon-Sat) Hot-pink walls, butterfly chairs and artworks made from beach junk...this Afro-chic cafe is totally groovy. Staff keep the good vibes and food coming – from breakfasts (€14.60) to ostrich burgers, samosas and steaks sizzling hot from the grill. It also does a good line in coffee, rooibos teas, juices and cakes.

Hagenauerstuben

AUSTRIAN $$

(☎0662-84 26 57; www.hagenauerstuben.at; Universitätsplatz 14; 2-course lunch €7.90, mains €9-21; ⏱11am-8pm Mon-Wed, to 11pm Thu-Fri, 9am-11pm Sat) You'd be forgiven for thinking a restaurant tucked behind Mozarts Geburtshaus would have 'tourist trap' written all over it. Not so. The baroque-contemporary Hagenauerstuben combines a stylishly converted vaulted interior with a terrace overlooking the Kollegienkirche. Pull up a chair for good old-fashioned Austrian home cooking – spinach *Knödel* (dumplings), suckling pig with wild mushrooms, goulash and the like.

Gasthof Schloss Aigen

AUSTRIAN $$

(☎0662-62 12 84; www.schloss-aigen.at; Schwarzenbergpromenade 37; mains €18-25, 4-course menu €56; ⏱11.30am-2pm & 5.30-9.30pm Thu & Fri, 11.30am-9.30pm Sat & Sun) A country manor with an elegantly rustic interior and a chestnut-shaded courtyard, Gasthof Schloss Aigen excels in Austrian home cooking. The Forstner family's house speciality is 'Wiener Melange', different cuts of meltingly tender Pinzgauer beef, served with apple horseradish, chive sauce and roast potatoes, best matched with robust Austrian wines. Bus 7 stops at Bahnhof Aigen, a 10-minute stroll away.

M32

FUSION $$

(☎0662-84 10 00; www.m32.at; Mönchsberg 32; 2-course lunch €16, mains €23-40; ⏱9am-1am Tue-Sun; 🍴) Bold colours and a veritable forest of stag antlers reveal architect Matteo Thun's imprint at the Museum der Moderne's ultra-sleek restaurant. The food goes with the seasons with specialities like organic local beef with sautéed porcini and lime-chilli risotto with roasted octopus. The glass-walled restaurant and terrace take in the full sweep of Salzburg's mountain-backed skyline.

St Paul's Stub'n

INTERNATIONAL $$

(☎0662-433 32 03; Herrengasse 16; mains €11-22; ⏱5-11pm Mon-Sat) Up the cobbled Herrengasse lies this gloriously old-world tavern, with a dark-wood interior crammed with antique curios, which attracts a regular crowd of locals. In summer, guests spill out into the beer garden to dig into authentically prepared classics such as roast pork in wheat beer sauce.

Triangel

AUSTRIAN $$

(☎0662-84 22 29; Wiener-Philharmoniker-Gasse 7; mains €12-34; ⏱11.30am-midnight Tue-Sat) The menu is market-fresh at this arty bistro, where the picture-clad walls pay tribute to Salzburg Festival luminaries. It does gourmet salads, a mean Hungarian goulash with organic beef, and delicious house-made ice cream.

Zum Fidelen Affen

AUSTRIAN $$

(☎0662-87 73 61; www.fideleraffe.at; Priesterhausgasse 8; mains €11-19.50; ⏱5pm-midnight Mon-Sat) The 'Jolly Monkey' lives up to its name with a sociable vibe. Presuming you've booked ahead, you'll dine heartily under vaults or on the terrace on well-prepared Austrian classics including goulash, *Salzburger Bierhendl* (chicken braised in dark beer) and sweet curd dumplings.

★Esszimmer

FRENCH $$$

(☑0662-87 08 99; www.esszimmer.com; Müllner Hauptstrasse 33; 3-course lunch €42, tasting menus €65-118; ⊗noon-2pm & 6.30-9.30pm Tue-Sat) Andreas Kaiblinger puts an innovative spin on market-driven French cuisine at Michelin-starred Esszimmer. Eye-catching art, playful backlighting and a glass floor revealing the Almkanal stream keep diners captivated, as do gastronomic showstoppers such as Arctic char with calf's head and asparagus. Buses 7, 21 and 28 to Landeskrankenhaus stop close by.

★Magazin

MODERN EUROPEAN $$$

(☑0662-841 584 20; www.magazin.co.at; Augustinergasse 13a; 2-course lunch €16, mains €27-41, tasting menus €71-85; ⊗11.30am-2pm & 6-10pm Tue-Sat) In a courtyard below Mönchsberg's sheer rock wall, Magazin shelters a deli, wine store, cookery school and restaurant. Chef Richard Brunnauer's menus fizz with seasonal flavours: dishes like marinated alpine char with avocado and herb salad and saddle of venison with boletus mushrooms are matched with wines from the 850-bottle cellar, and served alfresco or in the industrial-chic, cave-like interior.

Carpe Diem

FUSION $$$

(☑0662-84 88 00; www.carpediemfinestfingerfood.com; Getreidegasse 50; 3-course lunch €21.50, mains €27.50-36.50; ⊗8.30am-midnight) This avant-garde, Michelin-starred loungerestaurant has pride of place on Getreidegasse. A food-literate crowd flocks here for cocktails and finger-food cones, miniature season-inspired taste sensations with fillings like black cod, elderflower, basil and bell pepper, and *taglioni* of cep mushrooms with blueberries and celery. Mains swing from Breton lobster with coriander and peach to quail with cardamom and stuffed courgette flowers.

Ikarus

MODERN EUROPEAN $$$

(☑0662-21 97 77; www.hangar-7.com; Wilhelm-Spazier-Strasse 7A, Salzburg Airport; tasting menus €160-185; ⊗noon-2pm & 7-10pm) At the spaceage Hangar-7 complex at the airport, this glam Michelin-starred restaurant is the epitome of culinary globetrotting. Each month, Eckart Witzigmann and Martin Klein invite a world-famous chef to assemble an eight- to 12-course menu for a serious foodie crowd.

Blaue Gans Restaurant

AUSTRIAN $$$

(☑0662-842 491 50; www.blauegans.at; Getreidegasse 43; mains €19-27; ⊗noon-midnight) In the 650-year-old vaults of Arthotel Blaue Gans, this restaurant is a refined setting for regional cuisine, such as pike-perch with fennel compote, braised lamb shanks and *Marillenknödel* (apricot dumplings), which are married with full-bodied wines. The olive-tree-dotted terrace is popular in summer.

Riedenburg

MODERN EUROPEAN $$$

(☑0662-83 08 15; www.riedenburg.at; Neutorstrasse 31; mains €20-28, 3-/4-/5-course menu €45/56/67; ⊗noon-2pm & 6-10pm Tue-Sat) Helmut Schinwald works the stove at this gourmet restaurant with a romantic garden pavilion. His seasonally inflected flavours, such as homemade porcini ravioli with thyme butter and quail breast with pomegranate risotto, are expertly matched with top wines. The two-course lunch (€15) is a bargain.

🍷 Drinking & Nightlife

★Kaffee Alchemie

CAFE

(www.kaffee-alchemie.at; Rudolfskai 38; ⊗7.30am-6pm Mon-Fri, 10am-6pm Sat & Sun) Making coffee really is rocket science at this vintage-cool cafe by the river, which plays up high-quality, fair-trade, single-origin beans. Talented baristas knock up spot-on espressos (on a Marzocco GB5, in case you wondered), cappuccinos and speciality coffees, which go nicely with the selection of cakes and brownies. Not a coffee fan? Try the super-smooth coffee-leaf tea.

★Enoteca Settemila

WINE BAR

(Bergstrasse 9; ⊗5-11pm Tue-Sat) This bijou wine shop and bar brims with the enthusiasm and passion of Rafael Peil and Nina Corti. Go to sample their well-curated selection of wines, including Austrian, organic and biodynamic ones, with *taglieri* – sharing plates of cheese and *salumi* – salami, ham, prosciutto and the like – from small Italian producers.

★Augustiner Bräustübl

BREWERY

(www.augustinerbier.at; Augustinergasse 4-6; ⊗3-11pm Mon-Fri, from 2.30pm Sat & Sun) Who says monks can't enjoy themselves? Since 1621, this cheery, monastery-run brewery has been serving potent homebrews in beer steins in the vaulted hall and beneath the chestnut trees in the 1000-seat beer garden. Get your tankard filled at the foyer pump and visit the snack stands for hearty, beer-swigging grub like *Stelzen* (ham hock), pork belly and giant pretzels.

Sacher
CAFE

(www.sacher.com; Schwarzstrasse 5-7; ⊙ 7.30am-midnight) Nowhere is the chocolate richer, the apricot jam tangier and cream lighter than at the home of the legendary *Sacher Torte*. The cafe is pure old-world grandeur, with its picture-lined walls and ruby-red banquettes. Sit on the terrace by the Salzach for fortress views.

We Love Coffee
COFFEE

(www.we-love-coffee.at; Mozartsteg; ⊙ 7.30am-6pm Mon-Fri, 9am-6pm Sat & Sun) For a caffeine fix on the hoof, you can't beat this cute cafe in a converted Piaggio Ape, which parks up next to Mozartsteg. It knocks up a mean espresso, chai latte and flat white.

StieglKeller
BEER HALL

(Festungsgasse 10; ⊙ 11am-11pm) For a 365-day taste of Oktoberfest, try this cavernous, Munich-style beer hall, which shares the same architect as Munich's Hofbräuhaus. It has an enormous garden above the city's rooftops and a menu of meaty mains (€11 to €18) such as fat pork knuckles and schnitzel. Beer is cheapest from the self-service taps outside.

Die Weisse
PUB

(www.dieweisse.at; Rupertgasse 10; ⊙ pub 10am-midnight Mon-Sat, bar 5pm-2am Mon-Sat) The cavernous brewpub of the Salzburger Weissbierbrauerei, this is the place to guzzle cloudy wheat beers in the wood-floored pub and the shady beer garden out back. DJs work the decks in Sudwerk bar, especially at the monthly Almrausch when locals party in skimpy *Dirndls* and strapping Lederhosen.

220 Grad
CAFE

(www.220grad.com; Chiemseegasse 5; ⊙ 9am-7pm Tue-Fri, to 6pm Sat) Famous for freshly roasted coffee, this retro-chic cafe serves probably the best espresso in town and whips up superb breakfasts.

Café Bazar
CAFE

(www.cafe-bazar.at; Schwarzstrasse 3; ⊙ 7.30am-7.30pm Mon-Sat, 9am-6pm Sun) At this cafe, all chandeliers and polished wood, locals enjoy the same river views today over breakfast, cake and intelligent conversation as Marlene Dietrich did in 1936.

Mayday Bar
COCKTAIL BAR

(www.hangar-7.com; Wilhelm-Spazier-Strasse 7A, Salzburg Airport; ⊙ noon-midnight Sun-Thu, to 1am Fri & Sat) Peer down at Flying Bulls' aircraft through the glass walls at this crystalline bar, part of the airport's futuristic Hangar-7 complex. Strikingly illuminated by night, it's a unique place for a fresh fruit cocktail or 'smart food' appetisers served in Bodum glasses.

Café Tomaselli
CAFE

(www.tomaselli.at; Alter Markt 9; ⊙ 7am-7pm Mon-Sat, from 8am Sun) Going strong since 1705, this marble and wood-panelled cafe is a former Mozart haunt. It's famous for having Salzburg's flakiest strudels, best *Einspänner* (coffee with whipped cream) and grumpiest waiters.

Coffee House
CAFE

(Linzer Gasse 39; ⊙ 8.30am-9pm Mon-Sat; 🛜) Tucked away in a courtyard behind the Friedhof St Sebastian, this cafe is a trendy new addition to this side of the river, with its retro-cool interior, R 'n' B tunes and speedy free wi-fi. The coffee is decent and though the sign says 'self-service' they'll bring it over if they are not too busy.

Republic
BAR

(www.republic-cafe.at; Anton-Neumayr-Platz 2; ⊙ 8.30am-midnight Sun-Thu, to 4am Fri & Sat) One of Salzburg's most happening haunts, this back-lit lounge-bar opens onto a popular terrace on the square. By night, DJs spin to a 20-something, cocktail-sipping crowd in the club. Check the website for free events – from jazz, Latin and swing breakfasts to weekly salsa nights (9.30pm on Tuesdays).

Unikum Sky
CAFE

(Unipark Nonntal; ⊙ 10am-7pm Mon-Fri, 8am-7pm Sat) For knockout fortress views and a full-on Salzburg panorama, head up to this sun-kissed terrace atop the Unipark Nonntal campus, 300m south of Schanzlgasse in the *Altstadt*. It's a relaxed spot to chill over drinks and inexpensive snacks.

Köchelverzeichnis
WINE BAR

(Steingasse 27; ⊙ 5-11pm Mon-Sat) This is a real neighbourhood bar with jazzy music, antipasti and a great selection of wines. Taste citrusy Grüner Veltliners and rieslings from the family's vineyards in the Wachau.

Steinterrasse
COCKTAIL BAR

(Giselakai 3; ⊙ 7am-midnight Sun-Thu, to 1am Fri & Sat) Hotel Stein's chichi 7th-floor terrace attracts Salzburg's Moët-sipping socialites and anyone who loves a good view. It isn't cheap, but it's the best spot to see the *Altstadt* light up against the theatrical backdrop of the fortress.

Fingerlos
CAFE

(Franz-Josef-Strasse 9; ⊙7.30am-7.30pm Tue-Sun) Salzburgers rave about the dainty petits fours, flaky pastries and creamy tortes served at this high-ceilinged cafe. Join a well-dressed crowd for breakfast or a lazy afternoon of coffee and newspapers.

Humboldt Stub'n
BAR

(www.humboldtstubn.at; Gstättengasse 4-6; ⊙11am-2am; 🔊) Following a recent makeover, this rustic-cool bar is once again a prime gathering spot, with a pavement terrace for sipping a cold, foamy one.

☆ Entertainment

★ **Salzburger
Marionettentheater**
PUPPET THEATRE

(📋0662-87 24 06; www.marionetten.at; Schwarzstrasse 24; tickets €20-37; 📋) The red curtain goes up on a miniature stage at this marionette theatre, a lavish stucco, cherub and chandelier-lit affair founded in 1913. The repertoire star is *The Sound of Music*, with a life-sized Mother Superior and a marionette-packed finale. Other enchanting productions include Mozart's *The Magic Flute* and Tchaikovsky's *The Nutcracker*. All have multilingual surtitles.

Landestheater
THEATRE, OPERA

(📋0662-87 15 12; www.salzburger-landestheater. at; Schwarzstrasse 22; tickets €11-70; ⊙box office 9am-5pm Mon-Fri, to 1pm Sat; 📋) Opera, operetta, ballet and musicals dominate the stage at this elegant 18th-century playhouse. There's a strong emphasis on Mozart's music, with the Mozarteum Salzburg Orchestra often in the pit. There are dedicated performances for kids, and *The Sound of Music* musical is a winner with all ages.

Grosses Festspielhaus
THEATRE

(📋0662-804 50; Hofstallgasse 1) Designed by architect Clemens Holzmeister in 1956 and built into the sheer sides of the Mönchsberg, the cavernous Grosses Festspielhaus stages the majority of Salzburg Festival (p241) performances and can accommodate 2179 theatregoers.

ARGEkultur
LIVE MUSIC, PERFORMING ARTS

(www.argekultur.at; Ulrike-Gschwandtner-Strasse 5) This alternative cultural venue was born out of protests against the Salzburg Festival in the 1980s. Today it's a bar and performance hybrid. Traversing the entire arts spectrum, the line-up features concerts, cabaret, DJ nights, dance, poetry slams and world music. It's at the Unipark Nonntal campus, a five-minute walk east of the *Altstadt*.

SALZBURG FOR CHILDREN

With dancing marionettes, chocolate galore and a giant fairy-tale fortress, Salzburg is kid nirvana. If the crowds prove unbearable with tots in tow, take them to the city's adventure **playgrounds** (there are 80 to pick from); the one on **Franz-Josef-Kai** is centrally located.

Salzburg's sights are usually half-price for children and most are free for kids under six years of age. Many galleries, museums and theatres also have dedicated programs for kids and families. These include the **Museum der Moderne** (p230), which has workshops for kids and teens, and the matinée performances at the enchanting **Salzburger Marionettentheater**. The **Salzburg Museum** (p230) has lots of hands-on displays, from harp playing to old-fashioned writing with quills. Pick up 'Wolf' Dietrich's cartoon guide at the entrance.

Other surefire kid-pleasers around Salzburg include the following:

➡ Children will have a blast with natural history at the **Haus der Natur** (p235), with its fun facts on alpine crystals, dinosaurs, science and the human body. The highlight is the aquarium, with its clownfish and sharks.

➡ Salzburg's very own toy story, the **Spielzeugmuseum** (p235) is a rambling attic of toys old and new. There are even 'adult parking areas' where grown-ups can hang out while tots play.

➡ Take a whizz through Austrian farming life through the ages at the huge open-air **Freilichtmuseum** (p235), with animals to pet, crafts to explore and a big adventure playground to romp around in. For more animal-themed fun, head to the **Salzburg Zoo** (p251), near Schloss Hellbrunn.

Rockhouse
LIVE MUSIC

(www.rockhouse.at; Schallmooser Hauptstrasse 46) Salzburg's hottest live music venue, Rockhouse presents first-rate rock, pop, jazz, folk, metal and reggae concerts – see the website for details. There's also a tunnel-shaped bar that has DJs (usually free) and bands. Rockhouse is 1km northeast of the *Altstadt;* take bus 4 to Canavalstrasse.

Schlosskonzerte
CLASSICAL MUSIC

(www.schlosskonzerte-salzburg.at; ☺concerts 8pm) A fantasy of coloured marble, stucco and frescoes, Schloss Mirabell's baroque Marmorsaal (Marble Hall) is the exquisite setting for chamber-music concerts. Internationally renowned soloists and ensembles perform works by Mozart and other well-known composers such as Haydn and Chopin. Tickets costing between €31 and €37 are available online or at the box office (☎0662-84 85 86; Theatergasse 2; ☺10am-3pm Mon-Fri, to 1pm Sat).

Festspiele Ticket Office
TICKET OFFICE

(☎0662-804 55 00; info@salzburgfestival.at; Herbert-von-Karajan-Platz 11; ☺10am-12.30pm & 1-4.30pm Mon-Fri Sep–mid-July, 10am-6pm daily mid-Jul–Aug) This office sells tickets for the Salzburg Festival, which range in price from €11 to €430. Tickets sell like hot cakes – so either book well in advance (at least several weeks ahead) or try your luck last minute.

Mozarteum
CLASSICAL MUSIC, OPERA

(☎0662-87 31 54; www.mozarteum.at; Schwarzstrasse 26) Opened in 1880 and revered for its supreme acoustics, the Mozarteum highlights the life and works of Mozart through chamber music (October to June), concerts and opera. The annual highlight is **Mozart Week** in January.

Salzburg Arena
CONCERT VENUE

(☎0662-240 40; www.salzburgarena.at; Am Messezentrum 1) Under a domed wooden roof, this is Salzburg's premier stage for sporting events, musicals and big-name concerts (Santana and Bob Dylan have played here). The arena is 3km north of town; take bus 1 to Messe.

Jazzit
JAZZ

(☎0662-88 32 64; www.jazzit.at; Elisabethstrasse 11; ☺6pm-midnight Tue-Sat) Hosts regular concerts from tango to electro alongside workshops and club nights. Don't miss the free Tuesday-night jam sessions in the adjacent Jazzit:Bar. It's 600m north of the Mirabellgarten along Elisabethstrasse.

Das Kino
CINEMA

(www.daskino.at; Giselakai 11) Shows independent and art-house films from Austria and across the globe in their original language. The cinema hosts the mountain-focused **Bergfilmfestival** in November.

Sound of Salzburg Show
SHOW

(☎0662-231 058 00; www.soundofsalzburgshow.com; Griessgasse 23, Sternbräu; tickets with/without dinner €54/34; ☺dinner 6.30pm, show 8.30pm May-Oct) This all-singing show at the beer garden Sternbräu is a triple bill of Mozart, *The Sound of Music* and operetta faves performed in traditional costume. Kitschy but fun.

🔒 Shopping

Ploom
CLOTHING

(www.ploom.at; Ursulinenplatz 5; ☺11am-6pm Thu & Fri, to 5pm Sat) Embracing the *Tracht* (traditional costume) trend is Ploom, where designer Pflaum has playfully and successfully reinvented the *Dirndl;* her boutique is a wonderland of floaty femininity: a sky-blue bodice here, a frothy cotton blouse, a wisp of a turquoise *Schürze* (apron) or silk evening gown there.

Genussmanufaktur
FOOD, ALCOHOL

(Mozartplatz 4; ☺10am-7pm Mon-Fri, to 6pm Sat) Found next to the tourist office on Mozartplatz, this vaulted emporium is a terrific new place to stock up on all-Austrian goodies, from homemade pesto sauces, dressings, vinegars, mustards and chutneys to forest honey, chocolate with pumpkin or blueberry, wines and spices.

Zotter
CHOCOLATE

(Herbert-von-Karajan-Platz 4; ☺10am-6pm Mon-Fri, 9.30am-6pm Sat) Made in Austria, Zotter's organic, fair-trade chocolate – including unusual varieties like Styrian pumpkin, ginger-carrot and mountain-cheese-walnut – is divine. Dip a spoon into the choc fountain and try samples from the conveyor belt.

Fürst
CHOCLATE, FOOD

(www.original-mozartkugel.com; Getreidegasse 47; ☺10am-6.30pm Mon-Sat, 11am-5pm Sun) Pistachio, nougat and dark-chocolate dreams, the *Mozartkugeln* (Mozart balls) here are still handmade to Paul Fürst's original 1890 recipe and cost €1.20 per mouthful. Other specialities include cube-shaped *Bach Würfel* – coffee, nut and marzipan truffles dedicated to yet another great composer.

Spirituosen Sporer WINE, ALCOHOL
(Getreidegasse 39; ⊙ 9.30am-7pm Mon-Fri, 8.30am-5pm Sat) In Getreidegasse's narrowest house, family-run Sporer has been intoxicating local folk with Austrian wines, herbal liqueurs and famous *Vogelbeer* (rowan berry) schnapps since 1903.

Musikhaus Katholnigg MUSIC
(Sigmund-Haffner-Gasse 16; ⊙ 9.30am-12.30pm & 1.30-6pm Mon-Fri, 9.30am-5pm Sat) Housed in a 16th-century townhouse and a music shop since 1847, this is the place to pick up high-quality recordings of the Salzburg Festival. There's a huge selection of classical, jazz, chanson and folk CDs and DVDs.

Stassny CLOTHING
(www.stassny.at; Getreidegasse 30; ⊙ 9.30am-6pm Mon-Fri, to 5pm Sat) Upscale Stassny combines *Tracht*-making know-how with high-quality fabrics and age-old patterns (stag prints, polka dots, gingham etc).

Wenger CLOTHING
(www.wenger.at; Getreidegasse 29; ⊙ 10am-6pm Mon-Fri, to 5pm Sat) Wenger stocks figure-hugging Lederhosen for ladies and *Dirndls,* from below-the-knee Heidi to thigh-flashing diva creations trimmed with ribbons and lace.

Forstenlechner CLOTHING
(www.salzburg-trachtenmode.at; Mozartplatz 4; ⊙ 9.30am-6pm Mon-Fri, to 5pm Sat) For a fusion of modern and traditional *Trachten* outfits in myriad colours, try the midrange Forstenlechner.

Salzburger Heimatwerk CLOTHING, GIFTS & SOUVENIRS
(www.salzburgerheimatwerk.at; Residenzplatz 9; ⊙ 9am-6pm Mon-Fri, to 5pm Sat) As well as knocking fine fabrics into *Dirndls* and dapper traditional costumes, Salzburger Heimatwerk does a fine line in local handicrafts, schnapps, preserves and honeys.

Salzburg Salz GIFTS & SOUVENIRS
(Wiener-Philharmoniker-Gasse 6; ⊙ 10am-6pm Mon-Fri, to 4pm Sat) Pure salt from Salzburgerland and the Himalayas, herbal salts and rock-salt tea lights are among the high-sodium wonders here.

Lanz Trachten CLOTHING, HATS
(www.lanztrachten.at; Schwarzstrasse 4; ⊙ 9am-6pm Mon-Fri, to 5pm Sat) Lanz is just the place if it's a tight-fitting *Dirndl* or a snazzy felt hat you're after.

Alte Hofapotheke PHARMACY
(Alter Markt 6; ⊙ 8am-6pm Mon-Fri, to noon Sat) For a whiff of nostalgia and a packet of sage throat pastilles, nip into this wonderfully old-fashioned, wood-panelled pharmacy. Salzburg's oldest, it was founded in 1591.

Klosterladen St Peter GIFTS & SOUVENIRS, ALCOHOL
(St Peter Bezirk 1; ⊙ 10am-6pm Mon-Fri, to 5pm Sat) Sidling up to Stiftskirche St Peter, this monastery shop stocks everything from hand-carved angels and rosaries to gentian syrup, monastic beer, wine and liqueurs.

Bottle Shop FOOD & DRINKS
(www.beerbottle.eu; Mirabellplatz 7; ⊙ 10am-6pm Mon-Fri, to 1pm Sat) A real delight for craft beer and cider lovers, this tucked-away shop does a creative line in ales, porters, stouts and ciders, all set under atmospheric vaults.

ⓘ Information

Hospital (☑ 0662-44 82; Müllner Hauptstrasse 48) Just north of Mönchsberg.

Main Post Office (Residenzplatz 9; ⊙ 8am-6pm Mon-Fri)

Police Headquarters (☑ 0662-63 83; Alpenstrasse 90)

Salzburgerland Tourismus (☑ 0662-668 80; www.salzburgerland.com; Wiener Bundesstrasse 23, Hallwang bei Salzburg; ⊙ 8am-5.30pm Mon-Thu, to 5pm Fri) Has information on the rest of the province outside Salzburg.

Station Post Office (Südtiroler Platz 1; ⊙ 8am-8.30pm Mon-Fri, to 2pm Sat)

Tourist Office (☑ 0662-88 98 70; www.salzburg.info; Mozartplatz 5; ⊙ 9am-7pm Mon-Sat, 10am-6pm Sun) Helpful tourist office with a ticket-booking service (www.salzburgticket.com) in the same building.

ⓘ Getting There & Away

AIR

Salzburg airport (p229), a 20-minute bus ride from the centre, has regular scheduled flights to destinations all over Austria and Europe. Low-cost flights from the UK are provided by **Ryanair** (www.ryanair.com) and **EasyJet** (www.easyjet.com). Other airlines include **British Airways** (www.britishairways.com) and **Jet2** (www.jet2.com).

BUS

Salzburger Verkehrsverbund (☑ 24hr hotline 0662-63 29 00; www.svv-info.at) makes it easy to reach the province's smaller villages. Buses depart from just outside the *Hauptbahnhof* on Südtiroler Platz, where timetables are displayed. Bus information and tickets are available from the information points on the main concourse.

For more information on buses in and around Salzburg and an online timetable, see www.postbus.at.

Buses leave hourly for the Salzkammergut:

Bad Ischl €10.60, 1½ hours
Mondsee €6.70, 53 minutes
St Gilgen €6.70, 45 minutes
St Wolfgang €9.70, 1¾ hours

TRAIN

Salzburg has excellent rail connections with the rest of Austria from its recently revamped **Hauptbahnhof**.

Trains leave frequently for Vienna (€51.90, 2½ to three hours) and Linz (€26, 1¼ hours). There is a two-hourly express service to Klagenfurt (€39.50, three hours).

The quickest way to Innsbruck is by the 'corridor' train through Germany; trains depart at least every two hours (€45.50, two hours) and stop at Kufstein. Direct trains run at least hourly to Munich (€30.70, 1½ to two hours); some of these continue to Karlsruhe via Stuttgart.

There are also several trains daily to Berlin (€175.70, 8½ hours), Budapest (€90.80, 5¾ hours), Prague (€98.90 to €125.60, 7½ hours) and Venice (€59, six to nine hours).

For timetables, see www.svv-info.at.

❶ Getting Around

BICYCLE

Salzburg is one of Austria's most bike-friendly cities. It has an extensive network of scenic cycling trails heading off in all directions, including along the banks of the Salzach River. See www.movelo.com for a list of places renting out electric bikes (e-bikes).

A Velo (Mozartplatz; bicycle rental half-day/full day/week €12/18/55, e-bike €18/25/120; ☺9am-6pm mid-Apr–Oct) Just across the way from the tourist office.

BUS

Bus drivers sell single (€2.40), 24-hour (€5.30) and weekly tickets (€14). Single tickets bought in advance from machines are slightly cheaper. If you're planning on making several trips, *Tabak* (tobacconist) shops sell tickets even cheaper still (€1.60 each), but only in units of five. Kids under six travel for free, while all other children pay half-price.

Bus routes are shown at bus stops and on some city maps; buses 1 and 4 start from the *Hauptbahnhof* and skirt the pedestrian-only *Altstadt*.

Information and timetables are available at www.salzburg-verkehr.at.

CAR & MOTORCYCLE

Parking places are limited and much of the *Altstadt* is only accessible on foot, so it's easier to leave your car at one of three park-and-ride points to the west, north and south of the city. The largest car park in the centre is the Altstadt Garage under Mönchsberg (€18 per day); some restaurants in the centre will stamp your ticket for a reduction. Rates are lower on streets with automatic ticket machines (blue zones); a three-hour maximum applies (€3.90, or €0.60 for 28 minutes) from 9am to 7pm on weekdays.

For car hire, try **Avis** (www.avis.com; Ferdinand-Porsche-Strasse 7), **Europcar** (www.europcar.com; Gniglerstrasse 12) or **Hertz** (www.hertz.com; Ferdinand-Porsche-Strasse 7).

AROUND SALZBURG

Hellbrunn

Hellbrunn's biggest stunner is its extraordinary baroque palace, Schloss Hellbrunn, the flamboyant vision of Prince-Archbishop Markus Sittikus, set in manicured gardens. Factor in at least half a day for a visit. Salzburg Zoo is also a big draw for families

◉ Sights

★**Schloss Hellbrunn** PALACE
(www.hellbrunn.at; Fürstenweg 37; adult/child/family €12.50/5.50/26.50, gardens free; ☺9am-5.30pm Apr-Oct, to 9pm Jul & Aug; 🚼) A prince-archbishop with a wicked sense of humour, Markus Sittikus, built Schloss Hellbrunn in the early 17th century as a summer palace and an escape from his functions at the Residenz. The Italianate villa became a beloved retreat for rulers of state, who flocked here to eat, drink and make merry. It was a Garden of Eden to all who beheld its exotic fauna, citrus trees and trick fountains – designed to sober up the clergy without dampening their spirits.

Domenico Gisberti, poet to the court of Munich, once gushed: 'I see the epitome of Venice in these waters, Rome reduced to a brief outline.'

While the whimsical palace interior – especially the Oriental-style Chinese Room and frescoed Festsaal – is worth a peek, the eccentric **Wasserspiele** (trick fountains) are the big draw in summer. Be prepared to get soaked in the mock Roman theatre, the shell-clad Neptune Grotto and the twittering Bird Grotto. No statue here is quite as it seems, including the emblematic tongue-poking-out Germaul mask (Sittikus' answer to his critics). The tour rounds out at the 18th-century water-powered **Mechanical Theatre**, where 200 limewood figurines depict life in a baroque city. Tours run every 30 minutes.

Studded with ponds, sculptures and leafy avenues, the **palace gardens** are free and open until dusk year-round. Here you'll find the *Sound of Music* pavilion of 'Sixteen Going on Seventeen' fame.

Salzburg Zoo   ZOO
(www.salzburg-zoo.at; Hellbrunnerstrasse 60, Anif; adult/child/family €10.50/4.50/24.50; ☺9am-6.30pm Jun-Aug, shorter hours Sep-May; ♿) Kids can come face to face with lions, flamingos and alpine ibex at the Salzburg Zoo, near Schloss Hellbrunn at the foot of Hellbrunn's cliffs. The zoo is home to 140 animals from across the globe.

❶ Getting There & Away

Hellbrunn is 4.5km south of Salzburg, a scenic 20-minute bike ride (mostly along the Salzach River) or a 12-minute ride on Bus 25 (€2, every 20 minutes), departing from Mozartsteg/Rudolfskai in the *Altstadt*.

Hallein & Around

☑ 06245 / POP 20,380

Too few people visit Hallein in their dash north to Bavaria or south to Salzburg, but those who do are pleasantly surprised. Beyond its industrial outskirts lies a pristine late-medieval town, where narrow lanes are punctuated by courtyards, art galleries and boho cafes. Hallein's major family attraction, the Salzwelten salt mine, is actually located in Bad Dürrnberg, 6km southwest of town.

◉ Sights

★ Salzwelten   MINE
(www.salzwelten.at; Ramsaustrasse 3, Bad Dürrnberg; adult/child/family €21/10.50/53.50; ☺9am-5pm; ♿) The sale of salt filled Salzburg's coffers during its princely heyday. At Austria's biggest show mine, you can slip into a boilersuit to descend to the bowels of the earth. The tour aboard a rickety train passes through a maze of claustrophobic passageways, over the border to Germany and

down a 27m slide – don't brake, lift your legs and ask the guide to wax the slide for extra speed!

Keltenmuseum   MUSEUM
(Celtic Museum; www.keltenmuseum.at; Pflegerplatz 5; adult/child €6/2.50; ☺9am-5pm; ♿) Overlooking the Salzach, the glass-fronted Keltenmuseum runs chronologically through the region's heritage in a series of beautiful vaulted rooms. It begins with Celtic artefacts, including *Asterix*-style helmets, an impressively reconstructed chariot and a selection of bronze brooches, pendants and buckles.

Stille Nacht Museum   MUSEUM
(www.stillenachthallein.at; Gruberplatz 1; adult/child €2/0.70, free with entry to Keltenmuseum; ☺3-6pm Jul & Aug, 3-6pm Fri-Sun Sep-Jun) Hallein's festive claim to fame is as the one-time home of Franz Xaver Gruber (1787–1863) who composed the carol *Stille Nacht* (Silent Night). Joseph Mohr penned the poem in 1816 and Gruber, a schoolteacher at the time, came up with the melody on his guitar. The fabled guitar takes pride of place in Gruber's former residence, now the Stille Nacht Museum, next to Hallein's parish church. The museum tells the story of the carol through documents and personal belongings.

☂ Activities

Keltenblitz   ADVENTURE SPORTS
(Bad Dürrnberg; adult/child €9.60/6.60; ☺10am-6pm May–mid-Oct; ♿) In summer, families pick up speed on this toboggan run close to Salzwelten. A chairlift takes passengers up to the top of Zinken mountain, where they board little wheeled bobsleds to race 2.2km down hairpin bends. The ride is over in a flash and affords fleeting views of the Salzach Valley.

⌁ Sleeping

Pension Sommerauer   GUESTHOUSE $
(☑06245-800 30; www.pension-hallein.at; Tschusistrasse 71; s €47-61, d €75-98, tr €98-126, q €125-160; 🅿🏊) Housed in a 300-year-old farmhouse, the rustic rooms at this guesthouse are a bargain. There's a heated pool and conservatory as well as kiddie stuff like a playroom, sandpit and swings.

Pension Hochdürrnberg   GUESTHOUSE $
(☑06245-751 83; Rumpelgasse 14, Bad Dürrnberg; s/d/tr/q €45/60/70/100; 🅿) Surrounded by meadows, this farmhouse in Bad Dürrnberg

---

ⓘ FAST TRACK TO THE SALT MINES

All train stations in the region sell the money-saving **Salzwelten Hallein** ticket (adult/child €25.80/12.90), which covers a bus transfer to Bad Dürrnberg, plus entry to Salzwelten, the Keltenmuseum and Stille Nacht Museum.

---

has countrified rooms with warm pine furnishings and downy bedding. The furry residents (rabbits, sheep and cows) keep children amused.

Hotel Auwirt HOTEL **$$**
(✆ 06245-804 17; www.auwirt.com; Salzburgerstrasse 42; camp sites per adult/child/tent €10/7/6, s €60-95, d €90-165, q €149-255; P ☏) Auwirt's light-filled, wood-floored, Alpine-trimmed rooms are spacious and comfy; some superior rooms come with balconies. The hotel is a good family base, with a tree-shaded garden and playground. You can also pitch a tent here.

✖ Eating

Koi ASIAN **$**
(✆ 06245-731 13; Schanzplatz 2; lunch €8.90, dinner mains €9-16; ⊗ 8am-2am Mon-Sat; ✐) There's a cool breeze to be had on the raised terrace by the stream at this modern, upbeat cafe. The menu tempts with fresh-from-the-wok noodles, spring rolls and crunchy beansprout salads, which you can wash down with organic juices or an Illy coffee. Good-value lunch specials swing from Thai-style chicken to meatballs with mushroom curry and courgette noodles.

Esswerk INTERNATIONAL **$$**
(✆ 06245-705 09; www.esswerkhallein.at; Salzachtalstrasse 29; mains €10-18) Housed in an old paper factory, Esswerk is a contemporary, chilled-out spot for Austrian and international grub, or simply a drink at the bar. It does a line in pizzas, burgers, pasta dishes and salads, as well as more substantial mains like pike perch fillet with thyme and lime tagliatelle. Lunch specials cost between €5.90 and €7.90.

Toro Toro SPANISH, TAPAS **$$$**
(✆ 06245-842 23; www.toro-toro.at; Schloss Altendorffstrasse 2; 8-/12-course menu for two €108/128; ⊗ 6pm-1am Tue-Sat) Lodged in the vaults of an old castle on the fringes of town, Toro Toro is a little snippet of España in the Austrian Alps. The tapas and dishes – from clams cooked in sherry to paella – are expertly paired with Spanish wines. On warm summer evenings, the tree-fringed terrace is simply lovely. It's 3km northeast of town.

🍷 Drinking & Nightlife

Kurkurma CAFE
(www.cafe-kurkuma.at; Metzgergasse 9; ⊗ 8.30am-6pm Sun-Fri, to 3pm Sat) If you're seeking a coffee with a kick in Hallein, this is where you should head: it uses beans from 220°, a well-regarded roasting company. The bright, minimalist, vaulted interior has a relaxed vibe, and the cafe also does a fine line in breakfasts, cakes, muffins and homemade lemonade.

ⓘ Information

Tourist Office (✆ 06245-853 94; www.hallein.com; Mauttorpromenade 6; ⊗ 8.30am-5pm Mon-Fri) Hallein's tourist office is a good first port of call for information on the town and its surrounds.

ⓘ Getting There & Away

Hallein is close to the German border, 18km south of Salzburg via the B150 and A10/E55 direction Graz/Villach. It's a 25-minute train journey from Salzburg, with departures roughly every 30 minutes (€4.60, 20 minutes).

Werfen

✆ 06468 / POP 2965

The world's largest accessible ice caves, the soaring limestone turrets of the Tennengebirge range and a formidable medieval fortress are but the tip of the superlative iceberg in Werfen. Such salacious natural beauty hasn't escaped Hollywood producers – Werfen stars in WWII action film *Where Eagles Dare* (1968) and makes a cameo appearance in the picnic scene of *The Sound of Music*.

Both the fortress and the ice caves can be squeezed into a day trip from Salzburg; start early, visit the caves first and be at the fortress for the last falconry show.

◉ Sights

★**Eisriesenwelt** CAVE
(www.eisriesenwelt.at; adult/child €12/9, incl cable car €24/14; ⊗ 8am-4pm Jul & Aug, to 3pm May, Jun, Sep & Oct) Billed as the world's largest acces-

sible ice caves, Eisriesenwelt is a glittering ice empire spanning 30,000 sq metres and 42km of narrow passages burrowing deep into the heart of the mountains. A tour through these Narnia-esque chambers of blue ice is a unique experience. As you climb up wooden steps and down pitch-black passages, with carbide lamps aglow, otherworldly ice sculptures shaped like polar bears and elephants, frozen columns and lakes emerge from the shadows.

A highlight is the cavernous **Eispalast** (ice palace), where the frost crystals twinkle when a magnesium flare is held up to them. A womblike tunnel leads to a flight of 700 steps, which descends back to the entrance. Even if it's hot outside, entering the caves in any season is like stepping into a deep freeze – bring warm clothing and sturdy footwear.

In summer, minibuses (return adult/child €7/5) run at 8.18am, 10.18am, 12.18pm and 2.18pm from Werfentrain station to Eisriesenwelt car park, which is a 20-minute walk from the bottom station of the cable car. The last return bus departs at 4.32pm. Allow roughly three hours for the return trip (including the tour). You can walk the whole route, but it's a challenging four-hour ascent, rising 1100m above the village.

Liechtensteinklamm
GORGE

(Liechtenstein Gorge; www.liechtensteinklamm.at; adult/child €6/4; ⊗8am-6pm May-Sep, 9am-4pm Oct; 🚼) One of the deepest and longest ravines in the Alps, the Liechtensteinklamm is off the beaten track but well worth the detour. The jaw-dropping chasm was carved out during the last Ice Age; it's named after Johann II, Prince of Liechtenstein, who poured plenty of money into making the gorge accessible in the 19th century. Following raging waters flanked by vertical 300m-high cliffs, the footpath crosses bridges and passes through tunnels gouged into slate cliffs veined with white granite.

Burg Hohenwerfen
CASTLE

(Hohenwerfen Fortress; www.salzburg-burgen.at; adult/child/family €12/10.50/28.50, incl lift €15.50/13.50/36.50; ⊗9.30-5pm Jan-Apr & Oct-Dec, 9am-7pm May-Sep; 🚼) Slung high on a wooded clifftop and cowering beneath the majestic peaks of the Tennengebirge range, Burg Hohenwerfen is visible from afar. For 900 years this fortress has kept watch over the Salzach Valley; its current appearance dating to 1570. The big draw is the far-reaching view over Werfen from the 16th-century belfry, though the **dungeons** (displaying the usual nasties such as the iron maiden and thumb screw) are also worth a look.

🛏 Sleeping & Eating

Mariannenschlössl
PENSION $

(☑06468-420 93 80; wimmer.werfen@sbg.at; Poststrasse 10; d €60-64) What a view! A five-minute uphill trot from the centre of the village, this family-run guesthouse offers an entrancing vista of the fortress and of the Tennengebirge's magnificent rock turrets and spires – both from its garden and the sweet, spotlessly kept rooms. A generous breakfast is served in a room adorned with hunting trophies.

Weisses Rössl
PENSION $

(☑06468-52 68; hofer.r@sbg.at; Markt 39; s/d/tr/q €38/67/84/96; P🐕) In the village centre, this good-value pension has great views of the fortress and the Tennengebirge from its rooftop terrace. Rooms are a blast from the 1970s, but all are large and cosy, with sofas and cable TV.

Camping Vierthaler
CAMPGROUND $

(☑06468-565 70; www.camping-vierthaler.at; Reitsam 8; camp sites per adult/child/tent €6/3/6.50, bungalows d/tr/q €29/38/47; ⊗mid-Apr–Sep) This lovely campground on the bank of the Salzach River has a back-to-nature feel. Facilities include a snack bar and playground. Bungalows with kitchenettes, patios and barbecue areas are also available.

Oedlhaus
AUSTRIAN $$

(www.oedlhaus.at; Eishöhlenstrasse 30; snacks €3.50-8, mains €8-12.50; ⊗9am-3.45pm May, Jun, Sep & Oct, to 4.45pm Jul & Aug) Next to Eisriesenwelt cable-car top station, this woodsy hut at 1574m fortifies walkers with mountain grub such as *Gröstl* (pan-fried potatoes, pork and onions topped with a fried egg). The terrace has views to rave about: you can see across the Salzach Valley to the chiselled limestone peaks of the Hochkönig range.

★ Obauer
MODERN EUROPEAN $$$

(☑06468-52 12; www.obauer.com; Markt 46; 3-course lunch €38, dinner menus €40-125; ⊗noon-2pm & 7-9pm Wed-Sun; 🚼) Culinary dream duo Karl and Rudi Obauer run the show at this highly regarded, ingredient-focused restaurant. Sit in the rustic-chic restaurant or out in the garden, where most of the fruit and herbs are grown. Signature dishes such as meltingly tender Werfen lamb and flaky trout strudel are matched with the finest of Austrian wines.

ℹ Information

Tourist Office (🖰 06468-53 88; www.werfen. at; Markt 24; ⊙ 9am-noon & 1-6pm Mon-Fri) The friendly tourist office hands out information and maps.

ℹ Getting There & Away

Werfen is 45km south of Salzburg on the A10/ E55 motorway. Trains run frequently to Salzburg (€8.70, 40 minutes).

SOUTHERN SALZBURG PROVINCE

Filzmoos

🖰 06453 / POP 1460

Theatrically set amid the jagged limestone spires of the Dachstein massif, rolling pastures and the aptly named Bischofsmütze (Bishop's Mitre) peaks, Filzmoos is quite the alpine idyll. Despite some wonderful hiking and skiing, the resort's out-of-the-way location deters the masses and the village has kept its rural charm and family-friendly atmosphere.

🏃 Activities

Dachstein Circuit HIKING
Heading up to an elevation of 2995m, the eight-day, 126km Dachstein Circuit is a phenomenal introduction to this jagged limestone range. It takes in the entire spectrum of Alpine landscapes: glaciers and high mountains, forests, karst, raging rivers and flower-dotted meadows.

Gosaukamm Circuit HIKING
This spectacular two-day, 23km circuit gets you up close and personal with the ragged Gosaukamm range, sometimes dubbed 'Salzburg's Dolomites' because they are similar in size and scale. The highlight in every sense of the word is the 2012m **Steigl Pass**, an exposed, fixed-cable route involving some scrambling. Pick up the Freytag & Berndt map *WK 281: Dachstein* (1:50,000).

Ski Amadé SKIING
(🖰 06452-20 20 20; www.skiamade.com; full-region 6-day pass €232) Salzburgerland's Ski Amadé is Austria's biggest ski area, covering a whopping 760km of pistes in 25 resorts divided into five snow-sure regions. Among them are low-key Radstadt and family-friendly Filzmoos. Such a vast area means that truly every level is catered for: from gentle cruising on tree-lined runs to off-piste touring.

Dachsteinrunde CYCLING
(Dachstein Tour; http://dachstein.salzkammergut. at) For keen cyclists, the challenging 182km to 269km Dachsteinrunde (Dachstein Tour), taking in Salzburgerland, Upper Austria and Styria and passing through some classic Alpine terrain, is a must. Maps can be ordered online for €7.

★ Festivals & Events

Thanks to its central alpine location and stiff winds, Filzmoos has become something of a ballooning mecca. Balloons light up the winter skies in January at the highly photogenic **Hanneshof Hot Air Balloon Trophy** (www. ballonfahren-filzmoos.com; ⊙ Jan).

🛏 Sleeping & Eating

Pension Wieser PENSION **$**
(🖰 06453-83 56; www.wieser-filzmoos.at; Neuberg 123; d €92-100, incl full board €106-118) Handy for the slopes, this sweet, rustic pension sits opposite the Filzmoos-Neuberg chairlift. A fire blazes downstairs in winter and the spotless rooms come with mountain-facing balconies. It's worth shelling out extra for full board, which includes breakfast, a packed lunch, all-day soft drinks and a delicious three-course dinner. There's table tennis and a games room for kids.

★ **Bio-Hotel Hammerhof** HOTEL **$$**
(🖰 06453-82 45; www.hammerhof.at; Filzmoos 6; d €134-170; P �) ✎ Set in a beautifully converted 400-year-old farmhouse, this ecofriendly hotel is a find. Bathed in soft light, the rooms are decorated with natural wood and country touches; some have balconies and tiled ovens. The restaurant serves home-grown organic produce. Unwind in a herbal bath or saddle a horse to canter off into the hills. The owner, Matthias, arranges riding tours.

Haus Obermoos GUESTHOUSE **$$**
(🖰 0664 1261 403; www.hausobermoos.com; Neuberg 190; s/d €90/100, apt €150-260; P ﾞ) Lily and Stephen extend the warmest of welcomes at Haus Obermoos. Their love for this guesthouse shows in bright, immaculate rooms and apartments, tastefully done out

in wood, marble and earthy hues. A heated ski room and a spa area are welcome touches. Haus Obermoos is near the ski lifts, a 10-minute walk from the centre.

Fiakerwirt   AUSTRIAN $
(☑ 06453-82 09; www.fiakerwirt.co.at; Filzmoos 23; mains €6-13; ⊙ 10am-11pm Tue-Sun; 🖼) This rambling farmhouse and beer garden serves meaty fare such as schnitzel, goulash and pork roast. Kids love the pet goats, ducks and ponies. In winter, horse-drawn sleighs depart from here (€20 per person). They pass through the village and snowy forest en route to one of the surrounding *Almen* (alpine meadows).

ℹ Information

Tourist Office (☑ 06453-82 35; www.filzmoos. at; Filzmoos 50; ⊙ 8.30am-12.30pm & 2-6pm Mon-Fri, 8.30am-12.30pm & 3-6pm Sat, 10am-noon Sun) The centrally located tourist office provides stacks of information on activities in the region and will help book accommodation.

ℹ Getting There & Away

Filzmoos is a 10km detour from the A10/E55 Tauern-Autobahn motorway. Several train–bus connections operate daily between Salzburg and Filzmoos (€14.40, 1¾ to three hours); most require a change at Bischofshofen.

Radstadt

☑ 06452 / POP 4800
Low-key Radstadt has an attractively walled town centre, with round turrets and a *Stadtpfarrkirche* (town parish church) that's a potpourri of Gothic and Romanesque elements. The Alps that rear above the town are a vast playground for all manner of outdoor activities.

Most visitors come to Radstadt for the varied skiing and snowboarding. The resort is part of the vast Ski Amadé area, which is covered by a single ski pass and interconnected by ultramodern lifts and free ski buses.

The same mountains attract active types in summer, too, with more than 1000km of walking trails and opportunities for canyoning, climbing, white-water rafting and mountain biking.

Salzburger Sportwelt Tourist Office (☑ 06452-74 72; www.salzburgersportwelt.com; Stadtplatz 17; ⊙ 9am-noon & 2-6pm Mon-Fri, 9am-noon Sat) dishes out information and maps on the region.

Radstadt is on the route of a regular bus-train service running between Innsbruck (€41 to €60, 3¼ to four hours) and Graz (€40, three hours). Zell am See (€13.40, 1½ hours) and Bruck an der Mur (€33.20, three hours) are on this route.

From Radstadt, the B99 climbs to the dramatic Radstädter Tauern Pass (1739m), then over to Carinthia. Just to the west is the A10/E55, which avoids the high parts by going through a 6km tunnel.

Mauterndorf

☑ 06472 / POP 1780
A turreted castle high on a hill provides a backdrop ripe for a bedtime story in sleepy little Mauterndorf. Dotted with gabled houses and fountains, its streets are a pleasure to mooch around. While the surrounding high moors and exposed bluffs are set up for walking and skiing, its remote setting in the Lungau region keeps things quiet.

Looking every inch the fairy-tale castle with its setting atop a rocky outcrop and sturdy towers, medieval **Burg Mauterndorf** (adult/child €9.50/5.50; ⊙ 10am-6pm May-Oct) is the village's pride and joy. It was built in the 13th century by the archbishops of Salzburg on the site of a Roman fort. The castle now houses a regional **museum** and provides the backdrop for various cultural events.

ℹ Getting There & Away

Mauterndorf is on Hwy 99. Bus 780 runs from Radstadt to the Mauterndorf post office (€8.70, 48 minutes, three times daily).

HOHE TAUERN NATIONAL PARK

If you thought Mother Nature pulled out all the stops in the Austrian Alps, think again: Hohe Tauern National Park was her magnum opus. Welcome to Austria's outdoor wonderland and one of Europe's largest nature reserves (1786 sq km), which straddles Tyrol, Carinthia and Salzburgerland and is overshadowed by the 3798m hump of Grossglockner, the country's highest peak.

Try as we might, no amount of hyperbole about towering snow-clad mountains, shimmering glaciers, impossibly turquoise lakes and raging waterfalls can quite do this place justice. Go see it for yourself.

◉ Sights

National Park Worlds   MUSEUM, NATIONAL PARK
(Gerlosstrasse 18, Mittersill; museum adult/child
€10/5; ⊙9am-6pm; ⊞) For the inside scoop
on all things Hohe Tauern National Park,
factor in a stop at this terrific visitor centre.
The **museum** side of it showcases the park
in a nutshell, with exhibits on glaciers, avalanches, wild waters, farming life, mountain
forests, alpine animals and plants. A highlight for kids is the marmot burrow to clamber around in. The **shop** stocks a great array
of books and maps.

⚡ Activities

Ranger Walks   WALKING
(www.nationalparkerlebnis.at; ⊙Mon-Fri Jul-Sep)
To get the most out of Hohe Tauern National Park, consider signing up for one of the
guided walks led by well-informed rangers.
On weekdays from July to September, they
offer 30 hikes – several of which are free
with a guest card – covering everything from
herb discovery trails to high-altitude hikes,
around-the-glacier tours, gorge climbing
and wildlife spotting.

See the website for the program and prices.

Bergführer Kals   CLIMBING
(☑0664 416 12 89; www.bergfuehrer-kals.at; Köd-
nitz 18, Kals am Grossglockner; Grossglockner normal
route from €195, Grossvenediger from €100; ⊙office
3-7pm Jun-Oct) If you're seriously considering
a two-day ascent to Austria's highest of the
high, **Grossglockner** (3798m) or **Grossvenediger** (3666m), this team of mountain
guides provides expert assistance. Experience is essential. It also arranges other alpine
climbs (the Lienzer Dolomites, for instance)
as well as ski touring, free-riding, ice climbing and snowshoeing expeditions in winter
(but call ahead). The website has details.

⌷ Sleeping

Erzherzog-Johann-Hütte   HUT $
(☑04876-85 00; www.erzherzog-johann-huette.
at; dm/r €33/42, incl half board €52/61; ⊙mid-
Jun–Sep) Perched like an eyrie at 3454m, this
is the highest of Austria's alpine huts and a
mere two-hour climb from the summit of
mighty Grossglockner. As you might expect
at this giddy elevation, the wooden bunk
room is bare bones and there are no wash
rooms. The kitchen rolls out hearty grub –
goulash, schnitzel and wood-oven strudel,
for instance.

Hotel Tauernstern   CHALET $$
(☑04822-248; www.tauernstern.at; Winklern
24, Winklern im Mölltal; d/ste €116/128; ⓟ⍲)
Sweeping valley views extend from the
timber balconies of this mountain-set gem.
Four-poster pine-and-stone beds, in-room
fridges, a sauna and spa built from local
wood and slate, and an exceptional gour-
met restaurant using ingredients from local
farms all make Tauernstern a fabulous pit
stop before tackling the Grossglockner High
Alpine Road.

Matreier Tauernhaus   GUESTHOUSE $$
(☑04875-88 11; www.matreier-tauernhaus.
at; Tauer 22, Matrei in Osttirol; s/d/tr/q
€55/90/105/120; ⍲) Cowering in the shadow of some of Austria's highest peaks, this
is a mountain chalet in the classic mould,
with simple rooms, a heartfelt welcome and
children's playground. Run by the Brugger
family for the past five generations, it was
originally built for the Archbishop of Salzburg in 1207. It's a great base for an ascent
of Grossvenediger.

ⓘ Getting There & Away

CAR & MOTORCYCLE

To limit traffic through the park, many of the
roads have toll sections and some are closed
in winter. The main north–south road routes
are the year-round Felber-Tauern-Strasse
(B108) between Mittersill and Lienz, and the
spectacular Grossglockner Road (open May to
October).

The 5.5km-long Felbertauerntunnel is on the
East Tyrol–Salzburgerland border; the toll is
€11 for cars and €10 for motorbikes. Buses on
the Lienz–Kitzbühel route operate along this
road.

TRAIN

The main hubs for train services are Zell am See
(p261) (for services to Salzburg and points north
via St Johann im Pongau) and Lienz (p290), for
trains east and west into Tyrol and Carinthia.

ⓘ Getting Around

BUS

Train-bus combinations run four times daily
from Zell am See to Matrei in Osttirol (€14.10,
two hours), involve a change at Mittersill.

There are also regular bus services to Heiligenblut (p267), one of the most central bases for
exploring the park.

Zell am See

☑ 06542 / POP 9575

Zell am See is an instant heart-stealer, with its bluer-than-blue lake (Zeller See), pocket-sized centre studded with brightly painted chalets, and the snowcapped peaks of the Hohe Tauern that lift your gaze to postcard heaven. You can dive into the lake and cycle its leafy shores, hike and ski in the mountains and drive high on the Grossglockner Road. Every year, more than one million visitors from all round the world – from families to playboys in souped-up Mustangs – do just that, in search of the Austrian dream.

🏃 Activities

★ **Kitzsteinhorn Glacier**   SKIING, HIKING
(www.kitzsteinhorn.at; day pass adult/child €46/23, with guest card free) Winter or summer, the 3029m Kitzsteinhorn Glacier is one of Zell am See's must-do attractions, with enough snow for skiing and boarding 10 months of the year. A cable car (adult/child €40/20) whizzes up to top-station **Gipfelwelt 3000**, where two viewpoint platforms command phenomenal alpine views deep into the Hohe Tauern National Park – look out for the distinctive profile of Grossglockner. From mid-May to mid-September there are free **guided tours** at 10.30am and 1pm.

In summer you can hike the glacier trail, check out the **Ice Arena**'s deckchair-clad snow beach and slides, and buff up on local geology at the **Nationalpark Gallery**, which has some pretty impressive Hohe Tauern crystals on show. For downhill mountain biking, a 12km trail descends to the valley. The free Zell am See–Kaprun Card (p260) will get you admission to the glacier and one free return cable-car ride.

For the chill factor in winter, check out the **Ice Camp** with its spectacularly lit igloo bar, lounge and sundeck – perfect for cocktail sipping and listening to mellow beats after a hard day on the slopes.

Adventure Service   ADVENTURE SPORTS
(☑ 06542-735 25; www.adventureservice.at; Steinergasse 5-7) A one-stop daredevil shop, this offers a long list of adrenaline-charged activities from tandem paragliding (€120) and white-water rafting (€50) to canyoning (€59 to €95), climbing (€50 to €105) and guided half-day mountain-bike tours (€27). Less physically exerting are the 90-minute Segway tours (€40), taking in the lake and mountain scenery. Bike hire costs €13/23 per half-/full day.

Windsurfcenter Zell Am See   WINDSURFING
(☑ 0664 644 36 95; http://windsurfcenter.members.cablelink.at; Seespitzstrasse 13; 2hr beginner course €38; ☉ dawn-dusk May-Sep) Stiff mountain breezes create the ideal conditions for windsurfing and stand-up paddle boarding on Zeller See. This reputable windsurfing centre is 2km south of town; call for more information on its wide range of courses.

HIKING & CLIMBING IN HOHE TAUERN NATIONAL PARK

Hohe Tauern's deep valleys, towering peaks and plateaux are a Mecca to hikers and climbers. The reserve has treks to suit every level of ability, from gentle day walks to extreme expeditions to inaccessible peaks and ridges. Freytag & Berndt (www.freytag-berndt.com) produce detailed 1:50,000 walking maps covering the national park and surrounding areas, available online, at the **visitor centre** (p256) or in bookshops in larger towns. When planning a major trek, it's worth booking overnight stops in advance, as accommodation can be sparse the higher you go; local tourist offices can advise.

Popular hikes include the ascent of the eternally ice-capped **Grossvenediger** (3666m), flanked by glaciers. The closest you can get by road is the 1512m-high **Matrei-er Tauernhaus** (p256), at the southern entrance to the Felbertauerntunnel. You can park here and within an hour's walk gain fine views of the mountain.

Anyone with climbing experience and a reasonable level of fitness can climb the mighty **Grossglockner** (3798m) via the 'normal' route, though a guide is recommended. The main trail begins at the **Erzherzog-Johann-Hütte** (p256), a four- to five-hour hike from Heiligenblut. From here, the roughly two-hour route crosses ice and rocks, following a steel cable over a narrow snow ridge, to the cross at the summit. It's essential to have the proper equipment (maps, ropes, crampons etc) and to check weather conditions before setting out. For guides, contact the tourist office in Heiligenblut or check out the options with **Bergführer Kals** (p256).

You can also rent windsurfing/wetsuits/funboards for €12/18/25.

Rundfahrt Schmittenhöhe CRUISE
(adult/child €13.50/6.60; ☺10am-5pm Jun-Sep, 11am-4pm May & Oct) For a scenic spin on the lake – with cracking views of the Hohe Tauern mountains to boot (on cloudless days) – hop aboard one of these 45-minute panoramic boat tours.

✨ Festivals & Events

Zell am See swings into summer with live music, fireworks and sports events at its two lake festivals, held in mid-July and early August.

Zell Summer Night MUSIC, PERFORMING ARTS
(☺Wed Jul & Aug) The free Zell Summer Night festival draws bands, street entertainers and improvised theatre to streets and squares every Wednesday night in July and August.

🛏 Sleeping

Haus Haffner GUESTHOUSE $
(✔06542-72 39 60; www.haffner.at; Schmittenstrasse 29; s €25-34, d €48-68, apt €96-133; 🕸) Tucked down a quiet backstreet near the ski lift, this cheery guesthouse has spacious rooms and family apartments with rag rugs, kettles and chunky wood furniture (the owner is a cabinet maker).

Junges Hotel Zell am See HOSTEL $
(✔06542-571 85; www.hostel-zell.at; Seespitzstrasse 13; s/d/tr/q €42/71/99/133; P🕸) Right at the lake and beach, a 15-minute walk south of town, these family-friendly digs are a great budget deal. Rooms are simple but well kept, the mountain views dreamy and there's always plenty going on, from volleyball matches to weekly barbecues.

Seecamp Zell Am See CAMPGROUND $
(✔06542-721 15; www.seecamp.at; Thumersbacherstrasse 34; camp sites per adult/child/tent €9.90/6.40/7.60; P🕸) If waking up to views of the snowcapped Kitzsteinhorn mountains appeals, camp out at this tree-shaded site on the lakeshore. Facilities include a shop, restaurant and kids' club. Guided mountain-bike and hiking tours are available.

★ Pension Hubertus PENSION $$
(✔06542-724 27; www.hubertus-pension.at; Gartenstrasse 4; s €52-69, d €104-138; P) 🍃 Beate and Bernd extend a warm welcome at their eco-savvy chalet. Situated opposite the ski

lifts, the pension uses 100% renewable energy (solar and wind power), and organic produce and fair-trade coffee are served at breakfast. The bright, airy rooms are decked out country-style, with lots of pine, floral drapes and downy bedding.

Steinerwirt BOUTIQUE HOTEL $$
(✔06542-725 02; www.steinerwirt.com; Dreifaltigkeitsgasse 2; s €79, d €158-208; @🕸) A 500-year-old chalet turned boutique hotel, Steinerwirt has light-filled rooms tastefully done out in muted tones and untreated pinewood, with flat-screen TVs and DVD players. The rooftop whirlpool, mountain-facing sauna, library and art gallery invite relaxation. There are incredible views of Kitzsteinhorn glacier and Schmittenhöhe from the roof terrace.

Haus Wilhelmina PENSION $$
(✔06542-726 07; www.haus-wilhelmina.at; Schmittenstrasse 14; d €89, apt €89-180; P🕸) Just a joyous skip from the ski lift and centre, this friendly pension has simple but homey rooms with lots of pine, floral prints and balconies. There are also family-sized apartments, and a playground to keep the little ones amused.

Hotel Seehof HOTEL $$
(✔06542-726 66; www.seehof.at; Salzmannstrasse 3; s €79, d €138-150, f €185; P🕸) This lemon-fronted chalet is just steps from the lake. Rooms are cosy, if a tad small, with good beds and pine trappings. Light sleepers may hear the trains; rooms at the back are quieter but sacrifice the fine lake views. The family puts on a generous breakfast spread.

Schloss Prielau HISTORIC HOTEL $$$
(✔06542-72 91 10; www.schloss-prielau.at; Hofmannsthalstrasse 10; s €145, d €150-260; P@🕸) A once-upon-a-dream fairy tale of a hotel, this 16th-century castle was once the haunt of Bavarian prince-bishops. Wood panelling and antiques add a touch of romance to the rustic-chic rooms; many feature lake and mountain views. With its private beach, mini-spa and Michelin-starred restaurant, this is luxury all the way. It's 2.5km northeast of the centre along the lakefront promenade.

Romantik Hotel Zell am See HOTEL $$$
(✔06542-725 20; www.romantik-hotel.at; Sebastian-Hörl-Strasse 11; s €103-119, d €166-214; P@🕸🏊) This dark-wood chalet, ablaze with geraniums in summer, looks back on a 500-year history. Antique wood furnishings

Zell am See

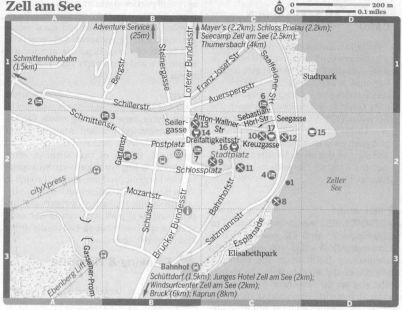

in the cosy rooms, a solar-heated pool with mountain views and a small spa with pampering treatments such as chocolate baths create an ambience of discreet luxury.

🍴 Eating

Heimatgold
CAFE $
(Bahnhofstrasse 1; snacks €5.50-12; ⊙9am-6pm Mon-Fri) This cracking deli-cafe is a fine place to stock up on regional products – sample some on the terrace while you're at it. Besides wholesome breakfasts, it does tasting plates of Salzburgerland cured hams and cheeses and Styrian-fruit juices.

Feinkost Lumpi
DELI $
(Seegasse 6; ⊙8.30am-6.30pm Mon-Fri, to 5pm Sat) This deli is picnic-central. Stop by for dense rye bread, Pinzgauer ham and cheese, homemade *Knödel* (dumplings) and local honey, herbs and liqueurs. The farm-fresh ice cream is superb, too.

Bio Burger Factory
BURGERS $
(📞06542-470 15; www.bioburgerfactory.at; Salzmannstrasse 2; burgers €9-13; ⊙noon-11pm; 🖉) This is a burger joint but not as you know it. Slick, contemporary and streamlined, this one has fabulous lake views and does a brisk trade in organic burgers with a gourmet touch – everything from the fries down to

the ketchup and mayo is homemade – and there are veggie options, too. Organic wine and beer make the perfect match.

ℹ ZELL AM SEE–KAPRUN CARD

If you're in town in summer, ask at your accommodation for the free **Zell am See–Kaprun Card**. The card gets you free entry to all major sights and activities in the region, including the swimming pools around the lake, **Wildpark Ferleiten** (p265) and the **Krimmler Wasserfälle** (Krimml Falls; p267). It also gives you a boat trip on the lake and one free ride per day on the cable cars that ascend to Schmittenhöhe and Kitzsteinhorn.

★ Steinerwirt   AUSTRIAN $$
(✆06542-725 02; www.steinerwirt.com; Dreifaltigkeitsgasse 2; lunch €12, mains €10-31.50; ☺7am-midnight) Whether you dine in the contemporary bistro or in the old-world ambience of the wood-panelled Salzburger Stube, you get the same great food and service at Steinerwirt. The Austrian menu emphasises locally sourced meat and fresh lake fish, accompanied by wines drawn from the 600-year-old cellar.

Deins & Meins   FUSION $$
(✆06542-472 44; www.deins-meins.at; Schlossplatz 5; mains €13-34; ☺5pm-2am Mon-Sat; 🛜🎵) Floor-to-ceiling glass, red velvet chairs and rotating exhibitions of modern art define this slinky lounge-restaurant. Local chef and confectioner David Fischböck has put his stamp on the Slow-Food menu: herby Mediterranean-inspired mains and spot-on steaks are followed by his delectable homemade desserts.

Zum Hirschen   AUSTRIAN $$
(✆06542-77 40; www.hotel-zum-hirschen.at; Dreifaltigkeitsstrasse 1; lunch special €10.90, mains €11.50-29; ☺11am-11pm) Warm pine panelling, flickering candles and friendly yet discreet service create an intimate feel in this smart restaurant. The chef makes the most of local ingredients, so expect dishes like organic Pinzgauer beef *Tafelspitz*, local trout with dill potatoes and Tyrolean mountain lamb on the menu.

Villa Crazy Daisy   INTERNATIONAL $$
(✆06542-725 26; www.villa-crazydaisy.at; Salzmannstrasse 8; 2-course lunch €8.50, mains €9-28; ☺10am-late; 🎵🛜) In a rambling villa opposite the Grand Hotel, Daisy hosts full-on après-ski parties in winter and has the most popular terrace in town in summer. Pizza, *gambas* (prawns) piri-piri and giant salads are on offer in the restaurant (where service can be hit or miss). Head upstairs for live music, DJs and a real party vibe. Has a kids' menu.

Mayer's   GASTRONOMY $$$
(✆06542-72 91 10; www.mayers-restaurant.at; Hofmannsthalstrasse 10; tasting menus €85-175; ☺6.30pm-midnight Wed-Sun) Andreas Mayer heads the stove at Schloss Prielau's refined restaurant, holder of two Michelin stars. Freshness is key, with home-grown vegetables and organic produce shining through in French-infused specialities such as goose liver with vanilla, rhubarb, strawberry and brioche, and local pork with cep mushrooms, scallops and bouillabaisse – all totally divine and creatively presented.

🍷 Drinking & Nightlife

Ginhouse   BAR
(www.ginhouse.at; Dreifaltigkeitsgasse 1; ☺4pm-2am) Move over Europop and shots – 'après chilling' is what the Ginhouse offers. It delivers, with 500 different varieties of gin, expertly mixed cocktails and mellow post-ski tunes, all in a kind of modern alpine pub.

Grand Café   CAFE
(Esplanade 4; ☺noon-6pm) You don't have to stay in the belle-époque finery of Grand Hotel Zell am See to appreciate the dreamy lake and mountain views from its tree-shaded cafe terrace. Watch ducks and boats glide by as you savour coffee with homemade cake and live piano music.

Seegasse   CAFE
(Seegasse 10; ☺8am-8pm Mon-Sat, 9am-8pm Sun; 🛜) With a pavement terrace, this sleek cafe is a relaxed spot for proper gelato or an espresso with a slice of homemade carrot cake.

Insider   BAR
(Kreuzgasse 1; ☺10am-3am) Join the cocktail sippers for a daiquiri or Cuba Libre at this upbeat, backlit lounge bar, which has occasional live music and DJ nights.

ℹ Information

Post Office (Postplatz 4; ☺8am-6pm Mon-Fri)
Tourist Office (✆06542-770; www.zellamsee-kaprun.com; Brucker Bundesstrasse 1a; ☺8am-6pm Mon-Fri, 9am-6pm Sat, 9am-1pm

Sun) Staff at this office will help you find rooms; there's also an accommodation board in the foyer with a free 24-hour telephone.

ℹ Getting There & Away

BUS
Buses leave from outside the *Hauptbahnhof* and from the **bus station** (Postplatz) behind the post office. They run to Kaprun (€3.50, 20 minutes, twice hourly) and Krimml (€10.60, 1½ hours, every two hours).

TRAIN
Hourly trains run from Zell am See to destinations including Salzburg (€15.70, 1½ to two hours), Kitzbühel (€12.90, 55 minutes) and Innsbruck (€31, 2½ hours).

ℹ Getting Around

BICYCLE
You can hire bikes to pedal around the lake at any of the sports shops in town, such as **Adventure Service** (p257) or **Carve In** (Postplatz 4; bike rental per day city/mountain/e-bike/children's €15/25/25/10).

Bad Gastein
📞 06434 / POP 4225
With belle-époque villas clinging to forest-cloaked cliffs that rise above thunderous falls, and views deep into the Gastein Valley, Bad Gastein is a stunner. The town runs both hot and cold, with first-class skiing, high-level hiking and hot springs still hailed for their miraculous healing properties. Though the damp is rising in places, the higgledy-piggledy resort has kept some of the grandeur of its 19th-century heyday, when Empress Elisabeth (Sisi) came to bathe and pen poetry here.

◎ Sights

★ Gasteiner Wasserfall   WATERFALL
Bad Gastein's star attraction is this 341m waterfall, which rages over rugged cliff faces and through thick forest to tumble into three turquoise pools. The waterfall's wispy, ethereal beauty captured the imagination of Klimt, Max Liebermann, Schubert and Empress Elisabeth. The stone **Wasserfallbrücke** (waterfall bridge) is the best vantage point and the trailhead for the **Wasserfallweg** (waterfall path) shadows the magnificent cataract and provides some great photo opportunities.

Gasteiner Museum   MUSEUM
(www.gasteinermuseum.com; Kaiser-Franz-Josef-Strasse 14, Grand Hotel de l'Europe; adult/child €5/free; ◎2.30-6.30pm Wed-Sun) Tap into the source of Bad Gastein at this museum, which spells out the town's history and the wonders of its thermal waters, from the bath-loving Romans to the Romantic painters inspired by its waterfall. The collection spans everything from *Krampus* (devil) costumes to vintage tourist posters and 19th-century oil paintings of Bad Gastein. English audio guides are available.

🏃 Activities

Ski Amadé   SKIING
(www.skiamade.com; day pass adult/child €50.50/25.50) The Gasteinertal's slopes and spas are a match made in heaven in winter. The 208km of varied pistes challenge confident beginning and intermediate skiers, with attractive wooded runs and some great carving opportunities. Mountain transport is not brilliant, though, and reaching the slopes in neighbouring resorts can be time consuming unless you have your own wheels.

The resort is part of the expansive Ski Amadé arena, which comprises 760km of slopes, with skiing and snowboarding centred on **Stubnerkogel** (2246m) and **Graukogel** (2492m). **Cross-country skiing** is also big in Bad Gastein, with 90km of prepared *Loipe* (tracks), including a floodlit trail at **Böckstein** (3km south of Bad Gastein).

★ Felsentherme Gastein   SPA
(📞06434-222 30; Bahnhofplatz 5; 3hr/day ticket adult €23/27.50, child €13.50/17.50; ◎9am-9pm) A glass elevator zooms from street level up to Felsentherme Gastein, where you can take the rejuvenating waters. The spa shelters grottoes, an adventure pool for kids and an outdoor thermal bath with pummelling massage jets and stellar views of the mountains. For those prepared to bare all, there are panoramic saunas and salty steam baths to test out.

Alpentherme   SPA
(📞06432-829 30; www.alpentherme.com; Senator-Wilhelm-Wilfling-Platz 1, Bad Hofgastein; 4hr ticket adult/child €25.50/15.50; ◎9am-9pm Sun-Wed, to 10pm Thu-Sat) This architecturally innovative spa is split into four different 'worlds', where experiences stretch from relaxing in radon-rich thermal baths to racing down

white-knuckle flumes. The sauna village comprises brine grottos, loft saunas, red-hot Finnish saunas and an ice-cold plunge pool. For some pampering, pop over to the beauty centre, which offers goat-milk wraps and silky smooth hot-chocolate massages.

Stubnerkogel & Graukogel   WALKING, HIKING
Both Stubnerkogel and Graukogel are excellent for summertime walking, with high-altitude trails traversing alpine pastures and craggy peaks. Stubnerkogel also has an impressive 140m-long suspension bridge, with big-top views of the Hohe Tauern range. The two-section **Stubnerkogelbahn cable car** is near Bad Gastein's train station and the **Graukogelbahn cable car** 300m northeast of the centre; both cost €24 return.

Gasteiner Heilstollen   SPA
(Gastein Healing Gallery; ☑06434-375 30; www.gasteiner-heilstollen.com; Heilstollenstrasse 19, Böckstein; trial session €30.90; ◷8am-5pm Mon-Fri, to noon Sat) Böckstein's medieval gold mine has been reinvented as a much-celebrated health centre. Visitors get a brief health check and board a small train that chugs 2km into the humid 38°C depths of Radhausberg mountain, where you absorb the healing radon vapours, said to cure everything from arthritis to fibromyalgia.

Flying Waters   ADVENTURE SPORTS
(☑0664 202 97 93; Villa Solitude, Kaiser-Franz-Josef-Strasse 16; adult/child €19.50/15; ◷10am-noon & 1.30-6pm mid-May–early Nov) The waterfall is but a blur on this exhilarating new zip line that threads 300m precariously over the Gastein Valley, from Villa Solitude to the parkland below.

Kaiser-Wilhem-Promenade   WALKING
There's no need to exert yourself for a view in Bad Gastein. Simply follow this balcony trail along Kaiserhofstrasse for deep views into the forest-cloaked, mountain-rimmed, villa-studded Gastein Valley. It's an easy-going, 45-minute walk, with prime photo ops at the **statue of Kaiser Wilhelm**, who gave Bad Gastein's curative waters the royal seal of approval by coming here 20 times in the late 19th century.

Thermalkurhaus   SPA
(☑06434-271 10; www.thermalgastein.com; Bahnhofsplatz 7; radon bath €20.50; ◷8am-noon & 2-5pm Mon-Fri, 8am-noon Sat) Curative massages, radon baths, *fango* mud packs, acupunc-

ture and electrotherapy are available at the Thermalkurhaus.

🛏 Sleeping

Euro Youth Hotel Krone   HOSTEL $
(☑06434-23 30; www.euro-youth-hotel.at; Bahnhofsplatz 8; dm €30-46, s €38-55, d €66-102, half board per person €11; P🅿🛜) With its well-kept, high-ceilinged rooms, this century-old manor has more charm than your average hostel. Backpackers praise the facilities, which include a restaurant, TV lounge and barbecue area. Staff can arrange adventure sports such as rafting, canyoning, paragliding, mountain biking and snowshoeing.

Kur-Camping Erlengrund   CAMPGROUND $
(☑06434-302 05; www.kurcamping-gastein.at; Erlengrundstrasse 6; camp sites per adult/child/tent €8.45/5.10/12.65; P🛜🏊) Close to a natural lake, this campground has shady pitches and, in summer, a heated pool. It's an hour's walk following the waterfall north of Bad Gastein to Kötschachdorf; bus 555 runs from the train station (€2.10, 15 minutes).

★ Alpenblick   HOTEL $$
(☑06434-20 62; www.alpenblick-gastein.at; Kötschachtaler Strasse 17; s €70-82, d €140-164, apt €210-255; P🅿🛜) The name says it all: the view of the Alps and deep into the Gastein Valley is phenomenal from this panoramically perched hotel at the foot of the Graukogel ski slope. The parquet-floored rooms are nicely traditional; the facilities are terrific, with a spa area, outdoor pool and gardens, plus a games room and playground for kids. Half-board included.

Hotel Miramonte   DESIGN HOTEL $$
(☑06434-25 77; www.hotelmiramonte.com; Reitlpromenade 3; s €105-200, d €140-220; P🛜) This hilltop hotel impressed the likes of *Vanity Fair* with its retro-chic design and phenomenal mountain backdrop. A terrace overlooking forested peaks, a thermal spa with pampering Aveda treatments and yoga classes draw a style-conscious crowd here. The studio-style rooms are all about pared-down glamour, with bare-wood floors, cowskin rugs and iPod stations. Breakfast is served until a snoozy 11am.

Villa Solitude   HISTORIC HOTEL $$$
(☑06434-51 01; www.villasolitude.com; Kaiser-Franz-Josef-Strasse 16; d €130-260, half board per person €20; P🛜) Once home to an Austrian countess, this belle-époque villa shelters six suites crammed with oil paintings and

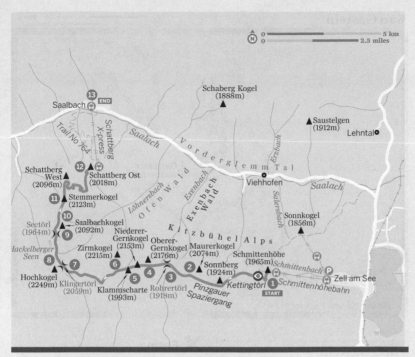

Walking Trail
Pinzgauer Spaziergang

START ZELL AM SEE
FINISH SAALBACH
LENGTH 19KM; FIVE TO SIX HOURS

This moderately challenging day hike affords magnificent views of the Kitzbühel Alps and Hohe Tauern range. Bring supplies and consider buying Kompass 1:35,000 map No 30 *Zell am See–Kaprun*.

At **1** **Schmittenhöhebahn** top station, begin a gradual descent from Saalbach/Pinzgauer Spaziergang, enjoying views of Zeller See and the glaciated Hohe Tauern range. The ever-narrowing path continues up an incline and passes through tarn-studded forest, occasionally drawing your gaze to shimmering Grossglockner and the Kitzsteinhorn Glacier to the south.

The landscape soon opens up as you wend through wildflower-streaked meadows and, after roughly an hour, contour the rounded summit of **2** **Maurerkogel**. Make a short, painless ascent to **3** **Rohrertörl** saddle, where you can contrast the limestone Kai-

sergebirge to the north with the icy Hohe Tauern peaks to the south.

Passing two junctions, follow a balcony trail that contours the base of **4** **Oberer-Gernkogel** and gently mounts **5** **Niederer-Gernkogel**. You'll soon reach the foot of **6** **Zirmkogel**, which, with will and expertise, can be climbed in little over an hour.

The rocky trail runs through high meadows and mottled mountains, passing a small hut near a stream. Around four hours from the trailhead, the path ascends a steepish incline to the **7** **Klingertörl** saddle, where a sign shows the way to Saalbach. Traverse the base of cliffs that sweep down from **8** **Hochkogel** and make a short descent to the grassy col of **9** **Seetörl**.

Walk north from here, either climbing over the **10** **Saalbachkogel** or skirting its western slopes. The same option is repeated for **11** **Stemmerkogel**. Descend the ridge and continue towards Schattberg, making a final ascent to the **12** **Schattberg X-press** gondola and then down to **13** **Saalbach**.

Bad Gastein

Bad Gastein

antiques. The intimate piano room downstairs is the place to slip into your role as lord or lady of the manor. Lutter & Wegner restaurant, with its fusion menu and cracking terrace, is next door.

🍴 Eating

Silver Bullet Bar   INTERNATIONAL $

(☎ 06434-22 53 60; www.silverbulletbar.com; Grillparzerstrasse 1; mains €9-15; ⊙ 3.30pm-2am winter, 3.30-10pm Mon, Wed, Thu & Sun, 3.30pm-midnight Fri & Sat rest of year; 🎴) Wagon wheels, a stuffed buffalo head and cow-print benches give this barn-style restaurant and bar a mock American Wild West look. Fingerlickin' snacks like 100% Austrian beefburgers are accompanied by a party vibe and regular live music. In summer, families gravitate here for the sunny terrace and activities such as a climbing wall, mini-golf and boules.

★ Ginger & Gin   ASIAN $$

(☎ 06434-304 51; www.gingerandgin.at; Kaiser-Franz-Joseph-Strasse 14; mains €16-26; ⊙ 6pm-2am Wed-Sat, to midnight Sun; 🍴) This swank new addition to Bad Gastein's dining scene puts a funky modern spin on the baroque opulence of the Grand Hotel de l'Europe. It pulls it off, with its chandeliers and clever backlighting, occasional live music, and Asian fusion cuisine from seared tuna with wasabi to chilli mussels and sushi. Some 99 sorts of gin go into creative cocktails.

Jägerhäusl AUSTRIAN $$
(☎06434-202 54; www.gastro-gastein.at; Kaiser-Franz-Josef-Strasse 9; mains €10-25; ⊙11am-11pm)
Besides wood-fired pizza, this galleried villa has Austrian faves such as schnitzel and venison goulash with dumplings. Pull up a chair on the maple-tree-shaded terrace when the sun's out. There's often live Tyrolean music on summer evenings (see the website for details).

Lutter & Wegner AUSTRIAN $$
(☎06434-51 01; www.villasolitude.com; Kaiser-Franz-Josef-Strasse 16; 3-course menu €23; ⊙6-9.30pm) Big on atmosphere, this smart restaurant at Villa Solitude has a fairy-tale tower setting, award-winning fusion cuisine and a terrace with knockout views over the Gasteinertal and the falls. Fine wines (choose from 150 bottles) are expertly matched with season-driven flavours like venison with spinach dumplings and red cabbage and trout with wild garlic.

Hofkeller AUSTRIAN $$
(☎06434-203 72 45; Grillparzerstrasse 1; mains €19-28; ⊙6-11pm Sun-Fri; ⊛) In winter, there's no place like this stone cellar beneath the Salzburger Hof hotel for warming up over fondue, a raclette cheese fest or hot-stone specialities. Kids' menus are available.

ⓘ Information

Post Office (Bahnhofplatz 9; ⊙8am-noon & 2-5.30pm Mon-Fri) Next to the train station.
Tourist Office (☎06434-339 35 60; www.gastein.com; Kaiser-Franz-Josef-Strasse 27; ⊙8am-6pm Mon-Fri) To get here, go left from the train station exit and walk down the hill. Staff will find you accommodation free of charge. There's information on the national park in the foyer.

ⓘ Getting There & Away

TRAIN
Trains trundle through Bad Gastein's station every two hours, connecting the town to points north and south, including Spittal-Millstättersee (€11.60, 35 minutes), Salzburg (€15.70, 1½ hours) and Innsbruck (€56, 3½ hours).
From Bad Gastein to Bad Hofgastein, sit on the right side of the train for the best views.

Grossglockner Road

Austria's best road trip bar none, the Grossglockner Road is phenomenally beautiful – provided, that is, that the weather is fine enough for you to enjoy the views of the

glacier-capped peaks, waterfalls and lakes you'll be driving past as you crunch gears on the hairpin bends. This marvel of 1930s engineering provides total immersion in Austria's highest Alps.

⊙ Sights

Wildpark Ferleiten WILDLIFE RESERVE
(www.wildpark-ferleiten.at; adult/child €7.50/3.50; ⊙8am-dusk May-Oct; ⊛) Wildpark Ferleiten is a 15-hectare reserve home to 200 alpine animals such as chamois, marmots and bears. Kids can let off steam in the playgrounds or on the mini-roller coasters.

ⓘ Getting There & Away

You can travel the Grossglockner Road by bus, but it's not as fast or as easy as having your own wheels. Bus 5002 runs frequently between Lienz and Heiligenblut on weekdays (€8.70, one hour); less frequently at weekends. From late June to late September, four buses run from Monday to Friday, and three at weekends between Heiligenblut and Kaiser-Franz-Josefs-Höhe (€5.90, 32 minutes).

Heiligenblut

☎04824 / POP 1185
One of the single-most striking images on the Grossglockner Road is Heiligenblut, the needle-thin spire of its pilgrimage church framed by the glaciated summit of Grossglockner. The village's iconic scenery and easily accessible mountains lure skiers, hikers and camera-toting tourists. The compact centre is stacked with wooden chalets and, despite an overload of yodelling-kitsch souvenirs, retains some traditional charm.

In summer, serious mountaineers head here to bag peaks in the Hohe Tauern National Park (p257). Enquire at the tourist office for details on mountain-bike trails in the park.

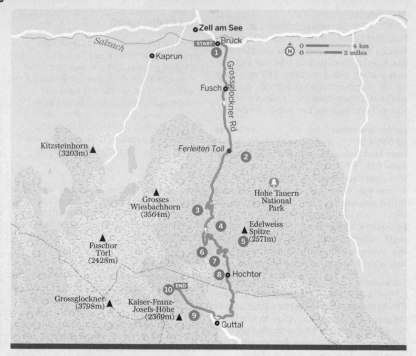

Driving Tour
Grossglockner Road

START BRUCK
FINISH BRUCK
LENGTH 96KM; FOUR TO SIX HOURS

Buckle up for one of Europe's greatest alpine drives. Grossglockner Road consists of 48 head-spinning, glacier-gawping, wow-what-a-mountain kilometres.

Leaving ❶ **Bruck**, enter the wild, mountainous Fuschertal (Fuscher Valley), passing Fusch and ❷ **Wildpark Ferleiten** (p265). Once through the tollgate, the road climbs steeply to ❸ **Hochmais** (1850m), where glaciated peaks including Grosses Wiesbachhorn (3564m) crowd the horizon. The road zigzags up to ❹ **Haus Alpine Naturschau** (2260m), which spotlights local flora and fauna. A little further along, a 2km side road (no coaches allowed) corkscrews up to ❺ **Edelweiss Spitze** (2571m), the road's highest viewpoint. Climb the tower for staggering 360-degree views of more than 30 peaks of 3000m. Refuel with coffee and strudel on the terrace at the hut.

Get your camera handy for ❻ **Fuscher Törl** (2428m), with super views on both sides of

the ridge, and gemstone of a lake ❼ **Fuscher Lacke** (2262m) nearby. Here a small exhibition documents the construction of the road, built by 3000 men over five years during the Great Depression, from 1930 to 1935.

The road wriggles on through high meadows to ❽ **Hochtor** (2504m), the top of the pass, after which there's a steady descent to ❾ **Schöneck**. Branch off west onto the 9km Gletscherstrasse, passing waterfalls and *Achtung Murmeltiere* (Beware of Marmots) signs – you may well spot one of the burrowing rodents.

The Grossglockner massif slides into view on the approach to flag-dotted ❿ **Kaiser-Franz-Josefs-Höhe** (2369m), with memorable views of the bell-shaped Grossglockner (3798m) and the rapidly retreating Pasterze Glacier. The 8km swirl of fissured ice is best appreciated on the short and easy Gamsgrubenweg and Gletscherweg trails. Allow time to see the glacier-themed exhibition at the visitor centre and the crystalline Wilhelm-Swarovski observatory before driving back to Bruck.

⊙ Sights

Wallfahrtskirche St Vinzenz　　CHURCH
(Hof 2; ⊙ dawn-dusk) As though cupped in celestial hands and held up to the mighty Alps, this 15th-century pilgrimage church lifts gazes, and spirits. Inside is a tabernacle which purportedly contains a tiny phial of Christ's blood, hence the village name (*Heiligenblut* means 'holy blood'). Legend has it that the phial was discovered by a saint named Briccius, who was buried in an avalanche on this spot more than a thousand years ago.

𝕏 Activities

Schareck　　SKIING
(www.gross-glockner.at; Kaiser-Franz-Josefs-Höhe; day pass €40, cable car adult/child 1 way €13.50/7 return €20/10; 🎿) Skiers can play on 55km of snow-sure slopes in the shadow of Grossglockner in Heiligenblut. This is perfect cruising terrain for beginners and easy-going intermediates, and families often choose the resort for its Snowland Kids' Club and gentle slopes. Most of the skiing takes place on the Scharcck (2604m) peak.

🛏 Sleeping

Jugendherberge　　HOSTEL $
(☎ 04824-22 59; www.oejhv.or.at; Hof 36; dm/s/d €22.50/30.50/52; P 🌐) Near the church, this chalet-style HI hostel has spacious dorms and handy extras, including ski storage and a common room. It's right next to the public swimming pool, sauna and climbing wall, too.

★ Chalet-Hotel Senger　　HOTEL $$
(☎ 04824-22 15; www.romantic.at; Hof 23; s €50-97, d €116-148; P 🌐) Colourful prayer flags flutter at this farmhouse, a tribute to the Tibetan monks who once stayed here. All cosy nooks, warm wood and open fireplaces, this is just the spot for a little mountain hibernation and soul-searching. Most of the snug rooms have balconies; room 24 offers Grossglockner views instead.

ℹ Information

Tourist Office (☎ 04824-27 00; www.heiligenblut.at; Hof 4; ⊙ 9am-6pm Mon-Fri, 2-6pm Sat & Sun) On the main street, close to the Hotel Post bus stop. Books mountain guides.

ℹ Getting There & Away

As well as buses running to/from Kaiser-Franz-Josefs-Höhe (€5.90, 32 minutes, three daily) from late June to September, there is a year-round service to/from Lienz (€8.70, one hour, eight daily).

Krimml
☎ 06564 / POP 840

A real crash-bang spectacle, the 380m-high, three-tier Krimmler Wasserfälle, Europe's highest waterfall, is the thunderous centrepiece of this tiny village. Those who look beyond the falls find even more to like about Krimml – gorgeous alpine scenery, fine mountain walks and farmstays that are great for tiptoeing back to nature for a few days.

⊙ Sights

★ Krimmler Wasserfälle　　WATERFALL
(Krimml Falls; ☎ 06564-72 12; www.wasserfaelle-krimml.at; adult/child €9.20/4.60 incl WasserWelten Krimml; ⊙ 9am-5pm May-Oct) Enshrouded in mist, arched by a rainbow, frozen solid – this waterfall always looks extraordinary, no matter the time of year. The **Wasserfallweg** (Waterfall Trail), which starts at the ticket office and weaves gently uphill through mixed forest, has numerous viewpoints with photogenic close-ups of the falls.

𝕏 Activities

Tauernradweg　　CYCLING, HIKING
(www.tauernradweg.at) Well-marked cycling and hiking trails fan out from Krimml into the surrounding Alps. The Tauernradweg is a 310km bike route through the mind-blowing scenery of the Hohe Tauern National Park to Salzburg and then to Passau; it covers some high-altitude stretches and demands a good level of fitness. The Krimmler Wasserfälle Wasserfallweg **walking trail** begins near the Tauernradweg's starting point.

Zillertal Arena　　SKIING
(www.zillertalarena.at; 1-/3-/6-day pass €50.50/139.50/242; 🎿) Krimml is part of the Zillertal Arena, which covers 143km of pistes that are mostly geared towards intermediates. Krimml also appeals to families and nonskiers in winter, with low-key activities such as tobogganing, snowshoeing and horse-drawn sleigh rides.

🛏 Sleeping

Hölzlahneralm　　HOSTEL $
(☎ 0664 402 68 78; www.hoelzlahner.at; Oberkrimml 66; dm €20, without breakfast €14; ⊙ May-Oct) 🌿 This wood-shingled farmhouse is a

superb budget choice. You'll need to do the legwork – it's a two-hour hike from Krimml via the Krimmler Wasserfälle – but that makes the *Kaspressknödel* (dumpling in gooey Pinzgauer cheese) all the more welcome. The ecofriendly chalet generates its own electricity, uses natural spring water and has comfy bunks for weary walkers upstairs.

Burgeck Panorama Hotel GUESTHOUSE **$$**
(☎ 06564-72 49; www.burgeck.com; Oberkrimml 79; d €90-99; P ⓢ) Scenically perched above the village and next to forest, this guesthouse is run by the kindly Bachmaier family and has terrific waterfall views. The recently renovated rooms are modern, while others are done out in rustic alpine style. Kids are well catered for with a playground and, in winter, an illuminated toboggan track right on the doorstep.

Hotel Klockerhaus HOTEL **$$**
(☎ 06564-72 08; www.klockerhaus.com; Oberkrimml 10; s/d incl half-board €73/136; P ⓢ ☒)

Plenty of pine keeps things cosy here, both in the rooms with waterfall views and in the lounge with an open fire. There's a small spa with a sauna, saline steam bath and treatments such as Tibetan massage, as well as an untreated outdoor pool.

ⓘ Information

Tourist Office (☎ 06564-72 39; www.krimml. at; Oberkrimml 37; ⓢ 8am-6pm Mon-Fri, 8.30-11.30am Sat) The tourist office is in the village centre next to the white church.

ⓘ Getting There & Away

The village is about 500m north of the Krimmler Wasserfälle, on a side turning from the B165. There are parking spaces near the path to the falls, which branches to the right just before the toll booths for the Gerlos Alpine Rd to Mayrhofen.

Buses run year-round from Krimml to Zell am See (€10.60, 1½ hours, every two hours).

Carinthia

Best Places to Eat

➡ Princs (p274)

➡ Dolce Vita (p275)

➡ Weinphilo (p290)

➡ Stand No. 17 (p274)

➡ Dolomitenhütte (p290)

Best Places to Sleep

➡ Camping Klagenfurt am Wörthersee (p272)

➡ Hotel Mosser (p277)

➡ Hotel Schloss Leonstain (p283)

➡ Villa Verdin (p284)

Why Go?

Few regions in Europe match the rugged beauty of Carinthia, and you'll find that travelling here is often a serpentine journey. Carinthia can also, at times, seem larger than life with its high peaks, gouged valleys and glistening lakes; the flamboyant show of opulence in the capital, Klagenfurt; and the resorts around the more famous of the region's 1270 pristine mountain lakes. The most popular of these lakes, such as the large Wörthersee, have waters warmed to a comfortable swimming temperature by thermal springs.

Carinthia's deep medieval heritage is another attraction – celebrated in picturesque walled villages such as Friesach and Gmünd, and impressive castles such as the hilltop fortress of Hochosterwitz. Many of the towns and villages nestled in Carinthia's rolling hills hold an annual summer festival, with roving performers coming from neighbouring Italy and Slovenia to take part alongside the locals.

When to Go

➡ Midsummer is the time to make the most of Carinthia's lakes and excellent mountain hiking. Because it gets more sunshine than elsewhere in Austria, lake temperatures are warmer.

➡ In winter the province morphs into one of Austria's best ski regions, despite having a shorter ski season than elsewhere due to the warmer temps.

➡ The shoulder season periods are less interesting here except for valley hiking or cycling – the winter or summer outdoor action seasons are the best time to visit.

Carinthia Highlights

1 **Weissensee** (p286) Cycling and hiking the forest trails.

2 **Eboard Museum** (p271) Visiting this Klagenfurt museum and playing vintage predigital keyboards – the largest collection in Europe.

3 **Strandbad Klagenfurt** (p272) Swimming the shores of the Wörthersee at Europe's largest lake baths.

4 **Bar Leon** (p283) Spritzing away the afternoon as swans glide by in Pörtschach.

5 **Heinrich Harrer Museum** (p282) Transporting yourself to the tranquil ambience of Tibet in Hüttenberg.

6 **Burg Hochosterwitz** (p282) Admiring the views from atop a spectacular medieval castle.

7 **Millennium-Express cable car** (p280) Skiing Nassfeld from the top of this 6km-long cable car.

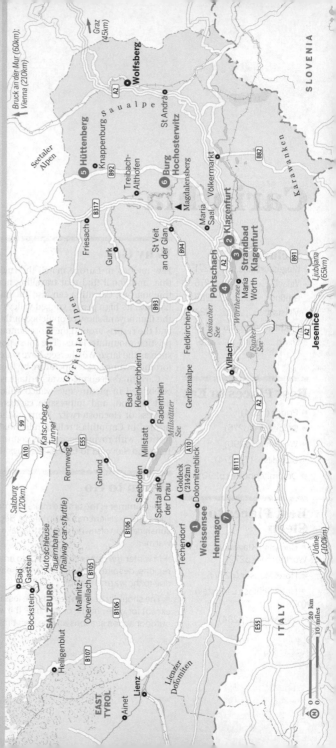

❶ Getting There & Away

Klagenfurt airport has cheap connections with the UK (Ryanair; www.ryanair.com) and Germany (Air Berlin; www.airberlin.com). Klagenfurt and Villach are the main hubs for trains from elsewhere in Europe, especially those from Italy.

❶ Getting Around

Carinthia is divided into regional zones for public transport, with either single tickets or passes that are valid for one day or longer. Ask what's cheapest when buying a ticket, or contact Kärntner Linien in Klagenfurt. Many of the lakes are served by boat services in summer.

The **Kärnten Card** (www.kaerntencard.at; 1-/2-week card €37/48) gives free or cheaper access to the province's major sights plus 50% discount on buses and trains. It's sold at hotels and tourist offices from mid-April to late October.

KLAGENFURT

✆ 0463 / POP 95,450

Klagenfurt may not be up there with Vienna or Graz in terms of urban lifestyle, but it's an enjoyable, vibrant and sunny city with a compact Inner Stadt and offers easy access to lakeside villages on and around the beautiful Wörthersee. At the city's western limit is the wide green space of Europapark along with Austria's largest bathing complex. It's a surprisingly lively place, both as a playground for partiers down at the lido in summer and as a university town the rest of the year.

◉ Sights

MMKK   GALLERY
(Museum für Moderne Kunst Kärnten; Map p273; www.mmkk.at; Burggasse 8; adult/child €5/free; ⊙10am-6pm Tue-Sun, to 8pm Thu) This gallery for modern and contemporary art stages three or four excellent temporary exhibitions a year based on its collection of Carinthian and mostly Austrian artists, including the likes of Arnulf Rainer and Hans Staudacher.

Dragon Fountain   MONUMENT
(Map p273) Neuer Platz, Klagenfurt's central square, is dominated by the 16th-century Dragon Fountain, the emblem of the city. The blank-eyed, wriggling statue is modelled on the *Lindwurm* (dragon) of legend, which is said to have resided in a swamp here long ago, devouring cattle and virgins.

Kärntner Botanikzentrum   GARDENS
(www.landesmuseum.ktn.gv.at; Prof-Dr-Kahler-Platz 1; ⊙9am-6pm daily May-Sep, to 4pm Mon-Thu Oct-Apr) FREE This small botanical garden is especially popular for its evocative landscape of small cliffs with alpine plants, and for another section with a waterfall and ponds. Adjoining it is the **Kreuzbergkirche**, perched on a hillock with some pretty mosaics of the Stations of the Cross on the path leading up to it. Take bus 60 or 61 from Heiligengeistplatz to Kreuzbergl.

Landhaus   HISTORIC BUILDING
(Map p273; www.landesmuseum.ktn.gv.at; Landhaushof 1; adult/child €4/2; ⊙9am-4pm Mon-Fri, to 2pm Sat Apr-Oct, closed Mon Nov-Mar) The Renaissance *Landhaus* (state parliament) building dates from the late 16th century and is still the centre of political power today. The stairs on the right (facing the portico) lead up to the **Grosser Wappensaal** (Heraldic Hall), with its magnificent trompe l'œil gallery painted by Carinthian artist Josef Ferdinand Fromiller (1693–1760).

Stadtgalerie   GALLERY
(Map p273; www.stadtgalerie.net; Theatergasse 4; adult/child €6/1; ⊙10am-6pm Tue-Sun) Thoughtfully curated program of modern and contemporary international and Austrian artists is shown at the Carinthian state gallery, which has a main venue on Theaterstrasse and a second nearby in the Alpen-Adria-Galerie im Stadthaus (p272).

Eboard Museum   MUSEUM
(✆ 0699 1914 4180; www.eboardmuseum.com; Florian Gröger Strasse 20; adult/family €10/20; ⊙2-7pm Sun-Fri, call ahead Sat) With the largest collection of keyboard instruments in Europe (more than 1300), this quirky museum is literally a 'fingers-on' experience: you are able play most of the organs, including rare items such as a Model A Hammond from 1934. Live bands perform on Friday nights (except July and August) at 8pm (€5 to €10).

Europapark   PARK
(Map p274; ♿) The green expanse and its *Strandbad* (beach) on the shores of the Wörthersee are centres for aquatic fun and especially great for kids. The park's biggest draw is Minimundus, a 'miniature world' with 140 replicas of the world's architectural icons, downsized to a scale of 1:25. To get here, take bus 10, 11, 12 or 22 from Heiligengeistplatz.

Minimundus   AMUSEMENT PARK
(Map p274; www.minimundus.at; Villacher Strasse 241; adult/child €18/10; ⊙9am-7pm Mar & Apr, to 8pm May-Sep; ⊡) Down near the Wörthersee in Europapark, Minimundus has around 140 replicas of some of the world's architectural icons, downsized to a scale of 1:25. By lying on the ground with a camera, you can later impress your friends at parties with great snaps of the Taj Mahal, Eiffel Tower or Arc de Triomphe. Guides in English (€4) are available.

Dom   CATHEDRAL
(Map p273; Domplatz 1; ⊙dawn-dusk) Klagenfurt's cathedral is a monolith with an ornate marble pulpit and a sugary pink-and-white stuccoed ceiling. The highlight is an altar painting by Paul Troger in one of the chapels.

Stadthauptpfarrkirche St Egid   CHURCH
(Map p273; http://st-egid-klagenfurt.at; Pfarrplatz; church free, tower adult/child €1/0.50; ⊙tower 10am-5.30pm Mon-Fri, to 11.30pm Sat Easter–mid-Sep) Climb the 225 steps of this baroque church's 45m-high tower for a bird's-eye view of town and the surrounding mountains.

Alpen-Adria-Galerie im Stadthaus GALLERY
(Map p273; www.stadtgalerie.net; Theaterplatz 3; adult/child €2.50/0.50; ⊙10am-6pm Tue-Sun) **FREE** Some excellent rolling art exhibitions are held in the Alpen-Adria-Galerie im Stadthaus, usually featuring local contemporary artists.

Landesmuseum Rudolfinum   MUSEUM
(Map p273; www.landesmuseum.ktn.gv.at; Museumgasse 2; ⊙10am-8pm Mon-Fri, to 5pm Sat & Sun) Carinthia's flagship museum has lots of exhibitions on natural and cultural history. It closed for restoration after severe water damage and is set to reopen in 2018.

Happ's Reptilienzoo   ZOO
(Map p274; ☑0463-234 25; www.reptilienzoo.at; Villacher Strasse 237; adult/child €14/8; ⊙8am-6pm May-Sep, to 5pm rest of year, closed Nov; P⊡) Crocodiles plus all manner of creepers, crawlers and slitherers are here for kids and adults to admire. Some signs are in English. It's located in Europapark.

🏃 Activities

★**Strandbad Klagenfurt**   SWIMMING
(Map p274; www.stw.at; Metnitzstrand 2; adult/child €4.50/1.80; ⊙8am-8pm Jun-Aug, to 7pm May & Sep, closed Oct-Apr; ⊡) Klagenfurt's wonderful lakeside beach is the largest complex in Europe and has cabins, restaurants and piers for basking like a seal. *Kästchen* (lockers large enough for day packs) in the *Strandbad* cost €2 plus €20 deposit. There's good swimming outside the buoys further south, past the relaxed Maria Loretto beach. You can also indulge in paddle or electric boat escapades. Admission drops to €3.20 after 3pm.

🎉 Festivals & Events

Vollmond Schwimmen   SPORTS
(Map p274; www.vollmondschwimmen.at; ⊙Jul or Aug) A beautifully simple summer celebration, swimmers and SUP-boarders take to the warm waters of the lake between Strandbad Loretto and Strandbad Maiernigg while the full moon rises, with DJs and other postswim entertainment.

Wörthersee Classics Festival   MUSIC
(www.woertherseeclassics.com; tickets €40-85; ⊙mid-Jun) Five world-famous composers, each of whom grew up during the latter years of the Austrian empire, also lived and worked at some point on Wörthersee: Gustav Mahler, Alban Berg and Anton von Webern from Vienna, the adopted Viennese Johannes Brahms from Hamburg, and Hugo Wolf. All are celebrated in this annual classical festival.

Klagenfurter Stadtfest   MUSIC, THEATRE
(www.altstadtzauber.at; ⊙Aug) Annual two-day music and theatre festival.

🛏 Sleeping

Lemon 7   HOTEL $
(Map p273; ☑0463-577 93; 10 Oktober Strasse 11; dm/s/d €28/49/75; ☎) Rooms are arranged around a plant-filled vaulted atrium at this small budget place in a 400-year-old building. Freshly renovated rooms are simple and modern and their wooden, almost ecclesiastical furnishings add warmth and character. A good budget find.

Camping Klagenfurt am Wörthersee   CAMPGROUND $
(Map p274; ☑0463-28 78 10; www.camping-woerthersee.at; Metnitzstrand 5; camp site per adult/child/tent €7.50/6.90/9.90; ⊙May-Sep; P☎⊠) This attractive, shady and well-organised camping ground offers free use of the *Strandbad* (a really good deal) and has bike rental. Rates are a few euros more in July and August.

Klagenfurt

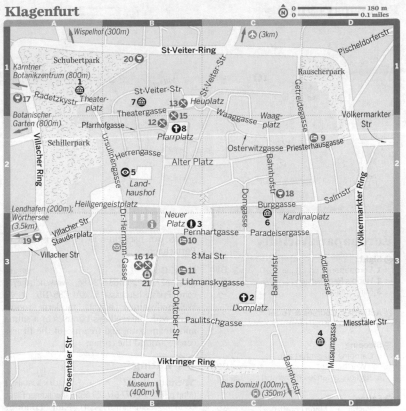

Klagenfurt

◉ Sights
1	Alpen-Adria-Galerie im Stadthaus	A1
2	Dom	C3
3	Dragon Fountain	B3
4	Landesmuseum Rudolfinum	D4
5	Landhaus	B2
6	MMKK	C3
7	Stadtgalerie	B1
8	Stadthauptpfarrkirche St Egid	B2

🛏 Sleeping
9	Hotel Geyer	D2
10	Hotel Palais Porcia	B3
11	Lemon 7	B3

✕ Eating
12	Bierhaus zum Augustin	B2
13	Dolce Vita	B1
14	Kochwerkstatt	B3
15	Princs	B2
16	Stand No. 17	B3

🍷 Drinking & Nightlife
17	Cafe Ingeborg Bachmann	A1
18	Kamot	C2
19	Lendhafencafe	A3
20	Park Haus Cafe	B1

🛍 Shopping
21	Bendediktinermarkt	B3

Jugendgästehaus Klagenfurt HOSTEL $
(Map p274; ☎0463-23 00 20; www.oejhv.or.at; Neckheimgasse 6; dm/s/d €22.50/30.50/53; P@🖃) The modern HI hostel is near Europapark, a great location in summer. To get here from the centre, take bus 81 from the train station or 10 from Heiligengeistplatz and get off at Jugendgästehaus or (depending on the bus route) Neckheimgasse.

Europapark Vicinity

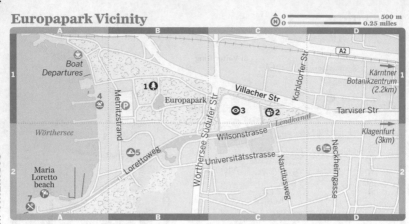

Europapark Vicinity

★**Das Domizil**　APARTMENT **$$**
(📞0664 843 30 50; www.das-domizil.at; Bahnhof-strasse 51; apt €98; 🅿🤶) This large, light and sweetly decorated apartment is in a grand 19th-century building just beyond the ring of the historic centre. It's extremely well equipped with a full kitchen, laundry facilities and lots of space. Owner Ingo Dietrich is a friendly and fashionable young local who is generous with his insider tips and time. Courtyard parking is €12 per day extra.

Hotel Palais Porcia　HOTEL **$$**
(Map p273; 📞0463-511 59 00; www.palais-porcia. at; Neuer Platz 13; s/d €125/150; 🅿🤶🌐🤶) This ridiculously ornate and old-fashioned hotel takes it to town with gilt, mirrors and red-velvet couches, and then a bit further with pink marble and gold taps in the bathrooms. It also has a private beach that

guests can use, close to its other hotel in Pörtschach.

Hotel Geyer　HOTEL **$$**
(Map p273; 📞0463-578 86; www.hotelgeyer. com; Priesterhausgasse 5; s/d €85/115; 🅿🤶) Well-maintained bright, modern rooms come with the wellness bonuses of a sauna and steam bath, and free use of the fitness centre around the corner.

✗ Eating

★**Stand No. 17**　ITALIAN, AUSTRIAN **$**
(Map p273; 📞0677 617 129 65; Benediktiner Platz; €8-14; ⊙8am-4pm Tue-Sat) Nini Loudon's kitchen springs into service from 11.30am to 2pm. Her small, market-fresh menu has beloved regional specialities but more often crosses the border to include seasonal Italian classics (white truffle risotto if you're lucky) as well as occasionally ranging further to include couscous and tagines.

Kochwerkstatt　INTERNATIONAL **$**
(Map p273; 📞0664 217 88 77; www.kochwerkstatt-am-markt.at; Benediktiner Platz 15; mains €11.50-12.50; ⊙9am-4pm Tue-Sat) Christian Cabalier plates up daily specials that usually, though not always, feature Asian vegetables, herbs and spices. The dishes sing with flavour and represent the city's freshest and most contemporary dining. As for all the restaurant stalls here, you can also drop in for a spritz and snack stop morning or early afternoon.

★**Princs**　INTERNATIONAL **$$**
(Map p273; 📞0676 470 06 76; www.princs.com; Heuplatz 1; mains €12.80-24.80; pizza €7.20-10.20; ⊙8.30am-midnight Mon-Wed, to 1am Thu-Sat)

The kitchen here sends out endless pizzas, plates of pasta and a large menu of 'street food'. The bar is also one of Klagenfurt's most popular and DJs play on weekends. You can take away pizza or pasta from €5.50.

Bierhaus zum Augustin
PUB FOOD $$

(Map p273; www.gut-essen-trinken.at; Pfarrhofgasse 2; mains €9.50-18; ⊘11am-midnight Mon-Sat) *Beisl* (bistro pub) Bierhaus zum Augustin is one of Klagenfurt's liveliest haunts for imbibers, with a particularly warm traditional pub atmosphere. There's a cobbled courtyard at the back for alfresco eating. The menu is as Carinthian as can be, with bar snacks of rye spread with a spicy meat paste, the delightful 'beer sandwich' or a trio of beef, brawn and aspic.

Restaurant Maria Loretto
AUSTRIAN $$

(Map p274; ☑0463-244 65; Lorettoweg 54; mains €18-28; ⊘10am-midnight Wed-Mon) Situated on a headland above Wörthersee, this restaurant is easily reached by foot from the *Strandbad* and has lots of lakeside character. It does good trout and fish grills, though don't expect Mediterranean lightness of touch, as it comes with a solid Austrian richness to all. Reserve for an outside table.

★ Dolce Vita
ITALIAN $$$

(Map p273; ☑0664 554 99; Heuplatz 2; lunch dishes €14-28, mains €21-28, 4-6 course menu €59-79; ⊘Mon-Fri) In a region strongly influenced by northern Italian cuisine, this restaurant is something of a local flagship. It offers an authentic seasonal menu revolving around fresh local produce and game; in summer lighter seafood specials like Venetian *Sarde in saor* (sardines in a marinade) and *brodetto* (fish soup) are also served.

Wispelhof
AUSTRIAN $$$

(☑0463-553 98; www.wispelhof.at; Feldkirchnerstrasse 29; mains €16-34) A pared-back rustic dining room is beautifully stylish and the perfect backdrop for a menu of Carinthian favourites – confit venison, fried liver and baked calf's head – along with Austrian standards and some nice Italian plates. Produce is usually from local farmers. Best beef tartare in town.

☕ Drinking & Nightlife

★ Lendhafencafe
BAR

(Map p273; www.lendhafencafe.at; Villacher Strasse 18; ⊘9am-1pm & 6pm-midnight Tue-Sat) This wonderfully rambling bar-cafe has a lovely outlook over the Lend Canal, along with a

REACHING EUROPAPARK

The large, green expanse of Europapark and the *Strandbad* (beach) on the shores of Wörthersee are centres for splashy fun and especially good for kids. Boating and swimming are usually possible from May to September. To get here, take bus 10 from Heiligengeistplatz via Minimundus to **Strandbad** (p272). To get to Wörthersee by bicycle, avoid Villacher Strasse and take the bicycle path running along the northern side of Lendl Canal. You can access it from the small streets running west from the junction of Villacher Ring and Villacher Strasse.

delightful ivy-clad internal courtyard. You can occasionally chance upon concerts and spill out to the pavillion downstairs where there is a range of edgy cultural events and parties.

Cafe Ingeborg Bachmann
BAR

(Map p273; ☑0463-50 10 70; www.kaffeehausingeborg-bachmann.at; Radetzkystrasse 3 (cnr Sterneckstrasse); ⊘7.30am-10pm Mon-Fri, 8am-2pm Sat) Klaus Kirchhauer, also known to Klagenfurt's party kids as DJ Barry Bahia, runs this original Klagenfurt *Kaffeehaus* (coffee house). A light, pretty sliver of a thing, it attracts the city's cultural set and is a good place to while away an afternoon with a book. Snacks are available, though limited to panini and cake.

Park Haus Cafe
BAR

(Map p273; www.park-haus.at; St-Veiter-Ring 10; ⊘7.30am-midnight Mon-Thu, to 2am Fri, 6pm-2am Sat) An all-day hang-out for Klagenfurt's young and interesting, with a lineup of sofas inside and a sunny terrace overlooking the park outside. While its by-day persona is very relaxed, at night it's partytime.

Kamot
BAR

(Map p273; www.kamot.at; Bahnhofstrasse 9; ⊘8pm-2am) This jazz venue hosts some of the top national names on the pub circuit, and it's a nice warm place for a drink anytime.

🔒 Shopping

Bendediktinermarkt
MARKET

(Fruit & Vegetable Market; Map p273; Benediktinerplatz) Produce and flower stalls fill this pretty market square on Thursday and Saturday mornings. During the rest of the week, there are great restaurant stalls to lunch in or grab coffee or wine.

ℹ Information

Main Post Office (Map p273; Dr-Herr-mann-Gasse 4; ⏱7am-6pm Mon-Fri, 8am-noon Sat)

Tourist Office (Map p273; ☏ 0463-537 22 23; www.visitklagenfurt.at; Neuer Platz 1, Rathaus; ⏱8am-6pm Mon-Fri, 10am-5pm Sat, to 3pm Sun) Sells Kärnten Cards and books accommodation.

ℹ Getting There & Away

AIR

Klagenfurt's **airport** (www.klagenfurt-airport. com; Flughafenstrasse 60-66) is 3km north of town. Ryanair connects Klagenfurt with London Stansted; Germanwings flies to Cologne-Bonn in Germany.

BOAT

The **departure point** (Map p274) for boat cruises on the lake is a few hundred metres north of the *Strandbad*.

BUS

Postbus services depart outside the Haupt-bahnhof, and there's a timetable board outside. Direct Österreiche Bundesbahn (Austrian Federal Railways; ÖBB) buses connect Klagenfurt with Graz (€27.50, two hours). At least four daily buses run via Villach to Venice (Italy; €28, 4¼ hours).

TRAIN

Two-hourly direct IC/EC (InterCity/EuroCity) trains run from Klagenfurt to Vienna (€52.60, 3¾ hours) and Salzburg (€41.25, three hours). Trains to Graz depart every two to three hours (€41.25, 2¾ hours), with a change at Leoben or Bruck an der Mur. Trains to western Austria, Italy, Slovenia and Germany go via Villach (€7.10, 25 to 40 minutes, two to four per hour).

ℹ Getting Around

TO/FROM THE AIRPORT

Klagenfurt Airport is a 10-minute walk from the train station Klagenfurt Annabichl, which is served by IC and S-Bahn trains (€2.80, five minutes). Better is bus 40 or 42 from Hauptbahnhof to the airport, which runs every 30 minutes to one hour (every two hours Sunday; €2.10, 30 minutes). A taxi costs about €12 from the centre of town.

BICYCLE

In summer the tourist office cooperates with a bicycle rental company. **Bicycles** (www.impulse.

co.at; 3-/24hr/weekly rental €7/12/45) can also be picked up and dropped off at various points around the lake. The tourist office has a brochure with locations.

BUS

Single bus tickets (which you buy from the driver) cost €1.40 for two or three stops or €2.10 for one hour. Drivers also sell 24-hour passes for €4.80. You can also buy tickets at the train station and from some hotels. Validate your advance tickets after boarding.

CENTRAL CARINTHIA

Carinthia's central region is wedged between the Saualpe in the east and the Nock Mountains in the northwest. Small, historic villages dot lakelands and alpine slopes: beyond the relatively lively city of Villach, this a profoundly rural and often very conservative place. Come here to get a taste of the Austrian landscape away from the crowds: a diverse landscape means a base in Villach can have you hiking snowcapped mountains in the morning and standup paddle boarding come afternoon.

Villach

☏04242 / POP 58,970

Although there are more picturesque cities in the region, and the town itself has little in the way of sights, Villach has long been a historically important junction between the Alps and southern Austria and is a lively and liveable city. Like its close neighbour Klagenfurt, the Italian influence here is strong. Consider using it as a base for activities and for exploring the region.

◉ Sights

Stadtpfarrkirche St Jakob   CHURCH
(Oberer Kirchenplatz 8; ⏱dawn-dusk) The Stadtpfarrkirche St Jakob dominates the old town and has frescoes, a stuccoed ceiling and a vast rococo altar in gold leaf, bedecked with fresh flowers. The walls are studded with the ornate memorial plaques of the region's noble families. Each summer a pair of falcons nests in the Stadtpfarrturm (p277).

Museum der Stadt Villach   MUSEUM
(☏04242-205 35 00; www.villach.at/museum; Widmanngasse 38; adult/child €4/free; ⏱10am-4.30pm Tue-Sun) This museum covers local history, archaeology and medieval art; it

Central Carinthia

also hosts occasionally interesting special exhibitions.

Relief Von Kärnten
MUSEUM

(Peraustrasse 14; adult/child €2.50/free; ⊘10am-4.30pm Mon-Sat, closed Nov-Apr) Relief Von Kärnten is a huge relief model of Carinthia housed in Schillerpark, south of the old town. It covers 182 sq metres and depicts the province at a scale of 1:10,000 (1:5000 vertically, to exaggerate the mountains).

Adler Flugschau
CASTLE

(Falconry Show; ☑04242-428 88; www.adlerflugschau.com; Schlossbergweg, Burgruine Landskron; adult/child €10/5; ⊘11am & 2.30pm May-Oct, closed Nov-Apr) Situated between Villach and the Ossiacher See, the castle ruins of Burg Landskron are home to the impressive Adler Flugschau, a 40-minute spectacle featuring falcons. Affenberg, a monkey reserve, is also here. Five to 11 buses (€2, nine minutes) leave daily from alongside Villach's train station stop in St Andrä, below the castle.

Stadtpfarrturm
TOWER

(adult/child & student €2.50/1.50; ⊘10am-6pm Jul & Aug, to 4.30pm May, Jun, Sep & Oct, closed Nov-Apr) A pair of falcons nests in the Stadtpfarrturm in summer; you can even follow their domestic life on a closed-circuit TV screen from the cafe across the street.

Villacher Fahrzeugmuseum
MUSEUM

(www.oldtimermuseum.at; Ferdinand-Wedenig-Strasse 9; adult/child €7/5; ⊘10am-6pm) Located 3km outside town, the Villach Automobile Museum focuses on icons of everyday motoring such as the Fiat Topolino, BMW Isetta and about 250 others. Take

bus 5179 from the train station to Zauchen (Bundestrasse stop).

🛏 Sleeping

Jugendherberge
HOSTEL **$**

(☑04242-563 68; www.hiyou.at; Dinzlweg 34; dm/s/d €34/46/80; P@) Located 1km west of the town centre, off Sankt-Martiner-Weg. Sauna facilities and a children's playground are on-site.

★Hotel Mosser
HOTEL **$$**

(☑04242-241 15; www.hotelmosser.at; Bahnhofstrasse 9; s €69-99, d €104-165, ste €190-220, apt €120-175; P@🛜) Some rooms in this friendly and efficient historic hotel have angled mirrors above the head boards; others have whirlpools for romantic interludes. Cheaper singles, in contrast, are functional and unremarkable. Obviously not one for the brokenhearted.

Romantik Hotel Post
HOTEL **$$**

(☑04242-261 01-0; www.hotel-villach.com; Hauptplatz 26; s €85-150, d €105-180, tr €134-199, ste €205-270; P@🛜) The corridors of this smart hotel offer a foretaste of its charms, which include chandeliers and oriental rugs. The wooden furnishings have a light and breezy feel, and the lift and some of the doubles joined by doors make it ideal for families.

Kramer Hotel-Gasthof
HOTEL **$$**

(☑04242-249 53; www.hotel-kramer.com; Italiener Strasse 14; s €49-69, d €94-106, tr €130; P@🛜) You'll find very good value among contemporary furnishings at this hotel just up the road from the Stadtpfarrkirche. Rooms are spacious and priced by size and demand.

Villach

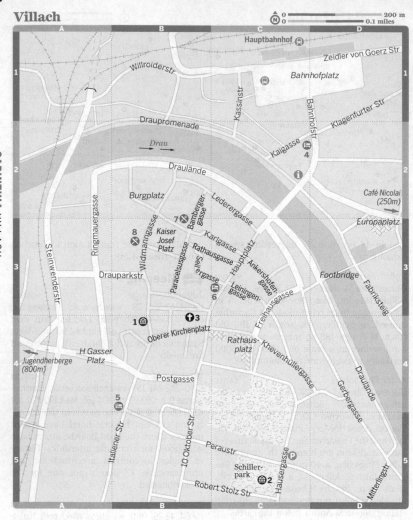

🍴 Eating

⭐ Trastavere
ITALIAN $$

(📞 04242-21 56 65; www.trastevere.at; Widmanngasse 30; pasta €8.90-12.80, pizza €7.80-11.80, mains €12.80-26; ⊙ 11am-midnight Mon-Sat) Book ahead for a courtyard table on weekend summer evenings in this trattoria situated in a lovely courtyard. It has a broad range of seafood dishes, excellent pizzas and a selection of Argentinian steaks.

⭐ Stern
INTERNATIONAL, STEAK $$

(📞 04242-247 55; www.stern-villach.com; Kaiser Josef Platz 5; mains €7.90-23.90, steaks €18.30-

22.30, lunch menu €4.90-6.90; ⊙ 7am-midnight Mon-Thu, to 2am Fri, 9am-2am Sat; 🛜) This lounge and restaurant is a perfect place to hang out over a drink, inside or outdoors on the square. Its speciality is steak, which you get by filling out a menu sheet.

Romantik Restaurant Post
AUSTRIAN $$

(www.stadtrestaurant.at; Hauptplatz 26; mains €14.50-23.50; ⊙ noon-2.30pm & 6-10pm; 🍴) The restaurant of the Romantik Hotel Post serves well-prepared regional specialities in a cosy atmosphere. The midday set menu is good value; there's also a healthy selection of salads.

Villach

◎ Sights
1 Museum der Stadt Villach B4
2 Relief Von Kärnten C5
3 Stadtpfarrkirche St Jakob B4
   Stadtpfarrturm .... (see 3)

🛏 Sleeping
4 Hotel Mosser C2
5 Kramer Hotel-Gasthof B4
6 Romantik Hotel Post C3

✘ Eating
   Romantik Restaurant Post .... (see 6)
7 Stern B3
8 Trastavere B3

ℹ Information

Tourismusinformation Villach-Stadt
(☑ 04242-205 29 00; www.villach.at; Bahnhofstrasse 3; ◷ 9am-7pm Mon-Fri, 10am-4pm
Sat) City tourist office, helps with accommodation; has a free city map and excellent free
city environs map, as well as a free internet
terminal.

ℹ Getting There & Away

BUS
Call ☑ 44410-15 10 or ☑ 0810 222 33 39 for
Postbus information. The **bus station** is oppo-
site the Hauptbahnhof. At least four InterCity
(IC) buses go to Venice daily (€25, 3½ hours).

TRAIN
Villach is situated on three Austrian IC/EC
(InterCity/EuroCity) rail routes, which serve
Salzburg (€31, 2½ hours, every two hours),
Lienz (€20, 1¾ hours, hourly) and Klagenfurt
(€7.20, 30 to 40 minutes, two to four per hour).
Direct services run to seemingly everywhere:
Munich (€70, 4½ hours, four daily) in Germany;
Ljubljana (€23, 1¾ hours, four daily) in Slo-
venia; Zagreb (€45, four hours, four daily) in
Croatia; and Belgrade (€82, 11 hours, one daily)
in Serbia.

Faaker See & Ossiacher See

Villach is blessed with two major nearby
lakes with low-key summer resorts. Both the
Faaker See, situated 6km east of Villach and
close to the Karawanken Range, and the Ossiacher See, 4km to the northeast, provide
plenty of camping, boating and swimming
opportunities. Above Annenheim and providing a backdrop to the Ossiacher See is

Gerlitzen (1909m), a popular ski area. Expect to pay about €40 for a ski pass here.

ℹ Information

Regional Tourist Office. (☑ 04242-420 00;
www.region-villach.at; Töbringer Strasse 1,
Villach; ◷ 8am-5pm Mon-Thu, to 4pm Fri)

ℹ Getting There & Away

Regular train and Postbus services leave
weekdays from the Villach bus station and train
station, running along the northern shore of
Ossiacher See via Annenheim (€2, 12 minutes)
and Bodensdorf (€3.40, 20 minutes). Regular
trains run to Faak am See (€3.40, 30 minutes),
and regular buses run to Drobollach (€2, 20
minutes), both on the Faaker See.

ℹ Getting Around

BICYCLE
You can explore the region by bicycle through
Das Radl (☑ 0664 226 95 40, 04242-269 54;
www.das-radl.at; Italiener Strasse 25; per day
€11; ◷ 8am-6pm Mon-Fri, 9am-noon Sat, bike
hire closed Oct-Apr). These can be hired in
Villach if you ring ahead, and at the Bodensdorf
(Ossiacher See) and Faak (Faaker See) train
stations; hotels and camp sites in the region hire
them out, too.

BOAT
On the Ossiacher See, **boats** (☑ 0699 15 077
077; www.ossiachersee-schifffahrtat; day ticket
adult/child €13.50/6.80, half-day lake boat tour
€9/4.50; ◷ up to 8 services daily Apr-Oct) run
by Drau Fluss Schifffahrt complete a crisscross
circuit between St Andrä and Steindorf (adult/
child €12.80/6.40, 2½ hours, approximately
hourly from May to October). Boats run by the
same company also navigate the Drau River
from Villach Congress-Center to Wernberg Bad
(one way adult/child €7.50/3.75, 45 minutes)
via St Niklas an der Drau (about 2km northeast
of the Faaker See) up to four times a day between early May and mid-October.

Dreiländereck
☑ 04255

Walkers and mountain bikers will find much
to do in the **Dobratsch** (2166m) area, in the
Villacher Alpen about 12km west of Villach.
Just south of here, hiking trails go from the
small town of Arnoldstein to the Dreilän-
dereck – the point where Austria, Italy and
Slovenia meet. At 1500m there's an **Alpine
Garden** (☑ 0664 914 29 53; www.alpengarten-
villach.at; adult/child €3/1; ◷ 9am-6pm daily
Jun-Aug) with flora from the southern Alps.

To reach the garden, follow the Villacher Alpenstrasse from town. This is a toll road (€16.50 per car), but it's free from about mid-November to mid-April, or free in summer if all occupants have the **Kärnten Card** (1-/2-week card €37/48; www.kaerntencard. at). Dobratsch is popular with cross-country skiers. Check the Alpenstrasse website (www. villacher-alpenstrasse.at) for road closures in bad weather.

The remote **Naturpark Dobratsch** (www. naturparkdobratsch.info) has a huge range of terrain. Hiking guides are available in English. See the website for summer and winter programs.

Buses run to Villacher Alpe Rosstratte in the Naturpark Dobratsch, via the Alpenstrasse and the alpine garden. Frequent trains connect Villach and Arnoldstein (€4.90, 25 minutes).

Hermagor

☑ 04282 / POP 7070

Situated about 50km west of Villach, Hermagor is popular as a base for skiing in the nearby Nassfeld ski slopes, where you can zip around 110km of pistes (day pass €43 to €46) and explore Nordic skiing trails and snowboarding runs; in summer it morphs into a low-key spot for hikers and mountain bikers. Hermagor is also the starting point for hiking the spectacular **Garnitzenklamm**, a narrow gorge some 2.5km west of town. Ask at the tourist office for advice.

This is a low-key place for skiing in the winter (both downhill and Nordic) and biking and hiking in the summer.

The **Millennium-Express Cable Car** (adult/child €20/12 return) climbs 6km up to Nassfeld, making it Austria's longest. The valley station is in Tröpolach, 8km west of town along the B111 and then B90; it can also be reached by train.

Situated on a lovely property about a 10-minute walk north of town along Radnigger Strasse, **Villa Blumegg** (☑04282-20 92; www.villa-blumegg.at; Neupriessenegg 2; s €52-59, d €84-104, apt €168-196; P) offers well-priced, comfortable rooms with and without balconies. There are also holiday apartments accommodating one to seven people.

The **Tourist Office** (☑04282-2043; www. hermagor.info; Göseringlände 7; ⊙8am-6pm Mon-Fri, 9am-2pm Sat, from 10am Sun) is about 400m west of the train station on the B111. It has

well-informed staff with information on skiing, guided and unguided hiking, alpine huts and mountain biking in the area.

Trains run to Hermagor from Villach (€10, 70 minutes) every one to two hours, some continuing to Tröpolach (€2.20, 10 minutes), complemented by bus services from Hermagor to Tröpolach.

EASTERN CARINTHIA

Friesach

☑ 04268 / POP 5180

Once a key staging post on the Vienna–Venice trade route, Friesach is Carinthia's oldest town. The hills on either side bristle with ruined fortifications, and the centre is surrounded by a moat (it's the only town in Austria that still has one) and a set of imposing, grey-stone walls. Once a year Friesach's gates are locked, everyone in town dresses up in medieval costumes and Friesach re-enacts its history.

◉ Sights

Friesach has four medieval fortress ruins set along the hills rising above Hauptplatz to the west, all offering excellent views (and all free). The northernmost is **Burg Geyersberg**; the furthest south are the **Virgilienberg** ruins. The middle two (**Rotturm** and **Petersberg**) are the most easily visited from the centre. There are lovely views from Peterskirche, accessible by paths ascending from the front of the Gothic Stadtpfarrkirche, with Romanesque elements dating from AD 927.

All fortresses are connected by the Burgwanderweg that winds through the bucolic landscape with views over town.

★☆ Festivals & Events

Spectaculum   CULTURAL
(⊙ Jul) On the last Saturday in July, electric lights are extinguished and the town is closed off and lit by torches and flares as jesters, princesses and armoured knights stroll around juggling, fire-eating and staging jousting tournaments and duels. Friesach reverts to the currency that made it famous, with medieval meals from street stalls being paid for with Friesach pennies.

Petersberg Fortress   THEATRE
(tickets €15-25) The site for open-air theatre in summer, where performances range from

Shakespeare to Brecht. Obtain details and tickets from the tourist office.

🛏 Sleeping & Eating

Metnitztalerhof HOTEL $$
(☑ 04268-251 00; www.metnitztalerhof.at; Hauptplatz 11; s €57, d €96-108; ⓟ @ 🤶) This pastel-pink edifice at the far end of the town square is the only four-star hotel in Friesach; rooms are modern and comfortable and have small balconies. There's a sauna, Jacuzzi and steam room on-site, plus a **restaurant** (mains €16 to €23.50; open Friday to Wednesday) that serves Austrian and Carinthian dishes.

Cafe Konditorei Craigher CAFE $
(www.craigher.at; Hauptplatz 3; ⊙ 7am-8pm Mon-Fri, 8am-7pm Sat & Sun) Connoisseurs of chocolate will love dipping into this place – all chocolate is made on the premises. Or come for coffee and cake in the 100-year-old *Kaffeehaus*.

Information

Tourist Office (☑ 04268-22 13 40; www.friesach.at; Fürstenhofplatz 1; ⊙ 8am-4pm Mon-Fri, 10am-3pm Sat & Sun, closed weekends Oct-May) Located a couple of minutes by foot north of Hauptplatz.

ⓘ Getting There & Away

Friesach has direct connections with Vienna's Meidling (€42.50, 3¼ hours, three daily), Villach (€15.30, 1½ hours, hourly), Bruck an der Mur (€23.10, 1¾ hours, 4 daily), St Veit (€7.20, 30 minutes, hourly) and Klagenfurt (€10.60, 60 minutes, hourly).

Gurk

☑ 04266 / POP 1290

This small town (Krka in Slovenian), some 18km west of the Friesach–Klagenfurt road, is famous for its former Dom, which still operates as a church. The frescoes in the Bischofskapelle, dating from around 1200, are all the more beautiful for the use of raw colours.

With its harmonious pillared crypt, the **Dom** (☑ 04266-82 36; Domplatz 11; tours €2.90-9, crypt entry €1.50; ⊙ 9am-7pm, Sunday service 10-10.45am, combined 70-minute tours dom, crypt & Bischofskapelle 10.30am, 1.30pm & 3pm), built between 1140 and 1200, is Austria's foremost church from the Romanesque epoch. Inside you will also find Gothic reticulated vaulting, and most of the church fittings are either baroque or rococo. The early-baroque high altar has 72 statues and 82 angel heads.

The small **Bischofskapelle** (Episcopal Chapel; adult/child €3.70/1.80; ⊙ guided tours 11.20pm, 2.20pm & 3.50pm) is part of the Dom and has unusually well-preserved late Romanesque paintings dating from 1263. One side is dedicated to the life of Mary, including the annunciation, the other to the birth of Jesus. You can also see the oldest surviving example Austrian stained glass here in the arched and round windows.

Visit on a weekday if using public transport – an 8.04am train from Klagenfurt to Treibach-Althofen connects with a bus (€12.70, 1¾ hours). Returning, the last bus from Gurk leaves at 6.06pm. With your own transport, take Hwy 93.

Hüttenberg

☑ 04263 / POP 1800

Step off the bus in the tiny mining village of Hüttenberg and you might be forgiven for thinking you've stumbled into Tibet, for here you see fluttering prayer flags rising up the cliff. Hüttenberg is the birthplace of Heinrich Harrer, who famously spent seven years in Tibet and was immortalised by Brad Pitt in film.

Outside the **Heinrich Harrer Museum** (☑ 04263-81 08 20; www.harrermuseum.at; Bahnhofstrasse 12; adult/child €14/8; ⊙ 10am-5pm May-Oct) you can sip on a bowl of butter tea and listen to the rush of water through wooden prayer wheels, before going inside the beautiful stone-and-wood building to see the huge collection of objects and photographs Harrer brought back from his world travels. The steep admission price includes the inconveniently located **Puppenmuseum** (Doll Museum) and the **Mineralienschaubergwerk** (Mineral Mining Museum) 3km away in Knappenberg.

Opposite the museum is the Lingkor, a metal walkway built up the cliff face as an aid to prayer and meditation. It closed in 2013 due to rockfall and may not be accessible for another couple of years.

ⓘ Getting There & Away

One direct bus runs to Hüttenberg weekdays from St Veit an der Glan (€9.70, one hour), and a train and bus connecting service operates from St Veit an der Glan via Treibach-Althofen (€17.30, 75 minutes). From Klagenfurt frequent buses run with a change either in Görtschitztal Vierlinden or in Mösel Ort (€12.10, one-1½ hours). Buses continue on to Knappenberg.

St Veit an der Glan

☎04212 / POP 12,600

St Veit was historically important as the seat of the dukes of Carinthia from 1170 until 1518. These days it's a mildly interesting, mid-sized town with a lovely baroque square.

The highlight on the town square is the 15th-century Gothic **Rathaus**, with its magnificent courtyard featuring sgraffito (a mural or decoration in which the top layer is scratched off to reveal the original underneath). St Veit's other main attraction is the Kunsthotel Fuchspalast. This surrealist structure was designed by mystical artist Ernst Fuchs, and has blue and red glass tiles in fantastical and astrological designs – a theme that you find throughout St Veit's best place to sleep.

Blue and red glass tiles in amazing, surreal designs decorate the exterior of the **Kunsthotel Fuchspalast** (☎04212-466 00; www.hotel-fuchspalast.at; Prof-Ernst-Fuchs-Platz 1; r €56 per person; P@🛜). Inside, surrealism gives way to fluted columns and jewel-like mosaics, while rooms have a simplicity that hints at art deco design. There's a sauna onsite and the reception doubles as the tourist office.

La Torre (☎04212-392 50; www.latorre.at; Grabenstrasse 39; mains €15.50-28, 6-course menu €69; ⏰noon-2.30pm & 6-10pm Tue-Sat) is a fantastic Italian restaurant set in one of the towers of the 14th-century town wall. As well as the smart, romantic interior, there's a beautiful, walled garden and terrace, and an Italian owner who exudes bonhomie.

ℹ Information

Tourist Office (☎04212-466 00; www.stveit.com; Hauptplatz 23; ⏰10am-4pm) This office inside the Kunsthotel Fuchspalast has an excellent map of town and the environs and hires out e-bikes (€20 per day; pick-up 8am, return 7pm) and electric cars (six hours €35, 8.30am-6.30pm). There's also an information screen with internet in the *Rathaus* (town hall).

ℹ Getting There & Away

St Veit is 33km south of Friesach and 20km north of Klagenfurt. Two-hourly express trains run to Villach (€14, 37 minutes), stopping at Klagenfurt (€4.70, 12 minutes). There are no left-luggage lockers at the station.

Burg Hochosterwitz

The fairy-tale **Burg Hochosterwitz** (www.burg-hochosterwitz.com; Hochosterwitz 1; adult/child incl tour €12/8; ⏰9am-6pm May-Sep, 10am-5pm Apr & Oct) claims to be the inspiration for the castle in *Sleeping Beauty* and drapes itself around the slopes of a hill, with 14 gate towers on the path up to the final bastion. These were built between 1570 and 1586 by its former owner, Georg Khevenhüller, to ward off invading Turks.

A Burgführer information booklet (in English; €4) outlines the different challenges presented to attackers by each gate – some have spikes embedded in them, which could be dropped straight through unwary invaders passing underneath. The castle also has a museum featuring the suit of armour of one Burghauptmann Schenk, who measured 225cm at the tender age of 16.

There's a small cafe serving sausages, soup, rolls and coffee at the top. Regional trains on the St Veit–Friesach route stop at Launsdorf Hochosterwitz station, a 3km walk from the car park and the first gate, where a lift (€6) ascends to the castle.

Wörthersee

The Wörthersee stretches from west to east between Velden and Klagenfurt and can be easily explored by bicycle on a 50km circuit. The southern shore is the most picturesque, but the northern shore has the best public transport access and is the busiest section.

A trip around the lake takes you past the genteel resort of Pörtschach, the nightlife hub of Velden and the small town of Maria Wörth. Five kilometres south of Velden is Rosegg, with its **Schloss** (☎04274-30 09; www.rosegg.at; Schloss Rosegg 1, Rosegg; adult/child €7/4.50; ⏰10am-6pm daily May-Sep, closed Mon Oct-Apr), and 8km southwest of Maria Wörth is the **Pyramidenkogel** (☎04273-24 43; www.pyramidenkogel.info; Linden 62, Keutschach am See; adult/child €11/5.50, slide ride/pass €4/20; ⏰9am-9pm Jun-Aug, 9am-8pm May & Sep, 10am-7pm Apr & Oct, 10am-6pm Mar), a hill topped by a 71m tower made of steel with wooden beams spiralling up its exterior. This vertiginous tower has three viewing platforms. Those with strong legs can climb the 400-odd steps; others can take the glass panorama lift. The relatively easy St Anna-Weg trail (90 minutes one-way) leads here through forest from Maria Wörth.

The **Strand Club** (☑ 04274-511 01; www.strandclub.com; Seepromenade 15, Velden; ☺ activities dawn-dusk Apr-Oct, bar 7am-midnight Apr-Oct) offers paragliding, water skiing, wakeboarding, and electric boat rental; prices include wetsuit hire. Afterwards, relax at the bar and adjoining cafe.

Hotel Schloss Leonstain (☑ 04272-28 16; www.leonstain.at; Leonstainerstrasse 1, Pörtschach; s €79-89, d €180-245) offers Austrian lakeside life at its most delightful, with hugely atmospheric rooms mixing rustic antiques with modern comfort. It's totally traditional but has a breezy, holiday feel to it all. The hotel's restaurant uses organic, local produce and the dreamy **Bar Leon** (Leon Beach; ☑ 04272-28 16; www.leonstain.at; cnr Kärntnerstrasse & Hauptstrasse, Pörtschach; mains €15-26; ☺ Apr-Sep) across the road gives you all-day lake access and more dining options. It's open to non-guests and affords a rare glimpse into the genteel summer pleasures of the Austrian well-to-do. Come for breakfast or lunch in the garden, dinner upstairs in the lantern-lit summer house or loll with a Lillet spritz on the lake deck as swans glide by.

❶ Information

Tourism Maria Wörth (☑ 04273-224 00; www.maria-woerth.at; Seepromenade 5; ☺ 8am-5pm Mon-Fri, 10am-12.30pm & 1-3.30pm Sat & Sun) Part of the Visit Wöthersee network of offices, this office has an accommodation booking service and information about events and activities, including yoga classes and retreats.

Tourism Pörtschach (☑ 04272-23 54; www.poertschach.at; Werzerpromenade 1; ☺ 9am-6pm Mon-Fri, 10am-6pm Sat, 10am-4pm Sun Jul & Aug, shorter hours rest of year) Helps with hotel bookings and activities.

Wörthersee Tourismus (☑ 04274-382 88; www.woerthersee.com; Villacher Strasse 19; ☺ 8am-6pm Mon-Sat, 9am-5pm Sun, closed Sun late Oct–mid-Apr) Wörthersee Tourismus can help with lists of bike stations on the lake. As well as regional information, they can advise on accommodation in Velden.

❶ Getting There & Away

Klagenfurt's excellent bus network extends to the Wörthersee resorts. The tourism offices in Klagenfurt or around the lake can help with timetables.

WESTERN CARINTHIA

Gmünd

☑ 04732 / POP 2630

Gmünd is an attractive 11th-century village with a delightful walled centre and a 13th-century hilltop castle, Alte Burg. From 1480, Hungarians conducted a seven-year siege of the city, breaking through and partially destroying the castle. Today it's the setting for plays and musical events, as well as two unusual museums.

⊙ Sights

Porsche Museum Helmut Pfeifhofer   MUSEUM
(www.auto-museum.at; Riesertratte 4a; adult/child €8/3.50; ☺ 9am-6pm mid-May–mid-Oct, 10am-4pm mid-Oct–mid-May) An unexpected sight in Gmünd is the Porsche Museum Helmut Pfeifhofer. A Porsche factory operated here from 1944 to 1950 and the first car to bear that famous name (a 356) was handmade here. One of these models on display (only 52 were built), together with about 15 other models and a couple of the wooden frames used in their construction. There's a 15-minute film (in German and English) on Dr Porsche's life and work.

Pankratium   MUSEUM
(☑ 04732-311 44; www.pankratium.at; Hintere Gasse 60; 1hr tour adult/child €9.50/5.90; ☺ 10am-5pm May-Oct) Gmünd's most atypical attraction is the Pankratium, an extraordinary space bringing together water, light and sound (ie vibration) in hands-on pieces designed for the senses. You can bring sound gadgets and all manner of instruments to life on a tour that culminates in bubble-blowing in the yard.

🛏 Sleeping

Gasthof Kohlmayr   GUESTHOUSE **$**
(☑ 04732-214 90; www.gasthof-kohlmayr.at; Hauptplatz 7; s/d/q €46/76/128; **P**) Gasthof Kohlmayr has cosy and affordable rooms in a 400-year-old building right in the heart of Gmünd. There's a restaurant (mains €8.90 to €17.90) serving tasty local fare.

❶ Information

Tourist Office (☑ 04732-22 22; www.familientral.com; Hauptplatz 20; ☺ 8am-5pm Mon-Fri, 9am-3pm Sat Jul & Aug, closed Sat Sep-Jun)

ⓘ Getting There & Away

One to two hourly buses connect Gmünd with Spittal an der Drau (€5.10, 30 minutes) from Monday to Friday. It is not on a rail route.

Millstatt

⏍ 04766 / POP 3410

The genteel lakeside village of Millstatt lies 10km east of Spittal an der Drau on the northern shore of the Millstätter See, a lake stretching 12km long but just 1.5km wide. It's the second-largest lake in Carinthia after the Wörthersee. Gouged out during the ice age about 30,000 years ago, the warm waters (about 22°C to 26°C in summer) lend themselves to sailing, kayaking and swimming. Millstatt is said to have got its name from a duke named Domitian, an early Christian convert who tossed *mille statuae* – a thousand heathen statues – into the lake from here.

◉ Sights

Stift Millstatt ABBEY
(www.stiftsmuseum.at; Stiftsgasse 1; adult/child €3.90/2.50; ⊙ 10am-4pm May-Oct) Apart from Lake Millstatt itself, the town's main attraction is its Romanesque Benedictine abbey, founded in 1070. This pretty complex consists of a moderately interesting Stiftsmuseum, the attractive 11th-century abbey **church**, a **graveyard**, and **abbey buildings** south of the church with lovely yards and arcades. If you walk downhill along Stiftsgasse from the church, you see on the left a **1000-year-old lime tree**. The abbey grounds and magnificent arcades and cloisters are free.

Stiftsmuseum MUSEUM
(Abbey Museum; ⏍ 0676 360 06 92; Stiftsgasse 1; admission adult/child €3.90/2.50, tours €6; ⊙ 10am-4pm May-Oct) The Stiftsmuseum, within the abbey Stift Millstatt, contains everything from documentation of the town's history to reliquaries and a geology collection.

🏃 Activities

Surf und Segelschule Millstatt WATER SPORTS
(⏍ 0676 751 19 39; www.surf-segelschulemillstatt.at; Seestrasse, alongside Villa Verdin; hire per hour windsurfing board & rig €17-23, kayak €10, sailing boats €10, e-boats €14; ⊙ 10am-5pm Mon-Fri, 12pm-5pm Sat-Sun Jul-Aug) This reliable outfit rents equipment and holds individual and group windsurfing, sailing and kayak courses.

Wassersport Strobl WATER SPORTS
(⏍ 04766-22 63; Seemühlgasse 56a; per hour e-boats €15) Wassersport Strobl has two landing stages where you can rent boats and canoes.

🛏 Sleeping

Früstuckspension Strobl PENSION $
(⏍ 04766-31 42; pension-hansstrobl@aon.at; Kaiser-Franz-Josef-Strasse 59; s €38, d €76; ☻) This budget hotel is back from the lake but has balcony views from most of the rooms. It's in a 400-year-old Gothic building that once belonged to the monastery.

★ Hotel See-Villa HOTEL $$
(⏍ 04766 2102; www.see-villa-tacoli.com; Seestrasse 68; s €76-90, d €170-200, ste per person €89-106; ℗ @ 🛜) This very comfortable turn-of-the-20th-century hotel has genuine historic charm. It is located right on the shore (perfect for sleeping with windows open), with a huge terrace restaurant, a private sauna and a swimming jetty. Its restaurant (mains from €14.50 to €20) is open daily for lunch and dinner.

★ Villa Verdin HOTEL $$
(⏍ 06990 1218 1093; www.villaverdin.at; Seestrasse 69; s €45, d per person €80; ℗ 🛜) This converted 19th-century villa-hotel mixes contemporary design style with antiques and interesting junk to create a comfortable, informal yet stylish atmosphere. It's gay-friendly and has a retro beach cafe. Wi-fi is in public areas.

✗ Eating

★ Fisch-Häusl Stark SEAFOOD $$$
(Kaiser-Franz-Josef-Strasse 134; mains €17-22, smoked trout about €8; ⊙ from 11am-6pm Jun-Sep) This small place serves delicious fish from the Millstätter See and the Weissensee, including smoked trout the owners will pack for a picnic. Grab a bread roll from the bakery across the street.

🍷 Drinking & Nightlife

★ Kap 4613 BAR
(www.kap4613.at; Kaiser-Franz-Josef-Strasse 330; ⊙ 9am-10pm Jun-Aug, shorter hours rest of year, closed Jan & Feb) Combining an atrium with a deck area and a beach bar extending over the water for summer sipping, this lakeside bar is easily Millstatt's best drinking venue.

ℹ️ Information

Infocenter Millstätter See (☎ 04766-370 00; www.millstaettersee.at; Thomas Morgenstern Platz 1; ⊙9am-5pm Mon-Fri) The central information office, Infocenter Millstätter See, is situated in a new building in Seeboden with an unusual curtain of water that parts as you enter. This symbolises 'touching the lake' (the curtain is tap water, though), a theme to bring people close to water. The Infocenter doubles as a call centre with English- and Italian-speaking staff, and there's a supermarket, cafe and ATM, as well as toilets, in or near the building.

Tourist Office – Bad Kleinkirchheim (☎ 04240-82 12; www.badkleinkirchheim.at; Dorfstrasse 30; ⊙9am-12pm & 3pm-5pm Mon-Fri) Helpful for ski information.

Tourist Office – Millstatt (☎ 04766-20 23 31; www.millstaettersee.com; Marktplatz 8; ⊙9am-6pm Mon-Fri, 10am-noon & 4-6pm Sat & Sun) Located inside Millstatt's *Rathaus*; has useful information on the town.

ℹ️ Getting There & Away

Postbus services to Millstatt depart from outside Spittal train station (€3.90, 20 minutes, two hourly), with some continuing to Bad Kleinkirchheim (from Spittal €7.60, one hour).

Spittal an der Drau

☑ 04762 / POP 15,900

Spittal is an important economic and administrative centre in upper Carinthia. Its name comes from a 12th-century hospital and refuge that once provided succour to weary travellers. Today it's a town with an impressive Italianate palace at its centre and a small but attractive park with splashing fountains and bright flowerbeds.

⊙ Sights

Goldeck   MOUNTAIN
(cable car one way/return €13/18, toll road cars & motorbikes €13, lift pass adult/child €36/18) In summertime, this peak (2142m) can be reached by either cable car or the Goldeckstrasse toll road (free with the Kärnten Card). The road stops 260m short of the summit. In winter, Goldeck is popular for skiing. The cable car doesn't operate from mid-April to mid-June or from mid-September to mid-December.

Schloss Porcia & Museum für Volkskultur   PALACE
(Local Heritage Museum; ☎ 04762-28 90; www.museum-spittal.com; Burgplatz 1; adult/child

€8/4; ⊙9am-6pm mid-Apr–mid-Oct, 1-4pm Mon-Thu mid-Oct–mid-Apr; 🎭) Boasting an eye-catching Renaissance edifice, Schloss Porcia was built between 1533 and 1597 by the fabulously named Graf von Salamanca-Ortenburg. Inside, Italianate arcades run around a central courtyard used for summer theatre performances. The top floors contain the enormous Local Heritage Museum, which has lots of displays about Carinthia and 3D projections, such as a virtual navigation through the Hohe Tauern National Park.

🛏️ Sleeping

Draufluss Camping   CAMPGROUND $
(☎ 04762-24 66; www.drauwirt.com; Schwaig 10; camp site per adult/child/tent/car €5/3/4/4, s/d incl breakfast €36/72; ⊙Jun-Sep) Spittal's campground is about 3.5km from the town centre on the southern bank of the Drau River. The *Gasthof* (inn) has six simple rooms.

★ Hotel Erlebnis Post   HOTEL $$
(☎ 04762-22 17; www.erlebnis-post.at; Hauptplatz 13; s €69-79, d €116-122, tr €166, ste €188; 🅿️🛜) Rooms in this unusual hotel might be described as *room-vertisements*, as they're sponsored by local companies (usually with the name inside). One non-sponsored room has beds from the local juvenile prison and an original cell door. Bonuses are the ski-storage room and transfers to the pistes.

Hotel Ertl   HOTEL $$
(☎ 04762-204 80; www.hotel-ertl.at; Bahnhofstrasse 26; s/d/tr/q €70/130/139/160; 🅿️@🛜♨️) Smack-bang across the road from the railway station, this comfortable hotel has the ochre colours of its Tex-Mex restaurant downstairs trickling into the interior design. The outdoor pool is about 25m in length.

🍴 Eating

★ Restaurant Zellot   AUSTRIAN $$
(☎ 04762-21 13; Hauptplatz 12; mains €11-19; ⊙11am-11pm Mon-Thu, to 4am Fri & Sat) This eccentric restaurant does good steak and Austrian favourites. Later in the evening it turns into a club and live venue, with part of the place decked out like a garage – its features become even more intriguing after your second drink.

Mettnitzer   AUSTRIAN $$
(☎ 04762-358 99; Neuerplatz 17; mains €16.90-26.90; ⊙noon-2pm & 6-10pm Wed-Sun) This is a class act that serves a small range of classic, local and seasonal dishes in a formal setting.

ⓘ THE AUTOSCHLEUSE TAUERNBAHN

If you're driving to Bad Gastein from Spittal an der Drau, you'll need to use the **Autoschleuse Tauernbahn** (Railway Car Shuttle Service; www.gasteinertal.com/autoschleuse) through the tunnel from Mallnitz to Böckstein. The fare for cars is €17 one way or €30 return (valid for two months). For motorcycles, the price is €16/28. For information, call ☑ 05 717. Departures are every 60 minutes, with the last train departing at 11.20pm heading south, and 10.50pm going north. The journey takes 11 minutes.

ⓘ Information

Post Office (Egarterplatz 2; ☺ 8am-6pm Mon-Fri, 9am-noon Sat)

Tourist Office (☑ 04762-565 00; www.spittal-drau.at; Burgplatz 5; ☺ 8.30am-noon Mon-Fri) On one side of Schloss Porcia, with maps and lots of useful information.

ⓘ Getting There & Away

BUS

One- to two-hourly Postbuses leave from outside the train station, Spittal-Drau Zentrum and Neuer Platz to Gmünd (€5.10, 30 minutes) from Monday to Saturday, but none on Sunday. Call ☑ 0180 222 333 for schedule information. Postbus services to Millstatt depart from outside Spittal train station (€3.90, 20 minutes, two hourly), with some continuing to Bad Kleinkirchheim (from Spittal €7.40, one hour).

TRAIN

Spittal-Millstättersee is an important rail junction: two-hourly IC/EC services run north to Bad Gastein (€12.20, 40 minutes); at least hourly regional services run west to Lienz (€12.80, one hour) and to Villach (€7.90, 35 minutes), 37km to the southeast. The railway line north via Mallnitz-Obervellach clings spectacularly to the valley walls.

Weissensee

Wedged within a glacial cleft in the Gailtal Alps with mountain ridges flanking its northern and southern shores, Weissensee is Austria's highest swimmable glacial lake, the least developed of Carinthia's large lakes, and a spectacular and peaceful nature reserve. It stretches as a turquoise-and-deep-blue slither for almost 12km and in most parts is about 1km wide. Because it's at an altitude of 930m, the water is cooler than the Wörthersee, but in July and August you can expect temperatures of above 20°C in most parts.

🏃 Activities

Bergbahn Weissensee   CHAIRLIFT
(☑ 04713-22 69; Techendorf; one-way adult/child €9.20/5.80; ☺ 9am-5pm, closed Mon May, Jun & Sep, closed early Mar–mid-May & early Oct-Nov) Depending on your head for heights, you'll either love the 12-minute ride on this open chairlift or see it as a necessary shortcut to reach Naggler Alm (p287) – a 10-minute walk from the top – and the start of some good walking trails above Techendorf. In winter it also services the ski fields. A hiking (1.5 hours) and mountain biking trail also leads to the top from Techendorf.

Yachtdiver   DIVING
(☑ 0664 460 40 80; www.yachtdiver.at; Techendorf 55; dives from €14, equipment rental from €30, courses from €38; ☺ 9am-6pm) You wouldn't usually associate the Alps with scuba diving, but the crystal-clear waters offer incredible visibility for dazzling views of the lake's 22 fish species. Yachtdiver runs trips for experienced divers and courses for beginners, as well as ice-diving expeditions in winter.

🛏 Sleeping & Eating

Hermagorer Bodenalm   FARMSTAY $
(☑ 0650 400 24 88; www.hermagorer-bodenalm.at; Bodenalm; per person half-board €38, Brettljause plus beer €17, mains €12; ☺ May-Sep) In an alpine meadow on the south side of Weissensee, this hut has comfortable basic rooms with shared bathrooms – bring warm pyjamas: the heating is from an oven on the ground floor. It makes its own cheeses, which are served along with cured meats to sustain hikers and mountain bikers during the day.

Kohlröslhütte   FARMSTAY $
(☑ 0664 8850 1860; www.kohlroesl.at; above Techendorf in Gail Valley Alps; per person full board €38, snacks €5-12; ☺ mid-May–mid-Oct; ▧) Few alpine meadow huts have views like this one: deep into the Gitsch Valley to Sankt Lorenz and the Alps in three countries from an altitude of 1534m. The only way up here is by foot (two hours from the chairlift mountain station) or mountain bike. Rooms with a shared bathroom are rustic and cosy.

Naggler Alm AUSTRIAN $
(☑ 0699 1036 1000; www.naggleralmut.at; Naggler Alm; mains €9-15, Brettljause €12; ☺ 9am-5pm Tue-Sun May-Oct) Situated a 10-minute walk from the top of the chairlift (p286), this *Gasthof* set in an idyllic meadow landscape has a good selection of organic vegetarian dishes, well-prepared mains, delicious homemade lemonade and a *Brettljause* (cold platter) for sustenance on a hike or ride. Thursday evening it does a fish platter from 6pm (reserve ahead) – you get a torch fire for the walk back down to Techendorf in the dark.

ℹ Information

Tourist Office (☑ 04713-222 00; www.weissensee.com; Techendorf-Süd; ☺ 8.30am-12.30pm & 1.30-5pm Mon-Fri, 9am-noon & 4-6pm Sat, 10am-noon & 4-6pm Sun, closed Sat & Sun mid-Sep–mid-June) Excellent activities brochures with map, helps with accommodation and also sells several detailed hiking and mountain biking maps for around €10.

ℹ Getting There & Away

The nearest train station is Greifenburg-Weissensee, 11km from the lake on the Villach-Spital an der Drau-Lienz line. From there **Mobil Büro Hermagor** (☑ reservations 0800 500 1905; www.mobilbuero.com; one-way €7.50; ☺ mid-May–late Sep & mid-Dec–Feb) runs a bus service to/from your place of stay on Weissensee. It's for overnight guests only. Book by telephone or online by 4pm one day before. Day guests can buy a day pass (€7.50) but only to Hotel Kreuzwirt, 4km from Techendorf. You can pick up the free but often infrequent Naturpark bus from there.

To reach the lake by car, take Bundesstrasse 87 from Greifenburg or Hermagor. From Spital an der Drau a road (L32) runs to the eastern end of the lake but ends there.

ℹ Getting Around

Boat services (www.schifffahrt-mueller.at; 1-8 stops €2-7.50, day ticket €12; ☺ up to 10 services daily mid-May–mid-Oct) Weissensee Schifffahrt runs boats to all stops between Techendorf and Dolomitenblick three to 11 times daily, peaking in July and August.

Lienz

☑ 04852 / POP 11,900

The Dolomites rise like an amphitheatre around Lienz, which straddles the Isel and Drau Rivers just 40km north of Italy. Those same arresting river and mountain views welcomed the Romans, who settled here some 2000 years ago and whose legacy is explored at medieval castle Schloss Bruck and archaeological site Aguntum. Looking up to the blushing Dolomites at sunset, it's easy to see why they were so taken with this region, which is an exclave of Tyrol.

⊙ Sights

Schloss Bruck CASTLE
(www.museum-schlossbruck.at; Schlossberg 1; adult/child €8.50/2.50; ☺ 10am-6pm Jul & Aug, to 4pm Tue-Sun Sep & Oct, to 6pm Tue-Sun Nov-Jun) Lienz' famous medieval fortress has a museum chronicling the region's history, as well as Roman artefacts, Gothic winged altars and local costumes. The **castle tower** is used for changing exhibitions; a highlight for art enthusiasts is the **Egger-Lienz-Galerie** devoted to the emotive works of Albin Egger-Lienz.

Aguntum MUSEUM, RUINS
(www.aguntum.info; Stribach 97; adult/child €7/4, combined admission with Schloss Bruck €11.50/9.50; ☺ 9.30am-4pm Jun-Sep, closed Sun May & Oct) Excavations are still under way at the Aguntum archaeological site in nearby Dölsach to piece together the jigsaw puzzle of this 2000-year-old *municipium*, which flourished as a centre of trade and commerce under Emperor Claudius. Take a stroll around the excavations, then visit the glass-walled museum to explore Lienz' Roman roots.

Stadtpfarrkirche St Andrä CHURCH
(Pfarrgasse 4; ☺ dawn-dusk) The town's main church has an attractive Gothic rib-vaulted ceiling, startling baroque altar, 14th-century frescoes and a pair of unusual tombstones sculpted in red Salzburg marble. Alongside is the solemn **Kriegergedächtniskapelle** (war memorial chapel) sheltering Albin Egger-Lienz's controversial frescoes, one depicting an emaciated Jesus post-resurrection, which in 1925 so scandalised the Vatican that religious activity was banned here for the next 60-odd years. Pick up the keys hanging on the door at Pfarrgasse 13 (across the bridge behind the Kirchenwirt restaurant).

🏃 Activities

Drau Radweg CYCLING
(www.drauradweg.com) A network of well-signposted mountain-bike trails radiates from Lienz, taking in the striking Dolomites landscape. The 366km Drau Radweg passes through Lienz en route to Maribor in Slovenia. Ask the tourist office for the free map *Rad*

CARINTHIA LIENZ

ℹ CABLE CARS & SUMMER PRICES

Cable cars to **Zettersfeld** and **Hochstein** go into hibernation from November to 8 December, and pause again after Easter. The Hochstein cable car starts running to the first station Hochstein 1 (return adult/child €10.50/7.50) from Thursday to Sunday from May to mid-June, after which all summer cable cars are back in full swing daily. Hochstein 2 is winter only. The return cost to Zettersfeld per adult/child is €11.50/6 (or €19/9.50 including the chairlift to 2214m). If you're planning on making several trips, it's worth investing in the Osttirol Card (adult/child €46/22).

und Mountainbike Karte Osttirol, which details cycling routes. **Probike Lienz** (☑04852-735 36; www.probike-lienz.at; Amlacherstrasse 1a; per day mountain bike €20, city bike €18, e-bike €28; ☺9am–noon & 2-6pm Mon-Fri, 9am–noon Sat) is the most central place to hire a bike.

La Ola   ADVENTURE SPORTS
(☑04852-611 99; www.laola.at; Mühlgasse 15) Thomas Zimmermann at La Ola organises everything from canyoning, kayaking and climbing in summer to ski touring, snowshoeing and ice-climbing in winter. Call for times and prices.

Dolomites Trails   WALKING
The tourist office (p290) sells walking (€4) and via ferrate (€1) maps, and can advise on the high-altitude trails that thread the steely peaks of the Dolomites.

Osttirol Adventures   ADVENTURE SPORTS
(☑04853-200 30, 0664 356 04 50; www.ota.at; Ainet 108b) Osttirol Adventures, with their basecamp in the small town of Ainet 8km west of Lienz, is the largest outdoor sports outfit in the region.

Bergstatt   CLIMBING
(☑0516-58 35; www.bergstatt.at; Kranewitweg 5; rock climbing trips per adult/child from €80/60) If you want to get up into the mountains, Bergstatt has guides who can lead you on half-day, full-day and multiday rock climbing, via ferrata or summit trips.

Hochstein   SKIING
(☑04242-570 47-0; www.topskipass.at; 1½-day ski pass €85, multiday passes for all East Tyrol lifts from €225) Slightly west of Lienz, Hochstein (2057m) is a ski area popular for its groomed pistes and 2.5km floodlit toboggan run; free buses link the train station to the cable-car valley stations in summer and winter high seasons.

Zettersfeld   SKIING
(www.topskipass.at; 1-day ski pass €41, multiday passes for all East Tyrol lifts from €83) Beginners and intermediates should find enough of a challenge on Lienz' 40km of pistes, which afford seductive views of the rugged Dolomites. Most of the action takes place around Zettersfeld, located slightly west of Lienz. A cable car and six lifts take skiers up to slopes reaching between 1660m and 2278m. Free buses link the Lienz train station to the cable-car valley stations.

Galitzenklamm   ADVENTURE SPORTS
(www.galitzenklamm.info; adult/child €4.50/3.50; ☺10am-5pm Jun-Sep) This vertiginous walkway clings to the sheer cliffs of a gorge that rises above the swirling waters of the Drau River. To get there, take bus 4421 to Leisach, 3km from Lienz.

🎊 Festivals & Events

Dolomiten Mann   SPORTS
(www.dolomitenmann.com; ☺mid-Sep) Lienz hosts the testosterone-fuelled Dolomiten Mann in September, a Red Bull–sponsored competition billed as the world's toughest team challenge. Headlining the program is the cross-country relay race, where teams of runners, paragliders, kayakers and mountain bikers battle it out for the title. Lively open-air concerts and parties complement the line-up.

🛏 Sleeping

Camping Falken   CAMPGROUND $
(☑0664 410 79 73; www.camping-falken.com; Eichholz 7; camp sites per adult/child/tent €7/5/11; ☺mid-Dec–mid-Oct; P 🛜) Wake up to Dolomite views at this leafy campground, a 20-minute walk south of the centre. There's a minimarket, restaurant and playground on site, and guests get free access to swimming pools in Lienz.

Goldener Stern   PENSION $
(☑04852-621 92; www.goldener-stern-lienz.at; Schweizergasse 40; s/d from €45/84; P) Framed by neat gardens, this 600-year-old pension has spacious, old-fashioned rooms. Breakfast is served in the tiny courtyard in summer.

Lienz

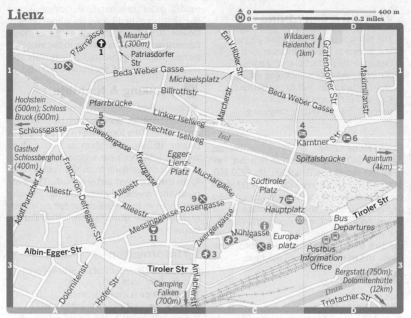

CARINTHIA LIENZ

Gasthof Schlossberghof HOTEL **$$**

(☏ 04852-632 33; schlossberghof.at; Iseltalerstrasse 21; s/d €65/100) The location of this simple, freshly renovated hotel might seem unprepossessing at first, but it's great if you're in a car (free parking and undercover parks for bikes), plus the ten-minute stroll into the centre takes you past Tyrolean 19th-century villas watched over by the Dolomites.

Wildauers Haidenhof HOTEL **$$**

(☏ 04852-624 40; www.wildauers.tirol; Grafendorferstrasse 12; s €75-90, d €145-170; P ⑤) Fringed by pear and plum orchards, Haidenhof is where rustic farmhouse meets Tyrolean chic. Rooms have plenty of natural light and stylishly done pine and there's a sauna and roof terrace with vistas of the Dolomites. Mostly everything in the restaurant (mains from €9.50 to €19.50) is home-grown. In winter there's a candle-lit basement; in summer a sunny Dolomites-facing terrace.

Goldener Fisch HOTEL **$$**

(☏ 04852-621 32; www.goldener-fisch.at; Kärntner Strasse 9; s/d €65/115; P ⑤) The chestnut-tree-shaded beer garden is a big draw at this family-friendly hotel. The rooms are light and modern – if not fancy – and you can wind down in the sauna and herbal steam baths.

Romantik Hotel Traube HOTEL **$$**

(☏ 04852-644 44; www.hoteltraube.at; Hauptplatz 14; s €75, d €145-210; P @ ⑤ ⑳) Right on the main square, Traube recalls the Biedermeier era with its high ceilings and antiquey rooms. The 10m pool and the wellness area afford lovely views over Lienz to the Dolomites.

RAFTING & CANYONING

The fast-flowing rivers, narrow gorges and forests of the Dolomites around Lienz are the perfect place for adrenalin-pumping sports, including rafting and canyoning. Expect to pay between €35 and €90 for rafting tours, and between €75 and €180 for canyoning.

Grand Hotel Lienz   HOTEL **$$$**
(☑ 04852-640 70; www.grandhotel-lienz.com; Fanny-Wibmer-Peditstrasse 2; s €105, ste €220-460; P 🛜 ❄) This faux fin-de-siècle hotel is Lienz's most upmarket choice. What it lacks in cool or historic texture, the Grand makes up for in luxury: impeccable service, a first-rate spa and pool, fine dining on a terrace overlooking the Isel River and Dolomites, nightly turn-down and in-room espresso machines.

✗ Eating

Da Leonardo   PIZZA **$**
(☑ 04852-699 44; www.daleonardo.at; Tiroler Strasse 30; pizza €7.80-15; ⊘ 11am-11pm) World champion pizza maker Leonardo Granata rests his dough for 24 to 48 hours, turning out authentic pizzas and running a 100% Italian operation with friendly, solicitous staff. Fabulous if you're missing *il bel paese*.

★ Dolomitenhütte   AUSTRIAN **$$**
(☑ 0664 225 37 82; www.dolomitenhuette.at; Amlach 39; mains €9.80-23.50) Clinging to a 1600m clifftop like an eagle's nest and watched over by jagged peaks, the Dolomitenhütte is extraordinary. With the Dolomites and larch woods as a mesmerising backdrop, it's like something out of a fairy tale. In summer, walkers and cyclists make the 12km jaunt south of Lienz for the enticing views from the terrace and the home cooking.

Kirchenwirt   AUSTRIAN **$$**
(☑ 04852-625 00; www.kirchenwirt-lienz.at; Pfarrgasse 7; mains €9.50-31; ⊘ 9am-11.30pm Sun-Thu, to 1.30am Fri & Sat) Up on a hill opposite Stadtpfarrkirche St Andrä, this atmospheric restaurant does a selection of local dishes under the vaults or on the streamside terrace.

Gösser Bräu im Alten Rathaus   AUSTRIAN **$$$**
(☑ 04852-721 74; Johannesplatz 10; mains €14-17.50; ⊘ 9am-1am Mon-Fri, to 2am Sat, 9.30am-mid-night Sun) Gather around a horseshoe-shaped bar at this vaulted brewpub, whose draught Gösser Brau beers go well with traditional favourites. In summer move to the vine-clad terrace for well-presented Italian daily specials and a menu of Austrian standards.

🍷 Drinking & Nightlife

★ Weinphilo   WINE BAR
(☑ 04852-612 53; www.weinphilo.com; Messinggasse 11; ⊘ 10am-10pm Mon-Fri, to 3pm Sat) A proper Italian wine shop and bar, where you can join locals for a glass of a beautiful small-producer wine from the Veneto, Friuli, Südtirol or even further south. There are meat and cheese platters and you can also pop in here in the morning for an expertly made coffee from Tuscany's Cafe Baratto beans.

ℹ Information

Post Office (Bozener Platz 1; ⊘ 8am-6pm Mon-Fri, 9am-noon Sat)

Tourist Office (Lienzer Dolimiten; ☑ 050 212 400; www.osttirol.com; Europaplatz 1; ⊘ 8am-6pm Mon-Fri, 9am-noon & 4-6pm Sat, 9.30-midnight Sun mid-June–end Sep, closed Sat afternoon & Sun Oct-May) Staff will help you find accommodation (even private rooms) free of charge. It also has hiking maps and brochures on all the adventure sports operators.

ℹ Getting There & Away

Regional transport in Tyrol comes under the wing of the **Verkehrsverbund Tirol** (VVT; www.vvt.at).

BUS

Buses pull up in front of the train station, where you'll find the **Postbus information office** (☑ 04852-9300 0187; Hauptbahnhof; ⊘ 8am-12.30pm & 1-2.30pm Mon-Fri). There are bus connections to regional ski resorts and northwards to the Hohe Tauern National Park. Buses to Kitzbühel (€15.80, 1¾ hours) are quicker and more direct than the train, but less frequent.

TRAIN

Most trains to the rest of Austria, including Salzburg (€37, 3½ hours, hourly), go east via Spittal-Millstättersee, where you usually have to change. The quickest and easiest route to Innsbruck (€23.50, 4½ hours) is to go west via Sillian and Italy, with a change in San Candido/Innichen and again in Fortezza/Franzensfeste.

Tyrol & Vorarlberg

Best Places to Eat

➡ Die Wilderin (p299)

➡ Schulhaus (p306)

➡ Museum Restaurant (p328)

➡ Restaurant Zur Tenne (p312)

➡ Breakfast Club (p299)

Best Places to Sleep

➡ Villa Licht (p312)

➡ Hotel Weisses Kreuz (p297)

➡ Hotel Garni Glockenstuhl (p309)

➡ Hotel Helga (p317)

➡ Gasthof Hirschen (p337)

Why Go?

There's no place like Tyrol for the 'wow, I'm in Austria' feeling. Nowhere else in the country is the downhill skiing as exhilarating, the après-ski as pumping, the wooden chalets as chocolate box, the food as hearty. Whether you're schussing down the legendary slopes of Kitzbühel, cycling the Zillertal or hiking in the Alps with a big, blue sky overhead, the scenery here makes you glad to be alive. Welcome to a place where snowboarders brag under the low beams of a medieval tavern about awesome descents; where *Dirndls* and lederhosen have street cred; and where *Volksmusik* (folk music) features on club playlists.

The Arlberg Alps give way to rolling dairy country in pleasingly low-key Vorarlberg. Spilling east to the glittering expanse of Bodensee (Lake Constance), this eastern pocket of the country swings happily between ecofriendly architecture on the cutting edge of design and deeply traditional hamlets with more cows than people.

When to Go

➡ In winter (December to early April), skiers flock to the Tyrolean Alps for snow and après-ski fun and prices soar, making advance booking essential. At Christmas, markets bring festive sparkle to towns and cities.

➡ In summer (June to September) room rates are lower in alpine resorts and this is prime time for high-altitude and hut-to-hut hikes, lake swimming and adventure sports such as rafting, paragliding and mountain biking. Zillertal rocks to summer folk music; the Bregenz Festival in mid-July lures opera fans to Bodensee.

➡ Crowds are few and room rates low in the shoulder seasons of April/May and October/November, though many places close in alpine resorts. Seasonal colour is at its best, with wildflowers in spring and foliage in autumn.

Tyrol & Vorarlberg Highlights

1 **Kitzbühel** (p311) Saving your best schuss for the slopes of Kitzbühel.

2 **Goldenes Dachl** (p294) Admiring the golden wonder of Innsbruck's late Gothic oriel.

3 **The Zillertal** (p304) Mountain biking in Tyrol's Alpine heartland.

4 **Aqua Dome** (p318) Peak-gazing and bathing at this spa in Längenfeld.

5 **St Anton am Arlberg** (p324) Partying in the rollicking après-ski bars.

6 **Hall in Tirol** (p302) Slipping back 500 years in this pristine medieval old town.

7 **Bodensee** (p333) Splashing and cycling at Europe's third-largest lake.

8 **Bregenzerwald** (p336) Enjoying pure mountain air in this off-the-radar region.

9 **Feldkirch** (p339) Tiptoeing back to medieval times in riverside Feldkirch.

10 **Bludenz** (p341) Gorging on Milka chocolate in Bludenz.

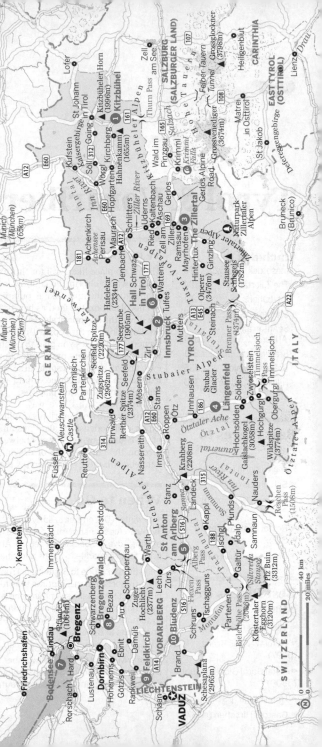

TYROL

Tyrol is as pure Alpine as Austria gets, with mountains that make you want to yodel out loud and patchwork pastures chiming with cowbells. After the first proper dump of snow in winter, it's a Christmas-card scene, with snow-frosted forests and skiers whizzing down some of the finest slopes in Europe. Summer is lower key: hiking trails thread high to peaks and mountain huts, while folk music gets steins swinging down in the valleys.

History

Despite its difficult Alpine terrain, Tyrol has been settled since the Neolithic age, verified by the discovery of a 5400-year-old body of a man preserved in ice in the Ötztal Alps in 1991. The Brenner Pass (1374m), crossing into Italy, allowed the region to develop as a north-south trade route.

Tyrol fell to the Habsburgs in 1363, but it wasn't until the rule of Emperor Maximilian I (1490–1519) that the province truly forged ahead. He boosted the region's status by transforming Innsbruck into the administrative capital and a cultural centre. In 1511 the emperor drew up the Landibell legislation, allowing Tyroleans to defend their own borders, thus creating the *Schützen* (marksmen militia), which still exists today. When the last Tyrolean Habsburg, Archduke Sigmund Franz, died in 1665 the duchy of Tyrol was directly ruled from Vienna.

In 1703 the Bavarians attempted to capture Tyrol in the War of the Spanish Succession. In alliance with the French, they reached the Brenner Pass before being beaten back by the *Schützen*. In 1805 Tyrol passed into Bavarian hands under Napoleon, a rule that was short-lived and troublesome. In 1809 South Tyrolean innkeeper Andreas Hofer led a successful fight for independence, winning a famous victory at Bergisel. The Habsburg monarchy did not support his heroic stance and Tyrol was returned to Bavaria later that year.

The Treaty of St Germain (1919) dealt a further blow to Tyrolean identity: prosperous South Tyrol was ceded to Italy and East Tyrol was isolated from the rest of the province.

A staunch ally of Mussolini, Hitler did not claim back South Tyrol when his troops invaded Austria in 1938. In the aftermath of WWII, Tyrol was divided into zones occupied by Allied forces until Austria proclaimed its neutrality in 1955. Since then Tyrol has enjoyed peace and prosperity, and tourism, particularly the ski industry, has flourished.

❶ Getting There & Away

AIR

Lying 4km west of Innsbruck's city centre, **Innsbruck Airport** (INN; ☏ 22 52 50; www.innsbruck-airport.com; Fürstenweg 180) caters to a handful of national (Vienna and Graz) and international flights (London, Amsterdam, Frankfurt, Hamburg, Palma and Antalya), handled mostly by Austrian Airlines, British Airways, easyJet, Niki and Lufthansa.

❶ Getting Around

Regional transport, covering buses, trams and ÖBB (Austrian federal railway) trains, is run by the Verkehrsverbund Tirol (www.vvt.at). Ticket prices depend on the number of zones you travel through; a single ticket costs €2, a day pass €4. Additionally, Tyrol is divided into overlapping transport zones. A regional pass covering one zone costs €10.20/35.90 per week/month.

Innsbruck

☏ 0512 / POP 124.580

Tyrol's capital is a sight to behold. The jagged rock spires of the Nordkette range are so close that within minutes it's possible to travel from the city's heart to over 2000m above sea level and alpine pastures where cowbells chime. Summer and winter activities abound, and it's understandable why some visitors only take a peek at Innsbruck proper before heading for the hills. But to do so is a shame, for Innsbruck is in many ways Austria in microcosm: its late-medieval Altstadt is picture-book stuff, presided over by a grand Habsburg palace and baroque cathedral, while its Olympic ski jump with big mountain views make a spectacular leap between the urban and the outdoors.

History

Innsbruck dates from 1180, when the little market settlement on the north bank of the Inn River spread to the south bank via an eponymous new bridge – Ynsprugg.

In 1420 Innsbruck became the ducal seat of the Tyrolean Habsburgs, but it was under the reign of Emperor Maximilian I (1490–1519) that the city reached its pinnacle in power and prestige; many of the emperor's monuments, including the shimmering

Goldenes Dachl, are still visible today. Maximilian was not the only Habsburg to influence the city's skyline: Archduke Ferdinand II reconstructed the Schloss Ambras, and Empress Maria Theresia the Hofburg.

Two world wars aside, Innsbruck has enjoyed a fairly peaceful existence over the centuries. More recently, the city held the Winter Olympics in 1964 and 1976, and the Winter Youth Olympic Games in 2012.

◎ Sights

★ Hofkirche CHURCH
(Map p298; www.tiroler-landesmuseum.at; Universitätstrasse 2; adult/child €7/free; ☉9am-5pm Mon-Sat, 12.30-5pm Sun) Innsbruck's pride and joy is the Gothic Hofkirche, one of Europe's finest royal court churches. It was commissioned in 1553 by Ferdinand I, who enlisted top artists of the age such as Albrecht Dürer, Alexander Colin and Peter Vischer the Elder. Top billing goes to the empty **sarcophagus of Emperor Maximilian I** (1459–1519), a masterpiece of German Renaissance sculpture, elaborately carved from black marble.

The tomb is embellished with Alexander Colins' white marble reliefs based on Dürer's *Ehrenpforte* (Triumphal Arch) woodcuts, depicting victorious scenes from Maximilian's life such as the Siege of Kufstein (1504). The twin rows of 28 giant bronze figures that guard the sarcophagus include Dürer's legendary King Arthur, who was apparently Emperor Maximilian's biggest idol. You're now forbidden to touch the statues, but numerous inquisitive hands have already polished parts of the dull bronze, including Kaiser Rudolf's codpiece!

Andreas Hofer (1767–1810), the Tyrolean patriot who led the rebellion against Napoleon's forces, is entombed in the church. In the **Silberkapelle**, a dazzling silver Madonna keeps watch over the marble tomb of Archduke Ferdinand II and his first wife, Philippine Welser.

★ Schloss Ambras PALACE
(www.schlossambras-innsbruck.at; Schlosstrasse 20; palace adult/child €10/free, gardens free; ☉palace 10am-5pm, gardens 6am-8pm; 🚲) Picturesquely perched on a hill and set among beautiful gardens, this Renaissance pile was acquired in 1564 by Archduke Ferdinand II, then ruler of Tyrol, who transformed it from a fortress into a palace. Don't miss the centrepiece **Spanische Saal** (Spanish Hall),

the dazzling **Armour Collection** and the gallery's Velázquez and Van Dyck originals.

The Spanische Saal is a 43m-long banquet hall with a wooden inlaid ceiling and Tyrolean nobles gazing from the walls. Also note the grisaille (grey relief) around the courtyard and the sunken bathtub where Ferdinand's beloved Philippine used to bathe.

Ferdinand instigated the magnificent Ambras Collection, encompassing three elements. Highlights of the Rüstkammer (Armour Collection) include the archduke's wedding armour – specially shaped to fit his bulging midriff! – and the 2.6m suit created for giant Bartlmä Bon. The **Kunst und Wunderkammer** (Art and Curiosity Cabinet) is crammed with fantastical objects, including a petrified shark, gravity-defying stilt shoes and the Fangstuhl – a chair designed to trap drunken guests at Ferdinand's raucous parties.

The **Portraitgalerie** features room upon room of Habsburg portraits, with paintings by Titian, Velázquez and Van Dyck. *Maria Anna of Spain* (No 126, Room 22) wins the prize for the most ludicrous hairstyle. When Habsburg portraits begin to pall, you can stroll or picnic in the extensive **gardens**, home to strutting peacocks.

Schloss Ambras is 4.5km southeast of the centre. The **Sightseer bus** (www.sightseer.at; adult/child day pass €14/9) runs every half-hour between the castle and central stops including the Hauptbahnhof and Hofburg.

★ Goldenes Dachl Museum MUSEUM
(Golden Roof Museum; Map p298; Herzog-Friedrich-Strasse 15; adult/child €4.80/2.40; ☉10am-5pm May-Sep, closed Mon Oct-Apr) Innsbruck's golden wonder and most distinctive landmark is this Gothic oriel, built for Holy Roman Emperor Maximilian I (1459–1519), lavishly festooned with murals and glittering with 2657 fire-gilt copper tiles. It is most impressive from the exterior, but the museum is worth a look – especially if you have the Innsbruck Card – with an audio guide whisking you through the history. Keep an eye out for the grotesque tournament helmets designed to resemble the Turks of the rival Ottoman Empire.

★ Hofburg PALACE
(Imperial Palace; Map p298; www.hofburg-innsbruck.at; Rennweg 1; adult/child €9/free; ☉9am-5pm) Grabbing attention with its pearly white facade and cupolas, the Hofburg was

Innsbruck

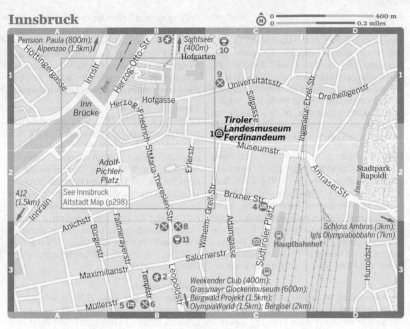

Innsbruck

Top Sights
1 Tiroler Landesmuseum
  Ferdinandeum C2

Activities, Courses & Tours
2 Inntour B3
3 Nordkettenbahnen B1

Sleeping
4 Grand Hotel Europa C2
5 Nala B3

Eating
6 Bistro Gourmand B3
7 Breakfast Club B3
8 Chez Nico B3
9 Himal C1

Drinking & Nightlife
10 Hofgarten C1
11 Theresienbräu B3

built as a castle for Archduke Sigmund the Rich in the 15th century, expanded by Emperor Maximilian I in the 16th century and given a baroque makeover by Empress Maria Theresia in the 18th century. The centrepiece of the lavish rococo state apartments is the 31m-long **Riesensaal** (Giant's Hall).

★ **Tiroler Landesmuseum Ferdinandeum** MUSEUM
(Map p295; ☎ 0512-594 89; www.tiroler-landes museum.at; Museumstrasse 15; adult/child €11/free; ◷ 9am-5pm Tue-Sun) This treasure-trove of Tyrolean history and art moves from Bronze Age artefacts to the original reliefs used to design the Goldenes Dachl. Alongside brooding Dutch masterpieces of the

Rembrandt ilk, the gallery displays an astounding collection of Austrian art including Gothic altarpieces, a handful of Klimt and Kokoschka paintings, and some shocking Viennese Actionist works.

Volkskunst Museum MUSEUM
(Folk Art Museum; Map p298; www.tiroler-landes museum.at; Universitätstrasse 2; adult/child €11/free; ◷ 9am-5pm) The Volkskunst Museum presents a fascinating romp through Tyrolean folk art from hand-carved sleighs and Christmas cribs to carnival masks and cow bells. On the 1st floor is a beautifully restored Gothic *Stube* (parlour) complete with low-ceiling, wood panelling and an antique tiled oven.

Bergisel VIEWPOINT
(www.bergisel.info; adult/child €9.50/4.50; ⊙9am-6pm Jun-Oct, 10am-5pm Nov-May) Rising above Innsbruck like a celestial staircase, this glass-and-steel ski jump was designed by much-lauded Iraqi architect Zaha Hadid. It's 455 steps or a two-minute funicular ride to the 50m-high **viewing platform**, with a breathtaking panorama of the Nordkette range, Inntal and Innsbruck. Tram 1 trundles here from central Innsbruck.

Dom St Jakob CATHEDRAL
(St James' Cathedral; Map p298; Domplatz; ⊙10.15am-6.30pm Mon-Sat, 12.30-6.30pm Sun) FREE Innsbruck's 18th-century cathedral is a feast of over-the-top baroque. The Asam brothers from Munich completed much of the sumptuous art and stucco work, though the Madonna above the high altar is by German painter Lukas Cranach the Elder. You'll have to fork out €1 for photography permission.

Alpenzoo ZOO
(www.alpenzoo.at; Weiherburggasse 37; adult/child €10/5; ⊙9am-6pm Apr-Oct, to 5pm Nov-Mar) Billing itself as a conservation-oriented zoo, this is where you can get close to alpine wildlife such as golden eagles, chamois and ibex. It's a 10-minute uphill walk from Innstrasse, or you can take Bus W from the Marktplatz or the Hungerburgbahn to the Alpenzoo stop.

Grassmayr Glockenmuseum MUSEUM
(www.grassmayr.at; Leopoldstrasse 53; adult/child €8/5; ⊙9am-5pm Mon-Fri, plus 9am-5pm Sat May-Sep) Showcases the Grassmayr family's 400 years of bell-making tradition. In addition to exhibits including some formidable Romanesque and Gothic bells, you can watch the casting process and have a go at ringing the bells to achieve different notes.

Stadtturm TOWER
(Map p298; Herzog-Friedrich-Strasse 21; adult/child €3.50/1.50; ⊙10am-8pm Jun-Sep, 10am-5pm Oct-May) Guards once kept watch over the city from this onion-domed tower, which was completed in 1450. Puff up 148 steps for 360-degree views of Innsbruck's rooftops, spires and the surrounding mountains.

🏃 Activities

Nordkettenbahnen FUNICULAR
(Map p295; www.nordkette.com; 1 way/return to Hungerburg €4.80/8, to Seegrube €17.30/28.80, to Hafelekar €19.20/32; ⊙Hungerburg 7am-7.15pm Mon-Fri, 8am-7.15pm Sat & Sun, Seegrube 8.30am-5.30pm daily, Hafelekar 9am-5pm daily) Zaha Ha-

did's space-age funicular runs every 15 minutes, whizzing you from the Congress Centre to the slopes in no time. Walking trails head off in all directions from **Hungerburg** and **Seegrube**. For more of a challenge, there is a downhill track for mountain bikers and two fixed-rope routes (*Klettersteige*) for climbers.

Olympiabobbahn ADVENTURE SPORTS
(☎0512-338 382 22; www.olympiaworld.at; Heilwasserweg, Igls; summer/winter €25/30; ⊙5-8pm daily Dec-Mar, 4-6pm Wed-Fri Jul & Aug) For a minute in the life of an Olympic bobsleigh racer, you can't beat the Olympiabobbahn, built for the 1976 Winter Olympics. Zipping around 10 curves and picking up speeds of up to 100km/h, the bob run is 800m of pure hair-raising action. You can join a professional bobsled driver in winter or summer; call ahead for the exact times. To reach it, take Bus J from the Landesmuseum to Igls Olympiaexpress.

OlympiaWorld SKIING
(3-/6-day ski pass €132/222) Innsbruck is the gateway to a formidable ski arena, the Olympia SkiWorld Innsbruck, covering nine surrounding resorts and 300km of slopes to test all abilities. The OlympiaWorld Ski Pass covers all areas; ski buses are free to anyone with an Innsbruck Card.

Inntour ADVENTURE SPORTS
(Map p295; www.inntour.com; Leopoldstrasse 4; ⊙9am-6pm Mon-Sat) Based at Die Börse, Inntour arranges all manner of thrillseeking pursuits, including canyoning (€80), tandem paragliding (€105), whitewater rafting (€45) and bungee jumping from the 192m Europabrücke (€140).

Nordpark SKIING
The most central place to pound powder is the Nordpark. Snowboarders are in their element at the Nitro Skylinepark, with its quarter-pipe, kickers and boxes, while daring skiers ride the **Hafelekar-Rinne**, one of Europe's steepest runs with a 70% gradient.

Nitro Skylinepark SNOW SPORTS
(www.skylinepark.at; ⊙9am-4pm) Boarders can pick up speed on the quarter-pipe, kickers and boxes at Nitro Skylinepark.

Nordkette Singletrail MOUNTAIN BIKING
(http://nordkette-singletrail.at; ⊙late May-early Nov) A magnet to hardcore downhill mountain bikers, this *very* steep, technically demanding track begins 200m below Seegrube. It's free to transport your bike on the cable

car but make sure the bike is clean. There is a special half-/one-day ticket costing €21/28 in case you want to ride it more than once.

Innsbrucker Klettersteig VIA FERRATA
(www.nordkette.com; adult/child incl cable car €29.30/16.10; ⊙ Jun-Sep) Hafelekar cable-car top station (2256m) is the starting point for Innsbruck's head-spinning, seven-hour via ferrata (fixed-rope route). The trail is not for the fainthearted – it traverses seven peaks and affords tremendous views of the Stubaier, Zillertaler and Ötztaler Alps. You can rent equipment at the sports shop at Seegrube.

✻✦ Festivals & Events

Christkindlmarkt CHRISTMAS MARKET
(www.christkindlmarkt.cc; ⊙ mid-Nov–6 Jan; 🖈) Innsbruck twinkles festively at Christmas markets in the Altstadt, Marktplatz and Maria-Theresien-Strasse from mid-November to Epiphany. Kids love the fairy-tale-themed Kiebachgasse and Köhleplatzl.

Vierschanzentournee SKIING
(Four Hills Tournament; http://vierschanzentournee.com; ⊙ Dec–Jan) Innsbruck sees in the New Year by hosting one of four World Cup ski-jumping events at Bergisel.

Promenadenkonzerte MUSIC
(www.promenadenkonzerte.at; ⊙ Jul) Every July Innsbruck hosts a series of free classical concerts set against the sublime backdrop of the Hofburg's inner courtyard. The full line-up is available online.

Festwochen der Alten Musik MUSIC
(Festival of Early Music; www.altemusik.at; ⊙ Aug) This festival brings baroque concerts to venues such as Schloss Ambras, the Landestheater, Goldenes Dachl and Hofburg.

Tanzsommer DANCE
(www.tanzsommer.at; ⊙ late Jun–mid-Jul) From classical ballet to gravity-defying acrobatics, dance takes the stage by storm at this festival.

🛏 Sleeping

Nepomuk's HOSTEL $
(Map p298; ☑ 0512-584 118; www.nepomuks.at; Kiebachgasse 16; dm/d from €24/58; 🛜) Could this be backpacker heaven? Nepomuk's sure comes close, with its Altstadt location, well-stocked kitchen and high-ceilinged dorms with homely touches like CD players. The delicious breakfast in attached Cafe Munding, with homemade pastries, jam and fresh-roasted coffee, gets your day off to a grand start.

Pension Paula GUESTHOUSE $
(☑ 0512-292 262; www.pensionpaula.at; Weiherburggasse 15; s €36-48, d €62-72; 🅿) This pension occupies an alpine chalet and has super-clean, homely rooms (most with balcony). It's up the hill towards the zoo and has great vistas across the city.

★ Hotel Weisses Kreuz HISTORIC HOTEL $$
(Map p298; ☑ 0512-594 79; www.weisseskreuz.at; Herzog-Friedrich-Strasse 31; s/d from €77/119, with shared bathroom from €41/75; 🅿 @ 🛜) Beneath the arcades, this atmospheric Altstadt hotel has played host to guests for 500 years, including a 13-year-old Mozart. With its wood-panelled parlours, antiques and twisting staircase, the hotel oozes history with every creaking beam. Rooms are supremely comfortable, staff charming and breakfast is a lavish spread.

Goldener Adler HISTORIC HOTEL $$
(Map p298; ☑ 0512-571 111; www.goldeneradler.com; Herzog-Friedrich-Strasse 6; s €147, d €167-220; 🅿 ✳ 🛜) Since opening in 1390, the grand Goldener Adler has welcomed kings, queens and Salzburg's two biggest exports: Mozart and Mrs Von Trapp. Rooms are elegant with gold drapes and squeaky-clean marble bathrooms. Downstairs there is a cracking traditional restaurant tucked under the arcades and spilling out on the cobbles.

Mondschein HOTEL $$
(Map p298; ☑ 0512-227 84; www.mondschein.at; Mariahilfstrasse 6; s €87-110, d €122-188; 🅿 ✳ @ 🛜) The moon beams down as you enter this riverside hotel, harboured in a 15th-century fisherman's house. Rooms painted in blues and sunny yellows give way to Swarovski crystal-studded bathrooms glittering like a night sky.

Weisses Rössl GUESTHOUSE $$
(Map p298; ☑ 0512-583 057; www.roessl.at; Kiebachgasse 8; s €70-110, d €100-160; @ 🛜) An antique rocking horse greets you at this 16th-century guesthouse. The vaulted entrance leads up to spacious rooms, recently revamped with blonde wood, fresh hues and crisp white linen. The owner is a keen hunter and the restaurant (mains €13 to €28) has a meaty menu.

Weinhaus Happ GUESTHOUSE $$
(Map p298; ☑ 0512-582 980; www.weinhaus-happ.at; Herzog-Friedrich-Strasse 14; s/d €75/110) Happ exudes old-world atmosphere. The rooms haven't been decorated in donkeys'

Innsbruck Altstadt

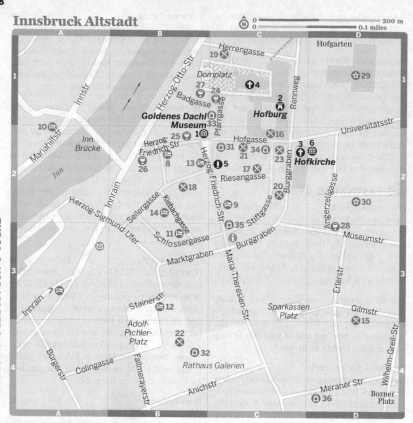

years, but its plus points are many: prime views of the Goldenes Dachl, a cavernous wine cellar and a wood-panelled restaurant dishing up gutsy mains (€9 to €17).

Basic Hotel
HOTEL $$

(Map p298; ☎0512-586 385; www.basic-hotel.at; Innrain 16; s €70-100, d €100-130; ☜) For central, simple digs bang in the heart of town, Basic Hotel takes some beating. It goes for a streamlined, ultramodern look in its bright, open-plan rooms and bistro, and has 24-hour self check-in. Breakfast is served at the in-house Stefan's bakery.

Grand Hotel Europa
LUXURY HOTEL $$$

(Map p295; ☎0512-59 31; www.grandhoteleuropa. at; Südtiroler Platz 2; s €114-154, d €129-219; ⓟ❋@☜) This luxurious pile opposite the station has been given a facelift. Pared-down chic now defines the rooms, though old-world grandeur lingers in the opulent Baroque Hall and wood-panelled restaurant.

Mick Jagger and Queen Elizabeth II are famous past guests.

Penz Hotel
HOTEL $$$

(Map p298; ☎0512-575 657; www.the-penz.com; Adolf-Pichler-Platz 3; s €145-265, d €185-295; ⓟ❋☜) Behind a sheer wall of glass, the Penz is a contemporary design hotel next to the Rathaus Galerien. The minimalist rooms in muted hues are spruced up with flat-screen TVs and shiny chrome fittings. At breakfast, a whole table is piled high with exotic fruits.

Nala
DESIGN HOTEL $$$

(Map p295; ☎0512-584 444; www.nala-hotel.at; Müllerstrasse 15; d €98-150, ste €200) Individualism trumps conformity at this slick design newcomer. Some of the rooms are on the small side of bijou, but they all reveal a razor-sharp eye for detail, with wood floors, Nespresso makers, mosaics and themes from 'Oriental' (with its ornamental tiles) to

Innsbruck Altstadt

naturalistic flourishes in 'Nightingale'. The roomier apartments and suites have terraces or balconies with uplifting mountain views.

✖ Eating

★ Breakfast Club
BREAKFAST $

(Map p295; www.breakfast-club.at; Maria-Theresien-Strasse 49; breakfast €5-13; ☉7.30am-4pm; 🐾🍴) Hip, wholesome and nicely chilled, the Breakfast Club does what it says on the tin: all-day breakfast and brunch. And boy are you in for a treat: free-range eggs, Tyrolean mountain cheese, organic breads, homemade spreads, cinnamon-dusted waffles with cranberries and cream, French toast, Greek omelette – take your pick. It also does fresh-pressed juices and proper Italian coffee.

Himal
ASIAN $

(Map p295; 🖉0512-588 588; Universitätsstrasse 13; mains €9.50-14.50; ☉11.30am-2.30pm & 6-10.30pm Mon-Sat, 6-10pm Sun; 🍴) Friendly and intimate, Himal delivers vibrant, robust Nepalese flavours. Spot-on curries (some vegetarian) are mopped up with naan and washed down with mango lassis. The two-course €8.10 lunch is cracking value.

Cafe Katzung
CAFE $

(Map p298; www.cafe-katzung.at; Herzog-Friedrich-Strasse 16; snacks €5-8; ☉8am-midnight Mon-Sat, from 9am Sun) Katzung attracts a faithful local following for its laid-back vibe, Goldenes Dachl–facing terrace and homemade cakes and ice cream. Menu favourites include all-day breakfasts, toasted sandwiches and wholesome soups.

Cafe Munding
CAFE $

(Map p298; www.munding.at; Kiebachgasse 16; cake €2-4; ☉8am-8pm) This 200-year-old cafe serves delicious cakes – try moist chocolate raspberry *Haustorte* or chocolate-marzipan *Mozarttorte* – and freshly roasted coffee.

★ Die Wilderin
AUSTRIAN $$

(Map p298; 🖉0512-562 728; www.diewilderin.at; Seilergasse 5; mains €9.50-20; ☉5pm-2am Tue-Sat, to midnight Sun) 🌱 Take a gastronomic walk on the wild side at this modern-day hunter-gatherer of a restaurant, where chefs take pride in local sourcing and using top-notch farm-fresh and foraged ingredients. The menu sings of the seasons, be it asparagus, game, strawberries or winter veg. The vibe is urbane and relaxed.

Chez Nico
VEGETARIAN $$

(Map p295; 🖉0650 4510624; www.chez-nico.at; Maria-Theresien-Strasse 49; 2-course lunch €14.50, 7-course menu €60; ☉6.30-10pm Mon & Sat, noon-2pm & 6.30-10pm Tue-Fri; 🍴) Take a petit bistro and a Parisian chef with a passion for herbs, *et voilà*, you get Chez Nico. Nicolas Curtil (Nico) cooks seasonal, all-vegetarian delights along the lines of tomato and argan oil consommé and watermelon and chanterelle carpaccio with pine nuts and parmesan. You won't miss the meat, we swear.

Dengg   INTERNATIONAL $$
(Map p298; ☑ 0512-582 347; www.dengg.co.at; Riesengasse 11; mains €13-23; ☺ 8.30am-midnight Mon-Sat) A cool curiosity shop of a bistro, with a minimalist, snow-white interior that contrasts strikingly with the old-fashioned kitchen appliances plastered to its walls, Dengg feels like a secret despite its Altstadt location. The chef rustles up regional-meets-Med taste sensations such as pike perch with red port sauce and fennel puree, and summer tiramisu with espresso sorbet.

Cafe Sacher   CAFE $$
(Map p298; www.sacher.com; Rennweg 1; mains €15.50-21.50; ☺ 8.30am-midnight) Sidling up to the Hofburg, this grand chandelier-lit cafe is the place to linger over chocolate *Sacher Torte*, salads or lunch. There are free classical concerts in the courtyard in summer. A mini torte (€14.90) to take home makes a great gift.

Fischerhäusl   AUSTRIAN $$
(Map p298; ☑ 0512-583 535; www.fischerhaeusl. com; Herrengasse 8; mains €9-23; ☺ 10am-1am Mon-Sat, 5pm-midnight Sun) The lemon-fronted Fischerhäusl has stood in this hidden spot between Domplatz and the Hofburg since 1758. On the menu is Tyrolean grub such as *Kaspressknödelsuppe*, cheesy dumplings swimming in broth, and *Gröstl*, a potato, bacon and onion fry-up. The terrace fills quickly on warm days.

Cafe Central   CAFE $$
(Map p298; www.central.co.at; Gilmstrasse 5; mains €8-16; ☺ 7am-10pm; ☑) Little has changed since this old-world, Viennese-style cafe opened in 1877. Come to lunch on schnitzel or goulash or to browse the daily papers over a slice of torte. There's live piano music on Sunday evenings in winter.

Stiftskeller   AUSTRIAN $$
(Map p298; www.stiftskeller.eu; Hofgasse 6; mains €10-20.50; ☺ 10am-midnight) A vaulted restaurant with a large beer garden for Augustiner Bräu beers and hearty fare such as pork roast with lashings of beer sauce, dumplings and sauerkraut.

Il Convento   ITALIAN $$
(Map p298; ☑ 0512-581 354; www.ilconvento.at; Burggraben 29; mains €13.50-25, 2-course lunch €17.50-18.50; ☺ 11am-3pm & 5pm-midnight Mon-Sat) Neatly tucked into the old city walls, this Italian newcomer is run with passion by Peppino and Angelika. It's a winner, with its refined look (white tablecloths, wood beams, Franciscan monastery views from the terrace) and menu. Dishes such as clam linguine, braised veal and salt-crusted cod are cooked to a T and served with wines drawn from the well-stocked cellar.

Lichtblick   INTERNATIONAL $$$
(Map p298; ☑ 0512-566 550; www.restaurant-licht blick.at; Maria-Theresien-Strasse 18, Rathaus Galerien; lunch €9.90-13, set menus €40-50; ☺ 10am-1am Mon-Sat) On the 7th floor of the Rathaus Galerien, this chic glass-walled restaurant has sweeping views over Innsbruck to the Alps beyond. Backlighting and minimalist design create a sleek backdrop for Mediterranean-inspired cuisine such as crayfish gazpacho and herby polenta with chanterelles, rocket and parmesan.

Bistro Gourmand   FRENCH $$$
(Map p295; ☑ 0512-580 356; www.bistro-gourmand.at; Templstrasse 4; mains €16-32.50; ☺ 6-10pm Tue-Sat, plus 11am-2.30pm Fri) Chef Thierry Aragona brings a dash of the French Mediterranean to Innsbruck at the aptly named Bistro Gourmand. Lemon walls and dark wood panelling set the scene for brilliantly cooked dishes such as Burgundy snails with hazelnut-garlic butter, sea bass bouillabaisse and Angus beef slow-cooked in onions and wine until meltingly tender.

🍷 Drinking & Nightlife

Tribaun   CRAFT BEER
(Map p298; www.tribaun.com; Museumstrasse 5; ☺ 6pm-2am Mon-Sat) This cracking new bar taps into craft-beer culture, with a wide variety of brews – from stouts and porters to IPA, sour, amber, honey and red ales. The easygoing vibe and fun-loving crew add to its appeal. For more insight, hook onto a 90-minute, seven-beer tasting (€19).

360°   BAR
(Map p298; Rathaus Galerien; ☺ 10am-1am Mon-Sat) Grab a cushion and drink in 360-degree views of the city and Alps from the balcony that skirts this spherical, glass-walled bar. It's a nicely chilled spot for a coffee or sundowner.

Moustache
BAR

(Map p298; www.cafe-moustache.at; Herzog-Otto-Strasse 8; ⊙11am-2am Tue-Sun; 🛜) Playing Spot-the-Moustache (Einstein, Charlie Chaplin and co) is the preferred pastime at this retro bolthole, with table football and a terrace overlooking pretty Domplatz. They knock up a mean pisco sour.

In Vinum
WINE BAR

(Map p298; www.invinum.com; Innrain 1; ⊙11am-midnight Mon-Sat, 4-9pm Sun) This snug Altstadt wine bar is a relaxed choice to sample Austria's finest wines, which start at €2.80 a glass; see the website for details of the regular tastings. If you get peckish, you can snack on local cheese and ham.

Elferhaus
PUB

(Map p298; Herzog-Friedrich-Strasse 11; ⊙10am-2am) Eleven is the magic number at Elferhaus, where you can nurse a beer beside Gothic gargoyles at the bar or take a church-like pew to hear live rock bands play. The haunt attracts an upbeat crowd that spills out onto Herzog-Friedrich-Strasse.

Theresienbräu
PUB

(Map p295; Maria-Theresien-Strasse 53; ⊙10am-1am Mon-Wed, to 2am Thu-Sat, noon-9pm Sun) Copper vats gleam and rock plays at this lively microbrewery, which opens onto a garden seating 120 beer guzzlers and pretzel munchers. The ceiling is studded with 10,000 dried roses.

Hofgarten
BAR

(Map p295; www.tagnacht.at; Rennweg 6a; ⊙6pm-4am Tue-Sat) DJ sessions and a tree-shaded beer garden are crowd-pullers at this trendy cafe-cum-bar set in the greenery of Hofgarten.

Weekender Club
CLUB

(www.weekenderclub.net; Tschamlerstrasse 3; ⊙9pm-3am Mon, 10pm-3am Fri & Sat) Happening warehouse club, with top DJs and gigs. It's a 10-minute walk south of Maria-Theresien-Strasse along Leopoldstrasse.

Dom Cafe-Bar
BAR

(Map p298; www.domcafe.at; Pfarrgasse 3; ⊙11am-1am Mon-Sat, 3pm-1am Sun May-Oct, 5pm-1am daily Nov-Apr) Chandeliers, vaulted ceilings and an HMV gramophone set the scene in this convivial Gothic-style bar.

☆ Entertainment

For entertainment options, pick up a copy of *Innsider*, found in cafes across town, or

---

visit www.innsider.at. Schloss Ambras hosts a series of classical concerts in summer.

OlympiaWorld
CONCERT VENUE

(www.olympiaworld.at; Olympiastrasse 10) This cutting-edge venue hosts big-name concerts, musicals and sports events from football to ice-hockey matches. Take Bus J from the Landestheater to Landessportcenter.

Treibhaus
ARTS CENTRE

(Map p298; www.treibhaus.at; Angerzellgasse 8; ⊙10am-1am) This cultural complex draws a boho crowd with its big terrace, regular DJs and live music. In August, it hosts an open-air cinema.

Tiroler Landestheater
THEATRE

(Map p298; 🗗 0512-520 744; www.landestheater.at; Rennweg 2; ⊙ticket office 10am-7pm Mon-Fri, to 6.30pm Sat) Innsbruck's imposing neoclassical theatre stages year-round performances of opera, dance, drama and comedy. Tickets cost between €4 and €70.

🔒 Shopping

Acqua Alpes
PERFUME

(Map p298; Hofgasse 2; ⊙10am-6pm) If you've ever wished to bottle the pure, fresh scent of the Alps, someone has already done it – fragrances inspired by those meadows, crisp air and wildflowers are sold at this vaulted, blue-and-white perfumery. Each of the four perfumes corresponds to the elevation of one of the peaks close by.

Swarovski Crystal Gallery   GIFTS & SOUVENIRS
(Map p298; Herzog-Friedrich-Strasse 39; ⊙8am-7.30pm) Swarovski's flagship store in Innsbruck is this gallery-style boutique, crammed with sparkling crystal trinkets, ornaments and jewellery.

Tiroler Heimatwerk   ARTS & CRAFTS
(Map p298; Meraner Strasse 2; ⊙9am-6pm Mon-Fri, to noon Sat) Great for traditional gifts, this place sells everything from *Dirndls* to hand-carved nativity figurines, stained glass and Tyrolean puppets.

Spezialitäten aus der Stiftsgasse   FOOD
(Map p298; Stiftsgasse 2; ⊙9.30am-6.30pm Mon-Sat) An Aladdin's cave of homemade goodies, this vine-clad shop stocks all-Austrian honeys, oils, preserves, wines and spirits from gentian liqueur to hay schnapps.

s'Culinarium   FOOD & DRINKS
(Map p298; http://culinarium-signor.at; Pfarrgasse 1; ⊙11am-7pm Mon-Wed, to 11pm Thu-Sat) The charming Herby Signor will help you pick an excellent bottle of Austrian wine at his shop-cum-bar. s'Culinarium also stocks other Tyrolean specialities from honey to schnapps.

Rathaus Galerien   MALL
(Map p298; www.rathausgalerien.at; Maria-Theresien-Strasse 18; ⊙8.30am-7pm Mon-Fri, to 6pm Sat; 🛜) High-street shops, boutiques and cafes line this swank glass-roofed mall, where you can break up shopping with a drink at 360° (p300).

ⓘ Information

Bergwald Projekt (☑0512-595 47 47; www.bergwaldprojekt.at; Olympiastrasse 37) Excellent volunteer work programs protecting and maintaining mountain forests in Austria, Germany and Switzerland. Generally, the Austrian programs last one week.

Innsbruck Information (Map p298; ☑0512-59 850, 0512-53 56-0; www.innsbruck.info; Burggraben 3; ⊙9am-6pm) Main tourist office with truckloads of info on the city and surrounds, including skiing and walking.

Landeskrankenhaus (☑50 40; Anichstrasse 35) The *Universitätklinik* (University Clinic) at the city's main hospital has emergency services.

Main Post Office (Map p298; Innrain 15; ⊙8am-6.30pm Mon-Fri, 9am-1pm Sat) Innsbruck's central main post office.

Post Office (Map p295; Südtiroler Platz 10; ⊙8am-6pm Mon-Fri) Handy to the Hauptbahnhof.

ⓘ Getting There & Away

BUS
The **bus station** (Map p295) is at the southern end of the Hauptbahnhof; its ticket office is located within the station.

TRAIN
Fast trains depart daily every two hours for Bregenz (€37.50, 2¾ hours) and Salzburg (€45.50, two hours). From Innsbruck to the Arlberg, the best views are on the right-hand side of the train. Two-hourly express trains serve Munich (€41.20, 1¾ hours) and Verona (€40.20, 3½ hours). Direct services to Kitzbühel also run every two hours (€15.80, 1¼ hours). There are roughly hourly connections to Lienz (€23.50, three to five hours); some pass through Italy while others take the long way round via Salzburgerland.

ⓘ Getting Around

PUBLIC TRANSPORT
Single tickets on buses and trams cost €2 from the driver, €1.80 if purchased in advance. If you plan to use the city's public transport frequently you're better off buying a 24-hour ticket (€4.40). Weekly and monthly tickets are also available (€13.90 and €45.20, respectively). Tickets bought in advance, which are available from ticket machines, *Tabak* (tobacconist) shops and Innsbruck Information, must be stamped in the machines at the start of the journey.

Hall in Tirol

📞 05223 / POP 13,590

Nestled beneath the Alps, just 9km east of Innsbruck, Hall is a beautiful medieval town that grew fat on the riches of salt in the 13th century. The winding lanes, punctuated by pastel-coloured town houses and lantern-lit after dark, are made for aimless ambling.

⊙ Sights

Burg Hasegg   CASTLE
(www.muenz-hall.at; Burg Hasegg 6; tower adult/child €5.50/4.50, mint €8/5.50, combined ticket €11.50/8; ⊙10am-5pm Tue-Sun; 🅿) Stepping south of the medieval centre is the Burg Hasegg, where a spiral staircase coils up to the 5th floor for far-reaching views over Hall. The castle had a 300-year career as a mint for silver *Thalers* (coins, the root of the modern word 'dollar'), and this history is unravelled in the **Münze Hall**, displaying

water-driven and hammer-striking techniques. Audio guides are included in the price and kids can mint their own coin.

Pfarrkirche St Nikolaus
CHURCH

(St Nicholas Parish Church; ⊘ dawn-dusk) This graceful 13th-century church is best known for its **Waldaufkapelle**, home to Florian Waldauf's grisly collection of 45 skulls and 12 bones, picked from the remains of minor saints. Each rests on embroidered cushions, capped with veils and elaborate headdresses, reminiscent of spiked haloes; the whole effect is both repulsive and enthralling.

✯ Festivals & Events

Haller Weinherbst
FOOD & DRINK

(⊘ early Sep) If you're in town for the Weinherbst festival on the first weekend in September, watch as the water in the Wilden Mannes fountain miraculously turns to wine.

🛏 Sleeping & Eating

Gasthof Badl
GUESTHOUSE $

(📞 05223-567 84; www.badl.at; Innbrücke 4; s €59-69, d €84-150; 🅿 🛜) A short dash across the Inn River, this gem of a guesthouse has immaculate rooms (most with river view) and a tavern that knocks up a great strudel. Children will love the playground and docile St Bernard, Max. Rent a bike here to pedal along the banks to Innsbruck.

Parkhotel
HOTEL $$

(📞 05223-537 69; www.parkhotel-hall.com; Thunfeldgasse 1; s €105-115, d €172-198; 🅿 🛜) It's a surprise to find such avant-garde design as this cylindrical hotel in tiny Hall. The mountains seem close enough to touch in the curvy glass-walled rooms, done out in minimalist style and earthy hues. Over-complicated lighting systems and curtains can be fiddly.

Goldener Löwe
AUSTRIAN $$

(📞 05223-415 50; www.goldenerloewe-hall.at; Obere Stadtplatz; mains €8-20; ⊘ 11am-2.30pm & 5.30pm-midnight Tue-Sat) The ambience is wonderfully cosy in this historic tavern on the main square. Join locals in a warren of dark wood-panelled rooms for Austrian comfort food such as *Tafelspitz* (boiled beef with horseradish) and sweet dumplings, paired with local wines.

Rathaus Cafe
CAFE $$

(Oberer Stadtplatz 2; snacks €3-6.50; ⊘ 8am-1am Mon-Thu, to 2am Fri & Sat, 9am-midnight Sun) Part of Hall's vaulted town hall has been transformed into this modern cafe. There's a terrace for people-watching over breakfast, a baguette or a drink.

ℹ Information

Tourist Office (📞 05223-455 44; www.region hall.at; Wallpachgasse 5; ⊘ 8.30am-6pm Mon-Fri, 9am-1pm Sat) Staff can point you in the direction of the town's attractions. They also organise guided tours.

ℹ Getting There & Away

The B171 goes almost through the town centre, unlike the A12/E45, which is over the Inn River to the south. The train station is about 1km southwest of the centre; it is on the main Innsbruck–Wörgl train line. Trains run frequently to/from Innsbruck (€3.60, eight minutes).

Wattens

📞 05224 / POP 7660

The quaint village of Wattens has but one claim to fame: it's the glittering heart of the Swarovski crystal empire. Call them kitsch or classy, but there is no doubting the pulling power of these crystals at the fantastical **Swarovski Kristallwelten** (Swarovski Crystal Worlds; http://kristallwelten.swarovski.com; Kristallweltenstrasse 1; adult/child €19/7.50; ⊘ 9am-7.30pm), one of Austria's most-visited attractions. A giant's head spewing water into a pond greets you in the park, where you will also find the attention-grabbing Crystal Cloud, embellished with 800,000 crystals and drifting above a mirrorlike pool and a crystalline-themed playground, tower and labyrinth for kids. Redesigned and expanded in 2015, other standouts are displayed in the five new Chambers of Wonder.

Trains run roughly half-hourly from Innsbruck to Fritzens-Wattens (€4.50, 16 minutes), 3km north of Swarovski Kristallwelten and on the opposite side of the river.

Schwaz

📞 05242 / POP 13,190

What is today a sleepy little town with pastel-washed houses and winding streets was once, believe it or not, Austria's second-largest city after Vienna. Schwaz wielded clout in the Middle Ages when its eyes shone brightly with silver, past glory that you can relive by going underground to the show silver mine.

◉ Sights

★ Silberbergwerk Schwaz
MINE

(Silver Mine; www.silberbergwerk.at; Alte Landstrasse 3a; adult/child/family €17/10/40; ⊙ 9am-5pm) You almost feel like breaking out into a rendition of 'Heigh-Ho' at Silberbergwerk Schwaz, as you board a mini train and venture deep into the bowels of the silver mine for a 90-minute trundle through Schwaz' illustrious past. The mine is about 1.5km east of the centre.

Altstadt
HISTORIC SITE

Schwaz hides a remarkably well-preserved Altstadt, built high on the riches of medieval silver. Taking pride of place on pedestrianised Franz-Josef-Strasse, the Gothic **Pfarrkirche** immediately catches your eye with its step-gabled roof bearing 14,000 copper tiles. Not far south is the Gothic-meets-baroque **Franziskanerkirche** (Gilmstrasse; ⊙ dawn-dusk).

Pfarrkirche
CHURCH

(Parish Church; ⊙ dawn-dusk) At the Gothic Pfarrkirche, your eye is immediately drawn to its steep roof bearing 14,000 copper tiles. The web-vaulted interior purportedly harbours the largest symphonic organ in Tyrol, which is put to good use at the summer organ festival at 8pm on Mondays in July and August.

Museum der Völker
MUSEUM

(www.hausdervoelker.com; St Martin; adult/child €9.50/5; ⊙ 10am-5pm Tue-Sun) Local photographer Gert Chesi set up this museum, showcasing a rich collection of African and Asian ritual art. Rotating exhibitions home in on elements of the collection, such as spiritual Tanzania or African textile art.

🍴 Sleeping & Eating

Gasthof Einhorn Schaller
GUESTHOUSE $

(☎ 05242-740 47; www.gasthof-schaller.at; Innsbruckerstrasse 31; s €50-60, d €82-112; ℗ 🐶 🛜) This super-central, family-friendly *Gasthof* (inn) combines modern rooms, done out in light pinewood and splashes of bright colour, with a traditional restaurant dishing up regional fare (mains €11 to €20) such as *Tiroler Käsespätzle*, eggy noodles topped with cheese and onions.

Villa Masianco
INTERNATIONAL $$

(☎ 05242-629 27; Münchner Strasse 20; lunch €5.50-6.50, pizza €6-10, mains €11-22; ⊙ 10am-midnight Mon-Fri, 11am-midnight Sat, to 11pm Sun; 🖘) A restaurant with pizza, pasta, steaks, Tex-Mex, Thai curry and Austrian classics on the same menu might cause foodies to raise a skeptical eyebrow. Yet this ambitious culinary globetrotter manages to consistently deliver quality, which has won it a faithful local following. The vibe is relaxed in the contemporary brasserie, with terrace seating in summer and a children's play area.

ℹ Information

The helpful **tourist office** (☎ 05242-632 40; www.silberregionkarwendel.at; Münchnerstrasse 11; ⊙ 9am-5.30pm Mon-Fri, 9am-noon Sat) provides information on sights and accommodation in Schwaz.

ℹ Getting There & Away

Schwaz is 30km east of Innsbruck and 10km west of the Zillertal on the A12 Inntal-Autobahn. There are frequent trains between Innsbruck and Schwaz (€6.40, 26 minutes).

The Zillertal

Sandwiched between the Tuxer Voralpen and the Kitzbüheler Alpen, the Zillertal (Ziller Valley) is storybook Tyrol. A steam train chugs through the broad valley, passing fertile farmland and wooded mountains, and affording snatched glimpses of snowy peaks and the fast-flowing Ziller River.

 Activities

🏃 Alpine Skiing

While Mayrhofen is the prime spot for serious skiing, there is plenty of downhill and cross-country skiing elsewhere. The Zillertaler Superskipass (two/four/six days €99.50/174/242) covers all 508km of slopes in the valley, including the snow-sure pistes at the Hintertuxer Glacier. Ski buses connect the resorts.

🏃 Summer Activities

In summer, the alpine valley morphs into excellent walking territory, with high-altitude trekking in the Tuxer Voralpen and myriad trails fanning out from the resorts of Ried, Kaltenbach, Aschau, Zell am Ziller and Ramsau. Mountain huts at elevations of around 1800m beckon weary hikers; visit www.alpenverein.at for details of huts in the valley. A detailed walking map covering the entire region is the Kompass *Zillertaler Alpen-Tuxer Alpen* (scale 1:50,000).

✈ Cycling in the Zillertal

The Zillertal is cycling nirvana, particularly for serious mountain bikers, many of whom limber up here before taking part in the gruelling three-day **Zillertal Bike Challenge** (www.zillertal-bikechallenge.com; ☉ late Jun/early Jul) in late June/early July. The wide, sunny valley and surrounding 3000m peaks are laced with 800km of well-marked routes that reach from easygoing two-hour jaunts along the valley floor to panoramic mountain passes, such as the notoriously tough 56km trail from Fügen to Kellerjoch, a test of stamina and condition.

You can access many of the high-altitude and downhill routes using the cable cars in the valley, and local trains will transport your bike for free. Bikes are available for hire at major stations throughout the Zillertal, including Zell am Ziller and Mayrhofen, for €9/13.50 per half-/full day; e-bikes cost €15/22 respectively. For free maps, detailed route descriptions and downloadable GPS bike tours, visit www.zillertal.at or www.best-of-zillertal.at.

✯ Festivals & Events

Almabtriebe   HERITAGE

(☉ late Sep-early Oct) The Zillertaler celebrate the coming home of the cows, which are adorned with elaborate floral headdresses and bells. The event is a valley-wide party with feasting, *Volksmusik* (folk music) and schnapps before another harsh winter.

ℹ Information

Practically every resort has its own tourist office, but the main **tourist office** (☏ 05288-871 87; www.zillertal.at; Bundesstrasse 27d, Schlitters; ☉ 8.30am-noon & 1-5.30pm Mon-Thu, 8.30am-noon Fri) covering the whole valley is in Schlitters, 6km from Jenbach. It stocks plenty of information on outdoor activities, along with the *Zillertaler Gästezeitung* (partially in English) magazine.

ℹ Getting There & Away

The Zillertal is serviced by a private train line, the Zillertalbahn (www.zillertalbahn.at), which travels the 32km from Jenbach to Mayrhofen. Those with a thirst for nostalgia can take a *Dampfzug* (steam train) along the valley. It runs at 9.47am from Jenbach to Mayrhofen and at 12.07pm from Mayrhofen to Jenbach. A one-way/return ticket for the 1¾-hour journey costs €13.60/19.80. If you just want to get from A to B, it's better to take the ordinary train (€7.40, 54 minutes), which runs twice hourly.

Zell am Ziller

☏ 05282 / POP 1768

Scenically located at the foot of knife-edge Reichenspitze (3303m), Zell am Ziller is a former goldmining centre. There's now less sparkle and more swoosh about this rural and deeply traditional little village, with its fine skiing and thrilling 7.5km floodlit toboggan run. In summer, active types come to hike in the mountains or pedal up the Gerlos Alpine Rd to Krimml in the Hohe Tauern National Park.

✈ Activities

Gerlos Alpine Road   SCENIC DRIVE

(www.gerlosstrasse.at; toll per car/motorcycle €9/6) Open year-round, the highly scenic Gerlos Alpine Rd links the Zillertal in Tyrol to Krimml in Salzburgerland, winding 12km through high moor and spruce forest, and reaching a maximum elevation of 1630m. The lookout above the turquoise *Stausee* (reservoir) is a great picnic stop, with a tremendous vista of the Alps. On the approach to Krimml near Schönmoosalm, there are bird's-eye views of the Krimml Falls.

Jodel Wanderweg   WALKING

(Yodel Hiking Trail; www.jodelweg.at; Wald-Königsleiten) If you've ever felt the urge to burst out into song Julie Andrews–style as you skip through meadows ablaze with wildflowers, you'll love the Jodel Wanderweg in Königsleiten, on the Gerlos Alpine Rd between Zell am Ziller and Krimml. You can practise your high notes at huts with giant cowbells, alpine horns and listen-repeat audio clippings.

Aktivzentrum Zillertal   ADVENTURE SPORTS

(☏ 0664 5059594; www.aktivzentrum-zillertal. at; Freizeitpark Zell; ⊕) Craving a little adventure? This specialist takes you paragliding (€55 to €130), rafting on the Ziller (€35), canyoning (€35 to €65), via ferrata climbing (€45 to €85) and – one for the kids – llama trekking (€20) in summer. Winter activities include snowshoe hikes (€35) and ski touring (€90).

Arena Coaster   ADVENTURE SPORTS

(www.zillertalarena.com; Zillertal Arena; adult/child coaster only €4.90/3, incl cable car €21.90/10.90; ☉ 9.30am-6pm late Jun-early Sep, shorter hours rest of year; ⊕) Feel your stomach do backflips with a whizzy, loop-the-loop ride on Zell's 1.5km rollercoaster bob. Kids love it.

❶ ZILLERTAL ACTIVECARD

If you're planning on spending a week or more in the valley between late May and mid-October, the value-for-money Zillertal Activecard (six/nine/12 days €61.50/84/105.50) covers public transport, one journey per day on any of the Zillertal cable cars and entry to swimming pools.

Freizeitpark Zell   SWIMMING
(www.freizeitparkzell.at; Schwimmbadweg 7; adult/child ice rink €6/3, swimming pool €7.50/4.50; ☺9am-7pm; ⊞) There's ice skating, tennis, football, bowling and a fun pool with plenty to amuse the kids at this riverside sports centre.

Goldschaubergwerk   MINE
(www.goldschaubergwerk.com; Hainzenberg 73; adult/child €13/6; ☺9am-6pm) Goldschaubergwerk is a two-hour tour of a gold mine, 2km east of Zell on the Gerlos road. The entry price covers a cheese tasting in the show dairy and a visit to the animal enclosure with deer, emus and llamas.

⚐ Festivals & Events

Gauderfest   BEER
(www.gauderfest.at; ☺early May) Over-strenuous activities are not recommended after a bellyful of super-strong Gauderbier (reputedly over 10% alcohol), brewed specially for this shindig. As well as eating, dancing and excessive drinking, there's a historical parade and alpine wrestling.

⊨ Sleeping & Eating

Enzianhof   FARMSTAY $
(☎05282-22 37; www.enzianhof.eu; Gerlosberg 23; s/d €35/58, half-board per person extra €11; ⓟ☎) High on a hilltop at 1272m, this rustic farmhouse is perfectly located for hiking and skiing, and has warm, spacious rooms. The farmer makes his own gentian schnapps and smokes his own ham, and you can fill up on Zillertaler specialities such as *Pressknödelsuppe* (Tyrolean dumpling soup) and goulash in the wood-beamed restaurant.

Gästehaus Brindlinger   PENSION $
(☎05282-26 71; Gaudergasse 4; d/apt €50/99; ⓟ☎) Tucked down a quiet lane, this chalet has bright rooms with plenty of pine, rag rugs and balconies affording mountain

views. Guests can wind down in the small sauna and Mrs Brindlinger lends out bikes free of charge.

Hotel Englhof   BOUTIQUE HOTEL $$
(☎05282-31 34; www.englhof.at; Zellbergeben 28; s/d €62/114; ☎) Beautiful blond-wood-panelled, white-linen-dressed rooms (many with balconies) and amenities including free DVD rental make Englhof a superb place to stay. But what really seals the deal is its in-house gourmet restaurant and world-class cocktail bar with Austria's second-largest collection of spirits (over 1400 varieties), mixing incredible cocktails like a Bloody Mary with frozen cherry tomatoes and barbecued black-pepper seasoning.

Gasthof Schulhaus   GUESTHOUSE $$
(☎05282-33 76; www.schulhaus.tirol; Zellberg 162; d €60-90,breakfast extra €12; ⓟ) Once a schoolhouse, Gasthof Schulhaus is now top of the hospitality class. You'll receive a warm welcome from the Geissler family at their hilltop abode in Zellberg, with stirring valley and mountain views and a restaurant championing Slow Food. The spacious rooms and apartments are done Tyrolean-style, and local farm-fresh goodies appear at breakfast.

★Schulhaus   AUSTRIAN $$
(☎05282-33 76; www.schulhaus.tirol; Zellberg 162; mains €18-25; ☺8am-10pm Thu-Sun) On its panoramic perch above Zell am Ziller, this old schoolhouse turned restaurant is Tyrolean through and through. The larch-wood interior is drenched in honeyed light, the terrace plays up the views deep into the valley and to the mountains beyond, while the succinct menu speaks of a family that believe in local sourcing and farm-fresh products.

❶ Information

The **tourist office** (☎05282-22 81; www.zell. at; Dorfplatz 3a; ☺8am-noon & 1-6pm Mon-Fri, 8.30-11.30am Sat) near the train tracks is a mine of information on walking, skiing and adventure activities in the area.

❶ Getting There & Away

Normal trains to Mayrhofen (€2.90, 11 minutes) and Jenbach (€6.40, 40 minutes) are cheaper than the steam train. Twice-hourly trains to and from Innsbruck (€12.10, 1½ hours) require a change at Jenbach.

Zell am Ziller is the start of the **Gerlos Alpine Road** (p305). By car between Zell am Ziller and

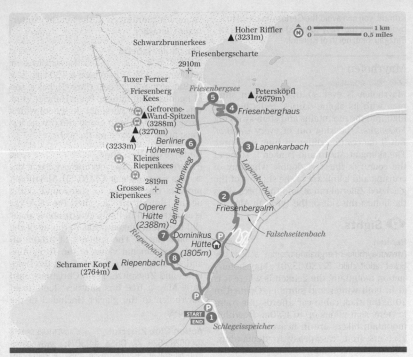

🏃 Walking Trail
Zillertal Circuit

START SCHLEGEISSPEICHER
END SCHLEGEISSPEICHER
LENGTH 11KM; FIVE TO SIX HOURS

This high-level circuit provides tremendous views to the startlingly turquoise Schlegeisspeicher and snowcapped Zillertal Alps. Though the trek involves 850m of incline, the path is well graded and mostly gentle; however, use care in bad weather. Kompass 1:50,000 map No 37 *Zillertaler Alpen-Tuxer Alpen* covers the walk in detail. Begin at the ❶ **Schlegeisspeicher**, ringed by rugged 3000m-high peaks. From the northeast end of the car park follow signs towards the Dominikus Hütte, bearing right towards Friesenberghaus alpine hut. The path emerges at the tree line near the alpine pasture of ❷ **Friesenbergalm** after about 45 minutes. It flattens to cross tarn-dotted pastures. Sidle around a shoulder and enter a valley overshadowed by Hoher Riffler.

Boulder-strewn meadows give way to scree patches and the ❸ **Lapenkarbach** stream. The trail winds uphill via long bends, then tight switchbacks, to the ❹ **Friesenberghaus** at the head of the valley around 1½ hours from Friesenbergalm. This is a scenic spot for a break.

Retrace your steps for 50m, following the signs right towards the Olperer Hütte and the Berliner Höhenweg. The trail descends slightly, crossing the outlet stream of ❺ **Friesenbergsee**, then makes a short, steep ascent up the rocky slope on the other side. Turn left when you reach a junction and contour the mountainside ahead. The next 1½ hours follow an easygoing balcony trail, part of the multiday ❻ **Berliner Höhenweg** route. It leads under the glacier-capped peaks of the Gefrorene-Wand-Spitzen.

About two hours from Friesenberghaus, cross a stream to reach ❼ **Olperer Hütte**, a great place for a drink. Then it's a steady descent to the reservoir, winding gently over grassy hummocks before zigzagging down beside the ❽ **Riepenbach** stream to the road (1½ hours from the Olperer Hütte). Turn left and head 1km to the parking area.

Krimml, you can avoid the Gerlos Alpine Rd toll by following the (easy-to-miss) signs to Wald im Pinzgau, 6km north of Krimml.

Mayrhofen

📞 05285 / POP 3858

Mayrhofen is ever so traditional in summer, with its alpine dairies, trails twisting high into the mountains and stein-swinging *Volksmusik* pouring out of every *Gasthof*. But it dances to a different tune in winter. The skiing at Ahorn and Penken is some of the country's finest, a double whammy of cruising and kamikaze in the shadow of the glaciated Zillertal range, and the après-ski is the hottest this side of the Tyrolean Alps.

◎ Sights

Penken   MOUNTAIN
(www.mayrhofner-bergbahnen.com; action day ticket adult/child €27.30/13.70) Mayrhofen's 'action mountain', the Penken is where it is at in both winter and summer. Opened in 2015, the slick cable car affords panoramic views as it glides up to 1790m. Downhill mountain bikers are in heaven here, with 21 tours from easy-peasy to demanding. The website www.mayrhofen.at has a virtual bike map. It's also a magnet for hikers, paragliders and climbers, and skiers and free-riders in winter, with the Harakiri and Vans Penken Park.

✗ Activities

Harakiri   SKIING
(Penken) With a 78% gradient, the Harakiri is Austria's steepest piste. This is half diving, half carving; a heart-stopping, hell-for-leather descent that leaves even accomplished skiers quaking in their ski boots. Only super-fit, experienced skiers with perfect (think Bond) body control should consider tackling this monster of a run.

Zillertal Arena   SNOW SPORTS
(www.zillertalarena.at; Tyrol; 2-/6-day Zillertal Superskipass €99.50/242) Mayrhofen is the showpiece of the Zillertal Arena, which covers 143km of slopes and 53 lifts (some pretty high-tech) in the highly scenic Zillertal, including the snow-sure pistes at the Hintertuxer Glacier. Ski buses connect the resorts. As well as being intermediate heaven, Mayrhofen has Austria's steepest black run, the kamikaze-like Harakiri, and appeals to freestylers for its fantastic terrain park. Even if snow lies thin in the

valley, it's guaranteed at the nearby Hintertuxer Gletcsher.

Skischule Habeler   SKIING
(📞05285-628 29; http://skimayrhofen.com; Hauptstrasse 458; ⊗8am-noon & 3.30-6pm Sun-Fri, 9am-noon & 1-7pm Sat) Chris Habeler, son of famous mountaineer Peter Habeler, runs this small, highly personal ski school with a passion. It offers both group and private lessons; prices are given on the website.

Hintertuxer Gletscher   SKIING
(Hintertux Glacier; www.hintertuxergletscher.at; day ski pass summer/winter €42.50/51) Mayrhofen provides easy access to year-round skiing on the Hintertuxer Gletscher; the cable car is an attraction in itself, gliding above sheer cliff faces and jagged peaks to the tip of the ice-blue glacier. The sundeck at 3250m affords phenomenal views of the Tuxer Alps and, on clear days, Grossglockner, the Dolomites and Zugspitze. From Christmas until early May, a free bus shuttles skiers from Mayrhofen to the glacier (included in the ski pass).

Action Club Zillertal   ADVENTURE SPORTS
(📞05285-629 77, 0664 4413074; www.action-club-zillertal.at; Hauptstrasse 458; ⊗9am-6pm) Action Club Zillertal is the place to go for adventure sports from rafting the raging waters of the Ziller River (€30) to canyoning (€35 to €85), tubing (€40), climbing (€60 to €120), guided mountain biking (€45 to €80) and tandem paragliding (€65 to €160).

Stocky Air   PARAGLIDING
(📞0664 3407976; www.stockyair.com; Hauptstrasse 456; ⊗9am-1pm & 3-6pm) This paragliding specialist will help you spread your wings in the surrounding Zillertaler Alps, with tandem flights costing between €80 and €150. It also rents out via ferrata equipment for €15.

Vans Penken Park   SNOWBOARDING
(www.vans-penken-park.com) Snowboarders are in their freestyle element in six areas with 11 kickers, 34 boxes and rails and a halfpipe at the Vans Penken Park in the Penken area, ranked one of Europe's best terrain parks.

★ Festivals & Events

Snowbombing   SKIING
(www.snowbombing.com; ⊗early Apr) The self-proclaimed greatest show on snow, Snowbombing in early April is Mayrhofen's biggest shindig. Some of the world's top

boarders compete on the slopes, but most people are just here for the party – six solid days of drinking and dancing to a cracking line-up of bands and DJs, plus fun from igloo raves to fancy-dress street parties in the mix.

🛏 Sleeping

⭐**Hotel Garni Glockenstuhl**   HOTEL **$$**
(☑05285-631 28; www.glockenstuhl.com; Einfahrt Mitte 431; s €55-58, d €98-112; P🢭) Good old-fashioned Austrian hospitality, dreamy alpine views, free bike rental and a relaxing spa make this chalet stand head and shoulders above most in town. If you can drag yourself out of the comfiest of beds, you'll find a delicious breakfast with fresh eggs on the table.

Alpenhotel Kramerwirt   HOTEL **$$**
(☑05285-67 00; www.kramerwirt.at; Am Marienbrunnen 346; s/d incl half-board €99/174; P🢭) Ablaze with geraniums in summer, this rambling 500-year-old chalet has corridors full of family heirlooms, spacious rooms and an outside whirlpool. At the restaurant (mains €8 to €21) try asking for the tasty *Zillertaler Bauernschmaus* (farmers' platter with meat, dumplings and sauerkraut).

Hotel Rose   HOTEL **$$**
(☑05285-622 29; www.hotel-rose.at; Brandbergstrasse 353; s €52-58, d €91-103; P🢭) In the capable hands of the fourth-generation Kröll family, this place has spacious rooms with chunky pine furnishings and balconies. There's a little sauna and whirlpool for après-ski relaxing. The garden pumps to live *Volksmusik* daily in summer.

Alpin Hotel Garni Eder   HOTEL **$$**
(☑05285-506 03 69; Zillergrundweg 572; d/tr €116/165) Huddled away in a serene part of town yet close to the ski lifts, this alpine chalet gets the hotel-as-home concept spot on and the location is unbeatable. You're made to feel like one of the family: the pine-trimmed rooms are spacious and beautifully kept, the owners go out of their way to help, and breakfasts are copious.

🍴 Eating

Cafe-Konditorei Kostner   CAFE **$**
(Hauptstrasse 414; snacks & mains €4-12; ⊙6.30am-6pm) 🥐 This candyfloss-pink villa has a popular terrace when the sun shines. The bakery side of it rolls out great spelt and rye bread, while the cafe rustles up tasty breakfasts, ice cream, speciality coffees and

homemade cakes, alongside salads, toasties and heart-warming dishes such as goulash.

Metzgerei Kröll   DELI **$**
(Scheulingstrasse 382; snacks €3-8; ⊙7.30am-1pm & 2.30-6pm Mon-Fri, 7am-noon Sat) This family-run butchery is famed for its unique *Schlegeis-Speck* ham, cured in a hut at 1800m for three months to achieve its aroma. There are a handful of tables where you can sample this speciality and the delicious homemade sausages.

Gasser   BURGERS **$**
(Hauptstrasse 475; snacks €3-7; ⊙7am-6pm Mon-Fri, to 5pm Sat) This award-winning butcher is the perfect spot to grab a snack on the way down from the slopes. It does a mighty fine bratwurst, as well as burgers, sandwiches and smoked hams. Vegetarian options are also available.

Gasthof Perauer   AUSTRIAN **$$**
(☑05285-625 66; www.perauer.at; Ahornstrasse 854; mains €15-26; ⊙11am-10pm; 🢭) With its tiled oven and all-wood interior, this *Gasthöf* is as gorgeously Tyrolean as they come. Both the setting and home cooking will warm the cockles. On the meaty menu are tried-and-trusted favourites including schnitzel and *Zwiebelrostbraten* (fried beef with onions), plus excellent steaks. Save an inch for the platter of regional cheeses.

Wirtshaus Zum Griena   AUSTRIAN **$$**
(☑05285-62 778; www.wirtshaus-griena.at; Dorfhaus 678; mains €8-16; ⊙11am-midnight Wed-Mon; 🢭) Set in high pastures, this woodsy 400-year-old chalet is the kind of place where you pray for a snow blizzard, so you can huddle around the fire and tuck into *Schlutzkropf'n* (fresh pasta filled with cheese).

🍷 Drinking & Nightlife

Mayrhofen's après-ski scene rocks; most bars go with the snow and open from mid-December to early April. In summer, it's all about the *Volksmusik,* so bring a *Dirndl* or a snazzy pair of lederhosen if you want to fit in.

White Lounge   BAR
(www.white-lounge.at; Ahorn; ⊙10am-4.30pm) Kick your skis off and chill over cocktails at this 2000m ice bar, with a big sunny terrace for catching rays. Things heat up with DJs and night sledding at Tuesday's igloo party (begins 8pm).

Ice Bar
BAR

(Hauptstrasse 470, Hotel Strass; ⊙ 3-9pm) A loud, lary, anything-goes après-ski haunt brimming with boot-stomping revellers, Europop beats and, occasionally, go-go polar bears (we kid you not!). Arena nightclub is under the same roof.

Scotland Yard
PUB

(www.scotlandyard.at; Scheulingstrasse 372; ⊙ 6pm-3am Tue-Sat) Scotland Yard is a British pub with all the trimmings: Guinness, darts and a red phone box where expats can pour their hearts out to folk back home after a pint or three.

Mo's
BAR

(Hauptstrasse 417; ⊙ 10am-1am Sun-Fri, 9am-1am Sat) An American-themed bar with an upbeat vibe, great cocktails, finger food and burgers, and regular live music. DJs work the decks on Wednesday and Friday nights.

☆ Entertainment

Brück'n Stadl
LIVE MUSIC

(Ahornstrasse 850, Gasthof Brücke; ⊙ 3pm-4am Dec-Apr) For year-round *Spass* (fun), you can't beat this lively barn and marquee combi. Lederhosen-clad folk stars get beer glasses swingin' in summer, while plentiful schnapps and DJ Mütze fuel the après-ski party in winter.

ⓘ Information

Tourist Office (✆ 05285-67 60; www.mayrhofen.at; Dursterstrasse 225; ⊙ 9am-6pm Mon-Sat, to 1pm Sun; 🛜) The ultramodern tourist office stocks loads of information and maps on the town. Look for the comprehensive *Info von A-Z*; it's free and written in English. There is a handy topographic model of the surrounding Alps, a 24-hour accommodation board and free wi-fi.

ⓘ Getting There & Away

By the normal train that runs twice hourly, it's €7.40 each way to Jenbach (52 minutes). For the Zillertal Circuit, buses run between Mayrhofen and the Schlegeisspeicher reservoir (one way €6.40, one hour, seven daily).

Ginzling

✆ 05286 / POP 400

For a taste of what the Austrian Alps looked like before the dawn of tourism, head to Ginzling, an adorable little village 8km south of Mayrhofen.

The main draw for hikers in Ginzling is the **Naturpark Zillertaler Alpen** (www.naturpark-zillertal.at), a 379-sq-km nature park and pristine alpine wilderness of deep valleys and glaciated peaks. It runs 200 excellent themed guided hikes, most costing between €5 and €7, from May to October. The extensive program includes everything from llama trekking to sunrise photo excursions, herb walks and alpine hikes.

The most charming place to stay is **Gasthaus Alt-Ginzling** (✆ 05286-202 96; www.ferienwohnungen-ginzling.at; Ginzling 240; d €80-96, apt €85-145; 🅿🛜), once a wayside inn for smugglers travelling to Italy. The 18th-century farmhouse oozes history from every creaking beam and the low-ceilinged, pine-panelled rooms are supremely cosy. The restaurant serves local rainbow trout.

In winter, free ski buses run frequently to Mayrhofen; otherwise there is an hourly service (€3.60, 21 minutes). A road (toll car/motorcycle €12/8) snakes on from Ginzling up the valley to the Schlegeisspeicher reservoir, the trailhead for the stunning Zillertal Circuit.

Achensee

The fjord-like Achensee is Tyrol's largest lake and one of its loveliest, flanked by thickly wooded mountains. Days here unfold with boat tours of the lake or jaunts up to Erfurter, which opens up an Alpine playground, with hiking, paragliding, ziplining and a via ferrata.

🏃 Activities

Rofanseilbahn
CABLE CAR

(www.rofanseilbahn.at; adult/child return €20/12, incl Airrofan Skyglider €28/17.50; ⊙ 8.30am-5.30pm Apr-Oct) Sweeping views over Achensee and the surrounding peaks can be had from Erfurter (1831m), which is easily reached by the Rofanseilbahn cable car from Maurach. To up the thrill factor, test out the Airrofan Skyglider, a kind of giant, multi-person zipline. Other adventure pursuits include paragliding and flirting with climbing on the five-peak, six- to eight-hour via ferrata.

Achensee Boat Tours
BOATING

(www.tirol-schiffahrt.at; adult/child €20/10; ⊙ May-Oct) These two-hour spins of the fjord-like Achensee are a soothing way to take in the scenery.

❶ Getting There & Away

The **Achenseebahn** (www.achenseebahn.at; one way/return €23/29.50), a private cogwheel steam train, trundles to the lake from Jenbach between May and October. Normal trains also run regularly between Jenbach and Maurach/Achensee Seespitz (€4.50, 26 minutes).

Kitzbühel

☑ 05356 / POP 8135

Ask an Austrian to rattle off the top ski resorts in the country, and Kitzbühel will invariably make the grade. Ever since Franz Reisch slipped on skis and whizzed down the slopes of Kitzbüheler Horn way back in 1893, so christening the first alpine ski run in Austria, Kitzbühel has carved out its reputation as one of Europe's foremost ski resorts. Legends have been made and born on these pistes, not least three-time Olympic medallist Toni Sailer.

Kitzbühel began life in the 16th century as a silver and copper mining town, and today continues to preserve a charming medieval centre despite its other persona as a fashionable and prosperous winter resort. It's renowned for the white-knuckled Hahnenkamm-Rennen downhill ski race in January and the excellence of its slopes.

◉ Sights

Alpine Flower Garden GARDENS
(⊙8.30am-5pm May-Sep) **FREE** Arnica, edelweiss and purple bellflowers are among the 400 alpine blooms flourishing at this quiet garden atop Kitzbüheler Horn. It's a four-hour (14km) hike one way, or a speedy cable-car ride. A highly scenic road also twists up to the mountain (toll per car/motorcycle €10/5, plus €3 per person).

Museum Kitzbühel MUSEUM
(www.museum-kitzbuehel.at; Hinterstadt 32; adult/child €6.50/free; ⊙10am-5pm Fri-Wed, to 8pm Thu Apr-late Sep, reduced hours late Sep-Mar) This museum traces Kitzbühel's heritage from its Bronze Age mining beginnings to the present day. The big emphasis is on winter sports, and the permanent collection pays tribute to homegrown legends including ski racing champ Toni Sailer and winter landscape painter Alfons Walde.

🏃 Activities

Streiff SKIING
The mind-bogglingly sheer, breathtakingly fast Streif downhill course lures hardcore

---

❶ KITZBÜHEL AREA SKI PASSES

One-/three-/six-day passes cost €53/147/256 in the high winter season and €47.50/132.50/230.50 at all other times. Passes cover lifts, cable cars and ski buses as far south as Thurn Pass. If you plan to cover a lot of terrain, the **Kitzbüheler Alpen AllStarCard** (www.allstarcard.at; 1-/3-/6-day pass €55/155/265;) is your best bet; it spans the whole region, including Kitzbühel, Wilder Kaiser-Brixental, Saalbach-Hinterglemm and Zell am See-Kaprun (some 1088km of pistes).

---

skiers to Kitzbühel – even experts feel their hearts do somersaults on the Mausefalle, a notoriously steep section with an 85% gradient. Jumps reach up to 80m and speeds can top 140kmph, which is sheer insanity on skis. One of the most terrifying World Cup courses, this is the stuff of legend. Ski it at least once if you dare.

Hahnenkammbahn CABLE CAR
(Hahnenkamm Cable Car; adult/child return €23/13) This cable car whisks you up to the summit of 1712m Hahnenkamm, a magnet for hikers and downhill bikers in summer and hardcore skiers – many attempting the mythical Streif race – in winter.

Element 3 ADVENTURE SPORTS
(☑05356-723 01; www.element3.at; Klostergasse 8; ⊙9am-noon Mon-Fri) A ski school in winter, in summer this is a one-stop shop for adventure sports, including canyoning (€60 to €110), paragliding (€125) and via ferrate (€110). Mountain and electric bike (e-bike) tours cost €45 to €60.

Ski Safari SKIING
Confident intermediates up for a challenge can tackle the incredibly scenic 35km Ski Safari, linking the Hahnenkamm to Resterhöhe/Pass Thurn. The alpine tour is marked by elephant signs and is a good introduction to the entire ski area.

Kitzbüheler Hornbahn CABLE CAR
(Kitzbüheler Horn Cable Car; adult/child return €23.50/13) Hitching a ride on this cable car brings you to the Alpine Flower Garden. Hiking and mountain-biking trails fan out from the summit. A panoramic pick is the 2.4km Karstweg circuit, which affords

impressive glimpses of the surrounding karst landscape. In winter, Kitzbüheler Horn is a magnet for beginners, with gentle cruising on sunny slopes.

Snowpark Hanglalm
SKIING

(www.snowpark-kitzbuehel.at) Snowpark Hanglalm is boarder and freeskier heaven with its rails, kickers, boxes, tubes and 35 obstacles. The snowpark can be reached by taking the cable car from Mittersill base station.

✿✿ Festivals & Events

Hahnenkamm-Rennen
SPORTS

(www.hahnenkamm.com; ⊗ Jan) Perhaps the most enthralling of all FIS Alpine World Cup stages, this is the mother of all downhill ski races.

Snow Polo World Cup
SPORTS

(www.kitzbuehelpolo.com; ⊗ mid-Jan) International polo teams battle it out on ice at this event, which brings a spritz of glamour to the winter calendar.

🛏 Sleeping

Snowbunny's Hostel
HOSTEL $

(☑ 067 67940233; www.snowbunnys.co.uk; Bichlstrasse 30; dm €22-25, d €66; @ 🖤) This friendly, laid-back hostel is a bunny-hop from the slopes. Dorms are fine, if a tad dark; breakfast is DIY-style in the kitchen. There's a TV lounge, a ski storage room and cats to stroke.

★ Villa Licht
HOTEL $$

(☑ 05356-622 93; www.villa-licht.at; Franz-Reisch-Strasse 8; apt €120-210; P@🖤🏊) Pretty gardens, spruce modern apartments with pine trappings, living rooms with kitchenettes, balconies with mountain views, peace – this

---

> ### ℹ LOCAL DISCOUNT CARDS
>
> Stay in Kitzbühel and you'll automatically receive the Red Card (guest card), which entitles you to hook onto half-day guided hikes arranged by the tourist office for free. Engelbert and Madeleine are the hiking guides that run the tours at 8.45am (summer) and 9.45am (winter) from Monday to Friday.
>
> You can save in summer by investing in the Kitzbüheler Alpen Summer Card (three-day pass with/without bus €55.80/48), which covers 31 lifts and cable cars. Children pay half-price.

---

charming Tyrolean chalet has the lot, and owner Renate goes out of her way to please. Kids love the outdoor pool in summer.

Hotel Edelweiss
HOTEL $$

(☑ 05356-752 52; www.edelweiss-kitzbuehel.at; Marchfeldgasse 2; d incl half-board €120-150; P 🖤) Near the Hahnenkammbahn, Edelweiss oozes Tyrolean charm with its green surrounds, alpine views, sauna and cosy interiors. Your kindly hosts Klaus and Veronika let you pack up a lunch from the breakfast buffet and also serve delicious five-course dinners.

Pension Kometer
PENSION $$

(☑ 05356-622 89; www.pension-kometer.com; Gerbergasse 7; s/d €65/114; P 🖤) Make yourself at home in the bright, sparklingly clean rooms at this family-run guesthouse. There's a relaxed lounge with games and DVDs. Breakfast is a treat with fresh breads, fruit and eggs.

Hotel Erika
HISTORIC HOTEL $$$

(☑ 05356-648 85; www.erika-kitz.at; Josef-Pirchl-Strasse 21; d incl half-board €182-212; P 🖤🏊) This turreted art-nouveau villa has luxurious high-ceilinged rooms and polished service. The rose-strewn garden centres on a vine-clad pagoda and pond that are illuminated by night. Unwind with treatments from thalassotherapy to hay baths in the spa.

✕ Eating

★ Restaurant Zur Tenne
AUSTRIAN $$

(☑ 05356-644 44-0; www.hotelzurtenne.com; Vorderstadt 8-10; mains €18-43; ⊗ 11.30am-1.30pm & 6.30-9.30pm) Choose between the rustic, beamed interior where an open fire crackles and the more summery conservatory at Hotel Tenne's highly regarded restaurant. Service is polished and the menu puts a sophisticated twist on seasonal Tyrolean dishes such as catfish with wild garlic pasta and artichokes.

Huberbräu Stüberl
AUSTRIAN $$

(☑ 05356-656 77; Vorderstadt 18; mains €9-18; ⊗ 8am-midnight Mon-Sat, from 9am Sun) An old-world Tyrolean haunt with vaults and pine benches, this tavern favours substantial portions of Austrian classics, such as schnitzel, goulash and dumplings, cooked to perfection.

Lois Stern
FUSION $$

(☑ 05356-748 82; www.loisstern.com; Josef-Pirchl-Strasse 3; mains €25-33; ⊗ 6pm-midnight Tue-Sat) Lois works his wok in the show kitchen of this bistro, with an understated chic decor of wood floors and caramel-hued

Kitzbühel

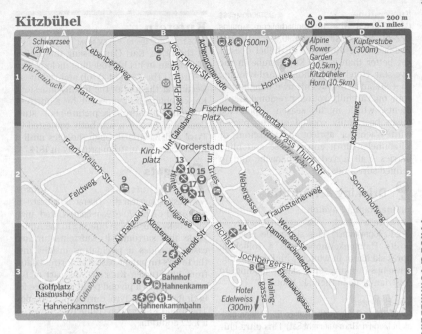

Kitzbühel

banquettes. Clean, bright flavours such as tempura of wild gambas and Thai-style ceviche with chilli-lime salsa shine on the Asian-Mediterranean crossover menu.

s'Kitz
AUSTRIAN $$

(☎05356-753 26; www.skitz.at; Bichlstrasse 7; mains €9-23; ⊙9.30am-midnight Mon-Sat) A real local's haunt, s'Kitz reels in a lively crowd with its beer garden terrace and laid-back vibe. The food is good honest Austrian home cooking: goulash, lentil stew, *Schlutzkrapfen* (Tyrolean-style ravioli filled with cheese and spinach) and lighter options such as roast beef salad with Styrian pumpkin oil. Lunch specials go for a reasonable €8.70.

Centro
ITALIAN $$

(☎05356-658 62; www.centro-kitzbuehel.at; Vorderstadt 12; 2-course lunch €7.80, pizza €6-14.50, mains €15.50-25.50; ⊙9am-midnight Mon-Sat, 2-11.30pm Sun; 🛗) On a sunny evening, it seems as though the whole of Kitzbühel congregates on the street-facing terrace of Centro to chat and people-watch over Italian salads, wood-fired pizzas, pasta and grilled fish. The slick vaulted interior entices in winter. It's popular, so best to book ahead.

Kupferstube
GASTRONOMY **$$$**

(📞 05356-631 81; www.tennerhof.com; mains €22-39, 4-/7-course menu €90/125; ⊘ 7-9pm Wed-Sun) Fine dining in Kitzbühel doesn't get better than at the Kupferstube in the five-star Hotel Tennerhof. Award-winning chef Stefan Lenz puts his own imaginative spin on carefully sourced regional ingredients, which might, season depending, mean beautifully cooked organic pigeon with Wachauer apricot and hazelnut or Kitzbüheler Horn curd cheese and blueberries – all served with panache and in refined surrounds.

🍷 Drinking & Nightlife

Hahnenkamm Pavillon
BAR

(www.pavillon-kitz.at; Hahnenkammstrasse 2; ⊘ 2-10.30pm winter) This slope-side pick opposite Hahnenkammbahn is a rollicking après-ski haunt in winter, with DJs, singing, schnapps-drinking and skiers jiggling to Austrian beats in their ski boots.

Leo Hillinger
WINE BAR

(📞 05356-202 51; Rathausplatz 5; ⊘ noon-midnight Mon-Fri, 11am-midnight Sat) This ultra-chic wine bar and shop has a terrace that is great for people-watching over fine wines and small plates.

Bergsinn
BAR

(www.bergsinn.at; Vorderstadt 21; ⊘ 8am-midnight Mon-Thu, to 1am Fri & Sat, 10am-midnight Sun; 🛜) This slinky, backlit lounge bar has a happy hour (6pm to midnight) on Sundays when cocktails are €5, a buzzy terrace, DJ nights and free wi-fi.

ℹ Information

Post Office (Josef-Pirchl-Strasse 11; ⊘ 8am-6pm Mon-Fri) The post office is midway between the train station and tourist office.

Tourist Office (📞 666 60; www.kitzbuehel.com; Hinterstadt 18; ⊘ 8.30am-6pm Mon-Fri, 9am-6pm Sat, 10am-noon & 4-6pm Sun) The central tourist office has loads of info in English and a 24-hour accommodation board.

ℹ Getting There & Away

Kitzbühel is on the B170, 30km east of Wörgl and the A12/E45 motorway.

The main train station is 1km north of central Vorderstadt. Trains run frequently from Kitzbühel to Innsbruck (€15.80, 1¼ hours) and Salzburg (€30.30, 2½ hours). For Kufstein (€10.20, one hour), change at Wörgl.

Kufstein

📞 05372 / POP 18,215 / ELEV 499M

In the 1970s, Karl Ganzer sang the praises of Kufstein in his hit yodelling melody 'Perle Tirols' (The Pearl of Tyrol) and rightly so. Resting at the foot of the mighty limestone Kaisergebirge and crowned by a fortress, Kufstein's backdrop is picture-book stuff. Control of the town was hotly contested by Tyrol and Bavaria through the ages until it finally became Austrian property in 1814.

◉ Sights

★Festung Kufstein
FORTRESS

(www.festung.kufstein.at; Oberer Stadtplatz 6; adult/child €11.50/7; ⊘ 9am-6pm) Lifted high on a rocky crag like an offering to the Alpine peaks that surround it, Kufstein's turreted castle provides a fascinating insight into the town's turbulent past. The fortress dates from 1205 (when Kufstein was part of Bavaria) and was a pivotal point of defence for both Bavaria and Tyrol during the struggles. The round Kaiserturm (Emperor's Tower) is a 1522 addition.

Römerhofgasse
HISTORIC SITE

A classic saunter leads along gingerbready Römerhofgasse, a reconstructed medieval lane that looks fresh-minted for a Disney film set with its overhanging arches, lanterns and frescoed facades. Even the crowds and souvenir kitsch – marmot ointment, *Dirndls*, strapping lederhosen, you name it – detract little from its appeal.

🏃 Activities

★Kaisergebirge
HIKING, SKIING

Rising like a sheer curtain of limestone to the east, the Kaisergebirge range reaches up to 2300m and stretches as far as St Johann in Tirol. It attracts walkers, mountaineers and skiers alike. The Kaisergebirge is actually two ranges, split by the east-west Kaisertal valley. The northern range is the **Zahmer Kaiser** (Tame Emperor) and the southern the **Wilder Kaiser** (Wild Emperor) – no medals for guessing which has the smoother slopes! Pick up a free *Wanderkarte* (walking map) from the tourist office.

Hechtsee
SWIMMING

(www.hechtsee.at; adult/child €4/1.60; ⊘ 9am-7pm late May–early Sep) This crystal-blue, mountain-rimmed lake sits 3km to the northwest of Kufstein. As well as a beach for swimming, there are also other activities such as rowing boats, table tennis and volleyball. A free city bus goes to Hechtsee in summer during fine weather (ask at the tourist office).

Stimmersee SWIMMING
(adult/child €4/1.60; ☉late May-early Sep) Stimmersee, 2.5km southwest of Kufstein, is hailed for having some of the cleanest waters in Austria. Rimmed by forest and ragged mountain peaks, the glassy green lake is fed by mountain streams. It has sunbathing lawns, cafes, hiking trails, beach volleyball and a playground for kids.

🛏 Sleeping

Camping Maier CAMPGROUND $
(☑05372-583 52; www.camping-maier.com; Egerbach 54, Schwoich; camp sites per adult/child/tent €5/3.50/7; ☒) Bordering woodland, this friendly campground 5km south of Kufstein has tree-shaded pitches, plus a playground and an outdoor pool.

★ Auracher Löchl HISTORIC HOTEL $$
(☑05372 621 38; www.auracher-loechl.at; Römerhofgasse 2-5; s €79-134, d €145-297; @☎) Squeezed between Römerhofgasse and the Inn River, this hotel marries medieval charm with 21st-century comfort; river or fortress views cost a little extra. Cross the footbridge to the low-beamed restaurant (mains €13 to €25), one-time haunt of Andreas Hofer, where creaking floors and grinning badgers create a rustic feel. Austrian classics such as *Schweinshaxe* (basically half a pig) are served in gut-busting portions.

Hotel Kufsteinerhof HOTEL $$
(☑05372-714 12; www.kufsteinerhof.at; Franz-Josef-Platz 1; s €54-64, d €108-118,; ℗☎) With its spacious, parquet-floored rooms in clean, contemporary style and substantial breakfasts, the Kufsteinerhof is one of the best central picks in Kufstein. It's just a three-minute walk from the fortress.

✗ Eating

Egger Bräustüberl AUSTRIAN $$
(☑05372-610 90; www.braeustueberl-kufstein.at; Oberer Stadtplatz 5a; day special €8, mains €8.50-14; ☉10am-2.30pm & 4.30pm-midnight Mon-Fri, 10am-midnight Sat; ☒☲) As traditionally Austrian as they come, this brewpub-restaurant dishes up satisfying Tyrolean and Bavarian grub, from schnitzel as big as a boot to goulash and bratwurst with lashings of sauerkraut – all of which go well with the freshly tapped brews. The atmosphere is laid-back and the terrace has castle views. Gluten-free, vegetarian and children's options are also available.

Purlepaus FUSION $$
(☑05372-636 33; www.purlepaus.at; Unterer Stadtplatz 18; lunch €6.90-8.20, mains €11-18; ☉11am-10pm; ☒) This is a perennially popular choice with a stylish vaulted interior and a big chestnut tree-shaded terrace. The wordly menu skips from pasta and tarte flambée to Thai curries and Tyrolean grub. Vegetarian picks are also available.

🍷 Drinking & Nightlife

Fritz Wein Cafe WINE BAR
(www.fritz-wein-cafe.com; Unterer Stadtplatz 18; ☉4pm-midnight Tue-Fri, 11am-midnight Sat) Adding a dash of urban slickness to Kufstein's after-dark scene, this wood-floored wine bar, lit by globe lights, has a terrific assortment of Austrian wines, which pair nicely with the day specials, tapas and cheese tasting plates on offer.

ℹ Information

At the **tourist office** (☑05372-622 07; www.kufstein.com; Unterer Stadtplatz 8; ☉9am-6pm Mon-Fri, 9am-1pm Sat), staff will hunt down accommodation without charging commission. If you stay overnight, ask for the Gästekarte, which has different benefits in summer and winter.

ℹ Getting There & Away

The frequent trains to Kitzbühel (€10.20, one hour) require a change at Wörgl. The easiest road route is also via Wörgl. Kufstein is on the main Innsbruck–Salzburg train route. Direct trains to Salzburg (€31, 1¼ hours) run at least every two hours; those to Innsbruck (€14, 40 minutes) are half-hourly. Buses leave from outside the train station.

Söll
☑ 05333 / POP 3535 / ELEV 703M

Söll is a well-known ski resort 10km south of Kufstein. Once a favourite of boozy, raucous visitors in the 1980s, the resort has successfully reinvented itself and is now a family-oriented place with myriad outdoor activities.

The highest skiing area overlooking the resort is Hohe Salve at 1828m.

⚡ Activities

Hohe Salve
WALKING

(www.hohe-salve.com; cable car 1 way/return €13/17.50; ⊙9am-5pm; 🚡) Walkers and paragliders are drawn to the heights of Hohe Salve in summer. At the first stage of the cable car climbing the mountain is **Hexenwasser**, a walking trail dotted with fun family activities. Along the route are water obstacles, sundials, playgrounds, a working mill and bakery and an apiary. Throughout the summer you can see (and sample) bread, schnapps and cheese made the traditional way.

The same slopes swish to the sound of skis in winter.

Skiwelt
SKIING

(www.skiwelt.at) Straddling the ragged limestone mountains of the Wilder Kaiser Brixental, Skiwelt comprises 284km of pistes, most of which are easy or moderate. Passes are €42.50 for a day in the high season. Cross-country skiing is also a popular winter pastime, with trails running as far as St Johann in Tirol.

🛏 Sleeping & Eating

Eggerwirt
HERITAGE HOTEL $$

(🕿05333-52 36; www.eggerwirt.cc; Dorf 14; s €49-62, d €82-92,; 🎈🐕) The welcome is heartfelt at this family-run, chalet-style hotel, with fine mountain views and a lounge warmed by an open fire in winter. The warm-hued rooms come with pine trappings. In summer, the outdoor pool and sun terrace are big draws, while the sauna area is great for a post-ski steam in winter. Bike rental is available on request.

Auf da Mühle
AUSTRIAN $$

(🕿05333-205 90; www.aufdamuehle.at; Dorf 89; mains €9.50-30; ⊙10am-2pm & 4.30pm-midnight Mon & Wed-Fri, 10am-midnight Sat & Sun; 🌱) Chipper staff bring sizzling, top-quality steaks, salads, wok dishes and pizza to the table at Auf da Mühle, bang in the centre of Söll. The look is contemporary, with sleek contours and smooth wood panelling, and a long list of cocktails fuels the buzzy vibe. Day specials go for €7.50 (vegetarian) to €8.50 (with fish or meat).

ℹ Information

The **tourist office** (🕿050-509 210; www.wilder kaiser.info; Dorf 84; ⊙8am-noon & 1-6pm Mon-Fri, 3-6pm Sat, 9am-noon Sun), in the centre of the village, provides information on activities and will help you find accommodation.

ℹ Getting There & Away

Söll is on the B178 between Wörgl and St Johann in Tirol. It's not on a train line, but there are plenty of buses from Kufstein (€4.50, 27 minutes).

Seefeld

🕿05212 / POP 3370 / ELEV 1180M

Seefeld sits high on a south-facing plateau, ringed by the fearsome limestone peaks of the Wetterstein and Karwendel Alps. While most Tyrolean resorts are crazy about downhill, Seefeld's first love is *Langlauf* (cross-country skiing), and fans of the sport flock here to skate and glide along 279km of prepared trails in winter.

Seefeld was the proud co-host of the Winter Olympic Games in 1964 and 1976 and the Winter Youth Olympics in 2012. It's currently gearing up to host the FIS Nordic World Ski Championships 2019.

◉ Sights

Pfarrkirche St Oswald
CHURCH

(Dorfplatz; ⊙8am-7pm) Seefeld's trophy sight is this late-Gothic parish church, the supposed location of a miracle. The story goes that Oswald Milser gobbled a wafer reserved for the clergy at Easter communion here in 1384. After almost being swallowed up by the floor, the greedy layman repented, but the wafer was streaked with blood – not from foolish Oswald but from Christ, naturally. You can view the **Blutskapelle** (Chapel of the Holy Blood), which held the original wafer, by climbing the stairway.

⚡ Activities

Seefeld's raison d'être is cross-country skiing. Well-groomed *Loipen* (trails) criss-cross the sunny plateau to Mösern, 5km away, where there are fine views of the Inn River and the peaks beyond.

The 48km of downhill skiing here is best suited to beginners and intermediates. Your pass to the slopes is the multiday Happy Ski Card (three-day pass adult/child €120.50/72.50), covering all lifts in Seefeld. The two main areas are Gschwandtkopf (1500m) and Rosshütte (1800m); the latter connects to higher lifts and slopes on the Karwendel range.

For some challenging walks, cable cars ascend nearby Seefeld Spitze (2220m) and

Reither Spitze (2374m); consult the tourist office for more information or join one of its regular guided walks.

🛏 Sleeping & Eating

★Hotel Helga
HOTEL $

(☑ 05121-23 26; www.hotel-helga.at; Haspingerstrasse 156; incl half-board s €75-110, d €120-150; P 🛜) Helga and Franz bend over backwards to please at this homely chalet, with sweet and simple rooms dressed in traditional Tyrolean style, with lots of wood and florals. Stay here for the mountain views, the terrific four-course dinners, the familiar atmosphere and the silence needed for a sound night's sleep. A sauna takes the chill out of winter.

Central
HOTEL $$

(☑ 05212-26 88; www.central-seefeld.at; Münchnerstrasse 41; s/d €92/144, half-board €16; P 🛜) 🍴 Friendly service, an attractive spa and kids' play areas make the Central a good choice. The well-lit rooms with balconies are contemporary Tyrolean in style, with light birch wood and earthy hues. The food makes the most of local products and there are organic options at breakfast.

Waldgasthaus Triendlsäge
AUSTRIAN $$

(☑ 05121-25 80; www.triendlsaege.at; Triendlsäge 259; mains €10-22; ⊙ 11.30am-10pm Thu-Tue) A romantic slice of Tyrolean rusticity, this woody restaurant, named after its sawmill, hides in the forest, a 20-minute walk north of town. Or reach it on cross-country skis or by horse-drawn carriage in winter. Sit by the open fire or on the terrace for regional dishes that play up seasonal, farm-fresh ingredients, from trout to game and wild mushrooms.

ℹ Information

The central **tourist office** (☑ 05-088 050; www.seefeld.com; Klosterstrasse 43; ⊙ 8.30am-6.30pm Mon-Sat, 10am-12.30pm & 3-5pm Sun) has stacks of info on accommodation and outdoor activities.

ℹ Getting There & Away

Seefeld is 25km northwest of Innsbruck, just off the Germany-bound B177. The track starts climbing soon after departing Innsbruck, providing spectacular views across the whole valley. Trains run to/from Innsbruck (€5.40, 36 minutes), Mittenwald (€5.20, 20 minutes) and Garmisch-Partenkirchen (€9.10, 42 minutes) in Germany.

Stams

📍 05263 / POP 1380 / ELEV 672M

The pride and joy of tiny Stams is its striking Cistercian abbey. **Stift Stams** (www.stiftstams.at; Stiftshof 3; tours adult/child €5.50/3; ⊙ guided tours hourly 9-11am & 1-5pm Mon-Sat, 1-5pm Sun Jun-Sep, 4pm Thu Oct-May) is one of Tyrol's true architectural highlights. The ochre-and-white Zisterzienstift was founded in 1273 by Elizabeth of Bavaria, the mother of Konradin, last of the Hohenstaufens. Set in pristine grounds, the monumental facade stretches 80m and is easily recognised by its pair of silver cupolas at the front, which were added as a final flourish when the abbey was revamped in baroque style in the 17th century.

The abbey is by far the biggest draw, but should you wish to linger in this peaceful corner of the Inn Valley, there are some lovely walking trails heading up into the surrounding hills and oak woods.

With its atmospheric stone vaults and cosy niches, **Orangerie Stams** (☑ 05263-202 08; www.orangeriestams.at; Stiftshof 7; lunch €7.90, mains €8.50-15; ⊙ 10am-10pm Mon-Sat, to 6pm Sun; 🚸), within the abbey complex, is big on charm. The menu emphasises high-quality regional produce. Snag a table to dig into dishes such as South Tyrolean beef tartare, Styrian chicken salad with pumpkin oil or *Stamser Pfandl*, grilled pork with garlic butter, root vegetables and roast potatoes. Vegetarian options are available.

Stams is on the train route between Innsbruck and Landeck (both €8.40, 40 minutes). Both the A12 and B171 pass near the abbey.

The Ötztal

POP 12,000

Over millennia, the Ötztal (Ötz Valley) has been shaped into rugged splendour. No matter whether you've come to ski its snow-capped mountains, raft its white waters or hike to its summits, this valley is all about big wilderness. Guarding the Italian border and dominated by Tyrol's highest peak, Wildspitze (3774m), this is one of

WORTH A TRIP

STUBAI GLACIER

One of Austria's biggest glacier skiing areas, the Stubai Glacier is just 40km south of Innsbruck. Thanks to its elevation, topping out at around 3300m, there's some form of skiing and boarding available year-round. Other activities include hiking, paragliding, tobogganing and cross-country skiing. Villages sprinkle the valley that unfurls below it.

Guesthouses, holiday apartments and chalet hotels are strung along the Stubaital, with the highest concentration in Neustift, a fine base if you want a head-start to the glacier in the morning before the crowds descend. Visit www. stubai.at for listings.

Buses from Innsbruck journey to Neustift im Stubaital Mutterbergalm at the foot of the glacier (€9.30, 1½ hours) twice hourly.

three river valleys running north from the Ötztaler Alpen to drain into the Inn River.

◉ Sights

Ötzi Dorf   MUSEUM
(www.oetzi-dorf.at; Umhausen; adult/child €7.50/3.70; ☉9.30am-5.30pm May-Oct; ☷) This small open-air museum brings to life the Neolithic world of Ötzi the ice man. A visit takes in traditional thatched huts, herb gardens, craft displays and enclosures where wild boar and oxen roam. Multilingual audio guides are available.

Stuibenfall   WATERFALL
From Ötzi Dorf it's a beautiful 20-minute forest walk to Tyrol's longest waterfall, the wispy Stuibenfall, cascading 159m over slate cliffs and moss-covered boulders. You can continue for another 40 minutes up to the top viewing platform and hanging bridge. A thrilling 450m *Klettersteig* (via ferrata) takes you right over the waterfall; bring your own karabiner and helmet.

🏃 Activities

★ Aqua Dome   SPA
(☑05243-6400; www.aqua-dome.at; Oberlängenfeld 140, Längenfeld; 3hr card adult/child Mon-Fri €20/10.50, Sat & Sun €23/13.50, sauna world €14; ☉9am-11pm, sauna world 10am-11pm) Framed by the Ötztaler Alps, this crystalline spa looks otherworldly after dark when its trio of flying saucer-shaped pools are strikingly illuminated. And there's certainly something surreal about gazing up to the peaks and stars while floating in a brine bath, drifting around a lazy river or being pummelled by water jets.

Area 47   ADVENTURE SPORTS
(☑05266-876 76; www.area47.at; Ötztaler Achstrasse 1, Ötztal Bahnhof; water park adult/child/family €22/13/54; ☉10am-7pm May-Sep; ☷) Billing itself as the ultimate outdoor playground, this huge sports and adventure park is the Ötztal's flagship attraction, dramatically set at the foot of the Alps and on the edge of a foaming river. The place heaves with families and flirty teenagers in summer.

Timmelsjoch Pass   SCENIC DRIVE
(www.timmelsjoch.com; car/motorbike €16/14, with Ötztal Card free; ☉7am-8pm Jun-Oct) Often nicknamed the 'secret pass to the south', this little-driven but nevertheless startlingly beautiful pass road wiggles from the Ötztal and the Passeier Valley in the Italian South Tyrol. Known since the Stone Age, the route attracted traders and smugglers in the Middle Ages. Negotiating 30 hairpin bends, its highest point is 2509m, where a tavern awaits.

Sölden   SKIING
(www.soelden.com; 1-/6-day pass €52/269) An Alpine Ski World Cup venue, Sölden is a snow-sure ski resort with a high-speed lift network and fun-loving après-ski scene. The resort's 145km of slopes attract confident intermediates and are complemented by glacier skiing at Rettenbach and Tiefenbach. For many, the highlight is the 50km **Big 3 Rally**, a four-hour downhill marathon which begins at Giggijoch gondola and takes in three 3000m peaks.

Obergurgl & Hochgurgl   SKIING
(www.obergurgl.com; day ski pass €50; ☷) Around 14km south of Sölden is family-friendly Obergurgl (1930m), Austria's highest parish, with skiing largely aimed at beginners and intermediates. Obergurgl is actually at the head of the valley, but the road doubles back on itself and rises to Hochgurgl (2150m), where the pistes are steeper and the views equally impressive.

🛏 Sleeping

★ Hotel Rita   SPA HOTEL $$
(☑05253-53 07; www.hotel-rita.com; Oberlängenfeld 44a, Längenfeld; incl full board s €94-104, d €168-208, ste €192-226; ℗☲☷) The Lengler family extend a heartfelt welcome at this

pretty chalet hotel, a five-minute walk from Aqua Dome. Set in gardens with mountain views, Hotel Rita has spacious, contemporary rooms and a terrific spa area with an indoor pool, whirlpool, herb-scented saunas and hammam. It's all about the details here: from lovingly prepared six-course dinners to free guided hikes and bicycle, map and walking-pole rental.

Nature Resort Ötztal   RESORT $$
(☑05252-603 50; www.nature-resort.at; Piburgerstrasse 6, Ötz; incl half-board s €112-132, d €184-224; 🅿@🛜) 🏊 This riverside retreat has eco-chic chalet rooms, warmly decorated in sustainable pine. It's a solid family choice, with free activities such as guided mountain hikes and bike tours, plus deals on rafting and canyoning. That's if you can tear yourself away from the saunas and open fire in the spa.

Hotel Garni Granat   HOTEL $$
(☑05254-20 62; www.hotel-granat.at; Gemeindestrasse 2, Sölden; d €98-126, tr €180; 🅿@🛜) This friendly pension in Sölden is near the ski lifts in winter and runs free guided hikes in summer. Many of the bright, traditional rooms have whirlpool bath-tubs. A playground and sandpit occupy kids, and guests have free use of the pool, sauna and tennis court at the nearby leisure centre.

ℹ Information

The valley's main **tourist office** (☑057200; www.oetztal.com; Gemeindestrasse 4, Sölden;

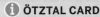

> ### ℹ ÖTZTAL CARD
>
> You can save in summer by investing in the **Ötztal Card** (www.oetztalcard.oetztal.com; 3/7/10 days €52/73/93;), which is half-price for children. From mid-June to September the pass covers public transport and cable cars in the valley, attractions such as Ötzi Dorf, activities from outdoor swimming pools to bike rental, plus one free entry to Aqua Dome and Area 47.

⊙8am-6pm Mon-Sat, 9am-noon & 3-6pm Sun) is in Sölden, though there are others in villages such as Ötz and Längenfeld. All can arrange accommodation and have brochures on activities in the area.

ℹ Getting There & Away

From Ötztal Bahnhof, buses head south roughly hourly to destinations including Umhausen (€4.50, 30 minutes) and Sölden (€8.40, one hour).

With your own wheels you should be able to get at least as far as Hochgurgl all year, but the road beyond into Italy via the high-alpine 2509m **Timmelsjoch Pass** (p318) is often blocked by snow in winter.

Trains arrive at Ötztal Bahnhof at the head of the valley and run frequently to Innsbruck (€10.20, 22 to 49 minutes), Imst-Pitztal (€3.60, nine minutes) and Landeck (€6.40, 26 minutes).

TYROL & VORARLBERG THE ÖTZTAL

ICE MAN

In 1991 German hiker Helmut Simon came across the body of a man preserved within the Similaun Glacier in the Ötztaler Alpen, some 90m within Italy. Police and forensic scientists were summoned to the scene. Carbon dating revealed that the ice man, nicknamed 'Ötzi', was nearly 5400 years old, placing him in the late Stone Age and making him the oldest and best-preserved mummy in the world.

Ötzi became big news, more so because his state of preservation was remarkable; even the pores of his skin were visible. In addition, Ötzi had been found with 70 artefacts, including a copper axe, bow and arrows, charcoal and clothing. Physiologically he was found to be no different from modern humans. X-rays showed he had suffered from arthritis, frostbite and broken ribs.

Not everybody was worried about these finer points, however. Several Austrian and Italian women contacted Innsbruck University shortly after the discovery and asked to be impregnated with Ötzi's frozen sperm, but the all-important part of his body was missing.

Ötzi was relinquished to the Italians to become the centrepiece of a museum in Bolzano in 1998. In September 2010 the family of the late Helmut Simon were rewarded €175,000 for his groundbreaking discovery. In 2016 Ötzi was in the news again as researchers studied a particular strain of his stomach bacteria to shed light on the history of human migration from north Africa.

Imst

📞 05412 / POP 9550

Beautifully situated in the wide Gurgltal (Gurgl Valley) and spreading towards a range of thickly wooded mountains, Imst is famous for its many springs. While the town itself won't keep you long, its surrounding meadows, rugged peaks and gorges might. Imst makes a fine base for hiking and skiing in the nearby Ötztal.

◎ Sights

★Rosengartenschlucht
GORGE

(Rose Garden Ravine; 🚶) An easygoing family hike is the 5km (approximately three-hour) loop through the dramatic 200m-high Rosengartenschlucht, where boarded walkways make for a gentle ascent and afford sterling views of a waterfall. At the top, the walk continues through forest and along a trail overlooking the Lechtaler Alps. You can't miss the **Blaue Grotte**, a cave pool that is a startling shade of blue.

Starkenberger Biermythos
BREWERY

(📞 05412-662 01; www.starkenberger.at; Griesegg 1, Tarrenz; tour adult/child €7/free; ⊗ 10am-5pm daily May-Oct, 10am-noon & 1-4pm Mon-Fri Nov-Apr) Housed in a medieval castle, this 200-year-old brewery sits 3km north of Imst in Tarrenz. A visit dashes through the brewing process and includes a beer tasting. If you can't get enough of the stuff, you can even bathe in it by calling ahead – it does wonders for the complexion, apparently.

Haus der Fasnacht
MUSEUM

(www.fasnacht.at; Streleweg 6; adult/child €4/1; ⊗ 4-7pm Fri) Every four years, Imst plays host to a Shrovetide festival, the Unesco-listed **Schemenlaufen** (ghost dance); the next takes place on 9 February 2020. The highlight is the vibrant parade of characters, from hunchback *Hexen* (witches) to *Spritzer* that squirt water at spectators. This museum homes in on this centuries-old tradition and exhibits many of the hand-carved ghost masks.

✦ Activities

Alpine Coaster
ADVENTURE SPORTS

(Hoch-Imst; adult/child €7.10/4.90; ⊗ 10am-5pm; 🚶) The Alpine Coaster is billed as the world's longest Alpine roller coaster and offers a thrilling ride down the mountains. A gondola shuttles passengers uphill to the starting point, where they board self-controlled bobs to catapult 3.5km downhill, negotiating tricky bumps and hairpin bends.

🛏 Sleeping

Romedihof
HOSTEL $

(📞 05412-222 12 10; www.romedihof.at; Brennbichl 41; dm €21-24, d €52; @ 🖥) Lodged in a 16th-century farmhouse, Romedihof is a terrific base for hiking, cycling and skiing. The interiors have been carefully restored, with beams, fireplaces and stucco adding a historic edge. Room rates include bread delivered fresh from a local baker for preparing your own breakfast in the shared kitchen. Take the train to Imst-Pitztal then walk 10 minutes; see the website for a detailed map.

Hotel Hirschen
HOTEL $$

(📞 05412-69 01; www.hirschen-imst.com; Thomas-Walch-Strasse 3; s €70-82, d €108-140; 🅿 @ 🖥 ⛱) This central guesthouse has comfy rooms, an indoor pool and modern spa area (check out the water beds in the relaxation room for a post-hike snooze). A plate of venison ragout is never far away in the wood-panelled restaurant (mains €10 to €18), where stag heads stud the walls.

❶ Information

The **tourist office** (📞 69 10-0; www.imst.at; Johannesplatz 4; ⊗ 8am-6pm Mon, 9am-6pm Tue-Fri, 10am-1pm Sat; 🖥) is highly informed on accommodation and activities in Imst and its surrounds; there's also free wi-fi.

❶ Getting There & Away

The town is slightly to the north of the main east–west roads (the A12 and B171), and is served by frequent buses and trains (from Innsbruck €12.10, 40 minutes).

❶ Getting Around

Adults may feel slightly silly boarding the Imster Bummelbär (adult/child €3/2, three daily) tourist train, but it's handy for reaching nearby sights including Starkenberger Biermythos.

The tourist office has a list of outfits with bike and e-bike rental.

Ehrwald

📞 05673 / POP 2665

Nudging the German border, this bijou town is dwarfed by colossal peaks, including the craggy limestone peaks of the Wetterstein range and Germany's highest of the high – 2962m Zugspitze. In summer, its hiking trails thread high to waterfall-laced mountains, while in winter it offers well-groomed slopes for beginner and intermediate skiers.

◉ Sights

Zugspitze VIEWPOINT

(www.zugspitze.at; cable car 1 way/return €28.50/42) Ehrwald's crowning glory is the glaciated 2962m Zugspitze, Germany's highest peak, straddling the Austro-German border. From the crest there's a magnificent panorama of the main Tyrolean mountain ranges, as well as the Bavarian Alps and Mt Säntis in Switzerland. North of Zugspitze is Garmisch-Partenkirchen, Germany's most popular ski resort.

ⓘ Information

For information on accommodation and activities, contact the **tourist office** (☏ 20 000 208; www.ehrwald.com; Kirchplatz 1; ☺ 8.30am-6pm Mon-Fri, 9am-5pm Sat, 9am-noon Sun) in the heart of the town. Staff will help find rooms free of charge.

ⓘ Getting There & Away

Trains from Innsbruck (€14, 1¾ hours) to Ehrwald pass through Germany; you must change at Garmisch-Partenkirchen. Austrian train tickets are valid for the whole trip.

Landeck

☏ 05442 / POP 7780

Landeck is an ordinary town with an extraordinary backdrop: framed by an amphitheatre of forested peaks, presided over by a medieval castle and bordered by the fast-flowing Inn and Sanna Rivers. The town makes a good-value base for outdoor activities and exploring the nearby Inntal and Patznauntal valleys.

◉ Sights

Schloss Landeck CASTLE

(www.schlosslandeck.at; Schlossweg 2; adult/child €7.70/2; ☺ 10am-5pm mid-Apr–late Oct, 1-5pm mid-Dec–early Jan; 🖈) Standing sentinel above Landeck, this 13th-century hilltop castle is visible from afar. The 1st-floor **museum** showcases everything from Celtic figurines to hand-carved *Krampus* masks, as well as a wonderful mechanised nativity scene during Advent. Climb the dizzying staircase to the tower for sweeping views over Landeck and the Lechtaler Alps.

Stanz VILLAGE

(www.brennereidorf.at) If all the fresh air and activity of Landeck have worked up a thirst, pop over to Stanz, 3km away. Set on a sunny plateau dotted with apple and plum orchards, the village has 150 houses and a whopping 60 schnapps distilleries. There are a number of rustic huts where you can kick back and taste the local firewater before rolling back down to the valley.

Zammer Lochputz GORGE

(www.zammer-lochputz.at; adult/child €4/3; ☺ 9.30am-5.30pm May-Sep, 10am-5pm Sat-Mon Oct) A roller coaster of water thrashes the limestone cliffs at Zammer Lochputz gorge just outside of Landeck. Leading up through pine forest, a trail passes viewpoints and some interesting rock formations – look out for the head of a bull and a nymph.

⚐ Activities

Landeck attracts the odd skier to its 22km of mostly intermediate slopes (a day ski pass costs €32), but is better known for its hiking trails. The magnificent **Adlerweg** (Eagle Trail) stops off in Landeck on its 280km journey through Tyrol. Many footpaths can be accessed by taking the **Venet** (www.venet.at; adult/child one way €14.40/8.20, return €16.50/9.80; ☺ 8am-5pm) cable car up to Krahberg (2208m).

Sport Camp Tirol ADVENTURE SPORTS

(☏ 05442-626 11; www.sportcamptirol.at; Mühlkanal 1; 🖈) This is a one-stop action shop for activities including paragliding (€110), canyoning (€79 to €95), white-water rafting (€36 to €62) and climbing (€59). You can also rent mountain bikes here (half-/full day €18/22) to head off on one of the tourist office's free GPS tours or tackle the downhill Inn Trail.

⎙ Sleeping

Gasthof Greif GUESTHOUSE $

(☏ 05442-622 68; www.gasthof-greif.at; Marktplatz 6; s €47-52, d €70-80; 🅿) Greif sits on a quiet square above the main street just down from the castle. Its 1970s-style rooms are large and tidy, and its restaurant (mains €9 to €16) serves solid Tyrolean cuisine.

Hotel Mozart HOTEL $$

(☏ 05442-642 22; www.mozarthotels.at; Adamhofgasse 7; s/d/f incl half-board €82/144/215; 🅿 ☒) It's amazing how far Amadeus travels in

ⓘ GLETSCHERPARK CARD

The Imst tourist office sells the good-value Gletscherpark Card (three/five days €59/79), available from mid-June to mid-October, which covers all public transport, cable cars and most attractions in the region.

Austria. This particular Mozart pleases with big sunny rooms opening onto balconies and broad mountain views. The flowery gardens and indoor pool with a little spa area invite relaxation, and there's ample bike storage.

Tramserhof   HOTEL **$$**
(☑ 05442-622 46; www.tramserhof.at; Tramserweg 51; s/d incl half-board €65/130; P 🖙 ≋) 🖉 Nestled among trees, this is a calm retreat 20 minutes' walk from central Landeck. The rooms are country-style with loads of natural light and warm pine. The spa shelters a whirlpool and sauna. Tuck into organic produce at breakfast.

✖ Eating

Cafe Haag   CAFE **$**
(Maisengasse 19; snacks €3.50-6; ⊙ 7.30am-6.30pm Mon-Fri, 8am-12.30pm Sat) Local plums, nuts and honey go into this cafe's divine chocolate, made with the milk of Tyrolean grey cattle, and the cakes are just the sugar kick needed for the uphill trudge to the castle.

Schrofenstein   AUSTRIAN **$$**
(☑ 05442-623 95; Malserstrasse 31; mains €15-30; ⊙ 11am-11pm; 🖗) With a generous helping of Austrian heartiness and a dash of Mediterranean lightness, Schrofenstein's elegantly rustic restaurant swings with the seasons: from spring asparagus to summer berries and mushrooms and autumn game. Dishes such as local sheep's-cheese creme brûlée with olive cake and basil pesto, and veal shank with truffle polenta and plums hit the mark every time.

ⓘ Information

The friendly staff at the **tourist office** (☑ 05442-656 00; www.tirolwest.at; Malserstrasse 10; ⊙ 8.30am-noon & 2-6pm Mon-Fri, 9am-noon Sat; 🖗) can help book accommodation and have a list of local pensions.

ⓘ Getting There & Away

Trains run roughly hourly to Innsbruck (€14, 46 minutes) and at least every two hours to Bregenz (€25.40, 1¾ hours). Buses depart from outside the train station and/or from the bus station in the centre. The train station is 1.5km to the east; to get into town walk left on leaving the station and stay on the same side of the river.

The A12 into Vorarlberg passes by Landeck, burrowing into a tunnel as it approaches the town. The B171 passes through the centre of town.

ⓘ Getting Around

Venet (p321) In summer, the Venet cable car zooms up to Krahberg (2208m), where there is a web of marked footpaths.

Inntal

POP 11.250

Shadowing the turquoise, swiftly flowing Inn River, the Inntal (Inn Valley) has few major sights but the scenery is beautiful, particularly around Pfunds with its jagged peaks and thickly forested slopes. Many of the ornately frescoed houses here are similar in design to those found in the Engadine in Graubünden, Switzerland, further up the Inntal.

South of Pfunds, you have a choice of routes. If you continue along the Inn you'll end up in Switzerland (infrequent buses). Alternatively, if you bear south to castle-crowned Nauders you'll soon reach South Tyrol (Italy) by way of the Reschen Pass (open year-round).

ⓘ Getting There & Away

Buses run roughly hourly from Landeck to Pfunds (€7.40, 42 minutes) and Nauders (€9.30, one hour), where it's possible to head on with public transport to Merano in Italy, but at least three changes are required.

Ischgl

☑ 05444 / POP 1560 / ELEV 1377M

Ischgl becomes a quintessential powdersville in winter, with snow-sure slopes and a boisterous après-ski scene. The resort is a bizarre combination of rural meets raunchy; a place where lap-dancing bars, folk music and techno happily coexist. That said, summer here can be *tote Hose* (totally dead) and you may prefer to base yourself in one of the more authentic neighbouring villages.

Activities

Silvretta Arena
SKIING

(www.silvretta.at; full-region 1-/6-day pass €52/281.50) Ischgl is the centrepiece of the vast Silvretta Arena, offering fabulous skiing on 238km of groomed slopes, ultramodern lifts (heated seats and all) and few queues. Suited to all except absolute beginners, the resort has great intermediate runs around Idalp, tough black descents at Greitspitz and Paznauer Taya, and plenty of off-piste powder to challenge experts.

Skyfly
ADVENTURE SPORTS

(adult/child €35/21; ☺12.30-4.30pm) The mountains are but a blur on this high-flying addition to Iscghl, which opened in summer 2016. The 50m-high, 2km-long zipwire whisks you above the valley and it's seriously fast – picking up speeds of up to 84 km/h. Kids should be at least eight years old and 1.2m tall; under 10-year-olds need to be accompanied by an adult.

Silvretta Mountain Bike Arena
MOUNTAIN BIKING

Few Austrian resorts can match Ischgl for mountain biking. The mammoth Silvretta Mountain Bike Arena features 1000km of bikeable territory, ranging from downhill tracks to circular trails. Pick up a free map of the area at the tourist office.

For bike rental, try **Intersport Bründl** (www.bruendl.at; Dorfstrasse 64; ☺8.30am-6pm Mon-Sat, 8.30am-12.30pm Sun) or **Silvretta Bike Academy** (www.silvretta-bikeacademy.at; Paznaunweg 15; ☺9am-6pm).

Toboggan Track
SNOW SPORTS

(adult/child €13/7.50) The 7km toboggan track offers a bumpy downhill dash through the snow from Idalp to Ischgl, which is particularly scenic when floodlit on Monday and Thursday nights from 7pm to 8.30pm. Toboggans can be hired at the mountain station for €8.50/4 for adults/children.

Klettersteige
WALKING

A step up from the alpine hikes heading out from Ischgl is the more ambitious scrambling on the *Klettersteige* (fixed-rope routes) at 2872m Greitspitz and 2929m Flimspitze.

Festivals & Events

Top of the Mountain
MUSIC

(☺late Nov & late Apr) This winter-season opening and closing concert has welcomed a host of stars, including English rock band Muse, in recent years.

Ironbike
SPORTS

(☺Aug) Super-fit mountain bikers compete in this 79km obstacle course of a race, involving steep climbs and exhilarating descents.

Sleeping

Hotel Alpenstern
HOTEL $

(☏05444-512 01; www.alpenstern.at; Versahlweg 5; d €68; ℗🛜) Nice surprise: one of Ischgl's sweetest hotels is also among its cheapest. The friendly Walser family keeps the modern alpine-style rooms spotless and serves generous breakfasts. In winter, the spa is great for post-ski downtime.

AlpVita Piz Tasna
HOTEL $$

(☏05444-52 77; www.piztasna.at; Stöckwaldweg 5; s €76, d €132-146, half-board €15; ℗@🛜🏊) Picturesquely set on a slope, Piz Tasna gets rave reviews for its heartfelt welcome, big, comfy rooms with fine mountain views, and superb food that places the accent on regional, organic ingredients (half-board is worth the extra). The spa has an indoor pool, saunas, herbal steam rooms and a relaxation zone with hay and water beds.

Hotel Verwall
HOTEL $$

(☏05444-52 74; www.verwall.at; Dorfstrasse 125; incl half-board s €68, d €102-116; ℗🛜) This handsome chalet in central Ischgl is a cracking choice, with spacious, warm-hued rooms, decked out with pine trappings – the pick of which have balconies. There's a cute spa for a post-hike or -ski unwind, and the kitchen makes the most of regional ingredients. Dairy products from the family's farm land on the breakfast table.

Eating

Kitzloch
INTERNATIONAL $$

(☏05444-56 18; http://kitzloch.at; Galfesweg 3; mains €18-27; ☺8-11pm Dec-Apr) Wild après-ski shenanigans with DJ Boris at Kitzloch (fancy dress and all) should work up an appetite for dinner in the rustic, fire-warmed restaurant. Go for the famous sticky spare ribs or a pot of bubbling fondue. Portions are very generous.

ⓘ TIROLWESTCARD

If you're staying overnight in summer, pick up the TirolWestCard (www.tirol-west.at) for free access to the major sights, outdoor pools and the bus network. In summer, the Landeck tourist office arranges guided walks from herb strolls to mountain hikes (free with the TirolWestCard), and can advise on activities from llama trekking to via ferrate.

Paznaunerstube   GASTRONOMY **$$$**
(☑ 05444-600; www.trofana-royal.at; Hotel Troyana Royal, Dorfstrasse 95; menus €60-120; ☺ noon-10pm Mon-Sat) Much-lauded chef Martin Sieberer turns every meal into a gastronomic event at this hotel restaurant. In a refined wood-panelled parlour, regional specialities such as milk-fed Galtür lamb are given an inventive twist, served with panache and paired with top wines.

🍷 Drinking & Nightlife

The snow doesn't get hotter than in Ischgl, famous Europe-wide for its pumping après-ski scene. Oompah-playing barns, raunchy go-go bars and chichi clubs shake the resort. Most places go with the snow and open in winter only.

Trofana Alm   BAR
(www.trofana-alm.at; Dorfstrasse 91; ☺ 3-8pm) A huge wooden barn with live Austrian bands and potent apple schnapps working the crowd into a singing, dancing, drunken frenzy.

Schatzi Bar   BAR
(Fimbabahnweg 4, Hotel Elizabeth; ☺ 4-8pm) This rollicking après-ski bar is full of *Schatzis* (little treasures) in the form of go-go dancing girls in skimpy *Dirndls* that look like they've shrunk in the wash. Madness.

Kuhstall   BAR
(www.kuhstall.at; Ischgl 80; ☺ 3pm-midnight) *The* place for slope-side socialising to gear up for a big night out in Ischgl.

Madlein VIP Club   CLUB
(www.madlein-vipclub.com; Madleinweg 2, Hotel Madlein; ☺ 10pm-6am Dec-Apr) Celebrities and would-be celebrities are often spotted at this uber-glamorous club brimming with beautiful people.

ⓘ Information

The **tourist office** (☑ 050-990 100; www.ischgl.com; Dorfstrasse 43; ☺ 8am-6pm Mon-Fri, to 5pm Sat, to 1pm Sun) stocks heaps of literature on hiking, biking and skiing in the area, plus accommodation brochures.

ⓘ Getting There & Away

Bus 4240 operates hourly between Ischgl and Landeck (€7.40, 44 minutes).

Arlberg Region

The wild and harshly beautiful Arlberg region, shared by Vorarlberg and Tyrol, comprises several linked resorts and offers some of Austria's finest skiing. Heralded as the cradle of alpine skiing, St Anton am Arlberg is undoubtedly the best-known and most popular resort.

St Anton am Arlberg

☑ 05446 / POP 2425 / ELEV 1304M
Once upon a time St Anton was but a sleepy village, defined by the falling and melting of snow and the coming and going of cattle, until one day the locals beheld the virgin powder on their doorstep and discovered their happy-ever-after... In 1901 the resort founded the first ski club in the Alps and downhill skiing was born, so if ever the ski bug is going to bite you it will surely be here. Nestled at the foot of 2811m-high Valluga and strung out along the northern bank of the Rosanna River, St Anton am Arlberg is a cross between a ski bum's Shangri-La and Ibiza in fast-forward mode – the terrain fierce, the nightlife hedonistic.

◉ Sights

St Anton Museum   MUSEUM
(www.museum-stanton.com; Rudi-Matt-Weg 10; adult/child €4/2; ☺ noon-6pm Tue-Sun) Set in attractive gardens above St Anton and housed in a beautiful 1912 villa, this nostalgic museum traces St Anton's tracks back to the good old days when skis were little more than improvised wooden planks.

🏃 Activities

Winter Activities
St Anton is the zenith of Austria's alpine skiing, and the brand-new, state-of-the-art cable cars connecting it to over-the-mountain Lech and Zürs has further improved con-

THE PAZNAUNTAL

Grazing the Swiss border and running west of the Inntal, the Paznauntal (Paznaun Valley) is a dramatic landscape overshadowed by the pearly white peaks of the Silvretta range. The villages are sleepy in summer, a lull that is broken in winter when skiers descend on party-hearty resorts such as Ischgl.

Activities

The Paznauntal is undoubtedly one of Austria's best ski areas, despite (or because of) its relative isolation. The Silvretta Ski Pass (two-day pass adult/child €103/58) covers Ischgl, Galtür, Kappl and Samnaun, a duty-free area in Switzerland. Its summer equivalent is the Silvretta Card, which is free when you stay overnight in the valley, comprising cable cars, lifts, public transport over the Bielerhöhe Pass into Vorarlberg, and numerous swimming pools in Ischgl and Galtür.

Getting There & Away

Only a secondary road (B188) runs along the valley, crossing into Vorarlberg at the Bielerhöhe Pass (toll cars/motorcycles €14/11), where the views are sensational. This pass, closed in winter, rejoins the main highway near Bludenz. Regular buses travel as far as Galtür (€8.40, one hour) from Landeck.

ditions. The terrain is vast, covering 305m of slopes, and the skiing challenging, with fantastic backcountry opportunities and exhilarating descents including the **Kandahar** run on Galzig.

Cable cars ascend to **Valluga** (2811m), from where experts can go off-piste all the way to Lech (with a ski guide only). For fledglings, there are nursery slopes on **Gampen** (1850m) and **Kapall** (2330m). **Rendl** is snowboarding territory with jumps, rails and a half-pipe. A 10-minute stroll east of St Anton is **Nasserein**, where novices can test out the nursery slopes. Further east still are the quieter slopes of **St Jakob**, easily accessed by the Nasserein gondola.

A single ski pass (one-/three-/six-day pass €52/148/262) covers the whole Arlberg region and is valid for all 87 ski lifts.

Summer Activities

Walking in the mountains is the most popular summertime activity, and the meadows full of wildflowers and grazing cattle are pure Heidi. A handful of cable cars and lifts rise to the major peaks. If you're planning on going hiking, pick up a detailed booklet and map from the tourist office.

The tourist office also produces a small booklet with a number of suggested **cycling** trails in the area.

★**H2O Adventure**   ADVENTURE SPORTS
(📞05472-66 99; www.h2o-adventure.at; Bahnhofstrasse 1, Arlrock; rafting €47-90, canyoning €63-140, mountain biking €39-59; ⊙May–mid-

Oct) H2O Adventure is a one-stop adventure shop. A team of pros takes you whitewater rafting on the turbulent waters of the Inn River, canyoning deep in the surrounding gorges, tubing and mountain biking. It has dedicated tours geared towards families, including a high-rope adventure course. Bike rental costs €15/25 per half-/full day.

Ski Arlberg   SNOW SPORTS
(www.skiarlberg.at; 1-/3-/6-day pass €52/148/262) Ski Arlberg is one of Austria's most famous skiing regions and deservedly so. Its centrepiece is St Anton am Arlberg, a mecca to expert skiers and boarders, with its great snow record, challenging terrain and terrific off-piste; not to mention the most happening après-ski in Austria, if not Europe. Its over-the-valley neighbours are the resorts of Lech and Zürs in Vorarlberg.

Run of Fame   SKIING
An epic run if ever there was one, St Anton's Run of Fame is a 65km marathon ski, covering an altitude difference of 18,000m. The run covers the entire Arlberg skiing area and takes the best part of a day, so brace yourself (and your legs) for one hell of a burner.

Rodelbahn   SNOW SPORTS
(adult/child €11.50/6, sled rental €9) Fancy a twilight dash through the snow? Every Tuesday and Thursday evening in winter, the 4km-long Rodelbahn toboggan run from Gampen to Nasserein is floodlit. Simply grab your sled and away you go! Sleds can be rented at the Talstation base station.

St Anton am Arlberg

N

0   400 m
0   0.2 miles

Putzenalm (8km);
St Jakob (1km);
Landeck (28km)

NASSEREIN

Nassereiner-
str

Hotel Garni
Ernst Falch
(500m)

Nassereinergasse

Rossanna

Arlbergstr

Rodelbahn
(Illuminated Bob
Sled Run)

Nassereinbahn

Dorfstr

Kirchegasse

20

Kindisfeld

7

18

Fangbahn

Mulden

Hannes-Schneider-Weg

Bahnhof

See Enlargement

Dorfstr

Rossanna

OBERDORF

6

Sesselbahn Gampen

Galzigbahn

1

17
Rudi-Matt-Weg

Rendlbahn

Arlbergstr

Alte Arlbergstr

Rendl
(2.2km)

10

OBERDORF

Gampen
(1846m)

5

MOOS

23

24

GASTIG

Unterer Mooserweg

Mooserweg

Dengertstr

21

25

Galzig (1.3km);
Valluga (4.4km)

Striissbach

St Christoph (6km);
Lech (18km)

Enlargement

0   200 m
0   0.1 miles

14

8

6

Stocklweg

Im Gries

Markstr

Dorfstr

Arlbergstr

Rossanna

Bahnhof

3

19

16

22

13

12

Gemeindegasse

Schüler-Weg

Walter-
Schneider-Weg

Hannes-Schneider-Weg

2

4

15

Kandaharweg

i

St Anton am Arlberg

⊙ Sights
1 St Anton Museum C3

⊕ Activities, Courses & Tours
2 Arlberg Well.com F3
3 Arlrock...G4
   H2O Adventure.............................(see 3)
4 Intersport Arlberg...............................F4
5 Rodelbahn...A1
6 Run of Fame D4
7 Ski Arlberg D2

🛌 Sleeping
8 Altes Thönihaus G3
9 Himmlhof G3
10 Lux Alpinae......................................B4
11 Piltriquitron Shelter E2
12 Rundeck...F4

🍴 Eating
13 Bodega F4
14 Fuhrmann Stube...............................G3
15 Galzig Bistro F4
16 Hazienda F3
17 Museum Restaurant..........................C3
18 Rodelalm..D1

🍷 Drinking & Nightlife
19 Bar Cuba F3
20 Fanghouse..E1
21 Heustadl...B3
22 Horny Bull F3
23 Krazy Kanguruh B3
24 Mooserwirt..C3
25 Sennhütte A3
   Taps...(see 23)

Arlrock   ADVENTURE SPORTS
(www.arlrock.at; Bahnhofstrasse 1; adult/child climbing wall €9/5, boulder wall €6.50/5; ⊙9am-8pm) This striking leisure centre by the train station has climbing and boulder walls, kids' play areas, a bowling alley and tennis courts. It's also the home base of H2O Adventure, offering adrenalin-based activities from rafting on the Sanna River to canyoning, ziplining and downhill mountain biking.

🎆 Festivals & Events

Mountain Yoga Festival   SPORTS
(⊙early Sep) Do you know your downward-facing dog from your tree pose? If the answer is yes, head on over to Mayrhofen's Mountain Yoga festival. Held for the first time in 2016 against the stunning backdrop of the Arlberg Alps, the four-day festival attracts yoga instructors from all over the world.

🛏 Sleeping

Hotel Garni Ernst Falch   GUESTHOUSE $
(☎05446-28 53; www.hotelfalch.at; Ing-Gomperz-Weg 26; r €78; 🛜) Rainer and his kindly mum are the heart and soul of this wonderful B&B, perched above St Anton, a five-minute stroll from the Nassereinbahn. The homely rooms are bright, immaculately kept and pine-clad, with balconies for soaking up the alpine views. Nothing is too much trouble for the family, so whether you need a pick-up from the station or Nordic poles for a hike, just say the word.

Altes Thönihaus   GUESTHOUSE $
(☎05446-28 10; www.altes-thoenihaus.at; Im Gries 1; s/d €36/64; 🅿🛜) Dating to 1465, this listed wooden chalet oozes Alpine charm from every last beam. Fleecy rugs and pine keep the mood cosy in rooms with mountain-facing balconies. Downstairs there's a superb little spa and restored *Stube* (parlour).

★Himmlhof   GUESTHOUSE $$
(☎05446-232 20; www2.himmlhof.com; Im Gries 9; d €108-130, ste €128-228; 🅿@🛜) This *himmlisch* (heavenly) Tyrolean chalet has wood-clad rooms brimming with original features (tiled ovens, four-poster beds and the like). An open fire for afternoon tea and a cosy spa with a grotto-like plunge pool beckon after a day's skiing.

Rundeck   HOTEL $$
(☎05446-31 33; www.hotelrundeck.at; Arlbergstrasse 59; d €110-120, ste €120-140; @🛜) Clean lines, earthy tones and nutwood panelling define the streamlined rooms at design-focused Rundeck. There's a sleek spa and a backlit bar with an open fire for relaxing moments, plus a playroom for the kids.

Lux Alpinae   DESIGN HOTEL $$$
(☎05446-301 08; www.luxalpinae.at; Arlbergstrasse 41; d incl half-board €170-440; 🅿🍽) This design hotel wings you into the 21st century with glass-walled rooms that bring the mountains indoors and industrial-chic interiors blending concrete, wood and steel. Personalised service (including a driver to take you to the slopes), a first-rate restaurant and a spa add to its appeal. Lux Alpinae is only open in winter.

Piltriquitron Shelter   GUESTHOUSE $$
(☎0676 7400908; www.piltriquitron.com; Kirchgasse 10; s/d €41/84) One for serious outdoor-lovers, this Nordic-cool guesthouse is super central. Jacob, the Danish owner, is

a terrific host and his incredible photography of the Alps and Patagonia adorns the communal lounge, where complimentary tea and coffee are available. A keen mountaineer and expeditioner, he can provide tips and help arrange hiking, trail running, climbing, fly fishing, kayaking and more.

🍴 Eating

Putzenalm
AUSTRIAN $

(Putzen Alpe; snacks €1.50-9; ⊘8am-8pm mid-Jun–mid-Sep) A beautiful 8km uphill hike from St Anton, this mountain hut sits in a tranquil Alpine meadow, where you can often spot marmots if you look carefully. It does a great *Brettljause* (tasting platter), featuring the cheese from its 50 cows, which you can, incidentally, see coming down from the pastures around 5pm, their clanging bells resonating through the valley.

★Museum Restaurant
AUSTRIAN $$

(📞05446-24 75; www.museum-restaurant.at; Rudi-Matt-Weg 10; mains €23.50-32.50; ⊘noon-9pm Tue-Sun) Arlberger hay soup with smoked wild boar and lavender served in a bread bowl, and the most succulent Tyrolean beef and trout fished fresh from the pond outside land on your plate at this intimate wood-panelled restaurant, housed in the picture-perfect chalet of the St Anton Museum.

Galzig Bistro
BISTRO $$

(📞05446-425 41; http://galzigbistrobar.at; Kandaharweg 2; mains €14-25; ⊘10am-1am Thu-Tue, 9am-1am Wed) Winningly fresh produce is the secret to the bistro-style dishes served at Galzig, which stretch from gourmet salads (wild herb and berry, for instance) to pasta with king prawns, capers and endives, and rack of suckling pig. It's uniformly delicious. The slick, contemporary interior and terrace attract a style-conscious, cocktail-sipping crowd after dark.

Fuhrmann Stube
AUSTRIAN $$

(📞05446-29 21; Dorfstrasse 74; mains €10-16; ⊘10am-10pm) When snow blankets the rooftops, this is a cosy hideaway for tucking into *Knödel* (dumplings), a carnivorous *Tiroler Bauernplatte* (Tyrolean farmers' platter) or a generous helping of strudel.

Bodega
TAPAS $$

(📞05446-427 88; Dorfstrasse 40; tapas €4.50-12.50; ⊘3pm-1am) Excellent tapas, vino and live music reel in the crowds to this buzzy Spanish haunt. You can't book, so be prepared to wait for a table.

Hazienda
INTERNATIONAL $$

(📞05446-29 68; www.m3hotel.at; Dorfstrasse 56; mains €16-33; ⊘cafe 8am-midnight year-round, restaurant 6pm-1am winter) A prime people-watching terrace fronts this smart restaurant-cafe hybrid. Thai-style Argentine beef fillet, herby homemade pasta with sheep's cheese, proper Italian espresso – everything here strikes a perfect balance.

Rodelalm
AUSTRIAN $$

(📞0676 886486000; www.rodelalm.com; Nassereinerstrasse 106; mains €14.50-21.50; ⊘10am-11pm, closed Wed; 🚠) With glowing faces and frosty fingers, most sledders heading down Rodelbahn stop at this hut located halfway, to warm up with schnapps and a big plate of *Schweinshaxe* (pork knuckles), *Gröstl* (Tyrolean potato, egg, bacon and onion fry-up) or cheese fondue. An open fire keeps things toasty in the pine-panelled interior.

🍸 Drinking & Nightlife

St Anton is Austria's unrivalled après-ski king. Dancing on tables, *Schlager* sing-alongs, Jägermeister after Jägermeister – it's just an average night out in St Anton, where people party as hard as they ski. Pace yourself.

Mooserwirt
BAR

(www.mooserwirt.at; Unterer Mooserweg 2; ⊘3.30-8pm) One word: *craaaazy*. Come teatime Mooserwirt heaves with skiers guzzling beer (the place sells around 5000L a day), dancing to DJ Gerhard's Eurotrash mix and sweating in their salopettes. The first challenge is to locate your skis, the second to use them to get back to St Anton in one piece.

Sennhütte
BAR

(Dengerstrasse 503; ⊘3-6pm) A sunny terrace, feisty schnapps, locals jiggling on the tables, live bands – what more après-ski could one ask for? In summer, there's a wonderful herb garden, treehouse and cow-themed walking trail for kids.

Heustadl
BAR

(www.heustadl.com; Dengerstrasse 625; ⊘9.30am-6.30am) Just north of Sennhütte, this shack is always fit to bursting with beery throngs. There's live music from 3pm to 6pm daily. Yes, the bar stools have legs; yes, you are still sane if not sober.

Krazy Kanguruh
BAR

(www.krazykanguruh.com; Mooserweg 19; ⊘10am-8pm) Owned by St Anton ski legend and two-time slalom world champion Mario Matt, this slopeside hot spot is loud, fun and jam-packed after 5pm. One too many tequilas will indeed send you bouncing (on skis) back to the valley.

Taps BAR
(Mooserweg 15; ⊙11am-8pm) Taps is a pumping après-ski place with the cheapest beer on the mountain and DJs keeping the party in full swing. There's a huge sun terrace for chilling and often free homemade schnapps (mind-blowing stuff) doing the rounds.

Fanghouse BAR
(www.fanghouse.com; Nassereinerstrasse 6; ⊙10am-11.59pm) At the base of the slopes in Nasserein, this laid-back hangout has a big sunny terrace, fun staff (including the crazy Swedish owner, Hasse) and lethal Jägermeister shots served at -17°C. The pub occasionally hosts events such as live music and quiz nights.

Horny Bull CLUB
(www.hornybull.com; Dorfstrasse 50; ⊙10pm-4am) Yes, we know, the name... But don't let it stop you from venturing into this club – when the après-ski ends, it takes over with international DJ-spun beats.

Bar Cuba BAR
(Dorfstrasse 33; ⊙4pm-2am) Live music, Wednesday-night fancy-dress parties, chipper bar staff and cocktails named Cuban Cocaine and Love Juice – say no more.

ℹ Information
You can check emails for free in most ski shops. The centrally located **tourist office** (☎05446-226 90; www.stantonamarlberg.com; Dorfstrasse 8; ⊙8am-6pm Mon-Fri, 9am-6pm Sat, 9am-noon & 2-5pm Sun) has information on outdoor activities and places to stay as well as maps and free wi-fi. There's an accommodation board and free telephone outside

ℹ Getting There & Away
The ultramodern train station is on the route between Bregenz (€12.80, 1¼ hours) and Innsbruck (€16.80, 1¼ hours), with fast trains every one or two hours. St Anton and St Christoph are close to the eastern entrance of the Arlberg Tunnel (cars and minibuses €8.50), the toll road connecting Vorarlberg and Tyrol. You can avoid the toll by taking the B197, but no vehicles with trailers are allowed on this winding road.

Buses depart from stands southwest of the tourist office.

ℹ Getting Around
Bicycles can be rented (half-/full day €16/23) from **Intersport Arlberg** (www.intersport-arlberg.com; Dorfstrasse 1; mountain bike/e-bike/ski rental per day €23/29/35; ⊙8.30am-7pm).

Free local buses go to outlying parts of the resort (such as St Jakob). Buses run to Lech (€4.70, 27 minutes) and Zürs (€3.80, 23 minutes) in Vorarlberg; they are hourly (until about 6pm) in winter, reducing to four a day in summer.

A minibus taxi can be shared between up to eight people; the trip from St Anton to Lech costs €37/55 in the day/night. Local **taxis** (☎0664 2302618) are also available.

Lech & Zürs
☎05583
Mountains huddle conspiratorially around the snow-sure slopes of the rugged Arlberg region, one of Austria's top ski destinations. The best-known villages are picture-postcard Lech (1450m) and its smaller twin Zürs (1716m), 6km south. Because of their relative isolation, fabulous skiing and five-star hotels, the resorts are a magnet to royalty (Princess Diana used to ski here), celebrities and anyone who pretends to be such from behind Gucci shades.

🏃 Activities
Remember Bridget Jones hurtling backwards down the mountain on skis in *The Edge of Reason?* That was filmed on Lech's scenic, forest-streaked runs. The terrain is best suited to beginners and intermediates, with off-piste possibilities and the famous 21km Weisse Ring (White Ring) appealing to more advanced skiers.

In winter 2016/2017 the resorts in Western Arlberg were finally linked to St Anton over the mountain, opening up Austria's biggest integrated ski area, with a whopping 305km of slopes to carve – from easy-peasy to pitch

ⓘ ST ANTON SUMMER & PREMIUM CARD

St Anton wings its way into summer with the fantastic Summer Card, free from your hotel or guesthouse when you stay overnight. It yields some excellent benefits, including one day of cable car use, one entry to **Arlberg Well.com** (http://wellness.arlberg-well.com; Hannes-Schneider-Weg 11; adult/child €7.50/4, incl sauna €15; ⊙9am-9pm), one guided walk, one green fee, entry to the **museum** (p324), one other activity (these range from yoga to e-bike tours), children's activities, plus free transport on buses between Landeck and St Christoph.

Upgrade to a Premium Card (three/five/seven days €55/66/77, children pay half-price) and you get daily use of the pool at Arlberg Well.com, cable cars and all activities for the duration of your stay. Activities can be prebooked at the tourist office or online at www.sommer-karte.at.

black – and 87 ski lifts. A one-/three-/six-day pass will set you back €52/148/262.

🛏 Sleeping

⭐ Hotel Gotthard   HOTEL $$

(☑05583-35 60; www.gotthard.at; Omesberg 119, Lech; s €75-86, d €144-170, ste €206-228; P🖨🛜🏊) It's the little touches that make all the difference at this chalet hotel, such as the oven-warm bread at breakfast (owner Clemens is a baker) and yoga room for Zen moments. Splashes of fuchsia and forest green jazz up the contemporary, pine-wood rooms, most of which have balconies, DVD players and iPod docks. There's a spa, an indoor pool and a children's playroom.

Theodul   HOTEL $$

(☑05583-23 08; www.theodul.at; Omesberg 332; s €85, d €144-176, ste €156-182; P🛜) The Walch family make you feel instantly at ease at this chalet hotel, handily positioned for the slopes. Rooms are decorated in classic alpine style, with white bedding, pine furnishings and mountain views. Slip into your bathrobe for a post-ski or -hike steam and unwind in the spa. Organic produce and speciality teas kick off the day healthily at breakfast.

Hotel Garni Lavendel   PENSION $$

(☑05583-26 57; www.lavendel.at; Dorf 447, Lech; s €50-65, d €90-120, apt €90-210; P🛜) The affable Mascher family make you feel at home at this cosy pension next to the ski lifts. Many of the spacious, immaculate rooms and apartments sport balconies and there's a little spa for a post-hike or après-ski unwind.

🍴 Eating

Hûs Nr 8   AUSTRIAN $$

(☑05583-332 20; www.hus8.at; Lech 8; mains €9-20; ⊙11am-1am) Raclette, fondue and crispy roast chicken are the stars of the menu at this rustic chalet, going strong since 1760. Snuggle up in an all-wood interior in winter or sit on the patio when the sun's out.

Fux   FUSION $$$

(☑05583-29 92; www.fux-mi.net; Omesberg 587, Lech; mains €29-46.50; ⊙4pm-3am; 🖋) Asian art gives a decadent touch to Fux, a steakhouse-restaurant hybrid. The food is top notch, whether you go for succulent charcoal-grilled steaks daubed with herb butter or Asian signatures such as yellow fin tuna with wok vegetables. The award-winning wine list comprises 2700 bottles.

ⓘ Information

The central **tourist office** (☑05583-216 10; www.lech-zuers.at; Dorf 2, Lech; ⊙8am-6pm Mon-Sat, 8am-noon & 3-5pm Sun) has bags of info on skiing and walking possibilities, and an accommodation board.

ⓘ Getting There & Away

Buses run between Lech and Zürs (€1.40, seven minutes); both resorts have connections to St Anton am Arlberg (€4.70, 30 minutes).

One kilometre south of Zürs is the Flexen Pass (1773m), occasionally blocked off by snow in winter, after which the road splits: the western fork leads to Stuben (1407m), the eastern one to St Anton am Arlberg in Tyrol. In summer, Lech can also be approached from the north, via the turning at Warth (1494m).

VORARLBERG

In Austria's far west, the Vorarlberg nudges up against Germany, Switzerland and Liechtenstein. Parts of it remain gloriously off-the-radar, with narrow valleys carving up mighty peaks and forests. The snow-capped heights of the Silvretta-Montafon give way to the wavy hills and lush dairy country of the Bregenzerwald, which in turn fall to the Bodensee (Lake Constance). Though renowned Austria-wide for its innovative architecture, this remains a remarkably peaceful and deeply traditional corner of the country.

History

Vorarlberg has been inhabited since the early Stone Age but it wasn't until the Celts arrived in 400 BC, followed by the Romans in around 15 BC, that lasting settlements were maintained. Brigantium, the forerunner of Bregenz, was a Roman stronghold until around the 5th and 6th centuries, when the raiding Germanic Alemanni tribes increased their influence and effectively took over.

Peace reigned in the province until the early 15th century, when it suffered substantial damage during the Appenzell War with the Swiss Confederation. Relations with its neighbour later improved to such an extent that in 1918 Vorarlberg declared independence from Austria and sought union with Switzerland. The move was blocked by the Allied powers in the postwar reorganisation of Europe; fears that an even smaller Austria would be easily absorbed by a recovering Germany were certainly founded. Today, Vorarlberg still looks first towards its westerly neighbours, and then to Vienna, 600km to the east.

❶ Getting There & Around

AIR

Friedrichshafen airport (②2840; www.fly-away.de), in Germany, is the closest major airport serving domestic and European destinations.

PUBLIC TRANSPORT

Vorarlberg is broken down into *Domino* (individual zones). A Maximo pass, costing €12.80/39.10, covers the entire province. Single *Domino* tickets cost €1.40 and a day pass is €2.70 – these cover city transport in Bregenz, Dornbirn, Götzis, Feldkirch, Bludenz, Lech and Schruns/Tschagguns. Information and timetables are available from the Verkehrsverbund Vorarlberg (www.vmobil.at).

Bregenz

②05574 / POP 28,410 / ELEV 427M

What a view! Ah yes, the locals proudly agree, Bregenz does indeed have the loveliest of views: before you the Bodensee, Europe's third-largest lake, spreads out like a liquid mirror; behind you the Pfänder

(1064m) climbs to the Alps; to the right you see Germany, to the left the faint outline of Switzerland. Just wow.

Whether contemplating avant-garde art and architecture by the new harbour, sauntering along the promenade on a summer's evening or watching opera under the stars at the much-lauded *Festspiele* (festival), you can't help but think – clichéd though it sounds – that Vorarlberg's pocket-sized capital has got at least a taste of it all.

◉ Sights

★**Vorarlberg Museum** MUSEUM
(www.vorarlbergmuseum.at; Kornmarktplatz 1; adult/child €9/free; ⊙10am-6pm Tue, Wed & Fri-Sun, to 8pm Thu) Following a three-year, €34 million makeover, the Vorarlberg Museum reopened in June 2013 to much acclaim. Its striking new home is a white cuboid emblazoned with what appears to 16,656 flowers (actually PET bottle bases imprinted in concrete). The gallery homes in on Vorarlberg's history, art and architecture in its permanent exhibitions, including one on the Roman archaeological finds of Brigantium. It also stages rotating exhibitions, such as recent ones spotlighting the Bregenzer Festspiele and mining in the Eastern Alps.

★**Pfänder Cable Car** CABLE CAR
(www.pfaenderbahn.at; Steinbruchgasse 4; adult/child 1 way €7.30/3.70, return €12.50/6.30; ⊙8am-7pm) A cable car whizzes to the 1064m peak of the Pfänder, a wooded mountain rearing above Bregenz and affording a breathtaking panorama of the Bodensee and the snowcapped summits of the not-so-distant Alps. At the top is the Alpine Game Park Pfänder .

★**Kunsthaus** GALLERY
(www.kunsthaus-bregenz.at; Karl-Tizian-Platz; adult/child €9/free; ⊙10am-6pm Tue, Wed & Fri-Sun, to 8pm Thu; ♿) Designed by Swiss architect Peter Zumthor, this giant glass and steel cube is said to resemble a lamp, reflecting the changing light of the sky and lake. The stark, open-plan interior is perfect for rotating exhibitions of contemporary art – the work of Chicago-based installation artist Theaster Gates and the myth-inspired marionettes of Egyptian artist Wael Shawky have recently featured. Check the website for details on everything from guided tours to kids' workshops.

Bregenz

Bodensee
(Lake Constance)

Pfänder Cable Car

OBERSTADT

Kunsthaus

Vorarlberg
Museum

Rathausstr

Sparkassenplatz

Seepromenade

Seestr

Reichsstr

Am Steinenbach

Schillerstr

Bergstr

Eichholzstr

Kornmarktstr

Anton-Schneider-Str

Brandgasse

Bergmannstr

Belruptstr

Am Brand

Weissenreuteweg

Am Brand

Eponastr

Thalbachg

Leutbühel

Kirchstr

Römerstr

Kaiserstr

Montfortstr

Bahnhofstr

St Anna Str

Klostergasse

Römerstr

Augasse

Quellenstr

Bahnhofstr

Mehrerauerstr

Stadionstr

Strandweg

Wotteggstr

Steinbruchgasse

Alpine
Game Park
Pfänder
(200m)

Pipeline (600m);
Lochau (6km);
Lindau (8km)

Rheindelta/Strandbad
Hard (8.5km)

Camping Mexico
(1.5km)

Nasha Kulinarisches (200m);
Schwärzler (1.1km)

1 17

3

9

20

11

12

2

7

6

5

15

16

13

18

19

4

8

10

14

200 m
0.1 miles

0
0

Bregenz

Rheindelta   NATURE RESERVE
(www.rheindelta.org; Hard) Easily explored on foot or by bike, this nature reserve sits 5km south of Bregenz, where the River Rhine flows into the Bodensee. The mossy marshes, reeds and mixed woodlands attract more than 300 bird species, including curlews, grey herons and rare black-tailed godwits.

Alpine Game Park Pfänder   NATURE RESERVE
(www.pfaender.at; Pfänder; ◔ sunrise-sunset) 𝗙𝗥𝗘𝗘 At the top of the Pfänder, a 30-minute circular trail brings you close to deer, wild boar, ibex and whistling marmots at the year-round Alpine Game Park Pfänder.

Festspielhaus   LANDMARK
(🖉 05574-41 30; www.festspielhausbregenz.at; Platz der Wiener Symphoniker 1) Even if you can't bag tickets for the Bregenzer Festspiele, the Festival Hall is a must-see. All tinted glass, smooth concrete and sharp angles, this is one of Bregenz' most visible icons. Many festival performances are held on the semi-circular Seebühne stage jutting out onto the lake.

Oberstadt   HISTORIC SITE
Slung high above the lake is the Oberstadt, Bregenz' tiny old town of winding streets, candy-coloured houses and flowery gardens. It's still enclosed by defensive walls and the sturdy **Martinstor** (St Martin's Gate).

Martinsturm   TOWER
(St Martin's Tower; www.martinsturm.at; Martinsgasse; adult/child €3.50/1; ◔ 10am-4pm Tue, Wed & Fri-Sun, to 9pm Thu) Not far past Martinstor is this baroque tower, topped by the largest onion dome in Central Europe. It's worth seeing the 14th-century frescoes in the

chapel before climbing up to the small military museum for fine views over Bregenz' rooftops.

🏃 Activities

Everybody who arrives in Bregenz is bewitched by the Bodensee, Europe's third-largest lake, straddling Austria, Switzerland and Germany. In summer, the lake becomes an autobahn for lycra-clad *Radfahrer* (cyclists); shoulder seasons are considerably more peaceful. Other activities on the lake include **sailing** and **diving** at Lochau, and **swimming**. For those that would prefer to kick back and enjoy the view, there are numerous boat companies that ferry passengers across the lake from April to mid-October.

Other lakeside activities include sailing and diving at Lochau, around 6km north of town, and swimming at the **Pipeline**.

Bodensee Cycle Path   CYCLING
(www.bodensee-radweg.com) When the sun's out, there's surely no better way to explore Bodensee than with your bum in a saddle. The well-marked Bodensee Cycle Path makes a 273km loop of the Bodensee, taking in vineyards, meadows, orchards, wetlands and historic towns. There are plenty of small beaches where you can stop for a refreshing dip in the lake. Visit the website for itineraries and maps.

Vorarlberg Lines   BOATING
(www.vorarlberg-lines.at; Seestrasse; ◔ early Apr–mid-Oct) This is one of a number of companies taking you out onto the lake from April to mid-October. There are two-hour Bodensee panorama cruises (adult/

child €18.40/9.10), one-hour Bregenz trips (€11.50/5.50) and regular boat transfers to lake destinations including Lindau, Mainau, Friedrichshafen and Konstanz.

Strandbad Hard
SWIMMING

(www.hard-sport-freizeit.at; Hard; adult/child €4.40/2.20; ⊗9am-8pm early May-early Sep) A lakefront contender 5km south of town, this lido has outdoor pools, barbecue areas, minigolf and a secluded *FKK* (nudist) beach for skinny-dippers.

Strandbad Bregenz
SWIMMING

(Strandweg; adult/child €4.90/2.40; ⊗9am-8pm early May-early Sep; ⊕) Packed with bronzed bods, overexcited kids and flirty teens in summer, this central lido has a lakeside beach, several outdoor pools with waterslides, and activities including volleyball and table tennis.

★ Festivals & Events

Bregenzer Festspiele
FESTIVAL

(Bregenz Festival; ✆05574-40 76; www.bregenzerfestspiele.com; ⊗mid-Jul–late Aug) The Bregenzer Festspiele is the city's premier cultural festival. World-class operas, orchestral works and other highly imaginative productions are staged on the open-air Seebühne, a floating stage on the lake, in the Festspielhaus and at the Vorarlberger Landestheater. Information and tickets (€30 to €130) are up for grabs about nine months before the festival.

⊨ Sleeping

JUFA Gästehaus Bregenz
HOSTEL $

(✆05708-35 40; www.jufa.eu; Mehrerauerstrasse 5; dm €28, s/d €68/108; P🖤) Housed in a former needle factory near the lake, this HI hostel now reels backpackers in with excellent facilities including a common room and a restaurant. It's welcoming to families, too, with a playroom, a playground and bike rental.

Camping Mexico
CAMPGROUND $

(✆05574-732 60; www.camping-mexico.at; Hechtweg 4; camp sites per adult/child/tent €8.50/4.50/6; ⊗May-Sep; 🖤) ✐ This eco-labelled camp site by the lake uses solar energy, recycles waste and serves organic food in its restaurant. The leafy pitches offer plenty of shade.

Schwärzler
HOTEL $$

(✆05574-49 90; http://schwaerzler.s-hotels.com; Landstrasse 9; s €98-116, d €160-214; P🖤🗐) This turreted, ivy-clad place is a far cry from your average business hotel. Contemporary rooms are done out in earthy hues

and blonde wood, with comforts including bathrobes, flat-screen TVs and minibars. Regional produce from organic farms features on the breakfast buffet, and there's a 400 sq metre pool and a sauna area.

Hotel Weisses Kreuz
HOTEL $$

(✆05574-498 80; www.hotelweisseskreuz.at; Römerstrasse 5; s €109-119, d €126-186; P🖤) Service is attentive at this central pick, with a cocktail bar and a restaurant (p335) rustling up seasonal Austrian fare. The smart rooms sport cherry-wood furnishings, flat-screen TVs and organic bedding.

Hotel Bodensee
HOTEL $$

(✆05574-423 00; www.hotel-bodensee.at; Kornmarktstrasse 22; s/d €70/129; P🖤) Right in the thick of things, this hotel's best rooms are spacious, tastefully decorated in muted tones and sport flat-screen TVs. Breakfast is a wholesome fresh fruit, muesli and regional produce affair.

✕ Eating

Buongustiao
DELI, ITALIAN $

(✆05574-581 29; www.buongustaio.at; Anton-Schneider-Strasse 10; lunch incl glass of wine €13.40; ⊗9am-7pm Tue-Fri, to 2pm Sat; ⊕) For an authentic Italian lunch or picnic goodies, drop by this deli-restaurant. The split-level, open-plan interior is a sociable setting for homemade pasta or a glass of prosecco with antipasti. The €24.90 Saturday brunch, with wood-oven bread, Italian salumi, cheese and *dolci* (sweets) is legendary.

Cafesito
CAFE $

(www.cafesito.at; Maurachgasse 6; bagels €2.50-4.50; ⊗7.45am-6.30pm Mon-Fri, 9am-4pm Sat; ✐) ✐ Tiny Cafesito does the best bagels, brownies and smoothies in town. Bright-hued, art-plastered walls create a boho-cool backdrop for a light lunch or cup of fair-trade coffee.

Nashia Kulinarisches
VEGETARIAN $

(✆0699 11787125; Gallusstrasse 12; ⊗10.30am-2pm & 4.30-7pm Mon-Thu, 10.30am-2pm Fri; ✐) Nashia works wonders with spices and purely vegetarian ingredients at this sweet, tucked-away cafe. Her specialities range from feisty banana curries to dhals, biryanis and South African stews. It's all healthy, wholesome and tasty.

Kornmesser
AUSTRIAN $$

(✆05574-548 54; www.kornmesser.at; Kornmarktstrasse 5; 2-course lunch €8.90, mains €14-30; ⊗9.30am-midnight Tue-Sun) Dine on local favourites in the vaulted interior or chestnut-shaded beer garden of this 18th-century baroque *Gasthaus*. These include pork knuckle with bread dumplings and potato salad, roast local trout with parsley potatoes, boiled beef with horseradish, pasta with picked-the-same-day chanterelles, and an 'emperor's pancake' (with stewed plums).

Wirtshaus am See
AUSTRIAN $$

(✆05574-422 10; www.wirtshausamsee.at; Seepromenade 2; mains €13-31; ⏰9am-midnight; 🅿) Snag a table on the lakefront terrace at this mock half-timbered villa, dishing up local specialities such as buttery Bodensee whitefish and venison ragout. Vegetarian options are abundant. It's also a relaxed spot for quaffing a cold one. Service can be hit and miss.

Goldener Hirschen
AUSTRIAN $$

(✆05574-428 15; www.hotelweisseskreuz.at; Kirchstrasse 8; lunch €7.60, mains €8.50-21; ⏰11am-10pm Wed-Mon) Austrian through and through, this restaurant in the Weisses Kreuz has bags of rustic charm, with its high beamed ceilings and jovial crowd of locals. The kitchen rolls out well-prepared classics such as Carinthian cheese noodles, boiled beef with horsradish, homemade dumplings with sauerkraut and pork roast with cumin-beer sauce. There's a garden courtyard for fine-weather dining.

🍷 Drinking & Nightlife

Beach Bar Bregenz
BAR

(www.beachbar-bregenz.com; Seepromenade 2; ⏰4pm-midnight Mon-Fri, from 2pm Sat, from 11am Sun late Apr-early Sep) Cool cocktails, palm trees, chilled DJ beats – it's the Costa del Bodensee every summer at this lakefront beach bar. Work your relaxed look in a *Strandkörbe* (wicker basket chair). It also stages occasional events, such as silent open-air cinema sessions.

Cuba
BAR

(www.cuba-club.at; Bahnhofstrasse 9; ⏰11am-4am Mon-Fri, from 2pm Sun) Glammed up with chandeliers and a sweeping staircase, this gallery-style bar attracts trendy types with Latin and soul tunes and a top line-up of DJs. Signature cocktails include Cubata (Havana Club, coke and lime) and Lilly (Lillet, rose tonic and dried rose petals).

Wunderbar
BAR

(Bahnhofstrasse 4; ⏰11am-midnight Mon-Thu, to 4am Fri & Sat, 2pm-midnight Sun; 🌐) Bordello meets neobaroque at the Wunderbar, where candles illuminate blood-red walls, cherubs and velvet sofas. Browse the papers, bag a swing on the terrace or sip cocktails as smooth funk plays.

ℹ️ Information

Bodensee-Vorarlberg Tourism (✆05574-434 43; www.bodensee-vorarlberg.com) Free regional accommodation booking service.

Landeskrankenhaus (✆05574-40 10; Carl-Pedenz-Strasse 2) Provincial hospital with emergency ward.

Main Post Office (Seestrasse 5; ⏰8am-6pm Mon-Fri, 9am-noon Sat) Also has a *Bankomat*.

Tourist Office (✆05574-49 59; www.bregenz.travel; Rathausstrasse 35a; ⏰9am-6pm Mon-Fri, to noon Sat) Information on the city and the surrounding area and help with accommodation.

ℹ️ Getting There & Away

BICYCLE

Fahrradverleih Bregenz (www.integra.or.at/fahrradverleih-bregenz; Seepromenade; per day city bike €15, e-bike €27; ⏰9am-noon & 4-7pm Mon-Fri, 9am-7pm Sat & Sun Apr-Oct) rents quality bikes and has free Bodensee cycling maps.

TRAIN

Four direct trains daily head for Munich (€49.20, three hours) via Lindau (€2.90, 12 minutes), while trains for Konstanz (€26.60, two hours) go via the Swiss shore of the lake and may be frequent, but require up to four changes. There are frequent departures for Zürich (€39, two hours), all of which call in at St Gallen (€15.40, 47 minutes). There are roughly hourly trains to Innsbruck (€37.50, 2½ hours), calling en route at Dornbirn (€2.90, nine minutes), Feldkirch (€6.50, 46 minutes) and Bludenz (€10.10, one hour).

Dornbirn

✆05572 / POP 46,885 / ELEV 437M

Ragged, thickly wooded limestone pinnacles are the dramatic backdrop to Dornbirn, Vorarlberg's largest city. While nowhere near as appealing as Bregenz, it's worth a visit for its refreshing lack of tourists and its museums.

Hohenems, 6km south of Dornbirn, sheltered a large Jewish community in the 17th century. Their numbers dwindled in the 1860s, when Jews were eligible to live anywhere under Habsburg rule.

◉ Sights

Inatura
MUSEUM

(www.inatura.at; Jahngasse 9, Dornbirn; adult/child/family €11/5.50/25.30; ⏰10am-6pm; 👶)

Dornbirn's biggest draw is this hands-on museum. It's a wonderland for kids who can pet (stuffed) foxes and handle (real) spiders, whip up tornadoes, conduct light experiments and generally interact with science, nature and technology. There's also a climbing wall and 3D cinema.

Altstadt HISTORIC SITE
(Dornbirn) Dornbirn's compact old town centres on the Marktplatz, where your gaze is drawn to the crooked, 17th-century **Rotes Haus**, which owes its intense red hue to an unappetising mix of ox blood and bile. Next door, the neoclassical columns and free-standing Gothic belfry of **Pfarrkirche St Martin** catch your eye.

Rolls-Royce Museum MUSEUM
(www.rolls-royce-museum.at; Gütle 11a; adult/child €9/4.50; ⏲10am-6pm daily Jul & Aug, 10am-6pm Tue-Sun Feb-Jun & Sep-Nov) Situated at the bottom of Rappenlochschlucht in a 19th-century cotton mill, this museum harbours the world's largest collection of Rolls-Royces. Highlights include a reconstruction of Royce's Cooke St factory in Manchester and a hall of fame showcasing vintage Rollers that once belonged to the likes of Queen Elizabeth, Franco and George V. Stay for tea in the ever-so-British rosewood tearoom.

Jüdisches Museum Hohenems MUSEUM
(www.jm-hohenems.at; Schweizer Strasse 5, Hohenems; adult/child €8/free; ⏲10am-5pm Tue-Sun) Housed in the Rosenthal villa in Hohenems, 6km south of Dornbirn, this museum zooms in on Hohenems' long-defunct Jewish community with photos, documents and religious artefacts. The Rosenthals built up a considerable textile business in the town, and part of their wealth – especially gorgeous period furniture – is also on show.

Activities

Rappenlochschlucht WALKING
(Rappenloch Gorge; www.rappenlochschlucht.at) Just 4km south of Dornbirn is the narrow Rappenlochschlucht, gouged out by the thundering Dornbirner Ache. A 10-minute walk leads up to a good viewpoint and a 30-minute trail to the **Staufensee**, a turquoise lake ringed by forest.

Sleeping & Eating

Hotel Hirschen HOTEL $$
(☎05572-263 63; Haselstauderstrasse 31; s €85, d €126-135; P 📶) Heading into its third generation with the same family, the Hirschen's contemporary, minimalist-style rooms come with appealing personal touches – starry ceilings or wood-burning stoves, wind chimes made by local creatives and DVD players. There's even a pillow menu (sheep's wool, pine and the like) and hot-water bottles to ensure a sound night's slumber. City/e-bike rental costs €5/10 per day

Vienna House Martinspark DESIGN HOTEL $$
(☎05572-37 60; www.viennahouse.com; Mozartstrasse 2; s €103-115, d €130-145; P ❄ 📶) 🌿 Winging Dornbirn into the future, this architecturally innovative, eco-friendly hotel makes quite a design statement in central Dornbirn. The pared-back, parquet-floored rooms are contemporary in style, and the restaurant makes good use of regional produce.

Pasta Fresca da Giovanni ITALIAN $$
(☎05572-20 21 97; www.pastafresca.co.at; Riedgasse 11; pasta €11-16, mains €19-30; ⏲11am-2pm & 5.30-11pm Mon-Sat; 👪) Hailing from Southern Italy, Giovanni helms the kitchen at this slick Italian job. As the name suggests, the big deal is the superb homemade pasta – from ravioli with king prawns, cherry tomatoes, herbs and rocket to *penne alla Norcina* (minced meat, Parmesan and truffle oil). It's a great prelude to simply grilled fish or flavour-packed mains such as veal osso bucco.

Information

Tourist Office (☎05572-221 88; Rathausplatz 1a; ⏲9am-6pm Mon-Fri, to noon Sat)

Getting There & Away

Dornbirn has frequent connections to Bregenz (€2.90, nine minutes) and Hohenems (€2, seven minutes) on the Bregenz–Innsbruck railway line. Bus 47 departs from Dornbirn train station and passes by the Rappenlochschlucht (€2, 21 minutes, nine daily).

Bregenzerwald

The wooded limestone peaks, cow-nibbled pastures and bucolic villages of the Bregenzerwald unfold to the south of Bregenz. This rural region is great for getting back to nature for a few days, whether cheese-tasting in alpine dairies, testing out hay and herbal treatments in spa hotels, or curling up by the fireside in a cosy farmhouse. One lungful of that good clean air and you'll surely want to grab your boots, slip into your skis or get on your bike and head outdoors.

◉ Sights

★ **Angelika Kauffmann Museum**   MUSEUM
(www.angelika-kauffmann.com; Brand 34, Schwarzenberg; adult/child €7.50/2; ⊙10am-5pm Tue-Sun May-late Oct) This ultramodern museum houses a permanent collection in winter and rotating exhibitions in summer of Swiss-Austrian neoclassical painter Angelika Kauffmann's works. The artist had strong connections to the village where her father was born. A ticket covers entry to the neighbouring Heimat Museum (Heritage Museum), a pristine alpine chalet. Displays of traditional painted furniture, extraordinary headwear, hunting paraphernalia and filigree iron crosses focus on rural 19th-century life.

Käsekeller Lingenau   SHOW DAIRY
(www.kaesekeller.at; Zeihenbühel 423, Lingenau; ⊙10am-6pm Mon-Fri, 9am-5pm Sat, shorter hours in winter) Step into the foyer of this modern cheese-maturation cellar to glimpse robots attending to wagon wheel–sized cheeses through a glass wall. It's famous for its tangy *Bergkäse* (mountain cheese). A tasting of cheeses with wine and bread costs from €6.80 to €10.90.

Käse-Molke Metzler   SHOW DAIRY
(☑05512-30 44; www.naturhautnah.at; Bruggan 1025, Egg; ⊙8am-noon & 1.30-6pm Mon-Fri, 8am-noon Sat) This architecturally innovative dairy churns out fresh *Wälderkäsle* ('forest cheese'), arranges farm tours and tastings (€16.50) and runs four-hour cheese-making workshops (€69). See the website for exact dates and times; booking is essential.

⚡ Activities

The hills buzz with hikers, climbers and cyclists in summer. Local tourist offices also arrange **themed walks**, including some geared towards families. **Paragliders** can launch themselves off mountains in Andelsbuch, Bezau and Au-Schoppernau; tandem flights cost around €100.

Downhill Skiing

Though lesser known than other Austrian ski regions, the Bregenzerwald has fine downhill skiing on 268km of slopes, well suited to beginners, intermediates and ski tourers (three-valley three-/six-day pass adult €131/221, child €66/111. Lift queues are virtually nonexistent and free ski buses shuttle between resorts. Nonskiers can shuffle through snowy forests on cross-country or snowshoe

trails, go winter hiking or bump downhill on toboggan runs in Au and Damüls.

★ Festivals & Events

Schubertiade   MUSIC
(☑05576-720 91; www.schubertiade.at) The highly acclaimed Schubertiade festival brings the *Lieder* (songs) and chamber music of the great Austrian Romantic composer Franz Schubert to atmospheric venues in Schwarzenberg (mid-June to early September) and Hohenems (dates in May, July, August, September and October). Tickets are like gold dust and should be booked well in advance.

🛏 Sleeping

Kräuterbauernhof   FARMSTAY $
(☑05515-22 98; www.kuhforyou.at; Argenau 116, Au; d/tr/q €45/56/67) This 300-year-old farmhouse is a fantastic place to stay, with spacious apartments full of woody charm, a herb garden and plenty of dairy goodness at breakfast.

★ **Gasthof Hirschen**   HISTORIC HOTEL $$
(☑05512-29 44; www.hirschenschwarzenberg.at; Hof 14, Schwarzenberg; s €104-119, d €188-208; P🐾🛜) This is a 250-year-old dream of a *Gasthof*. The wood-shingle facade is festooned with geraniums, while antique low-ceilinged corridors lead to antique-filled nooks and individually designed rooms. *Dirndl*-clad waitresses serve up spot-on regional fare such as saddle of venison in a walnut crust and *Bregenzerwälder Käsknöpfle* (cheese noodles) in the restaurant (mains €14 to €27).

Bio-Pension Beer   PENSION $$
(☑05515-23 98; www.bio-pension.at; Gräsalp 357, Schoppernau; d €66-74; 🛜) 🌿 The light, cheery rooms at this pension are done out in sustainable wood from the Beer family forest. You'll feel right at home at this eco-friendly country retreat, complete with pure spring water, clucking chickens and organic produce at breakfast.

Hotel Gasthof Gams   BOUTIQUE HOTEL $$$
(☑05514-22 20; www.hotel-gams.at; Platz 44, Bezau; d €206-246, ste €310-350; P🛜♨) A real glamour puss of a hotel, the Gams (chamois) whispers romance from every last gold-kissed, heart-strewn, candlelit corner. An open fire in the dreamlike Da Vinci spa, starry ceilings, a whirlpool with mountain views, a gourmet restaurant (seven-course

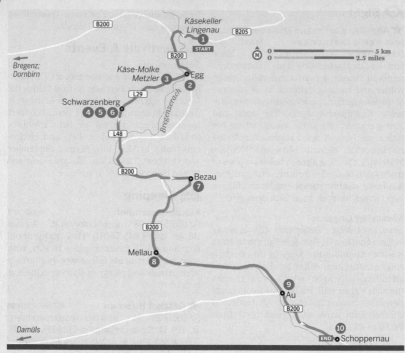

Driving Tour
Bregenzerwald

START KÄSEKELLER LINGENAU
END SCHOPPERNAU
LENGTH 35KM; FOUR HOURS

The Bregenzerwald's rolling dairy country is best explored on the Käsestrasse (Cheese Road). This tour (40 minutes' driving without stops) threads through quaint villages and stopping en route for silo-free buttermilk and cheese at local *Sennereien* (dairy farms). Spring through autumn is the best time to visit. See www.kaesestrasse.at for details.

Take a peek inside the huge cellars of the ultramodern ❶ **Käsekeller Lingenau** (p337) to see how cheese is matured, and taste flavoursome *Bergkäse* ('mountain cheese') with a glass of local wine. Hit the pretty, church-topped village of ❷ **Egg**, where the Bregenzerach flows swiftly, and, 2.5km west, ❸ **Käse-Molke Metzler** (p337), an avant-garde dairy and farmhouse duo. Here you can sample creamy *Wälderkäsle* ('forest cheese'), made from cow's and goat's milk, or call ahead to join a cheese-making workshop.

Veer southwest to the village of ❹ **Schwarzenberg**, where old farmhouses tiled with wood shingles and studded with scarlet geraniums crowd the narrow streets. Contemplate art in the ❺ **Angelika Kauffmann Museum** (p337) before lunching on cheese-rich *Kässpätzle* (egg noodles) in the wood-panelled parlour or garden at ❻ **Gasthof Hirschen** (p337).The narrow country lane now wends its way gently to ❼ **Bezau**, 7km southeast, where the Bregenzerach river flows swiftly past forest-cloaked slopes rising to jagged limestone crags. The village has a handful of dairy shops where you can buy cheese, honey, herbs and schnapps. Continue southeast towards the Arlberg and mountainous ❽ **Mellau**, where the tourist office organises cheese walks in summer.

Driving southeast brings you to peaceful ❾ **Au**, affording deep views into a U-shaped valley, particularly beautiful on a golden autumn day. Round out your tour with total cheese immersion at the ❿ **Bergkäserei Schoppernau**, where you can try the famous *Bergkäse*.

menu €115) with a walk-in wine tower – this is definite honeymoon material.

ℹ️ Information

The **Bregenzerwald tourist office** (☑ 05512-23 65; www.bregenzerwald.at; Impulszentrum 1135, Egg; ⊙ 9am-5pm Mon-Fri, 8am-1pm Sat) should be your first port of call for details on the region's sights, activities and accommodation. The shelves are well stocked with maps and brochures.

ℹ️ Getting There & Away

Buses run roughly twice hourly to Bezau (€5.60, one hour) from Bregenz, but for most other destinations a change at Egg is required. From Dornbirn, Schwarzenberg (€3.80, 30 minutes), Bezau (€4.70, 46 minutes), Mellau (€4.90, 50 minutes), Au (€7.40, 70 minutes) and Schoppernau (€7.40, 80 minutes) can all be reached a couple of times daily (times vary from season to season). For Damüls (€12.80, two hours), a change at Au is required.

Feldkirch

☑ 05522 / POP 30,660 / ELEV 458M

On the banks of the turquoise Ill River, Feldkirch sits prettily at the foot of wooded mountains, vineyards and a castle-crowned hill. It's a joy to stroll the well-preserved old town, which wings you back to late-medieval times with its cobbled, arcaded lanes, towers and pastel-coloured town houses. The town springs to life in summer with pavement cafes and open-air festivals.

⊙ Sights

★ **Schloss Schattenburg**   CASTLE
(www.schattenburg.at; Burggasse 1; adult/child €7/3.50; ⊙ 9am-noon & 1.30-5pm Mon-Fri, 10am-5pm Sat & Sun Apr-Oct, shorter hours rest of year) This 13th-century hilltop castle is storybook stuff with its red turrets and creeping vines. It's a steep climb up to the ramparts, which command far-reaching views over Feldkirch's rooftops. Once the seat of the counts of Montfort, the castle now houses a small **museum** displaying religious art, costumes and weaponry.

★ **Domkirche St Nikolaus**   CATHEDRAL
(Domplatz; ⊙ 8am-6pm) Identified by a slender spire, Feldkirch's cathedral has a large, forbidding interior complemented by late-Gothic features and dazzling stained glass. The painting on the side altar is by local lad Wolf Huber (1480–1539), a leading member of the Danube school.

Wildpark   WILDLIFE RESERVE
(Ardetzenweg 20; ⊙ dawn-dusk; 🚶) **FREE** Facing the castle across the town is Ardetzenberg (631m), a heavily forested hill. At its northern end is this wildlife park, with a woodland trail, adventure playground, barbecue areas, and animal-friendly enclosures home to marmots, ibex and wild boar.

🏃 Activities

Dreiländerweg   CYCLING
(Three Country Trail) The Feldkirch region is criss-crossed with cycling trails, including the 30km Dreiländerweg, taking in beautiful scenery in Austria, Switzerland and Liechtenstein. Pick up the free *Feldkircher Radwegkarte* map from the tourist office.

🎉 Festivals & Events

Poolbar Festival   CULTURAL
(http://poolbar.at; ⊙ early Aug) If you're in town during the Poolbar Festival festival be sure to check out the top-notch line-up of mostly free events, skipping from concerts, dance and poetry slams to juggling shows and DJ nights.

Gauklerfestival   FESTIVAL
(⊙ late Jul) Jugglers, fire-eaters and clowns entertain the crowds at this enormous street party.

Montfortspektakel   FESTIVAL
(⊙ early Jun) Feldkirch revisits the Middle Ages with troubadours, knights and nonstop feasting.

🛏️ Sleeping

Junges Hotel Feldkirch   HOSTEL $
(☑ 05522-731 81; www.oejhw.at; Reichsstrasse 111; dm/d €15.50/45; 🅿 🛜) A 700-year-old infirmary has been converted into this HI hostel, which exudes charm with its creaking beams, vaulted lounge and ivy-clad courtyard. A spiral staircase twists up to light-filled dorms with pine bunks. Buses 59, 60 and 68 stop here.

Gutwinski Hotel   BOUTIQUE HOTEL $$
(☑ 05522-721 75; www.gutwinski.cc; Rosengasse 4-6; s/d €102/172, ste €392; @ 🛜) Hidden down a quiet old-town backstreet, this 16th-century merchant's house has a touch of old-fashioned romance, with its lime-shaded garden and Biedermeier salon. The rooms

Feldkirch

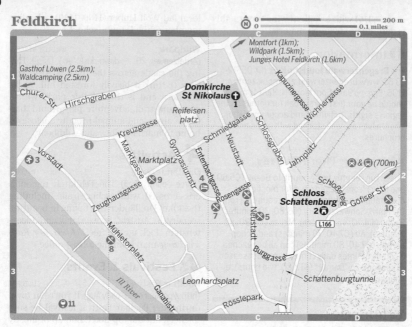

Feldkirch

◉ Top Sights
1 Domkirche St Nikolaus	C1
2 Schloss Schattenburg	D2

◉ Activities, Courses & Tours
3 Dreiländerweg	A2

◉ Sleeping
4 Gutwinski Hotel	B2

◉ Eating
5 April	C2
6 Dogana	C2
7 Gutwinski	C2
8 Papa Chadha's Kitchen	B3
9 Rauch Cafe	B2
10 Wirtschaft Zum Schützenhaus	D2

◉ Drinking & Nightlife
11 Poolbar	A3

blend contemporary and classic – think lots of polished wood, muted colours and flat-screen TVs. The suite ramps up the luxury with its own whirlpool. Modern riffs on Austrian classics feature on the restaurant menu.

Montfort HOTEL $$
(☎05522-721 89; www.montfort-dashotel.at; Galuragasse 7; s/d €109/159; P🖥) Run by the friendly Oberhöller family, Montfort is a business hotel with personality. Set in attractive gardens, the hotel has bright, contemporary rooms with flat-screen TVs and monochrome bathrooms. It goes the extra mile at breakfast, with freshly baked croissants, eggs and bacon, salmon and antipasti. Montfort is a 10-minute stroll northeast of the centre.

✖ Eating

★April CAFE $
(www.aprilcafe.at; Neustadt 39; breakfast €4.10-13.70, lunch €10.50; ⊙9am-6pm Thu-Mon; 🖊) 🌿 Bright flower pots and upside-down watering cans guide the way to this wholesomely hip and wonderfully laid-back cafe. Bag a spot on one of the sofas or on the pocket-sized terrace for a latte adorned with flowers or butterflies (Ingo is a 'coffee artist'). Lavish breakfasts, open sandwiches, Ayurvedic dhals and dips and vegan cakes feature on the all-organic menu.

Papa Chadha's Kitchen AUSTRIAN $$
(☎05522-390 07; www.papachadhaskitchen.com; Mühletorplatz 2; mains €15-30; ⊙10.30am-2.30pm & 5.30-10.30pm Tue-Sat) Right on the banks of the Ill River and with a terrace that's a real magnet on warm evenings, Papa Chadha's places the accent on quality,

regional produce. This shines through in brilliant home cooking – be it *Spinatknödel* (spinach dumplings), *Schlutzkrapfen* (Tyrolean crescent-shaped pasta) or venison medallions with porcini mushrooms in port-wine cranberry sauce.

Rauch Cafe
CAFE **$$**

(☑ 05522-763 55; www.rauchgastronomie.at; Marktgasse 12-14; 2-course lunch €9.40, mains €14-32; ☺ 9am-1am Wed-Sat & Mon, 10am-1am Sun) This vaulted cafe-restaurant opens onto a buzzy terrace. Breakfasts consist of dark bread, fresh juice and local cheeses and hams. The menu is a medley of Austrian staples, homemade pasta and season-driven dishes like venison with chanterelles and shallots. DJs spin house here after dark.

Wirtschaft Zum Schützenhaus
AUSTRIAN **$$**

(☑ 05522-852 90; www.schuetzenhaus.at; Göfiser Strasse 2; mains €11.50-17.50; ☺ 5pm-midnight Mon, Thu & Fri, 11.30am-9.30pm Sat, 11.30am-8.30pm Sun; 🍴) *Schiessen und Geniessen* (shoot and enjoy!) is the motto at this half-timbered tavern, where Lederhosen-clad staff bring humungous schnitzels to the table. The tree-shaded beer garden has prime views of the castle and a pet corner with fluffy rodents to keep kids amused.

Dogana
INTERNATIONAL **$$**

(☑ 05522-751 26; www.dogana.com; Neustadt 20; 2-course lunch €9.40, mains €9-27; ☺ 8.30am-1am Tue-Sat) This slinky lounge-bar-restaurant has a popular terrace for alfresco dining and imbibing. The menu has Mediterranean overtones, with antipasti, summery salads (try the curried chicken *kikeriki*), pasta, steaks and fish dishes.

★ Gutwinski
AUSTRIAN **$$$**

(☑ 05522-721 75; www.gutwinski.cc; Rosengasse 4-6; mains €20-34, 4-course menu €57; ☺ noon-2pm & 6-10pm Tue-Sat) In fine weather, head to Gutwinski's delightful tree-shaded terrace to dine on classics such as Wiener schnitzel with parsley potatoes and cranberry compote, or brighter, more inventive dishes such as mango-basil soup, chicken with peach, sage and chanterelles, and lavender panna cotta. When it's chilly, the candlelit interior makes an ideal refuge.

🍸 Drinking & Nightlife

Poolbar
BAR

(www.poolbar.at; Reichenfeldgasse 9) Feldkirch's old public swimming pool in the Reichenfeld district has been born again as the ul-

tra-hip Poolbar, the venue of the summertime Poolbar Festival.

ⓘ Information

The helpful **tourist office** (☑ 05522-734 67; http://www.feldkirch.travel; Montfortplatz 1; ☺ 9am-6pm Mon-Fri, 9am-noon Sat) has stacks of information and free town maps.

ⓘ Getting There & Away

Trains head north to Bregenz (€6.50, 46 minutes) and Dornbirn (€4.70, 28 minutes), and southeast to Bludenz (€4.70, 20 minutes).

Bludenz
☑ 05552 / POP 13,745 / ELEV 588M

The Alps provide a spectacular backdrop to Bludenz, the only town in Austria – perhaps the world – that can lay claim to having purple cows; the Milka ones churned out from the Suchard factory. Gorging on chocolate aside, Bludenz' arcaded old town takes you back to its heyday as the seat of the Habsburg governors from 1418 to 1806. Bludenz also makes a good base for exploring the surrounding valleys.

⊙ Sights

St Laurentiuskirche
CHURCH

(Mutterstrasse; ☺ 9am-5pm) Climb the covered staircase to this Gothic parish church, dominated by an octagonal onion-domed spire. There are stellar views over the town's rooftops to the Alps beyond from up here.

🏃 Activities

To explore Bludenz' attractions, join a free city tour organised by the tourist office, departing at 10.15am on Friday from mid-May till October.

There are 15 skiing areas within a 30km radius and ski bus transport to/from Bludenz is sometimes included in the price of ski passes. Walking and cycling are other popular activities; the tourist office has thick booklets on summer and winter outdoor pursuits.

Muttersberg
WALKING

(www.muttersberg.eu; Hinterplärsch; cable car adult/child 1 way €8.40/5.40, return €13.50/8.50; ☺ cable car 9am-5pm) About 1km north of the town centre, a cable car rises up to this 1401m peak, the starting point for numerous hiking, Nordic-walking and cycling trails. If you don't want to walk it, catch Bus 1 from in front of the train station to the cable-car station.

Kletterhalle
CLIMBING

(Untersteinstrasse 5; adult/child €5/3; ⊘hall 6am-10pm, ticket office 8am-noon & 1-5pm Mon-Fri) Practise clambering up boulders before tackling the real thing in the Alps at this excellent hall, run by the Austrian Alpine Club. The ticket office is on the 1st floor.

🎉 Festivals & Events

Milka Chocolate Festival
FOOD & DRINK

(www.milkaschokofest.at) Bludenz' sweetest event is the Milka Chocolate Festival in July, when 1000kg of *Schokolade* is up for grabs in prizes. There's also music and games, and plenty of kids full of sugar.

🛏 Sleeping

Schlosshotel Dörflinger
HISTORIC HOTEL $$

(☑ 05552-630 16; www.schlosshotel.cc; Schloss-Gayenhof-Platz 5; s €79-105, d €130-130; P @) Clinging to the cliffs above Bludenz, this smart hotel shelters modern rooms, many with balconies. There's a mountain-facing terrace for warm evenings, free mountain-bike hire for guests and a smart restaurant (mains €10 to €25) dishing up Austrian fare.

Gasthof Hotel Löwen
HOTEL $$

(☑ 05552-322 70; www.loewen-bludenz.at; Mutterstrasse 7; s €69-73, d €95-99; P 🛜) This peach-fronted pick sits right in the centre of town. Rooms sport parquet floors, crisp white bedding and walk-in showers. Fresh, seasonal produce makes its way onto the generous spread at breakfast.

Val Blu
SPA HOTEL $$

(☑ 05552-631 06; www.valblu.at; Haldenweg 2a; s/d €75/126; P 🛜 ⛲) Glass walls and smooth contours define this ultramodern spa hotel, a 10-minute walk east of the centre along Untersteinstrasse. The functional, minimalist-style rooms feature wi-fi and flat-screen TVs.

🍴 Eating

Remise
CAFE $

(www.cafe-remise.at; Am Raiffeisenplatz 1; lunch €7-8, snacks €4-8; ⊘10am-midnight Mon-Sat, 1-8pm Sun; 👶) This contemporary cafe attracts arty types and serves snacks from toasties to creative salads. The cultural centre next door regularly hosts exhibitions, film screenings and concerts. There's a kids' playground outside.

Wirtshaus Kohldampf
AUSTRIAN $$

(☑ 05552-653 85; www.fohren-center.at; Werdenbergerstrasse 53; mains €8-16; ⊘11am-10pm) A five-minute amble west of the centre lies this cavernous brewpub-cum–beer garden. Meaty grub such as schnitzel, pork roast and goulash is washed down with Fohrenburger beer from the brewery opposite.

🛍 Shopping

Milka Shop
CHOCOLATE

(Fohrenburgstrasse 1; ⊘9am-noon Mon & Sat, to 4.30pm Tue-Fri) You can stock up on the chocolate made by purple cows – and discover how it is made – at Milka's flagship shop.

ℹ️ Information

Bang in the heart of the historic centre, the **tourist office** (☑ 05552-302 27; www.vorarlberg-alpenregion.at; Rathausgasse 12; ⊘8am-5.30pm Mon-Fri) is well stocked with information on Bludenz and the surrounding region.

ℹ️ Getting There & Away

Bludenz is on the east–west InterCity express rail route to Innsbruck (€27.90, 1¾, every two hours) and Bregenz (€10.10, one hour, hourly).

The A14 motorway passes just south of the Ill River and the town centre. Buses run down all five valleys around Bludenz.

Montafon

POP 16,545

The Montafon's pristine wilderness and potent schnapps had Ernest Hemingway in raptures when he wintered here in 1925 and 1926, skiing in blissful solitude and penning *The Sun Also Rises*. Silhouetted by the glaciated Silvretta range and crowned by the 3312m arrow of Piz Buin, the valley remains one of the most serene and unspoilt in the Austrian Alps.

Partenen marks the start of the serpentine 23km Silvretta Hochalpenstrasse, which wends its way under peaks rising to well over 2500m before climbing over the 2036m Bielerhöhe Pass via a series of tight switchbacks.

⊙ Sights

Silvretta Stausee
LAKE

Glittering at a giddy 2030m above sea level, this startlingly aquamarine reservoir mirrors the snowcapped diamond of 3312m Piz Buin on bright mornings. The lake is the start and end point of the fabulous but challenging

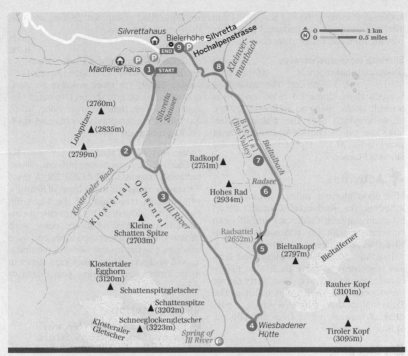

☆ Walking Trail
Radstattel Circuit, Bielehöhe

START SILVRETTA STAUSEE
END BIELERHÖHE
LENGTH 15KM; FIVE TO SIX HOURS

This is one of Vorarlberg's most spectacular hikes, exploring two valleys linked by a pass and taking you high into the realms of 3000m mountains and glaciers. Best tackled in July or August, the route demands a moderate level of fitness. The Alpenvereinskarte 1:25,000 map No 26 *Silvrettagruppe* covers the trail in detail.

From the **1 Silvretta Stausee** car park, walk over the dam to join the well-worn path skirting the western shore of the turquoise reservoir. Stick to the shoreline around the southern end of the lake, crossing one bridge over the **2 Klostertaler Bach**, then another over the fast-flowing **3 Ill River**. At the junction, turn right up the trail signed to the Wiesbadener Hütte.

An amphitheatre of glistening blue, heavily crevassed glaciers appears as you gradually gain height. Continue your steady ascent, stopping for refreshment on the sunny terrace of the **4 Wiesbadener Hütte** after two to 2¼ hours. At the back of the hut, veer left towards the Radsattel on a red-and-white-marked trail that becomes increasingly narrow and rough underfoot. The path zigzags steeply up the slope and over a small stream. Keep right and ascend a rise topped by a large cairn. Cross a shallow pool outlet before the final steep climb to the 2652m **5 Radsattel**, where a sign marks the Vorarlberg–Tyrol border, one to 1½ hours from the hut.

Drop steeply down the boulder-strewn eastern side of the pass, keeping an eye out for ibex. You will pass several small lakes including the jewel-like **6 Radsee** as you take the small path down to the remote meadows of the **7 Bieltal** (Biel Valley). Follow the path along the west bank of the babbling **8 Bieltalbach** stream and continue west to the Silvretta Stausee, turning right along the reservoir. Back at the main road, turn left and walk 300m to return to **9 Bielerhöhe** (1½ to two hours from the Radsattel).

Radsattel Circuit, a five- to six-hour, 15km hike that traverses the Radsattel at 2652m, crossing from one valley to another.

Silvretta Hochalpenstrasse   AREA
(www.silvretta-bielerhoehe.at; car/motorcycle €15/12; ☉ early Jun-late Oct) The 23km-long Silvretta High Alpine Rd twists and turns beneath peaks rising to well over 2500m before climbing over the 2036m Bielerhöhe Pass via 34 knuckle-whiteningly tight switchbacks. At the top of the pass is the Silvretta Stausee.

🏃 Activities

Mile upon glorious mile of alpine trails, including the **Radsattel Circuit**, attract hikers in summer. Cable cars and lifts can be accessed with the regional Montafon-Silvretta-Card (three/seven days €41/55).

In winter, Montafon is a magnet for families who come to carve its 246km of uncrowded pistes and go cross-country skiing, snowshoeing, ski touring and sledding. The Skipass-Montafon (three-/seven-day pass €120/237) covers public transport and the 61 lifts in the valley.

🛏 Sleeping

Posthotel Rössle   HISTORIC HOTEL $$
(☏ 05558-833 30; www.posthotel-roessle.at; Dorfstrasse 4, Gaschurn; d incl half-board €140-190; P ☒) Hemingway once stayed in this 200-year-old chalet – whether with his mistress or wife remains a mystery. The friendly Kessler family will show you the guestbook he signed and the bed he slept in. Within easy reach of the Silvretta Nova ski arena, the hotel has well-kept rooms, a superb

wood-panelled restaurant, indoor and outdoor pools, and a spa.

Silvrettahaus   HUT $$
(☏ 05558-42 46; www.silvretta-bielerhoehe.at; s/d €67/107, incl half-board €72/118; ☉ Jul–mid-Oct & mid-Dec–Easter) For more creature comforts at 2000m, check into the architecturally innovative Silvrettahaus at Bielerhöhe, which has bright, contemporary rooms and spellbinding mountain views.

Löwen Hotel Montafon   HOTEL $$$
(☏ 05556-71 41; www.loewen-hotel.com; Silvrettastrasse 8, Schruns; s €174, d €288-328; P ☎ ☒) This swish chalet sits in the heart of Schruns, with the big mountains of the Montafon right on the doorstep. The ultra-chic rooms put a modern spin on alpine rustic, with dark wood panelling, muted tones and huge windows playing up the views. A panoramic pool and spa, which uses local herbs in its treatments, are welcome post hiking or skiing.

ℹ Information

Montafon Tourism (☏ 050 6686; www. montafon.at; Silvrettastrasse 6, Schruns; ☉ 8am-6pm Mon-Fri, 9am-4pm Sat & Sun) has the low-down on accommodation and activities in the valley.

ℹ Getting There & Away

Trains run frequently from Bludenz to Schruns (€2.90, 19 minutes), from where up to five buses daily continue onto Partenen (€3.80, 38 minutes) at the base of the Silvretta pass. From mid-July to mid-October, eight buses daily climb from Partenen to the Silvretta Stausee (€3.80, 31 minutes).

Understand Austria

Austria Today

With resurgent extreme-right politics getting a grip on the nation, unemployment creeping steadily up and voting irregularities forcing Austrians to the polls twice in the 2016 presidential elections, the country is living turbulent times. But it isn't all bleak: there has been a boom in tourism and Vienna is topping quality of life surveys once again. Not to mention the forward-thinking chancellor and foreign minister – all little rays of hope that suggest the country can weather the storm.

Best on Film

The Third Man (1949) Classic film noir set in Vienna.
The Piano Teacher (2001) Masterpiece directed by Michael Hanecke about a masochistic piano teacher.
Metropolis (1927) Industry and prescient futuristic grunge by director Fritz Lange.
Amour (2012) Michael Hanecke directed and wrote the screenplay of this film about an elderly couple's tested love.
The Dreamed Ones (2016) Ruth Beckermann's literary film homes in on the love of poets as expressed through passionate postal exchanges.

Best in Print

Radetzky March (Joseph Roth; 1932) Chronicles the decline of the Austro-Hungarian Empire.
The World of Yesterday (Stefan Zweig; 1942) Posted to his publisher the day before he committed suicide, Zweig's moving memoir as a Jew in exile is set against the rise of Nazi power.
Danube (Claudio Magris; 1986) Italian travel journal covering the river's length.
Last Waltz in Vienna: The Destruction of a Family 1842–1942 (George Clare; 1982) Autobiographical account of a Jewish family's fate.

Tables Turn on Immigration

As elsewhere in Europe, the hot talking point of the moment is the migrant crisis and its social and economic ramifications. Historically, Austria has a good track record of welcoming refugees and asylum seekers, for instance during the Balkans War in 1995 when thousands fled here from war-torn Yugoslavia. When the crisis reached its borders in 2015, Austria initially expressed its solidarity by assisting refugees who entered the country via Hungary with their onward journey. At Vienna's Hauptbahnhof, a Train of Hope was set up, with volunteers helping refugees. In tune with neighbouring Germany's open-door policies, Austria accepted 90,000 asylum applications in 2015 – one of Europe's highest per capita. Then in August 2015, public opinion changed following the grim discovery of a truck containing the badly decomposing bodies of 71 migrants in the east of the country.

By 2016, the tables were turning. No longer able to cope with the influx of migrants and struggling to successfully integrate and find jobs for them amid rising unemployment, the country capped the maximum number of migrants at 37,500. Following the first round of presidential elections in April 2016, it introduced a highly controversial bill to allow 'a state of emergency', permitting the rejection of the vast majority of refugees at borders should numbers suddenly surge. A 4km fence was erected on the Slovenian border, and talks are in the pipeline about building further fences on the Hungarian and Italian (Brenner Pass) borders. The UN and asylum experts have condemned such actions as flouting human rights laws.

Presidential Elections: A Nation Divided

Another big talking point is the presidential elections (the role of Austria's president, however, is largely ceremonial). For the first time since WWII, neither of the country's two main centrist parties made it to the second presidential run-off in May 2016. Instead, the vote swung between two unlikely neck-and-neck candidates: Alexander van der Bellen, an independent backed by the Greens, and Norbert Hofer, a member of the far-right populist Freedom Party (FPÖ). Van der Bellen won by a hair's breadth, but ripples of shock shook the nation when the result was overturned by constitutional court due to ballot irregularities. Van der Bellen then increased his majority in the December re-vote.

Right vs Left

The 2016 presidential elections clearly indicated that populism in Austria is on rise. The reasons for this are complex, but issues such as the handling of the migrant crisis, disillusionment with the mainstream political parties and fears for the future (unemployment currently stands at 8.6%) are all key topics.

In this climate of uncertainty, Hofer's popularity has gone from strength to strength. Though critics see him as a wolf in sheep's clothing, the 45-year-old family man's message about 'putting Austria first' has struck a chord with many.

On the other side of the fence is progressive Green candidate Alexander van der Bellen, a 72-year-old retired economics professor, who dreams of a border-free 'United States of Europe'.

Silver Linings

Austria may have some clouds looming overhead, but some political silver linings are giving the country hope. The former CEO of Austrian Federal Railways (ÖBB), Christian Kern of the SPÖ, became chancellor in May 2016 (in Austria, the federal chancellor is the true head of government). He oversaw the mass influx of refugees by rail and after election called for an EU shakeup in the wake of Brexit.

The nation's focus is also on 30-year-old Sebastian Kurz, a member of the Austrian People's Party (ÖVP) and the world's youngest foreign minister. Seeing the recent presidential elections as a catalyst for change, he has called for a better control of EU borders. With his bold thinking and frank speaking, he believes in helping immigrants by giving them what they need to integrate successfully.

Oh Vienna!

Rising unemployment and political tussles aside, Vienna has every reason to celebrate. Its recently completed Hauptbahnhof has given the capital a new sheen, while Eurovison 2015 put it in the continent's spotlight. And the tourism boom that has swept across the country has been particularly spectacular here, thanks in part to a raft of new flights.

In terms of living standards, Vienna remains at the top of the class: in 2016 global consulting firm Mercer ranked it as the world's most liveable city for the seventh year in a row.

POPULATION: **8.7 MILLION**

AREA: **83,879 SQ KM**

PER CAPITA GDP: **$48,098**

UNEMPLOYMENT: **8.6%**

AVERAGE MONTHLY WAGE: **€2555**

if Austria were 100 people

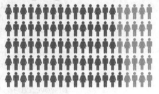

77 would be Austrian
23 would be foreign citizens

belief systems
(% of population)

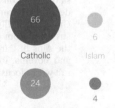

66 Catholic
6 Islam
24 Other
4 Protestant

population per sq km

AUSTRIA USA GERMANY

= 35 people

History

Although Austria's territorial heartland has always been modest in size, its monarchy ruled an empire that spanned continents and was once the last word in politics and high culture. Austria's history is a story of conflated empires and powerful monarchs, war and revolution, cultural explosion, Austro-Fascism, occupation by foreign powers and stable democracy.

Civilisations & Empires

The alpine regions of Austria were cold, inhospitable places during the last ice age 30,000 years ago and virtually impenetrable for human and beast. So it's not surprising that while mammoths were lumbering across a frozen landscape, the more accessible plains and Danube Valley in Lower Austria developed into early centres of civilisation. Several archaeological finds can be traced back to this period, including ancient Venus figurines that are today housed inside Vienna's Naturhistorisches Museum. The starlet among the collection is the Venus of Willendorf, discovered in 1908 in the Wachau region of the Danube Valley. The diminutive and plump 11cm figurine is made of limestone and estimated to be around 25,000 years old.

A proto-Celtic civilisation known as the Hallstatt Culture – named after the town of Hallstatt in the Salzkammergut where there was a burial site – took root in the region around 800 BC. These proto-Celts mined salt in the Salzkammergut and maintained trade ties with the Mediterranean. When other Celts settled in the late Iron Age (around 450 BC) from Gaul (France) they chose the valley of the Danube River, but also the salt-rich regions around Salzburg, encountering Illyrians who had wandered there from the Balkan region as well as the Hallstatt proto-Celts. Gradually an Illyric-Celtic kingdom took shape, known as Noricum, that stretched from eastern Tyrol to the Danube and the eastern fringes of the Alps in Carinthia, also extending into parts of Bavaria (Germany) and Slovenia. Today the towns of Hallstatt and Hallein have exhibits and salt works focusing on the Hallstatt Culture and these Celtic civilisations.

TIMELINE	30,000–25,000 BC	3300 BC	800–400 BC
	The 30,000-year-old Venus of Galgenberg (aka Dancing Fanny) and the 25,000-year-old buxom beauty the Venus of Willendorf are crafted – both are now in Vienna's Naturhistorisches Museum	The Neolithic 'Ötzi' dies and is mummified in a glacier in the Ötztal. After discovery in 1991, several Austrian and Italian women ask to be impregnated with his frozen sperm.	The Iron Age Hallstadtkultur (Hallstadt culture) develops in southern Salzkammergut, where settlers work salt mines. Around 450 BC Celts arrive in the region and build on this flourishing culture

Romans

The Romans, who crossed the Alps in force in 15 BC and settled south of the Danube River, carved up regions of Austria into administrative areas and built *Limes* (fortresses) and towns such as Carnuntum, Vindobona (the forerunner of Vienna), Brigantium (Bregenz), Juvavum (Salzburg), Flavia Solva (Leibnitz in Styria), Aguntum and Virunum (north of Klagenfurt). However, the Western Empire created by the Romans collapsed in the 5th century, leaving a vacuum that was filled by newly arriving tribes: the Germanic Alemanni in Vorarlberg, Slavs who pushed into Carinthia and Styria, and Bavarians who settled south of the Danube in Upper and Lower Austria, Tyrol and around Salzburg. The Bavarians proved to be the most successful, and by the 7th century they had most regions of Austria in their grip, creating a large German-speaking territory.

The Carolingian Empire

Once the Roman Empire had collapsed in the 5th century, it was difficult to talk about fully fledged empires. This changed in Europe and in Austria itself with the growth of the Carolingian Empire in the 6th century. This was Europe's most powerful empire in its day. It originated in western France and Belgium, grew into a heavyweight under Charlemagne (747–814) and took its inspiration from the Romans. Significantly for future Austria, Charlemagne created a buffer region in the Danube Valley, later dubbed Ostmark (Eastern March), which shored up the eastern edge of his empire, and in 800 he was crowned kaiser by the pope.

Early Habsburg Monarchy

The rise of the Habsburgs to rule was shaky at first. The period directly leading up to the election of Rudolf I was known as the Interregnum, a time when the Holy Roman Empire failed to produce an unchallenged and enduring monarch. After Rudolf died in 1291, the crown slipped out of Habsburg hands for a few years until the non-Habsburgian successor was slain by the Hungarians and Rudolf's eldest son, Albert I, was elected to head the empire in 1298.

The Habsburgs initially suffered some humiliating setbacks, including at the hands of the Swiss, who had begun forming political unions to help maintain peace following the death of Rudolf I. These unions subsequently fought the Habsburgs on numerous occasions and created the basis for greater autonomy and, much later, Swiss independence from the Habsburgs.

In Austria itself, however, the Habsburgs managed to consolidate their position: Carinthia (as well as Carniola in Slovenia) lost its independence and was annexed in 1335, followed by Tyrol in 1363. These foundations

The patron saint of Austria is Saint Leopold III of Babenberg (1096–1135).

15 BC–AD 600	AD 8	795	976 & 996
Romans establish relations with Celts and Nordic tribes. Roman occupation begins in the provinces of Rhaetia, Noricum and Pannonia. Slavic, Germanic and other tribes later overrun the territories.	Vindobona, the forerunner of Vienna's Innere Stadt, becomes part of the Roman province of Pannonia.	Charlemagne creates a buffer region in the Danube Valley, later dubbed Ostmark (Eastern March) by the Nazis; this shores up the eastern edge of his empire.	The Babenbergs are entrusted with the Ostmark in 976 and administer it as margraves; in 996 this appears for the first time in a document as Ostarrîchi.

allowed Duke of Austria Rudolf IV (1339–65) to forge ahead with developing his lands: he founded the University of Vienna in in 1365 and he created Vienna's most visible landmark today by ordering the building of Gothic Stephansdom in 1359, justifiably earning himself the moniker 'Rudolf the Founder'.

Keeping it Habsburg

Marriage, not muscle, was the historic key to Habsburg land gains. The Hungarian king Matthias Corvinus (1443–90) once adapted lines from Ovid when he wrote: 'Let others wage war but you, lucky Austria, marry! For the empires given to others by Mars are given to you by Venus.'

The age of the convenient wedding began in earnest with Maximilian I (1459–1519), whose moniker was the Last Knight because of his outdated predilection for medieval tournaments. His other loves were Renaissance art, his own grave (which he commissioned during his life time) and Albrecht Dürer (1471–1528), whom Maximilian commissioned to work on the very same grave before he stepped into it. It is now in Innsbruck's Hofkirche.

But it was Maximilian's affection for Maria of Burgundy (1457–82) that had the greatest influence on the fortunes of the Habsburgs. The two married, and when Maria fell from a horse and died as a result of a miscarriage in 1482, Burgundy, Lorraine and the Low Countries fell into Habsburg hands. In their day, these regions were the last word in culture, economic prosperity and the arts. However this began a difficult relationship with France that stuck to the Habsburg shoe for centuries.

The 'Spanish Marriage' in 1496 was another clever piece of royal bedding. When Maximilian's son Philipp der Schöne (Philip the Handsome) married Juana la Loca (Johanna the Mad; 1479–55), Spain and its resource-rich overseas territories in Central and South America became Habsburgian. When their son Ferdinand I (1503–64) married Anna of Hungary and Bohemia (1503–47), fulfilling a deal his grandfather Maximilian I had negotiated with King Vladislav II (1456–1516), Bohemia was also in the Habsburg fold. In the same deal, Maria von Habsburg (1505–58) married into this Polish-Lithuanian Jagiellonen dynasty, which traditionally purveyed kings to Poland, Bohemia and Hungary at that time. By 1526, when her husband Ludwig II (1506–26) drowned in a tributary of the Danube during the Battle of Mohács against the Turks, Silesia (in Poland), Bohemia (in the Czech Republic) and Hungary were all thoroughly Habsburg.

Under Karl V (1500–58), the era of the universal monarch arrived, and the Habsburgs had added the kingdom of Naples (southern Italy, including Sicily). That was about as good as it got.

1137	1156	1192	1246–78
Vienna is first documented as a city in the Treaty of Mautern between the Babenbergs and the Bishops of Passau.	As consolation for relinquishing Bavaria, Austria becomes a duchy (Privilegium Minus) and the Babenberg ruler Heinrich Jasomirgott (1107–77) becomes Austria's first duke, residing in Vienna.	Styria is given to Babenberg Leopold V (1157–94) on the condition that it stays part of Austria forever. Styria then includes chunks of Slovenia and Lower and Upper Austria.	Last Babenberg dies in 1246. Habsburg Rudolf I is elected king of the Holy Roman Empire in 1273; he defeats Bohemian Ottokar II in the 1278 Battle of Marchfeld.

The distended lower jaw and lip, a family trait of the early Habsburgs, is discreetly downplayed in official portraits.

Reformation & the Thirty Years' War

The 16th century was a crucial period in Austria during which the country came to terms with religious reformation brought about by Martin Luther, Counter-Reformation aimed at turning back the clock on Luther's Church reforms, and a disastrous Thirty Years' War that saw the Habsburgs' German territories splinter and slip further from their grasp.

In the German town of Wittenberg in 1517, theology professor Martin Luther (1483–1546) made public his 95 theses that questioned the papal practice of selling indulgences to exonerate sins. Threatened with excommunication, Luther refused to recant, broke from the Catholic Church, was banned by the Reich, and whilst in hiding translated the New Testament into German. Except in Tyrol, almost the entire population of Austria had become Protestant. In 1555 Karl V signed the Peace of Augsburg, which gave the Catholic and Protestant churches equal standing and allowed each local prince to decide the religion of their principality. The more secular northern principalities of the German lands adopted

AUSTRIA & THE HOLY ROMAN EMPIRE

The Holy Roman Empire was Europe's oddest 'state'. Its foundations were laid when the Carolingian king, Pippin, rescued a beleaguered pope and became *Patricius Romanorum* (Protector of Rome), making him Caesar's successor. The title 'kaiser' is derived from 'Caesar'. Pippin, with Italian spoils on his hands (one being the present-day Vatican), gave these to the pope. Pippin's son, Charlemagne, continued this tradition as protector (which meant he had the title kaiser), and in 962, with the crowning of Otto I (912–73) as Holy Roman Emperor, the empire was officially born.

Kings in the empire were elected in political horse-trading by a handful of prince electors, but for a king to take the next step and become kaiser (and protector of the pope), he had to be crowned by the pope. Depending on how feisty the pope happened to be, this brought other troubles. In 1338 enough was enough and the electors threw the pope overboard, deciding they could elect their own kaiser.

In 972, just before Otto I died, borders of the empire included present-day Austria, Slovenia, Czech Republic, Germany, Holland, Belgium and much of the Italian peninsula. These borders ebbed and flowed with the times. When Rudolf I arrived in 1273, all – or what remained of it – belonged to the Habsburgs.

The empire was formally buried in 1806 when Napoleon Bonaparte tore through Europe, and by the time the Austro-Hungarian Empire (a dual monarchy of Austria and Hungary) took shape in 1867, it was little more than a dim and distant reminder of medieval times.

1335 & 1363	1420–21	1496	1517
Bavarian Ludwig IV (1314–47) gives Carinthia to the Habsburgs in 1335; territories include Austria (Ostarrîchi), Styria and Carinthia. In 1363 Margarethe Maultasch (1318–63) dies and Tyrol is added.	Under Duke Albrecht V, the first large-scale persecution of Jews (known as the *Wiener Geserah*) in Austria's capital takes place.	Habsburg Philipp der Schöne (Philip the Handsome) marries Juana la Loca (Johanna the Mad) in the 'Spanish Marriage': Spain and its resource-rich Central and South American territories became Habsburg.	Theology professor Martin Luther sparks the Reformation when he makes public his 95 theses that call into question corrupt practices of the church, and most of Austria becomes Lutheran (Protestant).

Lutheran teachings, while the clerical lords in the south, southwest and Austria remained Catholic or adopted Catholicism. Not only does this explain the patchwork of Protestant and Catholic religions today in many regions that used to be part of the Holy Roman Empire, but it also made a mess of one Habsburg vision: Emperor Karl V had dedicated his life to creating a so-called universal Catholic monarchy. Seeing the writing clearly on the wall, he abdicated in 1556 and withdrew to a monastery in Spain to lick his wounds and die.

The spoils were divided up among the Habsburgs. The brother of Karl V, Ferdinand I, inherited Austria as well as Hungary and Bohemia, and Karl V's only legitimate son, Philip II (1527–98), got Spain, Naples and Sicily, the Low Countries, and the overseas colonies. To bolster Catholicism in Austria, Ferdinand I invited the Jesuits to Vienna in 1556; in contrast, his successor Maximilian II was extremely tolerant of Protestantism and the ideas of the Reformation. When the fanatically Catholic Ferdinand II took the throne in 1619 and put his weight behind a Counter-Reformation movement, the Protestant nobles in Bohemia finally rebelled in an armed conflict that quickly spread and developed into the pan-European Thirty Years' War; Sweden and France had joined this by 1635. In 1645 a Protestant Swedish army marched to within sight of Vienna but did not attack.

Calm was restored with the Peace of Westphalia (1648) but it left the Habsburgs' Reich – embracing more than 300 states and about 1000 smaller territories – a nominal, impotent state. Switzerland and the Netherlands gained formal independence, and the Habsburgs lost territory to France.

Turks & the Siege of Vienna

The Ottoman Empire viewed Vienna as 'the city of the golden apple', but it wasn't *Apfelstrüdel* they were after in their great sieges. The first, in 1529 during the reign of Karl V, was begun by Süleyman the Magnificent, who advanced into Hungary and took Budapest before beginning an 18-day siege to capture Vienna. This was the meeting of two powers almost at their peaks, but – for reasons that are unclear today – the Ottomans suddenly withdrew back to Hungary. The Turkish sultan died at the siege of Szigetvár, yet his death was kept secret for several days in an attempt to preserve the morale of his army. The subterfuge worked for a while. Messengers were led into the presence of the embalmed body, which was placed in a seated position on the throne. They then relayed their news to the corpse.

At the head of the second Turkish siege in 1683 was the general and grand vizier Kara Mustapha. Amid the 25,000 tents of the Ottoman army that surrounded Vienna's medieval centre, he installed 1500 concubines,

Historic Palaces

Schloss Schönbrunn, Vienna

Schloss Belvedere, Vienna

Schloss Eggenberg, Graz

Festung Hohensalzburg, Salzburg

1529	1556	1618–48	1670
The first Turkish siege of Vienna takes place, undertaken by Süleyman the Magnificent, but Süleyman's forces are not strong enough to take control of the city.	Abandoning the idea of uniting an empire under Catholicism, Karl V abdicates – the Spanish part goes to his son Philip II, and Ferdinand I gets Austria, Bohemia and largely Turkish-occupied Hungary.	Anti-reformer Ferdinand II challenges Bohemia's confessional freedom. Habsburg counsels are thrown out of a window (the Prague Defenestration), triggering the Thirty Years' War.	Leopold I drives the Jews out of Unterer Werd in Vienna and the quarter is renamed Leopoldstadt, the name it bears today.

guarded by 700 black eunuchs. Their luxurious quarters contained gushing fountains and regal baths, all set up in haste but with great effect.

Again, it was all to no avail, even though Vienna was only lightly defended by 10,000 men. Mustapha's overconfidence was his downfall; failing to put garrisons on Kahlenberg, he and his army were surprised by a swift attack from this famous hill. Mustapha was pursued from the battlefield and defeated once again, at Gran. At Belgrade he was met by the emissary of Sultan Mehmed IV. The price of failure was death, and Mustapha meekly accepted his fate. When the Austrian imperial army conquered Belgrade in 1718 the grand vizier's head was dug up and brought back to Vienna in triumph.

Maria Theresia

Maria Theresia (1717–80), whose plump figure in stone fills a regal stool on Maria-Theresian-Platz in Vienna today, was something of the mother of the nation. Thrust into the limelight when her father died with no male heirs, she ruled for 40 years while also managing to give birth to 16 children – among them Marie Antoinette, future wife of Louis XVI. Maria Theresia's fourth child, Joseph II, weighed a daunting 7kg at birth.

Although Maria Theresia is famous for her many enlightened reforms, she was remarkably prudish for a family that had married and bred its way to power. One of her less popular measures was the introduction of the short-lived Commission Against Immoral Conduct in 1752, which raided private homes, trying to catch men entertaining loose women –

WHATEVER HAPPENED TO THE HABSBURGS

They're still around – about 500 of them, some 280 of whom still live in Austria. The current family head is Karl Habsburg-Lothringen (b 1961). He recently took on the job of heading Europe's most famous family after the death of his father Otto von Habsburg (1912–2011). Famous for his bon mots, Otto von Habsburg renounced his claims to the Habsburg lands in 1961, a step that allowed him to re-enter Austria and launch a career in European politics.

Once asked why his name never surfaced in the tabloids, the aged 'monarch' replied: 'I've not once attended a ball. I prefer to sleep at night. And if you don't go to nightclubs, you don't run into the gossip columnists'. He was something of a sporting man, too: when quizzed about whom he thought would win an Austria–Hungary football match, Otto reportedly replied, 'Who are we playing?'

Most poignant is perhaps a comment by German president Paul von Hindenburg to Otto von Habsburg in 1933 (the year Hitler seized power in Germany): 'You know, your majesty, there's only one person with hostile feelings towards the Habsburgs, but he's an Austrian'.

1683	1740–48	1751	1752
Turkish siege of Vienna. Christian Europe is mobilised and the threat persists until 1718, after which the Ottoman Empire gradually wanes.	Maria Theresia inherits Habsburg possessions, Prussia seizes Silesia (in Poland today) and the Austrian War of Succession starts a power struggle between Prussia and Habsburg-controlled Austria-Hungary.	Tiergarten Schönbrunn is established in Vienna, making it the world's oldest zoological garden.	Maria Theresia introduces the short-lived Commission Against Immoral Conduct, which pillages homes and attempts to snatch men entertaining loose women.

the commission even tried to snare Casanova during his visit to Vienna, throwing him out of the city in 1767.

Maria Theresia's low take on fornication (and Casanova's womanising and proclivity for urinating in public) was no doubt coloured by the conduct of her husband, Francis I, who was apparently very adept and enthusiastic when it came to fornication. Yet despite her husband's philandering, Maria Theresia felt she should remain loyal to her spouse, and when he died suddenly in 1765 she stayed in mourning for the rest of her life. She retreated to Schloss Schönbrunn in Vienna, left the running of the state in the hands of Joseph II (of 7kg fame) as co-regent, and adopted a low profile and chaste existence.

The period of the Enlightenment began under Maria Theresia and continued during the co-reign of Joseph II in the late 18th century. Vienna was transformed from being a place in which the Habsburgs lived and ruled into an administrative capital. A functioning bureaucracy was established for the first time and this was directly responsible to the monarchy. Joseph was mostly of the same mettle as his mother. He ushered in a period of greater religious tolerance and in 1781 an edict ensured Protestants would enjoy equal rights with Catholics. While decrees gave Jews much more freedom, paving the way for a more active role in trade and education, paradoxically he promoted assimilation of Jews into the Austrian mainstream, banning whatever customs he thought hindered this.

Napoleon, Revolution & Empire

Austria's greatest military hero, Prince Eugene of Savoy, was in fact French. Refused entry to the French army by Louis XIV, Eugene went on to humiliate him on the battlefield.

The French Revolution of 1789–99 was a political explosion that ushered in a new age of republicanism in Europe and challenged surviving feudalistic undertakings like the Holy Roman Empire. It also led to the rise of Napoleon Bonaparte (1769–1821), Europe's diminutive moderniser. His code of law, the Napoleonic Code, was the backbone of modern laws and was anathema to precisely those privileges of rank and birth that had allowed the Habsburgs to rule and govern for so long.

Austria played a role in virtually all the Napoleonic wars from 1803 to 1815, the year Napoleon was finally defeated at Waterloo. He occupied Vienna twice (in 1805 and 1809), during occupation of Austrian regions, Tyrol – which had fallen into the hands of Bavaria – was the scene of a discontent when innkeeper Andreas Hofer (1767–1810) led a rebellion for independence. For his troubles, Hofer was put on trial and executed at Napoleon's behest. His body is entombed in Innsbruck's Hofkirche.

Despite ultimately being defeated, Napoleon's ventures triggered the collapse of the Holy Roman Empire. Its ruler Franz II reinvented himself as Franz I of Austria, and the man he appointed to help draw up a post-Napoleon Europe, the chief minister Klemenz von Metternich, rose to dominate Europe's biggest diplomatic party, the Congress of Vienna,

1764	1789–99	1793	1804–05
Reformer Kaiser Joseph II (1741–90) takes the throne and the Age of Enlightenment that began under Maria Theresia is in full swing. The power of the church is curbed.	The French Revolution takes place, bringing a new age of republicanism to Europe and challenging feudalistic establishments such as the Holy Roman Empire.	Following a marriage to French king Louis XVI (1754–93), Maria Theresia's 15th child, Marie-Antoinette – whom the French call 'L'Autrichienne' (the Austrian) – is beheaded during the French Revolution.	Napoleon (1769–1821) occupies Vienna in 1805. The Holy Roman Empire is abolished; Franz II reinvents himself as Austrian Kaiser Franz I. In 1809 the Frenchman returns to retake Vienna.

held in 1814–15 to reshape the continent. The Habsburgs survived all this and in the post-Napoleon Vormärz (Pre-March) years, they dominated a loose Deutscher Bund (German Alliance) comprising hundreds of small 'states' cobbled together in an oppressive period of modest cultural flourish and reactionary politics called the Biedermeier period.

Revolutions of 1848

With citizens being kept on a short leash by their political masters in the first half of the 19th century, it's not surprising that they began to seek new freedoms. Klemenz von Metternich, who had become court and state chancellor, believed in absolute monarchy and his police took a ferocious approach to liberals and Austrian nationalists who demanded their freedom. Meanwhile, nationalism – one of the best chances of liberalising Austrian society at that time – was threatening to chip away the delicate edges of the Habsburg empire. On top of this, atrocious industrial conditions added fuel to fires of discontent.

The sparks of the Paris revolution in February 1848 ignited Vienna in March 1848. Reflecting the city–country divide, however, the uprising failed to take hold elsewhere in Austria except in Styria. A similar revolution in Germany meant that some Austrian revolutionaries were now in favour of becoming part of a greater, unified and liberal Germany. This was the difficult Grossdeutsch-Kleindeutsch (Greater Germany–Lesser Germany) question – Germany with or without Austria – and reflects the unsettled relationship between the Austrian and German nations.

The rebels demanded a parliament, and in May and June 1848 Kaiser Ferdinand I issued manifestos which paved the way for a parliamentary assembly a month later. He packed his bags and his family and fled to Innsbruck. This should have been the end of the Habsburgs. It wasn't. Parliament passed a bill improving the lot of the peasants, and Ferdinand cleverly sanctioned this, overnight winning the support of rural folk in the regions. Meanwhile, the Habsburgs received a popular boost when General Radetzky (1766–1858) won back Lombardy (Italy) in successful military campaigns.

In October 1848, however, the revolution escalated and reached fever pitch in Vienna. Although this uprising could be quashed, the Habsburgs decided to dispense with Ferdinand I, replacing him with his nephew Franz Josef I, who introduced his own monarchical constitution and dissolved parliament in early 1849. It would only be revived properly in 1867.

By September 1849 it was time to weigh up the damage, count the dead and, most importantly, look at what had been won. Austria was not a democracy, because the kaiser retained absolute powers that allowed him to veto legislation and govern by decree if he wished. The revolutions,

1809	1813 & 1815	1815–48	1818
In the midst of the Napoleonic occupation, Tyrol – which has fallen under Bavarian control – is the scene of another rebellion when innkeeper Andreas Hofer leads a bid for independence.	Napoleon is defeated in Leipzig in 1813 and, in his final battle, at Waterloo in 1815.	The Metternich system, aimed at shoring up the monarchies of Austria, Russia and Prussia, ushers in the stifling Biedermeier period.	The Austrian tailor Josef Madersperger invents the world's first sewing machine.

however, had swept away the last vestiges of feudalism and, by giving them a taste of parliamentary rule, made state citizens out of royal subjects.

Austro-Hungarian Empire

In 1867 a dual monarchy was created in Austria and Hungary. This was an attempt by the Habsburgs to hold onto support for the monarchy among Hungarians by giving them a large degree of autonomy. The Austro-Hungarian Empire would grow to include core regions of Austria, Hungary, the Czech Republic, Slovakia, Slovenia, Croatia and Bosnia-Herzegovina, as well as regions like the Voivodina in Serbia, and small chunks in northern Italy, Romania, Poland and Ukraine.

Generally it is known as the 'KuK' (*König und Kaiser*; king and kaiser) monarchy – the kaiser of Austria was also king of Hungary. In practice, the two countries increasingly went separate ways, united only by the dual monarch and a couple of high-level ministries like 'war' and 'foreign affairs'. This so-called Danube Monarchy or Austro-Hungarian Empire was the last stage of development in the Habsburg empire and would endure until 1918, when it collapsed completely.

Fin-de-Siècle Austria

Austria in the late 19th century followed a similar pattern of industrialisation and growth of political parties based around workers' movements that occurred in other continental European countries. The country's oldest political party, the Sozialdemokratische Partei Österreichs (SPÖ; Social Democratic Party of Austria), was founded as the Social Democratic Workers' Party in 1889, based on German models. By the turn of the 20th century, Austria – and Vienna in particular – was experiencing one of its most culturally exciting periods. The capital's population had almost doubled between 1860 and 1890, growing to more than two million inhabitants.

This was the political and cultural hub of an empire that spanned Austria and Hungary, but also included 15 other countries, proving a magnet for artists, architects, the persecuted and plain hangers-on who wanted to try their luck in the capital of an empire. In this empire, however, Austrians and Hungarians enjoyed a higher status than Slavs, leading to exploitation and often tensions in the capital.

Architecturally, Austria's capital was transformed by a spate of building and infrastructure projects that, among other large projects, saw it receive a metro system. The Secession movement, the Austrian equivalent of art nouveau, sprang up and rejected historicism. Villas sprouted out of the ground in Vienna and across the country, and the coffee houses, especially in the capital, became the centre of literary activity and music. In 1913 Arnold Schöneberg began developing his 'atonal' style of musical composition when he conducted his famous Watschenkonzert ('clip-over-the-ear

---

The roots of Austria's Österreichische Volkspartei (ÖVP; Austrian People's Party) go back to 1887; a forerunner of the Sozialdemokratische Partei Österreichs (SPÖ; Social Democratic Party of Austria) was founded a year later.

Women in Austria gained the right to vote in national elections in 1919.

1848	1850	1857	1866
Revolution topples Chancellor Klemens von Metternich, who flees disguised as a washerwoman. Franz Josef I abolishes many reforms. Austria's first parliament is formed.	Vienna's city limits are expanded, mostly to include the area within the Linienwall (today the Gürtel). Districts are numbered – the old city becoming the 1st, the Vorstädte (inner suburbs) the 2nd to 9th.	Vienna's city walls are demolished to make way for the creation of the monumental architecture today found along the Ringstrasse.	Austria and its allied principalities in Germany fight the Austro-Prussian War, which leads to victory for Prussia and creates the groundwork for a unified Germany that excludes Austria.

concert') in Vienna's Musikverein. For a public used to the primrose tones of Romanticism, it must have felt like an unmitigated aural assault.

Meanwhile, Sigmund Freud (1856–1939) had set up his practice in Vienna's Bergstrasse and was challenging the sexual and psycho-social mores of the previous century. He used the term *psychoanalysis* and explained the role of sexuality in human life. This was, in fact, a highly sexualised period, with writers such as Arthur Schnitzler and Expressionist artists like Egon Schiele, Gustav Klimt and Oskar Kokoschka taking sexuality as a major theme in their works. WWI brought all this to an end.

World War I

The assassination of Franz Ferdinand, the nephew of Franz Josef, in Sarajevo on 28 June 1914 triggered the first of Europe's two cataclysmic wars in the 20th century. Almost overnight, the cultural explosion of fin-de-siècle Austria was replaced by the explosion of shells. Austria responded to the assassination by declaring war on Serbia one month later, in what it believed would be a short, punitive campaign. Austria-Hungary was poorly equipped, however, and the war rapidly escalated into a pan-European affair in which Germany, Austria-Hungary and Turkey found itself pitted against a European power coalition made up of Russia, Britain, France and Italy. Halfway through the war Franz Josef died and was replaced by Karl I. Ultimately, military revolt by troops in Italy spread and caused the rest of the army to lay down its arms, bringing defeat and collapse of the empire. WWI resulted in about 1.4 million military casualties for Austria-Hungary, and another 3.5 million Austro-Hungarians were wounded. In the rest of Europe, it was perceived as unprecedented in the scale of destruction and suffering it caused, and so horrific that it was dubbed 'the war to end all wars'.

The First Republic

With defeat and the abdication of Karl I, Austria declared itself a republic on 12 November 1918, having been reduced to a small country of about 6.5 million inhabitants, most of whom spoke German. South Tyrol was carved off from the rest of Austria and given to Italy, and the perception at the time was that a country of Austria's size would have little chance of surviving. Austria was therefore caught between contrasting movements that either wanted to unite with Germany, return to a monarchical system, or simply break away and join another country, as was the case with Vorarlberg (which sought union with Switzerland). The loss of land caused severe economic difficulties. Whole industries collapsed and unemployment soared, fuelled by the return of ex-soldiers and the influx of refugees, but also by a huge number of bureaucrats who, with the collapse of the monarchy, now had no job to return to.

Carl E Schorske magically interlinks seven essays on the intellectual history of Vienna in his seminal work *Fin-de-Siècle Vienna*.

1867	1874	1878	1897
Weakened by loss against Prussia, Austria is now forced by Hungary to create a dual Austro-Hungarian monarchy (the Ausgleich). Austria establishes a democratic parliament.	Viennese privatier Jakob Zelzer is buried in Vienna Zentralfriedhof (Central Cemetery) as its first deceased resident; today there are about 2.5 million.	To prevent the Russians increasing their influence in the Balkans after they win the Russo-Turkish War of 1877–78, Austria-Hungary occupies Bosnia and Herzegovina.	The giant Ferris wheel (Riesenrad) is built in Vienna's Prater recreational area, which until 1766 had been a royal hunting ground for Habsburgs.

One of the most serious problems facing the new republic was the divide between the socialist-governed cities, especially 'Red Vienna', and the extremely conservative rural regions. The 30,000-strong army created to ensure the country's existence was an additional conservative force in the country. The weakness of this army was matched by a police force that was helpless in thwarting the creation of left- and right-wing paramilitary forces.

The Social Democratic Workers' Party created its Republican Defence League (Schutzbund), whereas on the other side of the political fence the Christlichsoziale Partei (Christian Social Party), a Catholic nationalist party that had emerged in the late 19th century and survived until 1934, fostered close ties with a number of ultra-conservative paramilitary groups.

By the mid-1920s armed paramilitary groups from both sides were roaming the streets of Vienna and elsewhere engaging in bloody clashes. When in 1927 a court in Vienna acquitted members of the right-wing paramilitary Frontkämpfer (Front Fighters) on charges of killing two people during demonstrations, left-wing groups rose up and stormed the city's Justizpalast (Palace of Justice). The police moved in and regained control of the building, but about 90 people died in the revolt and over 1000 were injured. Troubled times had come.

Jewish History in Austria

As Austria entered the 1930s, the threat to its Jewish population intensified and would culminate in cultural, intellectual and above all human tragedy.

Austrian Jewry enjoys a long and rich history. The first mention of Jews in Vienna was in 1194, when a minter by the name of Schlom was appointed by the crown. The very same man was subsequently murdered along with 16 other Viennese Jews by zealous crusaders on their way to the Holy Land. Gradually, a ghetto grew around today's Judenplatz in Vienna, where a large synagogue stood in the 13th century.

Historically, Jews could only work in some professions. They were seldom allowed into tradesmen's guilds or to engage in agriculture, and therefore earned a living through trading goods and selling, or through money lending, which explains many of the clichés of the past and present. Two 'libels' in the Middle Ages made life difficult for Jews. One of these was the 'host desecration libel', which accused Jews of desecrating Christ by acts such as sticking pins into communion wafers and making them weep or bleed. The second was the 'blood libel', which accused Jews of drinking the blood of Christians during rituals. In 1420 these libels culminated in one of Vienna's worst pogroms, during which many Jews committed collective suicide. The synagogue on Vienna's Judenplatz was destroyed and the stones of the synagogue were used to build the old university.

Vienna's population peaked at more than two million between 1910 and 1914. After WWI, Vienna was one of the world's five largest cities.

1900	1905	1908	1910
Vienna becomes the centre of the *Jugendstil* (art nouveau) movement through its association with Otto Wagner and related artists called Vienna's Secession.	Austrian writer and pacifist activist Bertha von Suttner becomes the first woman to win the Nobel Peace Prize.	Fatefully, Austria-Hungary is given a mandate to occupy and administer Bosnia and Herzegovina, with the expectation that it will later be annexed completely.	Vienna's population breaks the two million barrier, the largest it has ever been. The rise is mainly due to exceptionally high immigration numbers – the majority of immigrants are Czechs.

Jews were officially banned from settling in Vienna until 1624, but this law was regularly relaxed. It did mean, however, that Vienna's Jews had a particularly rough time of it, and in 1670 when Leopold I (1640–1705) drove them out of Unterer Werd, the quarter was re-christened Leopoldstadt, the name it bears today. They returned, however, and this district remained Vienna's largest Jewish quarter until WWII.

When money was tight following the 1683 Turkish siege, Jews were encouraged to settle in town as money lenders. Interestingly, once the threat subsided from 1718, Sephardic Jews from Spain arrived and were allowed to establish their own religious community. An edict from Kaiser Joseph II (1741–90) improved conditions for Jews, and after Kaiser Franz I remodelled himself into Austria's kaiser and allowed Jews to establish schools, some of Vienna's Jewry rose into bourgeois and literary circles.

The revolution of 1848 brought the biggest changes, however. Vienna's Jews were at the forefront of the uprising, and it brought them freedom of religion, press and schooling. Indirectly, it also led to the founding of the Israelitische Kultusgemeinde (Jewish Religious Community), more than a century after the Sephardic Jews had founded their own. Today this is the largest body that represents religious Jews in Austria.

In 1878 Jewry in Austria was shaken up again by the arrival from Budapest of Theodor Herzl (1860–1904), who founded political Zionism, a concept that brought together the ideas of the workers movement with support for a Jewish state. His book *Der Judenstaat* (The Jewish State; 1896) would later be crucial to the creation of Israel.

Beginning with Adolf Fischhof (1816–93), whose political speech on press freedom in 1848 helped trigger revolution, and continuing with Herzl and with the founding father of Austrian social democracy, Viktor Adler (1852–1918), Jews drove reforms in Austria and played a key role during the 'Red Vienna' period of the 1920s and early 1930s.

Hella Pick's *Guilty Victim: Austria from the Holocaust to Haider* is an excellent analysis of modern-day Austria.

Anschluss & WWII

Austria's role in WWII is one of the most controversial aspects of its modern history. Hitler was popular inside Austria, and Austria itself supplied a disproportionately large number of officers for the SS and the German army. What Hitler and the Nazis couldn't achieve through pressure, large numbers of Austrians themselves helped achieve through their active and passive support for Nazism and Hitler's war.

Austro-Marxism & Austro-Fascism

The worldwide economic depression triggered by the crash of stock exchanges in 1929 further fuelled the flames of discontent and division. About 25% of the working population was now unemployed. Austro-Marxism, which sought a third way between Russian Leninism

1914	1918	1920s	1934
Austrian archduke Franz Ferdinand is assassinated in Sarajevo by a Serbian nationalist, triggering WWI, which sees Austria-Hungary in alliance with Germany and the Ottoman Empire.	WWI ends and Karl I abdicates after the humiliating defeat; the First Republic is proclaimed in Vienna. The Habsburg empire is shaved of border nationalities; Austria keeps most German-speaking regions.	The Social Democratic Party of Austria controls 'Red Vienna', its heart set on Austro-Marxism, while the provinces are controlled by conservative forces.	Austrian politics is polarised, paralysed by paramilitary groups. In 1934 parliament is gridlocked and Austria collapses into civil war – hundreds die in three-day fighting culminating in Social Democrat defeat.

and the revisionism cropping up in some European social democratic movements, enjoyed a strong following in the cities. Key figures behind it – today reading like a who's who of street names in Vienna – were Karl Renner (1870–1950), Otto Bauer (1881–1938), Friedrich Adler (1879–1960), Max Adler (1873–1937) and Rudolf Hilferding (1877–1941). In contrast to revolutionary Marxism, leaders were committed to 'winning over minds, not smashing in heads' as Otto Bauer so aptly put it.

The first government of the Austrian Republic was a coalition of left- and right-wing parties under Chancellor Karl Renner. A key figure of the right was Ignaz Seipl (1876–1932), who was chancellor twice during the 1920s and saw his calling in opposing the Marxists.

In 1930 right-wing conservatives forced through a constitutional change that gave more power to the president and weakened parliament. In a radicalisation of politics, paramilitary groups close to the right formally backed homegrown Austrian fascism, and when Engelbert Dollfuss (1892–1934) became chancellor in 1932, Austria moved a step closer to becoming a fascist state.

During the chaos, in a parliamentary session in 1933 following strikes by workers and a harsh response by the government, Dollfuss declared his intention to rule without parliament. This marked the beginning of a period when socialists and social democrats were gradually being outlawed and the workers' movements weakened. In 1933, police forced their way into the headquarters of the (left-wing) paramilitary Schutzbund, triggering an uprising in Linz, Vienna and other industrial centres that virtually led to civil war. The army quashed the uprising. Leading social democrats were executed and the social democratic movement declared illegal, turning the fight against fascism into an underground movement.

In 1934 Dollfuss – a deeply religious man who was backed by the Italian dictator Benito Mussolini – was murdered in a failed putsch staged by Austrian Nazis, who he had also banned.

The report of the Historical Commission's inquiry into Austria during the Nazi era can be found at www.historikerkommission.gv.at.

While Hitler was seizing power in Germany in 1933 and subsequently closing down all opposition, across the border in Austria, an Austro-Fascist government lifted the ban on local chapters of Hitler's Nationalsozialistische Deutsche Arbeiterpartei (National Socialist Democratic Workers' Party; NSDAP), which was neither democratic, sympathetic to workers nor socialist. This was done under pressure from Hitler, allowing Austrian Nazis to make a power grab at home. On 12 March 1938, Hitler's troops crossed the border and occupied Austria, in the so-called Anschluss (annexation), according to which Austria became part of a greater Germany. This ended a a period of contradiction in which Austria's leaders had virtually set themselves up as dictators, but did not like the idea of becoming part of Hitler's Nazi Germany. A few days later,

1938	1938–9	1939–45	1948
Nazi troops march into Vienna; Hitler visits his beloved Linz, and Vienna to address 200,000 ecstatic Viennese on Heldenplatz. After a rigged referendum, Austria becomes part of Hitler's Reich.	In the Pogromnacht of November 1938, Jewish businesses and homes are plundered and destroyed across Austria. 120,000 Jews leave Vienna over the next six months.	War and genocide in Austria. Over 100,000 of Vienna's 180,000 Jews escape, but 65,000 die. In 1945 the Red Army liberates Vienna. Austria and Vienna are divided among the Allied powers.	Graham Greene flies to Vienna for inspiration for a film which becomes *The Third Man*, starring Orson Wells and featuring an iconic scene on the city's Riesenrad (Ferris wheel).

Hitler held his famous speech to a cheering crowd of tens of thousands on Vienna's Heldenplatz, declaring Austria part of the German nation.

The Holocaust

The events of the Nazi era, culminating in the Holocaust, are etched in the collective memory of Jews everywhere: the prohibitive Nuremberg Laws, the forced sale and theft of Jewish property, and Reichspogromnacht (also known as 'The Night of Broken Glass') on 9 and 10 November 1939 when synagogues and Jewish businesses were burnt and Jews were attacked openly on the streets.

The arrival of Hitler in Vienna in March 1938 raised the stakes among those Jews who had not yet managed to flee the country. Vienna's 'father' of modern psychoanalysis, Sigmund Freud, had not wanted to read the signs for a long time; in June that year, however, he fled to England. The 20th century's most innovative classical composer, Arnold Schönberg (1874–1951), lost his job as a lecturer in Berlin in 1933 and went to the US. They were just two of many prominent Austrian Jews forced into exile.

Others were not as fortunate. The Holocaust (or Schoa), Hitler's attempt to wipe out European Jewry, was a brutal and systematic act that saw some 65,000 Austrian Jews perish in concentration camps throughout Europe. It ruptured Jewish history in Austria dating back to the early Middle Ages, and even today it's not really possible to talk about a 'recovery' of Jewish culture in the country.

Because of atrocities perpetrated on the Jewish population by the Nazis, today the Jewish community is only a fraction of its former size. About 8000 religiously affiliated Jews live in Austria, and there are about another 3000 to 5000 who are not affiliated with a community. The number was boosted by the arrival of Jews from the former Soviet Union in the 1990s, and increasingly Jews from Hungary, where anti-Semitism is on the rise, are moving to Vienna.

Take a virtual tour through Jewish history in Austria from the Middle Ages to the present in the Jewish Virtual Library at www.jewish-virtuallibrary. org/jsource/vjw/ Austria.html.

Resistance & Liberation

With the annexation of Austria in 1938, opposition turned to resistance. As elsewhere, whenever Hitler's troops crossed a border, resistance from within was extremely difficult. Interestingly, Tyrolean resistance leaders often rallied opposition to Nazism by recalling the revolt of Andreas Hofer in 1809 when Tyrol's innkeeper led his rebellion for independence. An Österreichisches Freiheitsbataillon (Austrian Freedom Battalion) fought alongside the Yugoslav People's Liberation Army, and partisan groups in Styria and Carinthia maintained links with other partisans across the Yugoslavian border. Tellingly, unlike other countries, Austria had no government in exile.

1955	1955–66	1972–8	1979
Austrian *Staatsvertrag* (state treaty) is ratified. Austria declares sovereignty and neutral status, ending a decade of occupation. Post-WWII international bodies come to Vienna; the UN later sets up offices here.	'Grand coalitions' of major parties govern Austria based on a system of *Proporz* (proportion), whereby ministerial posts are divided among the major parties. This becomes a hallmark of Austrian politics.	Vienna's Donauinsel (Danube Island) is created to protect the city against flooding. Today it serves as one of the city's recreation areas, with parks, river beaches, trails and forest.	A third United Nations (UN) headquarters is opened up in Austria's capital. It is the headquarters for the International Atomic Energy Agency, Drugs & Crime office, and other functions.

Resistance increased once the war looked lost for Hitler. The Austrian Robert Bernardis (1908–44) was involved in the assassination attempt on Hitler by high-ranking officers on 20 July 1944 and was then executed by the Nazis. Another involved in that plot, Carl Szokoll (1915–2004), survived undetected. The most famous resistance group, however, was called 05, whose members included Austria's president from 1957 to 1965, Adolf Schärf (1890–1965).

With the Red Army approaching Vienna in 1945, the resistance group 05 worked closely with Carl Szokoll and other military figures in Operation Radetzky to liberate Vienna in the last days of the war. Although they were able to establish contact with the Red Army as it rolled towards the city, they were betrayed at the last moment and several members were strung up from street lanterns. The Red Army, not Austrians, would liberate the capital.

> When then-governor Arnold Schwarzenegger allowed an execution to go ahead in California in 2005, some Austrians wanted to revoke his Austrian citizenship. Austria first abolished capital punishment in 1787.

Austria after 1945

Soon after liberation Austria declared its independence from Germany. A provisional federal government was established under socialist Karl Renner, and the country was occupied by the Allies – the Americans, Russians, British and French. Vienna was itself divided into four zones; this was a time of 'four men in a jeep', so aptly depicted in Graham Greene's book and film *The Third Man*.

Delays caused by frosting relations between the superpowers ensured that the Allied occupation dragged on for 10 years. On 15 May 1955 the Austrian State Treaty was ratified, with Austria proclaiming its permanent neutrality. The Soviet Union insisted that Austria declare its neutrality as a condition for ending Soviet occupation in 1955. At the last minute, recognition of Austria's guilt for WWII was struck out of the state treaty.

The Allied forces withdrew, and in December 1955 Austria joined the UN. The economy took a turn for the better through the assistance granted under the Marshall Plan, and the cessation of the removal of industrial property by the Soviets. As the capital of a neutral country on the edge of the Cold War front line, Vienna attracted spies and diplomats: Kennedy and Khrushchev met here in 1961, Carter and Brezhnev in 1979; the UN set up shop in 1979.

Kurt Waldheim Affair

Austria's international image suffered following the election in 1986 of President Kurt Waldheim who, it was revealed, had served in a German *Wehrmacht* (armed forces) unit implicated in WWII war crimes. Austria seriously confronted its Nazi past for the first time. Accusations that Waldheim had committed these crimes while a lieutenant serving with

1981	1986	1995	1999
Hohe Tauern National Park is established as the first of seven national parks in Austria.	Presidential candidate Kurt Waldheim (1918–2007) is accused of war crimes. Waldheim wins a tough election but is stained. The Historians Commission finds Waldheim unhelpful, but no proof of crimes.	Austria joins the EU in 1995, but because of guarantees in 1955 to Moscow to remain neutral it forgoes NATO membership.	Austria introduces the euro and abolishes the Austrian schilling as its currency, having easily satisfied the criteria for the level of debt and the inflation rate.

the German army in the Balkans could never be proved, but Austria's elected president was unwilling to fully explain himself or express misgivings about his wartime role.

In 1993 Chancellor Franz Vranitzky finally admitted that Austrians were 'willing servants of Nazism'. Since then, however, Austria has attempted to make amends for its part in atrocities against the Jews. In 1998 the Austrian Historical Commission, set up to investigate and report on expropriations during the Nazi era, came into being, and in 2001 Vienna's mayor Dr Michael Häupl poignantly noted that after having portrayed itself as the first victim of National Socialism for many years, Austria now had to admit to its own active participation in the regime's crimes. This marked a more critical approach to Austria's role during the Nazi dictatorship.

'Westernisation' of Austria

According to the Hungarian political historian Anton Pelinka, Austria spent the first few decades of the Second Republic defining and asserting its own homegrown political and social path, but since the mid-1980s has followed a course of 'Westernisation'. Two features of this are its membership in the European Union since 1995 and adoption of the euro currency when it was introduced in 1999.

The political consensus that saw the two larger parties, the SPÖ and Österreichisches Volkspartei (ÖVP), completely dominate politics has given way to a polarisation. In 1986 Die Grünen (The Greens) party was founded, with close links to a similar ecologically focused party in Germany. On the other side of the political spectrum is the Freiheitliche Partei Österreichs (FPÖ; Freedom Party of Austria), which was founded in 1955 and had a high proportion of former Nazis in its ranks. In 1986, however, its charismatic leader Jörg Haider reinvented the party as a populist right-wing party with a focus on immigration issues, asylum laws and integration – issues that today figure strongly in its policies.

In 2000 the FPÖ formed a federal coalition for the first time with the ÖVP, resulting in regular 'Thursday demonstrations' against the FPÖ within Austria to protest its participation in government, and in sanctions imposed on Austria by other EU members. Splintering has continued in recent years, best exemplified by the formation in 2012 of Team Stronach, founded by Austria's most powerful industrialist, Frank Stronach, with a political platform bearing many of the hallmarks of right-wing populism.

Discover more about the history of Austria from the Babenbergs to the country's entry into the EU in *The Austrians: A Thousand Year Odyssey* by Gordon Brook-Shepard.

HISTORY AUSTRIA AFTER 1945

2003	2007	2008	2010
Styrian muscle man, actor and director Arnold 'Arnie' Schwarzenegger is elected governor of California after becoming a US citizen in 1983.	A grand coalition government of Social Democrats (SPÖ) and the Austrian People's Party is formed under Alfred Gusenbauer.	Austria co-hosts football's European Cup with Switzerland.	SPÖ preferred presidential candidate Heinz Fischer is re-elected with an overwhelming majority as an independent; populist right-wing candidate Barbara Rosenkranz is resoundingly defeated.

Architecture

Thanks to the Habsburgs and their obsession with creating grand works, Austria is packed with high-calibre architecture. The earliest 'architectural' signs are ancient grave mounds from the Iron Age Hallstatt culture outside Grossklein, and the marginally more recent Roman ruins of Vienna and Carnuntum. In later centuries and millennia, Romanesque, Gothic, Renaissance and especially baroque buildings popped up all over the show.

Baroque Rocks

Everywhere you look in Austria you'll see that the country adheres to that old adage – if it's baroque, don't fix it. The height of the baroque era of building was in the late 17th and early 18th century in Austria. It only moved into full swing once the Ottoman Turks had been beaten back from the gates of Vienna during the Turkish siege of 1683. It took the graceful columns and symmetry of the Renaissance and added elements of the grotesque, the burlesque and the saccharine.

A stellar example of such architecture is the Karlskirche (Church of St Charles) in Vienna. Here you find towering, decorative columns rising up on Karlsplatz, a lavish cupola embellished with frescoes and an interior replete with golden sunrays and stucco cherubs. The church was the brainchild of Habsburg Charles VI following the plague of 1713, and it was dedicated to St Charles Borromeo, who succoured the victims of plague in Italy. It is arguably the most beautiful of the baroque masterpieces.

Don't Miss...

Vienna: Hofburg, MuseumsQuartier, Karlskirche, Schloss Schönbrunn and Kunsthistorisches Museum

Graz: Kunsthaus and Schloss Eggenberg

Salzburg: Festung Hohensalzburg

Melk: Stift Melk

Innsbruck: Hofburg and Hofkirche

Bernhard Fischer von Erlach

The mastermind behind the Karlskirche was Johann Bernhard Fischer von Erlach (1656–1723). Fischer von Erlach was Austria's first, and possibly greatest, baroque architect. Born in Graz, he began working as a sculptor in his father's workshop before travelling to Rome in 1670 and spending well over a decade studying baroque styles in Italy. He returned to Austria in 1686 and in 1693 completed one of his earliest works in the capital, the magnificent Pestsäule, a swirling, golden, towering pillar commemorating the end of the plague.

Fischer von Erlach's greatest talent during these early years was his interior decorative work, and in Graz he was responsible for the baroque interior of the Mausoleum of Ferdinand II. In 1689 he began tutoring the future Kaiser Joseph I (1678–1711) in architecture, before being appointed court architect for Vienna in 1694. Despite his high standing and connections to the royal court, he found himself without commissions, however, and worked in Germany, Britain and Holland until his favourite student, Joseph I, elevated him in 1705 to head of imperial architecture in the Habsburg-ruled lands.

Although Fischer von Erlach's original plans for Schloss Schönbrunn in Vienna would be revised, the palace, built from 1700, is his pièce de résistance. It counts among the world's finest baroque palaces and landscaped gardens, embracing the palace itself, immaculately laid-out gardens, baroque fountains, mythological figures inspired from classical epochs and an area used for hunting game that today is Vienna's zoo.

Johann Lukas von Hildebrandt

Alongside Schloss Schönbrunn, Vienna's other baroque palace masterpiece, Schloss Belvedere, was designed by Austria's second starchitect of the era, Johann Lukas von Hildebrandt (1668–1745).

In his day, Hildebrandt was eclipsed by dazzling Fischer von Erlach. Like his renowned fellow architect, Hildebrandt headed the Habsburgs' Hofbauamt (Imperial Construction Office). His great works were not churches – although he built several of these – or grand abodes for the royal court, but primarily palaces for the aristocracy. He became the architect of choice for the field marshal and statesman Prince Eugene of Savoy, and it was Prince Eugene who commissioned Hildebrandt to build for him a summer residence in Vienna. Today the magnificent ensemble of palaces and gardens comprising Schloss Belvedere is Hildebrandt's most outstanding legacy.

Baroque Across Austria

Vienna's palaces and churches were a high point in the art of the baroque, but the style swept right across Austria. In Salzburg, when fire reduced the Romanesque cathedral to smithereens, the new Salzburger Dom (Salzburg Cathedral) – a baroque stunner completed in 1628 – replaced it. Meanwhile, in Melk on the Danube River, Jakob Prandtauer (1660–1726) and his disciple Josef Munggenast (1660–1741) worked their magic on the monastery Stift Melk between 1702 and 1738. In Graz, Schloss Eggenberg was commissioned in 1625 to the Italian architect Giovanni Pietro de Pomis (1565–1633), giving Austria another fine baroque palace and gardens.

Baroque Conversions

It is said that the baroque was a leveller of styles, which is ironic considering that its grandeur was also an over-the-top display of power and wealth. Once the fad caught on, churches almost everywhere were pimped up and brought into line with the style.

The baroque era in Austria, as elsewhere, had begun in architecture before gradually spreading into the fine arts. The fresco paintings of Paul Troger (1698–1762) would become a feature of the late baroque. Troger is Austria's master of the baroque fresco and he worked together with Munggenast on such buildings as Stift Melk, where he created the library and marble hall frescoes, using light cleverly to deliver a sense of space.

The Austrian kaisers Leopold I (1640–1705), Joseph I and Karl VI (1685–1740) loved the dramatic flourishes and total works of art of the early baroque. During the late 17th century the influence of Italy and Italian masters such as Solari (of Salzburger Dom fame), de Pomis (Schloss Eggenberg) and other foreigners was typical of

c AD 40

Romans establish Carnuntum and build military outpost Vindobona, today's Vienna.

11th Century

Gurk's Romanesque Dom (cathedral) and Benedictine abbey Stift Millstatt are built (both in Carinthia).

12th Century

Early versions of Vienna's Stephansdom rise up.

12th–15th Centuries

Gothic Stephansdom in Vienna, the Hofkirche in Innsbruck and the Domkirche in Graz are built.

16th Century

The Renaissance in Austria produces Burg Hochosterwitz and Burg Landskron in Carinthia, Schallaburg in Lower Austria, Schloss Ambras in Innsbruck and the Schweizer Tor in Vienna's Hofburg.

17th–mid-18th Centuries

The baroque era results in an overwhelming number of masterpieces throughout Austria, among them Vienna's Schloss Belvedere and Schloss Schönbrunn.

Mid-18th–mid-19th Centuries

Neoclassicism takes root and the Burgtor is built in Vienna and Schloss Grafenegg in Lower Austria.

1815–48

A Biedermeier style casts off some of the strictness of classicism, focusing on housing with simple yet elegant exteriors and on light, curved furnishings and interior decoration.

Friedensreich Hundertwasser abhorred straight lines. He claimed in his *Mould Manifesto* to have counted 546 on a razor blade. He moved towards spiritual ecology, believing that cities should be in harmony with their natural environment, a philosophy that is represented metaphorically in his 'wobbly' KunstHausWien and Hundertwasserhaus in Vienna.

the movement. Vorarlberg, however, was an exception, as here Austrians, Germans and Swiss played the lead roles. While the zenith of baroque was reached during the era of Fischer von Erlach from the early 18th century, during the reign of Maria Theresia (1717–80) from the mid-18th century Austria experienced its largest wave of conversion of older buildings into a baroque style. This, however, brought little in the way of new or innovative buildings. A neoclassicist movement was gaining popularity, and in Austria as elsewhere the movement left behind the saccharine hype and adopted a new style of strict lines.

Back to the Future – Neoclassicism & Revivalism

Walk around the Ringstrasse of Vienna today, admire the Burgtor (Palace Gate) fronting the Hofburg on its southwest side and dating from the early 19th century, the Neue Burg (New Palace) from the late 19th century, or the parliament building designed by the Dane Theophil von Hansen (1813–91) and you may feel as though you have been cast into an idealised version of ancient Greece or Rome. In Innsbruck, the 1765 Triumphpforte (Triumphal Arch) is an early work of neoclassicism in Austria and creates a similar impression.

In Austria, the love of all things classical or revivalist moved into full swing from the mid-19th century. The catalyst locally was the tearing down of the old city walls that had run around the Innere Stadt (Inner City), offering the perfect opportunity to enrich the city's architecture with grand buildings.

OTTO WAGNER – AUSTRIA SHAPES UP FOR THE MODERN

No single architect personifies the dawning of Austria's modern age in architecture more than Vienna-born Otto Wagner. Wagner, who for many years headed the Hofbauamt, ushered in a new, functional direction around the turn of the 20th century. When he was finished with Austria's capital it had a subway transport system replete with attractive art nouveau stations, he had given the flood-prone Wien River a stone 'sarcophagus' that allowed the surrounding area to be landscaped and part of it to be given over to the Naschmarkt food market, and he had given us the Postsparkasse building and a sprinkling of other interesting designs in Vienna and its suburbs.

Wagner's style was much in keeping with the contours of his epoch. He was strongly influenced in his early years by the architects of the Ringstrasse buildings and the revivalist style (which entailed resurrecting mostly the styles of ancient Rome and Greece), and he even (unsuccessfully) submitted his own plans for the new Justizpalast (Palace of Justice) in Vienna in a Ringstrasse revivalist style. Gradually, though, Wagner grew sceptical of revivalism and spoke harshly about his early works, characterising revivalism as a stylistic, masked ball. His buildings dispensed with 19th-century classical ornamentation and his trademark became a creative use of modern materials like glass, steel, aluminium and reinforced concrete. The 'studs' on the Postsparkasse building are the perfect example of this. Those who venture out to his 1907 Kirche am Steinhof will find another unusual masterpiece: a functional, domed art-nouveau church built in the grounds of a psychiatric institution.

One of Wagner's most functional pieces of design was the Vienna U-Bahn (subway) system. He developed the system between 1892 and 1901 during his long spell heading the construction office of Vienna and he was responsible for about 35 stations in all – stops like Josefstädter Strasse on the U6 and Karlsplatz on the U4 are superb examples. One interesting way to get a feel for Wagner's masterpieces is simply to get onto the U-Bahn and ride the U6 north from Westbahnhof. It's sometimes called Wagner's *Gesamtkunstwerk* (total work of art) – in this case, one you can literally sit on.

Ancient Greek Inspiration

The age of neoclassicism took root during the second half of the 18th century, and over the next 100 years buildings inspired by ancient civilisations would spring up across Austria and elsewhere in Europe. By the mid-19th century, an architectural revivalist fad had taken root that offered a potpourri of styles: neo-Gothic, neo-Renaissance, and even a 'neo' form of neoclassicism.

Since the early days of the Renaissance, architects had looked to the ancient Greeks for ideas. The architecture of Rome was well known, but from the 18th century, monarchs and their builders were attracted to the purer classicism of Greece, and some of these architects travelled there to experience this first-hand. One of the triggers for this newly found love of all things Greek was the discovery in 1740 of three Doric temples in southern Italy in a Greek-Roman settlement known as Paestum.

Ringstrasse

Vienna's medieval fortress had become an anachronism by the mid-19th century and the clearings just beyond the wall had been turned into Glacis (exercise grounds and parkland). In stepped Emperor Franz Josef I. His idea was to replace the Glacis with grandiose public buildings that would reflect the power and the wealth of the Habsburg empire. The Ringstrasse was the result. It was laid out between 1858 and 1865, and in the decade afterwards most of the impressive edifices that now line this busy thoroughfare were already being built. It is something of a shopping list of grand buildings: the Staatsoper (National Opera; built 1861–69), the Museum für Angewandte Kunst (MAK; Museum of Applied Arts; 1868–71), the Naturhistorisches Museum (Museum of Natural History; 1872–81), the Rathaus (Town Hall; 1872–83), Kunsthistorisches Museum (Museum of Art History; 1872–91), the Parlament (1873–83), Burgtheater (1874–88), and the Heldenplatz section of the Hofburg's Neue Burg (1881–1908).

Hansen's parliament, with its large statue of Athena out front, possibly best symbolises the spirit of the age and its love of all things classical, but also ancient Greece as a symbol of democracy. One of the finest of the Ringstrasse buildings, the Kunsthistorisches Museum, is not only a neo-Renaissance masterpiece but also a taste of movements to come. This museum, purpose-built by the Habsburgs as a repository for their finest collection of paintings, is replete with colourful lunettes, a circular ceiling recess that allows a glimpse into the cupola when you enter, and paintings by Gustav Klimt (1862–1918). WWI intervened and the empire was lost before Franz Josef's grand scheme for the Ringstrasse could be fully realised.

By then, however, Gustav Klimt and contemporaries of his generation were pushing Austria in new directions.

Secession & Art Nouveau

They called it a 'temple for bullfrogs' or a temple for an anarchic art movement. Other unflattering names for the Secession building were 'the mausoleum', 'the crematorium' or, because of the golden filigree dome perched on top, 'the cabbage head'. Others still, according to

Mid-19th Century Onward

Lingering neoclassicism spills over into other revivalist styles, giving 'neo' prefixes to Gothic, baroque, Renaissance and other architecture on Vienna's Ringstrasse and across the country.

Late 19th–Early 20th Century

Backward-looking historicism is cast aside for lighter, modern styles such as Vienna's Secession building.

20th Century

While the Secession can still be felt, the Rotes Wien (Red Vienna) period produces large-scale workers' housing, and later postmodernist and contemporary buildings like Graz' *Kunsthaus* spring up.

'People love everything that fulfils the desire for comfort. They hate everything that wishes to draw them out of the secure position they have earned. People therefore love houses and hate art.' Adolf Loos

today's Secession association, thought it looked like a cross between a greenhouse and an industrial blast furnace.

In 1897, 19 progressive artists broke away from the conservative artistic establishment of Vienna and formed the Vienna Secession (*Sezession*) movement. In Austria, the movement is synonymous with art nouveau, although its members had a habit of drawing upon a broad spectrum of styles. Its role models were taken from the contemporary scene in Berlin and Munich and its proponents' aim had been to shake off historicism – the revivalist trend that led to the historic throwbacks built along Vienna's Ringstrasse. At the time, the Kunstlerhaus (Artists' House) of Vienna was the last word in the arts establishment, and Secessionists, including Gustav Klimt, Josef Hoffman, Kolo Moser and Joseph M Olbrich, distanced themselves from this in order to form their association.

'Prose is architecture, not interior decoration, and the baroque is over.' Ernest Hemingway, inadvertently revealing to us what he thought of baroque architecture (and also why he wrote about bullfights and not, say, Austrian churches).

Olbrich, a former student of Otto Wagner, was given the honour of designing an exhibition centre for the newly formed Secessionists. The 'temple for bullfrogs' was completed in 1898 and combined sparse functionality with stylistic motifs.

Initially, Klimt, Olbrich and their various colleagues had wanted to build on the Ringstrasse, but the city authorities baulked at the idea of watering down their revivalist thoroughfare with Olbrich's daring design. They agreed, however, to the building being situated just off it – a temporary building where for 10 years the Secessionists could hold their exhibitions.

Because art nouveau was essentially an urban movement, the scenes of its greatest acts were played out in the capitals or large cities: Paris, Brussels, New York, Glasgow, Chicago and Vienna. Like the Renaissance and baroque movements before it, Secession broke down the boundaries between painting and architecture. But it was also a response to the industrial age (although it used a lot of metaphors from nature), and the new movement sought to integrate traditional craftsmanship into its philosophy. The British were its role models for the crafts, and in 1903 Josef Hoffmann and Kolo Moser founded the Wiener Werkstätte (Vienna Workshop), which worked together with Vienna's School of the Applied Arts and the Secession movement to promote their ideas.

Another feature of Secession is its international tone. Vienna was a magnet for artists from the Habsburg-ruled lands. The movement was also greatly influenced by Otto Wagner. The Secession building, for in-

ADOLF LOOS – 'EVERY CITY GETS THE ARCHITECT IT DESERVES'

In 1922 a competition was held to build 'the most beautiful and distinctive office building in the world' for the Chicago *Tribune* newspaper. The greats of the architectural world vied for the project, and one of them was Czech-born Adolf Loos (1870–1933). As fate would have it, a neo-Gothic design trumped Loos' entry, which resembled a Doric column on top of what might easily have passed for a car factory.

Loos studied in Bohemia and later Dresden, then broke out for the US, where he was employed as a mason and also did stints washing dishes. He was influenced strongly by Otto Wagner, but it is said that his time as a mason (less so as a dishwasher) heightened his sensitivity to materials. He detested ornamentation, and that's why he also locked horns with the art nouveau crew, whose flowers and ornamental flourishes (the golden cabbage-head dome of the Secession building, for instance) were anathema to his functional, sleek designs. Space, materials and even the labour used to produce a building ('Ornament is wasted labour and therefore a waste of good health') had to be used as fully as possible. Today, anyone who squeezes into Loos' miniscule American Bar in Vienna, with its mirrors, glistening onyx-stone surfaces and illusion of space, will get not only a decent cocktail but a good idea of what the architect was about.

stance, may have been domed by a floral 'cabbage', but its form had the hallmarks of Otto Wagner's strictness of lines.

Contemporary Icons

Austrian architecture is more than historic masterpieces. Up and down the country, a flurry of new-wave architects have revamped, constructed and envisaged some extraordinary contemporary designs in recent years to harbour museums, offices and events venues. Many of these slot neatly in between the grand old buildings – their architectural antithesis.

Schloss Grafenegg near the Danube Valley in the lush, rolling hills of Lower Austria is a fine instance of a postmodern concert location. Here a neoclassical palace on the shores of a lake – long a venue for classical-music events – was given a striking new addition: a 15m open-air stage called the Wolkenturm (Cloud Tower), designed by Viennese architects nextENTERprise. Set in a cleft in manicured parkland, this shiny, jagged, sculpture-like stage is a natural amphitheatre and takes on the hue of the surrounding parkland.

A similar reflection of surroundings is incorporated into the postmodern Loisium Weinwelt in Langenlois. This brings together a modern hotel complex and tours through historic cellars with an aluminium cube designed by New York architect Steven Holl. Meanwhile, further along the Danube River in Linz, the capital of Upper Austria, the Lentos Kunstmuseum is a cubic, postmodern construction with a glass facade that kaleidoscopically reflects its surroundings.

States of Flux

This idea of the modern building reflecting or absorbing the tones of its environment contrasts with another approach in modern Austrian architecture: a building that is in a state of flux. Also in Linz, the postmodern Ars Electronica Center received an addition alongside its original modern building. The added dimension of an LED facade encloses both buildings and lights up and changes colour at night. Another example of this style is the Kunsthaus in Graz, which quickly became a new trademark of Styria's capital. Sitting on the Mur River, this slug-like construction – the work of British architects Peter Cook and Colin Fournier – has an exterior that changes colour through illumination. The building's modernity seeks to create an 'aesthetic dialogue' with the historic side of Graz rising up on a bluff on the other side of the river. This dialogue is linked by the Murinsel (Mur Island), a swirl-shaped pontoon bridge situated in the middle of the river with a cafe, a children's playground and an amphitheatre for performance.

MuseumsQuartier

One of the most innovative architectural works of recent years has been the MuseumsQuartier in Vienna. The MuseumsQuartier has retained an attractive ensemble of 18th-century buildings that once served as the royal stables for the Habsburgs, added cafes and shops, and augmented these with new buildings, such as the dark-basalt Museum Moderner Kunst (MUMOK) and the Leopold Museum. These two museums are separated by the Kunsthalle and a bold public space that has grown to become a favourite gathering place in the inner city.

'Because ornamentation is no longer an organic part of our culture it no longer expresses our culture. An ornament created today has nothing to do with us, no connection to human beings and nothing to do with the world order. It's not capable of developing any further.'
Adolf Loos

ARCHITECTURE CONTEMPORARY ICONS

Visual Arts & Music

For a country of such diminutive proportions, Austria's impact on the arts has been phenomenal. The Hapsburgs left a legacy of historic paintings, sculptures, concert halls and the Vienna Philharmonic – one of the world's finest orchestras. This is where child prodigy Mozart excelled and where Strauss taught the world to waltz; it is also the birthplace of golden wonder Klimt and expressionist Schiele. Today, art and music are still ingrained in the weft and warp of the Austrian psyche.

Visual Arts

The Great Fresco Artists

Austria's tradition of fresco painting dates back to the mid-Romanesque era of the 11th century, when frescoes appeared for the first time in churches, depicting religious scenes. Around 1200 original Romanesque frescoes were painted inside the former Dom (cathedral) in Gurk in eastern Carinthia, and in 1270 these were revamped with a 'zigzag' style, giving naturalistic figures long, flowing robes with folds; you can see some of these in Gurk today.

In the Gothic era that followed from about the 14th century (as for instance in Vienna's Stephansdom), fresco painting reached spatial limits due to vaulted ceilings and large windows (this encouraged glass painting). The height of magnificent fresco painting was therefore achieved in the baroque period of the 17th and early 18th centuries, when fresco painting is associated with three major figures: Johann Michael Rottmayr (1654–1730), Daniel Gran (1694–1757) and Paul Troger (1698–1762). Today the works of these three greats predominate in Vienna and especially in Lower Austria.

Rottmayr and Gran were active during the high baroque, which spans the late 17th century and early 18th century. Paul Troger, however, produced most of his work during the late baroque or rococo period from the mid-18th century. Troger spent several years in Italy learning techniques there and worked in Salzburg before moving to Vienna, where Rottmayr had been setting the tone for fresco painting since 1696. Over time Troger became the painter of choice for churches and monasteries in Lower Austria, and fine examples of his work survive in Stift Melk, Stift Zwettl and Stift Altenburg, as well as in the Dom in Klagenfurt, where you can find a Troger altar painting. Schloss Schönbrunn in Vienna also has work by Troger.

Rottmayr was Austria's first and the country's foremost baroque painter. He spent his early years as a court painter to the Habsburgs in Salzburg before he moved to Vienna in 1696, dominating the scene there for the next three decades. He became the favoured fresco painter of the architect Johann Bernhard Fischer von Erlach and is often compared to the Flemish painter Peter Paul Rubens. His work brought together Italian and Flemish influences into a style that featured plenty of bouncy, joyous figures and bright colours. Fine frescoes from Rottmayr can be found in Vienna decorating the Karlskirche, where a glass lift ascends

The Habsburgs were avid supporters of the arts, commissioning fresco painters to lend colourful texture and new dimensions to their buildings and using music as an expression of their own power and pomp.

over 70m into the cupola for a close-up view. In Lower Austria his work adorns Stift Melk and Klosterneuburg.

Daniel Gran, the third in the triumvirate of baroque fresco greats, also studied in Italy, but unlike those of Troger and Rottmayr his style reined in the most extravagant features and offered a foretaste of neoclassicism – perhaps best illustrated by his ceiling fresco in the Nationalbibliothek (National Library) in Vienna.

Jugendstil & The Secession

Vienna's branch of the Europe-wide art nouveau movement, known as *Jugendstil* ('Youthful Style'), had its genesis from within the Akademie der bildenden Künste (Academy of Fine Arts). The academy was a strong supporter of neoclassicism and wasn't interested in supporting any artists who wanted to branch out, so in 1897 a group of rebels, including Gustav Klimt (1862–1918), seceded. Architects, such as Otto Wagner, Joseph Maria Olbrich (1867–1908) and Josef Hoffman (1870–1956), followed.

By the second decade of the 20th century, Wagner and others were moving towards a uniquely Viennese style, called Secession, which stripped away some of the more decorative aspects of *Jugendstil*. Olbrich designed the Secession Hall, the showpiece of the Secession, which was used to display other graphic and design works produced by the movement. The building is a physical representation of the movement's ideals, functionality and modernism, though it retains some striking decorative touches, such as the giant 'golden cabbage' on the roof.

Hoffman, who was inspired by the British Arts and Crafts movement, led by William Morris, and also by the stunning art nouveau work of Glaswegian designer Charles Rennie Mackintosh, ultimately abandoned the flowing forms and bright colours of Jugendstil in 1901, becoming one of the earliest exponents of the Secession style. His greatest artistic influence in Vienna was in setting up the Wiener Werkstätte design studio, which included Klimt and Kolo Moser (1868–1918), set out to break down the high-art-low-art distinction, and brought *Jugendstil* into middle-class homes. In 1932 the WW closed, unable to compete with the cheap, mass-produced items being churned out by other companies.

No-one embraced the sensualism of *Jugendstil* and Secessionism more than Gustav Klimt (1862–1918). Perhaps Vienna's most famous artist, Klimt was traditionally trained at the Akademie der bildenden Künste but left in 1897 to pursue his own colourful and distinctive, non-naturalistic style, which had revitalist flavours. Klimt's fascination with women is a common thread in his paintings, and his works are as resonant and alluring today as they were when he sent ripples of scandal through fin-de-siècle Vienna, with his exotic, erotic style. The use of gold-leaf and mosaic-like detail is typical of Klimt's golden period, which was inspired by the Byzantine imagery he saw on his travels to Venice.

VISUAL ARTS & MUSIC VISUAL ARTS

20 BC Roman

With the building of the fortress of Carnuntum in Lower Austria, the Romans use decorative mosaics, some of which survive today in Carnuntum's open-air museum.

8th–12th Century Romanesque

Salzburg becomes the centre for frescoes, many of which have Byzantine influences.

13th Century Early Gothic

A transition from Romanesque to Gothic occurs, exemplified by frescoes today found in the former cathedral of Gurk.

14th Century High Gothic

Ribbed Gothic interiors and high windows leave little space for frescoes but create new opportunities for glass painting. Altar painting establishes itself in churches.

16th Century Danube School

In the transition from late Gothic to the Renaissance, a Danube School of landscape painting arises from the early 16th century, later absorbed into the Renaissance.

1680–1740 High & Late Baroque

Fresco painting reaches dizzying heights of achievement in the age of Johann Michael Rottmayr, Paul Troger and Daniel Gran.

Early 19th Century Biedermeier

Amid a wave of neoclassical and revivalist painting, the Biedermeier painter Ferdinand Georg Waldmüller becomes Austria's best-known painter of the era.

Home to the world's largest Klimt collection, Vienna's Schloss Belvedere provides total immersion.

Schiele, Kokoschka & the Expressionists

Tulln is a sleepy town slaked by the waters of the Danube River, with one major claim to fame: it is the birthplace of Austria's most important expressionist painter, Egon Schiele (1890–1918), and a museum there tells the story of his life through a sizable collection of his paintings and sketches. Other works are held in Austria's foremost museum for expressionist art, the Leopold in Vienna's MuseumsQuartier, where Schiele's art hands alongside the expressionists Oskar Kokoschka, Klagenfurt-born Herbert Boeckl, as well as Gustav Klimt.

Egon Schiele

In his day, Schiele was one of the country's most controversial artists. He left Tulln in 1906 to attend the Vienna's Akademie der Bildenden Künste (Academy of Fine Arts), one of Europe's oldest academies. It is now famous, incidentally, for having turned down Adolf Hitler in 1907. Schiele cofounded a group in Vienna known as the Neukunstgruppe (New Art Group) and around that time his work began to resonate with the public. Although he was very strongly influenced by one of the leading forces behind the Secession movement and art nouveau in Austria, Gustav Klimt, he is much more closely associated with expressionism than Klimt.

Vienna's famous psychologist, Sigmund Freud, apparently felt no affinity with expressionists like Schiele, preferring classical art and its neoclassical incarnations, but both Freud and Schiele were bedfellows in one way: the concept of the erotic. While Freud was collating his theories on Eros and the unconscious, Schiele was capturing the erotic on canvas, often taking death and lust as his explicit themes.

He had come a long way from the conservative, idyllic Tulln countryside – a little too far, some thought. In 1912 Schiele was held in custody for three weeks and later found guilty of corrupting minors by exposing them to pornography. His arrest and imprisonment were the culmination of a series of events that saw the painter and his 17-year-old lover and model 'Wally' Neuzil flee the Vienna scene and move to Bohemia (Český Krumlov in the Czech Republic), from where the two soon fled again. Today the Tulln museum dedicated to Schiele has a reconstruction of the prison cell near St Pölton where he was imprisoned.

Oskar Kokoschka

Like Schiele, Oskar Kokoschka, the second of the great Austrian expressionists, was born on the Danube River. Kokoschka comes from Pochlarn, near Melk. Like Klimt, he studied at the Kunstgewerbeschule (School of Applied Arts) in Vienna. Like Schiele, he was strongly influenced by Klimt, but another of his influences was Dutch post-impressionist Vin-

WOULD IT HAVE CHANGED HISTORY?

Vienna's Academy of Fine Arts was famous not only for being a place Oskar Kokoschka unkindly described as 'a hotbed of conservatism and somewhere you went to become an artist in a velvet skirt and beret'. In 1907 an aspiring young Adolf Hitler sat the entry exam at the academy (the exam themes were Expulsion from Paradise, Hunting, Spring, Building Workers, Death – you get the idea). There were 128 applicants in Hitler's year and 28 were successful. Not Adolf. He desolately crawled back to Linz to lick his wounds and lived from his allowance as an orphan (his mother had died) before trying and failing a second time. Disillusioned, Hitler enlisted to fight on the Western Front in WWI. The rest is history.

cent van Gogh. From 1907 he worked in the Wiener Werkstatte (Vienna Workshop). His earliest work had features of the Secession and art-nouveau movements, but later he moved into expressionism. The Österreichische Galerie in Schloss Belvedere (Oberes Belvedere) has a collection of about a dozen of his oil paintings; some of these portraits highlight Kokoschka's skill for depicting the subject's unsettled psyche without in any way resorting to bleak colours.

Kokoschka's long life was punctuated by exile and travel. He moved to Prague in 1934 to escape the extreme right-wing politics of the day; once the Nazis came to power and declared his works 'degenerate' in 1937, seizing over 400 of them in German museums, Kokoschka packed his bags for Britain and became a UK citizen.

If Kokoschka was 'degenerate' and shocked the Nazis, it was a good thing the 'brown' men and women of the Thousand Year Reich were not around to see what would come later. It was called Viennese Actionism – and now even the mainstream art establishment was being sent into a state of shock.

Actionism Shocking the Republic

Art has always loved a juicy scandal. The expressionist Egon Schiele and the architect Adolf Loos were – rightly or wrongly – embroiled in moral charges that resulted in partial convictions. Kokoschka and Klimt explored themes of eroticism, homoeroticism, and adolescence and youth. One day in 1968, however, the stakes were raised significantly higher when a group of artists burst into a packed lecture hall of Vienna's university and began an action that became known as the Uni-Ferkelei (University Obscenity). According to reports, at least one member of the group began masturbating, smearing himself with excrement, flagellating and vomiting. Lovely, but was it art? One member was possibly singing the Austrian national anthem, another seemed to be rambling on about computers. Court cases followed, and so too did a couple of convictions and a few months in prison for two of those involved. It was all about breaking down social taboos.

If some of the art of the 1960s, like the Fluxus style of happenings (picked from a similar movement in the US), was theatrical and more like performance on an impromptu stage, Actionism took a more extreme form and covered a broad spectrum. Some of it was masochistic, self-abasing or employed blood rituals. At the hardcore end of the spectrum a picture might be produced in an orgy of dramatics with colour and materials being splashed and smeared collectively from various bodily cavities while the artists ascended into ever-higher states of frenzied ecstasy. At the more harmless end, a few people might get together and squirt some paint.

Actionism doesn't lend itself to the formal gallery environment. Some of it has been caught on video – salad-smeared bodies, close-ups of urinating penises, that sort of thing – and is often presented in Vienna's MUMOK (Museum Moderner Kunst). The Uni-Ferkelei action survives

1900 Art Nouveau

Vienna becomes the world's art nouveau capital, with the likes of Gustav Klimt, Hans Makart and Kolo Moser working in the city.

1910–20 Expressionism

Seeking a new language of art, expressionists Egon Schiele and Oskar Kokoschka move to the forefront of Austrian painting.

1918–1939 New Objectivity

Post-expressionism takes root and international movements such as surrealism, futurism and cubism reach Austria, while from 1925 Neue Sachlichkeit (New Objectivity) moves away from the 'subjective' approach of expressionism.

1960s Viennese Actionism

After the Nazi era (when little of lasting significance was achieved), a period of post-WWII fantastic realism adopted esoteric themes; later Viennese Actionism brings 'happenings': pain, death, sex and abasement move to the fore.

21st Century Contemporary

A neo-expressionist Neue Wilde (New Wild Ones) movement of the 1980s gives way to 21st-century explorations using digital graphics to complement conventional forms of painting.

The innovative composer Arnold Schönberg (1874–1951) stretched tonal conventions to snapping point with his 12-tone style of composition. The most influential of his pupils were Alban Berg (1885–1935) and Anton von Webern (1883–1945); both were born in Vienna and continued the development of Schönberg's technique.

only in a few photographs and a couple of minutes of film footage. Günter Brus (b 1938), one of the participants, was convicted of 'denigrating an Austrian symbol of state'. His colleague of the day, Oswald Wiener (b 1935), is now an author and respected academic who went on to win one of the country's most prestigious literary prizes. Meanwhile, Hermann Nisch (b 1938), who staged theatrical events in the early 1960s based on music and painting and leaned heavily on sacrificial or religious rituals, has advanced to become Austria's best-known contemporary Viennese Actionist. His work can be found in Vienna's MUMOK, the Lentos Museum in Linz and in St Pölten's Landesmuseum.

Music

Habsburg Musical Tradition

The Hapsburgs began patronising court musicians as far back as the 13th century, and by the 18th and 19th centuries they had created a centre for music that was unrivalled in the world. Many of the Habsburgs themselves were gifted musicians: Leopold I (1640–1705) composed, Karl VI (1685–1740) played violin, his daughter Maria Theresia (1717–80) played a respectable double bass, while her son Joseph II was a deft hand at harpsichord and cello.

Vienna Classic

Wiener Klassik (Vienna Classic) dates back to the mid- and late 18th century and very much defines the way we perceive classical music today. Music moved away from the celestial baroque music of the royal court and the church and brought forms of classical music such as opera and symphonies to the salons and theatres of the upper-middle classes of Vienna and Austria.

The earliest of the great composers was Joseph Haydn (1732–1809), who in his long career would tutor a budding young German-born composer by the name of Ludwig van Beethoven (1770–1827). Other well-known figures of the epoch include Franz Schubert (1797–1828), followed by a wave of classical composers in the 19th century, such as Franz Liszt (1811–86), Johannes Brahms (1833–97) and Anton Bruckner (1824–96).

That Mozart Magic

Wolfgang Amadeus Mozart (1756–91) was born in Salzburg. The ultimate child prodigy, he tinkled out his first tunes on the piano at the age of four years, securing a dazzling reputation as Austria's Wunderkind. Aged just six, he performed for a rapturous Maria Theresia in 1762 at Schloss Schönbrunn. According to his father, Leopold, 'Wolferl leapt onto Her Majesty's lap, threw his arms around her neck and planted kisses on her face.'

In the years following Mozart's meteoric rise, Salieri, an Italian composer, was appointed by the Habsburgs to head Italian opera at the royal court. The stage was set for rivalries and intrigue, eventually culminating in rumours that Salieri had murdered Mozart. We will never know whether he did or not (it's extremely unlikely that he did), but this is a moot point. The interesting thing is how much art has been born of the rumours. A recent artistic masterpiece is the film *Amadeus* (1984), directed by Miloš Formann (b 1932). It won eight Academy awards and is widely considered to be the best of its ilk.

Mozart was insanely prolific during his lifetime: he wrote some 626 pieces; among the greatest are *The Marriage of Figaro* (1786), *Don Giovanni* (1787), *Così fan tutte* (1790), and *The Magic Flute* (1791). The *Requiem Mass,* apocryphally written for his own death, remains one of the most powerful works of classical music. Have a listen to Piano Concerto

Nos 20 and 21, which comprise some of the best elements of Mozart: drama, comedy, intimacy and a whole heap of ingenuity in one easy-to-appreciate package.

When not composing, Mozart enjoyed billiards, heavy drinking sessions and teaching his pet starling to sing operettas. It has been speculated that he had Tourette's syndrome, which would have accounted for his sudden outbursts of rage and compulsive utterance of obscenities. But his genius is undisputed. Indeed, when a boy once asked him how to write a symphony, Mozart recommended he begin with ballads. 'But you wrote symphonies when you were only ten years old,' said the boy. 'But I didn't have to ask how,' retorted Mozart.

Vormärz & Revolutionary Ideas

The epoch of Wiener Klassik began losing momentum in 19th-century Vienna and, with Mozart, Salieri, Haydn, Beethoven and the other great proponents dead or dying off, Austrian society and Europe as a whole experienced a period of repressive conservatism that culminated in revolutions across the continent in 1848 aimed at liberal reform. The pre-revolutionary period was known as the Vormärz ('Pre-March' – the revolutions began in March 1848); the Vormärz sounded the final death knell for Wiener Klassik and produced a creative lull in music. It was only once the noise of the revolutions had died down that a new wave of composers – the likes of Franz Liszt, Johannes Brahms and Anton Bruckner – arrived on the scene to seize the reins of the Wiener Klassik and transform it into new and exciting forms.

Life After Mozart

Austria has some great musicians and contemporary acts. Although none so far has achieved the international fame of Falco (real name Hans Hölzel; 1957–98), whose 'Rock Me, Amadeus' topped the US charts in 1986, there are some great acts to check out.

Klagenfurt, the provincial capital of Carinthia, has brought forth some good musicians. While Penny McLean (born as Gertrude Wirschinger) gave the 1970s one of its iconic disco songs in the form of 'Lady Bump', the indisputable king is the crooner Udo Jürgens. He has been long seen as a Schlager singer (a broad genre of folksy soft pop with a sentimental edge), but he composed hits for US greats such as Shirley Bassey and Frank Sinatra, and his style is comparable with Sinatra's.

Naked Lunch (www.nakedlunch.de) is probably the best-known Austrian indie band. Going a bit deeper into the underground, the duo Attwenger (www.attwenger.at) has a large following for its music with flavours of folk, hip-hop and trance. Completing the triumvirate of relative old hands, Graz-based Rainer Binder-Krieglstein has gone from an eclectic blend of headz, hip-hop, groove and nujazz to concentrate on folk music today.

For pure hip-hop, Linz-based Texta (www.texta.at) is the most established in the art. The vocal groove project from Lower Austria Bauchklang (www.bauchklang.com) is remarkable for using acapella – only voices, no instruments – for its reggae- and ethnic-influenced hip-hop and trance. Other names to watch out for are funky pop duo Bilderbuch, drum 'n' bass duo Camo & Krooked and Fatima Spar, whose worldly beats shift from Balkan to Swing.

Those into electric swing might be familiar with Parov Stelar, a musician, producer and DJ from Linz. His clubby tracks blend jazz, house, electro and breakbeat.

For more on what's happening in contemporary music (rock, jazz, pop, electronic, world music, classical and everything between and beyond) check out Music Austria: www.musicaustria.at/en.

Kaffeehäuser – Austria's Living Rooms

Swing open the heavy wooden door of one of Vienna's *Kaffeehäuser* (coffee houses) and it's as though the clocks stopped in 1910. The waiters are just as aloof, the menu still baffles and newspapers outnumber smartphones. Outside life rushes ahead, but the coffee house is a world unto itself, immune to time and trends. The story of their evolution from the Turkish siege of Vienna to today is an interesting one sprinkled with not just a few grains of fiction.

Magic Beans

For total immersion into the scene, hook onto one of Space and Place's English-language Coffeehouse Conversation evenings, where visitors get the chance to chat to locals over dinner in a local coffee house.

Like many a good fairy tale, Vienna's coffee house culture began with some magic beans. Back in Vienna in 1683, the Ottoman Turks were conducting their second great onslaught to wrest control of the Occident, the Second Turkish Siege, that saw the Turkish general and grand vizier Kara Mustafa along with his eunuchs, concubines and 25,000 tents, huddle on the fringe of fortified central Vienna in the *Vorstadt* (inner suburbs; places like Josefstadt and Alsergrund today).

According to legend, a certain Georg Franz Koltschitzky dressed himself up as a Turk and brought a message behind Turkish lines from the field Marshal Karl I of Lothringen and was rewarded for his efforts with some war booty that included sacks of coffee beans. Legend also says that although some dismissed the beans as camel feed or dung, clever Koltschitzky sniffed the beans and knew they had struck gold. He saw his chance to establish Vienna's first *Kaffeehaus* and is said to have been the first person to mix milk and sugar into the exotic elixir.

The Hapsburgs went mad for it. *Kaffeehäuser* soon flourished in Vienna, where coffee was served with a glass of water. *Kaffeehäuser* in the 17th century also had a billiard table, but playing cards in them wasn't allowed until the late 18th century.

Coffee house etiquette? Wait to be seated in formal places, take your pick of the tables in casual coffee houses. You're welcome to linger over a single cup if you wish; the waiter shouldn't move you on until you ask for the *Rechnung* (bill).

Gradually, newspapers were introduced, and from the late 18th century the *Konzertcafe* (concert cafe) took hold – places where music was played. This cast the humble *Kaffeehaus* into a new role of being a place where the likes of Mozart, Beethoven and later Johann Strauss (the elder) could try out their works in the equivalent of open-stage or 'unplugged' performances.

When Austria adopted Napoleon's trade embargo against Britain in 1813 it lost almost its entire source of imported coffee beans. Although alternatives like chicory, rye and barley were tried, in the end the *Kaffeehäuser* started serving food and wine, which is why today you can still get a light meal or a drink in a traditional *Kaffeehaus*.

COFFEE CONUNDRUMS

Coffee really is rocket science here and you'll need to know your *Mokka* (black coffee) from your *Brauner* (black coffee with a tiny splash of cream) to order Viennese style. A quick glance at a menu will uncover a long list of choices, so brush up on the ones below. A good coffee house will serve the cup of java on a silver platter accompanied by a glass of water and a small sweet. The selection of coffee includes the following:

➡ **Brauner** Black but served with a tiny splash of milk; comes in *Gross* (large) or *Klein* (small)

➡ **Einspänner** With whipped cream, served in a glass

➡ **Fiaker** *Verlängerter* with rum and whipped cream

➡ **Kapuziner** With a splash of milk and perhaps a sprinkling of grated chocolate

➡ **Maria Theresia** With orange liqueur and whipped cream

➡ **Masagran, Mazagran** Cold coffee with ice and Maraschino liqueur

➡ **Melange** Viennese classic; served with milk, and maybe whipped cream too; similar to a cappuccino

➡ **Mocca, Mokka, Schwarzer** Black coffee

➡ **Pharisäer** Strong *Mocca* topped with whipped cream, served with a glass of rum

➡ **Türkische** Comes in a copper pot with coffee grounds and sugar

➡ **Verlängerter** *Brauner* weakened with hot water

➡ **Wiener Eiskaffee** Cold coffee with vanilla ice cream and whipped cream

Literary Coffee Houses

Come the late 19th century, elegant *Kaffeehäuser* sprang up along Vienna's Ringstrasse and everywhere a new 'literary coffee house' developed where writers could work in the warm. Café Grienstedl was the first, but Café Central, the favourite of writers Peter Altenberg and Alfred Polgar, and architect Adolf Loos, is the best-known literary *Kaffeehaus*.

The writer Stefan Zweig saw them as an inimitable 'democratic club' bearing no likeness to the real world, but your average *Kaffeehaus* did have a clear pecking order. At the bottom of the heap was the piccolo who set the tables and topped up the guests' water glass, while flirting like a gigolo with the grand ladies whenever a spare moment presented itself. The cashier (in the ideal case of coffee-house tradition, buxom, blonde and with jewellery dripping from her ears) wrote the bills and kept a watchful eye on the sugar.

At the top of the heap was the *Oberkellner* (*Herr Ober*, for short, or head waiter), who until 1800 used to be a ponytailed fellow with a dinner jacket, white tie, laced shoes, striped stockings and often a green apron. No *Herr Ober* dresses like this today (there are hints of the old garb, but none of the kinky stuff), but they do still rule the tables and the spaces between them in their dark attire.

Today you find more of a *Konditorei* (cake shop) atmosphere, and most continue to be the living rooms of the Viennese. These are places where you can drink coffee or wine, eat a goulash or light meal, read the newspapers or even enjoy a lounge vibe.

'The coffee house is a place where people have to go to kill time so that time doesn't end up killing them.' Writer Alfred Polgar (1873–1955)

'In Café Central there are creative people who can't think of anything to write; everywhere else, though, there are fewer of them.' Alfred Polgar

The Austrian Alps

For many people, Austria is the Alps and no wonder. After all, these are the alpine pastures where Julie Andrews twirled in *The Sound of Music*; the mountains that inspired Mozart's symphonies; the slopes where Hannes Schneider revolutionised downhill skiing with his Arlberg technique. Olympic legends, Hollywood blockbusters and mountaineering marvels have been made and born here for decades.

Speaking of Superlatives

Europe's highest waterfall: the 380m-high Krimmler Wasserfälle

....

The world's largest accessible ice caves: Eisriesenwelt, Werfen

....

The largest national park in the Alps: Hohe Tauern (1786 sq km)

....

The longest glacier in the Eastern Alps: the 8km Pasterze Glacier

....

Austria's highest peak: 3798m Grossglockner (literally 'Big Bell')

Alpine Landscapes

The Alps engulf almost two-thirds of the 83,858 sq km that is Austria. It's almost as though someone chalked a line straight down the middle and asked all the Alps to shuffle to the west and all the flats to slide to the east, so stark is the contrast in this land of highs and lows. Over millennia, elemental forces have dramatically shaped these mountain landscapes, etched with wondrous glaciers and forests, soaring peaks and gouged valleys.

The Austrian Alps divide neatly into three principal mountain ranges running in a west–east direction. The otherworldly karst landscapes of the Northern Limestone Alps, bordering Germany, reach nearly 3000m and extend almost as far east as the Wienerwald (Vienna Woods). The valley of the Inn River separates them from the granitic Central Alps, a chain which features the highest peaks in Austria dwarfed by the majestic summit of Grossglockner (3798m). The Southern Limestone Alps, which include the Karawanken Range, form a natural barrier with Italy and Slovenia.

From snow-melt streams to misty falls, water is a major feature of the Austrian Alps. Mineral-rich rivers like the Enns, Salzach and Inn wend their way through broad valleys and provide a scenic backdrop for pursuits like rafting in summer. Lakes, too, come in all shapes and sizes, from glacially cold alpine tarns to the famously warm (around 28°C) waters of Wörthersee in Carinthia.

SEASON'S GREETINGS

Spring When the snow melts, the springtime eruption of colourful wildflowers sets senses on high alert. Look out for bell-shaped purple gentian and startlingly pink alpine roses.

Summer Stay overnight in a mountain hut, bathe in pristine alpine lakes and bring your walking boots for some highly scenic hiking on passes above 2000m.

Autumn The larch trees turn a beautiful shade of gold in late autumn and you might spot rutting stags. Come in late September for the *Almabtrieb*, where cows adorned with flowers and bells are brought down from the pastures for the winter.

Winter Snow, snow and more glorious snow. Enjoy first-class skiing, crisp mountain air and cheese-loaded alpine food. Your snug wood chalet on the mountainside awaits.

FLORAL HIGH FIVE

➡ **Edelweiss** Star-shaped white flowers found on rocky crags and crevices.

➡ **Gentian** Bell-shaped blue flowers of the high Alps.

➡ **Alpine crowfoot** Early-flowering anemone-like blooms.

➡ **Arnica** Bright yellow daisy-like flowers found in alpine meadows.

➡ **Alpine roses** Hot-pink rhododendron-like flowers.

Wildlife in the Austrian Alps

Nature reigns on an impressive scale in the Austrian Alps. The further you tiptoe away from civilisation and the higher you climb, the more likely you are to find rare animals and plant life in summer. Besides a decent pair of binoculars, bring patience and a sense of adventure.

Alpine Flora

Below tree line, much of the Austrian Alps is thickly forested. At low altitudes you can expect to find deciduous birch and beech forests, while coniferous trees such as pine, spruce and larch thrive at higher elevations. At around 2000m trees yield to *Almen* (alpine pastures) and dwarf pines; beyond 3000m only mosses and lichens cling to the stark crags.

A highlight of the Austrian Alps is its wildflowers, which bring a riot of scent and colour to the high pastures from May to September. The species here are hardy, with long roots to counter strong winds, bright colours to repel some insects and petals that can resist frost and dehydration.

Spring brings crocuses, alpine snowbells and anemones; summer alpine roses and gentians; and autumn thistles, delphiniums and blue aconites. Tempting though it may be to pick them, these flowers really do look lovelier on the slopes and most are protected species.

Men once risked life and limb to pluck edelweiss from the highest crags of the Alps for their sweethearts. The woolly bloom is Austria's national flower, symbolising bravery, love and strength.

Watching Wildlife

Dawn and dusk are the best times for a spot of wildlife-watching, though a lot boils down to luck. High on the must-see list is the ibex, a wild goat with curved horns, which was at one stage under threat but is fortunately now breeding again. It is the master of mountain climbing and migrates to 3000m or higher in the Austrian Alps come July. The chamois, a small antelope more common than the ibex, is equally at home scampering around on mountain sides. It can leap an astounding 4m vertically and its hooves have rubber-like soles and rigid outer rims – ideal for maintaining a good grip on loose rocks.

At heights of around 2000m, listen and look out for marmots, fluffy rodents related to the squirrel and native to the Alps. This sociable animal lives in colonies of about two dozen members. Like meerkats, marmots regularly post sentries, which stand around on their hind legs looking alert. They whistle once for a predator from the air (like an eagle) and twice when a predator from the ground (such as a fox) is approaching and the whole tribe scurries to safety down a network of burrows.

Ornithologists flock to the Austrian Alps for a chance to see golden eagles, falcons and vultures – both bearded and griffin.

Endangered Species

A right pair of love birds, golden eagles stay together for life. See www.birdlife. at (in German) to find out more about these elusive raptors and other Austrian birdlife.

Austria's most endangered species is the *Bayerische Kurzohrmaus* (Bavarian pine vole), which is endemic to Tyrol and found only in six localities. Following close behind is the *Kaiseradler* (imperial eagle), at one time extinct in Austria but fortunately staging a comeback through re-immigration. The *Europäische Hornotter* (long-nosed viper) may be a venomous snake at home in Carinthia, but humans are a far greater threat to its survival than its bite will ever be to ours.

Teetering on the brink of extinction, the Austrian Alps' population of brown bears is very low (estimated at less than 10), boosted now and then by inquisitive souls arriving from Slovenia and Italy. They only really appear in the Karawanks (Karawanken), Karnisch Alps (Karnischen Alpen) and Gailtal Alps (Gailtaler Alpen) in Carinthia, as well as in Osttirol. The survival of local populations and safety of transitory bears very much depends on the efforts of organisations like Austria's Brown Bear Life Project and the WWF who have invested millions of euros into bringing the bear back to the Alps and fostering awareness.

For the lowdown on endangered species, consult the Rote Liste (www. umweltbundesamt.at, in German), collated by the Umweltbundesamt (Federal Environment Agency).

National Parks in the Austrian Alps

For an area of such mind-blowing natural beauty, it may come as a surprise to learn that there are just three national parks (Hohe Tauern, Kalkalpen and Gesäuse) as well as one major nature reserve (Nockberge) in the Austrian Alps. But statistics aren't everything, particularly when one of these national parks is the magnificent Hohe Tauern, the Alps' largest and Europe's second-largest national park, which is a tour de force of 3000m peaks, immense glaciers and waterfalls.

ALPINE NATIONAL PARKS

PARK (AREA)	FEATURES	FAUNA	ACTIVITIES	BEST TIME	WEBSITE
Hohe Tauern (1786 sq km)	classic alpine scenery with 3000m mountains, glaciers, lakes, high alpine pastures	ibex, chamois, marmots, bearded vultures, golden eagles	hiking, rock climbing & mountaineering, skiing, canyoning, paragliding	year-round	www.hohetauern.at
Gesäuse (110 sq km)	rivers, meadows, gorges, thick forest, limestone peaks	owls, eagles, falcons, deer, bats, woodpeckers	hiking, rafting, caving, mountain biking, rock climbing	spring, summer, autumn	www.nationalpark.co.at
Kalkalpen (210 sq km)	high moors, mixed forest, rugged limestone mountains	lynx, brown bears, golden eagles, owls, woodpeckers, butterflies	hiking, cycling, rock climbing, cross-country skiing	year-round	www.kalkalpen.at
Nockberge (184 sq km)	gentle rounded peaks, alpine pastures, woodlands	marmots, snow eagles, alpine salamanders, butterflies	walking, climbing, cross-country & downhill skiing	year-round	www.national parknock berge.at

WHAT A PICTURE!

Photo ops abound in the Austrian Alps, but capturing the moment can be tricky. Here are our tips for getting that mountain shot just right:

➡ Make the most of the diffused early morning and evening light. Stay overnight in an alpine hut to get a head start.

➡ To get *really* white snow, you may need to increase the exposure.

➡ Get close-up wildlife photos with a telephoto zoom lens; moving too close unnerves animals. Stay calm and quiet.

➡ Think about composition: a hiker or a cyclist in the foreground gives your photo scale and highlights the immensity of the Alps.

➡ A polariser filter can help you capture that true blue sky.

The national-park authorities have managed to strike a good balance between preserving the wildlife and keeping local economic endeavours such as farming, hunting and tourism alive. The website www.national parksaustria.at has links to all national parks and a brochure in English to download.

Aside from national parks, protected areas and nature reserves are dotted all over the Austrian Alps, from the mesmerising mountainscapes of Naturpark Zillertaler Alpen in Tyrol to the lakes of the Salzkammergut. See www.naturparke.at for the lowdown on Austria's nature parks.

www.umwelt bundesamt.at/ naturschutz is a one-stop shop for info on Austria's landscape, flora and fauna.

Austria's Alpine Environment

Given the fragile ecosystem of the Austrian Alps, conservation, renewable energy and sustainable tourism are red-hot topics. In the face of retreating glaciers, melting snow, dwindling animal numbers and erosion, the people of the Alps come face-to-face with global warming and human impact on the environment on a daily basis.

Measures have been in place for years to protect Austria's alpine regions, yet some forest degradation has taken place due to air and soil pollution caused by emissions from industrial plants, exhaust fumes and the use of agricultural chemicals.

The good news is that Austrians are, by and large, a green and nature-loving lot. Recently, everyone from top hoteliers in St Anton to farmers in Salzburgerland has been polishing their eco-credentials by promoting recycling and solar power, clean energy and public transport.

The government has moved to minimise pollutants, assist businesses in waste avoidance and encourage renewable energy, such as wind and solar power. Some buses are gas powered and environmentally friendly trams are a feature of many cities.

Best Places to (maybe) See...

Marmots: Kaiser-Franz-Josefs-Höhe, Grossglockner Rd

Golden eagles: Hohe Tauern National Park

Lynx: Nationalpark Kalkalpen

Falcons: Nationalpark Gesäuse

Ibex: Northern Limestone Alps

Global warming

With global warming a sad reality, 'snow-sure' is becoming more wishful thinking in resorts at lower elevations in the Austrian Alps. Every year, the snow line seems to edge slightly higher and snow-making machines are constantly on standby.

A United Nations Environment Programme (UNEP) report on climate change warned that rising temperatures could mean that 75% of alpine glaciers will disappear within the next 45 years, and that dozens of low-lying ski resorts such as Kitzbühel (762m) will be completely cut off from their slopes by 2030. Forecasts suggest that the snowline will shift from 1200m to 1800m by 2100. As well as the impact on Austria's tourist industry, the melting snow is sure to have other knock-on effects, including erosion, floods and an increased risk of avalanches.

ECO SNOW

In a bid to offset the impact of skiing, many Austrian resorts are taking the green run with ecofriendly policies.

➡ Lech in Vorarlberg scores top points for its biomass communal heating plant, the photovoltaic panels that operate its chairlifts and its strict recycling policies.

➡ Zell am See launched Austria's first ISO-certified cable car at the Kitzsteinhorn Glacier. It operates a free ski bus in winter and runs an ecological tree- and grass-planting scheme.

➡ Kitzbühel operates green building and climate policies, and is taking measures to reduce traffic and the use of nonrenewable energy sources.

➡ St Anton am Arlberg has created protected areas to reduce erosion and pumps out artificial snow without chemicals. Its excellent train connections mean fewer cars.

➡ Ischgl uses renewable energy; recycles in all hotels, lifts and restaurants; and has a night-time driving ban from 11pm to 6am.

➡ Mayrhofen operates its lifts on hydroelectricity, separates all waste and has free ski buses to reduce traffic in the village.

Skiing

Melting ice is a hot topic in the Hohe Tauern National Park. The Pasterze Glacier has shrunk to half its size over the past 150 years and is predicted to disappear entirely within 100 years.

Austria's highly lucrative ski industry has its own environmental footprint to worry about. As their very survival has become threatened by warming temperatures, resorts find themselves pressured to develop higher up on the peaks to survive. For many years, ski resorts have not done the planet many favours: mechanically grading pistes disturbs wildlife and causes erosion, artificial snow affects native flora and fauna, and trucking in snow increases emissions.

However, many Austrian resorts now realise that they are walking a thin tightrope and are mitigating their environmental impact with renewable hydroelectric power, biological wastewater treatment and ecological buildings.

Survival Guide

Directory A–Z

Accommodation

Booking Services

Local city and regional tourist office websites often have excellent accommodation booking functions.

Austrian Hotelreservation (www.austrian-hotelreservation.at) Find hotels Austria-wide by theme and/or destination.

Austrian National Tourist Office (www.austria.info) The Austrian National Tourist Office has a number of overseas offices. There is a comprehensive listing on the ANTO website.

Bergfex (www.bergfex.at) Hotels, guesthouses, hostels, B&Bs, farms and huts searchable by region.

Best Alpine Wellness Hotels (www.wellnesshotel.com) The pick of Austria's top family-run spa hotels.

Camping in Österreich (https://www.camping.info/österreich) Search for campgrounds by location, facilities or reviews.

Lonely Planet (lonelyplanet.com/austria/hotels) Recommendations and bookings.

Hotels & Pensions

Most travellers stay in either a hotel or a pension or *Gasthöf* (inn or restaurant, usually with accommodation). All are rated from one to five stars. Hotels invariably offer more services, including bars, restaurants and garage parking, whereas pensions and *Gasthöfe* tend to be smaller than hotels and have fewer standardised fixtures and fittings but sometimes larger rooms.

TWO STAR

Budget hotels or pensions consist of functional rooms with cheap furnishings. Most cost under €40/80 per single/double. Breakfast is unlikely to thrill. The shower is in the room, but might be a booth.

THREE STAR

Most accommodation in Austria is in this midrange category. The majority of singles cost about €60 to €70, doubles €120 to €130 (from about €70/140 for a single/double in Vienna). Expect good clean rooms and a decent buffet breakfast with cold cuts of meat, cheeses, eggs and bread rolls. Usually there will be a minibar and perhaps snacks will be offered; often you have a place to sit or a desk to write on. Internet and either wi-fi or cable LAN is available, often free or inexpensively. Some specialise in catering to seminar guests. Showers and TVs are in rooms.

FOUR & FIVE STAR

Rooms in a four-star hotel or pension are generally larger than a three star and should have better sound insulation as well as contemporary or quality furnishings. Expect decent wellness facilities in a four-star option, premium facilities in five-star hotels.

ECO-HOTELS

So-called *Bio-* or *Öko-* ('eco') hotels are widespread in Austria. Most are located outside towns in picturesque settings. Quite a few of the hotels have wellness facilities such as saunas and steam baths, and because of their rural location they often have winter skiing and activities. Generally, you will need to have your own wheels – a car or a bicycle – to reach these. Tourist offices keep lists or have a special section in their accommodation listings and on websites. The website www.biohotels.info also has a brief list.

SLEEPING PRICE RANGES

The following price ranges refer to a double room with a bathroom for two people, including breakfast.

$ less than €80

$$ €80–€200

$$$ more than €200

Camping & Holiday Parks

Austria has some 500 camping grounds that offer users a range of facilities such as washing machines, electricity connections, on-site shops and, occasionally, cooking facilities. Camping gas canisters are widely available. Camp sites are often scenically situated in an out-of-the-way place by a river or lake – fine if you're exploring the countryside but inconvenient if you want to sightsee in a town. For this reason, and because of the extra gear required, camping is more viable if you have your own transport. Prices can be as low as €5 per person or small tent and as high as €12.

A majority of the camp sites close in the winter. If demand is low in spring and autumn, some camp sites shut, even though their literature says they are open, so telephone ahead to check during these periods.

Free camping in camper vans is allowed in autobahn rest areas and alongside other roads, as long as you're not causing an obstruction. It's illegal to camp in tents in these areas.

While in the country, pick up camping guides in bookshops or from the Österreichischer Camping Club (www.campingclub.at) and the useful *Camping* brochure-map from the national tourism authority Österreich Werbung (www.austria.info), with international representatives.

Farmstays

If you have your own transport and want to get away from the towns, staying on a farm is a nice way to get away from it all. You will find lots of conventional *Bauernhöfe* (farmhouses) in rural areas. Most rent out apartments for a minimum of three nights, but some also have rooms accepting guests for one night. Depending on the region and type of accommodation, the cheapest cost from about €35 per person, going up to about €100 or more per night for a slick apartment with all mod cons.

In mountainous regions you will find *Almhütten* (alpine meadow huts), usually part of a farmstead. Some of these can be accessed by cable car and road, while the more isolated ones are accessible only by foot or mountain bike on forestry tracks. Most are closed from October to April or May. The huts serve snacks or meals to hikers and mountain bikers, and many offer simple, rustic rooms (usually with shared bathrooms). Full board is sometimes available.

The website www.urlaubaufderalm.com and www.farmholidays.com are good places to look for farmstays, whereas tourist offices can also help with local mountain-top *Almhütten*.

Hostels

Austria is dotted with *Jugendherberge* (youth hostels) and *Jugendgästehaus* (youth guesthouses). Facilities are often excellent: four- to six-bed dorms with shower and toilet are the norm in hostels, while many guesthouses have double rooms or family rooms; internet facilities, free wi-fi and a restaurant or cafe are commonplace.

Austria has over 100 hostels affiliated with Hostelling International (www.hihostels.com), plus a smattering of privately owned hostels.

Memberships cards are always required, except in a few private hostels, but nonmembers pay a surcharge of about €3.50 per night and after six nights the stamped Welcome Card counts as full membership. Most hostels accept reservations by telephone or email and are part of the worldwide computer reservations system through the HI website. Average dorm prices are about €22 per night.

HI hostels are run by two hostel organisations (either can provide information on all HI hostels). JUFA is a guesthouse organisation with a loose affiliation.

Österreichischer Jugendherbergsverband (ÖJHV; Map p94; ☑01-533 53 53; www.oejhv.at; 01, Zelinkagasse 12, Vienna; ☺11am-5pm Mon-Fri Apr-Aug, 11am-5pm Mon-Thu, to 3pm Fri Sep-Mar; ☒1, 31, ☑Schottenring)

JUFA (☑reservations 05 70 83 800; www.jufa.at; ☺8am-8pm Mon-Fri, 9am-1pm Sat) There are 40 JUFA guesthouses scattered around Austria, any of which can be booked by telephone on a local number, through the central booking service or online. They generally offer a higher standard of facilities than youth hostels and specialise in singles, doubles and family rooms. An average price is about €40 to €60 for a single room with bathroom and toilet, and €35 to €40 per person in a double or family room. No membership fees apply. Prices usually vary by demand.

Rental Accommodation

Ferienwohnungen (self-catering holiday apartments) are common in mountain resorts, though it is sometimes necessary to book these well in advance. Contact a local tourist office for lists and prices or book online if possible using the local tourist-office website.

BOOK YOUR STAY ONLINE

For more accommodation reviews by Lonely Planet authors, check out http://lonelyplanet.com/hotels/austria. You'll find independent reviews, as well as recommendations on the best places to stay. Best of all, you can book online.

Climate

Innsbruck

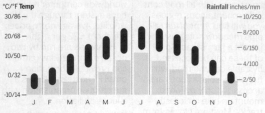

Salzburg

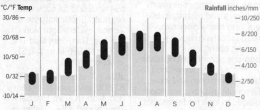

Vienna

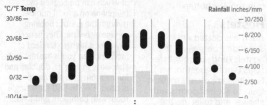

University Accommodation

Studentenheime (student residences) are available to tourists over university summer breaks (from the beginning of July to around the end of September). Some rooms have a private bathroom but often there's no access to the communal kitchen. The widest selection is in Vienna, but tourist offices in Graz, Salzburg, Krems an der Donau and Innsbruck can point you in the right direction. Prices per person range from €20 to €75 per night, sometimes including breakfast.

Children

With its parks, playgrounds and great outdoors, Austria has plenty to keep the kids amused.

➡ Regional tourist offices often produce brochures aimed directly at families.

➡ Museums, parks and theatres often have programs for children over the summer holiday periods, and local councils occasionally put on special children's events and festivals.

➡ Many lakes have a supervised beach area, with children's splash areas and slides and games for little ones.

➡ Family walks ranging from gentle to challenging abound, even in high Alpine terrain.

➡ Many museums in Vienna are free for those under 18 or 19 years.

For helpful travelling tips, pick up a copy of Lonely Planet's *Travel with Children*.

Customs Regulations

Austrian customs regulations are in line with all other EU countries. Items such as weapons, certain drugs (both legal and illegal), meat, certain plant materials and animal products are subject to strict customs control. All goods must be for personal use. The Ministry of Finance website (http://english.bmf.gv.at) has an overview of regulations.

Below are some key guidelines for anyone 17 years or older importing items from an EU or non-EU country. The amounts in brackets are for items imported from outside the EU; if tobacco products don't have health warnings in the German language, these too are limited to the amounts given in brackets.

➡ **Alcohol** Beer 110L (16L); or spirits over 22% 10L (1L); or spirits under 22%, sparkling wine, wine liqueurs 20L (2L); or wine 90L (4L).

➡ **Cigarettes** 800 (200); or cigarillos 400 (100); or cigars 200 (50); or tobacco 1kg (250g).

➡ **Money** Amounts of over €10,000 in cash or in travellers cheques (or the equivalent in cash in a foreign currency) must be declared on entering or leaving the EU. There is no limit within the EU, but authorities are entitled to request accurate information on the amount you are carrying.

Discount Cards

Various discount cards are available, many covering a whole region or province. Some are free with an overnight stay (eg Neusiedler See Card in Burgenland and Zell am See Card in Salzburgerland); others cost a few euros (eg Salzkammergut Erlebnis Card). Others, such as the Kärnten Card in Carinthia and the Innsbruck Card, must be purchased, but yield more substantial benefits such as free entry to museums and attractions as well as discounts on public transport.

➡ **Senior Cards** In some cases senior travellers will be able to get discount admission to sights, but local proof is often required. (It can't hurt to ask and show proof of age, though.) The minimum qualifying age for Austrians is 60 or 65 for men and 60 for women.

➡ **Student & Youth Cards** International Student Identity Cards (ISIC) and European Youth Card (Euro<26; check www. euro26.org for discounts) will get you discounts at most museums, galleries and theatres. Admission is generally a little higher than the price for children.

Electricity

220V/50Hz. Plugs are the European type with two round pins.

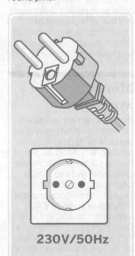

230V/50Hz

GLBTI Travellers

Vienna is reasonably tolerant towards gays and lesbians, more so than the rest of the country. Austria is these days close to Western European par on attitudes towards homosexuality.

Online information (in German) can be found at www.gayboy.at, www.rainbow.at, and www.gaynet.at. The *Spartacus International Gay Guide*, published by Bruno Gmünder (Berlin), is a good international directory of gay entertainment venues worldwide (mainly for men).

Health

Travelling in Austria presents very few health risks. The water everywhere can be safely drunk from the tap, while the water in lakes and streams is for the most part excellent and poses no risk of infection.

Before You Go
HEALTH INSURANCE

If you're an EU citizen, a European Health Insurance Card (EHIC), available from your healthcare provider, covers you for most emergency medical care in Austria.

Travellers from countries with reciprocal healthcare agreements with Austria will be covered for treatment costs here; travellers from those countries without reciprocal agreements – including the USA, Canada, Australia and New Zealand – will need to purchase travel health insurance for their trip.

Make sure you get a policy that covers you for the worst possible scenario, such as an accident requiring an emergency flight home. Find out in advance if your insurance plan will make payments directly to providers or reimburse you later for overseas health expenditures, and whether it covers all activities (like skiing or climbing).

VACCINATIONS

The World Health Organization (WHO) recommends that, regardless of their destination, all travellers should be covered for diphtheria, tetanus, measles, mumps, rubella and polio, as well as hepatitis B. A vaccination for tick-borne encephalitis is also highly advisable.

In Austria
AVAILABILITY & COST OF HEALTH CARE

A European Health Insurance Card (EHIC) will cover you for medical emergencies. Otherwise, expect to pay anything from €40 to €75 for a straightforward, non-urgent consultation with a doctor. Health care in Austria isn't cheap, and treatment for a skiing injury, for instance, can quickly amount to thousands, so ensure that you have adequate travel health insurance before travelling.

ENVIRONMENTAL HAZARDS

Wasps can be a problem in the countryside in midsummer but are only dangerous for those with an allergy or if you get stung in the throat. Look before you take a sip outdoors from a sweet drink.

Mosquitoes can be a nuisance around lakes.

INFECTIOUS DISEASES

Ticks can carry Lyme disease and encephalitis (TBE), and pose a serious outdoor hazard to health in many parts of Europe. They are usually found at altitudes below 1200m, in undergrowth at the forest edge or beside walking tracks.

Wearing long trousers tucked into walking boots or socks and using a DEET-based insect repellent is the best prevention against tick bites. If a tick is found attached to the skin, press down around the tick's head with tweezers, grab the tick as close as possible to the head and rotate continuously in one direction, without pulling, until the tick releases itself. Pharmacies sell plastic or metal tweezers especially for this purpose (highly recommended for hikers). Avoid pulling the rear of the body or smearing chemicals on the tick.

TAP WATER

Tap water in Austria is perfectly safe to drink – and it's actually of a very high standard in many mountainous parts of the country. Don't expect it to be free in restaurants, however; bottled water (either still or sparkling) is the norm.

Insurance

No matter how long or short your trip, make sure you have adequate travel insurance or are at least covered for the cost of emergency medical treatment. If you are not an EU citizen and your country doesn't have a reciprocal arrangement with Austria for treatment costs, don't leave home without travel health insurance (p387). (The USA, Canada, Australia and New Zealand don't have reciprocal agreements.)

Components of insurance worth considering include repatriation for medical treatment; burial or repatriation in the event of death; search and rescue; the cost of returning home in case of illness or the death of a close relative; personal liability and legal expenses; the loss of your passport; luggage loss or delay; and expenses due to cancellations for a variety of reasons.

Worldwide travel insurance is available at www.lonelyplanet.com/bookings. You can buy, extend and claim online anytime – even if you're already on the road.

Internet Access

Wi-fi This is available in most hotels, numerous cafes and bars, and (increasingly) for free in public spaces. Many tourist offices also have WLAN ('vee-lan') as it's called in German. A wi-fi icon in our listings means a venue has wi-fi access either for free or for a moderate charge.

Network (LAN) Cable Some hotels have wi-fi in the foyer and cable access or occasionally power LAN (through the electricity socket) in rooms. A cable is usually in the room or available from reception.

Internet Terminals Many hotels have internet terminals that guests can use for free or for a small cost. Icons in our listings indicate these places.

Public Access Prices in internet cafes vary from around €4 to €8 per hour. Small towns often won't have internet cafes but the local library will probably have a terminal.

Internet on Smart Phones Available but expensive if you are roaming. GPS and navigation work fine in most areas. If you don't want to use local hot spots you can buy prepaid SIM cards without formalities.

Hot Spot Resources See www.freewave.at/en/hotspots for free hot spots in Vienna, and www.freewlan.at for Austria-wide hot spots.

Legal Matters

Carry your passport or a copy of your passport with you at all times, as police will occasionally do checks. If you are arrested, the police must inform you of your rights in a language that you understand.

In Austria, legal offences are divided into two categories: *Gerichtsdelikt* (criminal) and *Verwaltungsübertretung* (administrative). If you are suspected of having committed a criminal offence (such as assault or theft) you can be detained for a maximum of 48 hours before you are committed for trial. If you are arrested for a less serious, administrative offence, such as being drunk and disorderly or committing a breach of the peace, you will be released within 24 hours.

Driving while drunk is an administrative offence, even if you have an accident. However, if someone is hurt in the accident it becomes a criminal offence. Possession of a controlled drug is usually a criminal offence. Possession of a large amount of cannabis or selling it (especially to children) could result in a five-year prison term. Prostitution is legal provided prostitutes are registered and have a permit.

Money

ATMs

Bankomaten are extremely common everywhere and accessible till midnight; some are 24 hours. Most accept at the very least Maestro debit cards and Visa and MasterCard credit cards. There are English instructions and daily withdrawal limits of €400 with credit and debit cards. Check with your home bank before travelling for charges for using a *Bankomat*; there's usually no commission to pay at the Austrian end.

Credit & Debit Cards

Visa and MasterCard (Euro-Card) are accepted a little more widely than American Express (Amex) and Diners Club, although a surprising number of shops and restaurants refuse to accept any credit cards at all. Up-market shops, hotels and restaurants will accept cards, though. Train tickets can be bought by credit card in main stations. Credit cards allow you to get cash advances on ATMs and over-the-counter at most banks.

For lost or stolen cards:

Amex ☑0810 910 940

Diners Club ☑in Vienna 01-501 35 14

MasterCard ☑0800 218 235

Visa ☑0800 200 288 followed by 800 892 8134

Currency

Like other members of the European Monetary Union (EMU), Austria's currency is the euro, which is divided into 100 cents. There are coins for one, two, five, 10, 20 and 50 cents, and for €1 and €2. Notes come in denominations of €5, €10, €20, €50, €100, €200 and €500.

Tipping

➡ **Bars** About 5% at the bar and 10% at a table.

➡ **Hotels** One or two euros per suitcase for porters and for valet parking in top-end hotels.

➡ **Restaurants** Tip about 10% (unless service is abominable). Round up the bill, state the amount as you hand the bill back or leave tip in the bill folder when you leave.

➡ **Taxis** About 10%.

Opening Hours

Banks 8am or 9am to 3pm Monday to Friday (to 5.30pm Thursdays). Many smaller branches close 12.30pm to 1.30pm.

Cafes Hours vary considerably: 7am or 8am to 11pm or midnight;

---

some traditional cafes close at 7pm or 8pm.

Offices & government departments Open 8am to 3.30pm, 4pm or 5pm Monday to Friday.

Post offices 8am to noon and 2pm to 6pm Monday to Friday; some open Saturday mornings; many are open all day weekdays.

Pubs & bars Close anywhere between midnight and about 4am.

Restaurants Generally 11am to 2.30pm or 3pm and 6pm to 11pm or midnight. Kitchens may closes an hour earlier in the evening.

Shops 9am to 6.30pm Monday to Friday (often to 9pm Thursday or Friday in cities); from 9am to 5pm Saturday.

Seasonal Opening Hours

➡ Opening hours can vary significantly between the high season (April to October) and winter – many sights and tourist offices are on reduced hours from November to March. Opening hours we provide

are for the high season, so outside those months it can be useful to check ahead.

Post

➡ Austria's postal system (www.post.at) is reliable, inexpensive and reasonably quick. Stamps are available at post offices and authorised shops and tobacconists. Post boxes and vans are bright yellow.

➡ The cost of sending a letter depends on its weight – letters weighing up to 20g cost €0.68 in Austria, and €0.80 to anywhere in the EU and €1.70 to the rest of the world.

Public Holidays

New Year's Day (Neujahr) 1 January

Epiphany (Heilige Drei Könige) 6 January

Easter Monday (Ostermontag) March/April

Labour Day (Tag der Arbeit) 1 May

Whit Monday (Pfingstmontag)
6th Monday after Easter

Ascension Day (Christi Himmelfahrt) 6th Thursday after Easter

Corpus Christi (Fronleichnam)
2nd Thursday after Whitsunday

Assumption (Maria Himmelfahrt) 15 August

National Day (Nationalfeiertag) 26 October

All Saints' Day (Allerheiligen)
1 November

Immaculate Conception (Mariä Empfängnis) 8 December

Christmas Day (Christfest) 25 December

St Stephen's Day (Stephanitag) 26 December

Safe Travel

Austria is a very safe country. Visitors will generally have no trouble walking around at night in cities.

➔ **Theft** Take usual commonsense precautions: keep valuables out of sight (on your person and in parked cars). Pickpockets occasionally operate on public transport and at major tourist sights.

➔ **Natural Dangers** Every year people die from landslides and avalanches in the Alps. Always check weather conditions before heading out; consider hiring a guide when skiing off-piste. Before going on challenging hikes, ensure you have the proper equipment and fitness. Inform someone at your hotel/guesthouse where you're going and when you intend to return.

Telephone

➔ Austria's country code is ☎0043.

➔ Each town and region has its own area code beginning with '0' (eg '☎01' for Vienna). Drop this when calling from outside Austria; use it for all landline calls inside Austria except for local calls or special toll and toll-free numbers.

➔ Austrian mobile (*Handy*) telephone numbers begin with ☎0650 or higher up to ☎0699 (eg ☎0664/plus the rest of the number). All ☎0800 numbers are free; ☎0810 and ☎0820 numbers cost €0.10 and €0.20 per minute (respectively); ☎0900 numbers are exorbitantly charged and best avoided. Some large organisations have '☎050' numbers, which do not need an area code (a local call from a landline, but more expensive from a mobile phone).

➔ Public telephones take phonecards or coins. Thirty cents is the minimum for a local call, which are charged by length of call (and by distance rates if not local). Call centres for domestic and international calls are also widespread, and many internet cafes are geared for Skype calls.

➔ There's a wide range of local and international *Telefonwertkarte* (phonecards), which can save you money and help you avoid messing around with change. They are available from post offices, Telekom Austria shops, call shops and *Tabak* kiosks.

Mobile Phones

Travellers from outside Europe will need a tri- or quad-band (world) mobile phone for roaming. Local SIM cards (about €15) are easily purchased for 'unlocked' phones.

ROAMING

The Handy (mobile phone) network works on GSM 1800 and is compatible with GSM 900 phones; it is not compatible with systems from the US unless the mobile phone is at least a tri-band model that can receive one of these frequencies. Japanese mobile phones need to be quad-band (world phone) to work in Austria. Roaming can get very expensive if your provider is outside the EU.

PREPAID SIM CARDS

Phone shops sell prepaid SIM cards for making phone calls or SIM cards capable of being used on smart phones for data (ie using internet apps) as well as making calls. Typically, you pay about €15 for a SIM card and receive about €10 free credit. To use one, your mobile phone must not be locked to a specific carrier.

WI-FI & DATA

Make sure your data transfer capability is deactivated while roaming. Austria has lots of wi-fi hot spots that can be used for surfing or making internet calls (such as on Skype) using smart phones with wi-fi capability.

International Calls

To direct-dial abroad, first telephone the overseas access code (00), then the appropriate country code, then the relevant area code (minus the initial '0' if there is one), and finally the subscriber number. International directory assistance is available on ☎0900 11 88 77.

Tariffs for making international calls depend on the zone. To reverse the charges (call collect), you have to call a free phone number to place the call. Some of the numbers are listed below (ask directory assistance for others):

Australia (☎0800-200 202)

Ireland (☎800-200 213)

New Zealand (☎0800-200 222)

South Africa (☎0800-200 230)

UK (☎0800-200 209)

USA (AT&T; ☎0800-200 288)

Time

Austria has summer and winter time. Daylight saving time (*Sommerzeit*) begins on the last Sunday in March; all clocks are put forward by one hour. On the last Sunday in October, normal Central European Time begins and clocks are put back one hour.

Note that in German *halb* (half) is used to indicate the half-hour **before** the hour, hence *halb acht* means 7.30, *not* 8.30.

Time Differences

When it's noon in Vienna (outside of daylight saving time):

Berlin, Stockholm & Paris	noon
London	11am
Los Angeles & Vancouver	3am
Moscow	2pm
New York	6am
Perth	7pm
Sydney	9pm

Toilets

➤ Public toilets are generally widely available at major stations and tourist attractions, but you'll always need a €0.50 coin handy (it helps to have a stash of these – exact change is required).

➤ Bars and cafes don't take kindly to passers-by using their facilities without buying a drink at least, but they might let you if you ask nicely.

Tourist Information

➤ Most towns and villages have a centrally situated tourist office and at least one of the staff will speak English. They go by various names – *Kurort, Fremdenverkehrsverband, Verkehrsamt, Kurverein, Tourismusbüro* or *Kurverwaltung* – but they can always be identified by a white 'i' on a green background.

➤ Staff can answer enquiries, from where to find vegetarian food to hotels with wi-fi in isolated areas. Most offices have an accommodation-finding service, often free of charge. Maps are available and usually free, often including some great hiking and cycling maps, too.

➤ The tourist office may have a rack of brochures hung outside the door, or there may be an accommodation board you can access even when the office is closed. Top hotels usually have a supply of useful brochures in the foyer.

Austria Info (www.austria.info) Excellent information on walking in Austria, from themed day hikes to long-distance treks. Also has details on national parks and nature reserves, hiking villages and special walking packages. Region-specific brochures are available for downloading.

Burgenland Tourismus (www.burgenland.info)

Kärnten Information (www.kaernten.at)

Niederösterreich Werbung (www.niederoesterreich.at)

Oberösterreich Tourismus (www.oberoesterreich.at)

Salzburgerland Tourismus (www.salzburgerland.com)

Salzkammergut (www.salzkammergut.at)

Steirische Tourismus (www.steiermark.com)

Tirol Info (www.tirol.at)

Tourist Info Wien (www.wien.info)

Vorarlberg Tourismus (www.vorarlberg-tourism.at)

Travellers with Disabilities

The situation in Austria for travellers with disabilities is good in Vienna, but outside the capital it's still by no means plain sailing. Ramps leading into buildings are common but not universal; most U-Bahn stations have wheelchair lifts but on buses and trams you'll often be negotiating gaps and one or more steps. Download Lonely Planet's free Accessible Travel Guide from http://lptravel.to/AccessibleTravel.

For distance travel, **ÖBB** (Österreichische Bundesbahnen; Austrian Federal Railways; ☏24hr hotline 05 1717; www.oebb.at) has a section for people with disabilities on its website. Change to the English-language option, then go to the menu and select 'Accessible Booking'. Use the ☏05 1717 number for mobility assistance (you can do this while booking your ticket by telephone). Staff at stations will help with boarding and alighting. Order this at least 24 hours ahead of travel (48 hours ahead for international services). No special service is available at unstaffed stations. Passengers with disabilities get a 50% discount off the usual ticket price.

The detailed pamphlet *Accessible Vienna* is available in German or English from **Tourist Info Wien** (www.wien.info). A comprehensive list of places in Vienna catering to visitors with special needs can be downloaded from www.wien.info/en/travel-info/accessible-vienna. In other cities, contact the tourist office directly for more information.

Some of the more expensive hotels (four-star or above, usually) have facilities tailored to travellers with disabilities; cheaper hotels invariably don't.

There is no national organisation for the disabled in Austria, but the regional tourist offices or any of the following can be contacted for more information:

Behinderten Selbsthilfe Gruppe (☏03332-654 05; www.bsgh.at; Sparkassenplatz 4, Hartberg, Styria) Maintains a database at www.barrierefrei-erurlaub.at listing hotels and restaurants suitable for those with disabilities.

Bizeps (☏01-523 89 21; www.bizeps.at; 02, Schönngasse 15-17, Vienna; Ⓤ Messe-Prater)

A centre providing support and self-help for people with disabilities. Located two blocks north of Messe-Prater U-Bahn station in Vienna.

WUK Faktor.i (Map p70; ✆01-401210; http://faktori. wuk.at; 09, Währinger Strasse 59, Vienna) Offers information to young people with disabilities. Located just north of the Pilgramgasse U-Bahn station.

Upper Austria Tourist Office (✆0732-22 10 22; Freistaedter Strasse 119) (www. barrierefreies-oberoesterreich. at) Information and listings for people with disabilities travelling in Upper Austria.

Visas

Austria is part of the Schengen Agreement. A visa generally isn't necessary for stays of up to three months, but some nationalities need a Schengen visa.

Visas for stays of up to three months are not required for citizens of the EU, the European Economic Area (EEA), much of Eastern Europe, Israel, USA, Canada, the majority of Central and South American nations, Japan, Korea, Malaysia, Singapore, Australia or New Zealand. All other nationalities, including Chinese and Russian travellers, require a visa; the Ministry of Foreign Affairs website (www.bmaa.gv.at) has a list of Austrian embassies where you can apply for one, and the Austrian embassy in Washington (www. austria.org/going-to-austria/ entry-a-residence-permits) lists all visa-free nationalities. Apply at least three weeks in advance.

If you wish to stay longer than three months you should simply leave the country and re-enter. For those nationalities that require a visa, extensions cannot be organised within Austria; you'll need to leave and reapply. EU nationals can

stay indefinitely but are required by law to register with the local *Magistratisches Bezirksamt* (magistrate's office) if the stay exceeds 60 days.

The Schengen Agreement includes all EU states (minus Britain and Ireland) and Switzerland. In practical terms this means a visa issued by one Schengen country is good for all the other member countries and a passport is not required to move from one to the other (a national identity card is required, though). Austrians are required to carry personal identification, and you too will need to be able to prove your identity.

Visa and passport requirements are subject to change, so always double-check your home country's foreign travel or Austrian embassy website before travelling.

Volunteering

Volunteering is a good way to meet people and get involved with local life, with projects lasting anything from a week to 18 months or more. In Austria, maintaining hiking trails is popular, but other volunteer projects range from joining a performance group on social issues to repairing school fences outside Vienna. Hook up with the networks in your home country and/or, if you speak German, approach an Austrian organisation directly.

Bergwald Projekt (✆0512-595 47 47; www.bergwaldprojekt. at; Olympiastrasse 37) Excellent volunteer work programs protecting and maintaining mountain forests in Austria, Germany and Switzerland. Generally, the Austrian programs last one week.

Freiwilligenweb (www.freiwilligenweb.at) Official Austrian government portal for volunteer work.

International Voluntary Service Great Britain (www.ivsgb.org)

The UK organisation networked with the Service Civil International (SCI).

International Voluntary Service USA (www.sci-ivs.org) The US organisation networked with the SCI.

International Volunteers for Peace (www.ivp.org.au) An Australian organisation networked with the SCI.

Service Civil International (SCI; www.sciint.org) Worldwide organisation with local networks.

Work

➡ EU, EEA and Swiss nationals may work in Austria without a work permit or residency permit, though as intending residents they need to register with the police.

➡ Non-EU nationals need both a work permit and a residency permit, and will find it pretty hard to get either unless they qualify for a Red-White-Red Card, which is aimed at attracting highly skilled workers. Your employer in Austria must apply for your work permit. You must apply for your residency permit via the Austrian embassy in your home country.

➡ Teaching is a popular field for expats; look under 'Sprachschulen' in the Gelbe Seiten (yellow pages) for a list of schools. In professions outside of that and barkeeping, you'll struggle to find employment if you don't speak German.

Some useful job websites:

Arbeitsmarktservice Österreich (www.ams.or.at) Austria's Labour Office

Monster (www.monster.at)

StepStone (www.stepstone.at) Directed towards professionals.

Virtual Vienna Net (www.virtual vienna.net) Aimed at expats, with a variety of jobs, including UN listings.

Transport

GETTING THERE & AWAY

Austria is well connected to the rest of the world. Vienna and several regional capitals are served by no-frills airlines (plus regular airline services). Europe's extensive bus and train networks crisscross the country and there are major highways from Germany and Italy. It's also possible to enter Austria by boat from Hungary, Slovakia and Germany.

Flights, cars and tours can be booked online at lonely planet.com/bookings.

Entering the Country

Paperwork A valid passport is required when entering Austria. The only exception to this rule is when entering from another Schengen country (all EU states minus Britain and Ireland, plus Switzerland); in this case, only a national identity card is required.

Border procedures Formal border controls have been abolished for those entering from another EU country or Switzerland, but spot checks may be carried out at the border or inside Austria itself.

Air

Vienna is the main transport hub for Austria, but Graz, Linz, Klagenfurt, Salzburg and Innsbruck all receive international flights. Flights to these cities are often a cheaper option than those to the capital, as are flights to Airport Letisko (Bratislava Airport), which is only 60km east of Vienna, in Slovakia. Bregenz has no airport; there are limited flights to nearby Friedrichshafen in Germany and much better connections at Zürich in Switzerland.

Airports & Airlines

Austrian Airlines (www.austrian. com) is the national carrier, based in Vienna; it's a member of

Star Alliance (www.staralliance. com).

Among the low-cost airlines, Air Berlin and Niki fly to Graz; Air Berlin, Transavia, easy-Jet and Niki to Innsbruck; Eurowings and Ryanair to Klagenfurt; Ryanair to Linz; Air Berlin, Transavia, easyJet, Eurowings and Ryanair to Salzburg; and Ryanair to Bratislava (for Vienna). Air Berlin, easyJet, Niki and Eurowings fly to Vienna Airport.

Airport Bratislava (BTS; ☎02-3303 3353; www.bts.aero; Ivanská cesta) Nine kilometres northeast of the centre. Connections to Italy, Germany, Spain, Greece, UK cities and more.

Blue Danube Airport Linz (LNZ; ☎07221-60 00; www. linz-airport.at; Flughafenstrasse 1, Hörsching) Austrian Airlines, Lufthansa, Ryanair and Air Berlin are the main airlines servicing the Blue Danube Airport, 13km southwest of the centre. There are flights to Vienna, Salzburg and Graz, as well as to Berlin, Frankfurt, Düsseldorf, Stuttgart

---

CLIMATE CHANGE & TRAVEL

Every form of transport that relies on carbon-based fuel generates CO_2, the main cause of human-induced climate change. Modern travel is dependent on aeroplanes, which might use less fuel per kilometre per person than most cars but travel much greater distances. The altitude at which aircraft emit gases (including CO_2) and particles also contributes to their climate change impact. Many websites offer 'carbon calculators' that allow people to estimate the carbon emissions generated by their journey and, for those who wish to do so, to offset the impact of the greenhouse gases emitted with contributions to portfolios of climate-friendly initiatives throughout the world. Lonely Planet offsets the carbon footprint of all staff and author travel.

and Zürich. Ryanair serves London Stansted.

Graz Airport (GRZ; ☏0316-290 20; www.flughafen-graz.at) Located 10km south of the centre and is served by carriers including Air Berlin and Niki.

Innsbruck Airport (INN; ☏22 52 50; www.innsbruck-airport.com; Fürstenweg 180) EasyJet and Niki fly to Innsbruck Airport, 4km west of the city centre.

Kärnten Airport (www.klagenfurt-airport.com; Flughafenstrasse 60-66) Klagenfurt's airport is 3km north of town and served by the low-cost airline Germanwings.

Salzburg Airport (☏0662-858 00; www.salzburg-airport.com; Innsbrucker Bundesstrasse 95; ☏) A 20-minute bus ride from the city centre, this airport has regular scheduled flights to destinations all over Austria and Europe.

Vienna International Airport (VIE; ☏01-700 722 233; www.viennaairport.com; ☏) Has good connections worldwide. The airport is in Schwechat, 18km southeast of Vienna.

Land

Border Crossings

There are numerous entry points by road from Germany, the Czech Republic, Slovakia, Hungary, Slovenia, Italy and Switzerland. Liechtenstein is so small that it has just one border-crossing point, near Feldkirch in Austria. The Alps limit the options for approaching Tyrol from the south (Switzerland and Italy). All border crossing points are open 24 hours.

Bus

Travelling by bus is a cheap but less comfortable way to reach Austria from other European countries. Options include Eurolines, Busabout and ÖBB Intercity Bus.

EUROLINES

Eurolines (☏0900 128 712; www.eurolines.at; 03, Erdbergstrasse 200; ☏office 8am-6pm; Ⓤ Erdberg) Buses pass through Vienna, with stops in Austria including Graz, Linz, Salzburg, Klagenfurt and Innsbruck. It also serves numerous cities in neighbouring Italy, Germany, the Czech Republic and

Hungary. For other destinations see www.eurolines.com.

London Buses connect London (Victoria coach station) and Vienna Erdberg (one-way/return €82/160, 24 hours); anyone under 26 or over 60 gets a 10% discount on most fares and passes.

Prague Buses (one-way/return €24/46, four hours) run twice daily.

Bratislava From Vienna 14 buses run daily (one-way/return €7.50/15, 65 to 80 minutes).

Eurolines passes are priced according to season: a 15-day pass is €225 to €320 for adults; a 30-day pass is €340 to €425 (cheaper for those under 26 and over 60). A pass covers 53 cities across Europe (including Vienna).

BUSABOUT

London-based **Busabout** (☏+44 8450 267 576; www.busabout.com) offers hop-on/hop-off passes for travel to about 50 European cities from May to late October. It splits stops into various 'loops', which you can combine. The **Northern Loop** includes Vienna and Salzburg, as well as Prague, Amsterdam, Paris and several German cities. See its website for other deals.

ÖBB INTERCITY BUS

An **ÖBB** (Österreichische Bundesbahnen; Austrian Federal Railways; ☏24hr hotline 05 1717; www.oebb.at) Intercity bus connects Klagenfurt via Villach and Udine with Venice (€26, 4¼ hours, three times daily).

Car & Motorcycle

To enter Austria by car, you'll need proof of ownership and third-party insurance (p400), as well as a sticker on the rear of the vehicle clearly displaying the country of origin. You will also need a *Vignette* (motorway tax) if you plan on using the autobahn (p400).

All border crossing (p394) points are open 24 hours,

INTERNATIONAL RAIL CONNECTIONS

ROUTE	PRICE (€)	DURATION (HR)
Belgrade–Villach	82	11
Budapest–Graz	76	6
Dortmund–Linz	169	9 (departs Vienna, changes in Würzburg for northern Germany)
Ljubljana–Graz	31	3 (some services continue to Zagreb & Belgrade)
Ljubljana–Villach	16	1¾
Munich–Graz	91	6 (via Salzburg)
Munich–Innsbruck	41	2
Munich–Salzburg	37	1¾
Munich–Villach	75	4½
Prague–Linz	49	5½
Verona–Innsbruck	40	3½
Zagreb–Villach	48	4
Zürich–Innsbruck	70	3½

and petrol stations are usually handily located nearby.

Train

Austria benefits from its central location within Europe by having excellent rail connections to all important destinations. Passengers do not need to disembark at borders, but do need to ensure they have any necessary visas (p392).

TIMETABLES

European Rail Timetable (www.europeanrailtimetable. eu) Contains all train schedules, supplements and reservations information. The monthly edition can be ordered online. A digital edition and app is also available.

ÖBB (Österreichische Bundesbahnen; Austrian Federal Railways; 24hr hotline 05 1717; www.oebb.at) With national and international connections, plus online national train booking. The website also shows Postbus services.

Deutsche Bahn (www.bahn.de) Useful for finding special deals to/from Germany or to check connections (but not prices and bookings) in Austria.

TICKETS

International Rail (+44 (0)871 231 0790; www.internationalrail. co.uk) handles bookings for a minimum UK£10 surcharge by telephone and also online; tickets from many different countries can be booked through the website. It's often cheapest to book the continental Europe leg, then find the best Eurostar deal.

Deutsche Bahn (www.bahn. com) is also useful, especially for taking advantage of savings through early booking.

SERVICES

Extra charges can apply on fast trains and international trains, and it's a good idea (and sometimes obligatory) to make seat reservations for peak times and on certain lines. Prices we give for national and international trains can vary slightly according to the route and type of train.

VIENNA'S NEW HAUPTBAHNHOF

With its diamond-shaped translucent glass-and-steel roof, Vienna's new *Hauptbahnhof* (main train station) is an architectural triumph. Opened in December 2015, it was designed and built by acclaimed Austrian firm Strabag. Up to 1000 trains per day carrying some 145,000 passengers now pass through the station, which also has 84 shops, bars and restaurants; parking for 600 cars; three bike garages; electric bike-charging points; and two Citybike Wien bike-share rental stations.

Located 3km south of Stephansdom, the *Hauptbahnhof* handles all international trains, as well as services to/from all of Austria's provincial capitals, and many local and regional trains.

S-Bahn S-Bahn lines S1, S2 and S3 connect Hauptbahnhof with Wien Meidling, Wien-Mitte and Praterstern.

U-Bahn U1 serves Karlsplatz and Stephansplatz.

Tram 0 to Praterstern, 18 to Westbahnhof and Burggasse/Stadthalle. Tram D connects Hauptbahnhof-Ost with the Ringstrasse.

Bus 13A runs through Vienna's Vorstädte (inner suburbs) Margareten, Mariahilf, Neubau and Josefstadt, all between the Ringstrasse and the Gürtel.

→ Express trains are identified by the symbols EC (EuroCity, serving international routes) or IC (InterCity, serving national routes). RailJet national and international train services are faster than IC/EC trains and cost the same but have perks like free wi-fi (in many) and power outlets alongside all seats. The French Train à Grande Vitesse (TGV) and the German InterCityExpress (ICE) trains are high-speed; surcharges apply.

→ Overnight trains usually offer a choice between a *Liegewagen* (couchette) or a more expensive *Schlafwagen* (sleeping car). Long-distance trains have a dining car or snacks available.

River

The **Danube Tourist Commission** (www.danube-river. org) has a country-by-country list of operators and agents who can book river tours, including companies in Australia, New Zealand, the USA, Canada and various European countries.

Ensure you have any necessary visa (p392) before entering Austria.

Danube Cruises

Avalon Waterways (www. avaloncruises.co.uk) is an international cruise operator with a branch in the UK, as well as Australia (www. avalonwaterways.com.au), Canada (www.avalonwaterways.ca), and the USA (www. avalonwaterways.com). It can also handle bookings from other regions.

Typical cruises include eight days from Budapest to Vienna (from US$1589), nine days from Vienna to Munich (from US$2739) and 15 days from Amsterdam to Budapest (from US$5547). All prices exclude air connections.

International Services

Twin City Liner (01-904 88 80; www.twincityliner.com; 01, Schwedenplatz; one-way adult €20-35; 1, 2, Schwedenplatz) Runs two-way service

Austrian Railways

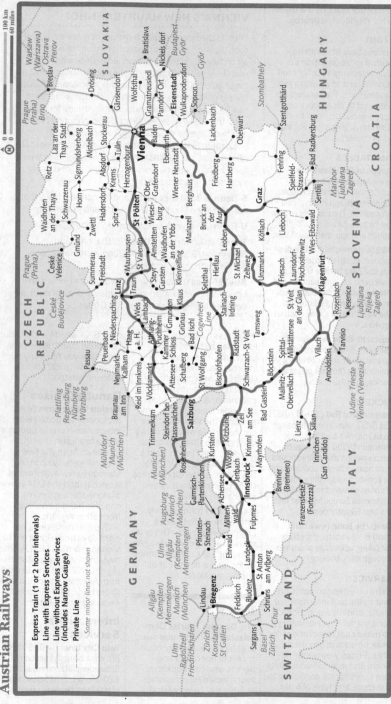

Legend:

Express Train (1 or 2 hour intervals)

Line with Express Services

Line without Express Services
(includes Narrow Gauge)

Private Line

Some minor lines not shown

100 km
60 miles

between Vienna and Bratislava (1¼ hours) three to five times daily from late March to early November. Ships dock at the Twin City Liner terminal on the Danube Canal.

LOD (☑in Slovakia 421 2 529 32 226; www.lod.sk; Schiffstation Reichsbrücke, Handelskai 265 (Vienna departure point); one-way/return €20/29; ☉late Apr-early Oct) Slovakian ferry company with hydrofoils between Bratislava and Vienna (1½ hours), running five to seven days per week from late April to late October. Best value is on weekends and for return trips. Booking is online, unless you call the office in Bratislava to reserve and then pay cash on the ship.

DDSG Blue Danube (☑01-588 80; www.ddsg-blue-danube. at; 02, Handelskai 265, Reichsbrücke; one-way €99-109, return €125; ☉9am-5pm Mon-Fri, 10am-4pm Sat & Sun, closed Sat & Sun Nov-Feb) Hydrofoil Vienna to/from Budapest (5½ to 6½ hours), running three to six times a week mid-May to late September.

GETTING AROUND

Public transport is excellent for reaching even remote regions, but it takes longer. Most provinces have an integrated transport system offering day passes covering regional zones for both bus and train travel.

Car Small towns and even small cities often have limited or no car-hire services, so reserve ahead from major cities.

Train & Bus Austria's national railway system is integrated with the Postbus bus services. Plan your route using the **ÖBB** (Österreichische Bundesbahnen; Austrian Federal Railways; ☑24hr hotline 05 1717; www. oebb.at) or **Postbus** (☑24hr hotline 0810 222 333; www. postbus.at) websites.

Air

Flying within a country the size of Austria is rarely necessary. The main exception is to/from Innsbruck (in the far west of Austria).

Austrian Airlines (www.austrian. com) The national carrier offers several flights daily between Vienna and Graz, Innsbruck, Klagenfurt, Linz and Salzburg.

Bicycle

Most regional tourist boards have brochures on cycling facilities and routes within their region. Separate bike tracks are common in cities, and long-distance tracks and routes also run along many of the major valleys such as the Danube, Enns and Mur. Others follow lakes, such as the bike tracks around the Neusiedler See in Burgenland and the Wörthersee in Carinthia. *Landstrassen* (L) roads are usually good for cyclists.

The **Danube cycling trail** is like a Holy Grail for cyclists, following the entire length of the river in Austria between the borders with Germany and Slovakia. The **Tauern Radweg** is a 310km trail through the mountain landscapes of Hohe Tauern National Park.

Mountain Biking

Austria's regions are well-equipped for mountain biking of various levels of difficulty. Carinthia (around Hermagor) and northern Styria (the Gesäuse, Schladming and Mariazell) are excellent places. The **Dachstein Tour** can be done over three days, whereas the **Nordkette Single Trail** in Innsbruck is one of the toughest and most exhilarating downhill rides in the country.

Hire

All large cities have at least one bike shop that doubles as a rental centre. In places where cycling is a popular pastime, such as the Wachau in Lower Austria and the Neusiedler See in Burgenland, almost all small towns have rental facilities. Rates vary from town to town, but expect to pay around €15 to €25 per day.

Bike Transport

It's possible to take bicycles on trains with a bicycle symbol at the top of its timetable. You can't take bicycles on bus services.

➡ You must purchase a ticket for your bicycle (10% the cost of your train ticket; a minimum fee of €2 applies).

➡ Weekly and monthly tickets are also available.

ELECTRIC BIKES

Touring electric bikes (e-bikes) are available in most regions. Pedal cleverly using energy-saving options and you can get well over 100km out of some models. A few places also rent e-mountain bikes (e-MBs) which cope with the hills and distances remarkably well. Taking advantage of energy options and the terrain on a good model, it's even possible to return an e-MB with almost as much juice as you set out with.

Movelo (www.movelo.com) This e-bike operator has a network of 250 partner outlets for hire and/or battery change in holiday regions of Austria. Typically, an e-bike costs €20 to €30 per day or 24 hours, depending on the station. You book the bikes directly through the stations (see the website for a list).

➡ It is not possible to reserve spaces on regional, regional express and S-Bahn train services – simply check if space is available.

➡ For long-distance trains (RailJet, Intercity, Eurocity and Euronight trains), you can reserve a space for your bicycle in advance for €3.50 at ÖBB ticket counters or by calling 📞+43 (0)5 1717.

➡ To make the journey run smoothly, ask train station staff where on the platform to wait so you'll be in front of the wagon with your reserved space when the train stops.

Boat

The Danube (p395) serves as a thoroughfare between Vienna and Lower and Upper Austria. Services are generally slow, scenic excursions rather than functional means of transport. Some of the country's larger lakes, such as Bodensee and Wörthersee, have boat services.

Bus

Rail routes are often complemented by **Postbus** (📞24hr hotline 0810 222 333; www. postbus.at) services, which really come into their own in the more inaccessible mountainous regions. Buses are fairly reliable, and usually depart from outside train stations.

➡ In remote regions plan a day or two ahead and travel on a weekday; services are reduced or nonexistent on Saturday, and often nonexistent on Sunday.

Pay attention to timetables on school buses in remote regions. These are excellent during the term (if a little loud and packed with kids) but don't operate outside school term.

➡ For online information consult www.postbus.at or www.oebb.at. Local bus stations or tourist offices usually stock free timetable brochures for specific bus routes.

➡ Reservations are usually unnecessary. It's possible to buy tickets in advance on some routes, but on others you can only buy tickets from the drivers.

➡ Oddly, travel by Postbus can work out to be more expensive than train, especially if you have a *Vorteilscard* for train discounts (only family *Vorteilscards* are valid on buses). The ÖBB intercity bus between Graz and Klagenfurt (€28.60, two hours) is cheaper, direct and slightly faster than the train. Generally, though, buses are slower.

Car & Motorcycle

➡ Autobahn are marked 'A', some are pan-European 'E' roads. You can only drive on them with a *Vignette* (motorway tax). *Bundesstrassen* or 'B' roads are major roads, while *Landstrassen* (L) are places to enjoy the ride rather than get quickly from one place to another.

➡ Some minor passes are blocked by snow from November to May. Carrying snow chains in winter is

highly recommended and is compulsory in some areas.

➡ Winter or all-weather tyres are compulsory from 1 November to 15 April.

➡ GPS navigation systems work well in Austria, but as elsewhere, use your eyes and don't rely on them 100%.

➡ Motorcyclists and passengers must wear a helmet. Dipped lights (lowbeams) must be used in daytime. You must carry a first-aid kit.

➡ The **National Austrian Tourist Office** (www.austria. info) has an *Austrian Classic Tour* brochure, which covers 3000km of the best roads for motorcyclists in the country.

➡ A number of train services allow you to transport a car with you.

Hire

It is much easier to hire cars in Austria in large cities. Small towns either have no hire companies or a very limited number of vehicles and can be expensive and booked out. If you've got time, shop around for small companies as they can be cheaper (but more restrictive conditions often apply).

Although companies accept any licence that is written in Roman letters, a translation or International Driving Permit (IDP) is required by the traffic police for any non-EU licence not in German.

MINIMUM AGE REQUIREMENTS

The minimum age for hiring small cars is 19 years; for prestige models, 25 years. A valid licence issued at least one year prior is necessary. If you plan to take the car across the border, especially into Eastern Europe, let the rental company know beforehand and double-check for any add-on fees and possible age requirements.

MOTORAIL TRAINS

ROUTE	PRICE (€)	TIME (HR)
Vienna–Feldkirch	78–98	9
Graz–Feldkirch	72–88	9
Villach–Feldkirch	66–78	8

ROAD DISTANCES (KM)

	Bad Ischl	Bregenz	Bruck an der Mur	Eisenstadt	Graz	Innsbruck	Kitzbühel	Klagenfurt	Krems	Kufstein	Landeck	Lienz	Linz	Salzburg	St Pölten	Vienna
Bregenz	432															
Bruck an der Mur	170	577														
Eisenstadt	297	704	127													
Graz	193	600	54	175												
Innsbruck	239	193	384	511	407											
Kitzbühel	191	300	275	469	400	113										
Klagenfurt	245	510	145	298	133	322	264									
Krems	222	626	175	132	229	433	372	320								
Kufstein	161	271	331	460	356	78	37	286	355							
Landeck	316	117	461	588	484	77	186	394	510	155						
Lienz	232	424	266	393	277	178	94	144	432	142	248					
Linz	103	507	190	246	237	314	247	253	145	236	391	359				
Salzburg	58	374	228	362	264	181	129	223	257	103	258	180	138			
St Pölten	206	610	140	123	194	417	356	285	32	339	494	416	129	241		
Vienna	266	670	145	50	191	477	420	316	79	399	554	411	189	301	66	
Villach	250	486	178	335	170	287	226	37	353	251	370	109	330	188	318	353
Wiener Neustadt	268	675	98	31	146	482	441	267	137	431	559	364	237	339	114	53

(Villach column value for Wiener Neustadt: 316)

INSURANCE

Third-party insurance is a minimum requirement in Austria. All companies offer personal accident insurance (PAI) for occupants and collision damage waiver (CDW) for an additional charge. (PAI may not be necessary if you or your passengers hold personal travel insurance.)

HIRE COMPANIES

Auto Europe (☏0800 723 9478; www.autoeurope.de) Books with other car-hire companies; prices can be at a lower rate than by going directly through a company.

Avis (☏0800 0800 87 57, in Vienna 601 87-0; www.avis.at)

Europcar (www.europcar.co.at)

Hertz (www.hertz.at)

Holiday Autos (☏in UK +44 20 3740 9859; www.holidayautos.com) Often offers very low rates and has offices or representatives in over 100 countries and regions. By booking early, you can find prices that are about 60% of those charged by the international companies.

Megadrive (☏05 01 05-4124; www.megadrive.at) Good network in major cities, with often cheaper rates.

Sixt (☏0810 97 74 24; www.sixt.at) Has offices all over Austria.

Bringing Your Own Vehicle

You'll need to have proof of ownership papers and third-party insurance. The car must also display a sticker on the rear indicating the country of origin.

DRIVING LICENCES

A driving licence and proof of ownership of a private vehicle should always be carried while driving. EU licences are accepted in Austria; all other nationalities require a German translation or an International Driving Permit (IDP). Translations can be obtained on the spot for a small fee from automobile associations.

Automobile Associations

Two automobile associations serve Austria. Both provide free 24-hour breakdown service to members and have reciprocal agreements with motoring clubs in other countries; check with your local club before leaving. Both have offices throughout Austria, and it is possible to become a member, but you must join for six months or a year; expect to pay around €38 or €75 respectively. For a small fee, the associations also translate non-German-language driving licences.

If you're not entitled to free assistance, you'll incur a fee for call-outs, which

AUTOBAHN TAX & TUNNEL TOLLS

A *Vignette* (motorway tax) is imposed on all autobahn; charges for cars below 3.5 tonnes are €8.80 for 10 days, €25.70 for two months and €85.70 for one year. For motorbikes expect to pay €5.10 for 10 days, €12.90 for two months and €34.10 for one year. *Vignette* can be purchased from motoring organisations, border crossings, petrol stations, post offices and *Tabak* (tobacconist) shops.

A toll (which is *not* covered by the motorway tax) is levied on some mountain roads and tunnels. For a full list of toll roads, consult one of the automobile associations (p399).

varies depending on the time of day.

ARBÖ (☏information 050 123 123, roadside assistance 123; www.arboe.at)

ÖAMTC (☏24hr emergency assistance 120, office 01-711 99 10200; www.oeamtc.at; Schubertring 1-3, Vienna; ☺8am-6pm Mon-Fri, 9am-1pm Sat)

Insurance

Third-party insurance is a minimum requirement in Europe and you'll need to carry proof of this in the form of a Green Card. If you're a member of an automobile association (p399), ask about free reciprocal benefits offered by affiliated organisations in Europe. The car must also display a sticker on the rear indicating the country of origin.

Road Hazards & Rules

Drive on the right-hand side of the road. The minimum driving age is 18.

Alcohol The penalty for driving while drunk – if you have over 0.05% BAC (blood-alcohol concentration) – is a hefty on-the-spot fine and confiscation of your driving licence.

Children Those under the age of 14 who are shorter than 1.5m must have a special seat or restraint.

Fines Can be paid on the spot, but ask for a receipt.

Giving way Give way to the right at all times except when a prior-

ity road sign indicates otherwise, or when one street has a raised border running across it (the vehicle entering from such a street must give way). Note: the 'give way to the right' rule also applies at T-junctions.

Helmets Compulsory for motorcyclists and their passengers (as well as for children under 13 years on bicycles).

Parking Most town centres have a designated *Kurzparkzone* (short-term parking zone), where on-street parking is limited to a maximum of 1½ or three hours (depending upon the place) between certain specified times. *Parkschein* (parking vouchers) for such zones can be purchased from *Tabak* shops or pavement dispensers and then displayed on the windscreen. Outside the specified time, parking in the *Kurzparkzone* is free.

Safety Carrying a warning triangle and first-aid kit in your vehicle is compulsory in Austria.

Seat belts Compulsory.

Speed limits During the day, it's 50km/h in built-up areas, 130km/h on autobahn and 100km/h on other roads. In some places, the speed on country roads is restricted to 70km/h. From 10pm to 5am – except for the A1 between Vienna and Salzburg and the A2 between Vienna and Villach – the speed limit on autobahn is 110km/h.

Trams Always have priority. Vehicles should wait behind while trams slow down and stop for passengers to alight.

Local Transport

Austria's local transport infrastructure is excellent, inexpensive and safe.

Buses & Trams Bus services operate in most cities and are complemented by a few night-bus lines. Tram and bus services in most places run from about 5am to 11pm or midnight. You usually need to press the stop-request button, even in trams.

Metro In Vienna, the metro runs all night on Friday and Saturday nights. From Sunday night to Thursday night it stops around midnight or 12.30am. No other towns have metro systems.

Taxis Austrians mostly call ahead or use taxi ranks. Flagging down a taxi usually works, though. Drivers always expect a 10% tip.

Tickets

Ticketing systems and prices vary from region to region. Often they're sold from machines at stops. Universally, tickets are cheaper from any *Tabak* shop, also known as a *Trafik*. Passes for single trips, 24 hours and several days or a week are usually available.

Fines are stiff if you don't have a ticket – about €60 to €100 is common – and checks are frequent, especially in the provincial capitals.

Train

While the country bemoans the state of its 'run-down' rail system, travellers praise it to the heavens. It's good by any standard, and if you use a discount card it's inexpensive.

The **ÖBB** (Österreichische Bundesbahnen; Austrian Federal Railways; ☏24hr hotline 05 1717; www.oebb.at) is the main operator, supplemented by a handful of private lines. You can call 24 hours to book a ticket or get information.

Buying tickets Tickets can be purchased by telephone (you'll be given a 12-digit collection code for printing the ticket at a machine or at the service desk). Other methods include online (with registration and self-printing), from staffed counters at stations and from machines at stations.

Reservations Cost €3.50 for most 2nd-class express services within Austria. If you haven't reserved ahead, check before you sit whether your intended seat has been reserved by someone else. Reservations are recommended for weekend travel.

Disabled passengers Call ☑05 1717 for special travel assistance (you can also do this while booking your ticket by telephone). Staff at stations will help with boarding and alighting. Order this at least 24 hours ahead of travel (48 hours ahead for international services).

Smoking Not allowed on trains.

Etiquette The ÖBB takes a strong stand on putting your feet on the seats. You can be fined for it.

Cost

Depending on the exact route, a fare can vary slightly.

➡ Tickets can be purchased online or by telephone with credit cards (Visa, Diners Club, MasterCard, Amex and JCB), and additionally with cash or a Maestro debit card at machines and service desks.

➡ EURegio tickets are discount return tickets between Austria and the Czech Republic, Hungary or Slovakia and can be great value for short visits.

➡ If you board and go immediately to the conductor to pay your fare, only a €3 surcharge will be applied to the normal price of the ticket. If you don't do this, a fee and fine totalling €95 will have to be paid (unless you board at an unstaffed station without a ticket machine or the ticket machine is out of order).

➡ Children aged six to 15 travel half-price; younger

kids travel free if they don't take up a separate seat.

➡ Kept in suitable containers, small pets travel free; larger pets travel half-price.

➡ One-way tickets for journeys of 100km or less are valid for only one day, and the journey can't be broken. For trips of 101km or more, the ticket is valid for one month and you can alight en route. This is worth doing, as longer trips cost less per kilometre. Return tickets of up to 100km each way are valid for one day; tickets for longer journeys are valid for one month, though the initial outward journey must still be completed within six days. A return fare is usually the equivalent price of two one-way tickets.

Rail Passes

Depending on the amount of travelling you intend to do in Austria and your residency status, rail passes can be a good deal. They can be purchased from any major train station.

VORTEILSCARD

These **ÖBB** (Österreichische Bundesbahnen; Austrian Federal Railways; ☑24hr hotline 05 1717; www.oebb.at) discount tickets can be purchased by anyone. They offer a 45% discount on inland trains for tickets purchased at the counter and 50% if you buy at a ticket machine. After purchasing one (bring a photo and your passport or other ID), you receive a temporary card and can begin using it right away. The plastic permanent card is posted to your home address. It's valid for one year, but not on buses. For more information visit the ÖBB website, and look under Tickets & Discounts.

Classic (€19) For those over 26.

Family (€19) Valid for up to two adults and any number of children. The children must be travelling with you. Children under 14 years travel free on this card. Also offers 50% discount

on Postbus services for adults and up to two children.

Jugend <26 (€19) For those under 26.

Senior (€29) For women or men over 60 years.

EURAIL PASS

Available only to non-European residents, Eurail passes are valid for unlimited 2nd-class travel on national railways and some private lines in 24 countries. You can also pay a supplement if you want to travel 1st-class. Those under 26 receive substantial discounts. See www.eurail.com for all options.

Global Pass Options for travelling 10/15 days within two months (€689/983), or continuous travel for a period from 15 days to one month (€585 to €926).

Eurail Select Pass Allows you to tailor a rail trip in two, three or four of 28 bordering countries (€255 to €418). For Austria, that means Slovenia and Croatia (classed as one Eurail Pass country), the Czech Republic, Germany, Hungary, Italy and Switzerland.

Two-Country Select Pass Combine Austria with Croatia/Slovenia, Germany, Hungary, the Czech Republic or Switzerland for four or five to 10 days within a two-month period.

INTERAIL

Passes are for European citizens (including UK) or anyone who has lived in Europe for at least six months. Those under 26 receive substantial discounts. See www.interrail-net.com for all options.

One-Country Pass Austria Adult 2nd-class three/four/five/eight days within a month €159/191/220/296.

InterRail Global Pass Valid for a certain number of days or continuously in up to 30 countries; five days' travel in 15 days costs €264, 10 days' travel in one month costs €374 and one month of continuous travel costs €626.

Language

The national language of Austria is German, though there are a few regional dialects. For example, the dialect spoken in Vorarlberg is much closer to Swiss German (Schwyzertütsch) – a language all but incomprehensible to most non-Swiss – than it is to the standard High German (Hochdeutsch) dialect. Nevertheless, Austrians can easily switch from their dialect to High German.

There are many words and expressions in German that are used only by Austrians, some throughout the country and others only in particular regions, although they'll probably be understood elsewhere. Most of these would not automatically be understood by non-Austrian German speakers. On the other hand, the 'standard' German equivalents would be understood by all Austrians. The greetings and farewells included in this chapter are specific to Austria.

Pronunciation

It's easy to pronounce German because almost all sounds are also found in English. If you read our coloured pronunciation guides as if they were English, you'll be understood.

Note that the vowel ü sounds like the 'ee' in 'see' but with rounded lips. As for the consonants, the kh sound is pronounced like a hiss from the back of the throat (as in the Scottish *loch*). The r sound is pronounced at the back of the throat, almost like saying a g sound, but with some friction – a bit like gargling.

WANT MORE?

For in-depth language information and handy phrases, check out Lonely Planet's *German Phrasebook*. You'll find it at **shop.lonelyplanet.com**, or you can buy Lonely Planet's iPhone phrasebooks at the Apple App Store.

As a general rule, word stress in German falls mostly on the first syllable. In our pronunciation guides the stressed syllable is indicated with italics.

BASICS

German has polite and informal forms for 'you' (*Sie* and *du* respectively). When addressing people you don't know well, use the polite form (though younger people will be less inclined to expect it). In this language guide the polite form is used unless indicated with 'inf' (for 'informal') in brackets.

Hello.	*Servus.*	zer·vus
Goodbye.	*Auf Wiedersehen.*	owf vee·der·zay·en
Yes.	*Ja.*	yah
No.	*Nein.*	nain
Please.	*Bitte.*	bi·te
Thank you.	*Danke.*	dang·ke
You're welcome.	*Bitte sehr.*	bi·te zair
Excuse me.	*Entschuldigung.*	ent·shul·di·gung
Sorry.	*Entschuldigung.*	ent·shul·di·gung

How are you?
Wie geht es Ihnen/dir? — vee gayt es ee·nen/deer (pol/inf)

Fine, thanks. And you?
Danke, gut. Und Ihnen/dir? — dang·ke goot unt ee·nen/deer (pol/inf)

What's your name?
Wie ist Ihr Name? — vee ist eer nah·me (pol)
Wie heißt du? — vee haist doo (inf)

My name is ...
Mein Name ist ... — main nah·me ist ... (pol)
Ich heiße ... — ikh hai·se ... (inf)

Do you speak English?
Sprechen Sie Englisch?   shpre·khen zee eng·lish

I don't understand.
Ich verstehe nicht.   ikh fer·shtay·e nikht

ACCOMMODATION

Do you have a room?
Haben Sie ein Zimmer?   hah·ben zee ain tsi·mer

How much is it per night/person?
Wie viel kostet es   vee feel kos·tet es
pro Nacht/Person?   praw nakht/per·zawn

air-con	Klimaanlage	klee·ma·an·lah·ge
bathroom	Badezimmer	bah·de·tsi·mer
campsite	Campingplatz	kem·ping·plats
double room	Doppelzimmer	do·pel·tsi·mer
guesthouse	Pension	pahng·zyawn
hotel	Hotel	ho·tel
inn	Gasthof	gast·hawf
single room	Einzelzimmer	ain·tsel·tsi·mer
window	Fenster	fens·ter
youth hostel	Jugend- herberge	yoo·gent· her·ber·ge

DIRECTIONS

Where's (a bank)?
Wo ist (eine Bank)?   vaw ist (ai·ne bangk)

What's the address?
Wie ist die Adresse?   vee ist dee a·dre·se

Can you please write it down?
Könnten Sie das bitte   kern·ten zee das bi·te
aufschreiben?   owf·shrai·ben

Can you show me (on the map)?
Können Sie es mir   ker·nen zee es meer
(auf der Karte) zeigen?   (owf dair kar·te) tsai·gen

at the corner	an der Ecke	an dair e·ke
at the traffic lights	bei der Ampel	bai dair am·pel
behind ...	hinter ...	hin·ter ...
far away	weit weg	vait vek
in front of ...	vor ...	fawr ...
left/right	links/rechts	lingks/rekhts
near	nahe	nah·e
next to ...	neben ...	nay·ben ...
opposite ...	gegenüber ...	gay·gen·ü·ber ...
straight ahead	geradeaus	ge·rah·de·ows

EATING & DRINKING

A table for (two) people, please.
Einen Tisch für (zwei)   ai·nen tish für (tsvai)
Personen, bitte.   per·zaw·nen bi·te

What would you recommend?
Was empfehlen Sie?   vas emp·fay·len zee

What's in that dish?
Was ist in diesem   vas ist in dee·zem
Gericht?   ge·rikht

I don't eat ...
Ich esse kein ...   ikh e·se kain ...

Cheers!
Prost!   prawst

That was delicious.
Das war sehr lecker.   das vahr zair le·ker

The bill, please.
Die Rechnung, bitte.   dee rekh·nung bi·te

Key Words

appetisers	Vorspeisen	fawr·shpai·zen
ashtray	Aschenbecher	a·shen·be·kher
bar	Kneipe	knai·pe
bottle	Flasche	fla·she
bowl	Schüssel	shü·sel
breakfast	Frühstück	frü·shtük
cold	kalt	kalt
cup	Tasse	ta·se
dinner	Abendessen	ah·bent·e·sen
drink list	Getränke- karte	ge·treng·ke· kar·te
food	Essen	e·sen
fork	Gabel	gah·bel
glass	Glas	glahs
grocery store	Lebensmittel- laden	lay·bens·mi·tel· lah·den
hot (warm)	heiß	hais
knife	Messer	me·ser
local speciality	örtliche Spezialität	ert·li·khe shpe·tsya·li·tayt
lunch	Mittagessen	mi·tahk·e·sen
main courses	Hauptgerichte	howpt·ge·rikh·te
menu	Speisekarte	shpai·ze·kar·te
market	Markt	markt
plate	Teller	te·ler
restaurant	Restaurant	res·to·rang
spicy	würzig	vür·tsikh
spoon	Löffel	ler·fel
vegetarian food	vegetarisches Essen	ve·ge·tah·ri·shes e·sen
with/without	mit/ohne	mit/aw·ne

Meat & Fish

bacon	Speck	shpek
beef	Rindfleisch	rint·flaish
brains	Hirn	heern

carp	Karpfen	karp·fen
chicken	Huhn	hoon
duck	Ente	en·te
eel	Aal	ahl
fish	Fisch	fish
goose	Gans	gans
ham	Schinken	shing·ken
hare	Hase	hah·ze
lamb	Lamm	lam
liver	Leber	lay·ber
minced meat	Hackfleisch	hak·flaish
plaice	Scholle	sho·le
pork	Schweinefleisch	shvai·n·flaish
salmon	Lachs	laks
tongue	Zunge	tsung·e
trout	Forelle	fo·re·le
tuna	Thunfisch	toon·fish

KEY PATTERNS

To get by in German, mix and match these simple patterns with words of your choice:

When's (the next flight)?
Wann ist (der van ist (dair
nächste Flug)? naykhs·te flook)

Where's (the station)?
Wo ist (der vaw ist (dair
Bahnhof)? bahn·hawf)

Where can I (buy a ticket)?
Wo kann ich (eine vaw kan ikh (ai·ne
Fahrkarte kaufen)? fahr·kar·te kow·fen)

Do you have (a map)?
Haben Sie (eine hah·ben zee (ai·ne
Karte)? kar·te)

Is there (a toilet)?
Gibt es (eine gipt es (ai·ne
Toilette)? to·a·le·te)

I'd like (a coffee).
Ich möchte ikh merkh·te
(einen Kaffee). (ai·nen ka·fay)

I'd like (to hire a car).
Ich möchte ikh merkh·te
(ein Auto mieten). (ain ow·to mee·ten)

Can I (enter)?
Darf ich darf ikh
(hereinkommen)? (her·ein·ko·men)

Could you please (help me)?
Könnten Sie (mir kern·ten zee (meer
helfen)? hel·fen)

Do I have to (book a seat)?
Muss ich (einen Platz mus ikh (ai·nen plats
reservieren lassen)? re·zer·vee·ren la·sen)

turkey	Puter	poo·ter
veal	Kalbfleisch	kalp·flaish
venison	Hirsch	hirsh

Fruit & Vegetables

apple	Apfel	ap·fel
apricot	Aprikose	a·pri·ko·ze
asparagus	Spargel	shpar·gel
banana	Banane	ba·nah·ne
beans	Bohnen	baw·nen
beetroot	Rote Rübe	raw·te rü·be
cabbage	Kohl	hawl
carrots	Karotten	ka·ro·ten
cherries	Kirschen	kir·shen
corn	Mais	mais
cucumber	Gurke	gur·ke
garlic	Knoblauch	knawp·lowkh
grapes	Trauben	trow·ben
green beans	Fisolen	fee·zo·len
mushrooms	Pilze	pil·tse
onions	Zwiebeln	tsvee·beln
pear	Birne	bir·ne
peas	Erbsen	erp·sen
peppers	Paprika	pap·ri·kah
pineapple	Ananas	a·na·nas
plums	Zwetschgen	tsvech·gen
potatoes	Kartoffeln	kar·to·feln
raspberries	Himbeeren	him·bee·ren
spinach	Spinat	shpi·naht
strawberries	Erdbeeren	ert·bee·ren
tomatoes	Tomaten	to·mah·ten

Other

bread	Brot	brawt
butter	Butter	bu·ter
cheese	Käse	kay·ze
chocolate	Schokolade	sho·ko·lah·de
cream	Sahne	zah·ne
dumplings	Knödel	kner·del
eggs	Eier	ai·er
honey	Honig	haw·nikh
jam	Marmelade	mar·me·lah·de
mustard	Senf	zenf
nut	Nuss	nus
oil	Öl	erl
pasta	Nudeln	noo·deln
pepper	Pfeffer	pfe·fer
rice	Reis	rais

salad	Salat	za·laht
salt	Salz	zalts
sugar	Zucker	tsu·ker

Drinks

beer	Bier	beer
coffee	Kaffee	ka·fay
(orange) juice	(Orangen-) saft	(o·rahng·zhen·) zaft
milk	Milch	milkh
red wine	Rotwein	rawt·vain
tea	Tee	tay
(mineral) water	(Mineral-) wasser	(mi·ne·rahl·) va·ser
white wine	Weißwein	vais·vain

EMERGENCIES

Help!
Hilfe!   hil·fe

Leave me alone!
Lassen Sie mich in Ruhe!   la·sen zee mikh in roo·e

I'm lost.
Ich habe mich verirrt.   Ikh hah·be mikh fer·irt

Call the police!
Rufen Sie die Polizei!   roo·fen zee dee po·li·tsai

Call a doctor!
Rufen Sie einen Arzt!   roo·fen zee ai·nen artst

I'm sick.
Ich bin krank.   ikh bin krangk

It hurts here.
Es tut hier weh.   es toot heer vay

I'm allergic to (antibiotics).
Ich bin allergisch gegen (Antibiotika).   ikh bin a·lair·gish gay·gen (an·ti·bi·aw·ti·ka)

Where is the toilet?
Wo ist die Toilette?   vaw ist dee to·a·le·te

SHOPPING & SERVICES

I'd like to buy ...
Ich möchte ... kaufen.   ikh merkh·te ... kow·fen

I'm just looking.
Ich schaue mich nur um.   ikh show·e mikh noor um

Can I look at it?
Können Sie es mir zeigen?   ker·nen zee es meer tsai·gen

How much is this?
Wie viel kostet das?   vee feel kos·tet das

That's too expensive.
Das ist zu teuer.   das ist tsoo toy·er

Can you lower the price?
Können Sie mit dem Preis heruntergehen?   ker·nen zee mit dem prais he·run·ter·gay·en

SIGNS

Ausgang	Exit
Damen	Women
Eingang	Entrance
Geschlossen	Closed
Herren	Men
Offen	Open
Toiletten	Toilets
Verboten	Prohibited

There's a mistake in the bill.
Da ist ein Fehler in der Rechnung.   dah ist ain fay·ler in dair rekh·nung

ATM	Geldautomat	gelt·ow·to·maht
PIN	Geheimnummer	ge·haim·nu·mer
post office	Postamt	post·amt
tourist office	Fremden-verkehrsbüro	frem·den-fer·kairs·bü·raw

TIME & DATES

What time is it?
Wie spät ist es?   vee shpayt ist es

It's (one) o'clock.
Es ist (ein) Uhr.   es ist (ain) oor

Half past one.
Halb zwei. (lit: 'half two')   halp tsvai

morning	Morgen	mor·gen
afternoon	Nachmittag	nahkh·mi·tahk
evening	Abend	ah·bent
yesterday	gestern	ges·tern
today	heute	hoy·te
tomorrow	morgen	mor·gen

Monday	Montag	mawn·tahk
Tuesday	Dienstag	deens·tahk
Wednesday	Mittwoch	mit·vokh
Thursday	Donnerstag	do·ners·tahk
Friday	Freitag	frai·tahk
Saturday	Samstag	zams·tahk
Sunday	Sonntag	zon·tahk
January	Januar	yan·u·ahr
February	Februar	fay·bru·ahr
March	März	merts
April	April	a·pril
May	Mai	mai
June	Juni	yoo·ni
July	Juli	yoo·li

August	August	ow·gust
September	September	zep·tem·ber
October	Oktober	ok·taw·ber
November	November	no·vem·ber
December	Dezember	de·tsem·ber

TRANSPORT

Public Transport

boat	Boot	bawt
bus	Bus	bus
plane	Flugzeug	flook·tsoyk
train	Zug	tsook

At what time does it leave?
Wann fährt es ab? — van fairt es ap

At what time does it arrive?
Wann kommt es an? — van komt es an

I want to go to ...
Ich mochte nach ... fahren. — ikh merkh·te nahkh ... fah·ren

Does it stop at ...?
Hält es in ...? — helt es in ...

I want to get off here.
Ich mochte hier aussteigen. — ikh merkh·te heer ows·shtai·gen

one-way ticket	einfache Fahrkarte	ain·fa·khe fahr·kar·te
return ticket	Rückfahrkarte	rük·fahr·kar·te
first	erste	ers·te
last	letzte	lets·te
next	nächste	naykhs·te
aisle seat	Platz am Gang	plats am gang
platform	Bahnsteig	bahn·shtaik
ticket office	Fahrkarten-verkauf	fahr·kar·ten·fer·kowf
timetable	Fahrplan	fahr·plahn
train station	Bahnhof	bahn·hawf
window seat	Fensterplatz	fens·ter·plats

QUESTION WORDS

How?	Wie?	vee
What?	Was?	vas
When?	Wann?	van
Where?	Wo?	vaw
Who?	Wer?	vair
Why?	Warum?	va·rum

NUMBERS

1	eins	ains
2	zwei	tsvai
3	drei	drai
4	vier	feer
5	fünf	fünf
6	sechs	zeks
7	sieben	zee·ben
8	acht	akht
9	neun	noyn
10	zehn	tsayn
20	zwanzig	tsvan·tsikh
30	dreißig	drai·sikh
40	vierzig	feer·tsikh
50	fünfzig	fünf·tsikh
60	sechzig	zekh·tsikh
70	siebzig	zeep·tsikh
80	achtzig	akht·tsikh
90	neunzig	noyn·tsikh
100	hundert	hun·dert
1000	tausend	tow·sent

Driving & Cycling

I'd like to hire a ...	Ich möchte ein ... mieten.	ikh merkh·te ain ... mee·ten
bicycle	Fahrrad	fahr·raht
car	Auto	ain ow·to
motorcycle	Motorrad	maw·tor·raht
child seat	Kindersitz	kin·der·zits
helmet	Helm	helm
mechanic	Mechaniker	me·khah·ni·ker
petrol/gas	Benzin	ben·tseen
pump	Luftpumpe	luft·pum·pe
service station	Tankstelle	tangk·shte·le

Does this road go to ...?
Führt diese Strasse nach ...? — fürt dee·ze shtrah·se nahkh ...

Can I park here?
Kann ich hier parken? — kan ikh heer par·ken

The car has broken down (at ...).
Ich habe (in ...) eine Panne mit meinem Auto. — ikh hah·be (in ...) ai·ne pa·ne mit mai·nem ow·to

I have a flat tyre.
Ich habe eine Reifenpanne. — ikh hah·be ai·ne rai·fen·pa·ne

I've run out of petrol.
Ich habe kein Benzin mehr. — ikh hah·be kain ben·tseen mair

Behind the Scenes

SEND US YOUR FEEDBACK

We love to hear from travellers – your comments keep us on our toes and help make our books better. Our well-travelled team reads every word on what you loved or loathed about this book. Although we cannot reply individually to your submissions, we always guarantee that your feedback goes straight to the appropriate authors, in time for the next edition. Each person who sends us information is thanked in the next edition – the most useful submissions are rewarded with a selection of digital PDF chapters.

Visit **lonelyplanet.com/contact** to submit your updates and suggestions or to ask for help. Our award-winning website also features inspirational travel stories, news and discussions.

Note: We may edit, reproduce and incorporate your comments in Lonely Planet products such as guidebooks, websites and digital products, so let us know if you don't want your comments reproduced or your name acknowledged. For a copy of our privacy policy visit lonelyplanet.com/privacy.

OUR READERS

Many thanks to the travellers who used the last edition and wrote to us with helpful hints, useful advice and interesting anecdotes:

Alessandra Furlan, Dean Walton, Jack Clancy, Javier de la Mata, Kendra Paice, William and Mary Lawrence

WRITER THANKS

Kerry Christiani

A heartfelt *Dankeschön* goes out to all the wonderful people I met on my Austria travels, not least Maggie Ritson, Shane Pearce in St Anton, and Chiara and Karin Juchem in Vienna. Thanks also go to all the pros who made the road to research smoother: Wilma Himmelfreundpointner, Martina Trumer, Helena Hartlauer, Bettina Jamy-Stowasser and many more. Finally, a big thank you to Eugene Quinn of Vienna's Space and Place for creative ideas and inspiration.

Catherine Le Nevez

Vielen Dank first and foremost to Julian, and to my co-authors Kerry Christiani and Donna Wheeler, as well as all the locals and fellow travellers in Vienna and throughout Austria for insights, information and good times. Huge thanks, too, to Destination Editors Helen Elfer and Dan Fahey, and everyone at Lonely Planet. As ever, *merci encore* to my parents, brother, *belle-sœur* and *neveu*.

Donna Wheeler

In Austria, gratitude goes to Anja Cervenka, Ingo Dietrich, Stephanie Tscheppe-Eselböck, and Andrea and Alexander Almásy, with special mentions to the incredibly welcoming and fascinating Peter and Sabine Eichinger, as well as Birgit Enge and Ingrid Enge for your kindness and local insights. Big thanks also to Sydney's Mike Bennie for sharing your knowledge of Burgenland's up-and-coming winemakers; to the best ever travel companion Joe Guario, and to Justin Westover, Gwen Jamois and Laura Lot for quality Paris R&R.

ACKNOWLEDGEMENTS

Climate map data adapted from Peel MC, Finlayson BL & McMahon TA (2007) 'Updated World Map of the Köppen-Geiger Climate Classification', Hydrology and Earth System Sciences, 11, 163344.

Cover photograph: Hallstätter See, Francesco Iacobelli/AWL©

THIS BOOK

This 8th edition of Lonely Planet's *Austria* guidebook was researched and written by Marc Di Duca, Kerry Christiani, Catherine Le Nevez and Donna Wheeler. The previous two editions were written by Anthony Haywood, Kerry Christiani, Marc Di Duca and Caroline Sieg. This guidebook was produced by the following:

Destination Editors Helen Elfer, Daniel Fahey

Product Editors Bruce Evans, Catherine Naghten

Senior Cartographer Anthony Phelan

Book Designer Clara Monitto

Assisting Editors Andrea Dobbin, Grace Dobell, Carly Hall, Victoria Harrison, Ali Lemer, Christopher Pitts, Jeanette Wall

Assisting Cartographer Rachel Imeson

Assisting Book Designers Fergal Condon, Gwen Cotter

Cover Researcher Naomi Parker

Thanks to Cheree Broughton, Jennifer Carey, Neill Coen, Daniel Corbett, Jane Grisman, Claire Naylor, Karyn Noble, Ellie Simpson, Tony Wheeler

Index

Map Legend

Sights

- 🏖 Beach
- 🐦 Bird Sanctuary
- ☸ Buddhist
- 🏰 Castle/Palace
- ✝ Christian
- ☯ Confucian
- 🕉 Hindu
- ☪ Islamic
- 卐 Jain
- ✡ Jewish
- ❶ Monument
- 🏛 Museum/Gallery/Historic Building
- ⊗ Ruin
- ⛩ Shinto
- ☬ Sikh
- ☯ Taoist
- 🍷 Winery/Vineyard
- 🦁 Zoo/Wildlife Sanctuary
- ⊙ Other Sight

Activities, Courses & Tours

- � Bodysurfing
- 🅾 Diving
- 🅾 Canoeing/Kayaking
- ● Course/Tour
- ♨ Sento Hot Baths/Onsen
- 🅾 Skiing
- 🅾 Snorkelling
- 🅾 Surfing
- 🅾 Swimming/Pool
- 🅾 Walking
- 🅾 Windsurfing
- 🅾 Other Activity

Sleeping

- 🛏 Sleeping
- 🅾 Camping

Eating

- 🅾 Eating

Drinking & Nightlife

- 🅾 Drinking & Nightlife
- 🅾 Cafe

Entertainment

- 🅾 Entertainment

Shopping

- 🅾 Shopping

Information

- 💲 Bank
- 🄌 Embassy/Consulate
- ➕ Hospital/Medical
- @ Internet
- 🅾 Police
- 🅾 Post Office
- 🅾 Telephone
- 🄍 Toilet
- ❶ Tourist Information
- ● Other Information

Geographic

- 🏖 Beach
- ⊢ Gate
- 🅾 Hut/Shelter
- 🅾 Lighthouse
- 🅾 Lookout
- ▲ Mountain/Volcano
- 🅾 Oasis
- 🅾 Park
-)(Pass
- 🅾 Picnic Area
- 🅾 Waterfall

Population

- ⊛ Capital (National)
- ◉ Capital (State/Province)
- ● City/Large Town
- ● Town/Village

Transport

- 🅾 Airport
- ⊗ Border crossing
- 🅾 Bus
- ⊷🅾⊷ Cable car/Funicular
- ⊸🅾⊸ Cycling
- ⊸🅾⊸ Ferry
- Ⓜ Metro station
- ⊸🅾⊸ Monorail
- 🅿 Parking
- 🅾 Petrol station
- 🅢 S-Bahn/Subway station
- 🅣 Taxi
- 🅣 T-bane/Tunnelbana station
- ⊷🅾⊷ Train station/Railway
- ⊸🅾⊸ Tram
- ⊸🅾⊸ Tube station
- Ⓤ U-Bahn/Underground station
- ● Other Transport

Note: Not all symbols displayed above appear on the maps in this book

Routes

- Tollway
- Freeway
- Primary
- Secondary
- Tertiary
- Lane
- Unsealed road
- Road under construction
- Plaza/Mall
- Steps
-)- = Tunnel
- Pedestrian overpass
- Walking Tour
- Walking Tour detour
- Path/Walking Trail

Boundaries

- International
- State/Province
- Disputed
- Regional/Suburb
- Marine Park
- Cliff
- Wall

Hydrography

- River, Creek
- Intermittent River
- Canal
- Water
- Dry/Salt/Intermittent Lake
- Reef

Areas

- Airport/Runway
- Beach/Desert
- + + Cemetery (Christian)
- × × Cemetery (Other)
- Glacier
- Mudflat
- Park/Forest
- Sight (Building)
- Sportsground
- Swamp/Mangrove

OUR STORY

A beat-up old car, a few dollars in the pocket and a sense of adventure. In 1972 that's all Tony and Maureen Wheeler needed for the trip of a lifetime – across Europe and Asia overland to Australia. It took several months, and at the end – broke but inspired – they sat at their kitchen table writing and stapling together their first travel guide, *Across Asia on the Cheap*. Within a week they'd sold 1500 copies. Lonely Planet was born.

Today, Lonely Planet has offices in Franklin, London, Melbourne, Oakland, Dublin, Beijing and Delhi, with more than 600 staff and writers. We share Tony's belief that 'a great guidebook should do three things: inform, educate and amuse'.

OUR WRITERS

Marc Di Duca

A travel author for the last decade, Marc has worked for Lonely Planet in Siberia, Slovakia, Bavaria, England, Ukraine, Austria, Poland, Croatia, Portugal, Madeira and on the Trans-Siberian Railway, as well as writing and updating tens of other guides for other publishers. When not on the road, Marc lives between Sandwich, Kent, and Mariánské Lázně in the Czech Republic with his wife and two sons.

Kerry Christiani

Vienna, Salzburg & Salzburgerland, Tyrol & Vorarlberg, Plan Your Trip, Understand Austria, Survival Guide Kerry's first encounter with real snow in Tyrol more than 15 years ago sparked her enduring love affair with the Austrian Alps – and she's been returning ever since. For this edition, she sweated out a heatwave in the Hohe Tauern Alps, grappled with white-water rapids in Tyrol, tested out radon cures and climbed (almost) every mountain. Kerry is an award-winning travel writer, and has authored/co-authored many of Lonely Planet's central and southern European titles. Follow her travels on her website https://its-a-small-world.com and tweets @kerrychristiani.

Catherine Le Nevez

Vienna, Upper Austria Catherine's wanderlust kicked in when she roadtripped across Europe from her Parisian base aged four, and she's been hitting the road at every opportunity since, travelling to around 60 countries and completing her Doctorate of Creative Arts in Writing along the way. She's written scores of Lonely Planet guides and articles covering Paris, France, Europe and far beyond. Her work has also appeared in numerous online and print publications.

Donna Wheeler

Vienna, Lower Austria & Burgenland, Styria, The Salzkammergut Carinthia Donna has written for Lonely Planet's *Italy, Norway, Belgium, Africa, Tunisia, Algeria, France, Austria* and *Melbourne* guidebooks. Born and bred in Sydney, Australia, Donna fell in love with Melbourne's moody bluestone streets as a teenage art student. She has divided her time between there and her home town for over two decades, along with residential stints in Turin, Paris, Bordeaux, New York, London and rural Ireland. Donna travels widely (and deeply) in Europe, North Africa, the US and Asia.

Published by Lonely Planet Global Limited
CRN 554153
8th edition – May 2017
ISBN 978 1 78657 440 4
© Lonely Planet 2017 Photographs © as indicated 2017
10 9 8 7 6 5 4 3 2 1
Printed in China